Comparative Government and Politics

COMPARATIVE GOVERNMENT AND POLITICS

Published

Rudy Andeweg and Galen A. Irwin
Governance and Politics of the Netherlands (2nd edition)

Tim Bale
European Politics: A Comparative Introduction

Nigel Bowles
Government and Politics of the United States (2nd edition)

Paul Brooker
Non-Democratic Regimes: Theory, Government and Politics

Robert Elgie
Political Leadership in Liberal Democracies

Rod Hague and Martin Harrop
Comparative Government and Politics (7th edition)

Paul Heywood
The Government and Politics of Spain

B. Guy Peters
Comparative Politics: Theories and Methods
[Rights: World excluding North America]

Tony Saich
Governance and Politics of China (2nd edition)

Anne Stevens
The Government and Politics of France (3rd edition)

Ramesh Thakur
The Government and Politics of India

Forthcoming

Tim Haughton and Darina Malová
Government and Politics in Central and Eastern Europe

Xiaoming Huang
Politics in Pacific Asia

Robert Leonardi
Government and Politics in Italy

Comparative Government and Politics
Series Standing Order
ISBN 0–333–71693–0 hardback
ISBN 0–333–69335–3 paperback
(*outside North America only*)

You can receive future titles in this series as they are published by placing a standing order. Please contact your bookseller or, in the case of difficulty, write to us at the address below with your name and address, the title of the series and an ISBN quoted above.

Customer Services Department, Macmillan Distribution Ltd
Houndmills, Basingstoke, Hampshire RG21 6XS, England

7th Edition

Comparative Government and Politics

AN INTRODUCTION

ROD HAGUE
and
MARTIN HARROP

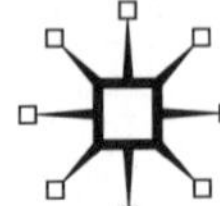

First edition 1982
Second edition 1987
Third edition 1992
Fourth edition 1998
Fifth edition 2001
Sixth edition 2004
Seventh edition 2007

First published 1982 by
PALGRAVE MACMILLAN

Palgrave Macmillan in the UK is an imprint of Macmillan Publishers Limited, registered in England, company number 785998, of Houndmills, Basingstoke, Hampshire RG21 6XS.

Palgrave Macmillan in the US is a division of St Martin's Press LLC, 175 Fifth Avenue, New York, NY 10010.

Palgrave Macmillan is the global academic imprint of the above companies and has companies and representatives throughout the world.

Palgrave® and Macmillan® are registered trademarks in the United States, the United Kingdom, Europe and other countries.

ISBN-13: 978–0–230–00636–2 hardback
ISBN-10: 0–230–00636–1 hardback
ISBN-13: 978–0–230–00637–9 paperback
ISBN-10: 0–230–00637–X paperback

This book is printed on paper suitable for recycling and made from fully managed and sustained forest sources. Logging, pulping and manufacturing processes are expected to conform to the environmental regulations of the country of origin.

A catalogue record for this book is available from the British Library.

A catalog record for this book is available from the Library of Congress.

10 9 8 7 6 5
16 15 14 13 12 11 10 09

Printed and bound in China

Summary of Contents

Contents

PART III

LINKING SOCIETY AND GOVERNMENT

PART IV

GOVERNMENT AND POLICY

List of illustrative material

Profiles

Spotlights

Debates

Timelines

Maps

Figures

Tables

Boxes

Preface

This edition retains the purpose of its predecessors: to provide a wide-ranging, contemporary and clearly written introductory text for courses in comparative politics and other introductory courses in politics and political science.

We have made four substantial changes to this new edition. First, we have recast our classification of governments. This edition is based on a division between liberal democracies, illiberal democracies and authoritarian states. While the previous distinction between established and new democracies served us well, it no longer carries much relevance for students with no memory of communism's collapse. In any case, we wanted to reflect the turn in the literature away from the study of transition towards an understanding of hybrid regimes that can no longer be credibly presented as emerging liberal democracies. By using the term 'illiberal democracy', rather than alternatives such as 'electoral authoritarianism', we hope to encourage Western students to contrast illiberal democracy with liberal democracy, thus facilitating an understanding that liberal democracy is itself a compromise between liberal and democratic principles.

The countries we have used most often as examples of illiberal democracy are Russia (especially under Vladimir Putin) and Venezuela (especially under Hugo Chávez). Because illiberal democracy is not a completely stable regime type, these countries will no doubt continue to evolve or, perhaps more likely, regress. We explore these issues in new sections on classifying governments in Chapters 1 and 3.

Second, we have added a new chapter on political economy, previously only available on our website (our thanks to those who provided feedback on the draft version). This new chapter enables us to address a number of themes well-suited to comparative political analysis: varieties of capitalism; convergence; the developmental state; the relationship between authoritarian rule and economic development; and the resource curse in rentier states. We have tried to write this chapter in a non-technical way, for a politics rather than an economics constituency, but our experience is that politics students do appreciate the significance of these topics for their understanding of the contemporary world.

Third, we have recast the discussion of authoritarian regimes, enabling us to focus more clearly on states of obvious international importance, such as China and Saudi Arabia. Although the book's institutional emphasis leads naturally to a primary concern with established liberal democracies, we do not see how any introduction to comparative politics can exclude non-democracies. After all, ten of the 45 largest countries by population are still governed by authoritarian means and those regimes control most of the world's remaining oil reserves. Some appreciation of politics within authoritarian states is surely an important foundation for understanding contemporary world politics.

Major changes in this edition

Chapter 1
New section
Classifying governments

Chapter 2
New section
Collapsed states and state building

Chapter 3
New section
Liberal and illiberal democracy

Chapter 4
Restructured

Chapter 8
New chapter
Political economy

Chapter 9
New section
Participation in political violence

Chapter 10
New section
Design and reform of electoral systems

Chapter 14
New section
What is multilevel governance?

Chapter 15
New section
Membership (including celebrity politicians)

Chapter 18
New section
Policy instruments

Fourth, we have given the entire text a thorough updating, adding eight new sections and subsections designed to address current and interesting topics. These include a section on collapsed states, which again provides a useful contrast for students more familiar with the hard states of European origin; a section on the members of legislatures, including some material on celebrity politicians; and a section on policy instruments which provides useful grounding for the rather airy notion of governance. The chapter on federal, unitary and local government has become multilevel governance; the bureaucracy has become public management and administration. To enhance clarity, the chapter on the comparative approach has been reordered. Most important, if perhaps least visible, we have tried throughout to capture a significant proportion of relevant recent research, with over 700 new references.

The country profiles now include a range of national rankings from sources such as Freedom House, the CIA and the World Bank. Such rankings are increasingly prominent and we introduce them below. In addition, each profile is now matched to a separate spotlight providing a case study relating that particular country to the chapter theme. Apart from the chapters on the comparative approach and public policy, which are rather more abstract in character, each chapter now includes a profile and a matching spotlight. We hope this arrangement will offer flexibility to those teachers incorporating a country-based element into their courses.

This edition is the work of many hands. At Palgrave Macmillan, we would like to thank Steven Kennedy for his continuing editorial advice and Stephen Wenham for steering the book from typescript to publication. We thank Keith Povey and Nick Fox for their copy-editing, Ian Wileman for designing the new livery, Thea Edwards for research assistance and Joanne Vasey for preparing the references. We owe a special debt to the publishers' anonymous reviewers for their careful but constructive comments and especially for putting us to rights on electoral systems. Any 'wrongs' that remain are of course solely our own responsibility.

Since its first publication 25 years ago, this book has sold well over 100,000 copies and been translated into many languages. We are grateful for the support reflected in these facts, as well as for the suggestions of the teachers who use the book. We also wish to thank the many students from around the world who have been kind enough to correct the inevitable mistakes of fact and interpretation which creep into each new edition. As ever, please feel free to contact Martin Harrop at:

School of Geography, Politics and Sociology
University of Newcastle
Newcastle upon Tyne
England
NE1 7RU
e-mail: Martin.Harrop@newcastle.ac.uk

ROD HAGUE
MARTIN HARROP

Guide to learning features

This book contains a range of features designed to aid your learning. These are outlined below.

Profiles

Profiles offer an outline of specific countries and regions to complement our thematic approach. For each country or region covered, our profile provides:

- A standard set of demographic, economic and political indicators;
- A capsule description of the country's main political institutions;
- A short account of its overall political configuration.

Spotlights

Spotlights follow on from profiles, providing a detailed case study of how the chapter theme plays out in the country profiled.

Learning resources

The learning resources at the end of each chapter offer guidance on exploring the topic in more depth. These sections should come in useful over the entirety of a politics degree. They cover:

- *Next step*: the one source which, in our opinion, represents your natural next move.
- *Further reading*: at least a dozen major publications on the chapter topic. Even a selection of these should provide highly detailed coverage.
- *Internet sources*: selected websites on the topic, often with a focus on factual or practical information which is useful for further research. For clickable links to these sources, visit our website.

Further reading on more detailed topics is also included in the debates, profiles and spotlights.

Note: All the references in this book are listed by chapter on our website, offering a comprehensive guide to the topic of each chapter.

Debates

Most chapters include a debate which presents in succinct form the main points for and against a particular perspective. These debates also enable the reader to ask, 'which position do I prefer (and why)?'

Definitions

The first time a technical term is used, it appears in **red** and is separately defined on the same page. In the index, these terms are also listed in **red** so that they can be located easily. All these definitions, and more, are also available in our on-line dictionary.

Boxes and tables

Boxes are used mainly to define, contrast and illustrate particular political processes. Tables display statistics, again usually with a comparative theme.

Hague and Harrop on the Web

Access to our website is free and unrestricted. Resources include:

- A new dictionary of comparative politics;
- Links to websites, by chapter;
- Interactive quizzes by chapter;
- Guide to comparative politics on the internet;
- Chapter summaries;
- Essay questions by chapter;
- The book's references listed by chapter.

http://www.palgrave.com/politics/hague

Guide to Profiles

In addition to profiles on the World and the EU there are 14 country profiles which include a number of figures, rankings and scales to indicate the social and political conditions of the country. These indicators and their sources are as follows.

A fuller discussion of these indicators is available in Box 2.5 (p. 33) and on our website.

Population (annual growth rate)

The median country's population is 4.5m. A high positive or negative growth rate can be destabilizing. Based on 2006 data.

Source: CIA (2006), itself based on US Bureau of the Census estimates

Income group

The World Bank's four-fold classification, based on 2005 data, is more precise than the traditional distinction between developed and developing countries:

- 55 *high* income countries (gross national income per head at least $10,726). Examples: Japan, USA.
- 40 *upper middle* income countries ($3,466–$10,725). Examples: Mexico, Russia.
- 58 *lower middle* income countries ($876–$3,465) Examples: Brazil, China.
- 54 *low* income countries ($875 or less). Examples: Nigeria, Pakistan.

Source: World Bank (2006a)

Human development index (HDI)

HDI is based on averaging three dimensions: life expectancy, education (enrolment, adult literacy) and gross domestic product per head. Of 177 countries ranked in the 2005 report, based on 2002 data, Norway scored highest (rank = 1) and Sierra Leone lowest.

Source: United Nations Development Programme (2005)

Regime type, political rights, civil liberties

Hague and Harrap classify governments as liberal democracies, illiberal democracies or authoritarian (as at 2006). Freedom House judges political rights and civil liberties, as at 2005, on a scale from 1 (most rights or liberties) to 7.

Source: Freedom House (2006a)

Freedom of the press

Freedom House assesses the freedom of print, broadcast and internet-based media in each country, based on the legal, political and economic environment for these media. Of 194 countries ranked in the 2005 report, based on 2005 data, Finland scored highest (rank = 1) and North Korea lowest.

Source: Freedom House (2006b)

Ease of doing business

The World Bank ranks economies for ease of doing business, based on such indicators as starting a business, employing (and dismissing) workers and enforcing contracts. Of 175 countries ranked in 2006, based on 2006 data, Singapore scored highest (rank = 1 for ease ofdoing business) and the Democratic Republic of the Congo lowest.

Source: World Bank (2006b)

Map P1 Locating the Profiles

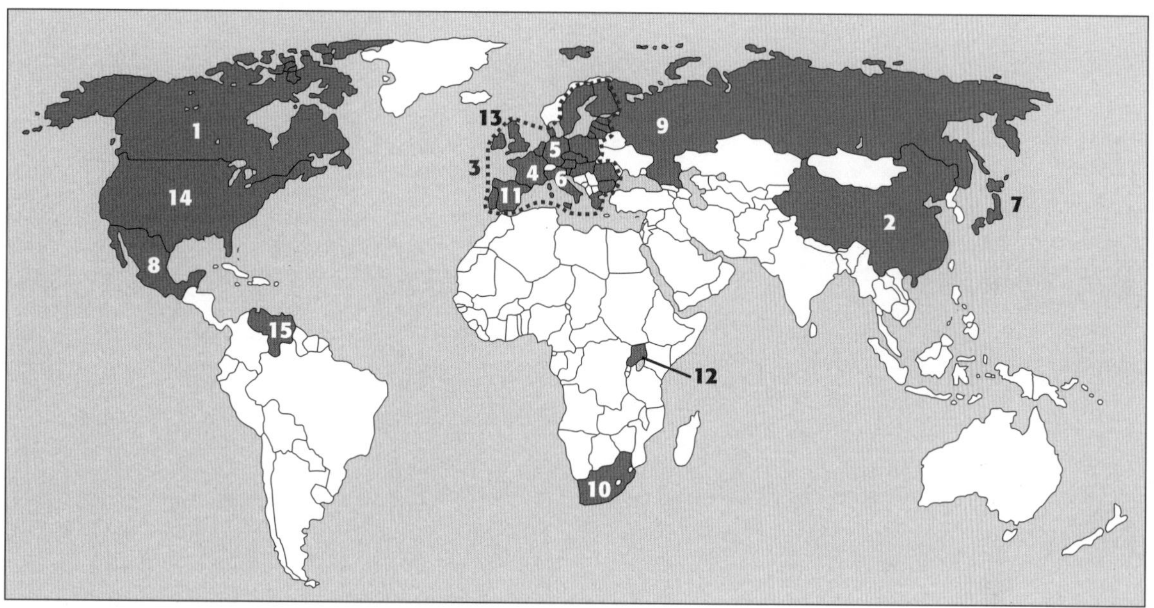

Areas features in the Profiles are shaded in the map and listed below

Note: The statement in each profile that a score of 1 'is best' is made purely to clarify interpretation of the scores themselves and is not meant as an unsubstantiated value judgement. It is, in fact, debatable whether 'freedom of the press' should be unlimited when its components include the freedom of journalists to invade individual privacy and protect their sources in all circumstances. Similarly, 'ease of doing business' is not necessarily desirable when it includes unlimited flexibility to dismiss workers.

Part I
FOUNDATIONS

The foundations of comparative politics lie in the concepts and methods through which we approach the subject. In this part, we introduce core ideas that are central to an understanding of politics of any kind, comparative or otherwise: for example, politics, government, governance, the state. More specifically, we examine the terms which are central to the comparative project, including the classification of governments used in this book: liberal democracy, illiberal democracy and authoritarian rule. The comparative approach is more important in the academic study of politics than in most other disciplines and our final task in this part is to outline the strengths and limits of the comparative method.

Accordingly, Chapter 1 outlines the key concepts of the subject, while Chapter 2 focuses on the state: its emergence, character and contemporary challenges. The subsequent chapters in this part discuss democracy (Chapter 3), authoritarian rule (Chapter 4) and the comparative approach (Chapter 5).

Chapter 1

Politics and government

This book examines the organization of politics in countries around the world. We focus on how nations solve the core problem of reaching collective decisions, paying particular attention to the institutions of government which serve this purpose. But we cannot jump straight into our subject. For just as what astronomers see in the sky depends on the type of telescope through which they peer, so too does any interpretation of politics depend on the concepts through which we approach the topic. Indeed, in politics it often seems as though everyone has his or her own telescope – and claims that their instrument is the best!

In politics, major concepts remain at the forefront of discussion in a way that does not normally apply to more scientific disciplines. Political analysis is far more than mere opinion; yet even so, conclusions vary with the analyst rather more than is comfortable for those who advocate a strictly scientific approach. Comparative politics, based on a range of countries, is especially suited to the task of revealing contrasting perspectives on our subject matter. So in this chapter we will discuss some central concepts of the discipline, not so much to establish correct definitions as to introduce our own interpretations.

Politics

To start at the beginning: what is **politics**? We can easily list, and agree on, some examples of political activity. When the American president starts his annual tussle with Congress over the federal budget, he is clearly engaged in politics. When people join a protest against a war, they are patently participating in politics. The heartland of politics, as represented by such examples, is clear enough. However, the boundaries of the political are less precise. When one country invades another, is it engaged in politics or merely in war? When a court issues a ruling about abortion, should its judgement be construed as political or judicial? Is politics restricted to governments or can it also be found in families, universities and even seminar groups?

A crisp definition of politics – one which fits just those things we instinctively call 'political' – is impossible. Politics is a term with varied uses and nuances. But three aspects of politics are clear:

> **Politics** is the activity by which groups reach binding collective decisions through attempting to reconcile differences among their members (Miller, 1991).

- Politics is a collective activity, involving people who accept a common membership or at least acknowledge a shared fate. Robinson Crusoe could not engage in politics.
- Politics involves reconciling an initial diversity of views and interests through discussion. Communication is therefore central to politics.
- Political decisions become authoritative policy for a group, binding

members to agreements that are implemented by force if necessary.

We will examine each of these features in turn. First, the collective nature of politics arises from our social nature. We live in groups that must reach collective decisions about sharing resources, about relating to other groups and about planning for the future. A family discussing where to take its vacation; a country deciding whether to go to war; the world seeking to limit the damage caused by pollution – all are examples of groups seeking to reach decisions which impact on their members. Groups must also reach a view on which aspects of life are to be left to private discretion: for example, is abortion a matter for individuals, society or both? So politics involves whether to decide as well as what decisions to reach.

The Greek philosopher Aristotle (384–322 BC) argued that 'man is by nature a political animal' (1962 edn, p. 28). By this he meant not just that politics is unavoidable but also that it is the highest human activity, the feature which most sharply separates us from other species. For Aristotle, people can only express their nature as reasoning, virtuous beings through participating in a political community. Politics, he claimed, is what we are for.

Second, politics involves reconciling differences of opinion and interests within the group. Members will rarely agree, at least initially, on what plan of action to follow. Even if there is agreement over goals, there may still be a skirmish over means. Often, differences of opinion reflect conflicting interests: a decision which benefits one person might bring disadvantages for others. Deciding to expand higher education may benefit society as a whole but those who obtain degrees benefit the most. Going to war may be in the national interest but some soldiers will not live to enjoy the peace. By itself, discussion can rarely dissolve such conflicts of interest but it can often identify a compromise between them. In any event, a decision must be reached, one way or the other, and politics is precisely the procedure through which contrasting views and interests are reconciled in an overall decision.

Note that the process of discussion should itself have desirable effects. The participants should become better informed about – and more committed to – the agreed choice. In this way, the quality of the final decision should improve. So in theory at least, good politics will facilitate public policy which is well-designed, well-supported and well-executed. In the longer term, too, deliberation should help citizens to become more informed about each other and about current affairs generally, thus laying the foundation for peaceful self-government (Crick, 2004; Mill, 1861).

Third, political decisions, once reached, commit all the group's members, including those who were not involved in their making, and they are implemented by force if necessary. In Easton's famous definition (1965a and b), 'politics is the authoritative allocation of values'. Taxes must be raised as well as set; wars must be fought and not merely declared. Public authority – ultimately, force – is used to implement collective decisions. If you break the rules, the authorities may put you in prison; at any rate, they are the only people empowered to do so.

What emerges, then, is a picture of the multifaceted nature of politics. The subject involves both shared and competing interests, both communication and force, and both the making of decisions and their execution. The essence of politics lies in the interaction between these dimensions. 'Pure conflict is war', wrote Laver (1983, p. 1). 'Pure cooperation is true love. Politics is a mixture of both.'

Government

Small groups can reach decisions without any special procedures. The members of a family or sports team can reach an understanding by informal discussion. And these agreements can be self-executing: those who make the decision implement it themselves. However, such simple mechanisms are impractical for larger units such as the countries which provide the focus of this book. Countries must develop special institutions for making and enforcing collective decisions. By definition, these decision-making bodies comprise the **government:** the arena for resolving political issues.

In popular use, 'the government' refers just to the highest level of political appointments: to presi-

A **government** consists of institutions responsible for making collective decisions for society. More narrowly, government refers to the top political level within such institutions.

dents, prime ministers and cabinet members at the apex of power. But in a wider sense government consists of all organizations charged with reaching and implementing decisions for the community. By this definition the police, the armed forces, public servants and judges all form part of the government, even though such people are not usually appointed by political methods such as election. In this broader sense, government provides the entire landscape of institutions within which we experience public authority.

The classic case for government was made in the seventeenth century by Thomas Hobbes (Box 1.1). His view was that government provides us with protection from the harm that we would otherwise inflict on each other in our quest for gain and glory. By granting a monopoly of the sword to a government, we transform anarchy into order, securing not only peace but also the opportunity for human endeavour, and indeed cooperation, to flourish.

In modern terms, a government offers security and predictability to those subject to it. In a well-governed society, citizens and firms expect laws to be durable, or at least not to be changed arbitrarily; they know that rules apply to other people as well as to themselves; and they have grounds for expecting that decisions will be enforced fairly.

An additional argument for government, much favoured by economists, is the efficiency to be gained by establishing a standard way of reaching and enforcing decisions (Coase, 1960). If every decision had to be preceded by a separate agreement on how to reach and apply it, politics would become tiresome indeed. These efficiency gains give people who disagree on what should be done an incentive to agree on a general mechanism for resolving disagreements. Although governments are often criticized for inefficiency, they are far more effective than no government at all.

Of course, establishing a government creates new dangers. The risk of Hobbes's commonwealth is that it will abuse its own authority, creating more problems than it solves. As one of Hobbes's critics pointed out, there is no profit in avoiding the dangers of foxes if the outcome is simply to be devoured by lions (Locke, 1690). And in the twentieth century the lions were hungry, killing over 100 million people in episodes ranging from arbitrary massacres to systematic genocides. Governments

BOX 1.1

Hobbes's case for government

The case for government was well-made by the English philosopher, Thomas Hobbes (1588–1679). His starting point was the fundamental equality in our ability to inflict harm on others:

> *For as to the strength of body, the weakest has strength enough to kill the strongest, either by secret machination, or by confederacy with others.*

So arises a clash of ambition and fear of attack:

> *From this equality of ability, arises equality of hope in the attaining of our ends. And therefore if any two men desire the same thing, which nevertheless they cannot both enjoy, they become enemies; and in the way to their end, which is principally their own conservation, and sometimes their own delectation, endeavour to destroy or subdue one another.*

Without a ruler to keep us in check, the situation becomes grim indeed:

> *Hereby it is manifest, that during the time men live without a common power to keep them all in awe, they are in that condition which is called war; and such a war, as is of every man, against every man.*

People therefore agree (by means unclear) to set up an absolute government to escape from a life that would otherwise be 'solitary, poor, nasty, brutish and short':

> *The only way to erect such a common power, as may be able to defend them from the invasion of foreigners, and the injuries of one another … is, to confer all their power and strength upon one man, or one assembly of men, that may reduce all their wills, by plurality of voices, unto one will …. This done, the multitude so united is called a COMMONWEALTH.*

Source: Hobbes (1651).

possess a unique capacity for murder; unlike individuals and small groups, they can kill by the million (Levene, 2005a, p. 53).

A key aim in studying comparative government is therefore to discover how to control Hobbes's common power while also securing its undoubted benefits. We can accept Hobbes's case for government without necessarily agreeing that the commonwealth should be granted absolute authority. We must keep in mind Plato's question of long ago: 'Who is to guard the guards themselves?'

Classifying governments

With 'government' defined, we can turn to the question of how governments are classified in comparative politics generally and in this book specifically. It is certainly true, as Huntington (1991, p. 8) advises, that 'political regimes will never fit neatly into intellectually defined boxes, and any system of classification has to accept the existence of ambiguous, borderline and mixed cases'. Even so, classification is an important tool of comparative politics, enabling us to group broadly similar cases together and to examine the origins and consequences of each type.

We must begin with the most influential classification ever devised: Aristotle's analysis of the 158 city-states of Ancient Greece. These were small communities showing considerable variety in their forms of rule during the period between approximately 500–338 BC. These settlements provided an ideal laboratory for Aristotle to consider which type of system provided what he sought in a government: namely, an optimal combination of stability and effectiveness.

Aristotle based his scheme on two dimensions (Box 1.2). The first was the number of people involved in the task of governing: one, few or many. This dimension captured the breadth of participation in a political system. His second dimension, more difficult to apply but certainly no less important, was whether rulers governed in the common interest ('the genuine form') or in their own interest ('the perverted form'). The significance of this second aspect is that a political system is likely to be more effective and stable when rulers govern in the long-term interests of the community, rather than in the narrow interests of their own social group.

Cross-classifying the number of rulers (one, few or many) with the nature of their rule (genuine or perverted) yields the six types of government shown in Box 1.2. It is worth outlining each cell in this highly influential table. In the case of rule by a single person, Aristotle took kingship as the genuine form and regarded tyranny as is its degraded equivalent. For government by the few, Aristotle distinguished between aristocracy (which he defined as rule by the virtuous) and its base form, oligarchy (rule by the rich). And within the category of rule by the many, he separated the ideal form of 'polity' – broadly equivalent to rule by the moderate middle class, exercised through law – from the debased form of 'democracy', which he interpreted unsympathetically as government by the poor in their own self-interest.

Modern classifications continue to be informed by Aristotle's work. Not surprisingly, however, Aristotle's categories now need supplementing to

BOX 1.2

Aristotle's classification of governments

		Rule by		
		One	*Few*	*Many*
Form	*Genuine*	Kingship	Aristocracy	Polity
	Perverted	Tyranny	Oligarchy	Democracy

Source: Aristotle (1962 edn) book 3, ch. 5.

yield a classification more sensitive to the modern world. In this book, we distinguish between liberal democracies, illiberal democracies and authoritarian regimes (Box 1.3). In Figure 1.1, the area of each category is shown in proportion to the number of governments in each group in 2005. Now we introduce the defining features of each type, leaving fuller discussion to the rest of this book, especially chapters 3 and 4.

Liberal democracy is perhaps the most familiar category. Here rulers are chosen through free, fair and regular elections. Nearly all citizens are entitled to vote and, to permit effective choice, electors can join and form political parties. Furthermore, an independent media allows electors to obtain an 'enlightened understanding' of the issues before as well as during election campaigns (Dahl, 1998, p. 39).

But – and here we reach the 'liberal' part – the government of a liberal democracy is subject to constitutional limits. Individual rights, including freedom of assembly, property, religion and speech, are effectively defended in independent courts. A clear boundary between public and private spheres keeps the elected government in its place. In office, rulers remain subject to clear, constitutional limits.

So the adjective 'liberal' in the phrase 'liberal democracy' is not used in the American sense, to denote a supporter of progressive, left-wing policies. Rather the term refers to the philosophy of liberalism, a doctrine which regards individual autonomy as the cardinal value. Thus, the constitution of a liberal democracy provides not only an accepted framework of political competition but also an effective shield for defending individual rights against government excess.

We now turn to the opposite end of Figure 1.1. **Authoritarian regimes** are neither liberal nor democratic. The absence of democracy lies precisely in the lack of any effective control by the population over its rulers. Elections may not take place at all, as in military regimes, or else the choice may be artificially restricted: vote for us or go to jail. Whole swathes of the population may be excluded from voting, as with the continued denial of the ballot to women in several Middle Eastern kingdoms. Political parties may be banned altogether; only one party may be permitted; or 'independent' parties may only be permitted if they do not challenge the existing order. In any event, the rulers manipulate the powers of office (and especially the media) to prevent a level playing field at elections. Communication between rulers and ruled is low in quantity and quality. Furthermore, the leaders of authoritarian regimes – unlike those of any type of democracy – are prepared to falsify the election result if necessary.

Although orthodox communist states have slipped into history and military rule is currently rare, authoritarian rule remains an important form of government. China, after all, is the world's most populous nation while the Middle East contains a clutch of significant authoritarian regimes (as well as most of the world's oil reserves).

We must also note, in parentheses, the distinction often drawn between authoritarian and totalitarian regimes (Linz, 2000). The latter term is frequently if controversially used to denote both communist and fascist regimes which sought tight control and total transformation of society. This penetration is in contrast to most authoritarian rulers, who seek to insulate themselves from the wider society. However, totalitarian regimes were primarily a phenomenon of the twentieth century only. We therefore use the term 'authoritarian rule' to refer to all forms of non-democracy and we discuss totalitarian regimes under this broader heading.

Finally, to the grey zone in Figure 1.1. Here lie the hybrid regimes which combine democratic and authoritarian principles. Many phrases have developed to capture this form of regime, including semi-democracy and even semi- or electoral authoritarianism. Simplifying decisively, the most important type of hybrid regime in today's world is what

Figure 1.1 A classification of the world's governments

Liberal democracies	Illiberal democracies	Authoritarian regimes

Note: The area of each category is based on the number of governments in Freedom House's comparable but not identical classification for 2005: free countries (89 of 192 countries, covering 44 per cent of the world's population); partly free (54 countries, 19 per cent of people) and not free (49 countries, 37 per cent of people of whom about half are in China). *See* Karatnycky (2006).

BOX 1.3

A classification of governments

	Characteristics	Examples
Liberal democracy	Representative and limited government operating through law provides an accepted framework for political competition. Regular elections based on near universal suffrage are free and fair. Individual rights, including freedom of expression and association, are respected.	Australia, Canada, France, Germany, India, Italy, Netherlands, New Zealand, Norway, Sweden, United Kingdom.
Illiberal democracy	Leaders are elected with minimal or no falsification of the count. However, the rulers exploit their position to prevent a level playing field. To keep their potential opponents off-balance, rulers interefere with the rule of law, the media and the market. Individual rights are poorly entrenched and the judiciary is weak.	Several post-military states in Latin America (e.g. Venezuela). Several Asian states (e.g. Malaysia). Some post-communist states (e.g. Russia).
Authoritarian regime	Rulers stand above the law and are free from effective popular accountability. The media are controlled or cowed. Political participation is usually limited and discouraged. However, the rulers' power is often constrained by the need for tacit alliances with landowners, industrialists, the military or religious leaders.	Examples include military governments, ruling monarchies and personal dicatators. Authoritarian rule is the most common form of rule in history.
	In the **totalitarian states** of the twentieth century, participation was compulsory but controlled as the government sought total control of society, justified by an ideology that sought to transform both society and human nature. These regimes placed heavy reliance on party members, the secret police and other informers as agents of social control.	Communist and fascist regimes subscribed to totalitarian thinking but the model was rarely fully implemented, except for a time in the Soviet Union. More recently, Iran after the Islamic revolution of 1979 showed some totalitarian characteristics.

we will call **illiberal democracy** – also known as electoral or delegative democracy (O'Donnell, 1994; Zakaria, 2003). Many low-income post-communist, post-military and post-colonial countries are of this form.

In an illiberal democracy, rulers run non-fraudulent but still controlled elections; they 'make' the result, even though they do not 'steal' it (Mackenzie, 1957). In Russia, for instance, President Putin's re-election victory in 2004 reflected his popularity; in that sense, Russia is at least an electoral democracy. Even so, no observer would describe contemporary Russia as a liberal democracy. As a graduate of the KGB, Putin showed a fine appreciation of the mechanics of power, dominating the broadcasting media, rewarding his friends and punishing his enemies. In the classic style of governance associated with illiberal democracies, Putin marginalized the opposition through effective, popular and ruthless leadership. Because elections in an illiberal democracy only rarely deliver a change in government, turnover arises more from resignation or – as in Russia and much of Latin America – from term limits.

Governance

Governance is an old word undergoing a revival in popularity. So how exactly does governance differ from government? Where government denotes the institutions of rule, governance covers the activity, process and quality of ruling. Governance directs our attention away from government's command-and-control function and towards the broader task of public regulation, a role which politicians in liberal democracies share with other actors. Because governance is a more abstract notion than government, we need here to clarify its meaning.

Jordan, Wurzel and Zito (2005, p. 478) observe that 'there is no universally accepted definition of governance'. However, the word does encourage us to focus on the wide range of actors involved in regulating contemporary societies. Depending on the particular sector, these actors might include employers, trade unions, the judiciary, professional employees, journalists and even academics. In areas such as health care and law, such expert participants form specialist networks delivering substantial self-regulation. Because such professions do not take kindly to instructions from government, institutions such as the executive and the legislature are just particular actors in these networks and by no means always the commanding players. Hence the need for the broader term.

Understood as the task of managing complex societies, governance involves the coordination of both public and private sector bodies; it is the ability to get things done without the capacity to command that they are done (Rhodes, 1996). Governance positions government as one actor in a network, rather than as a body with direct control over the levers of power. The term suggests a blurring or merging of public and private authority.

The concept of governance grew in popularity in the final two decades of the twentieth century as Western democracies lost some confidence in the ability of their governments to manage economic production and welfare provision directly. As a result, more emphasis was placed on government as a regulator (e.g. of privately owned telecommunications networks) rather than as a provider (e.g. through a state-owned telephone company).

The term 'governance' became especially popular in the United Kingdom, where the decline of direct state provision under Mrs Thatcher was particularly dramatic, and in the European Union, which relies almost exclusively on regulation and negotiation to influence its member states. In the United States, by contrast, the regulatory role of the federal government has long been prominent.

Because governance refers to the activity of ruling, it has become the preferred term when examining the quality and effectiveness of rule. In that context, governance refers to what governments do and to how well they do it. For example, many international agencies suggest that 'effective governance' is crucial to economic development in new democracies. Thus, the World Bank (1997, p. 1) argued in an influential report that 'the state is central to economic and social development, not as a direct provider of growth but as a partner, catalyst and

Governance denotes the activity of making collective decisions, a task in which government institutions may not play a leading, or even any, role. In international relations, many issues are resolved by negotiation: governance without government.

facilitator'. The focus here is on government policies, activities and achievements, not its internal organization or its direct provision of goods and services.

It is the field of international relations which offers the most striking examples of governance. The reason is clear: no world government exists to make enforceable decisions for the world as a whole. Even so, many aspects of global relations are regulated by agreement. One example is the internet, a massive network of linked computers beyond the control of any one government. Yet standards for connecting computers and data to the internet are agreed, mainly by private actors. Thus we can only speak of the governance, but not the government, of cyberspace (Goldsmith and Wu, 2006).

So the emerging pattern, in international and perhaps also in national politics, is rules without rulers, order without orders, steering without rowing, governing without government. In a word: governance (Rosenau, 1992).

Power

Power is the currency of politics. Just as money permits the efficient flow of goods and services through an economy, so power enables collective decisions to be made and enforced. Without power, a government would be as useless as a car without an engine. Power is the key political resource that enables rulers both to serve and to exploit their subjects.

Many authors go so far as to define politics in terms of power. Hay (2002, p. 3), for instance, suggests that politics is 'concerned with the distribution, exercise and consequences of power'. On such accounts, politics is found not just in governments but also in the workplace, the family, the university and indeed in any other arena in which power is exerted. Such a view is probably too broad; in reality, those who study politics are primarily interested in the flow of power in and around government. Morgenthau's interpretation of politics (1966, p. 63) as focused on the nature of power 'with special emphasis on the power of the state' comes closer to the mark. But the difference here is minor; all are agreed that power is central to politics. How then should this core term be understood?

The word itself comes from the Latin *potere*, meaning 'to be able'. In a general sense, then, power is simply the capacity to bring about intended effects (Russell, 1938). Thus, the greater our ability to determine our own fate, the more power we possess. In this sense, describing the United States as a powerful country simply means that it has the ability to achieve its objectives, whatever those may be. Similarly, to lack power is to fall victim to circumstances. Notice that the emphasis here is on power *to* rather than power *over* – on the ability to achieve goals, rather than the more specific exercise of control over other people or countries.

This 'power to' approach is associated with the American sociologist, Talcott Parsons (1902–79). Parsons interpreted power as the capacity of a government to draw on the obligations of its citizens so as to achieve collective purposes such as order and environmental protection. Just as an automobile requires gasoline, and an economy needs money, so power is the fuel of politics. Other things being equal, the more powerful the government, the more effective it will be at achieving community goals. For Parsons (1967), political power is a desirable collective resource which enables rulers to implement the common interest.

Power is the capacity to bring about intended effects. Thus, the term is often used as a synonym for influence, to denote the impact (however exercised) of one actor on another. But the word is also used more specifically to refer to the more forceful modes of influence: for example, threats.

In defining power as 'not just the ability to act but the ability to act in concert', the German-born political theorist Hannah Arendt (1906–75) adopted a similar perspective (1966, p. 44). A group whose members are willing to act together possesses more horsepower – an enhanced capacity to achieve its goals – than does a group dominated by suspicion and conflict. For Arendt, as for Parsons, to be in power is to be empowered by a group's members to pursue joint objectives. Thus Arendt viewed power and violence as enemies rather than siblings: 'power and violence are opposites; where the one rules, the other is absent. Violence can destroy power; it is utterly incapable of creating it' (1966, p. 56). For Arendt, a regime built on terror was prone to impotence rather than omnipotence.

The benign view of power developed by Parsons and Arendt has exerted some influence but it surely remains incomplete. Power is not just a technical task of implementing a vision shared by a whole society. It is also a struggle over what goals to pursue. The question of whose vision triumphs is surely relevant to any assessment of power. In large part, power consists in the ability to get one's way and to impose one's opinions, whether by force or persuasion. That is, one actor exercises power *over* others. In Dahl's famous definition (1957), power is a matter of getting people to do what they would not otherwise have done. Note that the underlying view of power here assumes conflict rather than consensus.

So far, we have presented power as a relationship of influence: power as the intended effects of one actor upon another. But this impact can, of course, operate through a variety of means, often operating together. The instruments of power include force (or more often just its threat), persuasion, negotiation and loyalty. Rather confusingly, the term 'power' is also used to denote the more forceful of such means: 'her power was so much greater than mine that I had no choice but to obey'. In this narrower sense, power refers to influence exerted by altering incentives rather than preferences. By contrast, if B obeys A from intrinsic commitment, rather than from the inequality in their resources, we would be more reluctant to refer to a power relationship (Haugaard, 2002).

The notion of power as the ability to alter what people do is clear and cogent. What though of manipulation: the power to mislead (Shapiro, 2006)? Power can consist not in changing how people behave but in denying them information which, if known, would have led them to act in a different way. Lukes (1986) gives the example of the manager of a nuclear power station who fails to inform local residents that his plant has discharged radioactivity into the surrounding community. Surely, he says, this is a case of power even though the residents continue with their ordinary lives, unaware of what happened? Developing this point led Lukes to a broader if less tangible interpretation of power: 'A exercises power over B when A affects B in a manner contrary to B's interests', even if B is unaware of the damage caused (1986, p. 37).

Authority and legitimacy

Authority is a broader notion than power. Where power is the capacity to act, authority is the acknowledged right to do so. It exists when subordinates acknowledge the capacity of superiors to give legitimate orders. Thus, a general may exercise power over enemy soldiers but his authority is restricted to his own forces.

When writers such as Parsons and Arendt argue that power is a collective resource, they mean, in part, that power is most effective when converted into authority. The German sociologist Max Weber (1864–1920) suggested that in a relationship of authority the ruled implement the command as if they had adopted it spontaneously, for its own sake (1922, p. 29). Yet authority remains more than voluntary compliance. To acknowledge the authority of rulers does not always mean you agree with their decisions; it means only that you accept their right to make decisions and your own duty to obey. As every soldier knows, relationships of authority are still hierarchical.

Authority is the right to rule. Authority creates its own power so long as people accept that the person in authority has the right to make decisions.

Just as there are various sources of power, so too can authority be built on a range of foundations. Weber provided a particularly influential analysis of the nature and evolution of authority in distinguishing three ways of validating political power: by tradition, by charisma and by appeal to legal–rational norms (Box 1.4).

Weber's first type, **traditional authority**, is based on 'piety for what actually, allegedly or presumably has always existed' (1923, p. 296). Traditional rulers do not need to justify their position; rather, obedience is required as part of the natural order. For example, monarchs rule because they always have done so; to demand any further justification would itself constitute a challenge to tradition. Traditional authority is usually an extension of patriarchy – the authority of the father or the eldest male. Weber offers numerous examples of such relationships:

> Patriarchy means the authority of the father, the husband, the senior of the house, the elder sibling

over the members of the household; the rule of the master and patron over the bondsmen, serfs, and freed men; of the lord over the domestic servants and household officials, of the prince over house- and court-officials (Weber, 1923, p. 296).

While such illustrations may seem old-fashioned, traditional authority does remain the model for many political relationships, especially in authoritarian regimes. In Arabic, for example, the term 'sheikh' refers to the head of both a kingdom and an extended family and carries positive overtones such as maturity, experience and wisdom. And indeed throughout the Middle East, 'government has been personal; both civil and military bureaucracies have been little more than extensions of the leader' (Bill and Springborg, 1999, p. 152). The leader looks after his followers and so on down the chain. When entire political systems operate on this principle of traditional, patriarchal authority, they are termed **patrimonial**.

In a **patrimonial** regime, rule is cemented through the distribution of resources on a personal, rather than rule-governed, basis. The president is father figure to the national family, occupying a benevolent but dominant position that affirms a relationship of inequality (patrimony is literally an inheritance from one's father).

BOX 1.4

Weber's classification of authority

	Basis	Illustration
Traditional	Custom and the established way of doing things	Monarchy
Charismatic	Intense commitment to the leader and his message	Many revolutionary leaders
Legal–rational	Rules and procedures. The office, not the person	Bureaucracy

Source: Weber (1922).

Charismatic authority is Weber's second form and one that contrasts sharply with authority based on tradition. In contrast to the foundation of traditional allegiance in the past, charismatic authority spurns history. The charismatic prophet looks forward, convincing followers that the promised land is within reach. Such leaders are obeyed because they inspire their followers, who credit their saviour with exceptional and even supernatural qualities.

Contrary to popular use, charisma is not for Weber an intrinsic quality of a leader. Rather, the term refers to how followers perceive such figures: as inspirational, heroic and unique. So there is little point in searching for the distinctive personal qualities of charismatic leaders; in fact, research suggests that their personalities are quite ordinary (Oakes, 1997). The key is demand rather than supply: what political conditions bring forth a requirement for authority to be expressed in such messianic terms?

Typically, charismatic leaders emerge in times of crisis and upheaval. Jesus Christ, Mahatma Gandhi, Martin Luther King and Adolf Hitler are illustrations. Yet the base of charismatic authority in an individual is also its weakness. Charismatic authority is short-lived: it fades either with the particular leader or with its transfer to a more permanent structure. This latter process is called the **routinization of charisma**. The religious leader founds a church; the politician, a party. 'It is the fate of charisma', wrote Weber (1922, p. 129), 'to recede with the development of permanent institutional structures.'

For example, Ayatollah Khomeini was a charismatic Muslim cleric and exiled hero who returned in triumph to his Iranian homeland to take over the government following the overthrow of the Shah in 1979. Khomeini succeeded in establishing a theocratic regime in Iran, dominated by the Islamic

The **routinization of charisma** is the process through which the individual authority of an inspirational leader is transferred to a permanent office or institution.

clergy, which outlasted his own death in 1989. But as memories of the regime's founder receded, so younger generations increasingly questioned the political authority of religious leaders. All charisma has long since gone but the regime's authority remains, though contested: a case, perhaps, of semi-routinization.

Legal–rational authority is the third and final foundation of Weber's scheme. Here obedience is owed to rules rather than individuals, resulting in government based on regulations, not tradition or charisma. Legal–rational authority inheres in a role or a position, not a specific person. Because it derives from the office rather than the person, we can speak of officials 'going beyond their authority'. Setting out the extent of an officeholder's authority reveals its limits and so provides an opportunity for redress. In this way, legal–rational authority offers a foundation for individual rights.

Weber judged that legal–rational authority was becoming predominant in the modern world, both in the political realm and beyond. A public servant proceeding in accordance with written rules, a banker deciding whether to offer a loan, a judge methodically applying the law – all are examples of individuals implementing an explicit rationality. In the political arena, Weber's German homeland is the best example of a regime founded on legal–rational authority. Germany is often described as a *Rechtsstaat*: a state based on law.

Returning to the broader notion of authority, we must now introduce its close cousin: **legitimacy**. The terms are similar in meaning but legitimacy is a broader concept. Where authority refers to a specific role, such as a judge, legitimacy refers to the wider system of government. When a regime is widely accepted by those subject to it, we describe it as legitimate. Thus we speak of the authority of an official but the legitimacy of a regime.

Although the word legitimacy comes from the Latin *legitimare*, meaning to declare lawful, legitimacy is much more than mere legality. Legality is a technical matter. It denotes whether a rule was made correctly – that is, following regular procedures. By contrast, legitimacy is a broader and more political concept. It refers to whether people accept the validity either of a specific law or of the political system as a whole.

Regulations can be legal without being legitimate.

A **legitimate** system of government is one based on authority: that is, those subject to its rule recognize its right to make decisions.

The majority black population in white-run South Africa considered the country's apartheid laws to be illegitimate, even though these regulations were made according to the existing constitution. The same could be said of many laws passed by communist states: properly passed and even obeyed but not accepted as legitimate by the people.

While legality is a topic for lawyers, political scientists are more interested in legitimacy: in how a regime gains and sometime loses public faith in its right to rule. Public opinion, not a law court, is the arena in which legitimacy is gained or lost.

The state and sovereignty

The **state** is now the dominant principle of political organization on the world's landmass. There are, of course, a few intriguing exceptions (Wilde, 2007). These include territories still under colonial control (e.g. Britain's Gibraltar); or administered by the United Nations (e.g. Bosnia); or voluntarily subject to partial external authority (e.g. Puerto Rico is affiliated to the United States); or granted substantial autonomy within a larger state (e.g. Hong Kong within China).

The **state** is a political community formed by a territorial population subject to one government.

Leaving such anomalies to one side, the world is parcelled up into separate states which, through mutual recognition and interaction, form the international system (Figure 1.2, p. 16). These units are the main focus of this book and for this reason we will devote the next chapter to an analysis of the state's evolution and significance. Here we focus on the simpler task of definition.

The state is a unique institution, standing above all other organizations in society. It alone claims not just the capacity but also the right to employ force. As Weber noted, the exclusive feature of the state is precisely this integration of force with authority: 'A state is a human community that (successfully) claims the monopoly of the legitimate use

GLOBAL PROFILE

THE WORLD

Population: 6.45 billion, increasing by 1.1 per cent per year.

Median age: 27.6 years.

Life expectancy: men 62.7 years, women 66.4 years.

Literacy: men 87 per cent, women 77 per cent.

Internet users (population aged 15+): 14 per cent.

Major languages: Mandarin Chinese, followed by English, Hindi and Spanish.

Major religions: Christian (33 per cent), Muslim (20 per cent), Hindu (13 per cent), Buddhist (6 per cent).

Labour force: agriculture (42 per cent), industry (21 per cent), services (37 per cent).

Gross domestic product (per head): $9500 (+4.4 per cent per year).

Inequality: the poorest 20 per cent receive about 2 per cent of the world's income.

Number of states: 193.

Total external debt (public and private): $36.9 trillion.

Total official development aid: $154 billion.

Note: Most statistics are from 2004–06.
Sources: CIA (2006), Comscore Networks (2006).

THE WORLD contains more people than ever and its population is growing at a rate of about 70 million per year – almost equivalent to the population of Germany. It took over a hundred years for the world's inhabitants to increase from one to two billion; the most recent increase of a billion occurred between 1988 and 2000. Another two and a half billion are expected by 2050.

The capacity of the planet to sustain these numbers, now and especially in the future, must be in doubt. Certainly, the challenge posed by the environment is sure to increase whatever measures are adopted now. Damage already inflicted has yet to reveal its full impact and recent generations have merely passed on risks such as disposing of nuclear waste to the future.

Environmental degradation is serious and increasing. Minerals, forests, soil, wetlands, vegetation, fossil fuels, animal species, plant diversity and the ozone layer are being depleted. The quality of air and water is falling. Global warming poses a particular danger as sea levels rise: half the world's inhabitants live in coastal areas. Some uninhabited atolls have already disappeared; low-lying islands such as Tuvalu and the Marshall Islands may provide the world's first climate refugees; and heavily populated delta regions in Bangladesh, China, Egypt and Louisiana are vulnerable to salt water intrusion. 'Sea level rise is not a fashionable scientific hypothesis,' said President Gayoom of the Maldives in 1998. 'It is a fact.' Global warming also causes heat stress; encourages the spread of diseases such as malaria; and increases the frequency of severe climatic events such as storms, posing unpredictable dangers to all countries.

Although climate change is inherently global, the contribution made by the world's national 'tenants' can be measured. Table 1.1 shows the largest contributors to the world's total carbon dioxide emissions over the second half of the twentieth century. The countries shown were responsible for a majority of these emissions and therefore owe a particular responsibility for mitigating contemporary effects. None of the big three (USA, China and Russia) can be said to have taken the lead in fulfilling its obligation.

Table 1.1 Cumulative carbon dioxide (CO_2) emissions, 1950–2000

	Share of global CO_2 emissions (per cent)
USA	16.9
China	9.9
Russia*	8.2
Indonesia	7.2
Brazil	6.1
Germany	4.3
United Kingdom	2.6
Canada	2.0

* formerly the Soviet Union.
Source: WRI (2007)

Further reading: Hardin (1999), Held *et al.* (2005).

SPOTLIGHT

A world of states

'Real communities of fate cannot be identified in exclusively national or territorial terms', writes McGrew (1997, p. 235). The problems of climate change and environmental degradation do not acknowledge national boundaries, creating a mismatch between nation-states and global problems. What, then, are the political hindrances that the world must learn to overcome if it is to heal itself?

Current political arrangements give states little incentive to take unilateral action since they know that their own efforts, however worthy, will not alter the global outcome. Inequality between states also hinders global cooperation, with developing countries arguing that they should not be prevented from industrializing by developed countries which managed to get their pollution in first. International competition is also a negative factor, with Asian countries such as China seeking to catch up with the West by prioritizing economic development.

In theory, a world government could put an end to free riding and interstate squabbling. Even a world federation of states could work, if a new authority could set priorities while relying on individual countries for implementation. To some extent, the European Union (EU) already performs these functions for its 25 member states that contain over 460 million people.

How likely is it, though, that a European-style confederation could be adopted for the whole world? We should be wary of dismissing this prospect. After all, the EU, like the United States before it, was created by a generation whose achievement was founded on determination. As Carr (1931, p. 87) wrote, 'Any sound political thought must be based on elements of both utopia and reality'.

Yet the current prospects of a world federation do seem remote. The EU was constructed on the institutional base provided by some of the strongest and most stable states in the world; this foundation is lacking elsewhere. Even in the EU, accusations of a democratic deficit now fly about, leading Dahl (1999, p. 32) to judge that at the larger global level 'international organizations are not and are not likely to be democratic'. Certainly, the United Nations – an underfunded, ineffective, decentralized and sometimes corrupt organization – seems unlikely to provide anything more than a forum in which its member states can discuss global issues.

The practical solution may lie in Dahl's further comment (1999, p. 32): 'to say that international organizations are not democratic is not to say that they are undesirable'. With this statement, a lifelong advocate of democracy returns to the idea of guardianship, implicitly acknowledging the capacity of international organizations to formulate, and commit their home governments to practical measures addressing specific environmental problems.

These networks of scientific experts, government officials, lawyers and pressure groups – from the International Council of Science to the World Wide Fund for Nature – operate at some remove from democratic and indeed political pressures, thus giving them the 'informality and confidentiality' needed for progress (Slaughter, 2003, p. 194). At the global level, it seems, the issue of democracy is a sideshow; when the health of the planet is at stake, whatever works best, is best.

Further reading: Dahl (1999), Held and McGrew (2003), Slaughter (2004).

The Stern Review on the Economics of Climate Change (2006)

In 2006, Sir Nicholas Stern published the conclusions of his review of the economics of climate change, commissioned by the British government so that it could 'understand more comprehensively the nature of the economic challenges and how they can be met, in the UK and globally'. His four central conclusions were:

- there is still time to avoid the worst impacts of climate change, if we take strong action now;
- the costs of stabilizing the environment are significant but manageable; delay would be dangerous and much more costly;
- a range of options exists to cut emissions; strong deliberate policy action is required to facilitate their take-up;
- climate change demands an international response, based on a shared understanding of long-term goals and agreement on frameworks for action.

Figure 1.2 Member states of the United Nations, 1949–2005

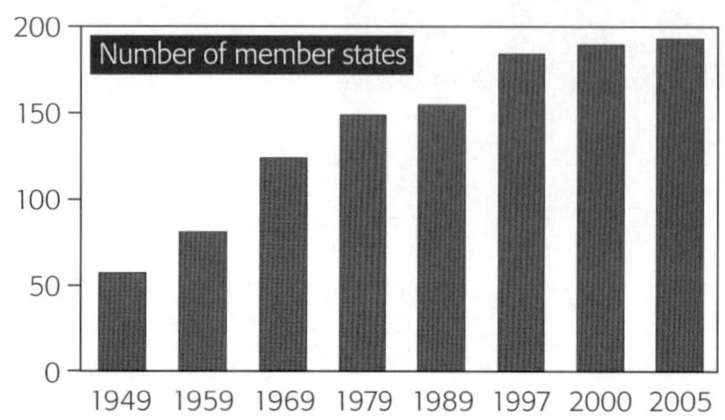

Note: Switzerland joined in 2002.
Source: United Nations (2005).

of physical force within a given territory' (Gerth and Mills, 1948, p. 78). When the state's monopoly of legitimate force is threatened, as in a civil war, its existence is at stake. As long as the conflict continues, there is no legitimate authority. Hence, in describing states as nothing more than 'bodies of armed men', the Russian revolutionary Vladimir Lenin (1870–1924) was only partly correct. Contrary to Lenin, a body of armed men does not suffice to form a state; for the law of the gun is no law at all.

How does a state differ from a government? The state defines the political community of which government is the managing agent. By successfully claiming a monopoly of authorized force, the state creates a mandate for rule which the government then puts into effect. This distinction between state and government is reflected in the characteristic separation of the roles of head of state and head of government. European monarchs, for example, symbolize the state but leave prime ministers to control the levers of government.

Much of the theoretical justification for the state is provided by the European idea of **sovereignty**. In describing the state, we must therefore unpack this related notion. As developed by the French philosopher Jean Bodin (1529–96), sovereignty refers to the untrammelled and undivided power to make laws. Echoing Hobbes, the English jurist William Blackstone (1723–80) also argued that 'There is and must be in every state a supreme, irresistible, absolute and uncontrolled authority, in which the right of sovereignty resides.'

The word 'sovereign' originally meant the one seated above. So the sovereign body is the one institution not subject to higher authority: the highest of the high. By definition, that body is the state. As Bodin wrote, the sovereign can 'give laws unto all and every one of the subjects and receive none from them'. Sovereignty originally developed in Europe to justify the attempt by monarchs to consolidate control over kingdoms in which authority had previously been shared with the feudal aristocracy and the Catholic church. Indeed, the British monarch is still known as the 'sovereign'. By consecrating central authority in this way, the legal concept of sovereignty contributed powerfully to the development of the European state.

But as democracy gained ground, so too did the belief that elected parliaments acting on behalf of the people are the true holder of sovereignty. The means of acquiring sovereignty evolved although the theoretical importance of Blackstone's 'supreme authority' remained unquestioned, especially in centralized European countries such as Britain and France. To this day, the notion of 'parliamentary sovereignty' remains a cornerstone of British political debate.

Sovereignty refers to the ultimate source of authority in society. The sovereign is the highest and final decision-maker within a community.

Beyond Europe, however, the notion of sovereignty remained weaker. In the federal 'United States', political authority is shared between the central and state governments, all operating under a constitution supposedly made by 'we, the people' and enforced by the Supreme Court. In these circumstances, the idea of sovereignty is diluted and so too is the concept of the state itself. Americans more often use the word 'state' to denote the 50 states of the union rather than the federal government in Washington.

Contemporary discussion distinguishes between **internal** and **external sovereignty**. External sovereignty is important because it allows a state to claim the right both to regulate affairs within its boundaries and to participate as an accepted member of the international order. In this way, the development of the international system strengthened the authority of states in the domestic sphere; indeed,

Internal sovereignty refers to law-making power within a territory. **External sovereignty** refers to international recognition of the sovereign's territorial jurisdiction.

internal and external sovereignty represent two sides of a single coin.

First and foremost, sovereignty is a theoretical construct. The formal right to make laws does not imply that in practice the sovereign is omnipotent. All sovereigns are influenced by events beyond and within their borders. For this reason, claims that sovereignty has become a myth in an interdependent world should be treated with caution. Sovereignty always was a myth; that is its nature and significance. Mexico depends more on the United States than vice versa but the two countries are equal as sovereign nations. A state's control over its destiny – its autonomy – is a matter of degree but its sovereignty is necessarily unlimited. The essence of sovereignty is an unqualified legal title:

> Constitutional independence, like marriage, is an absolute condition. People are either married or not married; they cannot be 70 per cent married. The same with sovereignty: a country either has the legal title of sovereignty or it does not; there is no in-between condition (Sørensen, 2004, p. 104).

Nations and nationalism

A **nation** is a more elusive term than a state. Nations are imagined communities and a nation is often viewed as any group that upholds a claim to be regarded as such (Anderson, 1983). In two ways, though, we can be a little more precise. First, nations are peoples with homelands. As Eley and Suny (1996, p. 10) put it, a nation – like a state – implies 'a claim on a particular piece of real estate'. Here the origin of the word 'nation', deriving from a Latin term meaning place of birth, is relevant. The link between nation and place is one factor distinguishing a nation from a tribe or ethnic group. A tribe can easily move home but a nation remains tethered to its motherland, changing shape mainly through expansion and contraction.

Second, when a group claims to be a nation, it asserts a right to self-determination within its homeland. It seeks sovereignty over its land, using or inventing a shared culture to justify this claim to autonomy. The assertion of self-rule gives the nation its political character. A group becomes a nation by achieving or seeking control over its own destiny, whether through independence or devolution. Nations have either achieved statehood or are states in waiting.

Some examples will illustrate how demands for nationhood integrate territory, culture and politics. To describe French-speaking Canadians as a separate nation, as opposed to a linguistic community, indicates a claim for autonomy if not independence for this culturally distinct and geographically concentrated group. Similarly, the broadening identity of the Palestinian people (which transformed what was an Arab refugee population in 1948 into the fully-fledged national grouping that exists today) formed part of the growing demand for a functioning Palestinian state. The campaign for a Palestinian state first required the invention of a Palestinian people and nation.

Because the concept of nation is political, nations need not be united by a common language, history or ethnicity. A common tongue certainly eases the task of cultural unification yet Switzerland is indisputably a nation even though French, German and Italian are used there. Similarly, speaking English does not suffice to qualify for membership of the English nation; if it did, the English would be the world's largest tribe.

'A portion of mankind may be said to constitute a **nationality** if they are united among themselves by common sympathies ... which make them co-operate with each other more willingly than with other people, desire to be under the same government, and desire that it should be government by themselves or a portion of themselves exclusively' (Mill, 1861, p. 391).

Why do nations exist? When and why did they come into being? Here debate centres on whether nations should be seen as ancient or modern. On the one hand, nations are frequently viewed as creatures of antiquity, emerging from the primeval soup of past times. Anthony Smith (1998, 1999) is the leading exponent of this position. He points out that several large ethnic groups ('nations'?) are indeed of distant origin; examples include the Greeks, Serbs and Chinese. For Smith, nations draw on a tradition – real or mythical – of a shared descent, history and culture. This position is the primordial view of nations, meaning existing from the beginning.

A modernist approach, on the other hand, links the idea of the nation to more recent notions of self-determination; nations are made rather than found. Even if nations do draw on ancient cultures, their core lies in justifying self-government amid a world of states. In pre-modern times, place of birth did not define identity to the same extent as today. Nations assert statehood and since states themselves are products of modernity, so too are nations.

A national identity also serves broader modern functions. It unites people who do not know each other but who nonetheless find themselves yoked together under common rulers and markets. Nationality provides an emotional bond for an increasingly rational world. It allows the losers from the transition to a market economy to take comfort in the progress of the country as a whole: 'rich and poor French people are equally French, sharing an inclusionary, involuntary and indivisible identity' (Lie, 2004, p. 15). In a similar way, national identity provides a rationalization for participation in war, encouraging people 'to die for the sake of strangers' (Langman, 2006).

This modernist view of the nation was first developed by the European philosopher, Ernest Gellner (1925–95). He argued forcefully that the nation 'preaches and defends continuity but owes everything to a decisive and unutterably profound break in human history' (1983, p. 125). Thus, an American identity only emerged to supplement loyalty to the 13 founding states after the creation of the USA following the Philadelphia convention of 1787. As Murrin (1987, p. 333) pointed out in an oft-quoted phrase, 'Americans erected their constitutional roof before they put up national walls'. In both France and the United States, national loyalties eventually succeeded in gluing large, dispersed populations together under a veneer of equality.

Certainly, many nations have been constructed in the course of recent struggles. In the nineteenth and especially the twentieth centuries, colonial peoples marched to independence under a nationalist banner. These assertions of national identity were often as artificial as the boundaries originally imposed by colonial rulers. Even so, 'the presence and power of the colonial regime stimulated the development of a national identity as the basis of resistance' (Calhoun, 1997, p. 108). In a process aptly termed nationalism from above, the leaders of independence movements established national movements which did indeed prove to be the grave-diggers of empire. Dating the precise origin of nations is impossible but, given such facts, their starring role in politics surely lies in modern times.

Even more than nations themselves, **nationalism** is a doctrine of modernity. Like some other 'isms', nationalism emerged in the nineteenth century to flourish in the twentieth. But unlike most ideologies, the principle of nationalism is reassuringly straightforward. It is simply the doctrine that nations do have a right to determine their own destiny – to govern themselves. Thus nationalism is the device that enables the territorial notion of a nation to transcend space and encompass the world; nations are universal even though each individual nation is unique. The significance of nationalism is that it offers one answer to a question beyond the reach of democracy: who are 'the people' who are to govern themselves?

Nationalism, the key ideology of the twentieth century, is the doctrine that nations are entitled to self-determination. Gellner (1983, p. 1) writes that nationalism 'is primarily a political principle, which holds that the political and national units should be congruent.'

The United Nations Covenant on Civil and Political Rights (UNHCHR, 1966) offers a succinct statement of the principle of national self-government:

> All peoples have the right to self-determination. By virtue of that right they freely determine their political status and pursue their economic, social and cultural rights.

This principle proved to be highly influential throughout the twentieth century. Early on, nationalism provided a justification for redrawing the map of Europe with the final collapse of the Austro-Hungarian Empire in 1918. And towards the century's end, the collapse of communism initiated a resurgence of national expression throughout the Soviet

DEBATE

SHOULD STATES PROMOTE MULTICULTURALISM?

In an age of terrorism, should governments still encourage a range of religious, ethnic and even national identities to flourish within their territory? Or should we revive the more traditional idea of a nation-state, in which citizens are offered equal rights under law in exchange for their primary allegiance to their country?

YES

Migration means that nearly all developed countries are multicultural. There is no realistic possibility of creating populations whose primary and exclusive loyalty is to their country. Rather, societies have fragmented into groups whose members wish to assert, and will assert, their particular ethnic, national, racial, religious, sexual and even global identities.

Such diversity should be celebrated. The cultural mosaic of global cities such as London and New York is an attractive feature to the inhabitants themselves; to employers seeking a labour market with a wide skills base; and to new immigrants wanting to find their feet in an unfamiliar country. Multiculturalism helps cities compete in a global world.

Besides, a liberal government should regard questions of identity and allegiance as matters for individuals and society, rather than the state. The state's duty is to respect difference and to promote the right of each group to sustain and develop its own identity, but not to impose a single model of citizenship on its entire population. In the twenty-first century, people from different cultures can nonetheless converge on the responsibilities of shared citizenship without needing the artificial glue of manufactured nationalism.

How, in any event, can governments control how people define themselves? Past attempts at assimilation to a dominant culture are hardly reassuring, sometimes amounting to cultural extermination. The treatment of indigenous groups in settler societies is a baleful example (Levene, 2005b).

NO

'Multiculturalism has failed', wrote José María Aznar, former prime minister of Spain (2005, p. 21). Noting that 'the 2004 terrorist attacks in Madrid and the attacks in London the following year were perpetrated by people who had lived in our countries for many years', Aznar judged that Europe must 'rediscover its Christian roots, setting aside the enormous error of multiculturalism'.

Following riots by Muslim youths in suburban slums in France in 2005, the French Prime Minister expressed a similar view, claiming that 'integration should be based on individuals, not communities' (*Financial Times*, 2005, p. 24). As Mill warned in the nineteenth century, we must not leave minorities to 'sulk on their own rocks' (1861, p. 395).

Similar voices have been heard in the United States. Huntington (2004, p. 366) suggests that America must decide whether to maintain the distinct Anglo-Protestant culture which has been the foundation of its success. He notes that 'The overwhelming bulk of the American people are committed to preserving and strengthening the American identity that has existed for centuries'.

Huntington cites state referendums rejecting bilingual education and reports evidence that immigrants themselves favour an education in English – the language of prosperity – for their own children.

The broader point is that when the practices of a particular group are unethical – arranged marriages, say, or homophobia – the government should not tolerate them in the name of multiculturalism.

ASSESSMENT

It remains to be seen how states themselves will resolve this debate, if indeed they do so. Balancing group and individual rights in liberal democracies is inherently difficult. External threats, and particularly the experience of war, may prove crucial. There is surely some significance, for example, in the fact that Wal-Mart sold 250,000 American flags in the United States on 12 September 2001, compared to just 10,000 on the same day a year earlier.

Further reading

Gagnon and Tully (2001), Huntington (2004), Kymlicka (1995), Nimni (2006).

Union and its satellite states. The end of the ideological war between communism and the West leaves politicians searching for alternative means of mobilizing public support; national identity is one such.

Yet even today nations and states continue to cut across each other in an untidy fashion. Whatever we might wish to be the case, we would err if we believed that each state contains only one nation, or that each nation is restricted to one state. Box 1.5 sets out four ways in which nations and states combine in practice. The first two rows in this box describe types of state (nation-state, multinational state) while the latter two rows denote additional possibilities for national groups (stateless nation, diaspora). To understand these categories is to appreciate some of the complexities of contemporary politics.

The first and most straightforward category is the traditional **nation-state**. Here each country contains only the people belonging to its nation. The French Revolution of 1789 established the idea that the state should articulate the interests and rights of citizens bound together by a shared national identity. The British philosopher John Stuart Mill (1806–73) was an early and influential advocate of the nation-state. He argued that 'where the sentiment of nationality exists in any force there is a *prima facie* case for uniting all the members of the nationality under the same government, and a government to themselves apart' (1861, p. 392). In today's world, Iceland is an example of a pure nation-state. Its population shares such a well-documented descent that the country's birth records provide a perfect laboratory for genetic research.

Even though few countries today are as homogeneous as Iceland, the nation-state is probably still an appropriate term when discussing the many countries in which one nationality remains politically and numerically dominant. In France, Germany and Israel, for instance, the state remains rooted in the soil of a strong national identity despite the presence of significant minorities: Algerians and Moroccans in France, Turks in Germany and Palestinians in Israel (Smooha, 2002). France, in particular, remains an archetypal nation-state; the government is expected to articulate the interests of the nation as a whole and all French nationals are deemed to share equally in the rights of citizenship.

The second category in Box 1.5 is the **multinational state**. Here, more than one nation is fundamental to a country's politics and assimilation to a dominant nationality is not a realistic option. International migration is moving many, perhaps most, states in this direction. Even so, we should not

BOX 1.5

Nations and states

	Type of	Definition	Example
Nation-state	State	A state with its own nation	Iceland
Multinational state	State	A state with more than one nation	The United Kingdom contains the Scottish and Welsh nations, as well as England and Northern Ireland
Stateless nation	Nation	A nation which lacks its own state and whose people are spread across several countries	Kurds, Palestinians
Diaspora	Nation	A nation dispersed beyond its homeland	Jews

regard the phenomenon of multinationalism as new. Britain, for instance, has long been divided between English, Welsh, Scottish and Irish nationals; Canada between English- and French-speakers; and Belgium between Dutch- and French-speakers. These examples demonstrate that multinational states can achieve internal peace and political stability but there are, of course, other cases where national divisions within a country have led to conflict. For instance, Balkan states such as Bosnia and Croatia experienced vicious conflicts between Croat, Muslim and Serbian national groups in the 1990s.

This book centres on states, whether nation-states or multinational in character. But there is a danger in such a state-centred approach: namely, that we ignore how national groups can cut across state boundaries. Our third category, the **stateless nation**, refers to just such a situation. Such a nation lacks a home state of its own. The Kurds, for example, have inhabited a mountainous region of Asia for over 4,000 years and their national identity is well-established. But their homeland of Kurdistan is divided between Iran, Iraq, Syria and Turkey, with little immediate prospect of an independent Kurdish state (Map 1.1). The 20 million Kurds seem likely to continue as the world's largest stateless nation.

By contrast, the Palestinian nation is in a stronger position to mount a successful claim to territorial statehood. Since the creation of Israel, the Palestinians have been an uprooted Arab people, living mainly in refugee camps not just in traditional areas of Palestine but also in other Arab countries such as Jordan. However, the Palestinian National Authority has already achieved some limited self-governance within the territories disputed with Israel and any final settlement of the Middle East seems likely to require the creation of a sovereign Palestinian state.

Our final category is the **diaspora**, defined by Esman (1996, p. 316) as 'a minority ethnic group of migrant origin which maintains sentimental or material links with its land of origin'. The term was originally associated with the dispersal of the Jews from their Palestinian homeland following their defeat by the Romans in 70 AD. The Jews are the archetypal case, with only a minority of the world's Jews now living in the ancient homeland. But there are other examples, notably in Asia. The Chinese 'commonwealth' in South East Asia links the Chinese homeland with economically important groups in Indonesia, Malaysia, the Philippines, Singapore and Thailand (Cheung, 2005). Similarly, India's 20 million NRIs (non-resident Indians) have become a powerful lobby for economic reform in the home country. Such transnational networks are growing in importance, encouraging the emergence of virtual nations and demonstrating the practicality of nationalism from a distance (Anderson, 1998).

Map 1.1 A stateless nation: the Kurds

Learning Resources for Chapter 1

Next step

Crick (2000) is a lively examination of the nature of politics.

Further reading

Leftwich (2004) offers an edited collection of perspectives on politics. On specific topics, governance is covered by Kooiman (2003) and Kjær (2004). On the classification of governments, see Dahl (2003) for democracy; Brooker (2000) and Linz (2000) for non-democracy; and Ottoway (2003) and Zakaria (2003) for points in-between. For the state, van Creveld (1999) traces the state's rise and alleged fall while Hay, Lister and Marsh (2005) focus on contemporary issues. Hinsley (1986), Hoffman (1998) and Krasner (1999) survey sovereignty from historical, sociological and international perspectives respectively. Calhoun (1997) provides an accessible overview of nationalism; Delanty and Kumar (2006) is a comprehensive handbook. On power, see Lukes (2005) for an updated account of a radical interpretation; for a review symposium on Lukes, see *Political Studies Review* (2006). Haugaard (2002) is an annotated collection on power. Watt (1982) introduces authority while Lipset (1960) provides a standard account of legitimacy.

Internet sources

Global Gateway, Library of Congress
Links to resources on the world's countries
http://www.loc.gov/rr/international/portals.html
IPSAportal
Top 300 sites in political science
http://ipsaportal.unina.it//final.html
Political Resources On The Net
Links to politics sites
http://www.political.resources.net
PolitInfo.com
Political resources, news, information and links
http://www.politinfo.com/
Richard Kimber's Political Science Resources, Keele University
Links to politics sites
http://www.psr.keele.ac.uk/
Working Paper Sites of Political Science
Links to online working papers in politics
http://www.workingpapers.org/
World Factbook, CIA
Country profiles, regularly updated
https://www.cia.gov/cia/publications/factbook/index.html
Zárate's Political Collections
World leaders since 1945
http://terra.es/personal2/monolith/home.htm
Documents Center, University of Michigan Library
Political science resources on the web
http://www.lib.umich.edu/govdocs/polisci.html

Chapter 2
The state

Although we now take for granted the division of the world into states, we should not assume that the state always was the dominant principle of political organization, nor that it always will be. There was a world before states and, as advocates of globalization tirelessly point out, there may be a world after them too.

Before the state, government consisted, in the main, of kingdoms, empires and cities. Although most such units were governed in a highly decentralized fashion, some were substantial in area and population. For example, the ancient Chinese empire 'proved capable of ruling a population that eventually grew into the hundreds of millions over a period of millennia – albeit control was not always complete and tended to be punctuated by recurring periods of rebellion' (van Creveld, 1999, p. 36). Ancient history quickly dispels the idea that all modern states are larger and more stable than every traditional political system.

Yet the modern state remains a unique political form, distinct from all preceding political formations. Today's states possess sovereign authority to rule the population of a specific territory, a notion which contrasts with the more personal and non-centralized rule of traditional kings and emperors. It is this difference which enables Melleuish (2002, p. 335) to suggest that 'the development of the modern state can be compared to the invention of the alphabet. It only happened once but once it had occurred it changed the nature of human existence for ever'.

This modern idea of the state developed in Europe between the sixteenth and eighteenth centuries, with the use of the word 'state' as a political term only coming into common use in Europe towards the end of this period (Dyson, 1980, p. 26). In this chapter, we portray some of the historical and contemporary forces shaping the state. Our aim is to present not just an abstract idea but also a force that has moulded, and is in turn shaped by, the modern world. We begin by reviewing the emergence, growth and partial retreat of the state in its Western heartland. We then examine its contrasting fortunes in those countries that have achieved independence from colonial rulers, looking in particular at the recent idea of a collapsed state. With that historical context established, we turn to the contemporary challenges facing the state.

Emergence

The state emerged from the embers of medieval Europe (*c.*1000–1500). In the Middle Ages, European governance had been dominated by the Roman Church and feudalism. The Church formed a powerful transnational authority placed above mere monarchs, with kings acting only as secular agents of the Church's higher authority. Even within their nominal territories, 'rulers' were limited by feudal noblemen who exerted extensive authority over men of lower rank within their domain. Sandwiched between these forces – the one supranational and the other subnational – monarchs occupied a far weaker position than do today's rulers. The problem before us, then, is to explain how modern states escaped from the dual constraints of church and feudalism to create the core political unit of the modern world.

War and reformation

If any single force was responsible for the transition to the modern state, that factor was war. As Tilly (1975, p. 42) writes, 'War made the state, and the state made war'. The introduction of gunpowder in the fourteenth century transformed military scale and tactics, as organized infantry and artillery replaced the knight on horseback. The result was an aggressive, competitive and expensive arms race. Between the fifteenth and eighteenth centuries, military manpower in France and England grew almost tenfold (Opello and Rosow, 2004, p. 50).

New technology forced fresh thinking from rulers. Kings needed administrators to recruit, train, equip and pay for standing armies, thus laying the foundation of a modern bureaucracy. Reflecting the new benefits to be secured from a large army, units of rule increased in size. Between 1500 and 1800, the number of independent political units in Europe fell from around 500 to just 25 as the medieval architecture of principalities, duchies and bishoprics gave way to a more recognizable framework of larger countries. (Note, however, that two major European states, Germany and Italy, did not unify until the second half of the nineteenth century.)

With the growth of bureaucracy, local patterns of administration and justice became more uniform. As feudal ties decayed, standard rules applying across a ruler's domain eased the growth of commerce. In addition, rulers began to establish formal diplomatic relations with their counterparts abroad, a core feature of the modern state system. The outcome of these changes was the more centralized monarchies which developed in England, France and Spain in the sixteenth century and went on to flourish in the seventeenth. In France, for instance, Louis XIV (reigned 1643–1715) became known as the Sun King: the monarch around whom the realm revolved.

Just as war-making weakened the feudal pillar of the medieval framework, so the Reformation destroyed its religious foundations. From around 1520, Protestant reformers led by Martin Luther condemned what they saw as the corruption and privileges of the organized Church. This reform movement exerted profound political consequences, shattering the Christian commonwealth as antagonism developed between Protestant and Catholic rulers, notably in the Thirty Years' War (1618–48) in German-speaking Europe.

This conflict was finally ended by the **Peace of Westphalia** (1648), an important if occasionally overstated chapter in the book of the state (Osiander, 2001). Westphalia is considered pivotal because it gave territorial rulers more control over the public exercise of religion within their kingdoms, thus rendering national secular authority superior to religious edict from Rome. The threat posed by Westphalia to papal supremacy doubtless explains the vigour of Pope Innocent X's reaction to it. He condemned the treaty as 'null, void, iniquitous, unjust, damnable, reprobate, inane, empty of meaning and effect for all time' (van Creveld, 1999, p. 82). But even this spirited tirade could not hold back the tide.

> The **Peace of Westphalia** (1648) is judged to be a significant moment in the emergence of the state. In bringing an end to the Thirty Years' War, the peace treaties gave territorial rulers more control over the exercise of religion within their boundaries, thus confirming the limited transnational authority of the Church.

Sovereignty, contract and consent

As central authority developed in Europe, so did the need for its theoretical justification. The crucial idea here was sovereignty, as later tamed by the notions of contract and consent. The French philosopher Jean Bodin made the key contribution to this new centralizing ideology. Bodin argued that within society a single authority should possess the untrammelled and undivided power to make laws. In his view, the sovereign should be responsible for legislation, war and peace, appointments, judicial appeals and the currency. Such a concentration of political authority is clearly far removed from the decentralized medieval framework of Christendom and feudalism.

Sharing Bodin's belief in the need for a powerful sovereign, the English philosopher Thomas Hobbes drove the argument forward. Without a central authority to enforce the peace, claimed Hobbes, society would regress to civil war. But where Bodin's sovereign still derived his authority from God, Hobbes's analysis was firmly and distinctively secular. He located the sovereign's authority in a contract between rational individuals seeking protection from each other's mischief. If the sovereign failed to deliver order, people would no longer be under any obligation to obey. In this way, the sovereign came to serve the people, no longer the other way round, and religion became entirely a matter of inner conviction. So, if Bodin was post-medieval in his thinking, Hobbes represents the first of the moderns. As Skinner (1978, p. 349) points out, 'By the seventeenth century, we may be said to enter the modern world: the modern theory of the state remains to be constructed, but its foundations are complete'.

The vision of a government made by and for the governed was further developed by John Locke, an English philosopher whose thinking shaped the liberal vision of the Western state that underpinned the American Revolution of the 1770s. Locke argued that citizens possess **natural rights** to life, liberty and property, rights that must be protected by rulers governing through law. Citizens consent to obey the laws of the land even if only by tacit means such as accepting the protection which law provides. But should rulers violate these natural rights, the people 'are thereupon absolved from any further Obedience, and are left to the common Refuge, which God hath provided for all Men against force and violence' – the right to resist (Locke, 1689, p. 412).

As if to mark the transition from traditional kingdoms to modern states, Locke further insisted that political rulers should not be viewed as traditional father figures caring for a notional household. He set out to 'shew the difference betwixt a Ruler of a Common-wealth, a Father of a Family, and a Captain of a Galley' (1689, p. 268). So in Locke's work we observe a modern account of the liberal state, with sovereignty limited by contract and consent. Society is now placed above rather than beneath government.

Natural rights (e.g. to life, liberty and property) are supposedly given by God or by nature; in either case, their existence is taken to be independent of government. In seventeenth-century political thought, natural rights functioned to limit the authority of government, thus establishing the basis for liberalism.

In contrasting ways, these ideas of sovereignty, contract and consent were reflected in the two most momentous affirmations of modernity: the American and French revolutions. In America, the colonists established their independence from Britain and went on to fashion a new republic, giving substance to Locke's liberal interpretation of the state. In Lockean fashion, the Declaration of Independence (1776) boldly declared that governments derive 'their just authority from the consent of the governed' while the American constitution (drafted 1787) famously begins, 'We, the people of the United States'.

However, it was the French Revolution of 1789 that made the most daring attempt to reinterpret sovereignty in democratic terms. Described by Finer (1997, p. 1516) as 'the most important single event in the entire history of government', the French experience mapped out the contours of modern democracy. Where the American federal government remained strictly limited in its authority, the French revolutionaries regarded a centralized, unitary state as the sovereign expression of a nation consisting of citizens with equal rights. Where the American revolution was liberal in design, built on distrust of power, the French revolutionaries favoured universal suffrage and a government empowered to pursue the **general will**. The principles of France's modernizing revolution were articulated in the Declaration of the Rights of Man and the Citizen, a document described by Finer as 'the blueprint of virtually all modern states' (Box 2.1). The Declaration served as

The **general will** is followed when citizens make decisions for the good of society as a whole rather than for the interests of particular groups and individuals within it. The term was central to the thought of the French philosopher Jean-Jacques Rousseau (1712–78) and still finds echoes in some distrust within France of special interests.

a preamble to the French constitution of 1791 and forms part of the country's current constitution.

True, these democratic pretensions were soon swept aside in France as violence, terror and war stimulated the return of authoritarian rule under Napoleon. However, the revolution in ideas was irreversible. As national identity joined forces with the state, so sovereignty – once the device used by monarchs to establish their supremacy over popes and princes – was decisively reinterpreted for a new democratic age.

Expansion and restructuring

With the French Revolution, the theoretical foundations of the Western democratic state were, in essence, complete. The detailed construction work was completed in the nineteenth and the first three quarters of the twentieth centuries, supported by growing nationalist sentiment. Only in the final decades of the twentieth century did the state begin to transform its shape, reducing its direct participation in the economy but expanding its regulatory role.

During the nineteenth century, the cage of the state became more precise, especially in Europe. Borders slowly turned into barriers as precise maps marked out defined frontiers. Lawyers established that a country's territory should extend into the sea by the reach of a cannonball and, later, above its land to the flying height of a hot-air balloon. Reflecting this new concern with national boundaries, passports were introduced in Europe during the First World War. To travel across frontiers became – as it had not previously been – a rite of passage, involving official permission as expressed in a passport stamp. Such documents remained necessary for overseas travel at least until some member countries of the European Union abolished mutual border controls through the Schengen Agreement of 1985.

Economically, too, the second half of the nineteenth century saw the end of an era of relatively liberal trade. Stimulated by economic depressions, many European actors introduced protectionist trade policies in the second half of the century. By the century's end, the United Kingdom was the only developed country practising free trade (Winham,

BOX 2.1

Declaration of the Rights and Duties of Man and the Citizen, France, 26 August 1789.

ARTICLES 1–6

1 Men are born and remain free and equal in rights. Social distinctions may be based only on considerations of the common good.

2 The aim of every political institution is the preservation of the natural and imprescriptible rights of man. These rights are liberty, property, security and resistance to oppression.

3 The source of all sovereignty lies essentially in the Nation. No corporation or individual may exercise any authority that does not expressly emanate from it.

4 Liberty is the capacity to do anything that does not harm others. Hence the only limitations on the individual's exercise of his natural rights are those which ensure the enjoyment of these same rights to other members of society. These limits can be established only by legislation.

5 The law is entitled to forbid only those actions which are harmful to society. Nothing not forbidden by legislation may be prohibited and no one may be compelled to do what the law does not ordain.

6 Law is the expression of the general will. All citizens have a right to participate in shaping it either in person, or through their representatives. It must be the same for all, whether it punishes or protects.

Note: Article 6 is an extract. For the Declaration's full text, see Finer (1997), p. 1538.

2005, p. 90). As national markets gained ground against local as well as international exchange, so the economy became more susceptible to regulation by central government. Internally, the domestic functions performed by the state began to expand. Many tasks we now take for granted as public responsibilities only emerged in the nineteenth century, including education, factory regulation, policing and gathering statistics (literally, 'state facts').

For most of the twentieth century, Western states bore ever deeper into their societies (Box 2.2). As with the original emergence of European states, this expansion was again fuelled by the demands of war. The 1914–18 and 1939–45 conflicts were **total wars**, fought between entire nations rather than just between specialized armed forces. To equip massive forces with the industrial weapons of tanks, planes and bombs required unparalleled mobilization of citizens, economies and societies. Such conflicts were also extraordinarily expensive. As a result, tax revenues as a proportion of national product almost doubled in Western states between 1930 and 1945 (Steinmo, 2003, p. 213). The twentieth century was an era of the state because it was also an age of war.

Total war requires the mobilization of the population to support a conflict fought with advanced weaponry on a large geographical scale. Total wars are fought between countries, not just between armed forces, with citizens mobilized in the name of nationalism. Total war requires state leadership.

Initially, the onset of peace in 1945 did not lead to a corresponding reduction in the state's role. Rather, Western governments sought to apply their enhanced administrative skills to domestic needs. In economic policy, many governments drew on the counter-cyclical policies recommended by John Maynard Keynes (1883–1946) to secure full employment. Throughout Europe, the warfare state gave way to the welfare state, with rulers accepting direct responsibility for protecting their citizens from the scourges of illness, unemployment and old age. In this way, the European state led a post-war settlement which integrated full employment and public welfare with an economy in which the private sector continued to play a substantial part.

Eventually, the post-war expansion of the state proved to be unaffordable. Warfare states are temporary but welfare states involve long-term commitments. By 1980, the average share of gross domestic product spent or transferred by the governments of 14 developed democracies reached 46 per cent, a substantial increase on the proportion just 10 years earlier (Table 2.1). With social democratic governments redistributing income in the name of greater equality, the top rate of income tax in Western countries reached an inhibiting 63 per cent by the mid 1970s (Steinmo, 2003, p. 221). As public employment continued to expand, so financial pressures mounted. Following the oil crises of the 1970s, speculation even began to emerge about whether governments might go bankrupt. Rather like the empires of old, no sooner had the Western state reached its full extent than it began to look overstretched.

In consequence, the 1980s and to a lesser degree the 1990s witnessed some significant restructuring. This refocusing was particularly pronounced in English-speaking countries, supported by the right-wing agenda of Ronald Reagan (American president, 1981–89) and Margaret Thatcher (British prime minister, 1979–90). Nationalized industries were sold, welfare provision was trimmed and the state increasingly sought to supply public services indirectly, using private contractors. Significantly, military demands were for once consistent with a diminished state: spending on the armed forces declined after the Cold War. Across the Western world as a whole, the state's share of total expenditure reached a plateau by 1980 (Table 2.1).

To be sure, the state's retreat was less pronounced in continental Europe than in the Anglo-American world. Even in the English-speaking democracies, the state's role in some ways evolved – from producer to regulator – rather than declined. But as the violent twentieth century approached its unusually peaceful end, some commentators discerned a fundamental shift in the approach of the state. Rather than waging war and providing welfare, governments began to focus on meeting the challenges of an increasingly open world economy (Waters, 2000). And the new century, of course, also crystallized the emerging global threats of terrorism and climate change. The state's work, it transpired, was far from over.

BOX 2.2

The Western state: expansion (1789–1974) and restructuring (1975–2000)

Aspect	Expansion (1789–1974)	Restructuring (1975–2000)
Centralization The penetration of central power over a specified territory	Emergence of national police forces. Introduction of border controls.	Migrants and asylum-seekers loosen border controls. Agreed elimination of border controls within some EU states.
Standardization Greater uniformity within society	Common language. Standard weights and measures. Consistent time zones.	Strengthening of regional autonomy and identities. Increased support for a multi-cultural society.
Force Strengthened monopoly of legitimate force	Emergence of national police forces, backed by the military.	
Mobilization Increased capacity to extract resources from society	Military conscription. Introduction of income tax. Increased public spending.	Reduced rates of income tax. Tax-payers' revolts in a few countries.
Differentiation State institutions and employees become increasingly distinct from society	The idea of 'public service' as the even-handed application of rules.	The idea of 'governance' as collaboration between state and society. Public employees encouraged to mimic private sector.
Functions Growth in the state's tasks and its intervention in society	War-making. Welfare provision.	Privatization reduces state's direct economic role. Welfare provision reduced modestly; some public tasks contracted out.
Size Expansion of the state's budget and personnel	Growth of public sector.	Public sector stabilizes. Fiscal deficits increase. Military spending falls.

Source: Adapted from Clarke (1995), table 1, p. 12.

Table 2.1 Total government expenditure in selected democracies as a proportion of gross domestic product, 1970–2004 (%)

	1970	1980	1990	2004
Sweden	43.3	61.6	60.5	57.3
Denmark	40.2	56.2	56.0	56.3
France	38.5	46.1	49.6	53.4
Finland	30.5	36.6	44.5	50.7
Belgium	36.5	50.7	50.8	49.3
Netherlands	43.9	57.5	49.4	48.6
Germany	38.6	48.3	43.8	46.8
Norway	41.0	48.3	52.3	46.4
United Kingdom	38.8	44.8	41.9	43.9
Canada	34.8	40.5	46.0	41.1
Japan	19.4	32.6	31.3	38.2
United States	31.6	33.7	33.6	36.5
Australia	26.8	33.8	33.0	36.2
Ireland	39.6	50.8	39.5	34.2
Average	36.0	45.8	45.2	45.6

Note: Gross domestic product is the total value of goods and services produced within a country over a year. The data in the final column are from 2003 for Australia, Canada and the USA. Averages are unweighted by size of economy.

Sources: adapted from Vartiainen (2004), table 7.1, and for 2004 from OECD (2005).

The post-colonial state

The state was born in Europe and then exported to the rest of the world by colonial powers, notably Britain, France and Spain. Countries without a history as a colony, leaving aside the ex-colonial powers themselves, are few and far between: principally China, Japan and Thailand in Asia, Ethiopia in Africa and Iran and Saudi Arabia in the Middle East. As Opello and Rosow (2004, p. 161) write, 'It is impossible to understand the development of modern states without taking into account the way European states constructed an interconnected global order by means of conquest, trade, religious conversion and diplomacy'.

Although the term 'post-colonial' is usually confined to states achieving independence in the aftermath of the Second World War, we should acknowledge that earlier settler societies such as Australia, Canada, New Zealand and the United States are also former colonies, albeit of a distinctive kind. In settler societies, the new arrivals sought to supplant, rather than exploit, indigenous communities, a goal they ruthlessly achieved. The founders brought with them segments of a European tradition which they recreated and adapted for a frontier environment. Even though the standing of the state in settler countries is less elevated than in Europe, their political organization remains recognizably Western. As Schlesinger (1998, p. 34) notes of the United States, 'the language of the new nation, its laws, its institutions, its political ideas, its literature, its customs, its precepts, its prayers, primarily derive from Britain'. Settler societies are from, though not in, Europe (Hartz, 1955; Huntington, 2004).

How then did non-settler colonies emerge into statehood? Described by Crawford (2002) as the largest single change in world politics over the last five hundred years, this process took place in four waves spread over two centuries (Box 2.3). The retreat from empire by European powers after 1945 was certainly the largest of these waves, stimulating a massive increase in the world's stock of states. However, each wave deposited particular kinds of state on the post-colonial shore.

The *first* wave of decolonization occurred early in the nineteenth century, in the Spanish and Portuguese territories of Latin America where colonial settlers had dominated, without eliminating, indigenous peoples. These early wars of independence occurred soon after the American and French revolutions but lacked their liberal, egalitarian basis. Rather, the Latin American cases took the form of republican movements against monarchical rule from Europe. New constitutions were produced but they were neither democratic nor even fully implemented. In reality, the movement for independence in Latin America was triggered by weakness in the imperial centre and was initiated by a Creole (native born of European origin) economic elite in the colonies.

So the outcome of the first wave of decolonization was not a Lockean constitutional state authorized by the citizens and subject to their consent. Liberal principles were invoked to justify independence but economic exploitation of native populations, the poor and the descendants of slaves continued in the post-colonial era. In the centre, power lay with autocrats; in the interior, where natural resources were gathered for export, strongmen known as **caudillos** held sway (McCreery, 2002). The resulting inequalities created endemic conflicts within Latin American societies which remain important to this day.

A **caudillo** is a political boss who rules the roost in a particular territory, providing order and expecting allegiance. These local strongmen remain important figures in Latin America, where they reflect and reinforce the weakness of state institutions.

The *second* wave of post-colonial states emerged in Europe and the Middle East with the final collapse of the multinational and religiously diverse Austro-Hungarian, Russian and Ottoman empires around the end of the First World War. The principle of national self-determination, espoused by American President Woodrow Wilson and reflected in nationalist sentiment within the imperial territories themselves, played a key role in this major redrawing of the European map.

Specifically, the Austro-Hungarian Empire dissolved into five separate states: Austria, Hungary, Poland, Czechoslovakia and Yugoslavia. Finland, Estonia, Georgia, Latvia, Lithuania and Ukraine achieved at least temporary independence following the Russian Revolution of 1917. Turkey, the historic core of the Ottoman Empire, became a sovereign state in 1923 although Ottoman territories in the Middle East, including Iraq and Palestine, were placed under British or French control by mandates from the new League of Nations.

However, with the exception of Turkey, strong and stable states failed to develop. Rather, international politics continued to intrude, preventing those countries on the European periphery from experiencing the continuous state development found in the continent's core. Most of the new states formed from the Austro-Hungarian Empire were incorporated into Hitler's Germany and, after the war, into the Soviet sphere of influence. Similarly, most of the Baltic states, together with Georgia and Ukraine, quickly returned to Russian control (Batt, 2003).

Only with the collapse of communism in the 1990s and the entry of many of these post-colonial countries into the European Union in 2004 was independent statehood finally achieved, creating new opportunities to construct effective states on the base provided by historic nations. In the Middle East, the former Ottoman territories of Iraq and Palestine remain immersed in internal division and great power politics.

The *third* and largest wave of state creation occurred after 1945, with the retreat from empire by European states diminished by war (Spruyt, 2005). Asian countries such as the Philippines (1946), India (1947) and Burma (1948) were the first to achieve independence; many other colonies in Africa, the Caribbean and the Middle East followed suit. This wave of decolonization grew into a veritable tsunami. Over 90 new independent states – almost half the world's current stock – were created between 1944 and 1984. Eighteen emerged in 1960 alone, a year in which the United Nations declared that lack of preparation for independence was no reason for delaying it (Mayall, 2005, p. 44).

But here it is crucial to distinguish between form and substance. The state form has been successfully exported from Europe but effective functioning has rarely followed. Most post-1945 countries lacked any previous experience as a coherent entity; rather, the state was superimposed on ethnic, regional and religious divisions that had themselves been strengthened by the rigid classifications of the colonialists.

Often, the state has become a prize for which the traditional leaders of such groups compete, resulting in a lack of autonomy from social interests. The prizewinners distribute the rewards to their own supporters, reinforcing circuits of personal rule which are incompatible with government by law. The state is both coercive and weak, lacking the drive of its European forebears. For such reasons, Davidson (1992, p. 188) suggests that the post-colonial state in Africa has proved to be the 'black man's burden' rather than 'Europe's last gift' to the continent.

The *fourth* and final wave of state formation occurred in the final decade of the twentieth century, triggered by the collapse of communism. The dissolution of the communist bloc previously dominated by the Soviet Union led to independence for the Baltic states and for a dozen Soviet satellites in Eastern Europe such as Hungary, Poland and Romania. In addition, the Soviet Union itself – in

BOX 2.3

States from empires: waves of decolonization

Wave of decolonization	Main imperial powers	Main locations of colonies and imperial territories	Approximate number of new states created by decolonization	Examples of newly independent states
1810–38	Spain, Portugal	Latin America	15	Argentina, Brazil
After the 1914–18 war	Ottoman, Russian and Austro-Hungarian empires	Europe (beyond its Western core), Middle East	12	Austria, Finland, Poland, Turkey
1944–84	UK, France, Belgium, Portugal	Mainly Africa, Asia and the Caribbean	94	Algeria, Congo, India, Philippines
1991	Russia	Soviet Union republics (East Europe, Central Asia)	15	Kazakhstan, Latvia, Ukraine

Sources: Adapted from Derbyshire and Derbyshire (1999) and Opello and Rosow (2004).

effect, a Russian empire – dissolved into 15 successor states, including the Ukraine, Uzbekistan and of course Russia.

The experience of these new post-communist states has again been mixed. The Baltic states gained economic and political stability from their proximity to, and now their membership of, the European Union. However, central Asian republics such as Uzbekistan reveal a more typical post-colonial syndrome: small size, ethnic divisions, a pre-industrial economy and autocratic rule. In the successor states to the Soviet Union, these problems are reinforced by the absence of pre-colonial experience as an independent state.

Overall, then, the contrasts between West European parent states and their post-colonial progeny are deep-rooted. Post-colonial states rarely possess the hard edge which their European predecessors acquired during their own development. This contrast can be seen in the treatment of borders. While European rulers were keen to mark off their own frontiers, they invented borders for their colonies which bore little relation to natural or social features. In the Middle East,

> Many of the new states exhibited a somewhat artificial appearance, with their new names, their new capitals, their lack of ethnic homogeneity and their dead-straight boundaries that were so obviously the result of a British or French colonial official using a ruler (Owen, 2000, p. 11).

Africa reveals a similar pattern. The boundaries of half its states contain at least one straight section and, reflecting the low value of land, many national borders are treated with indifference by governments and people alike. Some are completely unguarded, hardly the sign of a state concerned to demonstrate its territorial mastery. Sovereignty remains important as a title, securing international recognition and access to aid. But the label's significance is largely symbolic, with little to prevent the movement of people, soldiers and terrorists across boundaries. This point has long been recognised among African entrepreneurs themselves, as demonstrated by Davidson's conversation (1992, p. 202) with an ivory trader on the day Ghana came into existence as an independent state in 1957:

> I suggested that once despised colonial frontiers become proper national boundaries, it will no longer be practical to evade customs posts and officials. 'You will have to adjust your methods of trade.' I remember his smile of pity for my innocence, but he simply said, 'Ah, do you think so?' His skepticism was to prove well-justified. The official frontiers would be unofficially ignored.

The rulers of many post-colonial states – again, in Africa particularly – are constrained by limited penetration through their territory. Control may not extend far beyond the capital, with government outposts falling under the influence of local strongmen. Regional groups and leaders jostle to control central government outposts in their terrain (Migdal, 2001). The authority of political rulers is sometimes subject to further competition from other ethnic groups, organised criminal gangs and vigilante groups, all of which may operate across frontiers. As far as the state is concerned, Latouche's (1996) 'Westernization of the world' may be limited to form rather than substance.

Collapsed states and state building

As a counterpoint to our discussion of strong European states, it is useful to consider **collapsed states** and efforts to (re)build them. Western governments demonstrate a growing concern with what

BOX 2.4

Some cases of state collapse in Africa

	Year of independence	Start of collapse	Initiation of collapse
Uganda	1962	1979	The overthrow of the tyrant Idi Amin left a power vacuum
Chad	1960	1980	The collapse was brought about by factional conflict within the guerrilla movement that had itself overthrown the previous regime
Liberia	1847*	1990	A rebellion against the concentration of power under Samuel Doe who had himself led a military coup in 1980
Somalia	1960	1990	Opposition clans rose up against the governing clan led by the military ruler Siyad Barre

* Liberia was founded in 1821 by the American Colonization Society as a settlement for blacks repatriated from the southern United States.

Source: Adapted from Zartman (1995a) who includes a chapter on each example.

A **collapsed state** is often defined institutionally, to denote the crumbling of state organization and its effective replacement by private and subnational bodies. The concept of a **failed state** is closely related but is defined functionally, as the state's inability to perform its key role of monopolizing the legitimate use of force within its territory.

are variously termed collapsed, criminal, disrupted, failed, failing, fragile, fragmented, vulnerable, quasi-, weak or **failed states**. The USA's National Security Strategy, for instance, suggests that 'America is now threatened less by conquering states than we are by failing ones' (President of the United States, 2002, p. iv). Writing from a human rights perspective, Ignatieff (2002, p. 114) claims that 'the human rights dilemmas of the twenty-first century derive more from anarchy than tyranny'. In any event, examining collapsed states broadens our understanding of the state, avoiding the danger of focusing only on successes.

Where a revolution involves a temporary failure of state authority, based on a competition for the contract to rebuild, a collapsed state is a decayed regime that no longer fulfils its core task of securing order and welfare. In Zaire, for example, Reno (2003, p. 86) reports in a chilling sentence that 'expenditures on education and health care reached zero in 1992'. Collapse may not involve civil war and does not usually result in a new regime. Rather, order is typically retained but by private means rather than public. That is, wealthy people arrange their own protection and the black, informal or parallel economy takes over. Even some international trade is sustained as armed groups, sometimes led by the nominal political rulers themselves, control the export of natural resources such as timber, gems and drugs. Thus, against Hobbes, the disintegration of state institutions does not imply the triumph of disorder. Nor indeed does the economy become completely detached from global markets. A collapsed state need not entail a failed society.

Most examples of state collapse come from post-colonial Africa and especially from smaller countries with no pre-colonial experience as an independent entity. Seven out of the ten countries which top the *Foreign Policy* (2006) and Fund for Peace (2006) lists of failed states are in Africa. As Zartman (1995, p. 2) comments, such geographical concentration provides an opportunity 'not just to learn about Africa but to learn from Africa – a project of much wider importance'. Outside Africa, many instances of state 'collapse' are cases of state weakness rather than complete failure. In Afghanistan and Colombia, for instance, leaders may share authority with drug dealers and warlords but the state continues, at least as a lame leviathan.

(Re)building states after a period of collapse is a difficult exercise, showing in particular the danger of imposing a Western form in non-Western conditions. A state cannot be constructed like a factory. Rather, the state-building project cannot be imposed

BOX 2.5

Country indicators

The profiles in this book give a range of indicators for each country. This box discusses the nature of such ratings.

The collection of country-based political and social indicators has a substantial history in comparative politics (Taylor and Hudson, 1972). Such information is useful for academic, policy and political purposes alike.

Ideally, any measurement procedure employed should be based on *explicit* rules for giving countries a particular score. The procedure should be *reliable*: that is, different researchers applying the same rules should produce very similar results. The procedure itself should also be *valid*, providing a true indication of the concept we seek to measure (e.g. freedom of the press).

In practice, the underlying data are rarely error-free. Generally, information is more accurate for developed countries. Reducing an absolute measurement (e.g. size of economy) to a rank order can increase reliability because we can often be confident that country A scores higher than country B on a given variable even though we cannot be sure of the size of the difference between them. But the position of the country in a ranking can itself be strongly influenced by small differences in the underlying measurement.

COUNTRY PROFILE

UGANDA

Form of government ■ a unitary republic with 69 districts, many with substantial practical autonomy.

Legislature ■ the 332 current members of the unicameral Parliament include 215 constituency members and 79 district representatives reserved for women. Additional seats are reserved for groups such as the armed forces and workers. The president can appoint additional members. Members are elected for a renewable five-year term.

Executive ■ the president is both chief of state and head of government; he is assisted by the prime minister in supervising the cabinet. Semi-presidential elements notwithstanding, the system is effectively presidential. The president is directly elected for a five-year renewable term.

Constitution and judiciary ■ the current constitution dates from 1995. The judiciary is headed by the Court of Appeal whose members are appointed by the president and approved by the legislature. The legal system is based on English common law and customary law.

Electoral system ■ Single-member plurality.

Party system ■ the 1995 constitution was revised in 2005 to permit a multiparty system. President Yoweri Musevini's vehicle, the National Resistance Movement (NRM), won 207 seats in the 2006 parliamentary elections. The main opposition came from the Forum for Democratic Change (FDC), led by Dr Kizza Besigye, which won 37 seats. The FDC consists of figures who have fallen out with Musevini; they accuse him of 'corruption and nepotism, because of weak and dictatorial leadership' (FDC, 2007).

Population (annual growth rate)	28.2m (+3.4%)
World Bank income group	low income
Political Rights score	5
Civil Liberties score	4
Human development index (rank/out of)	146/177
Freedom of the press index (rank/out of)	99/194
Ease of doing business index (rank/out of)	107/175

Note: For meaning and sources of scales and indexes, see p. xvi. In all cases a score and rank of 1 is 'best'.

Located on a plateau in east Africa, **UGANDA** is a landlocked but fertile country with large freshwater lakes and rivers; Churchill referred to it as 'the pearl of Africa'.

By population, it is one of the largest countries in sub-Saharan Africa. Despite an effective anti-Aids campaign, about 500,000 people are still living with HIV/Aids. Reflecting the Aids factor, the population is exceptionally young, with a median age of just 15 (USA: 37).

The economy remains mainly agricultural, with coffee the main export but there are also substantial deposits of copper and cobalt. In 2006, the economy grew by 5 per cent.

Nonetheless, the level of human development remains comparatively low, with one in five men, and two in five women, still illiterate.

The country is a typical colonial construct, bringing together a wide variety of ethnic and language groups under a British protectorate consolidated during the 1890s from a series of traditional kingdoms.

The largest of these groups, but comprising no more than a fifth of the current population, is Buganda. Located in the centre and south of the country, Buganda's kingdom dates back to at least the fourteenth century ('Uganda' is a Swahili term for Buganda). The original colonial settlement was with the Kabaka, the king, and Buganda also opened the door to independence.

Aspirations for an independent Bagandan state have gone unfulfilled, however, and the position of Buganda within post-independence Uganda has been a major source of conflict, contributing to the country's recent history of instability and violence.

Further reading: Ocitti (2006), Tripp (2000).

SPOTLIGHT

State collapse and reconstruction in Uganda

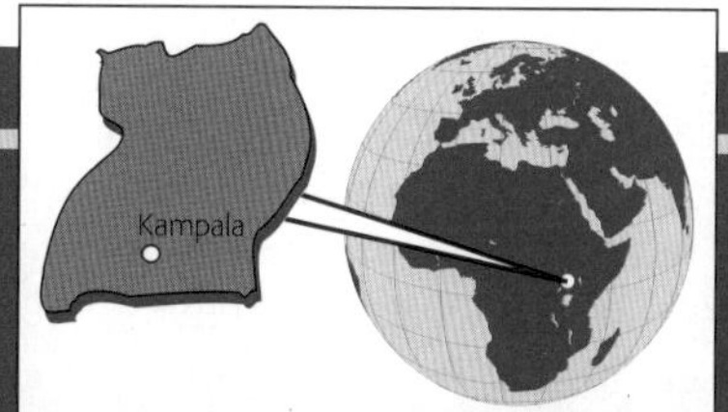

Uganda provides an interesting case of the difficulties and dangers of imposing the Western concept of the state on a region historically ruled in a more traditional and decentralized fashion. If European countries such as France provide us with archetypal examples of statehood, Uganda (like many other sub-Saharan countries) tells us about the concept's limits.

Independence in 1962 bequeathed to the new leaders 'a state groping with rudimentary tasks of broadening its authority over an uncertain territory, against a background of scarce resources and unrefined administration' (Khadiagala, 1995, p. 33). The first post-independence government was an alliance between the Kabaka, serving as ceremonial president, and Milton Obote, a member of the Lango tribe, who was executive prime minister. Obote soon became the dominant figure, with assistance from General Idi Amin, an ethnic Kakwa, only for Amin himself to seize power in 1971.

Amin was a crude military despot who ignored weak state institutions in creating a personal dictatorship that led to the deaths of about 300,000 people. With the economy in decay, Amin was himself removed from power in 1979 by a combined force of Ugandan exiles and an invading army from neighbouring Tanzania. The subsequent state collapse led to violent conflict between competing guerrilla groups, producing another 100,000 deaths and numerous internal refugees. It can surely be argued that had there been no state to begin with, many of these deaths would have been avoided.

Because state collapse lacks the self-limiting character of revolution, it poses the puzzle of whether, how and by whom public authority should be reconstructed. In the absence of established institutions, the key to state rebirth seems to be good domestic leadership.

Uganda illustrates the point. The country began to recover after Yoweri Museveni's National Liberation Army secured control in 1979. Under Museveni's skilled but increasingly authoritarian leadership, and with substantial international support, Uganda's economy recovered considerably. The country is praised by the World Bank as an example of successful development in fragile states (Manor, 2006).

Today, Uganda is best classified as an illiberal democracy – no small achievement given the country's history and continuing low standard of living. Freedom of speech and assembly are at least partially respected.

In 2005, however, parliament abolished a constitutional limit on presidential terms, paving the way for Museveni to win a third term in 2006 with 59 per cent of the vote. Such self-serving constitutional modifications are a sign of a president who stands above, rather than sits beneath, the constitution. Despite the reintroduction of political parties, the president's National Resistance Movement remains pre-eminent, with some harassment of opposition figures and groups. Although the European Union judged that the 2006 elections were generally well-administered and competitive, two FDC supporters were killed by an armed group during the campaign

Self-designation of 'Dada' Amin:

His Excellency President for Life Field Marshal Al Hadj Doctor Idi Amin Dada, VC, DSO, MC, Lord of All the Beasts of the Earth and Fishes of the Sea and Conqueror of the British Empire in Africa in General and Uganda in Particular

Above all, though, Uganda has still to finally resolve the problem of the Lord's Resistance Army (LRA), a violent northern cult whose members prey on the Acholi people, causing many to flee their homes and demonstrating thereby the continuing difficulty experienced by the central government in ensuring its control over all its territory.

Further reading: Keitetsi (2004), Manor (2006).

solely from outside; indeed, aid agencies providing services in a failed state may for that reason inhibit the growth of government (Fukuyama, 2004). It is one thing for external might to overthrow rulers such as the Taliban in Afghanistan and Saddam Hussein in Iraq. It is quite another to secure effective indigenous leadership and to build legitimate national institutions such as an army, a police force, a judiciary, a central bank, government departments, local administration, a tax collection agency and functioning education, transport, energy and health care systems. 'You, the people' is less compelling than 'we, the people'.

The difficulties of state building, particularly from outside, raise a fundamental question: does the effort make sense? Perhaps alternative forms of organization should be permitted to evolve in the developing world, finally ending the West's obsession with the state as a universal institution with secure boundaries.

Certainly, many contemporary 'states' seem to lack the capacity to achieve real autonomy. As many as 45 developing countries possess populations below 1.5 million, surely below the size needed to function with significant autonomy (Commonwealth Secretariat, 1997). Many are quasi-states, pretending to sovereignty and sometimes reduced to cashing in on its value by providing flags of convenience for the disreputable (Jackson, 1990).

In particular, many vulnerable island states possess no resilience to external shocks, no economic diversification, no military force, and limited capacity to participate in international organizations. Perhaps reflecting this reality, Australian-led intervention in the Solomon Islands in 2003 to improve security and policing garnered broad support across the South Pacific, reflecting a desire for a regional leader to rehabilitate what was becoming a bad neighbourhood (Reilly and Wainwright, 2005).

Some specialists on African politics have queried the value of statehood altogether. Clapham (2003, p. 29) suggests that territorial states are an expensive burden in an African setting where most national populations are widely scattered over infertile land. In these conditions, the traditional tribal model of an interdependent group united by a shared ethnic identity may be more appropriate than the imposed Western model of a territorial state governing a united citizenry. Clapham concludes that the project of attempting to restore universal statehood may be a pipe dream.

Similarly, Herbst (2004) invites the West to adopt a more flexible stance in responding to issues of boundaries and secession. In his view, the long-run solution is for the West to overcome its obsession with statehood and to encourage experiments in Africa with new (or old) models of political organization. His view is that when states collapse, we should 'let them fail'.

However, such radical views are not universally shared. In particular, Zartman (1995c, p. 268) argues that 'both the cause and remedy of state collapse relate to socio-political structures within a given sovereign territory and people, not to the shape of the state itself. It is better to reaffirm the validity of the existing unit and make it work.' Perhaps so, but we should remember that statehood developed in response to the conditions of early modern Europe and that the states that exist there today are themselves survivors of a competitive struggle. There is no necessary reason why the form should fit circumstances elsewhere.

Globalization and the state

In this final section, we return to Western states, asking whether the contemporary forces of **globalization** have reduced their autonomy and altered their functioning. Even accepting the blunt nature of the globalization concept, and its differential impact on large and small states, it is still worth asking how international and transnational connections impinge on domestic institutions, politics and policies. In the remainder of this chapter, we explore the overall effects on the state of international organizations, one of the more tangible forms of globalization. We divide our discussion into three parts, looking first at intergovernmental organizations (IGOs), then at regional organizations and finally at non-governmental organizations (NGOs).

Waters (2000) defines **globalization** as 'a process in which the constraints of geography on social and cultural arrangements recede and in which people become increasingly aware that they are receding'.

DEBATE

ARE STATES DINOSAURS WAITING TO DIE?

In his analysis of economic globalization, Ohmae (1995) claimed that in a world of regional markets, states had become 'dinosaurs waiting to die', overwhelmed by unconstrained movements of capital and corporations. Notwithstanding 9/11, the world economy became even more interconnected over the next ten years. In the face of such relentless globalization, are states doomed, even if not yet extinct?

YES

The image of a borderless world, no longer governed by states but patrolled instead by multinational corporations, international organizations and global markets, grew in importance with the expansion not just of trade but also of communications and environmental problems in the final third of the twentieth century.

States, it is argued, are anchored to land but it is now intellectual property that drives growth. Wealth creation comes from creativity, knowledge, software and science, none of which are constrained by borders.

Thus, Guéhenno (1995, p. 7) suggests that 'territory is of dwindling importance' in a weightless world economy where the value of a product bears no relation to its bulk.

In similar vein, Held (2005, p. 1) refers to 'a transformation in the scale of human organization that links distant communities and expands the reach of power relations across the world's regions'.

The argument is not only that traditional *inter*national processes, such as diplomacy, are becoming more intense. It is also that such familiar linkages are now supplemented by *trans*national processes which bypass the state.

Of course, states are not going to disappear altogether; some dramatic licence should be permitted. But globalization is reshaping states, forcing them to compete in the race to attract mobile corporations and skilled labour. States are globalization's servants, not its master.

NO

Growing interconnectedness should be seen as a long-term unfolding, not just as a phenomenon of the last 50 years (Robertson, 1992). Our species succeeded in spreading itself across much of the globe 30,000 years ago. Globalization in this deeper sense bears no particular relationship to states.

We can acknowledge that states are not self-contained silos – but then they never were. When we compare current reality against actual history, rather than against an imaginary world of independent states, we discover that the change initiated by the current phase of globalization is much less dramatic than is often claimed.

We should compare the internet to the telegraph; asylum seeking to the slave trade; and the war on terror to the world wars of the twentieth century.

Even in the contemporary era, globalization is overblown. For instance, most 'world' trade operates within the triad of Europe, the United States and Asia.

In addition, most 'globalization' is really regionalization. Refugees turn first to a country nearby; most multinational corporations only operate regionally; and most efforts at reducing trade barriers are between neighbouring countries (Keohane and Nye, 2000).

The state remains the decisive political actor, with democratic governments still possessing a unique legitimacy. Climate change may indeed be a global problem but who can solve it except states?

ASSESSMENT

The debate on globalization's impact concentrates on larger Western states. Small countries – and the population of most is below five million – have always been massively affected by their external environment. If all modern states really were 'dinosaurs waiting to die', then smaller countries such as Denmark, the Netherlands and New Zealand would have become extinct long ago. After all, their ratios of trade to gross domestic product have long exceeded even the current figures for larger economies such as the United Kingdom and the United States.

Further reading

Held (2005), Keohane and Nye (2000), Robertson (1992), Scholte (2005), Waters (2000).

Intergovernmental organizations

The majority of established states belong to most of the 250 or so **intergovernmental organizations** (IGOs) which now populate the international environment. They include single purpose entities (e.g. the International Telecommunications Union), regional organizations (e.g. the European Union) and universal bodies (e.g. the United Nations). Such bodies are an appropriate response to global problems by an international community lacking a world government. They perform useful functions for states, sharing information and coordinating policies. Everyone gains from a world telephone network and from a sustainable environment. Operating in an informal and flexible manner, with high levels of trust among participants, their distance from immediate democratic pressures may contribute to their efficacy.

> **Intergovernmental organizations** (IGOs) are bodies whose members include states. IGOs are established by treaty and usually operate by consent, with a permanent secretariat.

Our concern here is the impact of IGOs on states themselves. At the very least, belonging to so many IGOs complicates the task of governance. States must arrange to pay their subscriptions, attend meetings, identify their national interests, consult with domestic interest groups, initiate some proposals, respond to others and implement agreements. IGOs bore into the daily activities of national governments, posing a particular challenge for many small states. Even for large countries, IGOs dilute the distinction between domestic and foreign policy, giving an international dimension to many, perhaps most, government activities.

IGOs have affected the balance of forces within national political systems. Specifically, they tend to fragment domestic policy-making. Slaughter, in particular, has emphasised the segmenting effect of public officials communicating with colleagues from other countries. Noting how judges, administrators, regulators, central bankers, legislators, police forces and heads of state 'are all networking with their foreign counterparts', she suggests that

> The state is not disappearing; it is disaggregating into its component institutions. The primary state actors in the international realm are no longer foreign ministries and heads of state but the same government institutions that dominate domestic politics. The disaggregated state, as opposed to the mythical unitary state, is thus hydra-headed, represented and governed by multiple institutions in complex interaction with one another abroad and at home (Slaughter, 2003, p. 190).

In part this effect arises because a club-like spirit develops among ministers in 'their' IGO. For instance, finance ministers – never popular at home – are among friends at meetings of bodies such as the International Monetary Fund. The same applies, except more so, to farmers' groups. As a Dutch minister of agriculture said about the European Union,

> In the Dutch Council of Ministers I met the ministers from the departments, and I had to defend the farmers' interest against other interests, but in the European Council of Ministers [an EU body] I met only other ministers of agriculture, and we all agreed on the importance of agriculture (Andeweg and Galen, 2002, p. 169)

Given such fragmentation within national political systems, we must ask which governing institutions gain, and which lose, from such interdependence. Among the winners are the executive and the bureaucracy (Box 2.6). These bodies provide the representatives who attend IGO meetings and conduct negotiations; they therefore occupy pole positions. The judiciary is also growing in significance as a result of IGO activity, partly because some influential IGOs such as the World Trade

BOX 2.6

The impact of IGOs on national politics: winners and losers

Winners	Losers
Executive	Legislature
Bureaucracy	Parties
Judiciary	

TIMELINE

THE EUROPEAN UNION

The European Union is the world's most developed example of regional integration. It represents a deliberate attempt by European politicians to bring peace to a continent with a long history of war. From modest beginnings in the 1950s, the Union has developed its institutions, acquired considerable policy-making authority, reduced national barriers to trade, established a new currency and broadened its membership.

1951	Treaty of Paris signed by France, West Germany, Italy, Belgium, the Netherlands and Luxembourg. This Treaty set up the European Coal and Steel Community (ECSC) which included a supranational High Authority.
1957	The ECSC members sign the Treaty of Rome, establishing the European Economic Community (EEC) and Euratom.
1965	The Merger Treaty combines the ECSC, EEC and Euratom.
1973	Britain, Denmark and Ireland join the EEC.
1979	The European Monetary System (EMS) is agreed, linking currencies to the European Currency Unit (ECU). First direct Europe-wide elections to the European Parliament.
1981	Greece joins the EEC.
1986	Spain and Portugal join the EEC. Signing of the Single European Act, to streamline decision-making and set up a single market by 1992.
1992	Treaty of Maastricht launches provisions for Economic and Monetary Union (EMU) and replaces the EEC with the European Union (EU) from 1993.
1995	Austria, Finland and Sweden join the EU.
1997	Treaty of Amsterdam extends the Union's role in justice and home affairs and enhances the authority of the European Parliament.
1999	Launch of European Monetary Union (EMU), initially linking 11 national currencies to the euro. Launch of the euro as a virtual currency.
2000	Treaty of Nice agrees on institutional reforms to prepare for enlargement, including a reallocation of member states' voting power and a reduction in the issues requiring unanimity.
2002	The eurozone withdraws national currencies.
2003	Publication of a draft constitutional treaty for Europe.
2004	Cyprus, the Czech Republic, Estonia, Hungary, Latvia, Lithuania, Malta, Poland, Slovakia and Slovenia join the EU.
2005	Referendums in France and the Netherlands reject the constitutional treaty.
2007	Bulgaria and Romania join the EU.

Note: nomenclature of the 'European Union' has varied over time, reflecting institutional and constitutional developments. For a map, see p. 225.

Organization adopt a highly judicial style, issuing judgements on the basis of reviewing cases. In addition, national judges are increasingly willing to use international agreements to strike down the policies of their home government.

As for losers, the most significant is surely the legislature, which may only learn of an international agreement after the government has signed up to it. In some countries, Australia for one, international treaties are an executive preserve, enabling government to bypass the assembly by signing treaties on proposals opposed by parliament. Similarly, 'Europeanization has strengthened the central executive at the expense of parliaments, despite the increased involvement of the latter in EU policy-making' (Börzel and Sedelmeieir, 2006, p. 56).

Political parties, too, seem to have lost ground under pressure from IGOs. Like assemblies, their natural habitat is the state, not the international conference. While party groupings have developed in the EU, these are loose groupings lacking the cohesion and drive of parties operating on the national stage for which they were originally designed.

Regional organizations

Regional bodies are a specific form of IGO in which neighbouring governments join together for common purposes, most often trade. These agreements have multiplied in number and significance since the end of the Cold War as countries which once sheltered under the skirts of a superpower have turned to their neighbours to find a response to international economic pressures.

So how far do regional organizations impact on states? In comparison with at least some IGOs, the answer is very little. Most regional associations are simple free trade areas, with little prospect of institutional development. Their purpose is to secure gains from trade without compromising sovereignty. For that reason, any political impact is likely to be unplanned and indirect.

However, even setting up these free trade areas can cause domestic political controversy, dampening political interest in deeper integration. The North American Free Trade Agreement (NAFTA) is an example. For a 15-year period that began in 1994, NAFTA is seeking to eliminate trade tariffs between two developed states, the USA and Canada, and a developing economy, Mexico. Even though the agreement does not compromise traditional ideas of sovereignty, its establishment has occasioned considerable debate. American unions feared that free trade with Mexico would cause a migration of jobs to low-cost assembly sites on the Mexican side of the border. In a famous phrase, the independent politician Ross Perot referred to the 'great sucking sound' of jobs being pulled down to Mexico. When even simple free trade areas create such debate, attempts at formal political integration between neighbouring countries are likely to be impossible in most circumstances.

Even the European Union, the only developed example of regional integration, illustrates the domestic problems of deepening integration. Take the effort (ultimately successful) to establish a common currency among some member states. German citizens in particular judged that the introduction of the euro in 2002 provided an opportunity for businesses to put up prices, a perception that no doubt reflected traditional national pride in the Deutschmark. As always, the specific, short-term costs of change proved more visible than the general, long-term benefit.

Similarly, the defeat of referendums in France and the Netherlands in 2005 on a proposed constitution for Europe suggests that these electorates do not judge that the benefits of further integration outweigh a further reduction in national sovereignty.

Like other IGOs, most regional organizations lack the legitimacy that only direct election can provide. In contrast to established democracies, they suffer from a democratic deficit which limits their legitimacy and even their visibility to national populations (Dahl, 1999). Thus the European Union may prove to be a false model for the rest of the world. Certainly, it seems unlikely that the turn to economic regions in today's world will result in political regimes of the type established in Europe in the twentieth century. Moving towards a free trade zone does not require political integration.

Non-governmental organizations

As private and unofficial bodies lacking the status offered by a membership of governments, we might expect international non-governmental organizations (NGOs) to exert less influence than IGOs on domestic politics. This conclusion is probably justified, at least for the more powerful states. However NGO impact on post-colonial countries can be considerable. Leading NGOs such as the Red Cross and Médecins Sans Frontières can apply substantial pressure in countries where the international community is already engaged in supplying services as a result of civil war or humanitarian crisis (Adams, 2003).

International non-governmental organizations (usually called NGOs) are private institutions with members or groups drawn from more than one country. Examples include the International Red Cross, Greenpeace and the Catholic Church.

In such conditions, NGOs have become important actors as executors of IGO, especially United Nations, policy. By the mid 1990s, over ten per cent of all public development aid was distributed through NGOs, compared to less than one per cent in 1970 (Weiss and Gordenker, 1996). About ten super-NGOs, including CARE, Save the Children and Oxfam, dominate the distribution of aid in complex emergencies.

In acting as UN subcontractors, NGOs can partially substitute for government. For instance, NGOs coordinated primary education in northern Sri Lanka after civil war started there in 1987. As a channel for distributing aid and implementing associated policy, NGOs possess clear attractions to outside donors: they are more efficient and less corrupt than many domestic governments and they are also more sensitive than armies to local political conditions.

These points mean NGOs possess considerable clout in the least developed countries on which aid is concentrated. Fernando and Heston (1997, p. 8) go so far as to suggest that 'NGO activity presents the most serious challenge to the imperatives of statehood in the realms of territorial integrity, security, autonomy and revenue'. The danger is not only that NGOs inhibit the strengthening of the domestic government but that they become an economic force themselves, offering relatively well-paid jobs to the local population and supplying an injection of demand into the economy. If state-building really is the objective, NGOs – just like an invading army – also need an exit strategy.

Learning Resources for Chapter 2

Next step

Opello and Rusow (2004) is a wide-ranging but accessible historical introduction to the state.

Further reading

Van Creveld (1999) and Pierson (2004) examine the rise of the state but Finer (1997) offers the most monumental history of government. Both Sørensen (2004) and Paul (2004) examine the state's alleged transformation in the contemporary era. Davidson (1992) remains an engaging account of the impact of the state on Africa; see also Hyden (2006, ch. 3) and Jackson (1990) on quasi-states. Collapsed states and state building are covered in Chesterman, Ignatieff and Thakur (2005), Milliken (2003), Rotberg (2004) and Zartman (1995a). On globalization itself, Waters (2000) offers a clear introduction while Lechner and Boli (2003) is a wide-ranging reader. See Slaughter (2004) for emerging styles of world governance. Strange (1994) and the more sceptical Hirst and Thompson (1999) have each generated considerable debate on the autonomy of states in a global economy; see also Weiss (1998).

Internet sources

Europa, European Union
Gateway to the European Union
http://europa.eu

Fund For Peace
Profiles of failed states
http://www.fundforpeace.org/

Global Policy Forum
Useful material on nations and states
http://www.globalpolicy.org/

Human Development Report
Publishes the Human Development Index
http://hdr.undp.org/

Transparency International
Publishes the Corruption Perceptions Index
http://www.transparency.org/

Third World Network
Development and the Third World
http://www.twnside.org.sg

World Bank
Ranks countries by income and ease of doing business
http://www.worldbank.org

World Trade Organization
Administers the rules of international trade
http://www.wto.org

Chapter 3
Democracy

We live in an era of democracy; for the first time in history, most people in the world live under tolerably democratic rule. This fact reflects the dramatic transformation of the world's political landscape in the final quarter of the twentieth century. Over this short period, the number of democracies more than doubled – from less than 40 to more than 80. Democracy expanded beyond its core of Western Europe and former settler colonies to embrace Southern Europe (e.g. Spain), Eastern Europe (e.g. Hungary), Latin America (e.g. Brazil), more of Asia (e.g. Taiwan) and parts of Africa (e.g. South Africa). This expansion began before, but was accelerated by, the collapse of communism (Figure 3.1).

Now that the Cold War has passed, and the principle of unconditional state sovereignty has come into question, the promotion of democracy has become a more explicit objective of the West. International law, which previously had little to say on the subject, has begun to address the topic. The United States, in particular, has talked the talk: 'It is the policy of the United States to seek and support democratic movements and institutions in every nation and culture, with the ultimate goal of ending tyranny in our world' (White House, 2006).

As democracy continues to spread, so it becomes more varied. Understanding the forms taken by democracy in today's world is therefore a central task in comparative politics. We begin by exploring the origins of democracy in the fifth century BC in Athens. There, the Greeks invented a model of direct self-government which continues to influence contemporary discussions of deliberative democracy in particular. We then consider the emergence of representation as the device enabling a measure of democracy to be achieved in large states. Finally, we examine the two main forms of representative democracy in today's world – liberal and illiberal – and the waves of democratization leading to them.

Direct democracy

The core principle of democracy is self-rule; the word itself comes from the Greek *demokratia*, meaning rule (*kratos*) by the people (*demos*). In its richest sense, democracy refers not to the election of the rulers by the ruled but to the denial of any separation between the two. The model democracy is a form of self-government in which all adult citizens participate in shaping collective decisions in an environment of equality and open deliberation. In a direct democracy, state and society become one.

Democracy was born in ancient Athens. Between 461 and 322 BC, Athens was the leading *polis* (city-community) in ancient Greece. *Poleis* were small independent political systems, typically containing an urban core and a rural hinterland. Even though Athens only comprised about 40,000 citizens, it was one of the larger examples. Especially in its earlier and more radical phase, the Athenian *polis* operated on the democratic principles summarized by Aristotle (Box 3.2). This ethos applied to all institutions of government within the community. All citizens could attend meetings of the assembly, serve on the governing council and sit on citizens' juries. Because ancient Athens continues to provide the archetypal example of direct democracy, we will discuss its operation in more detail (Figure 3.2).

History has judged there to be no more potent symbol of direct democracy than the Athenian *Ekklesia* (People's Assembly). Any citizen aged at least 20 could attend assembly sessions and there address his peers; meetings were of citizens, not their representatives. The assembly met around 40 times a year to settle issues put before it, including the recurring issues of war and peace which were central to the *polis*'s prospects and prosperity. In Aristotle's phrase, the assembly was 'supreme over all causes' (1962 edn, p. 237); it was the sovereign body, unconstrained by a

Figure 3.1 The number of democratic countries in the world, 1946–2003

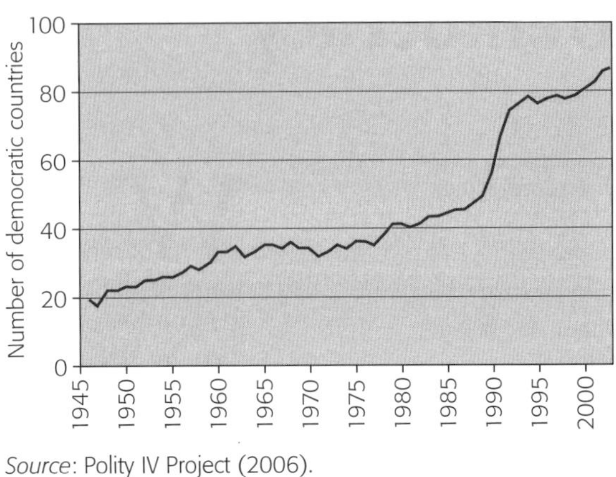

Source: Polity IV Project (2006).

BOX 3.1

Forms of democracy

	Definition
Direct democracy	The citizens themselves assemble to debate and reach decisions on matters of common interest.
Deliberative democracy	A perspective on democracy which emphasizes the value of public discussion among free, equal and rational citizens in giving legitimacy to decisions and in enhancing their quality.
Representative (indirect) democracy	Citizens elect a parliament and, in presidential systems, a chief executive. These representatives are usually held to account at the next election.
Liberal democracy	A version of representative democracy in which the scope of democracy is limited by constitutional protection of individual rights, including freedom of assembly, property, religion and speech. Free, fair and regular elections are based on universal (or near universal) suffrage.
Illiberal democracy	A version of representative democracy in which rulers, once elected, govern with few limits and little respect for individual rights. To assist re-election, the president ensures favourable media coverage and often harasses political opponents, precluding any need to falsify the count.

formal constitution or even, in the early decades, by written laws. As far as we can tell, meetings were lengthy, factional and vigorous, with the talking – and hence probably the subsequent show of hands – dominated by influential orators known as demagogues (Dahl, 1989, p. 21).

The assembly did not exhaust the avenues of participation in Athens. Administrative functions were the responsibility of an executive council consisting of 500 citizens aged over 30, chosen by lot for a one-year period. Through the rotation of members drawn from the citizen body, the council was regarded as exemplifying a principle of community democracy: 'all to rule over each and each in his turn over all'. Hansen (1991, p. 249) suggests that about one in three citizens could expect to serve on the council at some stage in their life, an astonishing feat of self-government entirely without counterpart in modern representative democracies.

A highly political legal system provided the final leg of Athenian democracy. Juries of several hundred people, again selected randomly from a panel of volunteers, decided the lawsuits which citizens frequently brought against those considered to have acted against the true interests of the *polis*. The courts functioned as an arena of accountability through which top figures (including generals) were brought to book.

Thus the scope of the Athenian democracy was extraordinarily wide, providing an enveloping framework within which citizens were expected to develop their true qualities. For the Athenians, politics was intrinsically an amateur activity, to be undertaken by all citizens in the interest of the community at large as well as to enhance their own development. Nevertheless, Athens's little democracy did possess serious flaws:

BOX 3.2

Aristotle's characterization of democracy

- All to rule over each and each in his turn over all;
- Appointment to all offices, except those requiring experience and skill, by lot;
- No property qualification for office-holding, or only a very low one;
- Tenure of office should be brief and no man should hold the same office twice (except military positions);
- Juries selected from all citizens should judge all major causes;
- The assembly should be supreme over all causes;
- Those attending the assembly and serving as jurors and magistrates should be paid for their services.

Source: Aristotle (1962 edn), book VI.

Figure 3.2 The direct democracy of ancient Athens

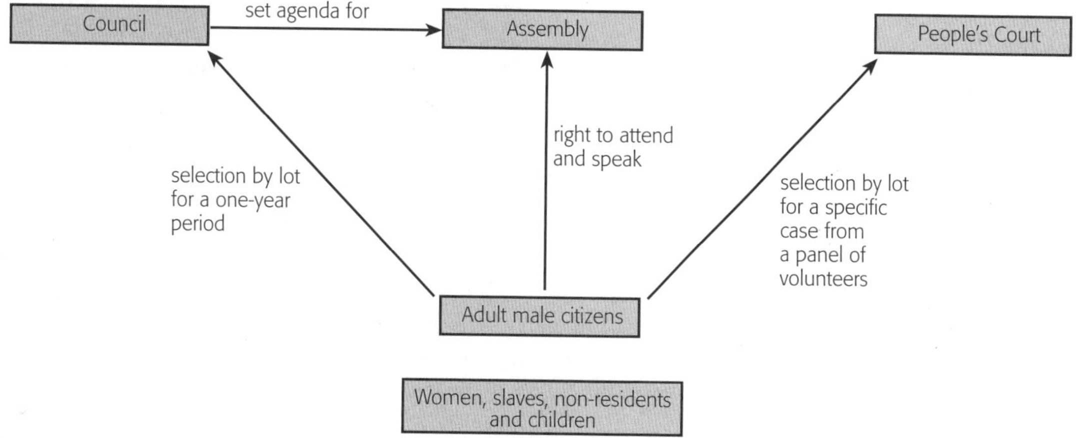

Note: citizenship was a birthright which could not normally be acquired by other means.

- Citizenship was restricted to men whose parents were themselves citizens. So most adults – including women, slaves and foreign residents – were excluded. Women played no significant public role and critics allege that slavery provided the platform from which the citizen elite could make time for public affairs (Finley, 1985).
- Participation was not in practice as extensive as the Athenians liked to claim. Most citizens were absent from most assembly meetings even after the introduction of a payment for attending.
- Athenian democracy was hardly an exercise in lean government. A management consultant would surely conclude that the system was time-consuming, expensive and over-complex, especially for such a small society. Its applicability to a modern world in which people are committed to paid work, and the affluence resulting therefrom, is questionable.
- The principle of self-government did not always lead to decisive and coherent policy. Indeed, the lack of a permanent bureaucracy eventually contributed to a period of ineffective government, leading to the fall of the Athenian republic after defeat in war.

Perhaps Athenian democracy was a dead-end in that it could only function on an intimate scale which precluded expansion and, worse, proved vulnerable to larger predators. Finer (1997, p. 368) adopts just such a position: 'The *polis* was doomed politically if it expanded and doomed to conquest if it did not. It had to succumb and it did'. Yet the Athenian democratic experiment prospered for over 100 years. It provided a settled formula for rule and enabled Athens to build a leading position in the complex politics of the Greek world. Athens proves that direct democracy is, in some conditions, an achievable goal.

Certainly, Finer (1997, p. 371) was correct in acknowledging the Athenian contribution to Western politics: 'The Greeks invented two of the most potent political features of our present age: they invented the very idea of citizen – as opposed to subject – and they invented democracy'.

Deliberative democracy

Although modern democratic government is representative rather than direct, the Greek tradition still finds echoes in the current concern with deliberative democracy. Because of this link, we will explore the contemporary notion of deliberative democracy here.

The German philosopher Jürgen Habermas is the key figure in this theoretical movement. He suggests that we should view democracy as a method of communication. Specifically, democratic legitimacy arises from free, public and rational discussion among

BOX 3.3

Deliberative democracy in America: Leib's proposal for a popular branch of government

- 525 citizens are to be selected at random for compulsory service in the new popular chamber. A fresh sample to be drawn for each topic;
- The chamber is to divide into 35 panels of 15 people;
- Each panel is to discuss the same topic face-to-face over several days;
- Topics are to emerge from an initiative signed by 10 per cent of the population or by a majority vote in the House of Representatives and Senate;
- Panels are to conclude their deliberations with a secret vote;
- Transcripts are to be published but anonymity is to be respected;
- If a two-thirds majority is achieved when the votes of all panels are combined, the proposal is to become law unless vetoed either by the House and Senate or by the courts;
- An administrative agency is to support the panels by, for example, summarizing materials. Some members of this agency are to be elected; others are to be chosen by political parties.

Source: Adapted from Leib (2004).

competent citizens deliberating in a context of openness and equality (Habermas, 1975). This ideal situation is expected to inculcate civic virtue in the manner hoped for, and perhaps partly achieved, by the Athenian *Ekklesia*. Cohen (1997, p. 79) summarizes the deliberative tenet: 'Outcomes are democratically legitimate if and only if they could be the object of a free and reasoned argument among equals'.

The underlying idea is straightforward. In an open debate, arguments based on private interests are soon recognized and discounted; public reason involves appeal to the public good. Free and sincere discussion delivers reasons on which all can agree, allowing the stronger argument rather than the stronger speaker to prevail. Authentic debate also enables public opinion to be formed and not merely expressed, thus providing a crucible for developing the collective will. In such conditions, a consensus should emerge about what is truly in the public interest, with reason triumphing over interests. Even if deliberation does not yield consensus, voting should follow the debate rather than serving as a substitute for it. In common with the ancient Greeks, deliberative democrats encourage the weighing of judgements among debaters rather than the crafting of compromises between interests.

Unfortunately, few advocates of deliberative democracy offer specific guidance on institutional arrangements to secure their objective. Indeed, some critics allege that, just as women, slaves and non-citizens were excluded from the *Ekkelsia*, so the voices of similar groups today will remain unheard in public discourse as long as society continues to be based on inequalities such as race, class and education. As the Greeks discovered, large meetings are always vulnerable to domination by mere rhetoric (Fontana, Nederman and Remer, 2004). So creating the conditions in which a debate can be truly free and open is by no means straightforward (Meehan, 1995).

Clearly, however, the theory points in the direction of discussion in small groups, perhaps building on formats such as university seminars and town meetings. In a world of large states, such aspirations may seem utopian. However, Leib (2004) has suggested a method of integrating deliberation among citizens within the existing framework of representative democracy. His proposed scheme – based on the United States but, he claims, with wider applicability – repays examination (Box 3.3).

Leib proposes the addition of an entirely new popular branch to the United States government. This popular chamber would consist of citizens selected at random so, unlike the existing chambers, its deliberations would truly articulate the voices of the people, albeit with a rather large sampling error. The new body would not however control its own agenda; rather, topics would be set by popular initiative or a reference from the existing chambers. Any proposal supported by a two-thirds majority in the popular house would become law unless vetoed by the legislature or the courts (Box 3.4).

Box 3.4

A range of democratic decision rules

Majority (simple majority)	More than half of those voting
Absolute majority	More than half of those entitled to vote
Plurality	The largest number of votes but not necessarily a majority
Qualified majority	More than a simple majority: typically, two thirds
Weighted majority	A majority after adjusting votes for differences in voting power
Concurrent majority	More than one majority required: for example, a double majority of voters and states in a federation
Unanimity	All to agree, assent or at least acquiesce

Why will Leib's scheme fail to progress? Leaving aside the difficulty of amending an entrenched constitution, the answer seems to be that deliberation is only one value among several we want to incorporate into our democratic designs. America's constitution has proved fit for purpose in providing a framework for encouraging compromises between interests and in contributing to stability. This success creates an understandable bias against radical reform: 'if it ain't broke, don't fix it'. In addition, a new chamber would further complicate policy-making in a system already fully loaded with checks and balances. Also, in contrast to the Ekklesia, only a trivial proportion of a population of about 300 million would be a member of the popular chamber even over a lifetime. In that respect, the new body would be a mechanism of representative rather than direct democracy.

Representative democracy

At national level, all contemporary democracies are **representative** rather than direct. The democratic principle has transmuted from self-government to elected government, with barely a nod to ancient tradition. To the Greeks, the very idea of a representative democracy would have seemed preposterous: how can the people be said to govern themselves if they are ruled by a separate government? As late as the eighteenth century, the French philosopher Jean-Jacques Rousseau propounded the same point: 'the moment a people gives itself representatives, it is no longer free. It ceases to exist' (1762, p. 145).

> A **representative** stands for another person, group or entity. A flag represents a nation, a lawyer represents a client and elected politicians represent their electors, districts and parties.

Yet as large modern states emerged, so too did the requirement for a new form of democracy. In contrast to the little democracy of Athens, any modern version had to be compatible with the much larger states found in today's world. In addition, citizenship ceased to be an elite status as it extended to the vast majority of the adult population, including women.

One of the first authors to graft representation onto democracy was Tom Paine (1737–1809), a British-born political activist who experienced both the French and the American revolutions. In his *Rights of Man* (1791/2, p. 180), Paine wrote:

> The original simple democracy . . . is incapable of extension, not from its principle, but from the inconvenience of its form. Simple democracy was society governing itself without the aid of secondary means. By ingrafting representation upon democracy, we arrive at a system of government capable of embracing and confederating all the various interests and every extent of territory and population.

Scalability has certainly proved to be the key strength of representative institutions. The conventional wisdom in ancient Athens was that the upper limit for a republic was the number of people who could gather together to hear a speaker. However, modern representative government allows massive populations (such as a billion Indians and 300 million Americans) to exercise some popular control over their rulers. And there is no upper limit. In theory, the entire world could become one giant representative democracy. To adapt Tom Paine's phrase, representative government has indeed proved to be a highly convenient form.

As ever, intellectuals were on hand to validate this thinning of the democratic ideal. Prominent among them was Joseph Schumpeter (1883–1950), an Austrian-born economist who became an academic in the United States. Schumpeter conceived of democracy as nothing more than party competition: 'Democracy means only that the people have the opportunity of refusing or accepting the men who are to rule them'. He wanted to limit the contribution of ordinary voters because he was sceptical of their political capacity:

> The typical citizen drops down to a lower level of mental performance as soon as he enters the political field. He argues and analyzes in a way that he would recognize as infantile within the sphere of his real interests. He becomes a primitive again (1943, p. 269).

Reflecting this jaundiced view, Schumpeter argued that elections should not even be construed as a device through which voters elect a representative to carry out their will; rather, the role of elections is simply to produce a government. From this perspective, the elector becomes a political accessory, restricted to selecting from broad packages of policies and leaders prepared by the parties. Representative democracy is merely a way of deciding who shall decide, a system far removed from the discussion in Athens's assembly, Habermas's debating forum and Leib's popular branch:

> The deciding of issues by the electorate [is made] secondary to the election of the men who are to do the deciding. To put it differently, we now take the view that the role of the people is to produce a government . . . And we define the democratic method as that institutional arrangement for arriving at political decisions in which individuals acquire the power to decide by means of a competitive struggle for the people's vote (Schumpeter, 1943, p. 270).

Liberal and illiberal democracy

Although all modern democracies are representative, the diffusion of democracy around the world has created a requirement for an additional distinction between liberal and illiberal democracies.

Like representative democracy itself, **liberal democracy** is a compromise. Specifically, it seeks to integrate the authority of democratic governments with simultaneous limits on their scope. By definition, liberal democracy is limited government. The goal is to secure individual liberty, including freedom from unwarranted demands by government. In this way, the population can be defended against its rulers and minorities can be protected from democracy's inherent risk: tyranny by the majority (Held, 2006).

In place of the all-encompassing scope of the Athenian *polis*, liberal democracies are governments of laws rather than men. Elected rulers are subject to constitutions that usually include a statement of individual rights. Should the government become overbearing, citizens can in theory use domestic and international courts to uphold their rights. In these respects, a liberal democracy is democracy disarmed. At the same time, rights to free speech and association permit political opinion to form and to receive expression through political parties, leading some authors to claim that 'without liberty, there can be no democracy' (Beetham, 2004, p. 65).

Liberal democracy is a settlement between individual liberty and collective politics which reflects the key issues involved in its emergence. These issues included the desire to entrench religious freedom and to secure property rights against encroachment by the poor. These elements were especially important to the design of the American system of government, the most liberal (and perhaps the least democratic) of all the liberal democracies.

With the collapse of communist and military rule in the final decades of the last century, **illiberal democracy** (also called electoral or semi-democracy) became a more common and recognized form. In this type of regime, the elected ruler or rulers pay little attention to individual rights, at least when dealing with political opponents. Ballot stuffing is avoided but democracy does not extend far beyond the election itself. Even the election outcome is conditioned by the ruler's influence over the media and by the use of state resources to favour his own organization, factors which exert their influence even before the formal campaign gets underway. The result is what Huntington (1991, p. 306) describes as 'democracy without turnover and competition without alternation'. Hence illiberal democracy is less democratic – as well as less liberal – than its liberal cousin. If, as Przeworski (1991, p. 10) maintains, liberal democracy 'is a system in which parties lose elections', illiberal democracy is a system in which they don't. Rather, change at the top usually results from a constitutional limit on tenure or the occasional resignation.

The illiberal character of these regimes emerges most clearly once an election is won. The government, typically dominated by a strong president, shows only a limited sense of constitutional restraint; such concepts as fair play and a loyal opposition barely register. O'Donnell (1994, p. 59) describes the format: 'Whoever wins election to the presidency is thereby entitled to govern as he or she sees fit, constrained only by the hard facts of existing power relations and by a constitutionally limited term of office'. Illiberal democracy authorizes power without limiting it.

Illiberal democracy is based on a powerful leader rather than strong institutions. In this respect, the

DEBATE

IS LIBERAL DEMOCRACY CEASING TO BE DEMOCRATIC?

'What we need in politics today is not more democracy but less', says Zakaria (2003, p. 248). It might seem surprising to question the scope of liberal democracy in this way. But even as democracy spreads around the world, so too does its reach quietly diminish within its Western heartland. As judges and regulators acquire more authority, so fewer decisions come to be made directly by elected politicians. So is the principle of self-government becoming ornamental, with governance by expert regulators replacing government by the people?

YES

Democracy was a political compromise allowing different classes to live together in peace. The working class secured the vote (the democratic element) but the rich secured their property (the liberal element). Now that this class war has abated, the battle of the parties which provided the lifeblood of democracy is over.

In its place, we observe a gradual resurgence of decisionmaking by unelected experts and regulators. With privatization, the scope of the market continues to grow, limiting the room for political and hence democratic influence over the economy.

Judges and regulators make more and more policy decisions, providing the stable, predictable environment beyond a democratic system based on elections. Who today really believes that noisy debate in parliament or on the campaign trail is the optimal way to solve complex problems?

Blinder (1997), for example, contrasts short-term decision-making in the White House with the higher quality of policy made by unelected officials at the Federal Reserve. Many other countries (including the UK) have now taken control of interest rates away from elected politicians, aware of the dangers of electoral manipulation.

Furthermore, a global economy, and even international organizations, provide an inhospitable ecology for democracy, which thrives only at the national level.

In short, Western politics is evolving a post-democratic style in which decisions come to be based on the merits of a case rather than the counting of votes.

NO

The instinctive belief that those who are subject to a decision should be involved in its making is universal. The principle of democracy, if not always its practice, is widely supported by contemporary electorates (Norris, 1999a).

Liberalism without democracy would wholly lack legitimacy. Even Alan Greenspan, Chairman of the United States Federal Reserve, 1984–2006, said that 'in a democracy, you cannot have central banks either fully or partly disassociated from the electoral process' (Greenspan, 1994, p. 253).

As education continues to expand, so voters' interest in broad political issues will grow. A sophisticated and educated electorate will insist on a political voice that will not be silenced by judges, experts and regulators.

As recent American elections show, politics will increasingly take the form of a debate over values rather than the economy – and the nature of value conflicts is that they must be resolved through democratic means, not by technical experts. There is no scientific solution to such issues as war, abortion and same-sex marriage. Political issues require political resolution.

Democracy is evolving rather than declining. Interest in politics remains high as does membership of specialist single-issue groups.

In any case, democracy is deepening, not fading. New avenues for democracy have developed such as referendums, elected mayors, regional elections and party primaries (Dalton, Scarrow and Cain, 2004).

ASSESSMENT

This debate encourages a distinction between the number of democracies (which is at an all-time high) and their depth or quality (which may be falling). Even more important, though, is the emergence of the question, 'what should democracies decide?' The notion of liberal democracy provided an answer to that question which helped to dissipate earlier conflicts over religious freedom and private property. But political philosophers have yet to work out how to balance democratic and regulatory authority.

Further reading

Dalton, Scarrow and Cain (2004); Inglehart (1997); Zakaria (2003).

format resembles authoritarian rule more than liberal democracy. Rather than serving as a representative agent, the president – or, less often, prime minister – plays the part of personal ruler, taking care of the people's needs and claiming their respect, deference and support in exchange. Having elected a saviour, the voters are expected to cheer from the stands, only entering the political field at their own risk. In view of this 'poisoned partnership' between ruler and ruled, some commentators prefer to speak of electoral or competitive authoritarianism rather than illiberal democracy (Korosteleva, 2004; Schedler, 2006). Yet if we set the bar too high, we may find it crashing down around us (Box 3.5).

Because the judiciary in an illiberal democracy is under-resourced, it is unable to enforce the individual rights documented in the constitution. The law is used selectively, as a tool of power. Political opponents are subject to detailed legal scrutiny but supporters find the law rarely intrudes on their activities ('for my friends, everything; for my enemies, the law', said Getúlio Vargas, President of Brazil, 1930–45, 1951–54). The state intervenes in the workings of the market, with political connections influencing economic rewards; politics occupies more space in an illiberal democracy than in a liberal one. And, in contrast to most authoritarian regimes, the leader often does provide effective governance, thus earning as well as manipulating his popular support.

Illiberal democracy is common in new democracies. Zakaria (2003, p. 61) notes how 'since the fall of communism, countries round the world are being governed by regimes like Russia's that mix elections

BOX 3.5

Is this country a liberal or an illiberal democracy? Which country is it?

- About 20 million adults living in this country are not entitled to vote;
- At most elections in this country, most of those entitled to vote abstain;
- Members of the legislature manipulate electoral boundaries to secure their own re-election, and the continued strength of their own party;
- Incumbents use public and private resources to ensure their re-election and are rarely defeated; challengers are systematically disadvantaged;
- The law protects the existing major parties against newcomers;
- The presidential candidate coming second in votes is sometimes deemed to have won the election;
- The president has no personal electoral accountability for up to half his tenure;
- The constitution of this country has never been ratified by vote of the people;
- A president of this country once said, 'In the working out of a great national program which seeks the primary good of the greater number, it is true that the toes of some people are being stepped on and are going to be stepped on. But these toes belong to the comparative few who seek to retain or to gain position or riches or both by some short cut which is harmful to the greater good.'

The country is, of course, the United States. Nonetheless, the USA is a clear example of a liberal democracy. The moral is this. Just as we do not expect a liberal democracy to be perfectly democratic, neither should we set an unrealistic standard in judging whether a country such as Russia qualifies as an illiberal democracy.

Note: 'In 2004, the voting-age population included 3.2 million ineligible felons and former felons and an estimated 17.5 million noncitizens' (Bardes, Shelley and Schmidt, 2006, p. 312). Second-term presidents cannot stand for re-election. The passage above from President Franklin Roosevelt was quoted by Vladimir Putin in his address to Russia's Federal Assembly in 2006. Putin added, 'These are fine words and it is a pity that it was not I who thought them up'.

and authoritarianism – illiberal democracy'. The form is particularly common in democracies with continuing poverty; with ethnic, religious or economic divisions; and facing real or imagined external threats. For instance, many Latin American countries are characterized by extreme inequality, with the urban poor seeking salvation through a strong, populist leader. Asian illiberal democracies such as Malaysia and Singapore combine an overriding commitment to further economic development with ethnic divisions between Chinese and Malays (Bourchier, 2006). Chávez in Venezuela and Putin in Russia claim to be engaged in projects to restore national prestige in a hostile international environment. In these circumstances, a national father figure or dominant party can be presented as a protector against external threats, a bulwark against domestic disintegration and an engine of development. The head, it is claimed, must be allowed to rule the body politic.

How widespread is illiberal democracy? According to Karatnycky (2006), 30 countries with competitive elections could only be classified as 'partly free' in 2005. Such countries included populous Islamic states such as Indonesia, Nigeria and Turkey. Indonesia's illiberalism, for instance, arises from a strong military presence in politics, weak media, a corrupt judiciary and limited protection of human rights, especially for minorities. Many other examples come from new democracies in Africa, Latin America and Asia.

To the extent that illiberal democracies are personal in character, they might be expected to be unstable in the long run. Huntington (1991, p. 137), for example, claims 'this half-way house cannot stand'. Yet we cannot wish illiberal democracies out of existence by just deeming them to be transitional. So far illiberal democracy seems to have provided a stable method of governing poor and unequal societies, particularly since the end of communism rendered blatant dictatorship less defensible. Once set, illiberal democracy can be a strong amalgam, not least in an Islamic setting where liberal democracy is equated with Western permissiveness. Crouch (1996, p. vii) shows how Malaysia's 'repressive-responsive' regime 'provides the foundation for a remarkably stable political order'. Similarly, Borón (1998, p. 43) argues that in the 'faulty democracies' of Latin America, democracy 'endures but does not consolidate'. When one strong leader departs, he may just be replaced by another.

Writing on sub-Saharan Africa, Herbst (2001, p. 359) judges that 'it is wrong to conclude that African states are travelling between democracy and authoritarianism simply because a majority of them belong to neither category. Rather, the current condition of African states could well prevail for decades'.

The heart of the matter is perhaps that illiberal democracy is a tacit, but stable, compromise between domestic elites and international organizations. Illiberal democracy is usually sufficient for the ruling elite to meet the conditions of aid set by the World Bank, the IMF and donor governments. While these international bodies may welcome democracy, in practice they give higher priority to economic reform. Non-fraudulent elections, even if neither completely free nor fair, are regarded as sufficient tests of democracy. Such reasoning led Case (1996, p. 464) to conclude that illiberal democracy is not 'a mere way station on the road to further democracy'.

Waves of democratization

When and how did modern democracies emerge? Here we review the historic transition to democracy, looking not just at the emergence of liberal democracy in such countries as the USA and the UK but also at the more recent transitions to both liberal and illiberal democracy. As with the phases of decolonization discussed in the preceding chapter, so too did democracies emerge in a series of distinct **waves** (Box 3.6).

First wave

The earliest liberal democracies emerged in the 'first long wave of democratization' between 1828 and 1926. During this first wave nearly 30 countries established at least minimally democratic national

> A **wave** of democratization is a group of transitions from nondemocratic to democratic regimes that occur within a specified period of time and that significantly outnumber transitions in the opposite direction during that period' (Huntington, 1991, p. 15).

BOX 3.6

Huntington's three waves of democratization

	Period	Examples
First	1828–1926	Britain, France, USA
Second	1943–62	India, Israel, Japan, West Germany
Third	1974–91	Southern and Eastern Europe, Latin America, parts of Africa

Note: The first wave partly reversed between 1922 and 1942 (e.g. in Austria, Germany and Italy) and the second wave similarly between 1958 and 1975 (e.g. in much of Latin America and post-colonial Africa). Many such reversals have now themselves reversed.

Source: Huntington (1991). For some criticisms of the wave approach, see Grugel (2002), pp. 32–7.

institutions, including Argentina, Australia, Britain, Canada, France, Germany, the Netherlands, New Zealand, the Scandinavian countries and the United States. However, some **backsliding** occurred as fledgling democracies were overthrown by fascist, communist or military dictatorships during Huntington's 'first reverse wave' from 1922 to 1942 (Linz and Stepan, 1978).

However, democracy did consolidate in the earliest nineteenth-century democratizations, including the United States and the United Kingdom. We will examine these two transitions in more detail, not least because they resulted in some subtle but persistent differences in how liberal democracies can operate.

The emergence of democracy in the United States was rapid but it was a transition nonetheless. The republic's founders had thought of political leadership in non-democratic terms, as the duty of a disinterested, leisured gentry. They favoured an elite-led republic, not an Athenian-style democracy. But the idea that citizens could only be represented fairly by those of their own sort quickly gained ground in the states, supported by the egalitarian spirit of a frontier society. The suffrage soon extended to nearly all white males. Of course, some groups had to wait until the twentieth century for the full franchise. Women were not offered the vote on the same terms as men until 1919 and the black franchise was not fully realized until the Voting Rights Act of 1965 (Dahl, 2001). In that sense America's democratic transition was completed only 40 years ago.

Backsliding occurs when a democratic transition is reversed, in whole or especially in part.

Today, the USA gives us the clearest picture of a liberal democracy in which the liberal dimension is entrenched by design. The Founding Fathers wanted, above all, to prevent a dictatorship of any kind, including tyranny by the majority. To prevent any government – and especially elected ones – from acquiring excessive power, the constitution set up an intricate system of checks and balances between institutions (Figure 3.3, p. 56). Because power is fragmented, the danger of any particular faction manipulating public authority for private ends is much reduced. Even the administration itself experiences difficulty in passing reforms which are widely recognized to be necessary but are opposed by an organized minority. The constitution placed government under law above government by the people. In this way, the liberal dimension of America's democracy emerged victorious over its representative aspect. Only during periods of external threat, including post-9/11, do individual liberties come under threat (Lyon, 2003).

In Britain, by contrast, the outcome of the transition was a less liberal implementation of democracy. By the eighteenth century, the power of the monarch had been checked by the growing authority of parliament. However, the rights of the individual citizen were never stated as clearly as in the USA. The widening of the suffrage also occurred more gradually in the United Kingdom, with each step easing the fears of the propertied classes about the dangers of further reform (Table 3.1, p. 57). As the House of Commons acquired democratic legitimacy, so both the monarchy and the non-elected House of Lords retreated into the background.

Yet where American democracy diffuses power across institutions, British democracy emphasizes

COUNTRY PROFILE

MEXICO

Form of government ■ a federal and presidential republic.

Legislature ■ the 500 members of the Chamber of Deputies are elected for a single three-year period and the 128 members of the Senate for a six-year tenure.

Executive ■ the president, directly elected for a non-renewable six-year term, heads both the state and the government, choosing the members of the Cabinet.

Judiciary ■ headed by the Supreme Court of Justice, the judicial system mixes American constitutional principles with the civil law tradition. In practice, both judicial independence and police enforcement of law have been weak.

Electoral system ■ 300 members of the Chamber represent single-member districts; the other 200 are elected by a list system of proportional representation. The Senate also operates a mixed electoral system.

Party system ■ dominated by the Institutional Revolutionary Party (PRI) until the 1990s. The conservative National Action Party (PAN), which formed part of Vicente Fox Quesada's successful Alliance for Change in the 2000 elections, retained the presidency in 2006 with a narrow and disputed victory over the left-wing Revolutionary Democratic Party (PRD).

Population (annual growth rate):	107.4m (+1.2%)
World Bank income group:	upper middle
Political Rights score:	2
Civil Liberties score:	2
Human development index (rank/out of):	53/177
Freedom of the press index (rank/out of):	95/194
Ease of doing business index (rank/out of):	43/175

Note: For meaning and sources of scales and indexes, see p. xvi. In all cases a score and rank of 1 is 'best'.

Although **MEXICO** achieved independence from Spain as early as 1821, the decisive moment in its history was the civil conflict that erupted in 1910 against a ruling oligarchy established by President Díaz. His powerful elite was supported by foreign capital and the military but provided few opportunities for an emerging middle class. The revolution was led by younger elements of this class though peasants and workers were eventually drawn in. The initial outcome was the constitution of 1917, a left-wing document which limited the authority of the Catholic Church, but the revolution's radical spirit was best expressed under the presidency of Lázaro Cárdenas in the 1930s. His administration undertook radical land reform, breaking up many large estates and granting land to over a million peasants.

Cárdenas also established the system of rule built round the Partido Revolucianario Institucional (PRI). Founded in 1929 in an attempt to rein in regional political machines, the PRI was transformed into a structured patronage organization capable of mobilizing and channelling mass support. The party was organized into three sectors, representing workers, peasants and 'popular' (mainly public sector) groups. Leaders of these sectors distributed favours to their members, creating incentives to continue supporting the party. As a ruling party, the PRI also used the considerable perks of office to further reward its clients. PRI rule also included a harder edge: it repressed opposition and manipulated election results, becoming 'one of the world's leading manufacturers of electoral fraud' (Schedler, 2005, p. 9).

Gradually, the PRI's left-wing principles weakened as it established a 'perfect dictatorship' based on its entrenched patronage networks. Especially in the 1950s and 1960s, the PRI seemed to have found the recipe for stable rule by a dominant party. However, three problems recurred:

- Continuing poverty for those excluded from the party's network, reflected in periodic revolts;
- Increasing opposition from the expanding urban middle class created by economic growth;
- Economic crises which sometimes occurred when the PRI placed its political objectives before sound economic policy.

Further reading: Crandall, Paz and Roett (2005), Lawson (2004).

SPOTLIGHT

Democracy in Mexico

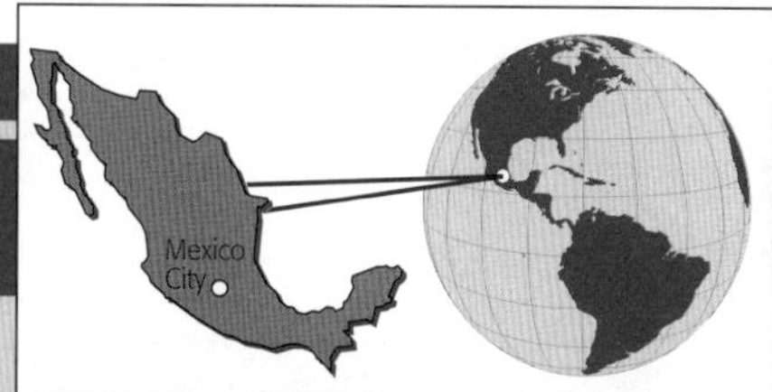

'Yes, it can be done,' shouted the crowds in Mexico City as they celebrated the downfall of the PRI after the presidential election of 2000. After 70 years in power, the PRI not only lost a presidential election for the first time but also ceased to control either house of the national legislature. The world's oldest ruling party had suffered an historic reverse, subsequently confirmed by its poor performance in 2006. This peaceful transfer of power decisively confirmed Mexico's status as a new democracy. For students of comparative politics, Mexico offers a remarkably successful example of democratization. How did this transition unfold?

With the political effectiveness of the PRI machine decaying, Carlos Salinas (president, 1988–94) initiated economic reforms, including privatizing major firms and opening the economy to international competition, not least through NAFTA. In contrast to the Soviet Union, where Gorbachev introduced political reform before economic change, in Mexico economic liberalization preceded political change.

As the PRI lost direct control of economic resources, so its powers of patronage declined and voters became free to support opposition parties, especially in the cities. Independent trade unions began to form outside the enveloping embrace of the PRI.

Eventually, the PRI itself introduced political changes that served to enliven a moribund opposition. By the 1990s, the party no longer felt able to manipulate election results. In 1997, it lost its majority in the Chamber of Deputies after relatively fair elections.

The next and decisive election, in 2000, was overseen by a powerful independent election commission, characterized by Lawson (2004, p. 146) as 'worthy of emulation by many established democracies'. The growing authority of the Federal Electoral Institute, backed by a specialized election count, sends a clear message that the era of PRI vote-rigging in federal elections has ended.

So the PRI's fall was partly self-induced: its leaders recognized that the tools needed to guarantee their party's continued grip on power were hindering the country's further development.

Mexico's gradual move to democracy seems to have avoided what Baer (1993, p. 64) described as 'the dilemma of all reforms from above, particularly in ageing regimes: how to avoid unleashing a revolution from below'. But it remains to be seen how far, and at what speed, democracy will deepen in Mexico. Vicente Fox proved to be a more effective campaigner than president; in power, he sustained economic stability but put through few reforms of what remains a highly regulated economy.

Mexico's continuing problems – peasant revolts, urban squalor, drugs, crime, corrupt judges, incompetent police and inadequate education – mean that it is premature to regard the country as a wholly secure and consolidated liberal democracy alongside the USA and Canada, its NAFTA partners. A close and controversial presidential election in 2006, when the defeated candidate of the left refused to accept the result, showed that the electoral process is not yet fully authoritative. As in South Africa, however, progress should be judged not against an ideal standard but rather against what came before.

Election to the Chamber of Deputies, 2006

	Votes (%)	*Seats*
National Action Party (PAN)	34.6	206
Party of the Democratic Revolution (PDR)	29.8	160
Institutional Revolutionary Party (PRI)	28.4	121
Others	7.2	13

Source: Adapted from Psephos (2006).

Further reading: Rubio and Purcell (2004), Shirk (2005).

Figure 3.3 Liberal democracy: checks and balances in American government

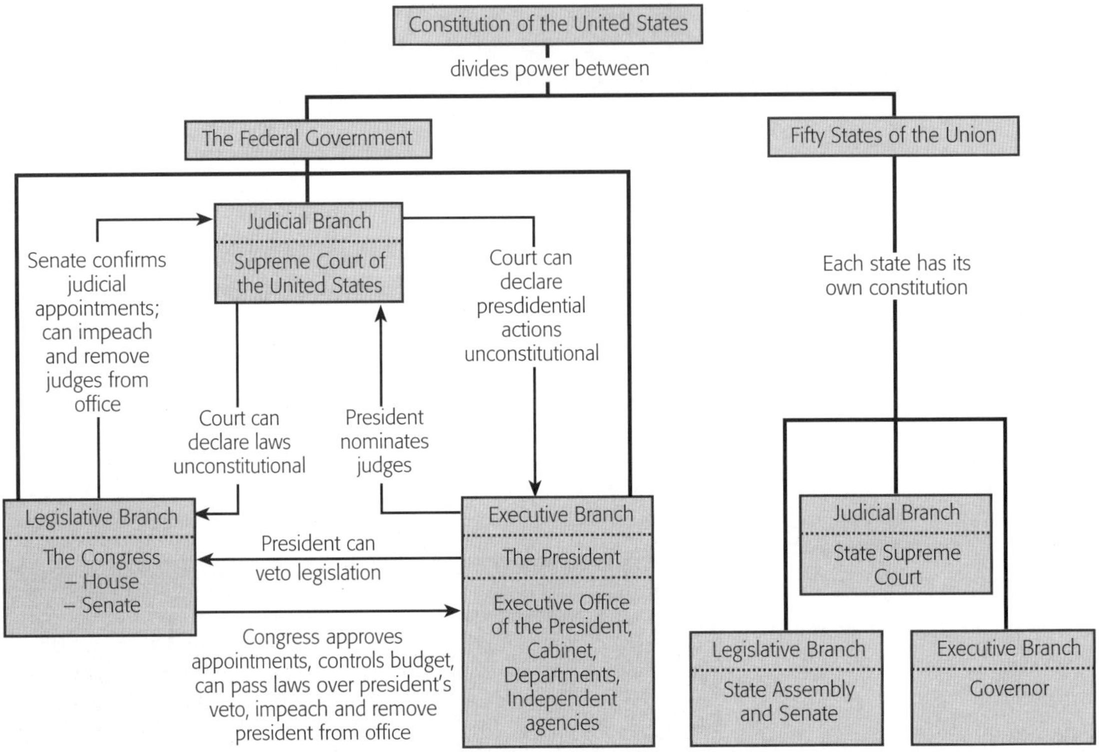

Constitution of the United States
divides power between
The Federal Government
Fifty States of the Union
Judicial Branch
Supreme Court of the United States
Senate confirms judicial appointments; can impeach and remove judges from office
Court can declare presdidential actions unconstitutional
Court can declare laws unconstitutional
President nominates judges
Legislative Branch
The Congress
– House
– Senate
President can veto legislation
Congress approves appointments, controls budget, can pass laws over president's veto, impeach and remove president from office
Executive Branch
The President
Executive Office of the President, Cabinet, Departments, Independent agencies
Each state has its own constitution
Judicial Branch
State Supreme Court
Legislative Branch
State Assembly and Senate
Executive Branch
Governor

the sovereignty of parliament. The electoral rules normally ensure a secure majority of seats for the leading party, which then forms the government. This ruling party retains firm control over its own members in the House of Commons, enabling it to ensure the passage of its bills into law. In this way, the hallowed sovereignty of Britain's parliament is leased to the party in office. Except for the government's sense of self-restraint, the institutions that limit executive power in the United States – including a codified constitution, the separation of powers and federalism – are absent.

Far more than the United States, Britain exemplifies Schumpeter's model of democracy as an electoral competition between organized parties. 'We are the masters now', trumpeted a Labour MP after his party's triumph in 1945; similar thoughts must have occurred to many Labour MPs after their party's equally emphatic victory in 1997. Certainly, the country's judiciary has now become more active, stimulated in part by the European Court of Justice. But from a comparative perspective, a winning party is still rewarded with an exceptionally free hand. Britain is one of the less liberal of liberal democracies

Second wave

Huntington's second wave of democratization began in the Second World War and continued until the 1960s. Like the first wave, some of the new democracies created at this time did not consolidate. For example, elected rulers in several Latin American states were quickly overthrown by military coups.

But established democracies did emerge after 1945 from the ashes of defeated dictatorships, not just in West Germany but also in Austria, Japan and Italy. These post-war democracies were introduced by the victorious allies, led by the USA, acting with the support of partners in the countries concerned. Such second-wave democracies did establish firm roots, helped by an economic recovery which was itself nourished by American aid. During this

Table 3.1 The British electorate as a percentage of the adult population, 1831–1931

Year	Electorate (percentage of population aged 20+)
1831	4.4
1832	First Reform Act
1832	7.1
1864	9.0
1867	Second Reform Act
1868	16.4
1883	18.0
1884	Third Reform Act
1886	28.5
1914	30.0
1918	Vote extended to women over 30
1921	74.0
1928	Equal Franchise Act
1931	97.0

Note: In 1969, the voting age was reduced from 21 to 18.

Source: Adapted from Dahl (1998), figure 2.

second wave, democracy also consolidated in the new state of Israel and the former British dominion of India.

How did these second-wave democracies differ from those of the earlier wave? Their liberal traditions were somewhat weaker as representation through parties proved to be the stronger suit. Parties had gone unmentioned in the American constitution but by the time of the second wave they had emerged as the leading democratic instrument. Like many recent constitutions, Germany's Basic Law (1949) goes so far as to codify their role: 'The political parties shall take part in forming the democratic will of the people'. In that respect, second-wave constitutions are built in the Schumpeter mould. However, in several cases effective competition was reduced by the emergence of a single party which dominated national politics for a generation: Congress in India, the Christian Democrats in Italy, the LDP in Japan and Labour in Israel.

Third wave

The third wave of democratization was a product of the final quarter of the twentieth century – within the memory of most people alive today. Its main and highly diverse elements were:

- The ending of right-wing dictatorships in Southern Europe (Greece, Portugal and Spain) in the 1970s;
- The retreat of the generals in much of Latin America in the 1980s;
- The collapse of communism in the Soviet Union and Eastern Europe at the end of the 1980s.

This third wave transformed the global political landscape. The predominance of democracy resulting from this wave provides an inhospitable environment for those non-democratic regimes that survive. Even in sub-Saharan Africa, presidents subjected themselves to re-election (though rarely to defeat). With the end of the Cold War and the collapse of any realistic alternative to democracy, the European Union and the United States became more encouraging of democratic transitions (while keeping a close eye on their shorter-term interests). Thus, although the third wave peaked in the early 1990s, some countries have continued to experience democratic or at least popular uprisings in the twenty-first century: for instance, Georgia's Rose Revolution in 2003 and Ukraine's Orange Revolution the following year (Wilson, 2006).

Within the third wave, the Southern European group provides the most secure cases of **consolidation**, aided by membership of the European Union and economic development. These same factors also encouraged democratic deepening in Eastern Europe, at least in countries seeking to join the European Union. Elsewhere, including much of Latin America and Africa, many democratic latecomers have not yet fully consolidated, if indeed they are to do so at all. Indeed, the category of illib-

> A democracy has **consolidated** when it provides an accepted framework for political competition. Huntington (1991, p. 266) suggested a two turnover test: that is, consolidation occurs when each of the two main sides has given up power to the other through an election. But Przeworski's broader definition (1991, p. 26) has proved to be more useful: 'Democracy is consolidated when . . . a particular system of institutions becomes the only game in town and when no-one can imagine acting outside the democratic institutions'.

eral democracy is becoming a more plausible perspective on many third-wave regimes. As the euphoria of transition fades, so the assumption that consolidation of liberal democracy is just a matter of time begins to wear thin (Carothers, 2002).

Reasonably competitive elections are one thing; a consolidated liberal democracy is quite another. Enforcing legal restraint on state power, protecting civil rights, establishing uncorrupt and effective bureaucracies, creating a market economy and imposing democratic control over the military and the security services are long-term tasks. As Pehe (2004, p. 41) writes, 'Qualities such as tolerance, a preference for open dialogue and respect for minorities cannot be conjured into being by even the best administered democratic procedures'.

Even over the medium term, the inheritance from the old regime is bound to limit progress. After all, ruling communist parties and military councils had brooked no interference from the judiciary and paid no heed to constitutions, including statements of human rights. Many such countries had no tradition of individual rights or formal restraints on rulers even before the emergence of communist and military dictatorships. In such conditions, an illiberal democracy is an unsurprising outcome.

Lower levels of affluence, often combined with highly visible inequalities, are particularly important. As Vanhanen (1997) notes, such conditions favour neither the diffusion of power resources nor the development of mutual toleration and compromise which foster the consolidation of liberal democracy. In addition, a long research tradition holds that economic well-being is the key to a stable liberal democracy. In *Political Man* (1960, pp. 48–9), for instance, Lipset famously concluded that 'the more well-to-do a nation, the greater the chances that it will sustain democracy'. Following Aristotle, Lipset believed that a large middle class opposed to extremism was most conducive to democracy.

More recent research confirms the correlation between affluence and stable democracy, despite exceptions such as poor but democratic India. Marks and Diamond (1992, p. 110) seem to be fully justified in describing the connection between affluence and democracy as 'one of the most powerful and stable relationships in the study of comparative national development'. Wealth, widely diffused, helps a liberal democracy to take root while an established liberal democracy itself allows a market economy to flourish. Yet clambering on board this virtuous circle remains a difficult assignment for countries with no tradition of either democratic politics or market economics.

Learning Resources for Chapter 3

Next step

Dahl *et al.* (2003) is a wide-ranging collection on the nature, conditions, procedures and impact of democracy.

Further reading

Dahl (1989, 1998) offers lucid accounts of democracy. The 1989 book is more advanced, the 1998 volume more introductory. Other overall assessments include Arblaster (2002) and Held (2006). For Athens, see Finley (1985) for an introduction and Hansen (1991) for more detail. Deliberative democracy is a more difficult and theoretical literature; see, for instance, Habermas (1978). In addition to Leib (2004), applied works include Mutz (2006), O'Flynn (2006) and Parkinson (2006). On illiberal democracy, O'Donnell (1994) set the scene; for more recent assessments, see Carothers (2002), Ottaway (2003), Schedler (2006), Zakaria (2003) and the *Journal of Democracy* generally. Democratization spawned an outstanding literature: Huntington (1991) and O'Donnell, Schmitter and Whitehead (1986) were influential while Pridham (1995) is a collection of classic articles.

Internet sources

Freedom House
Widely-used country ratings of democracy, civil liberties and the press
http://www.freedomhouse.org/

Democracy Coalition Project
Seeks open democratic societies around the world
http://www.demcoalition.org/2005_html/home.html

Direct Democracy, University of Geneva
An interdisciplinary approach to the study of direct democracy
http://c2d.unige.ch/

Journal of Democracy
Accessible scholarly articles on the curent position of democracy around the world
http://www.journalofdemocracy.org/

National Endowment for Democracy
'Supporting freedom around the world'
http://www.ned.org/

Rights & Democracy
Seeks to develop democratic practices, institutions and culture at national and regional levels
http://www.ichrdd.ca/site/

Chapter 4

Authoritarian rule

'The study of politics in **authoritarian** countries should be more valued by comparative scholars,' comments Posusney (2005, p. 2). And the reason is straightforward: 'non-democratic government, whether by elders, chiefs, monarchs, aristocrats, empires, military regimes or one-party states, has been the norm for most of human history' (Brooker, 2000, p. 1). As late as 1981, Perlmutter (p. xi) could still claim that 'the twentieth century is the age of political authoritarianism'. Certainly that brutal century will be remembered as much for the dictatorships it spawned – including Hitler's Germany, Stalin's Russia, Mao's China and Pol Pot's Cambodia – as for the democratic transitions at its close.

Studying non-democracies remains far more than a historical exercise. Ten of the forty-five largest countries by population are still governed by authoritarian means (Table 4.1). Several of these are of international significance. China is already one of the world's largest economies. Saudi Arabia provided most of the 9/11 terrorists. Pakistan and Uzbekistan became important allies of America as George W. Bush launched his war on terror. Iran's investment in nuclear technology projected the country to the centre of world politics in 2005. Despite generally low living standards, non-democratic countries control most of the world's remaining oil, with Saudi Arabia and Iran to the fore. Compared with most democracies such states possess younger and faster-growing populations (Figure 4.1). Geographically, most authoritarian states are located in an arc running through North Africa, the Middle East and much of Asia. This location overlaps, albeit imperfectly, with the Islamic crescent (Map 4.1, p. 64).

We should not assume that all authoritarian states place total, unlimited power in a despot who seeks to control the whole population through fear and surveillance. Even in the twentieth century, totalitarian regimes demanding controlled participation by the people in support of the supposed transformative goals of the supreme leader were the exception rather than the rule. Elements of the totalitarian method can still be found, particularly in the widespread use of the secret police for monitoring potential opposition. But with the possible exception of Islamic theocracies, totalitarian regimes are rarely observed today.

Most non-democracies, past and present, are authoritarian rather than totalitarian. That is, the rulers seek to maintain their own control (and increase their wealth) by limiting mass participation rather than by mobilizing the population. Ordinary people are unlikely to experience the knock on the door as long as they keep away from politics. Rulers operate within unspoken limits, recognizing the need to strike deals with other power holders in business, the church and the regions. Typically, government takes the form not of a single dominant leader but rather of an elite group such as a military council, with considerable internal jockeying. Ideology and

Authoritarian rule is a broad category, used here to cover any form of non-democratic rule. Some authors use the term in a more restricted sense, to distinguish authoritarian regimes from totalitarian states which sought total penetration of society in an attempt, notional or real, at transformation (Linz, 2000).

Table 4.1 The ten largest authoritarian states by population

	Population, million (annual growth rate)	Form of rule	World Bank income group	Oil reserves	Military spending	Corruption
China	1,306 (+0.6%)	Communist party	Lower middle	High	High	Medium
Pakistan	162 (+2.1%)	Civilianized military	Low	Medium	High	High
Vietnam	83 (+1.0%)	Communist party	Low	High	Medium	High
Egypt	77 (+1.7%)	Presidential	Lower middle	High	High	Medium
Iran	68 (+1.1%)	Contested theocracy	Lower middle	High	High	Medium
Burma	46 (+0.8)	Military junta	Low	High	Medium	High
Sudan	40 (+2.6%)	Presidential dictatorship (military links)	Lower middle	Medium		High
Algeria	32 (+1.2%)	Presidential (strong military influence)	Lower middle	High	High	Medium
Uzbekistan	27 (+1.7%)	Presidential dictatorship	Low	Medium	High	High
Saudi Arabia	26 (+2.2%)	Royal family	High	High	High	Medium

Note: The table shows the ten largest countries by population of those classified by Freedom House as 'not free' in every year, 2001–05. The Democratic Republic of Congo is excluded (in transition). High, medium and low designations for military spending (as a share of gross domestic product), proven oil reserves and perceived corruption are obtained by dividing into thirds the rank orders given in CIA (2006) and Transparency International (2005). Data are from 2006 or earlier.

indeed policy is often absent. In such a situation, as perhaps in some totalitarian cases, rulership is an uneasy combination of formally unlimited authority with considerable political vulnerability.

Since non-democratic leaders stand above the law, the constitutional architecture is roughly built and is an uncertain guide to political realities. Laws are vague and contradictory, creating a pretext for bringing any chosen troublemaker to court. Special courts, often in the form of military tribunals, are often used for sensitive cases. Parliaments and the judiciary are under-resourced, unprofessional and ineffective. Civil rights are poorly respected and the state often requires private organizations to be licensed. The absence of constitutional constraint leads to callous treatment of the powerless, including minority groups, non-nationals, prisoners and women. The absence of a clear legal framework to protect private property rights is one reason why authoritarian rule is often associated with economic stagnation. The price of the rulers securing a large slice of the pie is that the pie itself fails to grow.

Inherited monarchies apart, the absence of a clear succession procedure is a central weakness of authoritarian regimes, providing much of their political dynamic. Because competitive elections do not provide a mechanism for refreshing the leadership, authoritarian leaders may continue in post until well past their sell-by dates. For this reason, a decline into personal despotism is an inherent danger of authoritarian regimes – though, as Brooker (2000, p. 130) observes, 'Degeneration into personal rule is common among dictatorships, particularly among party regimes, but is far from being inevitable'. A

Figure 4.1 Young dictatorships, old democracies (per cent of population aged under 15, 2006)

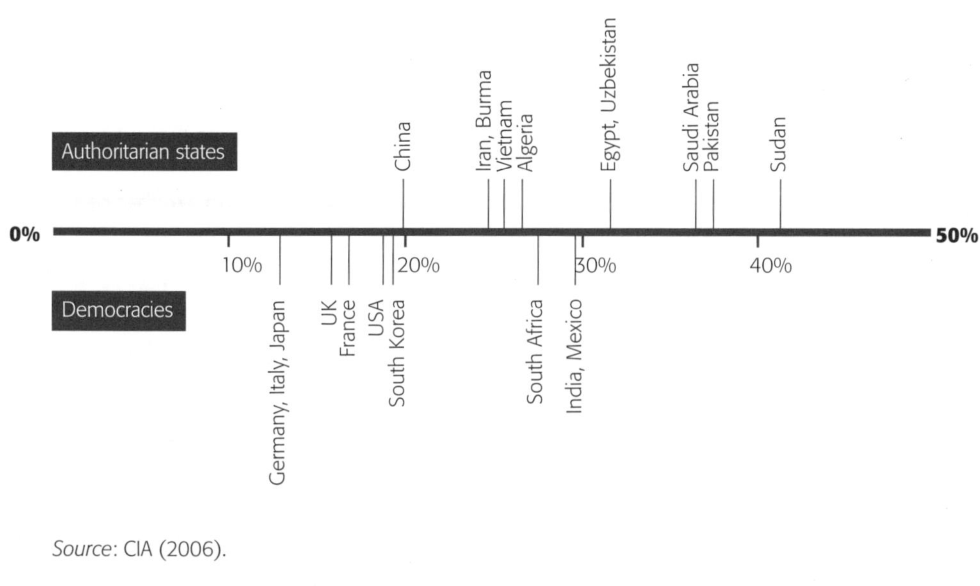

Source: CIA (2006).

more important consequence of uncertain succession is that authoritarian rulers can be removed by upstarts at any time, meaning that they must devote constant attention to shoring up their position.

Identifying how authoritarian leaders respond to these inherent political uncertainties brings us to the essence of non-democratic rule. Leaders rely on control of three key resources: the military, patronage and media. First, authoritarian rulers maintain a strong military and security presence. To sustain their position, they need to be perceived as willing to use this resource. The massacre of pro-democracy demonstrators in Tiananmen Square in Beijing in 1989 goes unmentioned in the Chinese media but, even today, its message is still understood. Similarly, Bellin (2005, p. 26) suggests that 'In the Middle East and North Africa, it is the stalwart will and capacity of the state's coercive apparatus to suppress any glimmers of democratic initiative that have extinguished the possibility of transition'.

High spending on the armed forces – often made possible by natural resource revenues – is typical of authoritarian states. Such investment buys off potential opposition, permits foreign adventures and provides the means for suppressing domestic dissent. Even when the military does not itself rule, it still provides a key support base for the political executive. Lavish treatment of the armed forces is therefore inevitable. Authoritarian regimes lack the separation of military and political spheres which characterizes liberal democracy (Feaver, 1999).

Second, authoritarian rulers maintain their position through an unofficial patronage network in which other power holders are incorporated by providing them with resources (such as control over jobs and access to money-making opportunities) which they can distribute, in turn, to their own supporters. In this way, allegiance to one's immediate patron, and indirectly to the regime, becomes the key to a successful career. These patron–client pyramids extend throughout society, providing a web of allegiances which overcome the public–private divide. As long as the clients are politically sound, their patrons will ignore shady behaviour, a fact which helps to explain why most authoritarian regime are corrupt. Institutions are weak but pragmatic alliances are strong.

This allocation of resources such as jobs, contracts and investment through private patronage leads to substantial misallocation of capital, a weak banking sector and reduced foreign investment. But as long as rulers continue to control the key economic commodity (such as oil), they can carry on purchasing political loyalty.

Map 4.1 The ten largest authoritarian states by population

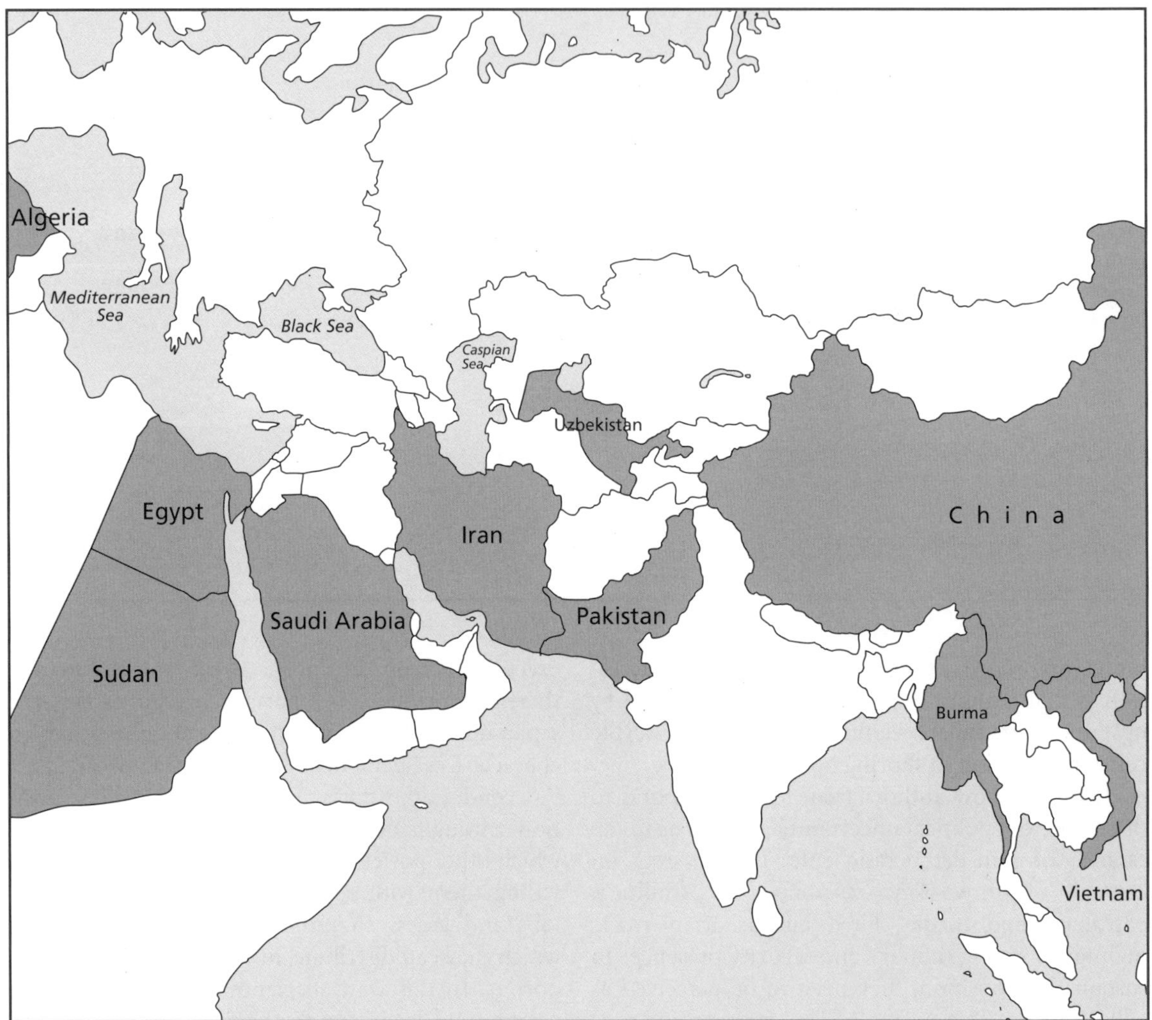

Third, the media are subject to close scrutiny. Communist and fascist states claimed they would use the mass media to build a new and improved human being, fully committed to the regime's objectives. Contemporary authoritarian rulers have more modest goals. They rest content with ensuring favourable media coverage of their own achievements while criticizing or ignoring their opponents. Censorship can be justified by catch-all offences such as threatening the dignity and effectiveness of the state. It is notable that even as the Chinese Communist Party introduced market mechanisms to many parts of its economy, it did not privatize the mass media (Esarey, 2006).

So authoritarian politics is typically driven by fear and vulnerability. The result is a repertoire of control mechanisms in which politics comes before economics and obedience before initiative. Communication is opaque, trust is lacking, government spending is misused, corruption is endemic, laws are ignored and foreign investors are scared away. In many cases, the outcome is a static society, an underperforming economy and a cynical population. In the long run, such a configuration may be a poor recipe for regime stability. Still, as the English economist John Maynard Keynes said in 1923, 'This long run is a misleading guide to current affairs. In the long run, we are all dead'.

The main forms taken by authoritarian rule are shown in Box 4.1. These are pure types; many contemporary authoritarian regimes are a mixture. For instance, an army general may take the post of president or the president may rule through a one-party system. Even so, we will use the scheme shown in the box to organize this chapter. We will proceed broadly historically, starting with regimes that belong, if not always exclusively, to the last century: communist and fascist states, personal dictatorships and military government. We will then examine in turn regimes based on a non-communist, non-fascist party; on a royal family, on organized religion; and – not least – on the presidential office itself.

Communist states

Unlike most authoritarian regimes, the totalitarian governments of the twentieth century were based on ideologies of transformation. Supposedly in pursuit of radical goals, communist and fascist regimes developed unprecedented mobilization and control of mass populations. The word 'totalitarian' emerged in the 1930s in an effort to capture this new and self-consciously modern form of centralized dictatorship. The term remained popular in the **Cold War**, perhaps as a way of linking communist regimes with disgraced fascism (Gleason, 1995). Here we discuss communist party states, and particularly the Soviet Union, leaving fascism to the next section.

> The **Cold War** refers to the competition between the United States and the Soviet Union which lasted from the late 1940s to the Soviet Union's collapse in 1991. In this era, the superpowers sought support wherever they could find it, showing little concern over an ally's internal politics.

Rise and fall

The 1917 October Revolution in Russia signalled the international advent of a regime, an ideology and a revolutionary movement which sought to overthrow the capitalist democracies of the West. Although communism failed to become a governing force in the affluent West, communist power did expand dramatically in Eastern Europe and Asia. The Union of Soviet Socialist Republics (USSR) – effectively a new Russian empire – was formed in 1924, extending from Ukraine in the west to the central Asian republic of Kazakhstan in the east. By area, the USSR became the largest country in the world. After 1945, Eastern European countries such as Poland and Romania became satellite territories of this new empire. Communism spread beyond the USSR to encompass other countries, such as China, North Vietnam and Cuba (*see* Timeline, p. 69). Until the decisive collapse of the communist order in the late 1980s and early 1990s, 23 regimes claiming Marxist inspiration ruled more than 1.5 billion people: about one in three of the world's population (Holmes, 1997, p. 4).

In seeking to understand communist rule, we should note the sharp contrast between ideology and practice. In his theoretical writings, Karl Marx (1818–83) had envisaged an equal, classless and stateless utopia in which goods would be distributed from each according to their ability to each according to their need. The state would be converted 'from an organ superior to society to one completely subordinate to it'. But in arriving at this golden age, Marx (1875) acknowledged that a temporary period of 'dictatorship of the proletariat' would be required:

> Between capitalist and communist society there lies the period of the revolutionary transformation of the one into the other. Corresponding to this is also a political transition period in which the state can be nothing but the revolutionary dictatorship of the proletariat.

Practical revolutionaries quickly seized on this rather vague observation. In particular, the Russian revolutionary Vladimir Lenin (1870–1924) developed the notion of a vanguard party. Lenin's proposition was that the Communist Party possessed a deeper understanding of the true interests of the working class than did the workers themselves. Accordingly, the party must place itself in the vanguard of the communist movement, leading the phase of dictatorship while the workers' revolutionary consciousness matured under the party's tutelage. Thus we arrive at an ironic position in which an ideology aimed at ending the existence of all classes is held to justify the creation of a new, if supposedly temporary, ruling class.

In power, of course, ruling 'communist' parties

BOX 4.1

Forms of authoritarian rule

	Definition	Examples
Communist states today	The communist party monopolizes political power but now allows party members, and others, to acquire private wealth.	China, Vietnam
Fascist state	An anti-liberal state which sought national renewal by aiming to rally people beyond an all-powerful leader. Never fully implemented.	Italy (Mussolini)
Personal despot	A single individual rules though fear and rewards, relying on a personal security force to maintain power.	Dominican Republic (Trujillo), Haiti (François Duvalier)
Military government	Government by the armed forces, often ruling through a junta comprising the leader from each branch.	Burma
Other party-based regimes	Rule by a single party, often combined with a strong president.	Many African states in the post-independence era. Pre-invasion Iraq under the Ba'ath Party.
Royal family	A ruling king emerges from the royal family, with other family members in key political and military posts.	Kuwait, Saudi Arabia
Theocracy	A rare form of rule in which religious leaders rule directly.	Iran
Ruling president	A president dominates politics (and the media), keeping opponents off-guard and the opposition marginalized. Power may rest with the particular leader but is still exercised through the presidency.	Uzbekistan

dominated all sections of society, wholly contradicting Marx's aspiration that society would come to prevail over the state. Lenin's view that the workers must be forced to be free simply resulted in no freedom whatever. Communist regimes were strongly authoritarian, brooking no opposition, stage-managing elections, acting above the law, rewriting constitutions, determining all major appointments to the government, controlling the media and spying on their populations.

The state, far from disappearing as anticipated by Marx, became an enveloping embrace. Economies were brought under public control as part of the push to industrialize; the elaborate five-year plans produced in the Soviet Union were undoubtedly the most ambitious, detailed and comprehensive attempts at economic planning the world has ever seen. Under state socialism, the party controlled and the government implemented – hence the compound term 'party state'.

This new form of dictatorship snuffed out independent social organization, creating a cultural wasteland of distrust in which true political beliefs could only be expressed safely within the family (and sometimes not even there). Not only was active opposition suppressed but explicit support – in the form of attendance at demonstrations, party-led meetings and elections – was required, particularly in the early decades of communist rule. This insistence on active if ritual support is one factor distinguishing totalitarian from merely authoritarian regimes.

As communist states retreat into history, we should be careful to avoid stereotyping their characteristics. Communist regimes varied among themselves and also over time. In parts of Eastern Europe, Poland for example, communist leaders governed with a lighter touch than in the Soviet Union. Similarly, communist states grew less totalitarian as they matured. In the Soviet Union, for instance, Nikita Khrushchev, the new party secretary, famously denounced Stalin's excesses in a secret speech to the party elite in 1956. Under Khrushchev's more moderate leadership, terror ceased to be a routine political tactic and the Soviet Union became, in Linz's phrase (2000, p. 5), post-totalitarian.

Yet far from stabilizing the party's control, the attempt to provide more orderly governance eventually proved to be communism's undoing. State-led planning was incapable of matching the advanced products and services found in the West. 'Advanced socialism' turned out to be a contradiction in terms. Communism reached its dead-end as the system rotted from within. As the party lost its mission, its language became wooden and predictable; in the end it ruled only because it ruled.

When Mikhail Gorbachev became General Secretary of the Soviet Communist Party in 1985, his intention was modernization but the outcome was dissolution. In Eastern Europe, communist rule fell apart in 1989 once the new Russian leader made clear that the USSR would no longer intervene militarily to protect the puppet rulers of its satellite states. The following year, the Soviet Union itself dissolved into 15 constituent republics. In Russia, by far the most important of these republics, the Communist Party was quickly outlawed, a humiliating fate for what had been the most powerful party on earth (Brown, 2004).

BOX 4.2

The totalitarian syndrome

Friedrich and Brzezinski's classic definition (1956, p. 9) identified six features of the totalitarian syndrome:

- An official ideology aimed at perfecting a new and final state of mankind;
- A single ruling party led by a dictator;
- Control by the secret police, based on terror;
- Monopoly of the mass media;
- Monopoly of armed force (no American 'right to bear arms');
- Central control and direction of the entire economy.

Communist states today

But what of those countries which continue to sail under the communist banner? With the exception of Castro's regime in Cuba (not without influence in Latin America), the surviving communist governments are clustered in Asia, far from the democratic hubs (Box 4.3). China, Vietnam and Laos were traditionally poor and agricultural societies in which communist rulers have, over the last two decades, loosened their control over the economy while retaining a firm grip on political power. They remain viable one-party states.

Whatever its theoretical persuasiveness, the reform strategy has delivered substantial if uneven growth, particularly in China and Vietnam. By unleashing entrepreneurial initiative, ruling parties have averted the inertia which led to the fall of communism in the Soviet Union and Eastern Europe. As a result, Asian communist parties can still expound the nationalist agenda of catch-up with the West and, partly for this reason, their position remains intact and indeed largely unchallenged. As its Marxist legacy fades,

BOX 4.3

Communist party states, 2006

	Official title	Communist rule established	Comment
China	People's Republic of China	1949	The Communist Party has retained tight political control while leading substantial and successful economic reform.
Cuba	Republic of Cuba	1961	A personal despotism led by Fidel Castro. Raúl Castro may succeed his elder brother.
Laos	Lao People's Democratic Republic	1975	An impoverished country with a partly liberalized economy and an ageing party leadership.
North Korea	Democratic People's Republic of Korea	1948	A totalitarian regime, based on a personality cult around the 'Dear Leader' Kim Jong-il, son of the 'Great Leader' Kim Il-sung.
Vietnam	Socialist Republic of Vietnam	1976*	As in China, the Communist Party has initiated economic reform while retaining a political monopoly.

* North Vietnam: 1954.

China may provide a model of development without democratization which may prove attractive to other low-income authoritarian states.

Historically, China is the most importance case of Asian communism. However, communism in the People's Republic has always possessed distinct national characteristics. Power has certainly been exerted through the Chinese Communist Party (CCP) but the party itself has been controlled by elite factions which have demonstrated considerable flexibility, especially in embracing the language of nationalism rather than class. As Mao Zedong advised his followers in 1938, 'we must discard our dogmatism and replace it by a new and vital Chinese style and manner, pleasing to the eye and to the ear of the Chinese people' (Gasster, 1976, p. 117). Park (1976, p. 148) judges that 'the success of Chinese communism lies primarily in its emphasis on nationalism'. The revolution itself was led by the People's Liberation Army as much as by the CCP, leading to Mao's famous observation that 'political power grows out of the barrel of a gun'.

Yet corruption, cronyism and cynicism remain endemic. As a result of reform, China possesses not so much a market economy as a political economy in which party members, local bureaucrats and army units are on the make alongside more conventional entrepreneurs. Commercial rationality in China is less focused on identifying market opportunities than on creating strong ties to local officials that will in turn guarantee those opportunities.

This reform ensemble has delivered early stage industrialization which may prove to be more successful than the Soviet Union in meeting the demands of an advanced economy and a well-

TIMELINE

COMMUNISM'S KEY DATES, 1848–2006

1848	Publication of the *Communist Manifesto*.
1917	October Revolution in Russia.
1922	Stalin becomes General Secretary of the Soviet Communist Party.
1928	Soviet Union introduces its first five-year plan.
1946–9	Communist rule established in Eastern Europe.
1949	Communist rule established in China.
1953	Stalin dies.
1954	Communist rule recognized in North Vietnam.
1956	Khrushchev denounces Stalin and tells the West, 'History is on our side. We will bury you'.* Soviet Union suppresses Hungarian uprising.
1959	Communist rule established in Cuba.
1966	Mao Zedong launches Cultural Revolution in China.
1968	Soviet Union suppresses uprising ('Prague Spring') in Czechoslovakia.
1976	Communist rule established in a reunited Vietnam. Mao Zedong dies.
1978	Deng Xiaoping begins economic reform in China.
1985	Gorbachev becomes General Secretary of the Soviet Communist Party.
1988	Gorbachev abandons Brezhnev doctrine of maintaining communist rule by force.
1989	China violently suppresses pro-democracy protests in Tiananmen Square, Beijing.
1989–91	Communist rule ends in Eastern Europe.
1991	Soviet Union disbands. Soviet Communist Party outlawed.
2001	China joins World Trade Organization.
2006	The Chinese Communist Party establishes a branch in the Wal-Mart store, Shenyang, NE China.

* This is the standard translation but Pearl (2003) suggests 'We will outlast you' is more accurate.

COUNTRY PROFILE

CHINA

Form of government ■ communist party state.

Legislature ■ the large National People's Congress (almost 3000 members chosen by provincial congresses and the armed forces) meets for only brief periods though its committees now make some contribution to national governance.

Executive ■ the State Council, headed by the premier, is the top executive body, supervising the work of the ministries. A president serves as ceremonial head of state.

Judiciary ■ China has been moving in the direction of rule by law but the judicial system remains a branch of the administration and is underdeveloped in comparison with any democracy. Extensive corruption.

Elections ■ Elections have been introduced to many of China's 930,000 villages since 1987 and, more recently and tentatively, to some townships. However, elected officials still operate under the party's supervision. Indirect election is usual at higher levels.

Population (annual growth rate): 1,313.9m (+0.6%)
World Bank income group: lower middle
Political Rights score: 7
Civil Liberties score: 
Human development index (rank/out of): 94/177
Freedom of the press index (rank/out of): 177/194
Ease of doing business index (rank/out of): 93/175

Note: For meaning and sources of scales and indexes, see p. xvi. In all cases a score and rank of 1 is 'best'.

THE PEOPLE'S REPUBLIC OF CHINA (PRC) has attracted considerable Western interest since its emergence at the start of the twenty-first century as a powerful force in the global economy. China's population is already the world's largest. Its increasingly open economy has grown tenfold since 1978 and continues to expand; it is likely to become the world's largest in the first half of the current century.

The country already employs around a quarter of the world's workers, with particular strengths in manufacturing and assembly. Its international competitiveness has created an enormous trade surplus with the USA, allowing China to build massive reserves of American dollars ('China lends while America spends'). Although the primary role of China's industry has been to serve as a low-cost subcontractor to the West, increasing technological sophistication will soon enable many of its producers to offer goods (if not services) of increased complexity and value.

The country's entry into the World Trade Organization in 2001 demonstrated its more outward-facing character, a trend confirmed by holding the Olympics in Beijing in 2008. China's burgeoning industrialization has required massive imports of raw materials, contributing to a global boom in commodity prices. Its policy-makers show few compunctions in importing resources such as oil from other authoritarian regimes. Rapid expansion combined with its sheer scale means that China is a major contributor to climate change without possessing the capacity to lead a global response. In all these ways, the world is learning the wisdom of Napoleon's observation from 1803: 'China is a sickly, sleeping giant. But when she awakes the world will tremble' (Safire, 1993).

In understanding China, it is crucial to recognize its internal diversity. A massive, increasing and destabilizing gulf exists between city and countryside; coastal zones and the interior; party and people; rich and poor; the corrupt and the honest; and between winners and losers. These inequalities have led to enormous population flows from rural areas to the cities, creating tensions within both importing and exporting regions. Environmental problems apparent within the country itself include air pollution, especially in the cities; water shortages in the north; water pollution from untreated waste; deforestation; soil erosion and desertification (CIA, 2006). Thus far, China's authoritarian rulers have ridden the country's transformation, and its effects, with both skill and difficulty. The longer-term political implications, for both China and the world, remain to be established.

Further reading: Dittmer and Liu (2006), Hutton (2006), Saich (2004).

SPOTLIGHT

Authoritarian rule in China

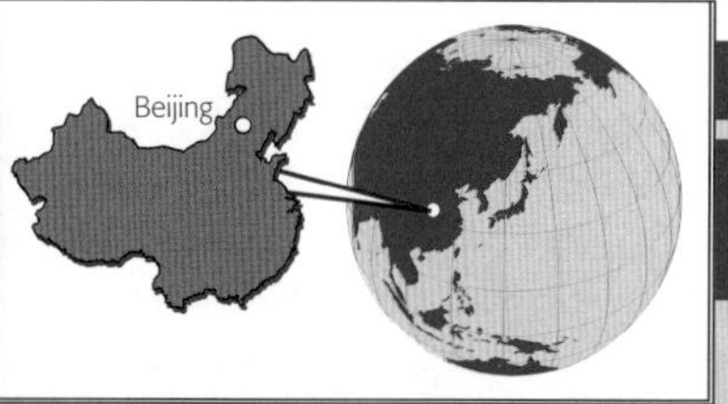

China's history differs fundamentally from that of the United States, where limits on central power were built into the republic, and from that of many Western European countries, where restraints on monarchical power were gradually imposed even before the transition to liberal democracy. China's political history is wholly non-democratic. Yet unlike the Soviet Union, the Chinese Communist Party (CCP) succeeded in jettisoning orthodox communist policies without destroying its own hold on power. So what is the formula that has enabled China to sustain an authoritarian political system in which the party retains a pre-eminent position?

The party's leaders devote considerable energy to maintaining its monopoly position. Even with nearly 70 million members, the party remains an elite force, supervising the government, the justice system and the mass media. Belonging to the party involves a continuing commitment but, in exchange, membership provides access to the contacts, information and patronage needed to acquire power and wealth. Even in the absence of ideology, ambition still glues the party together.

As communist governance has stabilized, so the party has become somewhat less intrusive and more supervisory. This revised role has allowed some expansion in the role of other institutions. For example, the National People's Congress remains weak but its leaders have acquired a role in supporting reform. Similarly, the notion of a distinct legal sphere has begun to emerge. The immature judicial system still approves public executions but a measure of 'socialist legality' now prevails.

However, the media are still tightly controlled, with about 30,000 officials censoring internet access for the country's 100 million or so users. Party members still occupy the key positions in all these institutions, providing an additional mechanism of control.

In the wider political system, the crucial reform, has been the reduction of central control from Beijing. In local communities, informal networks of power holders determine 'who gets rich first'. These collusive alliances are composed not just of well-placed men in the party but also of officials in the bureaucracy, local government and the army. Local officials can and do provide favoured businesses with contracts, land, favourable regulations, subsidies, supplies and transport, and other subsidies (Breslin, 2004). In many rural areas, local power holders also prey on peasants, creating explicit dissent.

> 'The continuing invocation of socialist values in an increasingly capitalist society has only deepened cynicism, allowing neither socialist nor capitalist values to gain a firm foothold' (Wang, 2002, p. 3).

So political and economic reform does not necessarily imply a shift towards a market economy operating within the rule of law. Currently, at least, reform empowers local elites to create a state-sponsored business class, whose members include public officials and party members.

The loosening of central political control has led to an explosion of corruption. In the new environment, public employees are quick to recognize opportunities to earn extra money from their official position.

In one port city, a smuggling racket responsible for about 10 per cent of China's total gasoline imports included the deputy mayor, the head of customs and over 100 other officials, six of whom were sentenced to death after the scheme was uncovered (Gong, 2002).

Here, perhaps, is one of the party's major dilemmas: it can only attract members by offering opportunities to acquire resources but the dubious manner in which these are obtained increases the distance between party and society.

Further reading: Breslin (2004), Brodsgaard and Yongnian (2006).

educated population. Even so, the policy-makers in Beijing face a long list of domestic challenges, including some arsing from economic development itself. These difficulties include environmental degradation, increasing inequality between provinces and between individuals, massive population movements from the countryside, an unruly peasantry, urban unemployment, an ageing population, inefficient allocation of capital, pervasive corruption and popular cynicism about the regime.

The management of such problems is more likely to involve choices from a menu which includes reform and repression but not democracy. Indeed, China's very success in entering the world economy has established the world's dependence on its goods, reducing international pressures for democratization.

Fascist states

Fascism was the twentieth century's second remarkable contribution to totalitarian thinking. Based on the idea of national unity rather than class conflict, fascist states nonetheless sought – like communist regimes – to dominate the societies they ruled. But fascist regimes were less common, stable and coherent than their communist equivalents.

Although we can still observe the consequences of communism in the twenty-first century, fascism's challenge ended with Germany's defeat in 1945. Fascist elements continued in Spain under General Franco (dictator, 1936–75) and in Portugal's 'New State' under António Salazar (dictator, 1932–68). But these were conservative authoritarian regimes rooted in the army and the church; they sought merely to recover traditional national glories rather than to build a new and self-consciously modern order (Linz, 2000).

Similarly, the right-wing anti-immigrant parties found in contemporary Europe do not embrace all aspects of the interwar ideology. Although these protest parties are frequently condemned as fascist, such a designation is little more than a term of abuse. Their essential character is post-fascist, with an appeal largely confined to a poorly educated, white, male underclass (Ignazi, 2006).

Even in its interwar heyday, fascist regimes were rare on the ground. Mussolini's leadership of Italy, lasting from 1922 until his deposition in 1943, is the main example. However, even Mussolini's dictatorship was fascist more by bombastic declaration than by institutional reality. In Hitler's Germany, the Nazi party espoused an ideology that certainly included fascist themes but these elements were blended with Aryan racism to form the crude amalgam known as national socialism.

What, then, was the doctrine expressed by these fascist regimes? Fascism was an extreme glorification of the state (in Italy) and the race (in Germany). Both regimes emphasized a traditional division of sexual labour, with politics a male preserve: 'war is to the man what maternity is to the woman', said Mussolini (Lee, 2000, p. 302). The notional purpose of fascism was to create an all-embracing warrior state to which the masses, of all classes, would show passionate commitment and submission. Democracy was dismissed as ignoring what Mussolini (1932, p. 49) called the 'irremediable, fruitful and beneficient inequality of men'. An autocratic ruler and a single party would lead and personify the state.

Under fascism, individuals find true meaning by serving the state; the liberal philosophy of individuals contracting to form a government is wholly rejected. Rather, the state defines and shapes the individual, providing him with his 'soul of the soul':

> For the Fascist, everything is in the State, and nothing human or spiritual exists, let alone has value, outside the State. In this sense, Fascism is totalitarian, and the Fascist State – the synthesis and unity of all values – interprets, develops and gives strength to the whole life of the people . . . In the Fascist State, the individual is not suppressed, but rather multiplied, just as in a regiment a soldier is not weakened but multiplied by the number of his comrades (Mussolini, 1932, p. 44).

Fascists sought to use the power of the state, as revealed by the First World War, to revive the countries defeated in that conflict. Religion, liberalism, parliamentary democracy and even capitalism were condemned as weak distractions from the key task of national renewal. In particular, fascism sought a strong national response to international groups (Jews) and movements (communism). Fascists claimed that a strong, self-sufficient state could mobilize the population more effectively, and in a more modern way, than any other ideology. Fascism was the nation-state taken to extremes (Griffin, 2004).

Even in Italy, fascism lacked the theoretical sophistication of communism; it offered an impulse more than a plan. 'Our doctrine is action', said Mussolini in 1919, commanding his followers to 'believe, obey, fight'. Unsurprisingly, therefore, fascist regimes governed very differently from ruling communist parties, even though both forms are often grouped under the totalitarian label. Certainly, fascist rulers were theoretically committed to energizing the population in an elite-led effort at national rebirth, just as communist parties claimed to be the vanguard for a new, classless society.

But fascism lacked the organized character of communist rule. It favoured the risky leader principle in which governance depended on a single individual rather than a well-developed party. Hitler, for one, never showed much interest in administration, preferring to leave his underlings to fight their own bureaucratic battles (Kershaw, 2000). A doctrine of constant movement and change, fascism never developed routines of rule comparable to those in mature communist states.

Fascist parties were essentially personal vehicles through which the leader managed his rise to power; unlike communist parties, the party lost significance once the state was won. In power, neither Mussolini nor even Hitler achieved the domination of society achieved under communism. Mussolini proved incapable of abolishing even the Italian monarchy while Hitler preferred to exploit rather than nationalize German industry. Noting the continuing separation of party and state in Nazi Germany, Friedrich (1970, p. 245) comments that party control of the government was 'not very effective'. Also, fascist regimes were less hostile to religion than were communist states.

For all its impact on the twentieth century, fascist practice often seemed to present politics as theatre: marches, demonstrations, symbols and speeches. It was no surprise that fascism's collapse in 1945 preceded that of its better-organized communist bogeyman.

Personal despots

In its original meaning, a despot is a barbaric and arbitrary ruler who treats his subjects as little more than slaves. The adjective 'personal' implies that the source of this power is the leader himself, together with his family, loyalists and bodyguards. In a personal despotism, links to a wider ideology and to social forces are at most intermittent. The leader retains discretion in his decisions, a resource which he uses to keep his opponents off-guard. He also takes care to fill not only his own boots but also those of his entourage.

Although personal despots have been most common in Central America and Africa, the syndrome was originally labelled 'sultanism' by the nineteenth-century German sociologist Max Weber (1978 edn, p. 231), a term also preferred by Chehabi and Linz (1998) in their wide-ranging study.

When we encounter the idea of authoritarian rule, an image of a personal despotism often springs to mind. However, this type of rule is uncommon in a pure form. It typically arose in small, post-colonial countries with agricultural economies, particularly during the few-questions-asked era of the Cold War. The dictatorships of Rafael Trujillo in the Dominican Republic, 1930–61, and of François Duvalier in Haiti, 1957–71, are archetypal cases, illustrating many standard characteristics.

In Dominica, Trujillo (known as The Goat) acquired power through a military coup in 1930. He established a brutal dictatorship, rationalized by an unsophisticated concoction of Catholic, anti-Haitian and nationalistic myths. Coming from a poor background, Trujillo accumulated enormous wealth, treating the sugar plantations as his own property. Torture was common. Like many despots, Trujillo was concerned with status as much as wealth. His statue was everywhere; schoolchildren prayed daily for 'God, country and Trujillo'. As Trujillo's abilities declined with age, so the repression became more arbitrary, the economy more impoverished and the wealthy more resentful. His circle of supporters narrowed, leading to his assassination, with American encouragement, in 1961 (Hartlyn, 1998).

The story of François 'Papa Doc' Duvalier in Haiti is fundamentally similar (Girard, 2006). Although Duvalier came to power through an election in 1957, his rule proved to be extraordinarily despotic and gruesome. He maintained a personal presidential guard and created the notorious Tontons Macoutes – the bogeymen – as an instrument of terror. Unpaid but exempt from prosecution, the members of this militia were in effect invited to prey upon the population. They did so. Again like Trujillo, Duvalier enriched himself and his family through corruption. If the government was short of money, Papa Doc would simply imprison a chosen businessman in the presidential palace until the victim signed a cheque. Duvalier achieved his ambition of retaining power until his death in 1971, when he was succeeded by his son, Baby Doc.

Other cases of personal despots include Fulgencio Batista (Cuba, 1933–58), Anastasio Somoza (Nicaragua, 1936–56), Ferdinand Marcos (Philippines (1965–86) and Mobutu Sese Seko (Zaire, now the Democratic Republic of the Congo, 1965–97). Some of these dictators sought, and for a period succeeded, in ensuring a family successor to their own rule. But the personal nature of such regimes, as well as their damaging exploitation of the economy, works against the establishment of a dynasty. Indeed, the virtual dismantling of any government institutions can result in a collapsed state. While the Cold War provided a hospitable environment for personal despots, the current international environment is less well-disposed to this type of rule.

Military government

In the second half of the twentieth century, military government became an important form of authoritarian rule in Africa, Latin America and parts of Asia. In most cases, the generals have now retreated to their barracks and military coups – such as the one in Thailand against a backdrop of political instability in 2006 – have once more become intermittent. However, a handful of direct military governments do remain, including a particularly repressive regime in Burma. Around a dozen countries, including Pakistan and several African states, are still ruled by presidents who originally came to power through a ***coup d'état***; these are more or less civilianized regimes. And even where authoritarian leaders come fron civilian backgrounds, the armed forces are usually a strong influence, leading in extreme cases to puppet governments (Box 4.4).

Although military governments shared the twentieth century with communist and fascist dictatorships, the contrasts between military and totalitarian rule are sharp. Most military coups came later in the century, between the 1960s and 1980s; more significantly they occurred in post-colonial countries where the state had not achieved the penetration found in Europe. Sub-Saharan Africa is the major arena, with 68 coups – including counter-coups against existing military governments – between 1963 and 1987 (Magyar, 1992). While fascist and communist parties sought to exploit the power of the modern state, many military coups (especially in smaller African countries) were made possible precisely because the state remained simple and underdeveloped. An ambitious general just needed a few tanks, driven by a handful of discontented officers, to seize the presidential palace and the single radio station.

A **military *coup d'état*** (or **putsch**) is a seizure of political power by the armed forces or sections thereof. Although the term conjures up images of a violent and unwelcome capture of power against civilian rulers, many coups replaced one military regime with another, involved little if any loss of life and were more or less invited by the previous rulers.

Why did military coups cluster in these post-war decades? The Cold War was the key. During this period, the United States and the Soviet Union were more concerned with the global chessboard than with how client countries governed themselves. So governing generals could survive through the political, economic and military backing of a superpower even though they might lack support in their own country.

The standard institutional form of an exclusionary military regime is the junta (council), a small group made up of the leader of each branch of the armed forces. In Chile, General Pinochet himself acted as chief executive while a classic four-man junta representing the army, navy, air force and national police took over other governance tasks.

Just as military governments prospered during the Cold War, so too did they shrivel after its close. By the 1990s, ruling generals could no longer rely on their sponsoring superpower; instead, conditionality ruled the roost. Aid and technical assistance flowed to civilian regimes adopting democratic forms and offering at least some commitment to civil rights. In addition, many military regimes discovered that governing was a complex task for which an army

BOX 4.4

Military influence in politics

	Nature of military influence	Comment
Burma	Military government	This impoverished South East Asian country has experienced virtually continuous military rule since 1962 when General Ne Win established a presidential dictatorship pursuing a state-dominated policy of national self-reliance. Elections were held in 1990 but the military refused to concede when the elections were won by Aung San Suu Kyi's National League for Democracy.
Pakistan	Civilianized military government	In this poor and corrupt country, the army sees itself as the guardian of the national interest. The current government dates from a coup in 1999 and is the fourth military regime since independence in 1947. In this putsch, General Pervez Musharraf suspended the constitution and appointed himself president, subsequently securing ratification of his position, first in a dubious referendum and then from the legislature. Musharraf governs, in part, through a 17-man National Security Council including the heads of the armed forces. Nonetheless, the government is far more extensive and less militarized than Burma's. A prime minister and elected parliament sit beneath the Council.
Algeria	Strong military influence on civilian government	'Every state has an army but in Algeria the army has a state', says Harbi (quoted in Bellin, 2005, p. 26). The army, the state and the leading party comprise a powerful elite ('*les décideurs*', '*le pouvoir*') forged in the fierce nationalist struggle against the French. After independence in 1962, a one-party state was established, committed to socialist industrialization. But this mission failed to incorporate the whole population, with the Islamic opposition gathering support from disadvantaged groups. When this opposition won a landslide victory in elections in 1991, the army cancelled the results, installing a new five-member High State Council in 1992. A vicious guerrilla conflict ensued between the security forces and Islamic groups; perhaps 150,000 people died in 'the Algerian night' (Hafez, 2005). With the Islamic opposition subdued by force, the state may now be securing more autonomy as a new generation of military officers emerges with no memories of the liberation struggle.

background provided poor preparation; many ruling generals began to yearn for the simplicity of life in the barracks. The last Latin American generals were back in their barracks by 1993; any coups since then have been short-lived affairs confined to smaller countries in the region (Figure 4.2).

What is the legacy of military rule for today's civilian leaders? The difficulty in answering this

Figure 4.2 The ending of military rule in Latin America

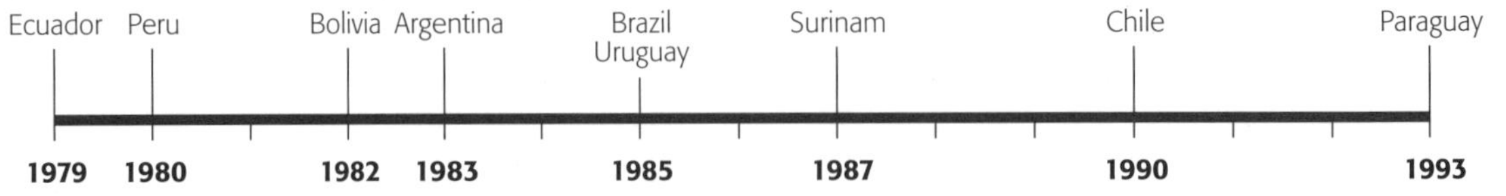

question lies in the problem of distinguishing the effects of military government specifically from the political role which the armed forces would have been expected to play even in the absence of a period in office. Furthermore, the legacy of a military regime is far from uniform; the stronger the position of the military government when it leaves office, the better the deal it can negotiate for the post-authoritarian order. Nonetheless, Agüero (2004, p. 252) notes that 'In none of the countries considered [in post-military Latin America] were the patterns of previous periods of democratic rule simply reproduced in the new democracies'. Rather, many of the new regimes were characterized by ugly birth defects which continued to fester even as the new order matured.

The main problem was that long periods of army rule led to an interweaving of civilian and military power. In many Latin American countries, senior officers had become accustomed to such privileges as guaranteed seats in the cabinet, a high level of military expenditure, sole control of the security agencies, personal profit from defence contracts, exemption from civilian justice and a formal role as guarantor of internal security. The ending of military government did not mean an end to these distortions. Indeed, some of these privileges were entrenched before military rulers could be persuaded to relinquish their occupancy of the state.

Chile illustrates the difficulties of full disengagement. Before returning power to civilians in 1980, General Pinochet ensured that the new constitution secured military autonomy. The armed forces were granted exemption from prosecution in civilian courts and retained their position as guarantors of 'institutional order' and 'national security'. Similarly, Ecuador's armed forces were guaranteed 15 per cent of the country's oil revenues until 2010. Such conditional transitions, characteristic of Latin America, helped the shift to, but weakened the depth of, the post-military democracy. Some of these conditions are now being unwound but they undoubtedly left a difficult bequest for new democracies.

Other party states

In theory, and occasionally in reality, single 'ruling' parties other than communist and fascist ones provide the basis for authoritarian rule. As Huntington (1970, p. 9) pointed out, 'unless it can guarantee a low level of political mobilization, an authoritarian regime may have little choice but to organize and develop a political party as an essential structural support'. An organised party is especially important in soft authoritarian regimes, where the rulers permit a measure of electoral competition; after all, even a controlled election needs a party to control it. In Mexico, the Partido Revolucionario Institucional performed this election-winning role until the country's democratic transition in 2000. In the Asian island state of Singapore, the People's Action Party continues to dominate elections.

But we must distinguish between the supports of power and power itself. Often, the party is the vehicle rather than the driver, with real power resting with a dominant president, military ruler or political elite. Once we move beyond communist and to an extent fascist states, we find only a limited number of cases where the single party sustains its position as an effective wielder of power.

The post-independence experience of many sub-Saharan countries shows the weakness of many 'ruling' parties. After independence, African presidents soon suggested that a single party – their party – would be the best means of expressing and encouraging national unity. But these one-party systems soon withered, if indeed they had ever flowered. They became little more than a vehicle for distributing patronage from the ruling ethnic group at the centre to its supporters in the regions. When

Kwame Nkrumah, leader of Ghana's Convention People's Party, was overthrown by a coup in 1966, his party effectively disappeared with him. These one-party systems were far weaker than in communist states.

Even when the single party does begin as an independent force, it can still be captured by a strong leader. In the Middle East, where parties in authoritarian regimes have generally retained more significance than in Africa, Iraq's Ba'ath party provides an example of this trajectory of decay. The Ba'ath began as a radical, secular, modernizing pan-Arab party with a strong, cellular organization. It provided the framework within which Saddam Hussein rose to power. But eventually Saddam stamped his authority on the party, building what became in part a personal despotism. His command was demonstrated at a party convention in 1979 when he read out the names of potential opponents and, as he did so, ordered each one to be taken out individually and shot. At the end of the meeting, in a speech given fulsome applause, the leader congratulated those remaining for their past and future loyalty.

Egypt is perhaps a more typical example of the role which a dominant party plays in non-communist authoritarian regimes. The National Democratic Party (NDP) forms part of an established, indeed ossified, structure of power based on a strong presidency and an extended bureaucracy. Within this framework, the NDP is the junior partner: 'the NDP has failed to serve as effective means to recruit candidates into the elite. Rather, persons who are already successful tend to join the party in order to consolidate their positions' (Lesch, 2004, p. 600). With its close links to the state, the NDP is an arena for furthering political and business careers but it is not a major policy-making force.

Royal families

Royal families remain a significant governing force in the Arab states of the Persian Gulf. Here, a leading tribe typically established a privileged relationship with the colonial power and exploited this connection to secure control of the Western-style state created at independence. These governing families or tribes continue to rule their countries in highly traditional fashion. Examples include Bahrain, Kuwait, Qatar, Oman, Saudi Arabia and the United Arab Emirates (UAE).

These Gulf states make few concessions to democracy. Thus, the constitution of Oman, issued by the Sultan in 1996, makes clear that the person of the Sultan 'is inviolable and must be respected and his orders must be obeyed'. Several of these kingdoms, notably Kuwait, have now established *majlis* (consultative assemblies), but this reform is unlikely to presage a transition to a constitutional monarchy (Herb, 2005). Beyond the Gulf, however, parliaments have made more ground in two other Arab monarchies: Jordan and Morocco.

In three ways, use of the term 'monarchy' to describe the traditional political systems found in the Gulf is imprecise. First, the titles used by Arab 'monarchs' reflect tribal or Islamic tradition: emir (leader or commander), sheikh (revered leader of the tribe) or sultan (a leader who possesses authority). Second, the leading members of the ruling dynasty, rather than a single monarch, often exercise authority. Governance is by princes, rather than just the king; these countries are run by family businesses rather than sole traders. Third, while the king typically designates a crown price as his preferred successor, custom requires that a family council meets after the monarch's death to confirm or indeed change this appointment. Herb (1999, p. 491) judges that this element of selection is the 'glue that holds the dynastic monarchies together'.

Weber's notion of patrimonial rule captures the nature of authority in these male-dominated Arab dynasties. Authority is owed to the ruler himself rather than to a more abstract entity such as a state or party. The people are subjects as much as citizens, and the ruler is constrained neither by law nor by competitive election. This authority flows from history and tradition, reinforced by a nomadic tribal tradition. For example, the Al Bu Said dynasty has ruled Oman for longer than the United States has existed as an independent entity. An Omani feels as an American would, had the USA been governed since its inception by the clan of Kennedy (or Bush).

Because the ruler is expected to take responsibility for his people, the right of ordinary people to petition the ruler on individual matters is well-established. But the petitioner requests benevolent treatment, not the implementation of constitutional rights. The abstract idea of a state linking rulers and citizens is weak, as are such modern notions as constitutions, rights, interest groups, the separation of powers and the rule of law. Politics is based on intrigue at the palace, with little distinction between public and private sectors.

We can use Saudi Arabia – the heartland of the Arab and Islamic worlds – to illustrate this style of governance. The country's political style reflects the influence of King Abdul Aziz Ibn Saud. He led the Saudi state from its inception in 1902 until his death in 1953. In true patrimonial style, Ibn Saud ran his kingdom as a gigantic personal household, using marriage as a vital political tactic. He took several hundred wives drawn from all the powerful families in the state, a stratagem which solidified his control.

The ruling royal family, led by an influential group of around 200 princes, still constitutes the core of government. The Basic Law promulgated in 1992 declared that Saudi Arabia is a monarchy ruled by the sons and grandsons of Ibn Saud. The crown prince, designated by the king, serves as the monarch's temporary successor. Reflecting Bedouin tradition, a permanent replacement is chosen through negotiation within the group. Family members occupy key positions on the Council of Ministers, serving in particular as a bridge between the government, the military and the active security forces.

The regime is authoritarian rather than totalitarian. The ruling family does not monopolize wealth but leaves space for lower-tier families. There is some separation of political and religious authority: 'the Al Saud have provided the sword and the purse while the Al Sheikh, the descendants of the founder of Wahhabism, have traditionally handled the religious establishment' (Seznec, 2003, p. 77). A tradition of consultation allows the royal family to incorporate other families, as well as technical experts, within its framework of rule.

Although political parties are still banned, some mechanisms of representation have emerged, adding an institutional veneer to what is still a traditional regime. The Basic Law of 1992, an innovation in itself, introduced a Consultative Council, with a non-princely and technocratic membership, to 'advise the King on issues of importance'. Although the Council is a strengthened form of a body which dates back to 1927, it remains at most a proto-parliament. The royal family, and the traditional rule it represents, remains pre-eminent.

Theocracy

Government by religious leaders is perhaps the rarest form of authoritarian rule. A religious society is one thing; a clerical government is quite another. Even Muslim countries typically separate religious and civil leadership within the context of an overall commitment to Islam. Indeed, in much of the Middle East, the mosque has become a source of opposition to authoritarian rulers, a divide which would not be possible if the religious and civil leaders were one and the same.

At least since the fall of the Taliban in Afghanistan, the Persian but non-Arab Islamic Republic of Iran stands alone as an example of a constitutional theocracy. Even here, rule by religious leaders (ayatollahs and mullahs) possesses limited legitimacy, especially among the young and educated.

Iran's theocracy was a child of the 1979 revolution, the last great insurrection of the twentieth century. In this revolution, Ayatollah Khomeini, a 76-year-old cleric committed to Islamic fundamentalism, overthrew the pro-Western Shah of Iran. In reaction, the revolutionaries advocated a traditional Islamic republic free from foreign domination; 'neither East nor West' was the slogan (Martin, 2003). In power, the ayatollahs created a unique Islamic state in which they governed directly rather than through oversight of secular rulers.

A **theocracy** is government by religious leaders. In ancient Israel, for example, God's laws were expounded and applied by holy men. Although most Islamic countries separate religious and political roles, the regime established in Iran after the overthrow of the Shah in 1979 is a recent example of a theocracy.

Iran's post-revolutionary constitution did incorporate a directly elected presidency and assembly. Yet real power lies with the clerics, expressed in part through a 12-member Council of Guardians which certifies that all bills and candidates conform with Islamic law. In strictly enforcing traditional, male-dominated Islamic codes, the ayatollahs permeate society in a manner reminiscent of totalitarian

DEBATE

SHOULD THE INTERNATIONAL COMMUNITY PROMOTE DEMOCRACY IN AUTHORITARIAN STATES?

'We cannot stand idly by as dictators develop weapons of mass destruction and fuel and support terrorism. It is time that these dangerous political relics went extinct. We must finally say enough is enough. We must join together to oust the last dictators and build universal democracy' (Palmer, 2003, p. 321). The international system has been based on non-intervention in sovereign states. International law, for example, makes little reference to how states should organize themselves internally. But the collapse of communism has opened new possibilities. So should the international community listen to Palmer's strictures and consider intervening in authoritarian states to promote or even enforce democracy?

YES

Democracy is a universal value: all peoples possess a right to govern themselves democratically, just as they embrace a right to self-determination.

Good governance is a democratic product. Democracies protect individual rights, facilitate economic growth, breed few terrorists and are more sympathetic to environmental concerns than are authoritarian states.

More importantly, democratic organization within countries encourages good relations between them. Democracies sign more trade pacts and are less war-like than authoritarian regimes. In particular, the democratic peace hypothesis suggests that democracies rarely go to war with each other.

These points show that the operation of the international system depends on how countries are organized internally. Given these connections, the distinction between national and international spheres is unsustainable.

Democracy promotion should not be stymied by the outdated theory of sovereignty. As Boutros Boutros-Ghali said when Secretary General of the United Nations, 'The time of absolute exclusive sovereignty has passed; its theory was never matched by reality'.

With the United Nations' Responsibility to Protect doctrine now justifying international intervention against governments which fail to protect their populations from ethnic cleansing, it is a logical next step to require governments to organize themselves by democratic principles.

NO

Ethics make poor politics. International politics operates on the basis of states pursuing their own interests. In reality, attempts to impose moral values such as democracy are likely to destabilize the system.

The invasion of Iraq in 2003 is an example. Toppling Saddam Hussein led to new violence within the country and the goal of a democratic Iraq remained elusive. In Iraq, Afghanistan and elsewhere, the first task is to build a state. Only then is democracy a feasible goal.

Claims that democracy is the best form of government anywhere and everywhere are imperious and inaccurate. Divided societies often find forms of political accommodation which bear little relation to democracy as conventionally understood. In traditional cultures, ideas of benevolent paternalism may be so entrenched that democracy is neither practical nor welcome.

Even if democracy is the best form of government for current conditions, these circumstances might change. Regime diversity, like genetic variation, retains flexibility in responding to altered conditions. The world should not put all its eggs in the basket of democracy.

Attempts to encourage and promote democracy should be left to non-governmental organizations. Certainly, the international community should reject any proposals to enforce democracy in authoritarian regimes. Democracy by force would be a rash folly, unlikely to achieve its object while remaining vulnerable to unforeseen consequences.

ASSESSMENT

After Iraq, democracy promotion by unilateral force will hardly be a feasible strategy. Nor should it be imagined that the United Nations, with its considerable number of non-democratic members, will take the lead. Still, international law is gradually taking more notice of democracy and the idea of democracy promotion is attracting more attention. Iraq notwithstanding, the debate is on the move at a theoretical level.

Further reading

Owen (2002), Palmer (2003), Rich (2001).

regimes. The Interior Ministry still makes extensive use of informants while the state employs arbitrary arrests and even assassination as a form of control through terror.

But as with many radical Islamic movements, Iran's revolution was backward-looking, offering no clear direction on such practical maters as economic development, monetary policy and overseas trade (Chehabi, 2001). Unsurprisingly, therefore, rule by ayatollahs has failed to deliver economic growth, even in a country awash with oil revenues. Instead, the clerics have grown wealthy by establishing *bonyads* – tax-exempt 'charitable' trusts – for their own benefit. Foundations monopolize many sections of an inefficient, state-dominated economy. Since Khomeini's death in 1989, Iran's theocratic establishment has consisted of competing factions of middle-aged to elderly men exploiting the revolutionary heritage in a successful effort to acquire and retain power and wealth. Neither a strong party nor a royal family exists to impose direction on these elements (Keshavarzian, 2005).

Unsurprisingly in a country where the median age is just 24 years (compared to 36 in the USA), this unprogressive regime has intensified the generational divide. Well-educated young people, including many female graduates, chafe at the restrictions imposed by a hypocritical establishment. 'I write a weblog so that I can shout, cry and laugh, and do the things that they have taken away from me in Iran today', said Lolivashe in her blog in 2004 (Alavi, 2005). The young rely on the internet, satellite television and mobile phones to circumvent official censorship, at some risk to themselves. To distance themselves from the regime, young people follow Western icons such as Mariah Carey that have long lost credibility in the West itself. Although a counter-revolution to 1979 currently seems highly unlikely, any resolution of the political, generational and gender conflicts in Iran will surely resonate throughout the Muslim world.

Ruling presidents

Our final category of authoritarian government is the ruling president. We have already met several strong presidents in this chapter but their power has derived from a source external to the executive office: in a monarchy, the army, the communist party or even the ruler's own family. But of course the office of president (or, less often, prime minister) can itself be the power base. Even if authority begins elsewhere, a president in an authoritarian system occupies a unique position, possessing a visibility which can be invested in an attempt to transfer the authority to his own post, typically by establishing a direct relationship through the media with the people he rules.

Thus, a ruling president usually contains a strong element of personal rule. However, in contrast to a personal despotism, the authority remains linked to a specific office which is likely to outlast the incumbent. The format is more institutional and thus better suited to larger and more complex societies.

The concentration of powers in the president is a familiar process in Latin America, where it is known as an ***autogolpe***. Typically, the president declares a state of emergency, removes the constitutional prohibition on re-election and extends his powers to govern by decree. In the Peruvian Fuji-coup of 1992, President Alberto Fujimori suspended the constitution, the judiciary and Congress before introducing a new constitution (subsequently ratified by referendum) permitting his re-election. Fujimori did not lack popular support; indeed, he was re-elected in 1995 and 2000 but resigned later in 2000 following allegations of corruption (Carriûn, 2006). The fascist-influenced dictatorship established by President Getulio Vargas in Brazil in 1937 is another example of an *autogolpe*.

> An ***autogolpe*** (self-coup) is a 'coup launched by the chief executive himself in order to extend his control over the political system in some extra-constitutional way' (Farcau, 1994, p. 2).

Although the concept of an *autogolpe* is Latin American in origin, examples can be found elsewhere, particularly if the notion is extended to include creeping centralization of power. Uzbekistan is a clear and significant case. The largest of the central Asian republics, Uzbekistan formed part of the Soviet Union until the collapse of communism, becoming an independent state in 1991. The country's politics are dominated by Islam Karimov, a former First Secretary of the Uzbek Communist Party. In effect, the establishment of Karimov's dictatorship in Uzbekistan was a coup against the party he once led. In 1994, he resigned from the communist successor party, claiming that only a non-partisan head of state could guarantee constitutional stability. By this route, he instituted a gradual change in the nature of authoritarian rule in the country.

To forestall the emergence of opposition, Karimov regularly dismisses ministers and replaces regional leaders. He keeps tight control of the media; uses a traditional institution of local governance (the *mahalla*) as an instrument of social control; and also relies on the National Security Service for surveillance. Like other leaders of secular regimes in Islamic societies, Karimov has sought to prevent the mosque from becoming an explicit site of opposition. Parties based on religious and ethnic groups are banned altogether. The regime's nervousness about Islamic opposition was demonstrated by its indiscriminate massacre of hundreds of Muslim demonstrators at Andijan in 2005. Karimov also maintains an infamous gulag at Jaslyk, known as the prison-of-no-return, where a Muslim inmate was boiled to death (Khatchadourian, 2004).

Although there are elements of personal despotism in Karimov's rule, his power is primarily based on the presidency. Melvin (2000, p. 34) provides a summary:

> As a result of the political change since independence, a system of one-man rule has been established in Uzbekistan. The President enjoys extensive powers including appointments and he resides at the pinnacle of a system of executive power that runs throughout the country and effectively subordinates all aspects of political life to its elements. The President takes all major, and many minor, decisions.

Learning Resources for Chapter 4

Next step

Linz (2000) is an influential and insightful guide to authoritarian rule.

Further reading

Brooker (2000) is a wide-ranging source on non-democracy while Palmer (2003) adopts a more practical approach, as shown by his title, *Breaking the Real Axis of Evil: How to Oust the World's Last Dictators by 2025.* Classic works on totalitarianism include Arendt (1966) and Friedrich and Brzezinski (1965); Gleason (1995) is a more recent review. For fascism, see Griffin (2004) and, for communist states, Harding (1984). Kershaw and Lewin (1997) compare these two forms of dictatorship. For twentieth-century authoritarianism, see Perlmutter (1981, 1997). Chebabi and Linz (1998) examine personal despotisms. On military government, see Finer (1962). For military disengagement, consider Howe (2001) for Africa, Cottey *et al.* (2001) for Eastern Europe and Silva (2001) for Latin America. Posusney and Angrist (2005) provide an excellent collection on authoritarian persistence in the Middle East. On China, Saich (2004) is a thorough guide. For authoritarian legacies, see Hite and Cesarinin (2004) on Latin America and Elster, Offe and Preuss (1998) on post-communist states.

Internet sources

The Central People's Government of the People's Republic of China
The Chinese government's website
http://english.gov.cn

Dictator of the Month
A rogue's gallery
http://www.dictatorofthemonth.com/English/English_welcome.htm

The Doctrine of Fascism
By Benito Mussolini, cowritten with Giovanni Gentile
http://www.worldfuturefund.org/wffmaster/Reading/Germany/mussolini.htm/

Marxists Internet Archive
Background on Marxist thinking
http://www.marxists.org/

Transparency International
Focuses on corruption, which inevitably overlaps with authoritarian rule
http://www.transparency.org/

Chapter 5
The comparative approach

The goal of comparative politics is to encompass the major political similarities and differences between countries. The task is to understand the mixture of constants and variability which characterizes the world's governments, bearing in mind the national and international contexts within which they operate. Given this definition of comparative *politics*, the comparative *approach* is simply the family of strategies and techniques which advances this goal.

Grander definitions are of course available. With justification, the comparative approach can be regarded as the master strategy for drawing inferences about causation in any area of study. After all, experiments and statistical analysis designed to uncover relationships of cause and effect must involve a comparison between observations; all investigations of cause and effect are by nature comparative.

But most political research has more modest ambitions. In the main, the challenge is to describe and to interpret rather than to explain. For example, identifying cross-national trends in electoral reform is itself a worthwhile exercise, involving the ability to engage with the politics of particular countries in order to identify broader themes. Nor is there anything limited about such generalized description; as King *et al.* observe (1994, p. 44), 'good description is better than bad explanation'.

This chapter proceeds from the general to the specific. We begin by outlining the strengths of comparison by asking the simple question, 'why compare?'. The chapter then continues with a discussion of the major levels or units of comparison – institutions, societies and states – before proceeding to an examination of the core techniques of case studies, focused comparisons and statistical analysis. We conclude on a cautionary but not discouraging note, describing some pitfalls of comparative research.

Why compare?

To begin, we will raise the obvious question: what is to be gained by comparing politics in different countries? Why comparative politics? The answer is that such an approach broadens our understanding of the political world, leading to improved classifications and giving potential for explanation and even prediction (Box 5.1). We discuss each of these advantages in turn.

The *first* strength of a comparative approach is straightforward: it enables us to find out more about the places we know least about. This point was well-stated by Munro (1925, p. 4). He described the purpose of his book on European governments as aiding 'the comprehension of daily news from abroad'. This ability to interpret overseas events grows in importance as the world becomes more interdependent. In an era of international terrorism,

BOX 5.1

The advantages of comparison

- Learning about other governments broadens our understanding, casting fresh light on our home nation;
- Comparison improves our classifications of political processes;
- Comparison enables us to test hypotheses about politics;
- Comparison gives us some potential for prediction and control.

no one can afford the insular attitude of Mr Podsnap in Dickens's *Our Mutual Friend*: 'Foreigners do as they do, sir, and that is the end of it'. In any case, Munro was perhaps a shade modest in stating his purpose. Even when the focus is just on one overseas country, an implicit comparison with the homeland contributes to the broadening of our horizons.

Understanding foreign governments not only helps to interpret new developments, it also assists with practical political relationships. For instance, British ministers have a patchy track record in negotiations with their European partners partly because they assume that the aggressive tone they adopt in the Commons chamber will also work in EU meeting rooms. Their assumption is incorrect, showing ignorance of the consensual political style found in many continental democracies. What works at home often fails when playing away.

Similarly, American students sometimes puzzle at how the British parliamentary system can deliver stable government when the prime minister, unlike their own president, is constantly at the mercy of a vote of confidence in the Commons. Because American parties are so decentralized, the tendency is to underestimate the ability of a British governing party to control its own members of parliament. Conversely, British students are so accustomed to the importance of party that they experience difficulty in understanding why Congress and the White House continue to quarrel even when the same party controls both institutions.

The general point is made by Dogan and Pelassy (1990): through comparison, we discover our own ethnocentrism and the means of overcoming it. In this respect, comparative politics is a virtual trip overseas – and the object of foreign travel, said the British critic G. K. Chesterton (1874–1936), is not so much to set foot overseas as to see one's own country as a foreign land.

A *second* advantage of comparison is that it improves our classifications of politics. For instance, we can group constitutions into written and unwritten ones, and electoral systems into proportional and non-proportional formulae. We can then search for the factors which incline countries to one form rather than the other. Similarly, once we classify executives into presidential and parliamentary systems, we can look at which type is more stable and effective. Classification is inherently comparative, turning what is a constant within a single country into a variable between them. In this way, classification provides the raw material from which explanatory ventures can be launched.

The potential for explanation is the *third* advantage of a comparative approach. Comparative researchers seek to understand a variety of political systems not just for their own sake but also to formulate and test **hypotheses**. Comparative analysis enables us to develop and scrutinize such questions as: do first-past-the-post electoral systems always produce a two-party system? Are two-chambered assemblies only found under federalism? Are revolutions most likely to occur after defeat in war?

A **hypothesis** is a relationship posited between two or more factors or variables: for example, between electoral and party systems, or between war and revolution.

Confirmed hypotheses are valuable nor just for their own sake but because they are essential for explaining the particular. Consider, for example, one specific question: why did a major socialist party never emerge in the United States? An obvious answer is because the USA was built on, and retains, a strongly individualistic culture. This explanation may seem to be particular but in fact it is quite general. It implies that other countries with similar values would also lack a strong socialist party. It also suggests that countries with a more collective outlook will be more likely to sustain a party of the left. These comparative hypotheses would need to be

BOX 5.2

Levels of analysis in comparative politics

	Definition	Examples
Institution-centred	How governments are organized and the relationships between these organizations.	The balance between president and legislature; the impact of constitutions and the judiciary.
Society-centred	How governments are influenced by the social context in which they operate.	Studies of political culture, elections, voting and social movements.
State-centred	The priorities and traditions of the state as a whole and how these impinge on society.	State functions and how these are performed; building the welfare state; regulating for economic competitiveness.

confirmed by looking at a range of countries before we could claim a full understanding of our original question about the USA. So explaining the particular calls forth the general; only theories explain cases.

Generalizations, once validated, have potential for prediction. Here we come to our *fourth* reason for studying politics comparatively. The ability to predict is not only a sign of systematic knowledge but also gives us some base for drawing lessons across countries. So, if we find that proportional representation (PR) does indeed lead to coalition government, we can reasonably predict at least one effect of introducing PR to countries such as Canada which still use the plurality method. Equally, if we know that subcontracting the provision of public services to private agencies raises the quality of delivery in one country, we can advise governments elsewhere that here is an idea at least worth considering.

In this way, lesson-drawing provides some capacity to anticipate and even to shape the future (Rose, 2004). Rather than resorting to ideology or guesses, we can use comparison to address 'what would happen if . . . ?' questions. This function of comparative politics was stated well by Bryce (1921, p. iv):

> Many years ago, when schemes of political reform were being copiously discussed in England, it occurred to me that something might be done to provide a solid basis for judgment by examining a certain number of popular governments in their actual working, comparing them with one another, and setting forth the various merits and demerits of each.

What to compare

The core unit of comparative politics is the country or state. But in reality most studies in comparative politics examine particular features of politics within countries, rather than comparing the whole political system. To be more precise, most comparative research uses one of three levels of analysis: the institutions of government, the social context of politics or the state as a whole (Box 5.2). Because the history of comparative politics is a story of shifts in the favoured level, we examine each of these three traditions of enquiry.

Comparing institutions

The study of governing **institutions** is a central purpose of political science in general and of comparative politics in particular. As Rhodes (1995, p. 43) writes,

> If there is any subject matter at all that political scientists can claim exclusively for their own, a subject matter that does not require acquisition of the analytical tools of sister fields and that sustains their claim to autonomous existence, it is of course, formal political structures.

Because virtually all countries possess an executive, legislature and judiciary, such institutions are natural units for comparative politics.

> An **institution** is a formal organization, often with public status, whose members interact on the basis of the specific roles they perform within the organization. In politics, an institution typically refers to an organ of government mandated by the constitution.

But how exactly should an 'institution' be understood? Usually, the term refers to the major organizations of national government, particularly those defined in the constitution. But the concept also radiates outwards in two directions. The first extension is to other governing organizations which may have a less secure constitutional basis, such as the bureaucracy and local government. And the second extension is to other important political organizations which are not formally part of the government, notably political parties.

However, as we move away from the heartland of constitutionally mandated structures, so the term 'organization' tends to supplant the word 'institution'. Implicitly, therefore, an emphasis on institutions in political analysis affirms the origins of political studies in the examination of constitutions and the state.

The starting point of institutional analysis is that posts within organizations matter more than the people who occupy them. This assumption enables us to discuss presidencies rather than presidents, legislatures rather than legislators and the judiciary rather than judges (Ridley, 1975). So the capacity of institutions to affect the behaviour of their members means that politics, like other social sciences, is more than a branch of psychology. In that sense, institutions are formal rules for interaction among their members. These rules provide the skeleton to which members attach informal practices of their own.

But institutions can also be conceived as possessing a history, culture and memory, frequently embodying traditions and founding values and often simply growing 'like coral reefs through slow accretion' (Sait, 1938, p. 18). They often possess legal personality, acquiring privileges and duties under law.

Why do institutions exist? Their value – in politics as elsewhere – lies in their capacity to make long-term commitments which are more credible than those of any single employee, thus building up trust. For example, governments can borrow money at lower rates than are available to individual civil servants. Similarly, a government can make credible promises to repay its debt over a period of generations, a commitment that would be beyond the reach of an individual debtor. Institutions offer predictability: when we visit a government office, we do so with expectations about how the member of staff will behave without knowing anything about the individual concerned. A shared institutional context eases the task of conducting business between strangers. So in and beyond politics, institutions help to glue society together, extending the bounds of what would be possible for individuals acting alone (Johnson, 2001). Where the institutions of government are weak, so too is the capacity of the state.

An institutional approach implies that organizations do indeed shape behaviour. Crucially, institutions provide career progression and therefore shape the interests of their staff. Employees acquire interests such as defending their organization against outsiders and ensuring their own personal progress within the structure. As March and Olsen (1984, p. 738) conclude in their influential restatement of the institutional approach:

> The bureaucratic agency, the legislative committee and the appellate court are arenas for contending social forces but they are also collections of standard operating procedures and structures that define and defend interests. They are political actors in their own right.

Further, institutions bring forth activity which takes place simply because it is expected, not because it has any deeper political motive. When a legislative committee holds hearings on a topic, it may be more concerned to be seen to be doing its job than to probe the topic itself. Much political action is best understood by reference to this **logic**

of appropriateness rather than a **logic of consequences**. For instance, when a president visits an area devastated by floods, he is not necessarily seeking to direct relief operations or to achieve any purpose other than to be seen to be performing his duty of showing concern. In itself, the tour achieves the goal of meeting expectations arising from the actor's institutional position. 'Don't just do something, stand there', said Ronald Reagan, a president with a fine grasp of the logic of appropriateness.

> The **logic of appropriateness** refers to actions which members of an institution take to conform to its norms. For example, a head of state will perform ceremonial duties because it is an official obligation. By contrast, the **logic of consequences** denotes behaviour directed at achieving an individual goal such as promotion or re-election.

Institutions are far more than the theatre within which the political drama unfolds: they also shape the script (Peters, 1999). This emphasis within the institutional framework on the symbolic or ritual aspect of political behaviour contrasts with the view of politicians and bureaucrats as rational, instrumental actors who define their own goals independently of the organization they represent.

Comparing societies

In the 1960s and 1970s, the focus of comparative politics moved from institutions to the social context within which institutions operate. One factor here was decolonization. This process spawned many new nations in which the formal structures of government proved fragile. The failure of newly designed democratic institutions to take root in former colonies led naturally to a concern with the social foundations of democracy. Institutions seemed irrelevant to the question, 'why did democratic institutions fail to consolidate?'. Government institutions also proved to be of little importance in communist states where the ruling party was the real wielder of power. So, in seeking to understand politics beyond Western democracy, political scientists sought a wider lens.

In this transition to a more society-centred approach, Easton's systems model of the **political system** led the way (1965a and b). Although few political scientists explicitly use Easton's framework

> As defined by Easton (1965a and b), the **political system** is 'a set of interactions abstracted from the totality of social behavior, through which values are authoritatively allocated for a society'. This definition interpreted politics as a task or function, thus moving attention away from a focus on the institutions of government.

today, his work still forms part of the vocabulary of political analysis. In particular, 'the political system' has become a widely used phrase.

Easton conceived politics in functional rather than institutional terms. Specifically, the task of politics is to make an authoritative allocation of values. This function is performed by taking selected demands from society and converting them into concrete laws, policies and decisions. These allocations then feed back to society, thus influencing the next cycle of demands. All being well, this continuous process of adjustment maintains a broad equilibrium between the political system and the wider social system.

For Easton, the particular institutions that perform the task of making authoritative judgements are secondary: 'there are certain basic political processes characteristic of all political systems even though the structural forms through which they manifest themselves vary considerably in each place and age' (1965a, p. 49). In practice, however, Easton's model proved to be too static, premised on the achievement of, or continual movement towards, equilibrium between inputs and outputs. It offered little insight into political change and was a little too neat. Still, it provided an alternative view of politics to the traditional institutional approach.

Society-centred analyses formed part of the behavioural revolution in politics, an approach which offers a further contrast with institutional analysis. The central tenet of **behaviouralists** was that 'the root is man' rather than institutions (Eulau, 1963). People are more than badges of the institu-

> **Behaviouralism** was a school of thought in political science which emphasised the study of individuals rather than institutions. The focus was on voters rather than elections, legislators rather than legislatures and judges rather than the judiciary. Its aim was to discover scientific generalizations about political attitudes and behaviour.

tion they work for: they possess some freedom to define their own role. The higher the position in an organization, the more flexibility the occupant possesses. Those at the very top can even reshape the institution itself.

Within the behavioural tradition, institutions were not ignored altogether but the study of assemblies, for instance, moved away from formal aspects (e.g. the procedures by which a bill becomes a law) towards legislative behaviour (e.g. how members define their career goals). Thus, researchers investigated the social backgrounds of representatives, their individual voting records and their own conception of their job (Wahlke *et al.*, 1962). In the study of the judiciary, too, scholars began to take judges rather than courts as their level of analysis, using statistical techniques to assess how the social background and political attitudes of justices shaped their decisions (Segal and Spaeth, 2002).

The disregard of institutions by much society-centred analysis of the 1960s now seems extreme but its effect in broadening horizons represents a positive legacy for comparative politics. For instance, the parts of this book examining the relationship between society and politics take up more space than the sections dealing with government institutions themselves. One legacy of society-centred analysis, and of the behavioural movement that went with it, is that the study of comparative government is now irreversibly embedded in the wider subject of comparative politics.

Comparing states

By the 1980s, the behavioural revolution had run its course and attention once more returned to the state. 'Bringing the state back in' became a rallying-cry in comparative politics (Evans *et al.*, 1985). Partly, this shift reflected a belated recognition that the state, not society, is the central concern of political study. In addition, statistical and behavioural studies had become highly technical, failing in particular to engage with political change.

Yet the new focus on the state represented more than a return to descriptive studies of government institutions. Rather, the state as a whole, rather than its specific manifestations in an executive, parliament and judiciary, now became the favoured level of analysis. The focus lay not so much on institutional detail but on the state as an active agent, shaping and reshaping society. Thus the state presents an additional level of analysis in comparative politics, distinct from both institutions and individuals.

Where society-centred analysis saw the state as embedded in society, the state-centred approach saw society as part of a configuration defined partly by the state itself. The state can act autonomously and is not just imprisoned by social forces. In particular, the state is seen as using its administrative capacity and monopoly of legitimate force to bring about fundamental social changes. For example, Skocpol (1979) showed how successful revolutionaries such as the Russian Bolsheviks and Iranian religious leaders used their control of the state to produce transformations of society.

But examples are not confined just to post-revolutionary situations. Throughout the world, states have played a large role in the shift to an industrial economy, most recently in Asian countries such as Japan and Singapore. Such large-scale transformations require a public effort going beyond the work of a particular institution or ministry. States have also led the introduction of mass education and welfare states, achievements that are again misread if they are attributed simply to specific branches of government.

State-centred analysts suggest that the uses to which public power has been put by those charged with its exercise cannot be understood by the routine analysis of specific institutions. Rather, the state itself must provide the unit of analysis. The interests of the state can be identified and analysed without declining into institutional detail, just as a country's 'national interest' is a useful guide to its foreign policy even though that policy is in practice the work of many hands.

Much state-centred thinking focuses on the functions of the state. Marxists, for example, judge that the state's core purpose is to protect the interests of capital. This role runs deeper than the manifest purpose of any particular organization within the state apparatus. Burnham (1982, p. 75) illustrates this perspective:

> Any state fulfils three basic functions. First, it defends the basic needs and interests of those who control the means of production within the society in question. Closely associated with this is the

second function of the state: achieving legitimacy for itself and ensuring social harmony. Finally, no state can survive if it cannot adequately defend itself, and the dominant powers in the economy and society, from external attack.

The state has also become a natural focus for scholars seeking to link the global and the national. With the expansion of global trade and finance since the 1980s, and the emergence of global environmental problems, questions have naturally been raised about how, if at all, states can and should respond to this global agenda. For instance, can the welfare state survive or should we move to a competition state in which the prime task of government is to prepare society for the challenge of global markets? (Cerny, 1990). These questions are typically framed as 'globalization and the state' rather than 'globalization and the government'. A focus on the state eases the task of linking comparative and international politics.

How to compare

This section turns from strategy to techniques. Comparative politics offers a wide repertoire of techniques and here we examine three major methods: case studies, focused comparisons and statistical analysis (Box 5.3). These devices range from intensive scrutiny of one (case studies) or a small number (focused comparisons) of countries to systematic analysis of variables drawn from a larger set of countries (statistical analysis).

Case studies

A case is an instance of a more general category. To conduct a case study is to investigate something with significance beyond its own boundaries. Lawyers study cases which are taken to illustrate a wider legal principle. Physicians study a case of a particular ailment because they want to learn how to treat similar instances in the future. So a project turns into a case study, and history or journalism becomes political science, only when it becomes clear what the study is a case *of*.

By definition, a case study examines only one example in detail. So strictly speaking, case analysis is not a comparative technique at all. But because a case study is by definition conducted with an eye to the wider class of which it is an example, it is conventionally accorded at least honorary membership of the comparative family. Even an exact thinker like Sartori (1991, p. 252) accepts that a case study 'may

BOX 5.3

Major techniques in comparative politics

	Number of cases	Case- or variable-centred?	Strategy
Case studies	One	Case	Intensive study of a single instance with wider significance
Focused comparisons (small-*N*)	A few	Case	Qualitative comparison of a few instances
Statistical analysis (large-*N*)	Many	Variable	Quantitative assessment of the relationships between variables

Note: *N* is the statistician's term for the number of cases.

have comparative merit even though it cannot be subsumed under the comparative method'. Guy Peters (1998, p. 62) makes the key observation: 'if it is well done, case analysis can be one of the more theory-driven forms of comparative analysis'. In reality, case studies provide the lion's share of articles published in journals of comparative politics (Hull, 1999).

So a single case offers a detailed illustration of a theme of wider interest. For instance, we could take the United States as an example of presidential government, Canada as an illustration of federalism and Sweden's Social Democrats as an example of a dominant party. We can trace the process through which these structures and organizations developed (with a focus on any turning points), examine how these entities operate today, and conclude with some general observations which could be taken up in explicitly comparative work (Pierson, 2004).

In the absence of overarching theory, case studies are the building blocks from which we construct our understanding of the political world (Yin, 2003). Rather like judges in common law systems, political scientists usually proceed by comparing cases rather than by making deductions from first principles. In consequence, much comparative political analysis takes the form not of relating cases to abstract theory, but simply of drawing analogies between the cases themselves. For instance: how did the process of state-building differ between post-colonial states of the twentieth century and the states of early modern Europe? What are the similarities and differences between the Russian and Chinese revolutions? Why does the plurality electoral system produce a two-party system in the USA but a multiparty system in India?

In practical politics, too, much practical reasoning operates by analogy. Decision-makers and analysts look for similar cases from earlier times or other countries, so that lessons can be learned and errors avoided. For instance, America's defeat in Vietnam served for a generation of policy-makers as a negative warning about the dangers of foreign entanglement (Khong, 1992). In domestic policy, schemes that work in one country – say, for improving reading standards in schools – may be emulated elsewhere. This strategy of learning from other cases reflects common sense; indeed, public policy would probably improve if it was tried more often (Rose, 2004).

But, of course, what worked then and there does not always work here and now. By its nature, a single case is embedded in its context; that is both the strength and weakness of the design. It is only when we try to draw lessons from abroad that we are in a position to distinguish between case and context. Typically, we discover that what worked so well in country A works less well in country B because of contextual differences we had not anticipated. The policy which worked like a dream in raising reading standards in country A registers no impact at all when emulated in country B. But at least we can now raise a focused comparative question: what differences between the countries explain why the same policy led to such contrasting results? In this way, case studies can encourage the search for more general knowledge.

A case study is a research strategy rather than a specific technique. In practice, case studies are multi-method, using the range of techniques in the political scientist's toolbag. The kit includes:

- reading the academic literature
- examining secondary documents (e.g. newspapers)
- searching for primary material (e.g. unpublished reports)
- conducting interviews with participants and other observers in the country, organization or other unit under scrutiny
- experiencing, or at least visiting, the unit under study

In other words, scholars of cases engage in 'soaking and poking, marinating themselves in minutiae' (King *et al.*, 1994, p. 38). Case studies aim to provide a description which is both rounded and detailed, a goal which the anthropologist Clifford Geertz (1973) famously defined as 'thick description'. Case analysis blends well with the current emphasis on interpretive explanation in politics.

By definition, all case studies possess broader significance, but this added value can be acquired in various ways. Box 5.4 outlines five types of case study. A case can be useful because it is representative, prototypical, deviant, archetypal or critical (or a combination of these).

Of these designs, the representative case is the most common. It is the workhorse of case studies, as useful as it is undramatic. Often researchers will use

BOX 5.4

Some types of case study

	Definition	Example
Representative	Typical of the category	Coalition government in Finland
Prototypical	Expected to become typical	The United States as a pioneering democracy
Deviant	The exception to the rule	India as a case of democracy in a poor country
Archetypal	Creates the category	The French Revolution
Critical	If it works here, it will work anywhere	Imposing democracy on post-invasion Iraq

Further reading: Yin (2003, 2004).

their own country as a representative case. For example, researchers may be interested in coalition formation in general but choose to study the phenomenon in their own country in detail. The home country is the research site but the hope is that the results will contribute to broader, comparative understanding. A collection of representative case studies will provide the raw material for later distillation.

By contrast, a **prototypical case** is chosen not because it is representative but because it is expected to become so. As Rose (1991, p. 459) puts it, 'their present is our future'. Studying an early example can help us to understand a phenomenon which is growing in significance elsewhere. In the nineteenth century, for instance, the French scholar Alexis de Tocqueville (1835, ch. 1) studied America because of his interest in the new politics of democracy. He wrote, 'my wish has been to find there [in the USA] instruction by which we [in Europe] may ourselves profit'. De Tocqueville regarded the United States as a harbinger of democracy and therefore a guide to Europe's own future.

The purpose of a **deviant case** study is very different. Here we deliberately seek out the exceptional and the untypical, rather than the norm: the countries which remain communist, or which are still governed by the military, or which seem to be immune from democratizing trends. Deviant cases are often used to tidy up our understanding of exceptions and anomalies: why is India an exception to the thesis that democracy presupposes prosperity? Why did tiny Switzerland adopt a federal architecture when most federations are in large countries? Why does turnout stay high in Denmark as it falls elsewhere (Elkit, Svensson and Togeby, 2005)? Deviant cases always attract interest and, by providing a contrast with the norm, can help our understanding of typical examples. But since the exceptional is always more exotic, the danger is overstudy. Comparative politics should be more than a collection of curios.

Reflecting the tendency for comparative politics to move from cases to theory, some of the most important examples in comparative politics are best conceived as **archetypal cases** or exemplars. An archetypal case serves to generate the category of which it is then taken, in a somewhat circular way, as representative. Archetypal cases are exemplars. For instance, the French Revolution altered the whole concept of revolution, reconstructing the idea as a progressive, modernizing force. In this way, the French Revolution made possible all the modern revolutions which followed. In similar fashion, the

American presidency does far more than illustrate the presidential system of government; it is the model which influenced later attempts to create similar systems, notably in Latin America.

Finally, a **critical case** (also called a crucial case), enables a proposition to be tested in the circumstances least favourable to its validity. The logic is simple: if true here, then true everywhere. For instance, attempting to introduce democracy to Iraq following the American invasion was a difficult assignment. If democracy could be imposed successfully in that case, it could surely also be imposed in more favourable situations, for example in countries with prior experience of democracy and fewer internal divisions. Thus Iraq provides a critical case for the proposition that democracy can be imposed. Similarly, if we find that political participation is low even among a sample of politics students, we can be fairly sure that it will be lower still among the wider population. So a critical case design seeks to build a potential for generalization into a single case study but at the risk of betting in advance that the relevant proposition will, in fact, be confirmed in unfavourable conditions.

Focused comparisons

Focused comparisons fall between case studies and statistical analysis. They are small-*N* studies concentrating on the intensive comparison of an aspect of politics in a few countries. Most often, the number of countries is either two, a paired or binary comparison, or three, a triangular comparison. The emphasis is on the comparison at least as much as on the cases; otherwise, the design would be a multiple case study. The concern with pre-defined aspects of the cases explains why George (1979) calls this method 'structured, focused comparison'. Countries are normally selected to introduce variation into the dependent variable, thus overcoming an inherent limit of the single case study.

To illustrate the technique, consider two examples using paired comparison. First, Kudrle and Marmor (1981) compared the growth of social security programmes in the United States and Canada. They sought to understand Canada's higher levels of spending and programme development, concluding that the elements of left-wing ideology and conservative paternalism found there were the key contrasts with the USA.

Second, a classic study by Heclo (1974) compared the origins of unemployment insurance, old age pensions and earnings-related supplementary pensions in Britain and Sweden. In both countries, Heclo concluded, the bureaucracy was the main agency of policy formulation. In contrast to Kudrle and Marmor, and indeed to many focused comparisons, Heclo's project was unusual in seeking to explain a similarity rather than a difference between the countries examined.

Focused comparisons such as these have proved to be the success story of comparative politics in recent decades (Collier, 1991). Like case studies, they remain sensitive to the details of particular countries and policies but in addition they demand the intellectual discipline inherent in the comparative enterprise. That is, the dimensions of comparison must be addressed, similarities and differences identified and some effort made to account for the contrasts observed.

Unlike many statistical studies, focused comparisons remain sensitive to history. Indeed, the format works particularly well when, as with Heclo, a few countries are compared over time, examining how they vary in their response to common problems.

How should countries be selected for a focused comparison? A common strategy is to select countries which, although differing on the factor under study, are otherwise similar. This is a **most similar** design. With this approach, we seek to compare countries which are as similar as possible in, say, their history, culture and political institutions, so that we can clearly rule out such common factors as explanations for the particular difference of interest to us. For instance, we might seek to explain why Britain managed a more peaceful transition to democracy than Germany, comparing two large countries with a common European heritage.

A **most similar** design takes similar countries for comparison on the assumption, as Lipset (1990, p. xiii) put it, that 'the more similar the units being compared, the more possible it should be to isolate the factors responsible for differences between them'. By contrast, the **most different** design seeks to show the robustness of a relationship by demonstrating its validity across diverse settings (Przeworski and Teune, 1970).

However, even with a most similar design many factors will remain as possible explanations for an observed difference and usually there will be no decisive way of testing between them. The problem of too many variables and too few countries cannot be sidestepped; in practice, the value of a focused comparison lies in the journey rather than the destination.

A **most different** design takes a contrasting approach. Here, the object is to test a relationship by discovering whether it can be observed in a range of different countries. If so, our confidence that the relationship is real, and not due to both factors depending on an unmeasured third variable, will increase (Peters, 1998).

For example, Rothstein (2002) examines the evolution of social and political trust in two contrasting democracies, Sweden and the United States, assuming that any trends shared between these two very different countries should also be observable in other democracies. In a similar way, if we were to find that the plurality method of election were associated with a two-party system in the diverse group of countries employing that method, our confidence in the robustness of this relationship would increase. A most different design is the basis of much statistical research, to which we now turn.

Statistical analysis

In comparative politics, statistical research is now less common than it was in the behavioural era but it remains a significant and worthwhile strand. In contrast to the techniques reviewed so far, the statistical approach is based on variables rather than cases. Specifically, the object is to explore the covariation between variables.

In such analyses, one variable is **dependent** while the others are **independent** or explanatory. Examples of such work in comparative politics include tests of the following hypotheses:

- The more educated a population, the higher its proportion of post-materialists;
- The higher a person's social status, the greater his or her participation in politics;
- The more affluent a country, the more likely it is to be a liberal democracy;
- Presidential government is less stable than parliamentary government.

> In a statistical analysis, the **dependent variable** is the factor we wish to account for; for example, party voted for. The **independent variable** is the factor believed to influence the dependent variable; for example, level of education.

To illustrate the statistical approach, consider an example. Figure 5.1 is a scatterplot showing the relationship between the number of members in a national assembly (the dependent variable) and a country's population, within the 10–60 million range (the independent variable). Such a plot displays all the information about these two factors for the countries surveyed. The graph reveals a **positive correlation**: the larger the population, the larger the assembly.

> The **correlation** coefficient measures the accuracy with which we can predict from one statistical variable to another. Correlations are scored from 0 to 1. Irrespective of its size, a correlation can be **positive** (when one variable goes up, so does the other) or **negative** (when one variable goes up, the other goes down).

However, the content of the graph can be summarized more precisely. This is achieved by calculating a **regression line**: that is, the line giving the best fit to the data. This line, also shown in the figure, is defined by a formula linking the variables. In this case, the formula reveals that, on average, the size of an assembly increases by 72 members for each increment of 10 million in a country's population. Given such an equation, we can use the population of any particular country to predict its assembly size; alternatively, and less precisely, we can use a ruler.

A regression equation allows us to identify **outliers**, also known as deviant or off-the-line cases. The greater the difference between the predicted and the actual assembly size, the greater the need for additional explanation, thus providing a link to case analysis. In our example, Cuba's National Assembly of People's Power is far larger than would be expected for a country with a population of just 11 million. How can we account for this outlier? The answer may be that communist states adopted large

> The **regression line** is the line of best fit in a scatterplot. **Outliers** are the observations furthest away from the value predicted by the regression line.

Figure 5.1 Population and assembly size, 2005, showing the line of best fit and highlighting two outliers

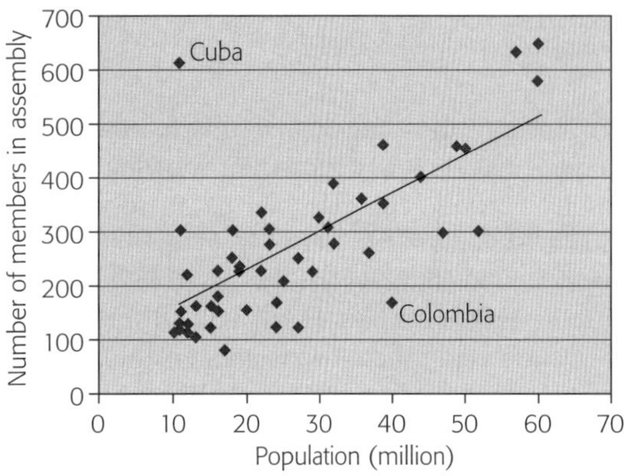

assemblies as a way of reducing any threat they might pose to the party's power. Such an interpretation offers a plausible starting point for further investigation, giving us a case selection strategy in which the case is nested within a statistical framework (Lieberman, 2005).

Statistical methodology can provide precise summaries of large amounts of data using standard techniques whose use can be checked by other researchers. But the approach carries two main risks. The first is that a strong correlation between two variables may arise simply because both depend on a third, unmeasured factor. For example, the tendency for multi-party systems to emerge in countries employing proportional representation (PR) might arise because both factors emerge in divided societies, not because PR itself increases the number of parties. Or the members of minority groups might exhibit low turnout at elections because they are concentrated among the poor, not because of their ethnic status as such.

In principle, the solution to spurious correlation is simple: include all relevant variables in the analysis, for statistical techniques can effectively control for such problems. In practice, not all the relevant variables will be known and spurious correlation is a continuing danger. However, even a spurious correlation may be a useful if risky basis for prediction.

The second risk is that even if a relationship is genuine, the direction of causation remains to be established. Suppose we find that liberal democracies secure higher rates of economic growth than authoritarian regimes. We still face a problem of interpretation. Does the correlation arise because democracies facilitate economic growth or because a high rate of growth fosters a stable democracy? A case can be made either way, or both, and by itself a statistical correlation will not provide the answer.

Worthwhile statistical analysis can be conducted even when the variables take the form of categories (e.g. yes/no) rather than numerical scores. For example, are federations less likely than unitary states to develop welfare states? Is proportional representation linked to coalition government? Are Christian countries more likely than Islamic ones to be democratic? A straightforward cross-tabulation is the qualitative equivalent of the scatterplot in Figure 5.1 and can be equally useful. Correlation-like statistics can also be estimated from tables (Pennings, Keman and Kleinnijenhuis, 2005).

Not all statistical work is concerned with estimating the impact of one factor on another. Simple counts provide a useful beginning. As Miller (1995) points out, asking the plain question 'how many of them are there?' is well worthwhile. For instance: how many federations are there? How many states are democratic? What was the probability that an authoritarian regime in 1980 had become democratic by 2005? Such questions must be answered if we are to achieve our objective of comprehending the variability of the political world. Just as straightforward case studies often contribute more to comparative politics than elaborate attempts at theory-testing, so simple counting can provide more useful results than sophisticated statistical analysis.

Avoiding the pitfalls

Any approach brings its own dangers and the breadth inherent in comparative politics brings its own risks (Box 5.5). We proceed by examining these difficulties one by one.

Knowledge requirements

By definition, any comparative study involves more than one country. A statistical analysis, such as an examination of the relationship between economic development and democracy, may draw on informa-

BOX 5.5

The difficulties of comparison

- By definition, comparative research demands knowledge of more than one political system;
- The 'same' phenomenon can mean different things in different countries, creating difficulties in comparing like with like;
- Globalization means that countries cannot be regarded as independent of each other, thus reducing the effective number of cases available for testing theories;
- The countries selected for study may be an unrepresentative sample, limiting the significance of the findings;
- Any pair of countries will differ in many ways, meaning we can never achieve the experimenter's dream of holding all factors constant apart from the one whose effects we wish to test.

tion from every country in the world. Clearly, the knowledge requirements for research in comparative politics can be substantial. One common solution is to form a team of researchers, each expert in at least one of the countries included in the study. In this way, knowledge deficits can be reduced.

Fortunately, the idea that knowledge requirements increase directly with the number of cases is a misconception, albeit an understandable one. In comparative research, the focus should be on the comparison as much as the countries. Breadth is at least as valuable as depth; indeed detail can often distract from the larger picture. One reason for engaging in large-*N* analysis is precisely to uncover relationships that apply across settings; in other words, the variables are deliberately extracted from their context.

For example, discussing the general trend towards proportional representation does not call for in-depth knowledge of the electoral system in every country. Similarly, we can draw conclusions about democratization in Latin America without understanding the intricacies of the transition in every case. And those who debate the relative merits of presidential and parliamentary government cannot possibly read all that has been written about the operation of the executive in every country where these forms of government have been tried.

The task in comparative politics is not to know all there is to know. Rather, the skill is to use specialist knowledge so as to produce new and more general observations. What matters is knowing what needs to be known and being able to find it out.

Understanding meaning

In comparing politics across countries, we should remember that the meaning of an action depends on the conventions of the country concerned. For instance, styles of political representation are highly variable. Where Nigerian politicians seek to impress by acts of flamboyant extravagance (such as seducing their competitors' female companions), Swedish politicians set out to affirm their very ordinariness (Chabal and Daloz, 2006). What works in Lagos would be disastrous in Stockholm and what succeeds in Stockholm would be met with indifference in Lagos. Similarly, when British MPs vote against their party in the House of Commons, their acts carry more significance than when American legislators do the 'same' thing in the less partisan Senate. In short, meaning varies with context.

Students of comparative politics must therefore be capable of understanding how politics is viewed in different countries. For example, is politics in a particular country based on class, race or religion? The answer can only be discovered by understanding how people in that country construct and interpret their political world. As Green (2002a, p. 6) puts it, 'actors have identities, world-views and cognitive frames, informed by culture, that shape perceptions and interests'. Perhaps all politicians everywhere are motivated solely by rational self-interest but, even so, what those interests are, and how they are pursued, will vary according to the particular environment in which politicians operate.

For some authors, interpreting how politics is constructed or interpreted in a particular country is no mere preliminary to a comparative project; rather, it is the stuff of comparative research itself. For instance, do politicians in a particular country view globalization as a danger to be resisted (a view many French politicians claim to support) or as a spur to essential domestic reform (as with Margaret Thatcher's administration in the United Kingdom)? From this perspective, there is no phenomenon of globalization independent of the ideas political actors hold about it (Hay, 2002, p. 204). At any rate, 'what is the meaning of it?' should always be the first, if not the only, question in comparative analysis (Yanow and Schwartz-Shea, 2006).

The implication of this **interpretive approach** is that we should be wary of starting comparative projects with excessively scientific pretensions. Our first task – some would say our main task – is to understand politics from the viewpoint of participants in the countries concerned.

> An **interpretive approach** to politics emphasizes the importance of grasping the ideas which political actors themselves hold about their activity. The assumption is that political reality does not exist independently of people's ideas; rather, political discourse in a particular country largely defines that reality (Bevir and Rhodes, 2002).

This problem of the meaning and significance of action is particularly important in politics because the activity is partly conducted through coded language. Were the people who attacked the World Trade Center and the Pentagon murderers, martyrs or both? Were American civil rights activists also black militants? Were active members of the Irish Republican Army terrorists or freedom-fighters? How such actors are described reflects existing political opinions, raising doubts about whether we can find, or should seek, a neutral language for interpreting our subject matter.

Globalization

Globalization poses a considerable challenge to comparative politics, understood as the comparison of separate states. Although 191 'independent' countries belonged to the United Nations by 2006, in reality far fewer cases are available to the student of comparative politics. Countries learn from, copy, compete with, influence and even invade each other in a constant process of interaction. As we saw in Chapter 2, even the states which provide the units of our subject did not develop separately; rather, the idea of statehood diffused outwards from its proving ground in Europe. As Dogan and Pelassy (1990, p. 1) say, 'there is no nation without other nations'. The major transitions of world history – industrialization, colonialism, decolonization, democratization – unfolded on a world stage. In that sense we have one global system rather than a world of independent states. Green (2002a, p. 5) puts the point well when he says the world is arranged 'as if national polities are in fact cells of a larger entity with a life all its own'. The implication is that we should study this larger organism rather than its component parts.

Specific institutional forms also reflect diffusion. The communist model was often imposed by force of Soviet arms; the presidential system in Latin America was imported from the United States; the ombudsman was a device copied from Sweden. The development of international organizations, from the United Nations to the European Union, also creates a newer layer of governance to which all member states must react.

Why do connections between states constitute a pitfall for students of comparative politics? The answer is provided by Tilly (1997): comparative politics traditionally presumes distinct and separate units of comparison, most often states, which can be treated as if they are independent. That assumption was always a simplification but in an interdependent world such a presumption has become positively misleading. Technically, treating countries as independent entities artificially inflates the sample size in statistical analysis, resulting in exaggerated confidence in the significance of the results obtained.

How students of comparative politics will react to the issue of globalization is a story still to unfold. It is one thing to agree with Jackson and Nexon (2002, p. 89) that it is 'difficult to clearly differentiate between the subject areas of comparative politics and international relations'. However, it is quite another to propose a merger between these two distinct fields, each with its own history and body of knowledge. How global processes interact with state forms is clearly an important theme for both disciplines. But this relationship flows in both directions: states shape the world at least as much as the world reshapes states.

Too many variables, too few countries

This is a major problem for those who conceive of comparative politics as a version of the experimenter's laboratory, in which researchers patiently seek to isolate the impact of a single variable. Even with nearly 200 sovereign states, it is impossible to find a country which is identical to another in all respects except for that factor (say, the electoral system) whose effects we wish to detect. For this reason, political comparison can never be as precise as laboratory experiments. We just do not have enough countries to go round.

To make the same point from another angle, we will never be able to test all the possible explanations of a political difference between countries. For example, several plausible reasons can be invoked to 'explain' why Britain and the USA were two of the countries most sympathetic to introducing the private sector into the running of public services during the 1990s. Perhaps the strength of these reforms reflected the right-wing ideology of Prime Minister Thatcher and President Reagan. Or perhaps the public sector in these English-speaking countries was vulnerable to reform because, unlike several democracies in continental Europe, its structure was not protected by the constitution and civil law codes.

Here we have two potential explanations for Anglo-American distinctiveness, one based on ideology and the other on law. Both interpretations are broadly consistent with the facts. But we have no way of isolating which factor is decisive. Ideally, we would want to discover whether the public sector had been reformed in those crucial countries where just one of the two factors applied. But at this point we typically discover that there are no such countries; we have run out of cases.

In such circumstances, we can of course resort to asking hypothetical 'what if' questions. Would public sector reform have progressed in Britain and the USA even without the right-wing leadership of Thatcher and Reagan? In general we should not shy away from such **counterfactuals**; they must form part of any attempt to estimate the impact of unique events. Although Tetlock and Belkin (1996) have developed useful guidelines for judging the plausibility of any particular counter-factual, by definition the outcome of such thought experiments can never be tested against reality.

Selection bias

We turn finally to a more technical difficulty in comparative politics which nonetheless has implications for all those who practise the art. **Selection bias** is a risk in any study in which the units of study (such as countries) are not sampled randomly; the point is not so much to eliminate such bias as to be aware of its continual presence.

> A **counterfactual** is a thought experiment speculating on possible outcomes if A had occurred rather than B. What would our world be like if Hitler had died in a car crash in 1932 or if his invasion of Russia had succeeded? (Rosenfeld, 2005).

This danger often emerges as an unintended result of haphazard selection. For example, we choose to study those countries which speak our language, or which have good exchange schemes, or in which we feel safe. As a result, large, powerful countries are studied more intensively than small, powerless ones. Similarly, current cases receive more attention than past examples, simply because political science focuses, perhaps excessively, on the present (Pierson, 2004).

One result of these biases in selection is that the findings of comparative politics become weighted towards contemporary liberal democracies, a rare form of government in the expanse of human history. A virtue of statistical designs covering a large number of countries is that they reduce the risk of selection bias. Indeed, if the study covers all current countries, selection bias disappears – at least so long as generalization is restricted to the contemporary world.

But, alas, the problem may just resurface in another form, through an unrepresentative selection of variables rather than countries. For example, much statistical research in comparative politics, including the scores used in the country profiles in this book, relies on existing data collected by governments and international bodies with different interests from our own. However, the priorities of these organizations tend to be economic rather than political. So the availability of data means that financial and economic variables receive more atten-

> **Selection bias** arises when the choice of what to study produces results that are unrepresentative of the wider class from which the cases and variables are drawn. Studies of English-speaking democracies may not be representative of all democracies; studies of communist parties that remain in power today may not be typical of ruling communist parties in the twentieth century.

tion than they justify, and politics runs the risk of being treated as a branch of economics.

A particularly important form of selection bias comes from examining only positive cases, thus eliminating all variation in the phenomenon we seek to explain. Because this is a common, noteworthy and avoidable mistake, it deserves careful consideration in any comparative design. King *et al.* (1994, p. 129) explain the problem:

> The literature is full of work that makes the mistake of failing to let the dependent variable vary; for example, research that tries to explain the outbreak of wars with studies only of wars, the onset of revolutions with studies only of revolutions, or patterns of voter turnout with interviews only of nonvoters.

When only positive cases of a phenomenon are studied, conclusions about the causes and consequences of the phenomenon are ruled out. Contrast is needed to give variation, so that we can then consider what distinguishes times of war from times of peace, periods of revolution from periods of stability and abstainers from voters. Without such variation, we can still identify common characteristics of the cases (which can itself be of great value) but we have no contrast to explore and explain. We do not know whether the conditions leading to revolution often exist without triggering a revolution, or whether the political cynicism we find among abstainers is equally prevalent among those who do turn out on election day (Geddes, 2003).

Survivorship bias is a particularly insidious form of this general problem. It arises when non-survivors are excluded, leading to biased results. Studying contemporary communist states or military governments as representative of the entire class of such regimes (past as well as present) is an error because those that have survived are likely to differ from those that disappeared. We should not treat those who complete a journey as typical of those who started out for to do so would be to ignore the casualties along the way. A tobacco company may defend its products by pointing to smokers who live to a ripe old age, and a university may advertise the number of degrees it awards while keeping quiet about its drop-out rate. But in comparative politics we should look through both ends of the telescope, at starters as well as finishers.

Learning Resources for Chapter 5

Next step

Peters (1998) is a thorough and judicious discussion of the comparative method.

Further reading

Dogan and Pelassy (1990) is a challenging account of the comparative approach, more philosophical than Peters but insightful even so. For general overviews, Lijphart (1971) and Mair (1996) are well worth reading. King *et al.* (1994) contribute much to comparative research strategy. Green (2002b) examines the interpretive approach, a theme also covered in the collection by Yanow and Schwartz-Shea (2006). For the institutional approach, see Peters (1999) and, for enthusiasts, Rhodes, Binder and Rockman (2006). For the state-centred approach, see Evans *et al.* (2003). Yin (2003) is the standard source on case studies; see also his selection of examples (2004). For case selection in political research, see George and Bennett (2005) and especially Geddes (2003). Focused comparisons are considered in Ragin (1987, 1994) and Ragin *et al.* (1996). Pennings, Keman and Kleinnijenhuis (2005) look at statistical methods in comparative politics. Pierson (2004) addresses the incorporation of history into political analysis. Comprehensive edited collections include Sica (2006) on the comparative method in the social sciences and Wiarda (2004b) on comparative politics.

Internet sources

Committee on Concepts and Methods
A research committee of the International Political Science Association
http://www.concepts-methods.org/

Comparative Methods in Political and Social Research
David Levi-Faur's course materials
http://poli.haifa.ac.il/~levi/method.html

Small-*N* Compass
Systematic cross-case analysis
http://smalln.spri.ucl.ac.be/

Society for Political Methodology
The political methodology section of the American Political Science Association
http://polmeth.wustl.edu/

Part II
POLITICS AND SOCIETY

The relationship between politics and society has always preoccupied political thinkers. Government does not operate in isolation, unaffected by the society of which it forms part, but rather both reflects and helps to shape the broader social framework. For example, the nature of rule is bound to differ significantly between Christian, Islamic and secular societies. Similarly, the presentation of politics through the media must surely influence popular perceptions of the political process. And the economic dimension of society plays an important part in structuring the public's assessments of government performance.

In this part, Chapter 6 looks at political culture, Chapter 7 discusses communication flows between politics and society, while Chapter 8 examines the important subfield of political economy.

Chapter 6
Political culture

Culture is defined by Unesco (2002) as 'the set of distinctive spiritual, material, intellectual and emotional features of society or a social group. It encompasses, in addition to art and literature, lifestyles, ways of living together, value systems, traditions and beliefs'. In other words, culture is the essential human characteristic, expressing our nature as aware social beings. Unlike nature (with which it is often contrasted), culture involves values, symbols, meanings and expectations. It tells us who we are, what is important to us and how we should behave. Any large country will contain a number of cultural groups, forming either a national culture and one or more subcultures or, when the balance is more even, a multicultural society.

A definition of **political culture** flows easily from this account of culture. It refers to the overall pattern of beliefs, attitudes and values in a society towards the political system. The concept can be usefully compared with political ideology. Political culture is a broader, more diffuse but also more widely applicable notion. Where an ideology refers to an explicit system of ideas, political culture comes closer to Linz's notion of mentalities: 'ways of thinking and feeling, more emotional than rational, that provide non-codified ways of reacting to different situations' (Linz, 2000, p. 162). With the decay of ideology, political culture has become a major highway into understanding the role of beliefs and attitudes in politics.

Gabriel Almond, the father of modern studies of political culture, teaches us that sentiments and mentalities can be an independent force in political life: 'political values, feelings and beliefs are not simple reflections of social and political structure . . . the political content of the minds of citizens and political elites is more complex, more persistent and more autonomous than Marxism and liberalism would suggest' (1993, p. 14). Mass attitudes towards government will of course reflect what the government has done in the past but – and here is Almond's point – these sentiments will in turn affect what the government can achieve in the present and the future. In this way, political culture connects government not just with society but also with its own history.

Political culture in liberal democracies

Political culture denotes 'the sum of the fundamental values, sentiments and knowledge that give form and substance to political processes' (Pye, 1995, p. 965).

Political culture is particularly important in liberal democracies, since the connections between society and government are especially strong in this type of regime. Cultural respect for restraints on power and individual rights are also a key factor separating liberal from illiberal democracies. In examining political culture in this context, we begin with Almond and Verba's classic account of the civic culture, a study based largely on democratic countries. We then turn to ideas that have attracted more recent attention: political trust, social capital and postmaterialism.

The civic culture

Almond and Verba's *The Civic Culture* (1963) sought to identify the political culture within which a liberal democracy is most likely to develop and consolidate. This landmark investigation became a political equivalent of Weber's attempt (1905) to discover the cultural source of modern capitalism. Where Weber located 'the spirit of capitalism' in protestant values, Almond and Verba find the source of stable democracy in what they call a civic culture.

Almond and Verba's argument is based on a distinction between three pure types of political culture: the parochial, the subject and the participant.

- In a *parochial* political culture, citizens are only indistinctly aware of the existence of central government, as with remote tribes whose existence is seemingly unaffected by central government. In liberal democracies, parochial elements can be found in isolated rural communities and in some inner city areas where first-generation immigrants do not speak the dominant language.
- In a *subject* political culture, citizens see themselves not as participants in the political process but rather as subjects of the government, as with people living under a dictatorship. In liberal democracies, subject attitudes may be growing among young people, many of whom remain distant from politics even though they recognize government's impact on their lives.
- In the familiar *participant* political culture, citizens believe both that they can contribute to the political system and that they are affected by its operation.

It is easy to assume that people with participant attitudes form the model citizen army of a stable liberal democracy. But the interest of Almond and Verba's study rests precisely in their rejection of such a proposition. The authors propose that democracy will prove most stable in societies blending different cultures in a particular mix they term the 'civic culture' (Figure 6.1). The ideal conditions for democracy, they suggest, emerge when subject and parochial attitudes combine to provide ballast to an essentially participant culture.

Figure 6.1 Almond and Verba's theory of the civic culture

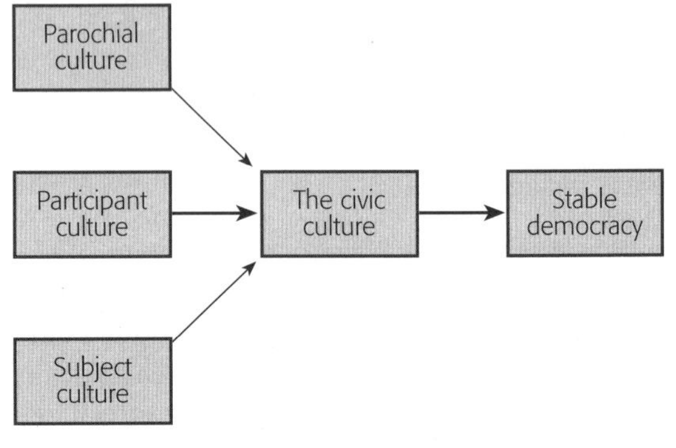

In this civic culture, many citizens are active in politics but the passive minority (whether parochials or subjects) stabilize the system. Further, participants are not so involved as to refuse to accept decisions with which they disagree. Thus the civic culture resolves the tension within democracy between popular control and effective governance: it allows for citizen influence while retaining flexibility for the government.

Armed with this theory, Almond and Verba set out to discover which countries in their study came closest to a civic culture. In 1959 and 1960, they conducted sample surveys in the USA, Britain, Italy, Mexico, the USA and West Germany. Of these countries, Britain and to a lesser extent the United States came closest to the civic ideal. In both countries citizens felt they could influence the government but often chose not to do so, thus conferring on the government its required agility. By contrast, the political cultures of Italy, Mexico and West Germany all deviated in various ways from the authors' prescription.

Like most original works, Almond and Verba's study attracted considerable scrutiny (Barry, 1988). Critics alleged that the whole notion of a national political culture is inherently vague and that the authors should have focused more on subcultures of race and class within the societies examined. Had they done so, suggests Macpherson (1977, p. 88), they would have discovered that the participants are the educated middle class while the parochials are the poorly educated working class. These critics claimed that the civic culture was simply a sanitized reformulation of class rule.

Nor did Almond and Verba offer a detailed account of the origins of political culture. In particular, it is possible that citizens believe they can affect government just because they can actually do so, a point that would suggest political culture reflects government more than it shapes it. Also, the authors initially had little to say about the evolution of political culture over time, a theme which – as we shall see – characterized much later discussion in this area, not least in Germany.

Political trust and social capital

Times move on. In the half century following Almond and Verba's study, many established democracies hit turbulent waters: Vietnam and student activism in the 1960s, the oil crisis of the 1970s, the anti-nuclear and ecology movements of the 1980s, privatization and cutbacks to the welfare state in the 1990s and terrorism in the 2000s.

As Almond and Verba (1980) noted in an initial update, such events left their mark on Western political cultures. More recent research in the area has therefore focused on whether liberal democracies have suffered a decline in political and social trust. And the answer, in general, is that they have, although the fall focuses on the public's confidence in the performance of democratic institutions rather than on the principle of democracy itself.

In a comparative study, Norris (1999a, p. 20) concluded that overall public confidence in such institutions as parliament, the civil service and the armed forces declined between 1981 and 1991 in each of the 17 countries she examined. Separate surveys show that European publics place less trust in the agencies of representation such as parties than in the forces of law and order, such as the military and the police (Inoguchi, 2002). Yet although electors have grown somewhat cynical about the operation of democracy, support for the underlying principle remains widespread even among today's disillusioned democrats. Democratic values now command widespread acceptance as an ideal, but at the same time citizens have often become more critical of the workings of the core institutions of representative democracy.

The United States dramatically illustrates the decline of trust in government. In 1964, three-quarters of Americans said that they trusted the federal government 'to do the right thing'; by 1994, at the bottom of the cycle, only a quarter did so (Figure 6.2). Much of this decline was brought about by specific events such as the Vietnam War and Watergate, though partial recoveries occurrred during periods of peace and prosperity. Thus, trust recovered somewhat as the economy and stock market boomed in the late 1990s.

Despite the intelligence failings exposed by 9/11, faith in government received a massive short-term boost following the attacks. In traditional fashion, Americans rallied round the flag (Brewer, Aday and Gross, 2003). But contemporary faith in national government remains well below the levels recorded

Figure 6.2 Americans' trust in the government in Washington, 1964–2004

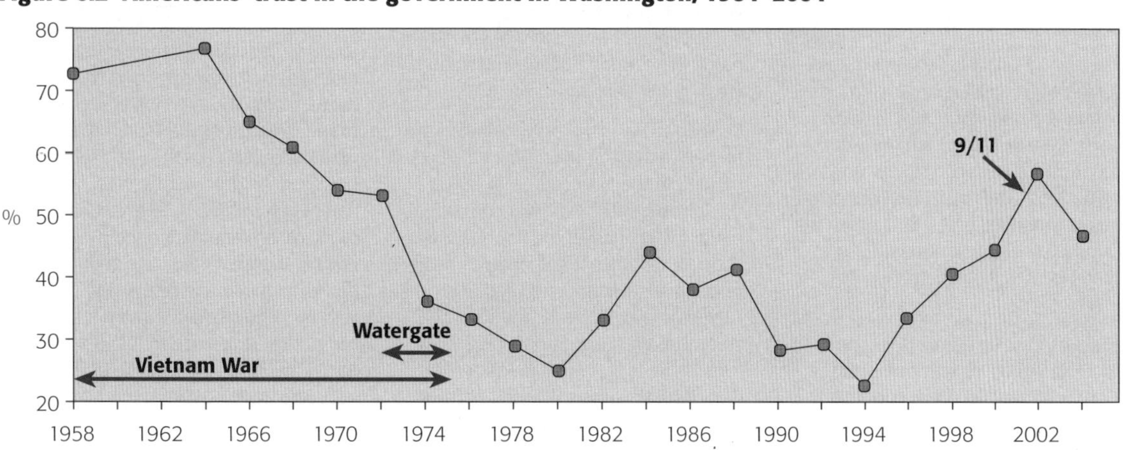

Note: Per cent trusting 'the government in Washington to do what is right' just about always or most of the time.
Sources: National Election Studies, University of Michigan; Mackenzie and Labiner (2002).

COUNTRY PROFILE

GERMANY

Form of government ■ a constitutional and parliamentary federal republic.

Legislature ■ the 614-member Bundestag is the lower house. The smaller and weaker upper house, the Bundesrat, represents the 16 federal Länder (states).

Executive ■ the chancellor leads a cabinet of between 16 and 22 ministers. A president serves as ceremonial head of state.

Constitution and judiciary ■ Germany is a state based on law (a Rechtstaat). The Federal Constitutional Court has proved to be highly influential as an arbiter of the constitution and, externally, as the model of a constitutional (rather than an American-style supreme) court.

Electoral system ■ the Bundestag is elected through the influential mixed-member proportional system which has now been adopted in over 20 countries. Members of the Bundesrat are nominated by the Länder, hence, the Bundesrat is never dissolved.

Party system ■ the leading parties are the SPD (Social Democratic Party) and the CDU (Christian Democratic Union). These parties formed a grand coalition after a close election in 2005. For the previous seven years, the SPD governed with the Greens. Previously, one of the leading parties typically ruled in conjunction with the liberal FDP (Free Democratic Party).

Population (annual growth rate): 82.4m (-0.02%)
World Bank income group: high income
Political Rights score: 1
Civil Liberties score: 1
Human development index (rank/out of): 19/177
Freedom of the press index (rank/out of): 20/194
Ease of doing business index (rank/out of): 21/175

Note: For meaning and sources of scales and indexes, see p. xvi. In all cases a score and rank of 1 is 'best'.

Among all the liberal democracies, **GERMANY** has experienced the most fragmented history. Although a German-speaking people has existed since time immemorial, Germany did not become a single entity until the formation of the German 'Empire' in 1871. Since then, the country's boundaries have been subject to frequent change, with losses of territory at the end of both world wars and a division of the remaining core into separate communist and democratic states in 1949. Germany was not reunited until 1990, when the communist east was successfully absorbed into the Federal Republic.

Aware of its difficult history, the FRG has been a motor for a united Europe in the post-war period. Its European commitment is entrenched in its constitution and for most of its existence (if less so now) the Federal Republic has been willing to support the EU with hard cash, to the detriment of its own budget. Because Germany naturally views European developments through the lens of its own system of government, the country's political institutions are of continental significance.

Seeking to avoid the political instability of the Weimar Republic, which had contributed to the Nazi seizure of power, the framers of the post-war constitution made the chancellor the key figure in the new republic. The chancellor determines government policy, appoints cabinet ministers, heads a staff of 500 and can be removed from office only when parliament simultaneously demonstrates a majority for a named successor. Within a parliamentary framework, Germany offers a distinctive form of 'chancellor democracy'.

Germany boasts the largest economy in Europe and the fifth largest in the world. Its skilled employees, working in capital-intensive factories, produce manufactured goods for export at premium prices. Germany is the world's largest exporter, ahead of the United States, China and Japan. By the late 1990s, however, the post-war German miracle had begun to fade. As the costs of reunification mounted, unemployment grew in the west while becoming entrenched in much of the east. The calls for reform became more insistent but cultural resistance to Anglo-American liberalism remained both wide and deep.

Further reading: Conradt (2005), Helms (2000).

SPOTLIGHT

Political culture in Germany

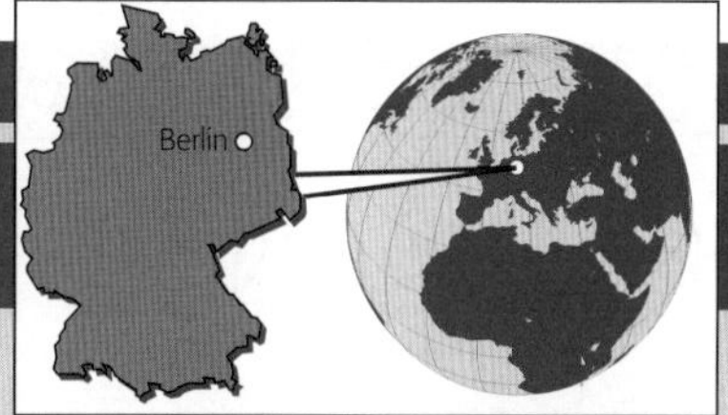

As well as studying the impact of political culture on government, it may be just as fruitful to examine how regimes affect values. As Almond (1993, p. 16) noted, 'the advocates of political culture recognise that causality works both ways: attitudes influence structure and behaviour, and structure and performance in turn influence political attitudes.' Here the post-war division of Germany provides a rare natural experiment, allowing us to gauge how the contrasting 'structure and performance' of the capitalist west and the communist east affected popular thinking.

Three main processes can be observed. The first is the positive impact of post-war economic recovery on political culture within the west. Between 1959 and 1988 the proportion of Germans in the FDR expressing pride in their political institutions increased from 7 to 51 per cent. Over a similar period, support for a multiparty system grew from 53 to 92 per cent. The emergence of a supportive public in the Federal Republic over this period certainly offers hope to other transitional countries seeking to build a democratic culture on an authoritarian history.

The second process is the impact of the communist German Democratic Republic on political culture. This effect can be estimated by comparing the attitudes of easterners and westerners immediately following reunification (Rainer and Sadler, 2006, who assume no differences in attitudes between east and west before 1949). Just after reunification, people in the east were significantly less trusting of parliament, the legal system and indeed each other than were people in western Germany. In 1991, for example, Germans who had lived under a totalitarian regime were 11 percentage points less trusting in these respects than their compatriots in western Gerrnany. The experience of living under a communist regime, and particularly one which engaged in such extraordinarily close surveillance of the population, seemed to have left its mark.

The third process is the impact of reunification on political culture in the former GDR. Here, there is strong evidence of declining contrasts between east and west. Trust in parliament and the legal system has increased dramatically in the east, leading Rainer and Sadler to project complete convergence in attitudes to these institutions by about 2010. Trust in other people among those in the east who have not experienced unemployment is also converging towards western levels. However, among easterners who have experienced unemployment since reunification, social trust seems to have declined rather than increased. Thus, the cultural reaction of east Germans to living in a liberal democracy is not uniform but varies with their success in coping with a market economy.

Broader cultural contrasts (and stereotypes) between east and west remain significant, however. Even in the decade after reunification, easterners and westerners remain, like Britons and Americans, divided by a common language. 'Ossis' tend to perceive 'Wessis' as bourgeois, patronising, materialistic and individualistic. Conversely, many westerners seem to look down on east Germans – and certainly are perceived to do so by easterners themselves.

Ostalgie, nostalgia for the German Democratic Republic, was a German cultural phenomenon of the early 2000s. It mocked Western seriousness by presenting a rose-tinted but also self-deprecating image of life in the communist East, focusing on such GDR icons as:

- *Ampelmänchen*: the little man on the traffic light.
- *Katarina Witt*: ice-skater and broadcaster.
- *Trabant cars*: bottled exhaust available.
- *Vita Cola*: fruity with notes of lemon.

Further reading: Berg-Schlosser and Rytlewski (1993), Kolinsky (2002), Rainer and Siedler (2006).

TIMELINE

GERMANY

1871	Germany is united under the leadership of the Prussian Chancellor, Otto von Bismarck.
1919	Treaty of Versailles imposes harsh conditions on Germany following its defeat in the First World War. The Weimar Republic, Germany's first experience with a fully democratic regime, is established.
1923	Hyperinflation begins. At its peak, prices doubled every 48 hours.
1931	Unemployment reaches six million. About one in two families were directly affected.
1933	Adolf Hitler is appointed Chancellor and institutes the Third Reich.
1941	Initiation of the holocaust in which at least five millions Jews are killed.
1945	Allies occupy Germany as the Third Reich collapses.
1949	The Federal Republic of Germany (FDR, West Germany) is established in the Western-occupied zone. The German Democratic Republic (GDR, East Germany) is established in the Soviet-occupied zone.
1990	Germany is reunited following the collapse of the GDR.
1999	The German capital moves from Bonn, in the west, to Berlin.
2005	The CDU and SPD form a grand coalition under Christian Democratic Chancellor Angela Merkel (CDU).

in the late 1950s, when Almond and Verba issued their positive appraisal of America's civic culture.

The long-term trend in political trust slopes downwards in other democracies too. In the UK, the proportion of people saying they would 'trust a British government of any party to place the needs of this country above the interests of their own political party' halved from 38 per cent in 1986 to 18 per cent in 2003 (BSA, 2006). So since Almond and Verba's study both the American and the British 'civic' cultures have witnessed a shift towards more sceptical and instrumental attitudes.

What are the consequences of falling confidence in political institutions? Putnam (2002) suggests that declining faith in government represents a deflation of the political culture, reducing the capacity of the political system to achieve shared goals. The argument here is that trust encourages solidarity among strangers. For example, as trust in government falls, so we might expect people to become less willing to: believe what their leaders say; vote at elections; pay taxes; fight in wars; and support any public projects in which they do not see a sure return for themselves (Hetherington, 2004).

By contrast, a culture of trust oils the wheels of collective action, enabling projects to be initiated which are impractical in a society where mutual suspicion prevails. It is ironic, suggest Putnam and Goss (2002, p. 1) that 'just at the moment of liberal democracy's greatest triumph, some fundamental social and cultural conditions for effective democracy may have eroded in recent decades, the result of a gradual but widespread process of civic disengagement'.

In an influential study using Italy as his laboratory, Putnam (1993) attempted to test such ideas by showing how a supportive political culture directly enhances the performance of a political system. In their original work, Almond and Verba had portrayed Italy as a country whose people felt uninvolved in, and alienated from, politics. At the time, Italy showed strong elements of the subject and parochial cultures. Putnam revisits Italy's political culture, paying more attention to diversity within the country. He demonstrates how cultural variations within Italy influenced the effectiveness of the 20 new regional governments created in the 1970s. Similar in structure and formal powers, these governments nonetheless varied greatly in performance. Some (such as Emilia-Romagna in the North) proved stable and effective, capable of making and implementing innovative policies. Others (such as Calabria in the South) achieved little. What, asks Putnam, explains these contrasts?

Putnam finds his answer in political culture. He argues that the most successful regions have a positive political culture: a tradition of trust and cooperation which results in high levels of **social capital**. By contrast, the least effective governments are found in regions lacking any tradition of collaboration and equality. In such circumstances, supplies of social capital run low and governments can achieve little.

Social capital refers to a culture of trust and cooperation which makes collective action possible and effective. As Putnam (2002) writes, it is the ability of a community to 'develop the "I" into the "we"'. A political culture with a fund of social capital enables a community to build political institutions with a capacity to solve collective problems.

But where does social capital itself come from? How does a community establish a foundation of mutual trust? Putnam's answer is historical: he attributes the uneven distribution of social capital in modern Italy to events deep within each area's history (Morlino, 1995). The more effective governments in the north draw on a tradition of communal self-government dating from the twelfth century. The least successful administrations in the south are burdened with a long history of feudal, foreign, bureaucratic and authoritarian rule. Thus, Putnam's analysis again illustrates how political culture can be a device through which the past influences the present. Although his interest in rebuilding trust might lead him to disagree, the implication seems to be that social capital is an inherited trait. It cannot be made to order.

Postmaterialism

One factor which helps to account for developments in political culture, at both mass and elite level, is postmaterialism. Along with the themes of political trust and social capital, this notion illustrates how political scientists have sought to incorporate change into their understanding of political culture.

From the late 1940s to the early 1970s, the Western world witnessed a period of unprecedented economic growth. 'You've never had it so good' became a cliché that summarized the experience of the post-war generation. This era was also a period of relative international peace, enabling cohorts to grow up with no experience of world war. In addition, the newly instituted welfare state (and increasing property prices in some countries) offered increased security to many Western populations against the demands of illness, unemployment and old age.

According to Inglehart (1971, 1997), this unique combination of affluence, peace and security led to a silent revolution in Western political cultures. He suggests that the priority accorded to economic achievement made way for increased emphasis on the quality of life: 'in a major part of the world, the disciplined, self-denying and achievement-oriented norms of industrial society are giving way to the choices over lifestyle which characterize post-industrial economies' (Inglehart, 1997, p. 28).

From the 1960s, a new generation of postmaterialists emerged: young, well-educated people focused on lifestyle issues such as ecology, nuclear disarmament and feminism. Where pre-war generations had valued order, security and fixed rules in such areas as religion and sexual morality, postmaterialists gave priority to self-expression and flexible rules, for themselves if not always for their own children. Postmaterialists were elite-challenging advocates of the new politics rather than elite-sustaining foot soldiers in the old party battles. They were more attracted to single-issue groups than to the broader packages offered by political parties.

Based on extensive survey evidence, Inglehart showed that the more affluent a democracy, the higher the proportion of postmaterialists within its borders. The United States was in the vanguard. In the early 1970s, American postmaterialists were concentrated among 'yuppies' – young, upwardly mobile urban professionals, especially those in the wealthiest state of all, California. Three decades later, this baby-boom generation retains a relatively progressive outlook despite its unparalleled affluence.

In Europe **postmaterialism** came first to, and made deepest inroads in, the wealthiest democracies such as Denmark, the Netherlands and West Germany. Norway apart, the affluent Scandinavian countries also proved receptive to these values (Knutsen, 1996). Postmaterialism was less common in poorer democracies with lower levels of education such as Greece.

> **Postmaterialism** is a commitment to radical quality of life issues (such as the environment) which can emerge, especially among the educated young, from a foundation of personal security and material affluence. Postmaterialists participate extensively in politics but are inclined to join elite-challenging promotional groups rather than traditional political parties.

If other things remain equal, postmaterial values will become more prominent. When Inglehart began his studies in 1970–71, materialists out-numbered postmaterialists by about four to one in many Western countries. By 2000 the two groups were much more even in size, a major transformation in political culture. Even allowing for the decay of radicalism with age, population replacement will continue to work its effect. As Inglehart (1999, p. 247) notes, 'as the younger birth cohorts replace the older more materialist cohorts, we should observe a shift towards the postmaterial orientation'.

The unerring expansion of education gives postmaterialism a further boost. Experience of higher education is the best single predictor of a postmaterial outlook. Indeed 'postmaterialism' can probably be best understood as the liberal outlook induced by degree-level education, especially in the arts and social sciences. These liberal values are then sustained through careers in professions where knowledge rather than capital or management authority is the key to success (Farnen and Meloen, 2000). The march of higher education, and the expansion of jobs in professional services, may be more important underpinnings of postmaterialism than the factors Inglehart himself emphasizes, namely peace, affluence and security.

Although postmaterialism is normally interpreted as a value shift among the general public, its most important effects may be on political elites. Inglehart's shock troops have moved into (and in some cases out of) positions of power, securing a platform from which their values could directly affect government decisions. For instance, the 1960s generation retained touches of radicalism even as it secured the seductive trappings of office. Thus, Bill Clinton (born 1946, the first president to be born after the war) offered a more liberal agenda to the American people than did his predecessor in the White House, George Bush (born 1924). These two men belonged to different parties, to be sure, but they also represented contrasting generations. A similar claim can be made about Britain by comparing Tony Blair (born 1953) with his predecessor John Major (born 1943).

However, the more recent political success of conservative leaders such as George W. Bush (born, like Clinton, in 1946) and Angela Merkel (born even more recently, in 1954) reminds us that postmaterialism may not carry all before it. Even if the diffusion of postmaterialism continues, this advance certainly does not rule out periods of conservative ascendancy. After all, the distinctive challenges of the twenty-first century include security issues such as terrorism, energy supply, global warming and pensions. These issues threaten individual security but also possess a clear collective dimension. Collective challenges to individual security may enable materialists and postmaterialists to converge on the same agenda.

Political culture in authoritarian states

In the mature democracies of the West, a supportive political culture still offers broad support to those charged with the task of ruling. By contrast, authoritarian rulers face characteristic problems arising from their unwillingness to confront the challenge of the ballot box. Lacking the legitimacy which flows from free election, such rulers must find other ways of responding to the political culture of the societies they govern. Broadly speaking, their options are threefold: to ignore, exploit or reconstruct the existing political culture.

The first option, ignoring political culture, is exemplified by many military regimes. Most military rulers rode to power on a tank and showed little concern for the niceties of political culture. Their task was to protect their own back against challengers seeking to supplant them. Far from seeking to draw support from the wider culture, military rulers typically sought to isolate the mass population from engagement with government, thus shrinking the political arena. 'We rule because we rule' remains the implicit message of many an authoritarian regime.

The second option, exploiting political culture, is much more common. As with democratic rulers, authoritarian leaders seek to emphasize those aspects of the culture that support their hold on power. In Pakistan, for instance, generals can exploit the perception that military men are less corrupt than civilian politicians. They can present themselves as outsiders, saving people from politics. 'Democracy works best in the long run' may have acquired the status of a self-evident axiom in Western liberal democracies but it is not yet a compelling proposition in cultures where political order and individual security are still a prime concern.

The other cultural resource available for exploitation by contemporary non-democratic rulers is, of course, religion. In many Islamic countries, political leaders can present democracy as an alien Western concept which in practice leads to licence rather than freedom; to an emphasis on material rather than spiritual values; and to the pursuit of individual self-interest rather than social harmony. In this way, authoritarian rule can be presented as an indigenous cultural tradition. Religion, then, continues to be a strong cultural force which can be used in defence of authoritarian rule.

The third option, seeking to reconstruct political culture, is both the least common and the most interesting response of authoritarian rulers. By definition, totalitarian rulers sought to transform the political values of their subjects. Nazi Germany, for instance, set itself 'the challenging task of manufacturing "new" men and women who were simultaneously fighters and obedient subjects' (Paxton, 2004, p. 143).

But it was communist regimes which made the most systematic and long-lasting effort at transforming political culture. Communist revolutions were, after all, originally intended as cultural revolutions. Almond (1983) describes the communist experience as a 'natural experiment in attitude change' in which the party set out to disprove the proposition that mass political culture resists transformation by the elite. If communist propagandists really could build a new communist personality, then political culture would clearly not possess the entrenched character attributed to it by authors such as Almond and Verba.

What then did the communist experiment reveal? Take the Soviet Union and China as examples. In both countries, propaganda was endlessly repeated not just in speeches but also in public arenas such as factories and schools. Most other ruling communist parties adopted a similar approach, though attempts at indoctrination were less extensive in Eastern Europe where communist rule resulted from invasion rather than revolution.

Yet the anticipated transformation of political culture never came about. Some idealism may have existed at first in the Soviet Union, at least among urban youth, but eventually mass participation took on a purely ritual form, based on passive obedience to power rather than active commitment to communism (Litvin and Keep, 2005). Fear created citizens who outwardly conformed but in reality adopted strategies designed to ensure their own survival: two persons in one body. People participated but only as subjects. Survival required a certain cunning in the pursuit of self-interest, wholly contradicting Marx's original vision of the flowering of cooperation under communism (Levada, 2001).

The endless repetition of lies became a way of demonstrating the party's ability to control public discourse rather than a genuine attempt to transform political culture. Under Stalin, indeed, the main function of the moral code of communism was simply to provide an excuse for liquidating those who were held to lack the required qualities.

Whatever legitimacy communist states possessed

seemed to owe more to traditional factors such as inherent patriotism and the party's successes at delivering industrialization, welfare services, public order and, in the case of the Soviet Union, superpower status. The new communist men and women never left the drawing board. Almond's conclusion regarding the twentieth century's largest experiment with political culture seems to be fully justified:

> What the scholarship of comparative communism is telling us is that political cultures are not easily manipulated. A sophisticated movement ready to manipulate, penetrate, organise, indoctrinate and coerce, and given an opportunity to do so for more than a generation, ends up as much or more transformed than transforming (Almond, 1983, p. 137).

Political culture in illiberal democracies

In illiberal democracies, presidents find themselves in an awkward position in relation to political culture. As elected leaders, they can hardly embrace the anti-democratic strategies associated with Marxist and many Islamic regimes. Yet neither can they embrace the full Western package of liberal democracy, with its emphasis on limited government, powerful institutions and individual rights. In practice, such rulers exploit the political culture by selectively emphasizing its authoritarian elements; their skill in doing so is often part of the reason for their political success. As O'Donnell (1994, p. 61) writes, such tendencies are widespread beyond the West: 'Whether it is called culture, tradition, or historically structured learning, the plebiscitary and *caudillista* tendencies toward delegative democracy are detectable in most Latin American (and, for that matter, many Central/East European, post-Soviet, African and Asian) countries'.

Traditions of deference, and of personal allegiance to powerful individuals, are a cultural resource which many leaders in Africa, Asia and Latin America exploit to the full. Loyalty to the national leader is presented as an outgrowth of the natural loyalty of the tribe to its leader; of the submission of the landless peasant to the powerful landowner; or of the unforced obedience of the child to its parent. In Africa, for example, Chabol and Daloz (2006, p. 30) boldly claim that 'most people in Africa conceive of "democracy" in terms of personalised politics and not in terms of institutionalisation'. Where institutional development facilitates liberal democracy, a culture of personal politics fosters at best illiberal democracy.

Once elected (and then re-elected), the ruler of an illiberal democracy functions as father and chief patron to the nation, providing security and stability but not day-to-day democratic accountability. Some authors view the cultural desire for a strong leader as the outgrowth of experience with authority within the family. In Asia, the argument has been made that strong family traditions encourage a group-centred style of adult politics in which deference to authority places a leading role (Pye, 1985). The child respects and accepts parental authority, leading – it is claimed – to similar deference to benevolent rulers later in life. The difficulty with the cultural expectation that the president will provide for his people is that he often lacks the means of doing so, producing an unstable cycle of high expectations, mass disappointment and the search for a new and equally personal saviour.

Post-communist Russia provides an example of a political culture which currently seems more consistent with an illiberal than a liberal form of democracy. Gitelman (2005, p. 248) writes that,

> the authoritarian traditions of Russia mean that people are not used to democratic behaviours and values, such as welcoming pluralism in thinking and behaving, tolerating dissent and supporting seemingly less efficient methods of democratic decision-making. They do not easily see the advantages of debate, discussion and non-conformity, and not deferring to a class of 'superiors'.

Inglehart (2000) also judges that Russian culture is exceptionally stony ground on which to nurture a liberal democracy. In analysing a comparative survey conducted in 1999/2000, he finds that Russians are less trusting, tolerant and happy than people in most other countries – features which were reinforced but not created by communist realities. Since he also argues that 'cultural factors are ultimately more decisive than economic ones', his conclusion is that the prospects for a transition from an illiberal to a liberal democracy in Russia are limited.

Yet the Russian case also illustrates the dangers of relying on a broad-brush notion such as political culture in explaining specific trends. When communism collapsed, some scholars doubted whether Russia's political culture was consistent with democracy of any kind (Eckstein, 1998b); now, with a post-communist constitution created and elections occurring on a regular basis, few would doubt that a regime with at least some democratic elements has been established. If internal order and economic growth continue, and in particular become taken for granted, it is surely possible that the culture itself will gradually become more sympathetic to a more liberal democracy. Here, then, is the wisdom of Almond's observation (1993, p. 16) that we quoted earlier: 'The advocates of political culture recognise that causality works both ways: attitudes influence structure and behaviour, and structure and performance in turn influence political attitudes'.

Elite political culture

Although the impact of mass political culture on political stability has been widely debated, the significance of elite political culture has been addressed less often. Yet in countries with a parochial or subject political culture, elite political culture is primary. Even where mass attitudes to politics are well-developed, as in liberal democracies, it is still the views of the elite which exert the most direct effect on political decisions. In this section, we examine elite political culture, again focusing on its consequences for political stability.

It is of course the case that in a liberal democracy, parties offer competing values and policies. Underlying these contrasts, however, we often find tacit agreements and shared understandings. Such perspectives are sometimes described as operational codes, cognitive maps, mindsets or worldviews. In defining his idea of an operational code, Leites (1960) also articulates well the notion of elite political culture: 'a set of general beliefs about fundamental issues of history and central questions of politics as these bear, in turn, on the problem of action' (George, 1969, p. 192).

Elite culture is far more than a representative fragment of the values of the wider society. The ideas of elites are distinct from, though they overlap with, the national political culture. For example, the leaders of liberal democracies generally take a more liberal line on social and moral issues. Stouffer's (1966) famous survey of American attitudes to freedom of speech, conducted in 1954, demonstrated this point. Stouffer showed that most community leaders maintained their belief in free speech for atheists, socialists and communists at a time when the public's attitudes were much less tolerant. It was crucial to the cause of free speech in the United States during the 1950s that a majority of the political elite resisted the strong pressure from Senator Joe McCarthy's populist anti-communist witch-hunt.

> **Elite political culture** consists of the beliefs, attitudes and ideas about politics held by those who are closest to the centres of political power. The values of elites are more explicit, systematic and consequential than are those of the population at large (Verba, 1987, p. 7).

One reason for the liberal and sophisticated outlook of political leaders is their education: in most democracies, politics has become virtually a graduate profession. The experience of higher education nurtures an optimistic view of human nature, strengthens humanitarian values and encourages a belief in the ability of politicians to solve social problems (Farnen and Meloen, 2000). Indeed the contrast between the values of the educated elite and the least educated section of the population is itself a source of tension in many political cultures.

In assessing the impact of elite political culture on political stability, three dimensions are crucial (Figure 6.3):

- Does the elite have faith in its own right to rule?
- Does the elite accept the notion of a national interest, separate from individual and group ambitions?
- Do all members of the elite accept the rules of the game, especially those governing the transfer of power?

The first and perhaps most vital component here is the rulers' belief in their own right to rule. To take an example from authoritarian regimes, the revolutions of 1989 in Eastern Europe dramatically illustrated how a collapse of confidence among the rulers themselves seemed to precipitate major political change. As Schöpflin (1990) points out, an authoritarian elite sustains itself in power not just through force and the threat of force but, more importantly, because it has some vision of the future by which it can justify itself to itself. No regime can survive long without some concept of purpose.

In the initial phase of industrialization, communist rulers in the Soviet Union and Eastern Europe had good reason to believe their new planned economies were producing results. By the late 1980s, however, progress had given way to decline; industrial planning had reached a dead end. As any remaining support from intellectuals faded, so party officials began to doubt their own legitimacy. Communist rulers were aware that they had become a barrier to, rather than a source of, progress. Elite values had ceased to underpin the system of government. By contrast, economic growth continues apace in contemporary China, sustaining the elite's confidence in its own legitimacy.

The second aspect of elite political culture is the conception of the national interest embedded within it. The issue here is the attitude of rulers to the government posts they hold. Is public service seen as just that – as a way of serving the national interest? Some national bureaucracies, from France to Pakistan, have seen themselves as guardians of the nation even to the point of protecting their country from 'mere politicians'. More often in the developing world, the state is seen by its ruling elite as a seam of scarce resources to be mined for the benefit of the rulers, their families, their constituents and their ethnic group. The cultural norm of leaders is, 'We've got the power, now we will fulfil our obligations to those who helped us to acquire it.'

The third dimension of elite political culture is the attitudes of politicians to the rules of the game. A range of possibilities exists here. Is elite competition absolute, as in divided societies such as Northern Ireland where gains to one side (Protestant or Catholic) were traditionally viewed as losses by the other? Alternatively, is strong party conflict moderated by agreement on the rules of the game, as entrenched in mainland Britain by the concept of Her Majesty's Loyal Opposition?

The consequences of these attitudes are highly significant for how the political game is played. As an example of unmoderated conflict, consider America's Watergate scandal (1972–73), during which President Nixon's Republican supporters engaged in illegal acts such as break-ins and phone-taps against their Democratic opponents. This unhappy episode reflected the President's own stark view of politics: us against them. Nixon was willing to dispense with the normal rules to ensure that his enemies 'got what they deserved'. In the USA, of course, most politicians do support the rules of the game as set out in the country's constitution. If Nixon's attitudes predominated among America's elite, its democracy would be far less secure.

Figure 6.3 How elite political culture affects political stability

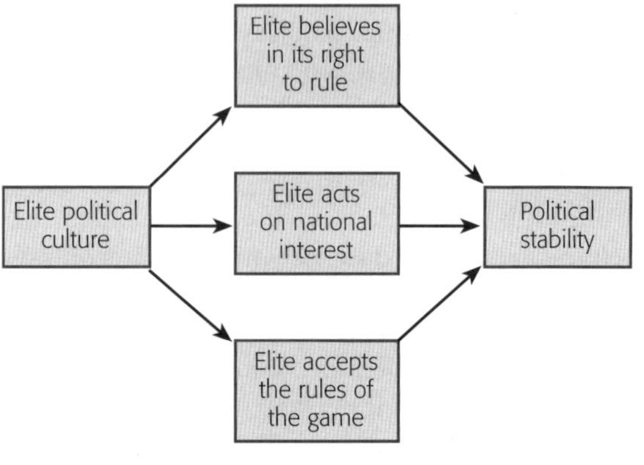

In political science, the classic analysis of elite political culture came from Arend Lijphart (1968, 1977, 2002). His concern was political stability in divided societies, a theme that remains of vital importance today in such areas as the Balkans, Iraq and Sri Lanka (Box 6.1).

Lijphart suggested that even a society separated into potentially hostile **pillars** can achieve political stability as long as party and group leaders are willing to compromise with each other at national level. Their agreements need not extend beyond the distribution of resources, with each group retaining autonomy over how it uses the resources it receives. This solution allows each community to continue to regulate itself on those matters not directly affecting other pillars (Figure 6.4). The outcome reflects a **plural society** arranged into separate cultures rather than a dominant culture with opposed subcultures.

Just such an accommodating attitude, Lijphart suggests, prevailed among group leaders in European **consociational democracies** such as

BOX 6.1

Elite political culture and political stability in divided societies: definitions

Consociational democracy A cooperative association between the separate communities or pillars of a plural society.

Pillars, depillarization Organized communities, typically based on religion (e.g. Catholic) or ideology (e.g. socialist). Depillarization refers to the weakening of the organized basis of such communities.

Elite accommodation An agreement between group leaders on distributing national resources without compromising the autonomy and distinctiveness of each pillar.

Plural society A society divided into separate groups which maintain an overall balance partly because of their separation. This term is most often used in the context of ethnic divisions specifically.

Figure 6.4 How elite compromise can deliver political stability to divided societies

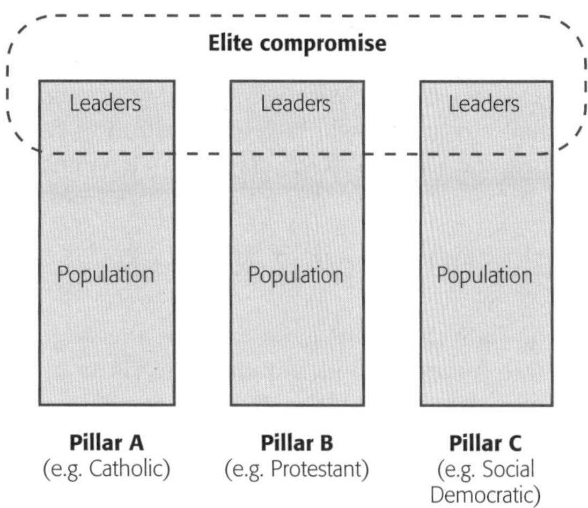

Austria (1945–66), Belgium (from 1919) and the Netherlands (1917–67). These were societies arranged into pillars by religion and ideology. In the Netherlands, for instance, Catholics and Protestants formed separate religious pillars while the Social Democrats and Liberals provided less densely organized secular groups. Andeweg and Galen (2002, p. 21) describe how religious pillars structured lives in the 1950s: a typical Catholic would have been born of Catholic parents in a Catholic hospital, received a Catholic education, joined the Catholic Boy Scouts, played soccer for a Catholic team, married another Catholic, joined a Catholic trade union, read a Catholic newspaper, died in a Catholic home for the elderly and been buried in a Catholic graveyard by a Catholic undertaker.

The leaders of all the pillars negotiated among themselves on how to slice the national pie. This **elite accommodation** operated on the basis of two informal rules: first, that distributions should reflect the relative population size of each group and, second, that each group should retain a minority veto over matters it judged vital to its own interests. Such discussions resembled international diplomacy, with the leaders of each pillar acting almost as if they represented a separate country. Discussions took place in secret and were treated for what they were: serious business.

As with the norm of non-intervention in the affairs of states, each pillar was left in control of the resources allocated to it. For example, the Catholic community might give priority to welfare; Protestants might allocate more money to schools; while the Social Democrats might develop their mass media. In this informal version of federalism, a culture of accommodation among the elite allowed separate communities to live together under the framework of a single state. The pillars supported the roof of the state while the roof protected the pillars.

Today, the pillars have crumbled as religious divisions have weakened. Despite **depillarization**, elite compromise remains a key theme in most post-consociational European democracies, including the Netherlands. Lijphart's formulation is a practical demonstration of how elite political culture can be detached from the wider group in a way that is nonetheless conducive to overall stability. Note, however, that the emphasis on elite culture means that consociational democracy is more than a matter of institutional arrangements and negotiating style. What worked for the Netherlands in the 1950s will not necessarily succeed elsewhere. Indeed, Lijphart (2002) suggests the device is most likely to succeed in smaller countries with a prior tradition of compromise and a shared awareness of a foreign danger.

A clash of civilizations?

To conclude this chapter, we examine the value of political culture in understanding the relationship between Islam and the West. Such a comparison has acquired added significance since 9/11 but also possesses two further advantages: first, it takes us beyond the state towards a more global perspective and, second, the comparison raises the topic of religion, a dimension of culture that we have not so far addressed. To what extent, then, should the current division between the Muslim and the Western worlds be viewed as a conflict of political cultures?

Huntington (1996) is the main proponent of the proposition that the division between Islam and the West is cultural or, to use his term, civilizational. Huntington's view derives from a broader analysis, published before September 11, 2001, in which he suggested that cultures based on civilizations rather than countries will become the leading source of conflict in the twenty-first century.

According to Huntington, the end of the cold war has not meant the end of cultural divisions. Rather the focus is shifting from a battle of ideologies to a clash of civilizations, including Islam and the West (Box 6.2). Since such groupings are supranational, Huntington (1996, p. 20) implies that political culture has escaped its national moorings to embrace wider but still competing identities:

> A civilization-based world order is emerging: societies sharing cultural affinities cooperate with each other; efforts to shift societies from one civilization to another are unsuccessful; and countries group themselves around the lead or core states of their civilization.

Between the contradictory worldviews of these civilizations, suggests Huntington, there is little common ground or room for compromise. He anticipates that as globalization proceeds, friction and conflict will intensify, reversing the 'McWorld' thesis – the proposition that the world will converge on American norms (Barber, 1995). Huntington notes, for example, how cultural kinship influenced the choice of sides in recent wars: 'in the Yugoslav conflicts, Russia provided diplomatic support to the Serbs . . . not for reasons of ideology or power politics or economic interest but because of cultural kinship' (1996, p. 28). In 2006, similarly, the Russian defence minister warned the West to steer clear of Belarus, citing cultural affinities: 'Belarusans and Russians are one people' (Shepherd, 2006, p. 19). Huntington is also sceptical of pragmatic efforts to switch civilizations, suggesting that the reason Australia failed to reinvent itself as an Asian country was simply that it's not.

Huntington draws on these civilizational themes in discussing the specific relationship between Islam and the West. The transnational character of civilizations is indeed exemplified by these religions, each of which predates the emergence of states. Thus, in medieval Europe, Christendom stood above kingdoms in the political hierarchy. Similarly, contemporary Muslim countries form an Islamic domain in which a shared religious commitment transcends national divisions. Although the origins

BOX 6.2

A clash of civilizations?

Huntington defines civilizations as the broadest cultural entities in the world; they are 'cultures writ large'. He divides the world into seven or eight major civilizations:

1 Western
2 Japanese
3 Islamic
4 Hindu
5 Slavic–Orthodox
6 Latin American
7 Chinese
8 (possibly) African

Source: Huntington (1996).

of the conflict between Islam and the West may lie in religion, Huntington argues that the contemporary division is cultural or civilizational rather than religious. With the Islamic world falling ever further behind the West in science, technology and wealth, it is no longer the West's Christian foundations which have become the target of Islamic criticism. Rather the Muslim critique rests on the West's secular character as exemplified by American materialism.

How do states relate to these civilizations? Huntington provides an intriguing classification though countries can fall into more than one category (Box 6.3). A core state leads a civilization, a member state is identified with a single civilization while a lone state either forms its own civilization or stands, like Haiti, in a class of its own. Perhaps the most interesting category is the torn state whose leaders attempt the difficult assignment of moving their country from one civilization to another. Turkey, an Islamic society whose leaders traditionally pursued a secular Western course, is the classic case. Russia, positioned between Western and Slavic–Orthodox civilizations, provides another example of perpetual ambivalence.

As would be expected for a civilizational divide, differences in education and upbringing underpin and perpetuate these cultural differences. Western education is avowedly secular, allowing schooling to concentrate on scientific knowledge and technical training. But in many Muslim countries, literal instruction in the Koran (Islam's holy text) remains a major theme, ill-preparing young people – male as well as female – for the modern world.

The upshot is that Huntington (1996, p. 217) portrays Islam and the West as civilizations locked in permanent cultural conflict:

> The underlying problem of the West is Islam, a different civilization whose people are convinced of the superiority of their culture and are obsessed with the inferiority of their power. The problem for Islam is the West, a different civilization whose people are convinced of the universality of their culture and who believe that their superior, if declining, power imposes on them the obligation to extend that culture throughout the world.

Many of Huntington's critics reject his essentialist reading of Islam which is focused on the religion's inherent characteristics and which assumes all believers speak with one voice. Stepan (2001, p. 234) is surely closer to the mark when he interprets Islam as multivocal, capable of varying its voice across place and time. In similar fashion, Gregorian describes Islam as 'a mosaic, not a monolith' while Fuller (2002) suggests that

BOX 6.3

Relationships between states and civilizations

Type of state	Relationship to civilization	Example (civilization)
Core state	The most powerful and culturally central state in a civilization	India (Hindu)
Member state	A state fully identified with a particular civilization	UK (Western)
Lone state	A state lacking cultural commonality with other societies	Japan (Japanese)
Torn state	The state's leaders want to shift their country to a different civilization	Turkey (from Islamic to Western)

Source: Huntington (1996), pp. 135–54.

DEBATE

IS A CLASH OF CIVILIZATIONS REMAKING THE WORLD?

'In the post-Cold War world, the most important distinctions among peoples are not ideological, political or economic. They are cultural. People and nations are attempting to answer the most basic question humans can face: who are we?' (Huntington, 1996, p. 21). Huntington's thesis that 'clashes of civilizations are the greatest threat to world peace' proved to be highly controversial, with the author reporting that 'people were variously impressed, intrigued, outraged, frightened and perplexed by my argument'. What matters, though, is not whether Huntington's proposition is controversial but whether it is true.

YES

The end of the cold war did not deliver everlasting peace. Most recent conflicts involve ethnic and religious identities, as between Islamic fundamentalists and the West. Huntington's ideas provide one interpretation of these divisions, an analysis worth supporting until and unless a superior perspective emerges.

Huntington recognizes the importance of divisions between rich and poor countries and between democratic and authoritarian states. But in his view even these contrasts possess cultural roots: 'East Asian economic success has its source in East Asian culture while Islamic culture explains in large part the failure of democracy to emerge in the Muslim world'. (p. 107)

In a similar way, the varying trajectories of post-communist countries can be attributed to their cultural and religious identity: 'Those with Western Christian heritages are making progress; the prospects in the Orthodox countries are uncertain; the prospects in the Muslim countries are bleak.' (p. 120)

As communication expands, so more contact takes place between civilizations, increasing the potential for friction. Asian economic expansion, and population growth in the Islamic world, will intensify tension with the West, a civilization that claims a universal prescription (e.g. 'human rights') but which also feels under threat.

Huntington is also well aware of diversity within the Muslim world. For the record, the section of his book on Islam is called, 'Consciousness without Cohesion'.

Huntington's analysis was published before 11 September 2001. What did those and later assaults signify if not an attack on Western civilization by people from a different and hostile culture?

NO

Huntington's notion of civilization conflates culture and religion. Some of his civilizations seem to have been made to fit the concept: is there really a single 'Latin American' or 'African' civilization?

Even the notion of an Islamic civilization encompasses such widely varying cultures and forms of government as Indonesia, Nigeria, Pakistan, Saudi Arabia and Turkey.

Huntington admits that his book is 'an interpretation, not social science'. Had he directly investigated the values of people in his 'civilizations', he would have discovered 'no significant differences between the publics living in the West and in Muslim religious cultures in support for democratic ideals and in support for strong leadership' (Norris and Inglehart, 2004, p. 146).

Such differences as do exist – for example, greater support in the West for gender equality – flow from higher Western levels of education, affluence and female employment. Values do not determine modernity; rather, modernity strongly influences values.

Huntington's thesis also lacks historical perspective. The relationship between Islam and the West has varied over the centuries, suggesting that there is nothing inevitable about a clash between them. Islam has the potential to become anti-Western but how this tradition is exploited depends on the politics of the time.

Finally, conflict has fallen since the cold war ended: 'At the peak in 1991, one in every three countries was experiencing some form of serious armed conflict. This had dropped to less than 15% in 2005' (Center for Systemic Peace, 2006). Can civilizations be clashing if the world is becoming more peaceful?

ASSESSMENT

Huntington's analysis is perhaps too sweeping. His thesis is pitched at a general level, showing insufficient sensitivity to diversity within civilizations. Just as Almond and Verba underplayed subcultures within the countries they surveyed, so Huntington discounts variation within civilizations, particularly Islam, and in the relationships between them over time.

Further reading

Huntington (1993, 1996), Norris and Inglehart (2004), Said (2001), Saikal (2003).

> Islam is not a butterfly in a collection box or a set of texts prescribing a single path. The real issue is not what Islam is but what do Muslims want. People of all sorts of faiths can rapidly develop interpretations of their religion that justify practically any quest.

Thus, both Turkey and Saudi Arabia are Muslim countries. However, Turkey's state is secular and substantially democratic whereas Saudi Arabia's authoritarian regime leads a society dominated by a severe form of Islam. The reaction to 9/11 confirms Islam's multivocal character: the hijackers undoubtedly drew on one anti-Western dialect within Islam but most Muslims, like most Christians, regarded the attacks as morally unjustified (Saikal, 2003, p. 17). Furthermore, any assumption of a monolithic Islam is invalidated by violent conflict between Sunni and Shia Muslims in post-invasion Iraq.

The political character of Islam, and its relationship with the West, has varied over time. The potential for conflict with the West may be inherent but this potential often remains latent. Saikal (2003, p. 24) writes that 'since the advent of Islam in the early seventh century, relations between its domain and the largely Christian West have been marked by long periods of peaceful coexistence but also by many instances of tension, hostility and mutual recrimination'. As long as civilizations are conceived as static, it is difficult to account for variability in the relationship between them. Huntington's expansive claim (1996, p. 210) that the West's problem is 'not Islamic fundamentalism but Islam' surely involves a breathtaking dismissal of entire centuries.

Rather than regarding the current wave of Muslim fundamentalism as an inherent feature of Islam, we should seek to locate its emergence in the events of the twentieth century, an approach which takes us away from political culture towards more specific themes in political history. Brzezinski's list (2002, p. 18), for instance, would be accepted by many:

> Arab political emotions have been shaped by the region's encounter with French and British colonialism, by the defeat of the Arab effort to prevent the existence of Israel and by the subsequent American support for Israel and its treatment of the Palestinians, as well as by the direct injection of American power into the region.

So political culture (or equivalent terms such as civilization) can only take us so far. Culture identifies the general climate but fails to offer specific forecasts. As Roy (1994, p. viii) observes, 'culture is never directly explanatory and in fact conceals all that is rupture and history: the importation of new types of states, the birth of new social classes and the advent of contemporary ideologies'. By itself, terms such as 'political culture' and 'civilization' are blanket explanations, offering wide coverage but also obscuring the intricate detail beneath.

Learning Resources for Chapter 6

Next step

Pharr and Putnam (2000) is an important comparative study of political culture in established democracies, focusing on increased dissatisfaction with the performance of government.

Further reading

Norris (1999b) is a useful supplement to Pharr and Putnam while Crothers and Lockhart (2002) is a wide-ranging reader on the concept of political culture. Almond and Verba (1963, 1980) remain a useful starting point; see Chabal and Daloz (2006) for a more interpretative perspective. For social capital, see Putnam (1993); Putnam (2002) is an interesting comparative attempt to apply the concept beyond the United States. The key source on postmaterialism is Inglehart (1971, 1990, 1997). On political culture in post-communist Europe, Pollack *et al.* (2003) is an extensive, survey-based collection. Norris and Inglehart (2004) study the relationship between religious and political values; Madeley (2003) is a comprehensive reader on religion and politics. Huntington (1993, 1996) is the main source on the clash of civilizations but see also more grounded works such as Saikal (2003) and even B. Lewis (2003).

Internet sources

Bowling Alone.com
The website of Putnam's book
http://www.bowlingalone.com/index.php3

Civic Practices Network
A learning collaborative for civic renewal
http://www.cpn.org/

Daniel Elazar Papers Index, Jerusalem Center for Public Affairs
Papers on American political culture
http://www.jcpa.org/dje/index-apc.htm

Saguaro Seminar, Harvard University
Building civic engagement in America
http://www.ksg.harvard.edu/saguaro/index.html

Chapter 7
Political communication

Society, and with it politics, is created, sustained and modified through communication. Without a continuous exchange of information, attitudes and values, society would be impossible. As Williams (1962, p. 11) wrote, 'What we call society is not only a network of political and economic arrangements, but also a process of learning and communication'. Communication is also a core political activity, providing opportunities to educate, inform, manipulate and persuade.

Awareness of the importance of communication led Aristotle (1962 edn) to provide the earliest systematic treatment of the topic, through his analysis of the rhetorical techniques used by orators in their speeches to the assembly and juries of ancient Athens. Where Aristotle asked how speakers influenced the reactions of their audience, contemporary scholars investigate who controls, and the influence of, the **mass media**. But in studies ancient and modern, the underlying assumption is the same: that communication is where politics does (and should) take place.

Assessments of the quality of political communication enter into the fundamental issue of classifying governments. A free flow of information is one test of several in discriminating between liberal democracies, illiberal democracies and authoritarian regimes. For example, Dahl (1998, p. 37) judges that a liberal democracy must provide opportunities for what he calls enlightened understanding: 'Within reasonable limits as to time, each member [of a political association] must have equal and effective opportunities for learning about relevant alternative policies and their likely consequences'. In an illiberal democracy, by contrast, dominance of major broadcasting channels is a tool through which the leader maintains his ascendancy over potential challengers. An authoritarian regime may permit no explicit dissent at all.

In examining political communication, it is useful to break the activity into its component parts. This task leads to what is known as the transmission model (Figure 7.1). This account interprets communication as consisting of who says what to whom, through which media and with what effects. So the model distinguishes five components:

- a sender: who?
- a message: what?
- a channel: how?
- a receiver: to whom?
- a presumed impact: with what effect?

For example, a local party (the sender) might distribute a leaflet (the channel) advocating voting at a forthcoming election (the message) to its own supporters (the receivers), with the result that turnout goes up (impact).

The **mass media** refer to methods of communication that can reach a large and potentially unlimited number of people simultaneously. These channels include blogs, books, cinema, magazines, newspapers, posters, radio, television and websites.

Figure 7.1 The transmission model of political communication

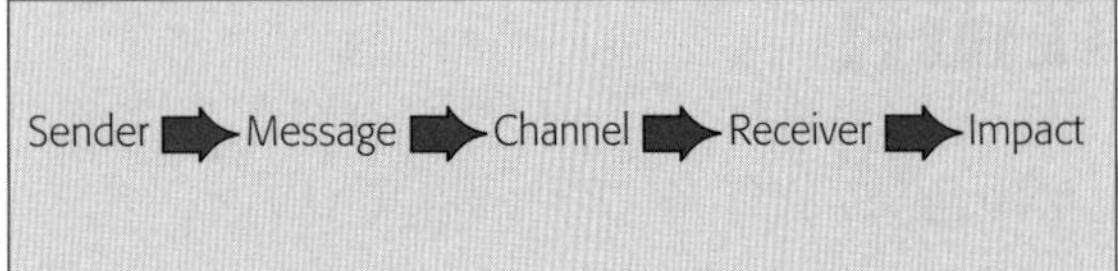

Even though most recent research in political communication focuses on one component only – namely the message and the meanings embedded within it – the transmission model still provides a helpful reminder of the existence of receivers and, sometimes, an impact. The danger of focusing solely on content is that we learn nothing about the receivers and even less about whether the communication has the slightest effect on them.

Development of the mass media

The intimate connections between communication and politics are revealed by examining the development of the media. Specifically, the expansion of communication facilitated the emergence of a common national identity and the growth of the state, especially in the nineteenth and twentieth centuries. The mass media, in particular, delivered a shared experience for dispersed populations, providing a glue to connect the citizens of large political units.

Table 7.1 outlines the major developments in the history of the media. The first innovation shown, namely writing, was of course the most important of all. Writing exerted profound effects on politics, permitting the record-keeping which is a foundation of the modern state. Without writing, states could not have penetrated society to the extent that they did. Writing also facilitated the expansion of empires, making possible the transmission of information, commands and values over large distances, as with the diffusion of Christianity through monasteries and church schools in medieval Europe (Mann, 1986, p. 335). Although the small democracy of ancient Athens was based on speaking rather than writing, the more extensive Roman Empire made use of writing.

In the fifteenth century, Gutenberg's invention of printing to paper using movable type provided the bridge to the era of modern communication. However, it was the later extension of literacy to the wider population that marked off the current era of both communication and states. Mass literacy in a common language was central to the successful development of contemporary states, facilitating the administration of large areas as well as encouraging a common identity. By the end of the eighteenth century, 'signing literacy' had reached about 80 per cent in innovative Sweden. Other European countries, and New England, achieved mass literacy in the nineteenth century, following the introduction of compulsory primary education. Mass literacy was a function, an achievement and an affirmation of the modern state, just as it has become an important success in many contemporary low income countries.

Widespread literacy in a shared language permitted the emergence of popular newspapers, the key development in political communication during the nineteenth and early twentieth centuries (Dooley and Baron, 2001). Advances in printing (e.g. the steam press) and distribution (e.g. the railway) opened up the prospect of transforming party journals with a small circulation into populist and profitable papers funded by advertising. By growing away from their party roots, papers became not just more popular but also, paradoxically, more important to politics.

In compact countries with national distribution, such as Britain and Japan, newspapers built enormous circulations which remain substantial to this day. Newspaper owners became powerful political figures. In interwar Britain, for example, four newspaper barons – Lords Beaverbrook, Rothermere, Camrose and Kemsley – owned newspapers with a total circulation of over 13 million, amounting to one in every two daily papers sold. True, these owners were more committed to circulation than to their favoured parties; under competitive pressure, they reduced political coverage. But they were also willing to use their organs to advocate particular causes, such as Rothermere's Anti-Waste Campaign. Stanley Baldwin, a prime minister of the time, famously described such proprietors as 'aiming at power without responsibility – the prerogative of the harlot throughout the ages' (Curran and Seaton, 2003, p. 64).

Table 7.1 The development of communication media

Date	Development
Fifth millennium BC	Writing systems develop in the earliest urban civilizations of the Near East, notably Phoenicia.
About 750 BC	The first modern alphabet, based on sounds rather than symbols, emerges in Greece.
AD 1450	In Mainz, Johannes Gutenberg invents printing with movable metal type. Book production is aided by new techniques for the mass manufacture of paper.
Nineteenth century	Compulsory primary education introduced, and mass literacy achieved, in Western states.
	The telegraph – a way of sending information across wires using electric signals – permits international dissemination of news, decisions and instructions.
Later nineteenth century and early twentieth century	Popular newspapers emerge, often with mass circulation. New railway networks allow national distribution.
1930s	Radio's golden age. For the first time, politicians broadcast directly into electors' homes.
1950s–1960s	Television becomes the most popular, and usually the most trusted, medium in Western countries. By regulation or state ownership, politicians secure access to the medium. Entertainment programmes from the USA are widely exported, diffusing American values.
1970s–1980s	The television audience begins to fragment, with an increase in the number and commercialization of channels, distribution by cable and satellite, and widespread use of video.
1990s	Internet access reaches more affluent and educated groups in Western societies, representing a further opening of international communication. Mobile telephony emerges.
2000s	The internet reaches the mass population in Western societies. Mobile telephony becomes standard in the West and provides the only form of telephony in many low-income countries. Media become more interactive (e.g. voting by viewers on entertainment shows) and personalized (e.g. downloading of content).

Although newspapers remain significant channels of political communication, in the twentieth century their role was of course supplanted by broadcasting. Cinema newsreels, radio and then television enabled communication with the mass public to take place in a new form: spoken rather than written, personal rather than abstract and, on occasion, live rather than reported. Oral communication reasserted itself though now in a form which could escape the confines of the small group.

In authoritarian states, the two major ideologies founded in the twentieth century – communism and fascism – consciously sought to mobilize popular support through exploiting these new broadcasting media. In these brave new worlds of total and totally controlled communication, the mass media would be used to create a mass society populated by individuals with the knowledge and attitudes specified by the political elite. Such visions proved to be fanciful but the very conception of a population controlled by Big Brother signalled awareness of broadcasting's potential impact.

By comparison, broadcasting's impact in Western liberal democracies was relatively benign. A small number of national channels initially dominated the airwaves in most countries, providing a shared experience of everything from national events to popular entertainment. By offering some common ground to societies which were, in these early post-war decades, still strongly divided by class and religion, the new media initially served as agents of national integration.

The impact of broadcasting on politicians was immediate. Politicians had to acquire new communication techniques. A public speech to a live audience encouraged expansive words and dramatic gestures but a quieter tone was needed for transmission direct to the living room. The task was to converse with the unseen listener and viewer rather than to deliver a speech to a visible audience gathered together in one place. The art was to talk to the millions as though they were individuals.

President Franklin Roosevelt's fireside chats, broadcast live by radio to the American population in the 1930s, exemplified this new, informal approach. The impact of Roosevelt's somewhat folksy idiom was undeniable. He talked not so much to the citizens but as a citizen and was rewarded with his country's trust. In this way, broadcasting – and the forgotten medium of radio specifically – transformed not just the reach but also the tone of political communication (Barber, 1992).

Broadcasting has also made a substantial contribution to political communication in most low-income countries but for different reasons. In the developing world, broadcasting (whether radio or television) possesses two major advantages over print media. First, it does not require physical distribution to each user and, second, it is accessible to people who cannot read. In low income countries, these factors initially encouraged the spread of radio. Villagers could gather round the shared set to hear the latest news, not least on the price of locally grown crops. Today, around half of the population in developing countries also has access to television; there are now more sets in China than in the USA.

Just as some developing countries are moving directly to mobile telephony, eliminating the need for an expensive fixed-wire infrastructure, so also have many poorer countries developed large broadcasting networks without passing through the stage of mass circulation newspapers. The capacity of ruling politicians to reach out to poor, rural populations through these radio and television networks is an important component of governance in illiberal democracies, particularly in Latin America.

The media: contemporary trends

In the first decade of the twenty-first century, the four major trends in communications in the developed world are commercialization, fragmentation, globalization and interaction (Box 7.1). The combined political effect of these developments is to reduce national political control over broadcasting and permit consumers either to choose their own political programming or increasingly to escape from politics altogether. If the mass media performed a nation-building function in the twentieth century, their emerging impact in the new century is to splinter the traditional national audience, fragmenting a shared experience and perhaps contributing thereby to the decline of participation in formal national politics.

Commercialization

Communication is increasingly treated as the important business it has become. By 2009, the average American is expected to spend ten hours a day with media of all kinds; communication is predicted to be the economy's fourth largest and fastest growing sector (Veronis, Suhler and Stevenson, 2005). Commercialization allows new media moguls, such as Rupert Murdoch, to build transnational broadcasting networks, achieving on a global scale the prominence which the newspaper barons of the nineteenth century acquired at national level.

In the Americas, Canada excepted, broadcasting had always been commercially led but in Western Europe commercialization has been a disputed political development. The first television stations in Europe had been national and publicly owned. The British Broadcasting Corporation (BBC) was a notable example. Typically, public-service broadcasters were controlled by public supervisory boards, funded by a special licence fee and motivated by a culture directed at education and even improvement, rather than just entertainment.

However the 1970s and 1980s saw the introduction of new commercial channels; in addition, advertising was added to many public stations. Even the BBC became more commercial, establishing numerous specialist channels and creating one of the world's most successful websites. Such develop-

BOX 7.1

Contemporary trends in mass communication

Commercialization	The decline of public broadcasting and the rise of for-profit media treating users as consumers rather than citizens
Fragmentation	More channels and an enhanced ability to download and consume programmes on demand
Globalization	Improved access to overseas events and media in the global village
Interaction	Increased use of interactive channels (e.g. e-mail, games), reducing passive exposure to politics through top-down communication

ments threatened previously cosy links between parties and broadcasters. They represented a shift to seeing the viewer in less political terms, as a consumer rather than a citizen. In this increasingly commercial environment, Tracey (1998) claims that public service broadcasting has become nothing more than 'a corpse on leave from its grave'.

In a similar way, McChesney argues in *Rich Media, Poor Democracies* (1999) that commercialization shrinks the public space in which political issues are discussed. Channels in search of profit will devote little time to serious politics. Certainly, profit-seeking media have no incentive to supply public goods such as an informed citizenry and a high electoral turnout, traditional concerns of public media. For those who view democracy as a form of collective debate, engaging most of the citizenry in matters of common concern, media commercialization is a challenge indeed. Against which, commercial broadcasters reply that it is preferable to reach a mass audience with limited but stimulating political coverage than it is to offer extensive but dull political programming which, in reality, only ever reached a minority with a pre-existing interest in public affairs (Norris, 2000).

Fragmentation

Consumers are increasingly able to watch, hear and read what they want, when they want. Long gone are the days when American viewers were restricted to the three large networks (ABC, CBS and NBC) and British viewers could choose only between the public BBC and the commercial ITV. Distribution by cable, satellite and telephone wire allows viewers to receive a greater range of content, local and overseas as well as national. Content can also be stored on a variety of recording devices for playback on demand, reducing reliance on what the broadcasters make available at a specific moment. Especially among younger age groups in the developed world, an increasing share of screen time is spent on the internet, further fragmenting the audience across a range of specialized virtual communities (Table 7.2).

The combined result of these developments is a more splintered audience. During the 1990s, for instance, the audience share of the big three American television networks dropped by a third. National newspaper circulations are also declining worldwide.

The political implications of this shift from broadcasting to narrowcasting are substantial. Governments, parties and commercial advertisers encounter more difficulty in reaching a mass audience when viewers can defend themselves by simply choosing another channel via their remote control. Exposure to politics falls as the electorate becomes harder to reach, forcing political parties to adopt a greater range and sophistication of marketing strategies, including the use of personalized but expensive

Table 7.2 World internet usage, 2006

	Percentage of population in region using internet	Percentage of world's internet users, by region
North America	69.7	21.5
Australia and Oceania	54.1	1.7
Europe	38.6	28.9
Latin America and Caribbean	15.4	7.9
Asia	10.3	35.2
Middle East	10.0	1.8
Africa	3.6	3.0
World	16.6	100.0

Source: Internet World Stats (2006).

contact techniques such as direct mail, e-mail and telephone.

In this more fragmented environment, politicians will have to communicate in a manner, and at a time, of the voters' choosing. They will have to continue their migration from television news to higher-rated talk shows, blurring the distinction between politician and celebrity (Jones, 2005). Politicians will find themselves in a competition for eyeballs with entertainers ranging from sports personalities to movie stars. The sound bite, never unimportant, will become even more vital as politicians learn to articulate their agenda in a brief interview or an even briefer commercial.

In short, just as the balance within the media industry has shifted from public service to private profit, so the emphasis within political communication will move from parties to voters. Politicians rode the emergence of broadcasting with considerable success in the twentieth century but they are experiencing tougher going in the new millennium of fragmented media.

Globalization

'The empires of the future will be empires of the mind,' said Winston Churchill in 1943. Certainly, in the global village, the world has been compressed into a television screen. In 1776 the English reaction to the American Declaration of Independence took 50 days to filter back to the United States. In 1950 the British response to the outbreak of the Korean War was broadcast in America after 24 hours. In 2003 British and American viewers watched broadcasts of the Iraq War at the same time. We now take for granted the almost immediate transmission of newsworthy events around the world.

Even wars have become, in part, battles of communication. During the conflict in Kosovo in 1999, television stations worldwide were supplied by NATO with video footage of high-tech weapons hitting specified targets. At the same time, Serbia offered pictures of civilians killed or injured by missiles destroying wrong targets. In the Iraq war of 2003, reporters were embedded in the coalition's military units, distributing live and occasionally dramatic coverage to viewers throughout the world.

It is now harder than ever for governments to isolate their populations from international developments. Even before the internet, communist states found it difficult to jam foreign radio broadcasts aimed at their people. Discussing the collapse of communist states, Eberle (1990, pp. 194–5) claimed that 'the changes in Eastern Europe and the Soviet Union were as much the triumph of communication as the failure of communism'.

Recent technological developments also facilitate underground opposition to authoritarian regimes. A small group with internet access now has the potential to draw the world's attention to political abuses, providing source material for alert journalists. Burma's military rulers, China's communist government and Saudi Arabia's ruling families have all suffered from overseas groups in this way. However, all three regimes remain in place (Atton, 2004).

Interaction

A particular aspect of fragmentation is the growing exposure to interactive channels of communication. Radio phone-ins allow ordinary people to listen to their peers discussing current issues, without mediation by a politician; blogs perform the same function in electronic space. E-mail and computer games are inherently interactive. Such media allow peer-to-peer interchanges which tend to crowd out top-down, one-way politician-to-voter communication.

DEBATE

WILL THE INTERNET REMAKE POLITICS?

The internet has become one of the most discussed communication channels, not just because of its explosive growth but also because of its inherently global character. But what will its political impact prove to be? Will it reshape politics, just as broadcasting did in the twentieth century, or are its political effects over-sold?

YES

The internet has spread more rapidly than previous innovations such as radio and television. Already, access has become routine in the developed world (Table 7.2). In the USA, the ratio of time spent watching television compared to the internet halved from 8:1 in 2000 to 4:1 in 2005 (Murrie, 2006). The internet is itself governed by technical committees, not states.

The internet goes further than any previous medium in overcoming distance, paying scant regard to national boundaries. Citizens in any country can access information from any other state, providing true globalization.

The internet weakens the hold of states over their populations and fragments political communication, allowing specialized communities (including exploited minorities) to present their views in a manner that overwhelms national boundaries.

Restrictions imposed by governments and traditional media are swept away as the democratic revolution reaches the information world. Internet access allows users, for the first time, to control their own information flow. Citizen reporters supplant traditional journalists. With over 100 million blogs, 'everyone is part of the story and everyone exerts influence' (Peskin and Nachison, 2006). Electronic voting at national, regional and global level cannot be far behind.

Authoritarian regimes that deny information to their citizens will find that censorship has become impractical.

The internet will also instigate the final triumph of business over politics: governments will be unable to control, let alone tax, international or even national e-commerce.

NO

The long-term political impact of the internet is exaggerated. Users can surf the world but how many Americans, in particular, will do so, given the predominance of American sites?

Most personal communication on the internet is not global but between people living within an hour's drive (Wellman, 2001).

Nor can a computer network overcome differences of language: secondary nets for languages other than English recreate rather than bypass linguistic divisions.

For all the talk of electronic democracy, official referendums by internet are nowhere to be found. Note, too, that in the past, newspapers, radio and television all improved coverage of far-off affairs but none succeeded in displacing the state. Why should the technical act of linking computers together be any different?

The internet delivers information overload. The heaviest users are those who are already informed and the apathetic stay away; the effect is simply to widen knowledge gaps.

Most sites, and nearly all blogs, have no impact of any kind. The examples typically quoted, such as as the online presence of Mexico's Zapatistas, are the exception, not the rule. No one cites the millions of unvisited sites and unread blogs. These non-communications are just catharses for the disengaged: the 'Daily Me'.

Citizens will eventually rebel against use of the internet for pornography, gambling and crime, forcing governments to regain control over what is currently, but only temporarily, a lawless region.

ASSESSMENT

Firm judgements are premature. The lesson of previous innovations in communication is that initial projections of their impact are wildly inaccurate. Some people thought radio would change the world; others said the telephone would never catch on. But one point is clear: technology does not determine content. The messages which travel over the internet will reflect forces beyond the net itself. Politics is more than technology and the message is more than the medium.

Further reading

Castells (2003), Chadwick (2006), Hall and Biersteker (2002), Olesen (2003).

Screen time is up but passive exposure is down, showing the error of referring to such an imprecise term as 'the media'.

In response to the threat from these new media, traditional broadcasters have added an interactive element to some of their output, notably in the internationally successful *Idol* series. These shows give many young people their first experience of voting yet, far from stimulating turnout in national elections, their freshness seems to give traditional participation though the ballot box a somewhat old-fashioned air.

The expansion of interactive channels sits uneasily alongside the rather passive role expected of most voters in a representative democracy. Implicitly, a young generation schooled on interactive media is raising an important question to which politicians have yet to find an adequate answer: why should we choose to listen to you?

The media in liberal democracies

The media possess a natural vitality in liberal democracies, where freedom of expression is legally protected. In this section, we discuss the vexed question of the media's impact before turning to the distinct character of television and newspapers, still the two main media. We then examine the media in elite politics, assessing the political game played between journalists and politicians in liberal democracies.

Media impact

What is the media's impact on those exposed to it? By virtue of its general nature, this question remains without an agreed answer. Clearly, politics would change substantially if all mass media were suddenly outlawed; for example, we would surely observe the de-nationalization of politics, with a revival of local campaigning in particular. But such mental experiments are as hypothetical as imagining a house without walls: there is perhaps more credibility in describing the media as the house within which many people (especially young people) live their political lives. Jones (2005, p. 17) expresses this viewpoint:

> Media are our primary point of access to politics – the space in which politics now chiefly happens for most people, and the place for political encounters that precede, shape and at times determine further bodily participation (if it is to happen at all). … Such encounters do much more than provide 'information' about politics. They constitute our mental maps of the political world outside our direct experience. They provide a reservoir of images and voices, heroes and villains, sayings and slogans, facts and ideas that we draw on in making sense of politics.

For example, the clutch of American movies about such topics as Vietnam, 9/11 and Iraq provide a stimulus for political discussion which is, in its way, as much a form of political participation as volunteering to take part in an election campaign or paying a subscription to an interest group.

Even so, it is worthwhile examining how scholarly thinking about specific media effects has evolved. Box 7.2 outlines four main mechanisms: reinforcement, agenda-setting, framing and priming. At various times since 1945, each of these has contributed to academic thinking about the impact of broadcast and print media.

In the 1950s, before television became pre-eminent, the **reinforcement** thesis – also known as the minimal effects model – held sway (Klapper, 1960). The argument here was that party loyalties initially transmitted through the family acted as a political sunscreen protecting people from media effects. People saw what they wanted to see and remembered what they wanted to recall. In Britain, where national newspapers were strongly partisan, many Labour supporters read left-wing papers while most Conservatives bought Tory papers. Given such self-selection, the most the press could do was to reinforce their readers' existing dispositions while also, perhaps, crystallizing the partisanship of some uncommitted readers.

The reinforcement theory proved its value half a century ago when voting was more stable than today. Even now, many studies of media impact on voting find only limited effects during the short period of an election campaign (Gavin and Sanders, 2003). The reinforcement thesis still offers effective medicine for the vast range of people and organizations blaming the 'biased' media for the unpopu-

BOX 7.2

Media effects

	Definition	Comment
Reinforcement	The media strengthen existing opinions	People read newspapers which support their existing outlook (selective exposure). In addition, people interpret information to render it consistent with their prior opinions (selective interpretation) and forget information that runs counter to existing beliefs (selective recall).
Agenda-setting	The media influence what we think and talk about	The compressed nature of news, especially on television, means coverage is highly selective. Reported events are widely discussed by the public but non-reported events lose visibility.
Framing	How an event is narrated as a coherent story highlights particular features of it	A frame focuses on particular aspects of a problem, its origins, remedies and evaluation. It encourages viewers and readers to interpret the topic in the same way.
Priming	Media coverage influences how we interpret events beyond those in the particular story	Priming extends media impact beyond the particular topic. For example, coverage of crime in the national media may encourage people to report crimes in their local area.

larity of their particular cause. Even so, the reinforcement account has surely become too limited as a contemporary perspective on media effects. Party loyalties have long been weaker, and television more pervasive, than in the 1950s. For this reason, the agenda-setting view of media impact gained ground in the 1970s and 1980s.

The **agenda-setting** perspective contends that the media (and television in particular) influence what we think about, though not necessarily what we think. The media write certain items onto the agenda and by implication keep other issues away from the public's gaze. As Lazarsfeld and Merton (1948) pointed out in an earlier era, 'To the extent that the mass media have influenced their audiences, it has stemmed not only from what is said but more significantly from what is not said.'

In an election campaign, for example, television directs our attention to the candidates and to the race for victory; by contrast, the issues are often treated as secondary. Walter Lippman's (1922) view of the press articulates well the agenda-setting account: 'it is like a beam of a searchlight that moves restlessly about, bringing one episode and then another out of the darkness and into vision'.

It is through their assumptions about newsworthiness that news editors resolve their daily dilemma of reducing a day's worth of world events to less than 30 minutes on the evening news. In deciding what to cover, in what order, and what to leave out, programme editors set the agenda and exert their impact.

Because news programmes focus on the exceptional, their content is invariably an unrepresentative sample of events. For example, policy fiascos receive more attention than policy successes. Similarly, corruption is a story but integrity is not. A fresh story gathers more coverage than a new development of a tired theme. Necessarily, agenda-setting creates a distorting mirror on the world. The shorter news bulletins become, the more selective the TV lens must be and the greater the distortion becomes.

But we should recognize that editors do not select stories on a whim (Box 7.3). In deciding what stories to pursue, editors take into account such factors as intrinsic importance and the likely impact of coverage on audience size and appreciation. Editors are paid to demonstrate their news sense; if they consistently fail to do so, they lose their job. It is therefore naïve to attribute agenda-setting power to editors simply because they make the front-line judgements about what is to appear on screen or the front page. The wider cultural context enters into their calculation of what to cover. Just as we do not blame the newsreader for the news, neither should we condemn the news selector for the agenda.

The **framing** of a story – the way in which reports construct a coherent narrative about an event – is a more recent attempt to address media impact. The idea here is a development of Plato's observation that 'those who tell the stories also rule society'. The journalist's words, as much as the camera operator's images, help to frame the story, providing a narrative which encourages a particular reaction from the viewer. For example, are immigrants presented as a stimulus to the economy or as a threat to society? Does the American media portray a war critically (Vietnam and perhaps Iraq, at least in their later stages) or positively (Iraq in the invasion phase)? Is a criminal sentenced to die facing his just deserts or cruel and unusual punishment? As the concept of a 'story' suggests, the journalist must translate the event covered into an organized narrative which connects with the receiver. The shorter the report, the greater the reliance on the shared, if sometimes simplistic, presuppositions termed consensus frames by Jamieson and Waldman (2003).

Finally, the media's agenda and frames may exert a **priming** effect, encouraging people to apply the criteria implicit in one story to new information and topics. This indirect, cueing effect may have been understated in research focused on direct media effects. For example, the more the media focuses its coverage on foreign policy, the more likely it is that voters will be primed to judge parties according to their policies in this area, and to vote accordingly. To take another example, it is possible that coverage of racist attacks may predispose or prime some individuals to engage in similar acts themselves, should the opportunity arise. Bear in mind, however, that priming is more often asserted than demonstrated – and that it is again often asserted by those who seek to blame the media for what they regard as undesirable behaviour.

BOX 7.3

Some tests used by journalists to determine newsworthiness

- Will the story have a strong impact on our audience?
- Does the story involve violence? ('If it bleeds, it leads')
- Is the story current and novel?
- Does the story involve well-known people?
- Is the story relevant to our audience?

Source: Adapted from Graber (2005), pp. 106–8, based on studies in the USA.

Television and newspapers

One danger in discussing the mass media lies in treating its various channels as uniform, as though television, press, films, books and radio are similar in their partisanship, reach and effects. As an antidote to such general treatments, in this section we contrast the two key channels of the mass media age: television and newspapers.

By the 1980s, television had become the pre-eminent mass medium in all liberal democracies. It is a visual, credible and easily digested format which reaches almost every household, providing the main source of political information. In election campaigns, the television studio has become the main site of battle. The party gladiators participate through appearing on interviews, debates and talk shows; merely appearing on television confirms some status and recognition on candidates. Ordinary voters consume the election, if at all, through watching television.

Local party activists, once the assault troops of the campaign, have become mere skirmishers. The British member of parliament who found that he could no longer canvass effectively on the doorstep because his constituents were too engaged with the campaign on television tells a plausible tale about the impact of television on local campaigning (Mitchell, 1982). Television has ceased to cover the campaign, it has become the campaign.

To say that the television studio is the site of battle is one thing; to say that it determines the outcome is quite another. It is difficult to demonstrate a strong connection between television coverage of campaigns and the voters' response. For instance, one frequent observation about the electoral impact of television is that it has primed voters to base their decision more on personalities, especially those of the party leaders. To which an obvious riposte is: compared to when? Before television, after all, came the now forgotten media of radio and in, some countries, cinema. Even the claim that the broadcasting media as a whole have led voters to decide on personality neglects the importance of personalized press coverage of the parties in the era before broadcasting.

To be sure, some studies have shown a modest increase in recent decades in the focus of media coverage of election campaigns on party leaders. However, it is far from proven that votes are increasingly cast on the base of leaders' personalities and even less clear that any such increase is attributable to television. Certainly, research does not support the proposition that television, even in the USA, has rendered the images of the leaders the key influence on electoral choice (King, 2002; Langer, 2006; Mughan, 2000).

Where television may have made a broader but larger contribution is in partisan dealignment: the weakening of party loyalties among electors. Because of the limited number of channels available in television's early decades, governments required balanced and neutral treatment of politics. The result was an inoffensive style that contrasted with the more partisan coverage previously offered in many national newspapers, especially outside the USA. As a result, television may have weakened party loyalties, particularly among generations growing up with the medium.

In the Netherlands, for instance, television helped to break down the separate pillars composing Dutch society in the 1950s, providing a new common ground for citizens exposed to the single national channel: 'Catholics discovered that Socialists were not the dangerous atheists they had been warned about, Liberals had to conclude that orthodox Protestants were not the bigots they were supposed to be' (Wigbold, 1979, p. 201).

Despite the primacy of television, it would be wrong to discount the political significance of the second mass medium, newspapers. Even today, quality newspapers possess an authority springing from their longevity. In nearly all democracies, newspapers are freer with comment than is television. In an age when broadcasters still lead the provision of instant news, the more relaxed daily schedule of the press allows print columnists to offer more interpretation and evaluation.

Television tells us what happened; at their best, newspapers place events in context. Broadcast news can only cover one story at a time whereas newspapers can be scanned for items of interest and can be read at the user's convenience. Newspapers offer a luxury which television can rarely afford: space for reflection. For such reasons, quality newspapers remain the trade press of politics, read avidly by politicians themselves. In countries with a lively press tradition, newspapers retain a political significance greatly in excess of their circulation.

Newspapers also influence television's agenda: a story appearing on TV's evening news often begins life in the morning paper. This agenda-influencing role, it is worth noting, does not depend on a newspaper's circulation. But when an elector does see a story covered both on television and in the press, the combined impact exceeds that of either medium considered alone.

In several liberal democracies – notably Britain, Germany, Japan, Korea, the Netherlands, Scandinavia and Switzerland – readership of national newspapers remains substantial (Norris, 2002, p. 130). In Japan, unusually, some studies indicate that the public still relies more on the national press than on television and that in consequence newspapers exert more influence over the electorate's agenda (Feldman, 1993, p. 24).

Throughout the world, though, national newspaper circulations are falling, especially among younger people. Those print media which are expanding, mainly free papers and specialist magazines, offer little political coverage. Those who regularly read about politics in newspapers have become, or are becoming, a minority, outnumbered by those

COUNTRY PROFILE

SPAIN

Form of government ■ a parliamentary liberal democracy, with strong regions and a hereditary monarch playing a largely ceremonial role.

Legislature ■ the bicameral legislature consists of the Congress of Deputies (350 members) and the Senate (259 members; 208 directly elected and 51 chosen by regional assemblies). Parliament is dominated by well-organized parties; the Senate is particularly weak.

Constitution and judiciary ■ the 1978 constitution establishes a 'social and democratic state based on the rule of law' and devotes extensive attention to the rights of individuals and regions. The Constitutional Court consists of 12 members appointed by parliament, the government and the judiciary itself. The legal system is based on civil law.

Electoral system ■ deputies are elected by PR with closed party lists. A small district magnitude gives large parties an advantage. For the directly elected members of the Senate, electors can vote for up to three candidates. The four obtaining the highest number of votes are elected.

Party system ■ the constitution states that parties 'express political pluralism', thus placing them at the centre of the new democracy. The party system has now stabilized, with the Spanish Socialists Workers' Party (PSOE) and the centre right People's Party (PP, Popular Party) securing 80 per cent of the vote in the 2004 elections to the lower chamber. As a result of this election, fought in the aftermath of the Madrid bombings, the PSOE replaced the PP in office.

Population (annual growth rate):	40.4m (+0.1%)
World Bank income group:	high income
Political Rights score:	1
Civil Liberties score:	1
Human development index (rank/out of):	20/177
Freedom of the press index (rank/out of):	48/194
Ease of doing business index (rank/out of):	39/175

Note: For meaning and sources of scales and indexes, see p. xvi. In all cases a score and rank of 1 is 'best'.

SPAIN's political transition following the death of General Franco in 1975 is one of democratization's great success stories. As Heywood (1995, p. 4) says, 'Franco's death was followed not by bloody conflict, as many had feared, but by a remarkably rapid and skilfully engineered transition to democracy.'

Favourable conditions included the country's location in Western Europe; the considerable economic modernization that had already taken place under the old regime; and the significant contribution made by King Juan Carlos.

Spain's delayed democratization came all the easier for its late arrival. All the *poderes fácticos* (de facto power centres such as the Catholic Church and the military) wanted to avoid reopening old conflicts, leading to the triumphant compromise of the 1978 constitution.

Spain is now a high income country with a growing economy and an increasingly diverse population. It is securely integrated into Europe, joining the European Union in 1986 and using the euro as its currency. Partly reflecting a highly regulated labour market, average living standards do however remain significantly below those of Europe's wealthiest economies.

Although Spain is one of Europe's oldest states, regional divergences remain central to its politics. The constitution established a complex mechanism by which regions could aspire to varying levels of autonomy within the state. The historic communities of the Basque Country and Catalonia quickly proceeded to the most autonomous level, with other regions offered the prospect of a later upgrade. In 2006, even greater devolution was agreed for Catalonia, including recognition of its status as a distinct nationality. In the same year, the Basque nationalist organization ETA ('Basque Homeland and Freedom') declared a 'permanent ceasefire', having killed about 900 people since the 1970s.

Spain has granted extensive devolution to historic regions and identities while retaining what is, in theory, a unitary rather than federal framework.

Further reading: Gunther, Montero and Botella (2004), Heywood (1995).

SPOTLIGHT

The media in Spain

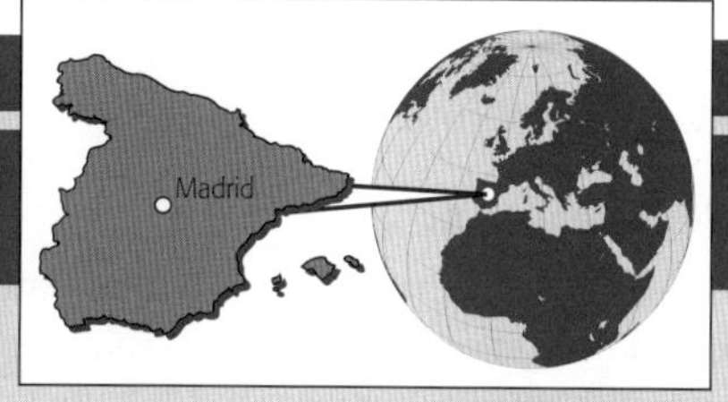

The development of the Spanish media over the era of democratization in some ways follows a typical pattern. The monotonous coverage offered under the dictatorship gives way to a flowering of free expression, followed by a media restructuring in which broadcasting increasingly dominates the press. Political communication comes to operate through television in particular, leading to political pressures on the broadcasters themselves.

Under the authoritarian Franco regime, the position of the media had been wholly subservient. Rigid censorship ensured that newspapers offered only the dullest of political coverage, largely confining themselves to reprinting official press releases. The fare provided by the broadcasters was little better. Monopoly channels under state control offered an innoffensive diet of operetta, sport and soap operas. The media formed an essential part of the dictatorship's 'culture of evasion' (Heywood, 1995, p. 76).

With liberalization, independent media burst into life, offering all shades of opinion through a diverse range of publications. As in many post-communist countries, television has established itself as the key medium in the new order. This pattern reflects not just the indifferent quality and poor reputation of the press but also the greater accessibility of television to an electorate with variable education: until the 1990s, illiteracy remained a significant issue in Spain.

The dominance of broadcasting over print in Spain is exceptional within Western Europe and more typical of the pattern found in the country's former colonies in Latin America. According to a 1995 survey, 91 per cent of Spaniards watch television daily while only 38 per cent read newspapers – and many of these confine themselves to the sports pages. In 1996, 66 per cent of respondents said that television was their main source of political information while only 17 per cent mentioned the press (Gunther, Montero and Botella, 2004, p. 146).

Media use in Spain

	Average time per day spent with each medium (minutes)
Television	222
Radio	95
Newspapers	18
Internet	6
Magazines	5

Note: Information dates from about 2000.
Source: Adapted from Press Reference (2006).

Reflecting an authoritarian and corporate tradition, membership of social organizations and political parties is low. When combined with reliance on television, the effect is an electorate which is mobilized cognitively rather than socially. That is, links between politicians and voters operate not so much through social networks such as trade unions and churches as through the mass media, especially television. The result is an individualized style of politics which gives considerable weight to the personality of party leaders (Magone, 2004, p. 39).

This pattern is common among new democracies but, in Spain, it has not led to an illiberal democracy in which one key politician dominates the airwaves. Rather, political parties now compete for influence over a pluralistic media environment in which large commercial media organizations coexist with diminished state channels.

The leading parties have sought influence over broadcasting, relying in part on a constitutional statement that interprets broadcasting as an essential public service requiring government regulation. In addition, antiterror legislation and large libel awards against newspapers have placed pressures on editorial freedom. Such difficulties lower the country's position in international rankings of media freedom but do not threaten Spain's status as an established and successful liberal democracy.

Further reading: Balfour (2005), Heywood and Closa (2004), Magone (2004), Preston (2004).

who either buy no paper at all or read titles with little political coverage.

The media game

One danger in examining the *mass* media is failing to acknowledge their central role in *elite* politics. The relationship between politicians and journalists remains central to the character of elite politics in contemporary, communication-rich democracies. Politicians make enormous efforts to influence coverage. Governing parties, in particular, devote considerable attention to informing, cultivating and seeking to manipulate the journalists whose reports achieve national coverage. The humble government press office, now populated by highly paid **spin doctors**, has never been more important.

> **Spin doctor** is a critical term applied to public relations experts working for politicians. The spin doctor's job is to facilitate favourable media coverage for a party or its leader. The term derives from the spins applied by baseball pitchers and was first applied to politics in 1977 by the novelist Saul Bellow.

Consider the media game played between government (say, a White House spokesperson) and journalists (say, a White House correspondent). This contest is classically political, mixing shared and competing objectives (Brams, 2004). The government needs coverage and the media must fill their space, creating a shared interest in news. But politicians seek favourable coverage while journalists are after a big story, objectives that are rarely consistent since, as every reporter knows, good news rarely makes the headlines. The game is further complicated by competition among journalists themselves, giving the administration leverage it can exploit by placing stories with compliant correspondents.

But as with so many political relationships, the game of government–media relations is repeated each day, allowing long-term norms of acceptable behaviour to develop. A spokesperson who gives out misleading information, or no information at all on a significant topic, loses credibility. So briefers accept that over the long run it pays to be accurate and even-handed in distributing information; the facts must be correct if rarely complete. Equally, competition among journalists reduces as they learn to hunt as a pack. Correspondents know that their key task is to avoid missing the story that everyone else has. Exclusives are optional.

Typically, stable routines develop which reduce the game of government–media relations to a few well-understood ground rules. The outcome is not so much collusion as contained competition; sometimes, not even that. Feeding off each other, but never entirely comfortable in doing so, journalists and politicians find themselves locked in an awkward embrace.

Of course, the government invariably has a head start over opposition parties in media presentation. Statements by presidents and prime ministers are always more newsworthy than those made by their political opponents. Journalists have no option but to cover a prime ministerial press release, even if they are fully aware of the partisan motives underlying its timing. Many a national leader has arranged a prestigious trip to the United States in the run-up to an election, keen to exploit the domestic impact of a handshake with the American president.

Public opinion

Especially in liberal democracies, politics is a battle for influence over the important but imprecise terrain of **public opinion**. Governments, parties and interest groups seek to persuade the public to adopt their agenda, their frame of reference and their policy preferences. Yet although the notion of public opinion remains somewhat opaque, it is an important element in political communication. In this section, we discuss the definition, measurement and impact of public opinion.

> **Public opinion** can refer to (1) 'the range of views on some controversial issue held by some significant portion of the population' or (2) the informed judgement of a community on an issue of common concern, where that judgement is formed in the context of shared political goals (Qualter,1991).

Defining public opinion

One definition is highly pragmatic: public opinion is simply what the public thinks about a given issue, nothing more and nothing less. This down-to-earth view was reflected in the definition offered by Sir

Robert Peel, twice prime minister of Britain in the nineteenth century. He referred to public opinion as 'that great compound of folly, weakness, prejudice, wrong feeling, right feeling, obstinacy and newspaper paragraphs' (Green, 1994, p. 213). In similar vein, Lippman (1922) famously interpreted the notion as the 'pictures inside our heads' of other people whose behaviour crosses ours. Lippman took pains to emphasize that these mental pictures have real effects, thereby providing the key argument for the political importance of the concept.

A second view of public opinion is more elaborate, linking the idea of a 'public' to the views of an informed community sharing basic political principles. This perspective was expressed by the British statesman W. E. Gladstone (1809–98): 'public opinion represents the sum or balance of the abstract moral principles of the persons forming the community' (quoted in Hare, 1873, p. xix). From this perspective, a community is only regarded as capable of a public opinion if its people are settled on the ends of government and the range of means for pursuing them Here public opinion is interpreted as the considered will of a cohesive group. This perspective derives from the model of a self-governing republic and treats public opinion as far more than an opinion poll finding. Within this framework, public opinion is judged to possess moral weight. In a divided society, by contrast, there would be more than one public and therefore more than one public opinion.

BOX 7.4

Measuring public opinion

- An **opinion poll** is a series of questions asked in a standard way of a systematic sample of the population. The term usually refers to short surveys on topical issues for the media. Polls are usually conducted face to face, by telephone or by email (Bishop, 2004).
- A **sample survey** is conducted using the same methods as an opinion poll but involves a more detailed questionnaire. Such surveys are often commissioned by government or academic researchers (Fink, 2005).
- A **focus group** is a moderated discussion among a small group of respondents on a particular topic. A focus group is a qualitative device used to explore the thinking and emotions lying behind people's attitudes. It is an open-ended technique that has found favour with party strategists (Krueger and Casey, 2000).
- In a **deliberative opinion poll**, or **citizens' jury**, people are briefed by, and can question, experts and politicians on a given topic before their own opinions are measured. This technique seeks to measure what public opinion would be if the public were fully informed on the issue (Fishkin and Laslett, 2003).

Measuring public opinion

The idea of public opinion has gained further currency as opinion polls, citizens' juries and focus groups have developed to study it. Indeed there are few areas where a concept is so closely linked to how it is measured. In modern democracies, public opinion is both measured by, and partly composed of, reports of investigations into its content (Box 7.4).

Consider **opinion polls** and **sample surveys**, the most accurate methods of identifying what people profess. Although the public itself remains resolutely sceptical of samples, their accuracy is now well-attested, at least in predicting election outcomes. In the United States, the average error in predicting the major parties' share of the vote at post-war national elections has been around 1.5 per cent. This accuracy is impressive even if not always sufficient for the television networks to pick the right winner on election night. Precision is similar in other democracies.

Counter-intuitive it may be, but 1,000 people carefully selected for an opinion poll can accurately represent the whole population. The key phrase here is 'selected carefully'. The selection must be by a systematic procedure. Self-selected samples such as viewers who respond to television polls, or constituents who contact their representative about their pet topic, are not a valid basis for estimating public opinion. An opinion poll must cover the non-attentive public as well as the **issue public**.

The **issue** or **attentive public** consists of the minority with a particular interest in or knowledge of a given topic.

Yet it would be wrong to overstate the reliability of opinion polls in measuring the opinions of individual respondents. Like students taking a test, interviewees in a survey are answering questions set elsewhere. Polls are commissioned by journalists and party officials in the capital city, not by the ordinary people who answer the questions. As a result, people may never have thought about a topic before they are invited to answer questions on it (Althaus, 2003). They may give an opinion when they have none or they may agree to a statement because it is the easiest thing to do ('yea-saying'). Certainly, one danger of opinion polls is that they help to construct public opinion even as they measure it.

In a **focus group**, a researcher gathers together a small group of people – typically eight to ten – for a general discussion of a topic in which the participants normally share a particular interest: for instance, lapsed Democrats, non-voters or protest participants. The idea is to explore in open-ended style the perspectives through which the participants view the issue. A focus group is a qualitative version of an opinion poll, smaller in scale and therefore potentially less representative, but aiming at a fuller understanding than is possible with the pre-coded answers used in an opinion poll (Krueger and Casey, 2000).

Because opinion polls do not give respondents a chance to discuss the issue before expressing their views, the technique is criticized by those who favour more ambitious interpretations of public opinion. Building on a richer view of public opinion, scholars have developed the idea of a **deliberative opinion poll** or **citizens' jury** (Fishkin, 1991). This technique involves exposing a small sample of electors to a range of viewpoints on a selected topic, perhaps through presentations by experts and politicians. With the background to the problem established, the group proceeds to a discussion and a judgement. Opinion is only measured when the issues have been thoroughly aired in this way. As Fishkin (1991, p. 1) explains,

> an ordinary opinion poll models what the public thinks, given how little it knows. A deliberative opinion poll models what the public would think, if it had a more adequate chance to think about the questions at issue.

Deliberative polling can therefore be used to anticipate how opinion might develop on new issues. It is also particularly useful on issues with a large technical content, for example global warming and genetic testing. In such areas, expert explanation can usefully precede an expression of opinion. Though not widely used, citizens' juries are an ingenious attempt to overcome the problem of ill-informed replies which bedevils conventional opinion polls.

The impact of public opinion

Because public opinion research is based on direct contact with the public, it goes behind group leaders claiming to speak on behalf of their members. Opinion polls, in particular, give even the most cocooned politicians an insight into the public mood. Given that public opinion is an important element of democratic politics, how exactly does it exert its influence? In a sense public opinion pervades all policy-making. It forms the environment within which politicians work, sitting in on many government meetings even though it is never minuted as a member.

In such discussions public opinion usually performs one of two roles, acting either as a prompt or as a veto. 'Public opinion demands we do something about traffic congestion' is an example of the former; 'public opinion would never accept restrictions on car use' illustrates the latter. So as Qualter (1991, p. 511) suggests, 'while public opinion does not govern, it may set limits on what governments do'.

Yet public opinion is never all-powerful, even in liberal democracies. It informs agendas rather than policy. Four factors limit its influence:

- Public opinion offers few detailed policy prescriptions. A few important objectives preoccupy the public but most policies are routine and uncontroversial. In detailed policy-making, expert and organized opinion matters more than public opinion.
- The public as a whole is often ill-informed, especially but not only on foreign policy. Asked before the Iraq invasion, 'To the best of your knowledge, how many of the September 11 hijackers were Iraqi citizens?' only 7 per cent of Americans gave the correct answer: none (Pryor, 2003).

- Public opinion can evade trade-offs but governments cannot, though they sometimes try. The public may want lower taxes, more government spending and a lower budget deficit simultaneously but rulers must choose between these objectives. Further, the risks associated with a policy are poorly assessed by the public but require close attention from decision-makers (Weissberg, 2002).
- Politicians typically respond to organized opinion rather than to public opinion. Their perceptions of the public's views are in any case often inaccurate, derived as they are from the distorting lenses of interest groups, the media and the natural tendency to project one's own views onto the wider electorate (Herbst, 1998).

Public opinion is most influential when it changes. Only foolhardy politicians disregard developments in the overall climate of opinion and many politicians are wisely sensitive to changes in the national mood (Stimson, 1991 and 2004).

The media in authoritarian states

Just as democracy thrives on the flow of information, so authoritarian rulers survive by limiting free expression, leading to media coverage which is subdued even when it is not subservient. Far from acting as the fourth estate, casting its searchlight into the darker corners of government, journalists in authoritarian states defer to political authority. Lack of resources within the media sector usually increases vulnerability to pressure. Official television stations and subsidized newspapers reproduce the regime's line while critical journalists are harassed and the entire media sector develops an instinct for self-preservation through self-censorship.

However, the consequence is that inadequate information flows to the top, increasing the gap between state and society and leading ultimately to incorrect decisions. Thoughtful rulers respond to this problem by encouraging the media to expose malfeasance at local level, either through journalistic investigation or by the time-honoured technique of letters to the editor. But there is no escape from the paradox of authoritarianism. By controlling information, rulers may secure their power in the short run but they also reduce the quality of governance, potentially threatening their survival over the longer term. The more developed the country, the more severe is the damage inflicted by an information deficit.

How exactly do authoritarian rulers limit independent journalism? The constraints are varied and often more subtle than explicit censorship. In her study of sub-Saharan Africa before the wave of liberalization in the 1990s, Bourgault (1995, p. 180) identified several mechanisms of control, including:

- Declaring states of emergency which formally limit media freedom;
- Licensing of publications and journalists;
- Heavy taxation of printing equipment;
- A requirement to post bonds before new publications can launch;
- Restricted access to newsprint;
- The threat of losing government advertising;
- Broad libel laws.

Lack of resources hold back the development of the media sector – and authoritarian states are, of course, most often found in low-income countries. Limited means stifle journalistic initiative and increase vulnerability. Sometimes, impoverished journalists are reduced to publishing favourable stories (or threatening to write critical ones) in exchange for money.

Pressures from authoritarian leaders are by no means restricted to Africa. In much of post-communist central Asia, large parts of the media remain in state hands, giving the authorities direct leverage. The state also typically retains ownership of a leading television channel. The outcome is subservience:

> From Kazakhstan to Kyrgyzstan and Tajikistan to Belarus and Ukraine, the story is a dismal one: tax laws are used for financial harassment; a body of laws forbids insults of those in high places; compulsory registration of the media is common. In Azerbaijan, as in Belarus, one-man rule leaves little room for press freedom (Foley, 1999, p. 45).

The justification for restricting the freedom of the media is typically built on an overriding national requirement for social stability, nation-building or economic development. The subtext is that we cannot be like the West until we have caught up, and perhaps not even then. In Egypt, for instance, the government expects that 'the press should uphold the security of the country, promote economic development, and support approved social norms' (Lesch, 2004, p. 610). A free press, like a competitive party system, is presented as a recipe for squabbling and disharmony.

Even though many of these justifications for controlling the media are simply excuses for authoritarian government, we should not assume that the Western idea of a free press has universal appeal. Islamic states, in particular, stress the media's role in affirming religious values and social norms. A free press is seen as an excuse for licence: why, the question is asked, should we import Western, and particularly American, ideas of freedom if the practical result is the availability of pornography? When society is viewed as the expression of an overarching moral code, whether Islamic or otherwise, the Western tradition of free speech appears alien and even non-ethical.

As with other aspects of politics, totalitarian states developed a more sophisticated approach to media. Mass communication was expected to play its part in the transformation of political culture. The media were therefore brought under tighter control than in other authoritarian systems. Unrelenting penetration of mass communication into everyday life was a core component of the totalitarian system. 'It is the absolute right of the state to supervise the formation of public opinion,' claimed Joseph Goebbels, Hitler's Minister of Propaganda. At the height of the Second World War, Goebbels's ministry employed 1900 people at national level, arranged into 17 divisions such as radio, press, film and theatre (Bytwerk, 2004, p. 60).

It is significant, however, that neither communist nor fascist regimes regarded the media, by themselves, as a sufficient means of ideological control. Communist states supplemented mass propaganda with direct agitation in places where people gathered together; fascist regimes valued direct control through public meetings as much as impersonal broadcasts through the media.

In communist states, the dual dimensions of political communication were **propaganda** and agitation. Propaganda explained the party's mission and instructed both the elite and the masses in the teachings of Marx, Engels and Lenin. To achieve their propaganda objectives, ruling communist parties developed an elaborate media network with radio, posters, cinema, television and 'socialist art' all reinforcing each other. While propaganda operated through the media, agitation operated at local level. The party sought to place an agitator in each factory, farm and military unit, encouraging the workers to ever greater feats of production. Together, propaganda and agitation dominated the flow of information; the theory being that the combined effect would be all the greater because, in the nature of a total regime, no dissenting voices were permitted.

> **Propaganda** is communication by an organization which seeks to promote support for its cause by influencing the attitudes and especially the behaviour of large numbers of people. The word is religious in origin: the Catholic Church established a College of Propaganda in1622 to propagate the faith.

What was the impact of the communist attempt to use the media as a tool for influencing the public? It seems to have helped with agenda-setting by disguising local problems such as accidents, poverty and pollution which could be hidden from people elsewhere in the country. It may also have scored some success in highlighting achievements such as industrialization (Oates, 2005, p. 118). And, just as advertising by parties in democracies is often aimed at their own activists, so communist propaganda may have helped party members to keep the faith.

But the communist experience also revealed the limits of media power. A cynical public was not easily fooled. Grandiose statements about national progress were too often contradicted by the grim realities of daily life. In any case, as communist states became inert, so propaganda became empty ritual. Eventually, its main purpose became that of showing the population that the party still ruled; the party's power was confirmed because no one was willing to dispute its lies.

It is noteworthy, however, that the remaining states with a nominal communist allegiance have kept close control over the means of mass communication. In China, access to information has traditionally been provided on a need-to-know basis. The country's rulers remain keen to limit dissenting voices even as the party's tolerance of non-political

BOX 7.5

China and the internet

This extract is summarized from *China's Public Pledge of Self-Regulation and Professional Ethics for the Chinese Internet Industry* (Internet Society of China, 2002). Yahoo and other Western providers signed this document despite the limitations it places on the free flow of information.

'We internet service providers pledge to abide by state regulations on internet information service management to fulfil the following disciplinary obligations:

- To refrain from producing, posting or disseminating pernicious information that may jeopardize state security and disrupt social stability, contravene laws and regulations and spread superstition and obscenity;
- To monitor the information publicized on websites according to law and remove harmful information promptly;
- To refrain from establishing links to websites containing harmful information.'

Further reading: Goldsmith and Wu (2006).

debate increases. Although the regime is keen to promote e-commerce, internet users who search for 'inappropriate' topics such as democracy or Tibetan independence will find their access to search engines withdrawn. The excuse offered is that the authorities are merely protecting Chinese people from unwholesome Western influence. Western companies themselves have gone along with such limitations in order to secure access to the large Chinese market (Box 7.5).

The media in illiberal democracies

In illiberal democracies, control over the media is far less extensive than in authoritarian states. Citizens who lived though a preceding era of communist or military rule become aware of the greater range and vigour of channels operating in a newly competitive sector. The press, in particular, is often left substantially alone, offering a forum for elite debate which is perhaps of value even to the rulers.

Yet the leading political force also dominates broadcast coverage, even where explicit or implicit censorship is absent. To some extent, such an emphasis reflects political reality: viewers are naturally most interested in those who exert most influence over their lives. Latin America provides a good example. In many countries on the continent, a tradition of personal and populist rule lends itself well to expression through broadcasting media which reach the many poor people who seek salvation through 'their' leader.

Foweraker, Landman and Harvey (2003, p. 105) describe the origins of this tradition in the twentieth century when 'populist leaders in Latin America made popular appeals to the people through mass media in newspapers and especially radio'. These authors comment that contemporary populism continues in the same vein, albeit now operating through television more than radio. Leaders hold out promises of 'a consumer lifestyle that is intimately familiar to their publics through television advertising and television soap operas' (p. 107).

The political style of Hugo Chávez, president of Venezuela since 1998, is a good example. Many callers to his weekly radio broadcast, *¡Aló, Presidente!*, petition the president for help in securing a job or social security benefit, usually citing in the process the callousness of the preceding regime. The president created a special office to handle all these requests. Aware of Chávez's communication skills, the opposition sought to restrict the president's access to state-owned broadcasting but the regime continues to intimidate journalists (Hellinger, 2003, p. 49). In Chávez, we see how the leader of an illiberal democracy can strengthen his authority through the media even against the opposition of many media professionals themselves.

Russia provides an example of a post-communist illiberal democracy where pressures on the media, from powerful business people as well as politicians, remain intense. This influence derives precisely from the centrality of television to political communication in Russia. As in Latin America, broadcasting is the main way of reaching a dispersed population for

BOX 7.6

The main television channels in Russia, 2004

	Ownership	Comment
Channel One	51 per cent state-owned	Supports Putin
Russian Television	State-owned	Supports Putin
TV-Centre	Main owner: City of Moscow	Supports Mayor of Moscow
NTV	Commercial interests friendly to the Putin government	Some support for Putin; avoids controversial topics
Culture	State-owned	Cultural channel
TV-6	Commercial	Sports channel

Source: Oates (2005), p. 124.

whom free television has more appeal than paid-for papers. In a 2004 survey, 82 per cent of Russians said they watched television 'routinely', compared to just 22 per cent who said the same about national newspapers (Oates, 2005, p. 124). The television audience in Russia for nightly news programmes is substantial indeed, matching that in the United States for the Super Bowl. For now, at least, the press and the internet are less important and less regulated.

Vladimir Putin's success in the presidential election of 2000 owed much to his control of public television, whose news broadcasts in the final days of the campaign portrayed his opponents as sympathetic to gays and Jews. Since then President Putin has taken steps to tighten his control over the main television channels, in some ways re-establishing an authoritarian level of dominance. Some channels are state-owned; others are controlled by friendly business interests; and one channel that did offer more independent coverage now finds itself covering sport only (Box 7.6). Particularly but not only during elections, television showcases the achievements of the administration and its favoured candidates; opposition figures receive less, and distinctly less flattering, attention.

With over 100 laws governing media conduct, and the occasional journalist still found murdered by unknown assailants, self-censorship – the voice in the editor's head which asks 'am I taking a risk in publishing this story?' – remains rife. Because editors know which side their bread is buttered, there is no need for politicians to take the political risk involved in explicit instruction. The internal censor allows the president to maintain deniability. 'Censorship? What censorship?' he can ask with a smile.

The interesting point – and one that is characteristic of illiberal democracy – is that the Russian public seems to prefer control of the media by established authority to the liberal model of independent journalists searching out the truth (Oates, 2005, p. 127). Russians regard state television as one of the most unbiased and reliable sources of information even though they are equally aware of what liberal democrats would regard as unwarranted interference in its coverage. Perhaps influenced by the communist era, most Russians raise no objections to the highly controlled treatment of the war in Chechnya or of the country's many social problems. These attitudes to the media reflect an underlying preference for order and in particular for a strong president who delivers it.

In many illiberal democracies, journalistic standards remain low, reflecting decades in which reporters just reproduced the platitudes of the ruling communist or military clique. Easy editorializing still takes priority over the hard graft of newsgathering. There is little tradition of media scrutiny of rulers to carry over from the pre-democratic era. Given these weak traditions, strong presidents can secure sufficient control without recourse to explicit censorship.

Learning Resources for Chapter 7

Next step

Norris (2000) offers an interesting comparative account of the media's role in Western democracies.

Further reading

Communication may be central to politics but the definitive contemporary treatment of the topic is still to be written. Williams's short but influential study (1962) is still relevant to students of politics. Mann's history of power (1986) includes considerable material on the development of communication. However, most modern studies focus on the media rather than communication generally. Gunther and Mughan (2000) and Esser and Pfetsch (2004) offer comparative collections; see also Bennett and Entman (2001) and Street (2001). On the USA, Graber (2005) is an authoritative text while Jamieson and Waldman (2003) look at the 'press effect' specifically. Norris *et al.* (2003) compare the frames used in media coverage of 9/11 with earlier terrorist incidents. On public opinion, Glynn *et al.* (1998) is a wide-ranging collection while Bishop (2004) examines whether it is fact or illusion. Away from Western democracies, McCargo (2002) examines the media in Asia, Bourgault (1995) discusses sub-Saharan Africa while Bytwerk (2004) looks at propaganda efforts at 'bending spines' in Nazi Germany and communist East Germany. Milton (2000) is an overview of the media in postcommunist states.

Internet sources

Communication, Cultural and Media Studies Infobase
A useful resource for students of communication
http://www.ccms-infobase.com/

Reporters without Borders
For press freedom
http://www.rsf.org/

Freedom House
Press freedom by country
http://www.freedomhouse.org

International Federation of Journalists
The world's largest organization of journalists
http://www.ifj.org/

Index on Censorship
For free expression
http://www.indexonline.org/

Pew Center for Civic Journalism
Advancing good journalism
http://www.pewcenter.org/

UNESCO Information and Communication
Communication from a cross-national and policy perspective
http://www.unesco.org

Chapter 8
Political economy

'The executive of the modern state is but a committee for managing the common affairs of the whole bourgeoisie,' wrote Marx and Engels in *The Communist Manifesto* of 1848. 'It's the economy, stupid,' proclaimed the notice famously displayed at Bill Clinton's campaign headquarters in 1992. These two statements are separated by space, time and ideology, yet both draw our attention to the close connections between politics and economics. Nearly everywhere, wealth helps to obtain power and, similarly, power is often an effective shortcut to wealth.

In liberal democracies, the disintegration of socialism means most elected governments now accept the sprit of a comment by Karl Schiller, Germany's Economics and Finance Minister in the 1960s: 'As much market as possible, as much state planning as necessary'. Yet how this balance is struck still varies significantly between, say, Germany and the United States or Japan and the United Kingdom. Understanding these national varieties of capitalism is the major aim of this chapter.

In authoritarian regimes and many illiberal democracies, politics generally takes precedence over the economy, limiting, or in communist states, abolishing the market. It is still worth reviewing the communist experience since this provides the world's most extensive attempt to develop an alternative to the market economy. More generally, our task in examining non-democratic regimes is to understand how authoritarian rulers use economic resources for political ends. This issue has attracted particular attention in discussions of the resource curse affecting commodity-based economies, notably in the Middle East.

This chapter also examines the important relationship between democracy and development. Sørensen (1997, p. 65) raises the key issue here, observing that 'in the twentieth century there was no case of successful economic development without comprehensive political action involving enormous state intervention in the economy'. Is this proposition still true today? If so, must we accept that non-democratic rule is an appropriate form of rule for low-income countries, at least until their living standards have improved? Discussing such questions will test the prevalent Western assumption that democracy is universally applicable and will also involve an introduction to the concept of the developmental state.

What is political economy?

In this section, we review the work of the central figures in the development of political economy: Adam Smith, Maynard Keynes and Milton Friedman. Between them, these scholars created the framework of the discipline,

BOX 8.1

Key thinkers in political economy

	Core prescription	Illustrative quotation
Adam Smith (1723–90)	Rely on the market's invisible hand to allocate resources to the areas where they will secure the highest return	'It is not from the benevolence of the butcher, the brewer, or the baker that we expect our dinner, but from their regard to their self-interest' (1776, p. 22)
John Maynard Keynes (1883–1946)	When demand is deficient, counter unemployment by boosting public spending	'If the Treasury were to fill old bottles with bank notes, bury them at suitable depths in disused coal mines which are then filled up to the surface with town rubbish, and leave it to private enterprise on well-tried principles of *laissez-faire* to dig the notes up again [. . .] there need be no more unemployment' (1936, p. 379)
Milton Friedman (1912–2006)	To bring inflation under control, restrict growth in the money supply	'Inflation is always and everywhere a monetary phenomenon' (1970, p. 16)

analysing technical economic issues but with a clear eye for both politics and policy.

The Scottish economist Adam Smith developed **political economy** as a field of study in the eighteenth century. He used the term to describe what is now called economics, proposing two objects for the subject: first, to enable the people to supply a plentiful revenue for themselves and, second, to endow the state with sufficient revenue to provide public services (Smith, 1776). Today, the term retains its focus not just on the relationship between politics and economics but also, and more specifically, on policies for improving economic performance.

The phrase **political economy** comes from seventeenth-century France when it referred to the financial management of the royal household. Today, the term refers to the area where politics meets economics, with a particular focus on economic policy.

The emergence of political economy in Smith's time reflected the rise of the modern state, thus linking the subject to the broader discipline of politics. As the idea of a modern state began to develop, so too did the desire to understand how wealth was created for society at large, rather than just for reigning monarchs. This shift in approach reflected the growth of a commercial society in which wealth was beginning to be created through trade as well as agriculture, and in which a country's assets were measured by broader tests than the mere accumulation of gold in the royal treasury. So the emergence of political economy, understood as the study of wealth creation for society at large, was an aspect of the broader transition to the modern era in which authority subsists in the community rather than solely in its ruling monarchs.

Adam Smith's own contribution, of course, lay in setting out how the invisible hand of the market could produce an efficient use of resources overall even though individual producers and consumers act only in their own interest. High profits in a given sector encourage new entrants until profitability declines; conversely, low profits encourage the less efficient providers to depart. Provided the market is genuinely competitive, the outcome is a system that allocates funds to projects earning the highest return.

As the British politician Gordon Brown points out, Smith's position is more balanced and sophisticated than his image as a ruthless free marketeer suggests (McLean, 2006). Smith was aware of the danger of business cartels and of the value of public investment in such market-friendly sectors as education and transport. His message to politicians, monarchs and other meddlers was similar to Schiller's, with one modification: 'as much market as possible, as little planning as necessary'.

While Smith's analysis still provides the theoretical basis for contemporary market economies, the circumstances of the twentieth century did require governments to attend to two major concerns: the rise of unemployment in the 1930s and of inflation in the 1970s. The first of these brought about an expanded role for government; the second, a reduction. The resolution of these issues extended the toolkit available to policy-makers, both at the time and today, and requires attention from students of politics as well as economics.

The English economist John Maynard Keynes provided a solution to the problem of unemployment, at least in the form it took in the 1930s. He suggested that in a depression, governments should prime the pump of recovery by increasing public spending. Through a multiplier effect, this injection of resources will circulate through the economy, gradually rebuilding confidence, demand, investment and finally the revenues flowing into the government's own coffers. However, Keynes's politics were liberal, not socialist; he sought to stimulate the market, not replace it.

This emphasis on governments' ability to manage aggregate demand held out the promise of solving what was still seen as capitalism's great weakness, at least compared to planned economies: the fluctuations of the business cycle. Indeed, Shonfield (1969, p. 64) suggested that 'control over the business cycle, which owes so much to Keynes's work, is probably the single most important factor in establishing the dynamic and prosperous capitalism of the post-war era'. Keynes seemed to have civilized the market, first demonstrating its superiority over totalitarian alternatives and then laying the foundations for post-war recovery. This was an achievement of the first order, and one demonstrating the political significance of economic ideas (Hall, 1989).

By the dismal decade of the 1970s, however, the Keynesian revolution appeared to have run its course. A new tangle of political and economic problems emerged: inflation, government budget deficits, high rates of personal taxation, declining productivity growth and powerful trade unions. At least some of these problems were exacerbated by the continuing application of Keynesian policies to an era when mass unemployment no longer obtained.

The solution, suggested the American economist Milton Friedman, lay in returning monetary policy to centre stage. In a contribution comparable in its impact to that of Keynes, Friedman (1970, p. 16) argued that 'inflation is always and everywhere a monetary phenomenon', in which 'substantial changes in prices are almost always the result of changes in the nominal supply of money' (money is usually defined to include bank deposits as well as cash). In the well-worn phrase, inflation results from too much money chasing too few goods. Friedman's research suggested that tightening the supply of money will reduce economic activity and employment in the short-run but cool inflation within 12 to 18 months as wage negotiators lower their expectations of future price increases (Friedman with Schwartz, 1963). In the long term, economic activity will recover in response to the stable and predictable environment which sound money provides.

Just as Keynes's deficit financing had advanced the cause of the left, so Friedman's monetarism gave an equivalent fillip to the right-wing administrations of Ronald Reagan and Margaret Thatcher. Like Keynes before him, Friedman's work modified the framework of economic policy-making, reinstating the importance of money. But where Keynes sought short-run solutions, Friedman's concern was with the long run. Friedman lacked Keynes's belief in the ability of policy-makers to fine-tune the economy; instead, he advocated a cautious, steady approach to the money supply.

Many liberal democracies do now give their central banks responsibility for achieving a target level or range for inflation (Clark, 2005). This duty is effected through manipulation of interest rates, rather than through what proved to be the excessively deflationary device of direct control over the supply of money. Delegating the execution of monetary policy to appointed officials reduces the risk of monetary manipulation by governing parties more concerned with the political short run than the economic long run. The outcome is a reduction in democratic control but a further increment to predictability, giving additional confidence to investors.

We can now use this foundation to review the political economies of contemporary liberal democracies, noting in particular the need to extend the discussion beyond the Anglo-American tradition established by these three leading figures.

Varieties of capitalism

Our purpose in this section is to compare the political economies of contemporary liberal democracies, identifying the contrasts which still exist within this group. Principally, this task requires a comparison of what are termed liberal market economies such as the USA with coordinated market economies such as Germany (Box 8.2). In addition, we will introduce the idea of the developmental state associated with several Asian economies, notably Japan in its high growth post-war decades.

Liberal and coordinated market economies

One traditional distinction within Western political economies is between pluralist and corporatist systems. In the former, the government acts as an umpire, arbitrating between numerous competing interests; in the latter, the state usually plays a more influential role, operating with and through groups representing capital and labour. Within the framework of political economy, Hall and Soskice (2001) have developed this analysis into a broader contrast between liberal market economies and coordinated market economies.

A liberal market economy corresponds to Adam Smith's construct as closely as can be expected from any system operating over three hundred years later. Competing firms operate in a flexible labour market, seeking to enhance profitability in order to satisfy the demands of their shareholders for a return. The government and the judiciary aim to ensure that contracts are enforced and disputes resolved but, as under pluralism, their function is to umpire rather than to play. Similarly, industry associations and trade unions seek to advise and support, but not to direct, their members. So economic actors, whether large corporations or individual employees, retain considerable autonomy, a feature which creates the potential for market-led restructuring when needed.

This liberal or pluralist model is exemplified by the United States but it is also now found in other English-speaking countries, notably Australia, Britain, Canada and New Zealand. Note, however, that the movement of these latter countries in a liberal direction since the 1980s confirms that states do not necessarily occupy a permanent position in relation to these models and that the position of Australia and New Zealand is further complicated by their distinctive strengths in agricultural production (Regini, 2003).

Consider the American exemplar. In the USA, **shareholder capitalism** predominates: the shareholders own the firm and expect a continuing return on their investment (though, in practice, managers often secure a generous share of profits). Expanding firms do not hesitate to take on additional labour, secure in the knowledge that staff can be dismissed should conditions worsen. Employees are mobile and willing to move for a better job. Hostile takeovers and corporate bankruptcies are interpreted as a signal from Adam Smith's invisible hand: they form 'the perennial gale of creative destruction' which Schumpeter (1943, p. 84) regarded as capitalism's essential strength. Failing companies may well declare themselves bankrupt but the managers can simply start another business, perhaps funded by venture capitalists whose function is to invest in young firms with good growth prospects.

In contrast to English-speaking liberalism, the political economies of continental Europe reflect a range of corporatist traditions. In the model coordinated market economy, the 'private' sector is seen less as an independent sphere of activity and more as an arena subject to control by social and political forces. In many countries, these forces have included

In **shareholder capitalism**, those who own the company seek to maximize the financial return on their investment and are willing to replace managers who fail to achieve this goal. This form is found in liberal market economies such as the USA.

BOX 8.2

Varieties of capitalism: liberal and coordinated market economies

	Liberal market economy	Coordinated market economy
Basis of relationships between firms	Mainly formal market contracts	Discussion within collaborative networks, often industry-based, is more significant
Cross-shareholding between firms?	Rare	Common
Source of capital for investment	Mainly shareholders	Banks and other companies more important
Priority of firms	Shorter-term profitability	Long-term profitability, and also market share, are more important
Hiring and firing staff	More flexible	Less flexible
Strength of trade unions and employer organizations	Low	High
Archetypal case	United States	Germany

Note: Coordinated economies are also described as organized market economies, social market economies or, with particular reference to Germany, Rhineland capitalism.

Source: Adapted from Hall and Soskice (2001).

not just a strong socialist party but also an influential Catholic church; neither institution has favoured the free play of the market. In societies divided by class, religion and ideology, economic competition has been subject to political control in order to deliver social stability. Social cohesion and solidarity are core values. The market operates in a constrained way, reflecting a shared desire to prevent Smith's invisible hand from becoming an invisible fist. The coordinating actors vary by country, including industrial associations in Germany, the dominant Social Democratic Party in Sweden and the state itself in France (Boyer, 1997).

In a coordinated economy, individual firms belong to influential industry-wide associations that provide a forum for exchanging information between leading firms. Companies hold shares in each other, forming a strong interlocking structure. Managers derive authority from their professional standing, not merely from the company they work for. Compared to liberal economies, more capital comes through long term funding from banks, thus limiting the pressure from shareholders for immediate returns. The employment relationship is conceived as long term, giving employees a greater stake in the business but also reducing the capacity for radical change. The state helps with coordination and the courts are prepared to intervene to ensure economic actors abide by broadly accepted standards, including civil law codes.

This coordinated or partnership model is exemplified by Germany but is also found in many other

BOX 8.3

Main level of wage negotiations in selected European countries, 2003

National level	Sectoral level	Company level
Belgium	Austria	Hungary
Finland	Germany	Poland
Ireland	Netherlands	United Kingdom

Source: Adapted from Avdagić and Crouch (2006), Table 11.2.

European economies, such as Austria, Belgium, Denmark, Finland, the Netherlands and Sweden. One indicator of a coordinated approach is that wage negotiations for specific types of job take place at national or sectoral level rather than within the firm (Box 8.3). At national level, a broad pact covering wages, prices and benefits may be agreed between the government and peak associations representing capital and labour. At sectoral level, the engineering union may negotiate a package with an employers' federation whose members include all the large firms in that industry.

Let us look at the German exemplar. The coordination here is formally structured, creating engineered capitalism for an engineering economy. **Stakeholder capitalism** rather than shareholder capitalism predominates. Companies recognize obligations to a wide variety of stakeholders, including trade unions, banks, industrial associations, other companies and all levels of government, and these interests are represented on supervisory boards (Box 8.4). Wage inequalities are contained at a lower level than in the Anglo-American world.

Reflecting Germany's guild traditions, industrial sectors are particularly important, a feature which has enabled post-war governments to remain in the background, avoiding comparisons with the interventionist Nazi era. Within industry, the focus is on enhancing existing strengths rather than building new ones. Stakeholders such as trade unions and even creditors are naturally risk averse; they do not gain as much as shareholders from successful new initiatives. Venture capital is less prominent and restructuring operates in a slower and more negotiated manner, with greater emphasis on fashioning a long-term solution acceptable to all partners (Padgett, 2003). In Germany, bankruptcies and takeovers are regarded negatively, as a sign of past coordination failures. A firm in difficulty is more likely to be absorbed into a larger enterprise than to be closed down.

In **stakeholder capitalism**, companies acknowledge – and often incorporate into their deliberations – a wide range of interests, including employees, trade unions, the local community and the government. This form is found in coordinated market economies such as Germany.

A coordinated economy is the industrial equivalent of the consensus politics which is found in most countries with this economic form. The representation of stakeholders within corporate governance parallels the power-sharing found in coalition governments. In both economic and political spheres, consensual governance reflects similar influences. These include the fear of instability induced by Europe's violent past; the desire to reconcile what were once divisive cleavages of class and religion; and, Scandinavia apart, Catholic distrust of a market society of sovereign individuals.

Coordination does bring several potential economic advantages, particularly in industrial economies needing to protect a legacy of past investment (Allen, 2006). Three strengths are particularly notable:

- Broadening the sphere of coordination from the individual firm to the industrial sector encourages investment both in training and in research and development. Germany's system of vocational training in engineering is unmatched in any liberal economy where the tendency is for firms to free-ride by poaching staff trained by their competitors.
- Organizing such features as pensions and medical insurance at the level of the sector (or even the state) rather than the company allows for a pooling of risk. If engineering companies form a single pensions scheme for all employees in their sector, individual workers will not lose their pension should their particular firm go bankrupt.

- Many coordinated economies operate under codified legal frameworks that set out detailed rules governing commercial practice in general and contracts in particular. In Germany, again, Article 242 of the extensive Civil Code establishes a norm of 'good faith' which the courts apply to all disputes. The existence of such commercial codes reduces the expense of doing business. By contrast, the tradition in liberal economies, notably the USA, is that contracting parties are free to insert into an agreement any conditions they wish. The result is a higher cost of doing deals - and more time in court (Casper, 2001).

The developmental state

We turn now away from the Western world and towards the contrasting notion of the **developmental state**. This term is used to describe the institutional foundations of the rapid economic growth achieved by many countries in East Asia in the post-war era. Such a regime takes the form of a highly coordinated market economy, in which the state's legitimacy derives from economic success as much as popular election. If we are to make a comparison with the West, it is certainly with German coordination rather than Anglo-American liberalism (Dore, 2000).

In a sense, the developmental state is a coordinated economy for an industrializing country, albeit with a more influential role for key politicians and bureaucrats and a more passive role for the population. We introduce this idea in the context of Japan but we should note that comparable strategies have been followed by South Korea (which did not democratize until the 1990s) and, to a lesser extent, by illiberal democracies such as Malaysia. We examine recent changes to the developmental state in the next section.

Chalmers Johnson developed the concept in *Japan: Who Governs? The Rise of the Developmental State* (1995). He suggested that after the Cold War the evident contrasts between Japanese and American capitalism no longer needed to be denied in the interests of anti-communist unity. Rather, the distinctive characteristics of Japan's political economy could be freely expressed.

According to Johnson, the state played an important coordinating role in Japan's post-war development. The bureaucracy targeted export-oriented manufacturing industries such as cameras and motorcycles. Close links between high-ranking government officials and senior managers in private firms sustained a powerful and cohesive elite, capable of containing popular pressures on government. Collaborative research at sectoral level provided a resource for the major firms in that industry. An undervalued currency encouraged exports while high tariffs and other trade barriers deterred imports, not least to protect an inefficient agricultural sector.

Compared with the West, wages and benefits were low but distributed more equally; job security was

The **developmental state** leads a society to rapid industrialization by combining a powerful bureaucracy, which formulates national economic targets, with private ownership of the means of production. The main examples are East Asian states such as Japan and Korea in the post-war decades.

BOX 8.4

Members of Volkswagen's Supervisory Board, 2007

- Ferdinand Piëch, Chairman;
- Prime Minister and Economics Minister, State of Lower Saxony;
- Chairman, Volkswagen Management Association;
- Two directors of Porsche AG;
- Three chairmen or presidents of other German companies;
- Five chairmen of Volkswagen Works Councils;
- Two members from IG Metall (metalworkers' union);
- Economist, Otto Brenner Foundation;
- President, German Shareholders' Association.

Note: Under the German format of codetermination, the supervisory board appoints and monitors the normal managing board as well as approving important decisions.

Source: Volkswagen AG (2007).

high, with the firm providing secure employment in exchange for life-long loyalty. Profits were reinvested rather than paid out to shareholders. Efficient production rather than profitability, and investment rather than domestic consumption, were judged the keys to catch-up. Johnson (1995, p. 68) summarized the central features of Japan's developmental state as 'a strong state, industrial policy, producer economics and managerial autonomy'. At the very least, this governed market, as Wade (1990) called it, proved consistent with high economic growth for almost thirty years after the war, allowing Johnson (1995, p. 68) to declare that 'Asian capitalism seems destined to lie at the center of what economists will teach their students in the next century.'

Convergence?

Our discussion so far has drawn attention to contrasts within the political economies of liberal democracies. To what extent, though, are these differences receding as coordinated market economies face the challenge of international competition and developmental states adjust to the more market-led approach associated with developed status? Is the **convergence thesis** correct in maintaining that advanced economies are coalescing around the American model of a liberal market economy?

The issues here arise, in part, from a familiar roster of post-war trends associated with the idea of a global economy. These factors include an expansion of international trade, an increase in cross-border investment, a growth in the number and scale of multinational corporations, the formation of regional trade agreements, the free flow of financial assets across borders since the early 1970s, and the founding of monetary unions, particularly the euro (Ravenhill, 2005).

> The **convergence thesis** maintains that all Western economies are adopting a common format. The proposition is that a more global environment is forcing a liberal, pro-market response from each national economy.

To be sure, Hirst and Thompson (1996, p. 2) have pointed out that 'the present highly internationalized economy is not unprecedented ... in some respects, the current international economy is less open and integrated than the regime that prevailed from 1870 to 1914'. But despite 11 September, 2001, the world economy has continued to become more integrated since Hirst and Thompson wrote these words and, in any case, the trends within the post-war period – and since the 1970s in particular – are undeniable.

It is no surprise, then, that the image of a global economy overwhelming historical differences in national capitalisms has gained ground. Strange (1997, p. 183) offers a crisp account of this global perspective. With some justification, she complains that 'comparative social scientists do not compare as much as they contrast. Their attention is mainly directed at differences rather than similarities. They seldom bother to inquire into the more important question – why is it that all these states adopted broadly similar policies and institutions at about the same point in their development?' Strange continues:

> Given that the seeds of capitalism grew to maturity in very different gardens, would the forces of global structural change allow these national differences to persist indefinitely? Or, alternatively, would the common logic of integrated world markets for more and more goods and services slowly but surely modify the old differences and bring national versions of capitalism ever closer to a common pattern? My bet was, and is, on the latter.

When we look at the current standing of coordinated market economies, in particular, we can certainly find support for Strange's position. The coordinated model is currently under stress. Since the 1990s, the performance of the German economy in particular has lagged behind that of the Anglo-American world. Germany is the world's largest exporter but overseas companies have been reluctant to invest in the country, citing over-regulation, high labour costs and an inflexible labour market. In 2003, Padgett (p. 142) judged that 'the capacity of the German model for reconciling economic efficiency with traditional values may have reached its limits'. Three years later, Angela Merkel, the new Christian Democratic chancellor, agreed: 'We need change. We must keep what has proven its worth but change what burdens us'. She emphasized, in particular, the need to revise Germany's elaborate system of employee representation on company boards.

Equally, developmental states have been losing distinctiveness. Japan entered a decade of deflation in the 1990s and the Asian region as a whole experienced a massive financial convulsion in 1997. One reading of these difficulties is that policies that aid industrialization become counter-productive once development is achieved. Collaboration between firms and government departments, which once seemed highly constructive, begins to appear as secretive collusion. The Japanese notion of 'excessive competition' was perhaps permissible in the building-up phase but seemed less appropriate once the economy had matured (Dore, 2000). Generally, developmental states can only place production before profit for so long. Banks must eventually go bankrupt if too many of their loans remain unpaid.

As Strange anticipated, the pressures on developmental states to reform also reflects the international environment. Exporting economies must eventually open their doors to imports, overseas investment must eventually be matched by inward investment, and economies that acquire greater weight in the world economy meet growing expectations to play responsibly by the liberal rules of the international trading regime.

On this account, then, the crisis of the developmental state resembles the crisis of communism: each hits the barrier of 'so far but no further'. In Weiss's summary (1998, p. 65), 'by being developmentally effective, the state ends up digging its own grave'. The implication is that there is one formula for catch-up but another – more liberal, more market-based, more American – for keep-up.

Certainly, the Japanese bureaucracy can no longer offer the same strategic direction to industry, given that the largest companies have gone on to achieve global significance and that some foreign companies have – with some difficulty – established a foothold in Japan. Matsuura *et al.* (2004, p. 151) report that 'industrial policy has undergone a marked shift as MITI (Ministry of International Trade and Industry) and its bureaucrats have declined in influence and importance and the JFTC (Japan Fair Trade Commission) has undertaken a more extensive and proactive role in enforcing competition'. The once-powerful MITI has now become part of a new ministry. So one traditional summary of Japan's developmental state – strong MITI, weak JFTC – has gone into reverse.

Yet convergence cannot be demonstrated by focusing on a single country. It is a comparative concept, implying a meeting of several states at a specific point. Even though the political economies of developmental states and coordinated market economies are surely moving in a liberal direction, liberal market economies such as the United Kingdom's have also become more liberal, implying therefore that cross-national differences may have remained constant. Indeed, the contrasts between Britain's liberal economy and Germany's coordinated approach may actually have increased, since the talk of reform in Germany has not yet led to decisive action – and may not do so at all, given the cautious policy-making approach of the grand coalition formed in 2005 between the Christian Democrats and Social Democrats.

Similarly, the distinctiveness of developmental states has declined but not dissolved. For Japan, Matsuura *et al.* (2004, p. 151) comment that 'much of the Japanese employment system remains intact for current workers' and that 'new institutional arrangements are emerging only slowly'. Change in South Korea has followed a comparable pattern: an evolution of the developmental state without convergence on the Anglo-American model of a liberal market economy. Despite democratization in the 1990s, Korea's political economy remains distinctive, leading Weiss (2004, p. 167) to postulate 'a more mature form of developmentalism: one that is now less propelled to catch up than by an emphasis on policies and institutions aimed at managing economic openness'.

So although Strange's convergence wager may yet come good, it does seem rather speculative. Prudence dictates that we avoid placing all our money on the superiority of one system of political economy. Even in the period since 1945, it is worth noting, notions of the most effective variant of a market economy have evolved rapidly. American scientific management, French industrial planning, German bank-funded investment, Japanese production techniques, Scandinavian training policies and Dutch corporatism have each enjoyed their moment in the sun. Just as orthodox economic theory suggests that countries should specialize in their areas of comparative advantage, so too may countries vary in the form of market organization best suited to their history, politics and culture.

In any case, we need to reserve judgement over whether Anglo-American capitalism will out-perform over the long run. Perraton and Clift (2004a, p. 202) point out that 'economic performance typically depends on the period of comparison chosen: different economies have appeared to be top dog at different times which in itself should indicate that there is no one superior model'. Adam Smith's logic may be universal but its institutional expression will surely continue to vary in ways that we cannot foresee. In all likelihood, the point on which states are supposedly converging will continue to move about and will never be reached.

The political economies of authoritarian states

Studying the political economies of non-democratic regimes quickly confirms the importance of distinguishing between different types of authoritarian government. At one extreme, many communist states developed a **command economy** without precedent in history; every communist state formulated clearer national goals and targets than any democracy. The result was an often decisive and generally ruthless commitment to a single goal, notably industrialization. At the other extreme, many military and personal rulers show immense concern about their own prosperity but none at all for their country's, with inadequate governance reinforcing an impoverished society. In this section, we will review the communist experience before turning to more contemporary authoritarian political economies, where we will focus in particular on the puzzle of low growth in resource-rich countries.

> In a communist **command economy**, also called a centrally planned economy, the national government sets quotas for state-owned production units and allocates resources to them. The bureaucracy then implements the plan.

Communist states

For much of the twentieth century, the issue of whether market or command economies were superior provided a topic for lively debate. The planned economies of communist states appeared to possess several advantages, including the ability to:

- Overcome the business cycle, and in particular the resulting unemployment, that is endemic to capitalism;
- Reduce inequality of income by adopting centrally determined wage rates;
- Abolish class inequalities by ensuring state ownership of the means of production;
- Achieve economies of scale since the state would become the only producer.

Yet we now know that planning eventually yielded economic stagnation, contributing to the collapse of communism in the Soviet Union and Eastern Europe. So why did command economies prove to be so uncommanding? What were the reasons for their failure? Answering these questions will help us to learn lessons from the twentieth century's most ambitious experiment in political economy.

The Soviet Union is the clearest example of a command economy because it became the most controlled economy on earth. Yet, paradoxically, the centrally planned economy was itself unplanned; Marx had left but the sketchiest account of his alternative to capitalism. As Sartori (1987, p. 401) writes, 'Soviet planning was Stalin's creature. Since Marx afforded no guidance, planning in the Soviet Union was improvised and imposed by the force of the sword'. Beginning in the 1920s, the Soviet Union became the land of The Plan. Gosplan, the State Planning Committee, drew up detailed five-year schedules which were given the status of law once they had received political approval. Implementation became the responsibility of ministries which controlled individual enterprises through a complex administrative network.

Detailed planning was essential to command economies. A factory could not buy its components on the market because there was no market. Instead, arrangements had to be made for another factory to manufacture the parts and deliver them on time. That factory, in its turn, had to be supplied with raw materials. In contrast to a market economy, no alternative suppliers existed. In prac-

DEBATE

IS AUTHORITARIAN RULE THE BEST FOUNDATION FOR ECONOMIC DEVELOPMENT?

Can authoritarian rule be defended as an effective method for economic development? If so, we will have a powerful critique of democracy's claims to be universally the best form of government. After all, we would nearly all prefer to eat under a dictator than to starve in a democracy. In addition, we could reasonably anticipate that democracy is unlikely to consolidate in poor countries over the long term if the cost is slower economic development.

YES

Industrialization requires massive investment in infrastructure such as transport, communications and education; initially, these can only be funded by the state. Authoritarian rulers generate the surplus for investment by resisting short-term pressures for immediate consumption. Simply put, they can kick-start development because they can ignore the squeals of those whose consumption is initially limited.

As Huntington and Nelson (1976, p. 23) said, 'Political participation must be held down, at least temporarily, in order to promote economic development'. Growth first, democracy later.

In a world which expects quick results, spontaneous industrialization in the style of Britain or the United States is no longer an option. In practice, development today must be state-led.

Consider some examples. The communist revolution in Russia initiated a remarkably rapid transformation from a rural to an industrial society. Similarly, for the half century after its establishment, growth in communist China has been at twice the rate achieved by democratic India.

In parts of Latin America, too, technocrats operating under more or less authoritarian governments succeeded in the final decades of the century in imposing coherent economic policy on unruly societies. Most of the East Asian developmental states began under authoritarian regimes; even today, few are liberal democracies.

NO

A few non-democratic regimes may initiate economic development but the majority do not. Many traditional rulers, such as the ruling families in the Middle East, continue to resist modernization. Other dictators, for example Nigeria's military 'lootocrats', set back economic development by decades.

A statistical study by Przeworski *et al.* (2000, p. 271) concludes that there is no 'cruel choice' to be made between democracy and development: 'we did not find a shred of evidence that democracy need be sacrificed on the altar of development'. Rather, authoritarian regimes depend more on expanding the labour force to achieve growth while democracies make more productive use of their inputs.

If industrialization does require forgoing consumption, rulers should attempt to persuade the people of the need for sacrifice, not impose dictatorial solutions. Besides, even if non-democratic rule can lead to industrialization, that point does not excuse the abuses of power and human rights which are an inherent danger of authoritarian regimes.

For example, China's path of communist modernization involved the brutality of the Great Leap Forward, in which around 40 million people died between 1958 and 1963 as a result of a bungled experiment in forced collectivization. Who is prepared to say – indeed, who is entitled to say – that economic growth is justified at such a massive human price?

ASSESSMENT

In the twentieth century, economic growth occasionally resulted in a stable authoritarian elite capable of extracting resources for investment and of providing state leadership for emerging private industries. But in the twenty-first century, globalization has given developing countries access to private capital through multinational corporations and overseas banks. To access these resources, developing countries must convince lenders that their economy is market-based and that their politics are tolerably democratic. So the twentieth century may prove to have been the pinnacle of the developmental state led by authoritarian rulers. In the new century, markets and democracy may come together in low-income as well as high-income countries.

Further reading

Halperin, Siegle and Weinstein (2005), Przeworski *et al.* (2000), Sørensen (1997).

tice, all sorts of informal and technically illegal deals had to be fixed up to ensure that arbitrary production quotas, based on quantities rather than quality, were met. The paradox was that The Plan's formal targets could only be met by informal collaboration outside its framework, creating a wedge between official statements and reality. The result was popular cynicism.

The underlying weakness was the absence of a price mechanism. This point was noted in an influential debate that took place among Western political economists even as the command economy was emerging. The Austrian-educated economist Ludwig Von Mises (1881–1973) declared, 'where there is no free market, there is no pricing mechanism, no economic calculation' (1920, p. 243). By definition, an efficient economy must allocate scarce resources to those uses that deliver the greatest return. In a market, this task is performed by price. But where planning is based on physical resources, as in a command economy, no practical method exists of comparing the return on all possible uses of capital (Hayek, 1935).

This limitation had huge practical consequences. Endemic misallocation created shortages and a black market. Necessarily, resources valued more highly by consumers than by planners were under-supplied. Scarcity encouraged corrupt swaps among individuals with access to resources: good cuts of meat in exchange for cigarettes, train tickets for university places. Those with little to offer, notably old people, just waited in line: by the 1980s, for an average of three hours a day in the Soviet Union (Macqueen, 1989). The command economy led to an equality of poverty for ordinary citizens but substantial wealth and privilege for a small minority with access to resources or the political clout to demand it.

The planned economy was not an unmitigated disaster. Notably in the USSR, it did prove successful at building the foundations of industrial development, albeit at a horrifying human price. Heavy industry was the great success of the planned economy, both in communist states undergoing industrialization for the first time and in those rebuilding after 1945. This success derived from the philosophy of the big push. The resources needed to meet the goal would be allocated to the priority area, whatever the impact on other sectors. The objective of the big push took precedence, deliberately overriding the allocations a market economy would have made. Goals determined budgets rather than vice versa.

The big push was a deliberately blinkered approach which ignored overall efficiency but often succeeded in achieving specific targets. Stalin's drive to industrialize Russia transformed a society of peasants into a world industrial power within a generation. However, economic growth in the Soviet Union resulted primarily from its capacity to mobilize ever more resources of labour, land and capital – for example, by engaging women in the formal workforce. In contrast to the market economies of liberal democracies, output per unit of resource barely increased. Indeed, by the 1970s Soviet productivity was falling; the same inputs were yielding fewer outputs (Table 8.1).

The ability of targeted planning to achieve specific goals, even if inefficiently, explains why liberal democracies introduce elements of a command economy during war. But the inherent weakness of any such scheme was spotted long ago by Adam Smith. He noted the folly of the 'man of system who seems to think he can arrange the different members of a great society with as much ease as the hand arranges the different pieces upon a chessboard' (quoted in Deane, 1989, p. 69).

Where, then, does the collapse of state planning leave the remaining communist states, principally China and Vietnam? In both countries, rulers have certainly reduced the importance of central planning yet they can hardly be said to have created the conditions for a market economy. Massive, and massively inefficient, state-owned enterprises still pervade the economy, soaking up labour and serving as an indirect welfare state. The expansion of the non-state sector has stimulated continued growth, unleashing massive entrepreneurial activity. Yet party contacts still determine access to economic opportunities. To most eyes, internal as well as external, the system is inherently corrupt; it is certainly technically inefficient in that political criteria distort economic decisions, leading to huge misallocations of capital. These errors must eventually unwind, with damaging consequences for state-owned banks with enormous bad debts.

This idiosyncratic model is still delivering growth in what remain, for the most part, poor countries. As long as economic growth continues, China's nomi-

Table 8.1 Average annual growth in productivity in the Soviet Union, 1930–85

Period	Average annual growth of productivity (%)
1930s	1.7
War	
1950s	1.6
1960s	1.5
1970s	–0.2
1980–85	–0.5

Source: Adapted from Cleaver (2002), Table 2.2, p. 34.

nally communist rulers may succeed in resolving the political tensions induced by corruption and increasing inequality. Judging by the experience of communism in Eastern Europe and the Soviet Union, however, that same growth will eventually deliver a demand for more fundamental political reforms.

Other authoritarian states

Some non-communist authoritarian regimes have also initiated economic development. Indeed, Sørensen (1997, p. 65) points out that 'in the twentieth century there was no case of successful economic development without comprehensive political action involving enormous state intervention in the economy'. Leaving aside the communist experience, examples include a few modernizing military regimes such as that of Abdel Nasser (president of Egypt, 1956–70) and Asian developmental states such as South Korea in its pre-democratic phase. Echoing the communist experience, the explanation for these successes rests with the potential capacity of non-democratic rulers to resist short-term pressures for immediate consumption, thereby generating resources for long-term industrialization.

But such cases are the exception. More often, non-communist authoritarian rule creates economic stagnation, leading to North's much-quoted comment (1981, p. 20): 'The existence of the state is essential to economic growth; the state, however, is the source of man-made economic decline'.

Inertia often results from a lack of motivation among the ruling elite. Often, the key task for non-elected rulers is to play off domestic political forces against each other to ensure that current leaders continue in office, an art developed to its highest level by the cautious but shrewd ruling families of the Middle East. When expensive patronage becomes the main political game, coherent economic development is bypassed. The public sector often becomes bloated, with poorly paid employees exploiting a host of regulations to enrich themselves at the expense of business. A firm's success, and its tax burden, depends on its political contacts more than its business strengths. Economics and politics form a single arena, as in European monarchies before the era of commerce.

Alternatively, the ruler may just want to enrich himself, his family and his ethnic group by taking resources out of the economy and often out of the country. Adam Smith's observation (1776, p. 446) from a pre-democratic era still applies to most non-democratic rulers today:

> Kings and ministers are always, and without exception, the greatest spendthrifts in the society. Let them look well after their own expense, and they may safely trust private people with theirs. If their own extravagance does not ruin the state, that of their subjects never will.

Leaving aside the characteristic economic distortions of authoritarian regimes, the **resource curse** provides an additional aspect of under-performance in those states 'blessed' with natural resources. Far from out-performing other developing countries, countries rich in resources such as oil achieve a lower rate of economic growth (Sachs and Warner, 1995b). Certainly, most Middle Eastern countries such as Saudi Arabia have escaped from low-income status. Nonetheless, their generous endowment seems to act as a brake on rather than a stimulus to sustained growth.

Why is it, then, that an abundance of natural resources seems to reduce economic growth? One answer, of particular relevance to sub-Saharan Africa, is that such resources comprise a honeypot

The **resource curse** refers to low economic growth in countries with an abundance of natural commodities such as oil, gas and scarce minerals.

which encourages internal conflict as local warlords compete for control of mineral-rich enclaves in areas remote from the capital. This account seems to be particularly relevant when resources can be easily extracted and dispersed: for instance, gems such as diamonds, and timber, rather than offshore oil (Englebert and Ron, 2004). Where central authority is already weak, such conflict over one of the few sources of available wealth can induce further instability, damaging overall economic performance and precluding the emergence of democratic politics.

However, the idea of the **rentier state** is an explanation with more widespread applicability, particularly to the Middle East. Rentier states obtain most of their revenue from exporting a natural resource, usually through licensing private, and often Western, contractors to secure the extraction. In economic terms, the government obtains a **rent** from owning an asset to which it adds little value. For example, agricultural commodities may be exported raw, with processing elsewhere. In the contemporary world, the purest rentier states are Middle Eastern countries with oil and gas reserves (Figure 8.1).

A **rentier state** obtains the bulk of its revenues from exporting such resources as oil and gas, and not by taxing the population. (**Rent** is simply a flow of income derived from control of an asset).

The governments of rentier states receive a direct income from overseas, reducing their need to raise taxes. A fast-growing economy is not required to bring in money for either the public purse or the leaders' personal bank accounts. Instead, a portion of the resource rent can be distributed to the population as handouts or through providing jobs in a swollen public sector. Broader issues of human development are ignored. For example, some rentier states have neglected education whereas Asian developmental states, lacking natural resources, made schooling a national priority. Further, what development does occur often takes the form of state-controlled prestige projects. Governments can borrow against future revenues, resulting in public sector deficits. The export of the resource can also hold back balanced growth as a result of **Dutch disease**. Even Norway, a petroleum-rich democracy which has invested much of its energy revenues for the long term, has not escaped these difficulties entirely.

Dutch disease occurs when a predominance of commodity exports causes a country's exchange rate to rise, handicapping other sectors with export potential and exposing domestic producers to cheaper imports. The mechanism is named after the decline in the Dutch manufacturing sector following the country's discovery of natural gas reserves in the 1960s.

The resource curse is politically important. Had Saudi Arabia become a mature industrial economy by 2000, the world politics of the early twenty-first century would surely have unfolded in a different way. And the evidence does support the proposition that the resource curse inhibits democracy by discouraging balanced economic development. Examining oil-rich states specifically, Ross (2001, p. 356) suggests that 'the oil-impedes-democracy claim is both valid and robust – oil does hurt democracy'. Herb (2005) is more cautious, doubting whether oil reserves are the only factor holding back the onset of democracy in the Middle East. Yet even Herb judges that the possibility that natural resources harm democracy 'cannot be dismissed'.

Figure 8.1 Rentier states: governments with the highest share of natural resource revenues in their income

Source: Adapted from Herb (2005, p. 299).

For the future, we can certainly imagine a world in which intensifying conflict over a diminishing supply of natural resources takes place between democracies and resource-rich authoritarian regimes. The Iraq invasion of 2003, for example, is sometimes interpreted in these terms. The resource curse may come to affect those living in liberal democracies as well as the inhabitants of those countries directly subject to it.

The political economies of illiberal democracies

In illiberal democracies, the operation of the economy is usually market-based but remains subject to political override. This intervention may take the form of a developmental regime, as in Asian countries such as Malaysia and Singapore. More often, the rulers of an illiberal democracy adopt an inconsistent approach, intervening in commercial decisions when political interests are at stake and, in particular, using the economy as a means of buying or rewarding loyalty. Thus the operation of the market is more arbitrary, and less efficient, than in liberal democracies where a network of institutions, developed over generations, provides a stable and credible framework for the conduct of business.

At the same time, economic intervention by the rulers of illiberal democracies is more limited than in authoritarian (especially communist) states. It is often contained to politically sensitive areas. After all, in an illiberal democracy in which re-election is permitted, a president must face the voters at election time. This task is more palatable when living standards are growing. The ruler's claim to extensive authority is based on the proposition, 'Only I can deliver'. In other words, an illiberal democracy creates a stronger alignment than does an authoritarian state between the interests of ruler and ruled.

In addition to these internal considerations, astute leaders realize the value of a functioning market economy in attracting foreign investment and in ensuring their credibility with international organizations such as the International Monetary Fund. In short, an illiberal democracy can align political interests with strong economic performance. As the example of Russia shows, even in low- or middle-income countries, an illiberal democracy with effective leadership can deliver economic growth.

The Russian economy has certainly experienced rapid fluctuations since the end of communism. When the communist ship sank in 1990, an entire method of organizing the economy (and society) went with it. Such an elaborate network could not be quickly replaced by market mechanisms. Rutland (2005, p. 188) comments that 'there was no such thing as a market for nuclear submarines or space stations – the items in which the Soviet Union had developed a comparative advantage during the Cold War'. A chaotic transition followed, in which a few new billionaires acquired the status of oligarchs, dominating the oil and metal industries and securing undoubted political influence during the Yeltsin era of 1991–2000.

After Vladimir Putin became president in 2000, economic policy became more orthodox. He modernized business law, improved tax collection, reduced inflation, increased foreign investment, ran a government budget surplus and generally provided a stable environment which enabled the economy to grow at an annual average of 6.7 per cent between 2000 and 2006 (Wagstyl, 2006, p. 2). At the very least, Putin provided a framework within which the economy could prosper from buoyant commodity prices. Even though most Russians have little sympathy for the subtleties of a market economy, Putin's record is such that he is judged to be a good tsar.

But the president is also an intensely political figure. Given the population's desire for strong leadership and the potential threat from the oligarchs, it is just as well that Putin's political skills are so finely honed. Just as he improved the environment for routine business transactions, so too did he extend the Kremlin's control over the crucial oil sector. It is this combination of policies – encouraging the market where possible but overriding it when politically necessary – which characterizes the economic management of illiberal democracies.

In 2003, for example, Putin launched a ruthless attack on Mikhail Khodorkovsky, head of the country's largest oil company, Yukos. Khodorkovsky's business ambitions for his company threatened

COUNTRY PROFILE

VENEZUELA

Form of government ■ a federal and presidential republic with 23 states.

Legislature ■ the 167 members of the National Assembly are elected for a five-year term. An opposition boycott of the 2005 election means that no deputies oppose the government.

Executive ■ the president, directly elected for a once-renewable six-year term, heads both the state and the government and chooses the members of the Council of Ministers.

Constitution and judiciary ■ the constitution dates from 1999. The judiciary is headed by the Supreme Tribunal of Justice whose members are elected by the National Assembly for a single 12-year term. Considerable political intervention.

Electoral system ■ Mixed member proportional. Voting is legally required but abstention is common.

Party system ■ President Hugo Chávez's party is the Fifth Republic Movement (MVR). The two traditional parties are Democratic Action (AD), a left-of-centre but not a class-based organization, and the Social Christian Party (Committee for Free Elections, COPEI), a Christian Democratic party offering a right-of-centre approach but without fully embracing market liberalism.

Population (annual growth rate): 25.7m (+1.4%)

World Bank income group: upper middle

Political Rights score:  4

Civil Liberties score: 4

Human development index (rank/out of): 68/177

Freedom of the press index (rank/out of): 158/194

Ease of doing business index (rank/out of): 164/175

Note: For meaning and sources of scales and indexes, see p. xvi. In all cases a score and rank of 1 is 'best'.

When Columbus arrived on the northern shores of Latin America in 1498, he was so impressed by the local buildings, constructed elegantly on stilts, that he was reminded of Venice – hence **Venezuela**. Today, a visitor to Caracas, the country's capital city, confronts a a modern if dilapidated city surrounded by ever-expanding *barrios* (shanty towns) climbing almost vertically on the ravines around.

This contrast expresses the fundamental fact about Venezuela and many other countries on the continent: inequality. In a country rated as upper-middle income, over 40 per cent of the population live in poverty. The rich possess considerable wealth, displayed through European cars, manicured suburbs, gated communities and even private planes (for which there is a waiting list).

Private affluence coexists with public squalor. Crime is endemic in most of this highly urban country, including Caracas. McCaughan (2004, p. 2) reports that 'the capital is literally falling apart as thieves filch metal from metro elevators, remove street lamps, dismantle apartment intercoms, steal electricity cables and even pickaxe cement barriers separating car lanes'. The point is not just the coexistence of poverty and crime but the simmering, and highly politicized, resentment connecting the two.

As part of Gran Colombia, full independence from Spain was achieved in 1819, with Venezuela becoming an autonomous country in 1830. 'The liberator' Simón Bolívar was the hero of the movement. Aspiring to create a Latin American federation which would entrench individual rights, Bolívar's revolutionary spirit and unfinished project are still frequently invoked by Latin America's left.

For the first half of the twentieth century, Venezuela was governed by military, civilian or mixed dictatorships: some brutal, some modernizing, some both. In 1958, however, democracy of a sort was established and has continued ever since. The 1958 Pact of Punto Fijo was an agreement between the two major parties to marginalize other parties and to keep divisive issues off the agenda. This cartel was corrupt and inefficient, and became more so, eventually enabling Hugo Chávez to launch his 'Bolivarian revolution'.

Further reading: Guevara (2005), McCaughan (2004).

SPOTLIGHT

Petro-populism in Venezuela

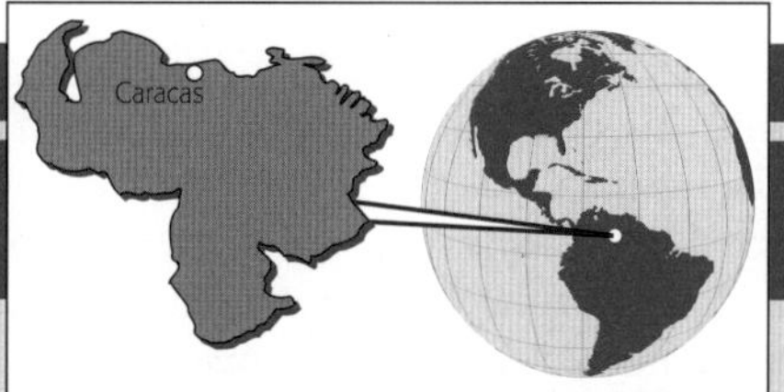

Oil was discovered in Venezuela in 1914 and has proved to be the dominating feature of the country's economy. Even today, the country's oil reserves are the seventh largest in the world. Petroleum generates a third of Venezuela's gross domestic product and about 80 per cent of its exports. The country is one of the USA's leading suppliers. The oil industry was nationalized in 1976 and now directly provides most government revenue. How, then, has this vital resource impinged on the regime of Hugo Chávez?

Oil rents sustained the Punto Fijo cartel, enabling the colluding parties to share out the receipts through patronage. But the oil curse was also at work. The economy became increasingly unbalanced and inefficient, fluctuating with the oil price. It was against this background that Hugo Chávez, a former paratrooper, was able to win the presidential election of 1998. He promised a Bolivarian revolution to bring social justice and clean government to the *barrios*: 'This is a different Venezuela, where the wretched of the earth know they can free themselves from their past. And this is a different Latin America'. The *Chavistas* cheered him on, especially but not only from the *barrios*.

Despite middle-class opposition, and many political twists and turns, Chávez has continued in power, winning a new term in 2006. A charismatic and intensely political figure, the president has retained considerable popular support while also marginalizing opposition through decisive and sometimes authoritarian influence over the military, the media and the justice system. He has sustained, but cannot institutionalize, his personalist illiberal democracy.

Chávez has proved to be as dependent on oil as the preceding regime. He has used the government's generous revenues to establish *misiones* (social programmes) in the slums. But easy money has led to an indifference to more fundamental economic reforms. Chávez has created grass-roots organizations that bypass rather than consolidate state institutions.

Corruption remains extensive. Rather like a boxer who cannot fight without an opponent, Chávez depends on his wealthy enemies on the right to sustain his own political momentum. His remarkable revolutionary energy will surely exhaust a society more concerned with economic growth than firebrand politics. Eventually, Chávez's instinctive left-wing populism will be revealed as a symptom of, not a solution to, the deep-seated inequalities of his country and continent. And oil will be shown once more to be a hindrance, not a help, to balanced economic and political development.

Further reading: Buxton (2001), Gott (2005).

TIMELINE

HUGO CHÁVEZ

1954	Born in Sabaneta, Venezuela.
1971	Enrols in the Academy of Military Sciences.
1975	Graduates from the Academy.
1982	Establishes a left-wing cell in the army.
1992	Leads a failed coup.
1994	Released from prison (where he studied Simón Bolívar).
1998	Elected president.
1999	Referendum ratifies new constitution.
2000	Re-elected president. Authorized by the assembly to legislate by decree for one year.
2001	National strike against decree laws.
2002	Removed from power by coup but returns two days later after street protests.
2004	Wins recall vote. Announces alliance with Cuba.
2006	Wins all seats in the National Assembly after opposition boycott. Informs the United Nations that George W. Bush is 'the devil'. Re-elected president. Announces plans for 'socialism for the twenty-first century'.

the government's command of the energy sector while his political ambitions concerned Putin. The businessman was jailed for fraud and later transferred to a Siberian penal colony located in a radioactive zone (Khodorkovsky, 2006). Yukos was dismembered and taken over by the state. As Rutland (2005, p. 199) writes, 'The arrest of Russia's richest man and the near destruction of its largest and most successful private company grabbed the attention of Western observers, who feared that Russia was turning its back on the market economy'. In an illiberal democracy, just as in a fully authoritarian state, industrialists must learn to avoid overstepping the mark.

Learning Resources for Chapter 8

Next step

Hall and Soskice (2001) is an informed and influential collection on the varieties of capitalist organization in established democracies.

Further reading

Shonfield (1969), Crouch and Streeck (1997) and Hollingsworth and Boyer (1997) provide earlier work on varieties of capitalism. Schmidt (2002) and Perraton and Clift (2004b) are also useful. On the general history of political economy, Heilbroner (1953) remains an outstanding account; see also Deane (1989) and Polanyi (1957). Hall (1989) is a comparative study of Keynes's impact. Friedman's monetarist counter-strike can be found in Friedman (1991); see Friedman (1962) for his underlying political perspective. Johnson (1995) is the classic work on the developmental state. See Sachs and Warner (1995b) for the resource curse. Rutland (2005) reviews the Russian economy under Putin.

Internet sources

Glossary of Political Economy Terms by Paul M. Johnson, Auburn University
A helpful glossary
http://www.auburn.edu/~johnspm/gloss/

International Forum on Globalization
Examines the 'restructuring of global politics and economics'
http://www.ifg.org/index.htm

Martin Wolf, Financial Times
Influential and accessible columns by a leading commentator
http://www.ft.com/comment/columnists/martinwolf

World Bank
An informative site on development policy
http://www.worldbank.org/

Part III

LINKING SOCIETY AND GOVERNMENT

In this part, we examine the mechanisms through which society, and the individuals within it, influence government. We begin with overall patterns of political participation before examining the specific linking device of elections, where we will explore the problem of falling turnout. We then turn to interest groups, discussing how such associations protect their own turf and, in some cases, promote their vision of the public good. And we conclude with an analysis of political parties, many of which originate in society but which are now facing a considerable decline in membership. The underlying theme of this part, then, is whether liberal democracies are facing a crisis or merely a change in representation as the traditional mechanisms of elections and parties lose their hold on contemporary populations.

Chapter 9

Political participation

Political participation refers to any of the many ways in which people can seek to influence the composition or policies of their government. Clearly, citizens contacting their representative and activists canvassing for their favoured candidate are participating in the formal political process. But participation can also take less conventional forms such as signing a petition, taking part in a demonstration or even engaging in terrorist acts against the state.

In a liberal democracy, people can choose whether to get involved in politics, to what extent and through what channels (Box 9.1). But participation is also found in many non-democratic regimes. Totalitarian states required citizens to engage in regimented demonstrations of support for the government. Other non-democratic regimes also demand at least a facade of participation, though this too is often manipulated so that it supports rather than threatens the existing rulers.

Participation in liberal democracies

In a renowned analysis, Milbrath and Goel (1977, p. 11) divided the American population into three groups, a classification which has since been applied to participation in other liberal democracies. These categories, based on involvement with conventional politics, were:

- A small proportion of gladiators (around 5–7 per cent of the population) who fight the political battle – for instance, the activist campaigners;
- A large group of spectators (about 60 per cent) who observe the contest but rarely participate beyond voting;
- A substantial number of apathetics (about one-third) who are unengaged in formal politics.

Milbrath and Goel's labels were based on an analogy with Roman contests at which a few gladiators performed for the mass of spectators but some apathetics did not even watch the show (Figure 9.1).

The most striking fact about political participation in liberal democracies is the small proportion of gladiators. Voting in national elections is normally the only activity in which a majority of citizens engages. Throughout the democratic world anything beyond voting is the preserve of a minority of activists. The gladiators are outnumbered by the apathetics: people who neither vote nor even follow politics through the media. With turnout and party membership falling in most democracies, even these traditional forms of engagement are becoming less common.

Political participation is activity by individuals formally intended to influence who governs or the decisions taken by those who do. Citizens can be classified by both the extent and the forms of their involvement.

In every democracy, furthermore, the gladiators are anything but a cross-

BOX 9.1

Patterns of political participation, by type of regime

	Amount of participation	Character of participation	Purpose of participation
Liberal democracy	Moderate but declining	Mainly voluntary	To influence who decides and what decisions are reached
Illiberal democracy	Limited	Mainly channelled through elections	To entrench and confirm the ruler's authority
Authoritarian regime (non-totalitarian)	Low	Manipulated	To protect rulers' power and to offer a democratic facade
Totalitarian regime	High	Regimented	In theory: to transform society In practice: to demonstrate rulers' power

section of society. In most democracies, participation is greatest among well-educated, middle-class, middle-aged, white men. The highest layers of political involvement show the greatest skew. As Putnam (1976, p. 33) put it,

> The 'law of increasing disproportion' seems to apply to nearly every political system; no matter how we measure political and social status, the higher the level of political authority, the greater the representation for high-status social groups.

Figure 9.1 Patterns of participation in liberal democracies

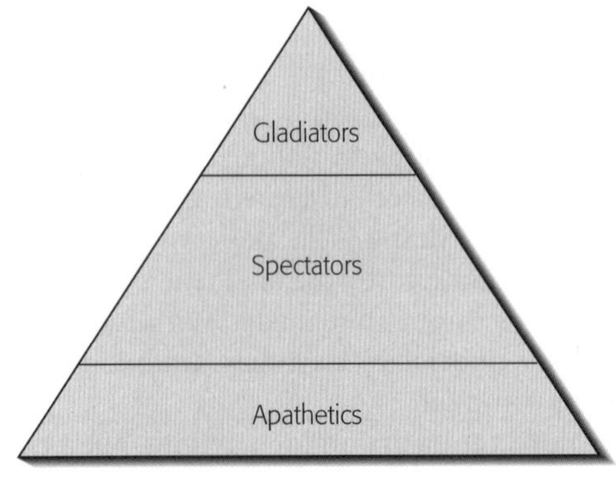

What explains this bias in participation towards upper social groups? Two factors seem to be particularly influential: political resources and political interest.

First, consider resources. People in high-status groups are equipped with such political assets as education, money, status and communication skills. Education gives access to information and, we trust, strengthens the ability to interpret it. Money buys the luxury of time for political activity. High status provides the opportunity to obtain a respectful hearing. And communication skills such as the ability to speak in public help in presenting one's views persuasively. Added together, these resources provide a useful toolkit for effective political intervention.

Second, high-status individuals are more likely to be interested in politics. They possess the motive as well as the means to become involved. No longer preoccupied with the daily struggle, they can take satisfaction from engagement in collective activity (Inglehart, 1997). The wealthy are also more likely to be brought up in a family, and to attend a school, where an interest in current affairs is encouraged. They will probably see how politics might impact on their own wealth. So upper social groups have an interest in politics – in both senses of 'interest' – and can afford to put their concerns into practice.

Table 9.1 Female representation in national legislatures, 1950s–2006

	Year of female suffrage	Current electoral system*	Female representation in the single or lower house (%)		Change (most recent election minus 1950s average)
			Average in the 1950s	Most recent election	
Sweden	1919	List PR	12	45	+33
Denmark	1915	List PR	8	38	+30
Finland	1906	List PR	13	38	+25
Norway	1913	List PR	5	38	+33
Netherlands	1919	List PR	8	37	+29
Germany	1918	MMP	8	32	+24
New Zealand	1893	MMP	4	28	+24
Australia	1902	AV	0.2	25	+25
Canada	1917	Plurality	1	21	+20
United Kingdom	1918	Plurality	3	20	+17
USA	1920	Plurality	3	15	+12
Ireland	1918	STV	3	13	+10
France	1944	Majority	4	12	+8
Italy	1945	PR	6	12	+6

* For definitions of electoral systems, see Box 10.1 (AV, alternative vote; MMP, mixed member proportional; PR, proportional representation; STV, single transferable vote).

Sources: IPU (2006a), McAllister and Studlar (2002).

These factors of political resources and political interest help to explain one continuing case of under-representation: why women are still in a minority at higher political levels even though in most countries they form a majority of electors (and often, these days, of voters). In 2006, women made up just 16 per cent of the world's legislators, double the figure 30 years earlier but still a large under-representation (Table 9.1).

There is no doubt that, as a group, women still possess fewer political resources than men. Across the world as a whole, they still have less formal education (even though this difference has reversed among the young in many liberal democracies). Further, interest in formal politics is sometimes limited by childbearing and homemaking responsibilities.

The emphasis of research on political participation is on explaining what distinguishes the gladiators from the spectators. But what about the apathetics, the people who do not participate at all? This group raises the problem of **political exclusion**. As Verba *et al.* (1995) write, the apathetics in effect exclude themselves – or perhaps are excluded – from the normal means by which citizens collectively shape their society.

A typical non-participant might be an unemployed young person with no qualifications, inhabiting a high-crime inner-city neighbourhood, often from a minority culture and perhaps not even speaking the dominant language. Such a profile may

Political exclusion refers to those people who are effectively excluded from participation in collective decision-making because they occupy a marginal position in society. Many migrant workers, prisoners, drug addicts and people who do not speak the native language are examples.

encourage radical activity among a few but, in general, a preoccupation with the daily struggle limits or eliminates formal political participation.

Just as higher social groups possess both the resources and the interest to over-participate, so a shortage of resources and lack of interest in the remote goings-on of national politics explain the under-participation of those near the bottom of increasingly unequal Western societies.

So studies of political participation demonstrate the tension within liberal democracy between strong principles and prosaic reality. The ideals of universal participation and political equality coexist alongside the facts of limited and unequal involvement. This gap provides room for concerned citizens to advocate measures to increase political involvement, a theme increasing in urgency as turnout and party membership decline. However, such efforts will not close the inherent gap between democratic aspirations and achievements. Because participation is an option rather than a requirement, it is unlikely ever to be equal; and because inequalities in participation are rooted in social differences in resources and interest, the active minority will remain unrepresentative of the passive majority.

Social movements

In 1996, 325,000 Belgians, 3 per cent of the country's population, marched through Brussels in a peaceful protest against an inadequate public investigation into a sexually motivated child murder. This White March (white was worn as a symbol of purity) was an example of a social movement, a form of participation that has come to mount a significant challenge to the 'official' political system in liberal democracies.

Social movements (also called popular movements) consist of people from outside the mainstream who come together to seek a common objective though an unorthodox challenge to the existing political order. The White March was a typical movement in that many participants considered themselves to be conventional citizens who would not ordinarily take an active part in politics. Their protest was simultaneously political and anti-political.

Social movements espouse a political style which provides distance from established channels, thereby questioning the legitimacy as well as the decisions of the government. The members of social movements adopt a wide repertoire of protest acts, including demonstrations, sit-ins, boycotts and political strikes. Some such acts may be illegal but, in contrast to other criminal behaviour, the actors' motives are political.

To appreciate the character of social movements, it is useful to compare them with parties and interest groups (Box 9.2). Movements are more loosely organized, typically lacking the precise membership, subscriptions and leadership of both parties and interest groups. Like parties whose origins lie outside the legislature, movements emerge from society to challenge the political establishment. However, unlike parties movements do not seek to craft distinct interests into an overall package; rather, they claim the moral high ground in one specific area.

Movements also possess both similarities and differences with interest groups. Like interest groups, social movements typically focus on a single issue: for example, nuclear disarmament, feminism or the environment. Again like interest groups, social movements do not seek state power; rather they seek to influence government, usually by claiming that their voice has previously gone unheard. But the contrasts are perhaps more important. Whereas protective interest groups seek precise regulatory objectives, movements are more diffuse, often seeking social as much as legislative change. For example, the gay movement might measure its success by how many gay people come out, not just by the passage of anti-discrimination legislation. By focusing on consciousness, culture and identity, movements adopt a broader interpretation of politics than do protective interest groups.

Social movements are sometimes described as 'new social movements' or as practising 'new politics'. Certainly, before the emergence of the modern state much protest activity was local rather than national, aimed at landlords, tax collectors and other authority figures. However, the transition to modernity soon created a favourable environment for the emergence of broader and more sophisticated forms of protest. Urbanization brings people together, education expands their concerns, the mass media enables information to circulate, civil rights allow people to express their opinions openly, representative institu-

BOX 9.2

Comparing social movements, political parties and protective interest groups

	Social movements	Political parties	Protective interest groups
Seek to influence the government?	Yes	Yes	Yes
Seek to become the government?	No	Yes	No
Focus on a single issue?	Yes	No	Yes
Formally organized, led and funded?	Not usually	Yes	Yes
Tactics used	Unconventional	Conventional	Conventional
Main levels of operation	Global, national, local	National	National

Note: On protective interest groups, see Box 11.3.

tions give people hope that their voice might be heard and, above all, the growth of government make politics a more important theme in ordinary lives.

Tilly (2004, p. 33) suggests that the British anti-slavery movement in the late-eighteenth and early nineteenth centuries should be regarded as the earliest example. The techniques adopted in this campaign, including petitions and boycotts, established a palette of protest activities soon emulated by other reformers. It is clear, at any rate, that while social movements are a product of the modern era, they are not an entirely new phenomenon.

Even though movements themselves are far from new, perspectives on them have evolved since 1945. In the 1950s, social movements (or mass movements, as they were then called) were perceived as a threat to the stability of liberal democracy. They were taken as a sign of a poorly integrated mass society 'containing large numbers of people who are not integrated into any broad social groupings, including classes' (Kornhauser, 1959, p. 14). Strong movements meant weak institutions and the inability of the political system to smoothly process inputs into outputs. Movements were judged to be supported by marginal, disconnected groups: unemployed intellectuals, isolated workers, the peripheral middle class. 'Until the 1960s,' say Goodwin and Jasper (2003a, p. 5), 'most scholars who studied social movements were frightened of them.'

The 1960s and 1970s were the decades of transition. The American civil rights movement could hardly be dismissed as irrational while Vietnam, and the draft specifically, propelled the educated American middle class into the anti-war lobby. As intellectuals became more critical of the government, so their treatment of social movements became more positive. Especially in the United States, movements were judged to be engaged in 'rational, purposeful and organized action', mobilizing resources in pursuit of specific political goals (Tilly, 1978). Like public-interest groups, they were regarded as part of the normal political process. Reviewing this changed perspective, della Porta and Diani (1999, p. 10) conclude that 'it is no longer possible to define movements in a prejudicial sense as phenomena which are marginal and anti-institutional. A more fruitful interpretation towards political interpretation of contemporary movements has been established'.

It is certainly worth noting that the movement activists of the era of protest in the West during the 1960s resembled the social profile of participants in orthodox politics. In the main, they were well-educated, articulate young people from middle-class backgrounds. And more than a few leaders of social movements switched to orthodox politics as they aged: many a protest activist of the 1960s turned into a party leader by the century's end. Prominent examples include Joschka Fischer, Germany's foreign minister between 1998 and 2005, and Peter Hain, a minister in Tony Blair's government in Britain. For all the stylistic contrast between mainstream and movement politics, one function of the movements has been to provide a training ground for future national leaders. Protest activism has entered the mainstream (Norris, 2002).

Compared to parties and interest groups, movements are more easily scalable, capable of expanding from the local to the national and even the international level (Tarrow and McAdam, 2005). Developments in technology are important here, allowing direct communication among sympathizers. Take the protest in Britain in 2000 against the country's high tax on petrol (Joyce, 2002). A diverse network of British farmers and road hauliers blocked petrol refineries in a coordinated series of protests, quickly creating a national fuel crisis. This movement's rapid expansion, albeit building on foundations previously established, owed much to mobile telephones. As Bennett (2005, p. 205) remarks, 'such applications of communication technology favour loosely linked distributed networks that are minimally dependent on central coordination, leaders or ideological commitment'.

Similarly, global communication enables coordinated participation across borders. The best example here remains the protest in February 2003 against the American-led war in Iraq. Over a single weekend, an estimated six million people took part in demonstrations in 600 or so cities throughout the world (Table 9.2). Bennett (2005, p. 207) reckons that this event 'may well stand as the largest simultaneous multinational demonstration in recorded history'. The ability of social movements to mushroom in this way, even without any central organization or leader, confirms their capacity to articulate authentic public concern at a transnational level. Social movements are a form of participation well-suited to a more global world.

Table 9.2 'Not in my name': the largest demonstrations against the Iraq War by city, 15–16 February 2003

City	Estimated number of protestors
Rome	Up to 3,000,000
Barcelona	1,300,000
London	1,000,000
Madrid	600,000
Berlin	500,000
Paris	200,000
Sydney	200,000
Damascus	Up to 200,000
Melbourne	160,000
New York	100,000

Note: Figures are estimates reported in the *Financial Times*, 17 February 2003.

Liberal democracies hold no monopoly over social movements. In the 1970s and 1980s, they also became a significant feature in many authoritarian regimes in lower-income countries. In contrast to liberal democracies, however, these movements have been the territory of the poor, as people facing acute problems of daily life collaborate to improve their living conditions in a hostile political environment. The urban poor organizing soup kitchens, the inhabitants of shanty towns lobbying for land reform, groups of mothers pressing for information on their sons who 'disappeared' under military rule – all were examples of this blossoming of popular political activity.

However, many community-based movements in low income countries have lacked the desire or the means to engage with national politics. A culture of anti-politics, also found in many post-communist countries, limits the movements' wider impact. Indeed the democratic transition has taken some wind from their sails. In Uruguay, for example, 'democracy brought, by a curious twist, the disappearance of many grass-roots movements that had been active during the years of dictatorship' (Canel, 1992, p. 290).

DEBATE

ARE AMERICANS BOWLING ALONE?

> 'Americans of all ages, all stations in life, and all types of disposition are forever forming associations . . . Thus the most democratic country in the world now is that in which men have in our time carried to the highest perfection the art of pursuing in common the objects of common desires' (de Tocqueville, 1835, p. 513).

In influential publications, Putnam (1993, 2000) questions whether de Tocqueville's thesis about the United States still applies. Putnam claims that 'something has happened in America in the past two or three decades to diminish social engagement and civic connectedness'. He says that Americans now spend more time watching *Friends* than making them and that the decay in social and political participation is damaging to the country and its people. Is Putnam right? If so, does his thesis also apply to other democracies?

YES

Putnam marshals considerable evidence to illustrate his theme. For instance, between the 1960s and the end of the 1980s:

- Voter turnout declined by nearly a quarter (and by rather more among young electors);
- The proportion of Americans claiming to have attended a public meeting 'in the last year' fell by more than a third;
- The proportion of people engaged in regular volunteer work dropped by a sixth;
- The proportion agreeing with the survey statement 'most people can be trusted' fell from a half to a third.

Putnam believes that the significance of these findings lies in their implications for social capital. Face-to-face communication nurtures commitment to the common good; allows networks to develop from which new projects can emerge; permits individuals to develop their skills, knowledge and understanding; and generally encourages the give-and-take which is a hallmark of democracy.

What kind of democracy awaits, asks Putnam, if most people are now bowling alone?

NO

All arguments that things are not what they were are suspect; most golden ages never existed at all.

In the 1920s, commentators worried that the automobile was reducing society to isolated family units (Lynd and Lynd, 1929). After the war, commentators bemoaned the rise of the 'lonely crowd', 'mass society' and the 'inner-directed personality' (Riesman, 1950).

It is much more likely that social activity has changed its form rather than its extent. As Putnam (2002) himself recognizes, some types of group, such as crime-watch groups, health clubs, support groups (e.g. of crime victims) and public interest groups have expanded.

With the advent of mobile phones, e-mail and the internet, people can associate with like-minded individuals elsewhere rather than face-to-face. As a result, they depend less on old-fashioned neighbours.

There is no reason to suppose that this change reflects any loss of social capital. Indeed, the ability to join, benefit from and then leave specific, instrumental and short-term networks in response to changing individual needs may increase the efficiency of social relationships compared to an era when people relied on whoever happened to live next door.

ASSESSMENT

Even if social participation is declining in the USA, it is difficult to see what can be done to reverse the trend. Any political implications need political solutions. If America is to solve its turnout problem, for instance, the solution surely lies in improved registration procedures, not in persuading people to invite their neighbours to a barbecue. In any extent, a revival of community may just reflect the onset of external crisis. For instance, the immediate effect of 9/11 was a rush of civic engagement, general togetherness and support for the government. At least in the short term, these factors reduced the extent to which Americans could be said to be bowling alone.

Further reading

Pharr and Putnam (2000), Putnam (1993, 2000, 2002).

Participation in authoritarian states

In contrast to liberal democracies, authoritarian rulers seek either to limit genuine participation in politics or, in the case of totalitarian states, to direct it through tightly controlled channels. In either case, the object is to minimize any threat which unregimented participation might pose to the regime. This section examines the role of patron–client networks as a form of limited and dependent participation in authoritarian regimes before turning to the directed participation demanded by totalitarian regimes.

We should be careful to avoid stereotyping here. Even in non-democracies, the limits and nature of participation are often subject to an implicit dialogue as activists test the boundaries of the acceptable. Non-democratic rulers may allow free space in those areas which do not directly threaten the central regime itself (e.g. local politics, university campuses). Further, as societies governed by authoritarian rulers grow more complex, so rulers often come to realize that responding to popular pressure on non-sensitive issues can enhance political stability.

Figure 9.2 A patronage network linking centre and periphery

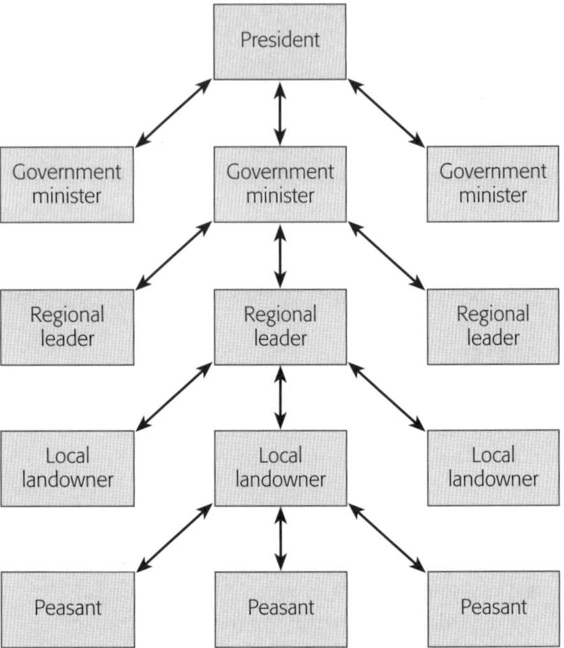

Note: Resources flow downwards, support flows upwards.

Patron–client networks

A major technique for controlling participation in authoritarian states is the patron–client network. **Clientelism**, as this practice is often called, is a form of political involvement which differs from both voluntary participation in liberal democracies and the regimented routines of totalitarian states. Although patron–client relationships are found in all political systems, authoritarian regimes offer the fullest expression of such relationships. Particularly in low income countries, personal networks of patrons and clients are the main instrument for bringing ordinary people into contact with formal politics and the central organizing structure of politics itself (Figure 9.2).

So what exactly are patron–client relationships? They are traditional, informal hierarchies fuelled by exchanges between a high-status 'patron' and 'clients' of lower status. The colloquial phrase 'big man/small boy' conveys the nature of the interaction. Patrons are landlords, employers, party leaders, government ministers or most often ethnic leaders. Lacking resources of their own, clients gather round their patron for protection and security. Political patrons control the votes of their clients and persuade them to attend meetings, join organizations or simply follow their patron around in a deferential manner. In Sri Lanka, for instance, patrons with access to the resources of the state largely decide how ordinary people vote (Jayanntha, 1991).

> **Clientelism** denotes politics substantially based on patron–client relationships. The patron provides protection to a number of lower-status clients who, in exchange, offer their unqualified allegiance and support.

Patron–client relationships are often traditional and personal, as in the protection provided to tenants by landowners in low-income countries. But they can also be more instrumental, as with the resources which dominant parties in American cities provided to new immigrants in exchange for their vote. In either case, the relationship affirms the inequality from which it springs.

In return for their clients' unqualified support, patrons offer access to jobs, contracts, subsidies, physical protection and even a guarantee of food in hard times. In other words, they provide an insurance policy for poor people who, lacking organized protection through collective insurance or the rule of law, would otherwise be in a position of extreme vulnerability. Instead of paying premiums to an insurance company, clients offer political support to a patron. The big man then exploits his local power-base to strike deals with ministers in the national government, offering the support of his clients in exchange for a share of the government's resources or simply a grant of a favourable licence. In this way, patronage networks grow and decline according to their patron's skill, just as more orthodox businesses rise and fall with the quality of their management.

The patron's power, and its inhibiting effect on democracy, is illustrated in this quotation from Egypt's President Abdul Nasser, interviewed in 1957 when he was still a reforming leader (Owen, 1993):

> We were supposed to have a democratic system between 1923 and 1953. But what good was this democracy to our people? You have seen the landowners driving the peasants to the polling booths. There they would vote according to the instructions of their masters. I want the peasants to be able to say 'yes' and 'no' without this in any way affecting their livelihood and daily bread. This in my view is the basis for freedom and democracy.

Participation through patronage is a device which appeals particularly in authoritarian settings because it links elite and mass, centre and periphery, in a context of inequality. Although inequality provides the soil in which patronage networks flourish, these relationships still act as a political glue, binding the 'highest of the high' with the 'lowest of the low' through membership of a patron's network. The glue often works particularly well when the patron presents himself as a traditional patriach.

By linking people across different levels within society, patron–client relationships limit the expression of solidarity among people at the same social level, such as peasants. The decay of such networks can be an indication of a transition to a more sophisticated society in which ordinary people have acquired sufficient resources to be able to organize their political participation in a more autonomous, voluntary fashion. Alternatively, patron–client relationships linking centre and region can disintegrate when the state itself collapses, often to be replaced as a form of social organization and insurance by gangs formed by people at the same social level.

Totalitarian governments

It is when we turn to totalitarian governments that we find the most ambitious attempts to develop mass participation in non-democratic systems. In communist and fascist states, participation was both more extensive and more regimented than in liberal democracies. **Regimented participation**, high in quantity but low in quality, was a central feature of totalitarian rule.

The most interesting examples come from communist states, particularly in their earliest and most vigorous decades. At first glance, participation in these regimes left liberal democracies in the shade. Under communism, citizen activity outscored the level found in today's democracies. Ordinary people sat on comradely courts, administered elections, joined para-police organizations and served on people's committees covering local matters. This apparatus of participation derived from the Marxist idea that all power at every level of government should be vested in soviets (councils) of workers and peasants.

However, the calibre of participation in communist states did not match its extent. To ensure that mass engagement always strengthened the party's grip, communist party members guided all the avenues of political expression. At regular meetings of women's federations, trade unions and youth groups, party activists would explain policy to the people. But communication flowed only from top to bottom. So the members of these groups eventually behaved as they were treated: passive recipients rather than active participants. Because the party controlled participation so tightly, cynicism soon replaced idealism. Only careerist diehards were prepared to invest their full energy in the charade.

Eventually, some ruling parties did allow more participation but only in areas that did not threaten their monopoly of power. Especially in Eastern Europe, industrial managers were given more say in

> **Regimented participation** is elite-controlled involvement in politics designed to express popular support for the notional attempt by the rulers to build a new society. Its supposed purpose is to mobilize the masses behind the regime, not to influence the personnel or policies of the government.

policy-making. Political participation also became more authentic on local matters. But these modest reforms were not matched in national politics. Because no real channels existed for airing grievances, people were left with two choices: to shut up and continue with life or to air their complaints outside the system. For all the notional participation, communist governments chose to ignore popular indifference to their rule.

The trajectory of participation in communist China illustrates these themes but with the added complexity caused by Mao Zedong's distrust of party routines. In the 1950s and 1960s, participation through accepted channels was required as a way of demonstrating active support for the party's goals. The question was not whether citizens participated but to what extent. This format was comparable with that of other communist states.

But Mao Zedong developed the doctrine of the 'mass line' by which party officials were expected to turn the ideas of the masses into plans which an enthused population would then put into action. This anti-bureaucratic philosophy of 'politics in command' led to the disaster of the Great Leap Forward, an unrealistic scheme launched in 1957 to improve national production. The outcome was a famine in which many millions died (Yang, 1996).

Mao remained dissatisfied with the caution of the party establishment. In 1966, he launched the Cultural Revolution, encouraging the masses to turn on corrupt power holders within the party, the workplace and the family. Even harmless intellectuals found themselves condemned as 'the stinking ninth category'. The outcome was an orgy of uncontrolled participation, including violent score-settling, which threatened the country's social fabric and caused permanent damage to the party's reputation. In 1969, Mao called on the army to restore order.

Following this remarkable episode, political participation developed along more predictable lines. After Mao's death in 1976, the leadership favoured economic reform over political purity, discouraging any form of participation which might threaten growth. Political passivity became acceptable. More recently, the party has opened some social space in which sponsored groups in areas such as education and the environment can operate with relative freedom. The level and pattern of participation has come to resemble that of an authoritarian rather than a totalitarian regime, with both the regimented routines and the political excesses of Mao's era consigned to the past.

However, channels for explicit opposition to the party remain closed. Memories remain of the Tiananmen Square massacre of 1989, when the army's tanks turned on pro-democracy demonstrators in Beijing. Local protests – against corruption, unemployment, illegal levies or non-payment of wages or pensions – continue to an extent which is unusual in an entrenched non-democratic regime. These under-reported episodes operate outside the framework of accepted participation but have been directed against local rather than national rulers.

Participation in illiberal democracies

The participation challenge facing illiberal democracies is considerable. The transition from authoritarian rule requires the population to learn new styles of political participation: votes must be cast, parties organized and leaders recruited to political office. Cynicism must give way to a measure of engagement. Yet the very nature of illiberal democracy means that political authority is delegated to a president who is expected to resolve severe national problems by dominating the political sphere.

Once the voting is done, the people return to their daily grind, called on only infrequently to express their support for the national leader in his battle against the enemies of the country and its people. Participation therefore tends to be intermittent, unstructured and predicated on political inequality: the leader leads and the masses follow. Individual needs are often met through the personal intervention of a local political figure or other patron, or by bribing a local official.

Consider, for example, post-communist democracies. The old style of regimented participation quickly disintegrated as communism fell apart, partly in response to dramatic street protests in the capital cities. Once new and nominally democratic institutions had been created, the task was to consolidate the new order by developing structured forms of voluntary participation through parties, elections and interest groups. This task has proved to be demanding. The populations of many Eastern European states had experienced regimented participation under communist rule and seen mass participation on television during its collapse. But this outburst of engagement did not last long. Few if any post-communist countries have established parties and interest groups with a large and stable membership.

The problem in illiberal democracies is the weakness of a **civil society** regulated by law but remaining separate from the state. Civil society provides opportunities for people to participate in collective activities that are neither pro-state nor anti-state but simply non-state. But developing such social capital is a conspicuous challenge in countries with a history of authoritarian rule. Under communist rule, for instance, civil society had been demobilized. It had been stood down so that the rulers could directly control the individual: 'everyone was supposed to be the same – working for the state, on a salary, on a leash' (Goban-Klas and Sasinka-Klas, 1992).

Civil society consists of those groups which sit above the personal realm of the family but beneath the state. The term covers public organizations such as labour unions, interest groups and, on some definitions, recreational bodies. However, companies are usually excluded because they are not voluntary bodies emerging from society.

The manipulated participation of the communist era left a bad taste, with 'the difficulties of starting afresh a major factor in accounting for the relatively low level of social and political participation' in the subsequent regimes (Rueschmeyer, Rueschmeyer and Wittrock, 1998, p. 270). There is a civic deficit rather than a civil society. An illiberal democracy, in which formal participation is largely confined to occasional voting at national elections, is an understandable response to this difficult legacy.

The weakness of civil society is a factor limiting orthodox participation in some of Latin America's illiberal democracies, especially the smaller ones. Social problems such as poverty, inequality, drugs, crime and limited education do not encourage either a sustained interest in national affairs or the development of means of political expression. Pervasive corruption breeds cynicism, further discouraging participation. Social organization often takes the form of self-help or even vigilante groups which define themselves in opposition to formal politics. Some such movements emerge from indigenous populations which are isolated from the political mainstream.

Consider, for example, the case of crime in Guatemala. Seligson (2005, p. 226) points out that 'one has to go back to fourteenth-century London to find historical homicide rates as high as those found in contemporary Guatemala'. Lynchings are common. No wonder more citizens say in surveys that 'a strong-hand government' is more important than the 'participation of everyone' in solving national problems. In these conditions, it is impossible to consolidate the patterns of formal political participation found in liberal democracies. Indeed, it is remarkable that amid such disorder, Guatemala, El Salvador and Colombia have retained the status of illiberal democracy (Hagopian and Mainwaring, 2005).

Despite the absence of a communist legacy, the story is similar in many of the African countries seeking to nurture new avenues of participation following the retreat of the generals in the 1980s. Again, the act of overthrowing the old order did stimulate significant mass participation, at least in major cities, providing echoes of the original struggle for independence in the 1950s and 1960s. Yet the difficulties of entrenching voluntary participation in Africa's illiberal democracies remain substantial. As Chazan *et al.* (1999, p. 101) comment, 'in few countries has a strong civil society emerged'.

As in Latin America, the core problem of poverty narrows horizons while illiteracy provides a barrier to voluntary participation. Further, the national government in many African states has limited functions and weak penetration outside the capital. The political culture remains strongly parochial. Such participation as emerges, at least beyond voting, is directed towards informal politics in ethnic groups and is contained through patron–client networks. These factors all suggest that voluntary participation in African illiberal democracies will remain limited.

Participation in political violence

The forms of participation we have examined so far operate within a broadly civil framework. Even when social movements engage in illegal acts, their protests take place within what has become an

COUNTRY PROFILE

RUSSIA

Form of government ■ a federation of 89 units, comprising 21 republics, 6 territories, 49 regions, 2 federal cities, one autonomous region and 10 autonomous republics.

Executive ■ formally semi-presidential but with a strong presidency. The prime minister heads the Council of Ministers and succeeds the president if needed (no vice president).

Assembly ■ the State Duma (lower house) contains 450 members elected by a mixed member majoritarian system for a four-year term. The Federal Council (upper house) contains two members from each federal unit.

Judicial branch ■ based on civil law and the constitution of 1993. Headed by a Constitutional Court and, for civil and administrative cases, a Supreme Court. Substantial lawlessness.

Population (annual growth rate): 142.9m (–0.4%)
World Bank income group: upper middle
Political Rights score: 6
Civil Liberties score: 5
Human development index (rank/out of): 57/177
Freedom of the press index (rank/out of): 145/194
Ease of doing business index (rank/out of): 96/175

Note: For meaning and sources of scales and indexes, see p. xvi. In all cases a score and rank of 1 is 'best'.

RUSSIA is a vast country with an imperial and authoritarian past. By area it is the largest country in the world, almost twice the size of the United States. Russia's rulers have in the past been autocratic empire-builders, basing their imperial expansion on control of a serf society and (until the communist era) a rural economy. Thus Russia's experience with communist dictatorship represented a culmination of a familiar authoritarian pattern.

In some ways, Russia is still best conceived as an empire whose leaders are concerned to extend the country's international influence. The Soviet Union's collapse led to the emergence of 25 million Russians living outside the country's new boundaries in 'the near abroad'. In the Kremlin, certainly, one objective seems to be to restore Russia's status as a Great Power. This goal is assisted by the country's huge reserves of oil, gas, timber and strategic minerals. These resources comprise about 80 per cent of Russia's exports. Vladimir Putin (president, 2000–08) sought to increase state leverage over these resources. As elsewhere, an economy based on commodity exports encourages corruption and rent-seeking, inhibiting both economic and democratic development (Fish, 2005).

The transition from communism in the 1990s was characteristically turbulent, involving a chaotic restructuring. Life expectancy and population fell as unemployment and alcoholism soared; even in 2006, male life expectancy remained 15 years below that in the USA. Many state-owned entities were in effect stolen, creating a few wealthy oligarchs but also a perceived link between capitalism and crime. This botched transition, for which naïve advice from Western economists was partly responsible, offers a powerful lesson: market economies must be underpinned by sound public institutions, including effective courts.

Russia is an illiberal democracy but its authoritarian tendencies have intensified under Putin, leading some authors to prefer the term 'electoral authoritarianism' to 'illiberal democracy'. Certainly, the latter designation sits uneasily alongside the country's low ratings by Freedom House for political rights and civil liberties. Exploiting the considerable powers accorded to his post under the 1993 constitution, Putin strengthened his control over television, the judiciary and the provinces while dealing ruthlessly with potential opponents. At the same time, his centralizing policies were at least partly directed towards producing a more law-governed society in which corruption would be less prominent and property rights more secure. Certainly, the economy recovered well under Putin's rulership and the president himself remained exceptionally popular. The regime's status is perhaps best characterized by its very ambiguity.

Further reading: Sakwa (2002), White, Gitelman and Sakwa (2005).

SPOTLIGHT

Participation in Russia

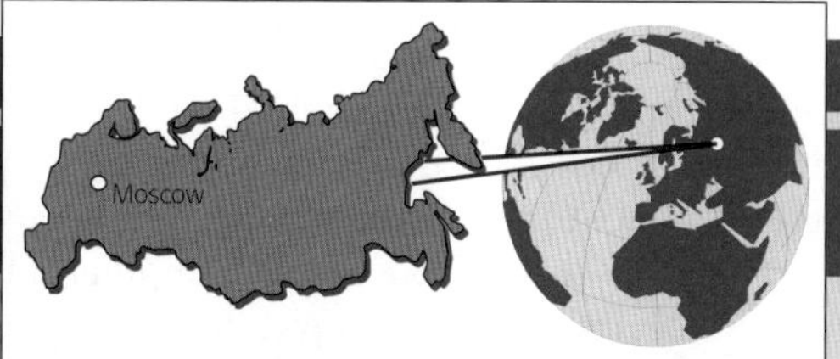

Russia presents a clear case of the limits of political participation in an illiberal democracy with a predominantly subject culture. On the one hand, Russia is an intensely political society with an educated people fully aware of national developments. On the other hand, political participation is extremely shallow, held back by pervasive cynicism about the capacity of ordinary people to make a difference. So how does political participation work in the setting of this large and important illiberal democracy?

Most Russians follow politics on television and in national and local newspapers. Two-thirds of Russians say they regularly or sometimes discuss the country's problems. Interest in politics follows through to participation in national elections. Sixty-four per cent turned out in the presidential election of 2004, a higher proportion than in the American presidential election of the same year.

Yet in one survey, most Russians said that the country is not a democracy and that their vote would not change anything. In another study, 85 per cent said they had no power to influence overall government decisions (Rose, 1999). Authoritarianism, past and present, pervades current attitudes, creating a country with a silent majority.

Suspicion of organizations is endemic, with more people distrusting than trusting even the highest-rated institutions: the army and the church. Trust remains contained within personal networks of friends and family.

Political parties come near the bottom of the trust list, perhaps explaining why so many of them choose bland names such as 'Russia's Choice' and 'United Russia'. At just 1 per cent, membership of parties remains well below even declining Western levels. The parties themselves have proved to be unstable, with an insecure social base. They are, in the main, creatures of politicians or even of the Kremlin itself.

Low membership of parties reflects limited participation in social organizations. Civil society remains poorly developed. Most Russians belong to no voluntary public organizations; membership of trade unions is low; regular church attendance is uncommon. Although some organizations that emerged during Gorbachev's era of *glasnost* (openness) have survived, few have acquired large memberships and others have been incorporated into the regime.

Particularly under President Putin, the government remained suspicious of non-governmental bodies, especially those with foreign links. In a pattern characteristic of illiberal democracies, and also of some of the more liberal democracies in Eastern Europe, mass political participation in Russia is concentrated on national elections, with few entities standing between citizen and state. Even in the post-communist era, participation is still constrained by the desire of the ruling elite to construct a powerful and stable state with a strong international preserve. The Russian people remain subjects first, participants second.

The paradox of participation in Russia

'When we examine the potential of conventional forms of political participation in Russia, it is quite high: 64 per cent of respondents are ready to participate in collective forms of political activities. At the same time, confidence in the effectiveness of various forms of public participation is rather low. Only a small share of respondents (between three and nine per cent) believe that any of the forms of public and political participation is efficient in the solution of problems.'

Source: Institute for Comparative Social Research (2003).

Further reading: Fish (2005), Remington (2004), Rose (1999).

accepted framework of dissent. Yet when orthodox politics leaves conflicts unresolved, and sometimes even when it does not, the outcome can be **political violence** – by citizens seeking to change government policy, by one social group against another and by the state against its own people. To appreciate the full repertoire of activities falling under the heading of political participation, we must also consider the role of violence in politics.

The events of 11 September, 2001 brought violence and **political terror** into focus (Lutz and Lutz, 2004). The assaults on New York and Washington were unprecedented terrorist acts in the number of their victims; but they built on a tradition of political violence that is as ancient as politics itself. Many terms used today in describing violence derive from these earliest instances. The Zealots (literally, those jealous on God's behalf) were Jewish activists who resisted Roman rule in Palestine. In the era of the Crusades, the Assassins (literally, hashish-eaters) were a Muslim sect who believed their religious duty was to hunt down Christians. The Thugs (literally, the deceivers) were religiously motivated bandits who operated in central and northern India between the seventeenth and nineteenth centuries. They specialized in befriending wealthy travellers during the day and strangling them at night, cutting up the corpses to aid disposal (van Woerkens, 2002).

> **Political violence** consists of 'those physically injurious acts directed at persons or property which are intended to further or oppose governmental decisions and public policies' (LaPalombara, 1974, p. 379). **Political terror** occurs when such acts are aimed at striking fear into a wider population than the immediate victims.

The central point about political violence is that it must be viewed through the conventional lenses of political analysis, not through a distorting filter that 'explains' violence as the product of the irrational fanaticism of the participants. As Clausewitz said of war, violence is 'a continuation of politics by other means'. The threat and use of force is a way of raising the stakes; it extends but rarely replaces conventional politics. Most political violence is neither random nor uncontrolled but tactical. When farmers block a road, or when the secret police beat up a student activist, or even when terrorists blow up an aircraft, the act carries a deliberate political signal.

Take the example of suicide missions, an extreme form of violent participation that has acquired significance since its resurgence in the Lebanon conflict of 1973–86. A focus on the characteristics and motivations of the perpetrators offers only limited purchase and is in any case a difficult research topic, since the subjects are dead (though those who fail to die in the act can be interviewed). As far as is known, the participants in these missions are not psychologically disturbed and would not otherwise be expected to kill themselves. A sociological profile is perhaps more promising: many are young, unmarried men with an above average education and social status (Gambetta, 2005a). Even so, only a minute proportion of those fitting this profile take part in terrorist acts and the profile can in any case vary as the participants come to be drawn from outside an organization's established membership (Pedahzur, 2005).

A broader political analysis is more appropriate. These missions typically arise when organized groups are in a weak position in a continuing conflict with a Western power (where the action will receive publicity). Suicide missions are adopted as a last resort, drawing on a cultural tradition of martyrdom and an underlying sense of hopelessness, within the community as much as the individual participant. An established organization provides the means for the intensive task of preparing the participants to complete the task successfully.

A similar conclusion arises when we examine participation in **genocide**. Confronting the genocide of the European Jews during 1941–45, or of the Tutsis in Rwanda in 1994, we naturally seek to understand why the people who carried out the killings did so. But in all such cases, the perpetrators appear to be normal people in abnormal situations. There is no no formula for predicting who will kill and who will refuse; indeed, there are often few refusals at all.

The Rwandan genocide is particularly revealing (Box 9.3). It was perpetrated by up to 200,000 Hutu

> **Genocide** is the deliberate and systematic extermination of a large proportion of a people, nation, race or ethnic group.

peasants armed with nothing more than machetes. Closely organized by political militias, the peasants hunted down and 'chopped' at least 500,000 Tutsis in 100 days. In a heavily populated country, many of the victims were known personally to the killers. Yet few Hutu refused to take part; even many women who stayed at home were happy enough to accept the loot obtained by their men. In this, as in other examples, the key question is political, not psychological: 'why were the orders given?' not 'why were the orders obeyed?'.

Revolution

Occasionally, political violence extends to the governing framework itself as the entire political order becomes a matter for dispute. When the existing structure of power is overthrown, leading to a long-term reconstruction of the political, social and economic order, we can speak of a **revolution**. Such episodes are rare but pivotal, inducing broad and deep alterations in society. The major instances – France, America, Russia, China, Iran – have substantially influenced the modern world. We therefore conclude this chapter with an assessment of the nature and causes of revolutions, focusing in particular on France and Russia.

Skocpol (1979, p.4) defines **revolutions** as 'rapid, basic transformations of a society's state and class structures; and they are accompanied and in part carried through by class-based revolts from below'. Goldstone (1991) suggests revolutions consist of three overlapping stages: state breakdown, the struggle for power and radical reconstruction of the state.

Although changes of the magnitude needed to qualify as a revolution usually require violence, it is debatable whether violence should be built into the definition of the term. The question is whether a 'peaceful revolution' is a contradiction in terms. On the one hand, we can make a case for the possibility of revolutions without violence. After all, the ancient world used the term 'revolution' just to refer to a circulation in the ruling group, howsoever induced. To 'revolve' is literally to move around, and in this traditional sense there is no necessary link between revolution and violent disorder.

BOX 9.3

Participation in genocide

Why do ordinary people participate in genocide? The main psychological device seems to be dehumanization, a mechanism encouraged by the organizers' propaganda. When Jews are presented as leeches, and Tutsis as cockroaches and snakes, genocide becomes a technical task of clearance. Many perpetrators believe or convince themselves that they are not killing normal human beings at all. As with any other form of political participation, people also respond to the circumstances around them. They kill because:

- Everyone else, including their friends, is doing so (social pressure);
- They will be punished if they do not take part (fear of sanctions);
- Participation often provides an opportunity to loot (prospect of rewards).

Three quotations from Hatzfeld's interviews with some perpetrators of the Rwanda genocide (2005, pp. 213, 67 and 89 respectively) illustrate these points:

- 'The jeering of colleagues is impossible to overcome if it gets round. You find it easier to ply the machete than to be stabbed by ridicule and contempt. This truth is impossible to understand for anyone who was not there beside us.'
- 'On the hills, many killed simply to get round their poverty. If they went along with the killings, they didn't risk fines, and besides it could pay off big on the way home. Whoever found a chance to sheet-metal his roof, how could he hesitate?'
- 'Others caught girls just to fool around with; they raped for a little while and then handed them over to be killed. Of course, a great number didn't do that, had no taste for misbehaving. Most said it was improper to mix fooling around and killing.'

Recent experience confirms that major political changes can occur without large-scale violence. The collapse of communism in Eastern Europe in 1989, leading to the fall of the Soviet Union in 1991, was a major reform initiated by peaceful means, with Czechoslovakia's Velvet Revolution a particular case in point. Yet 1989 surely qualifies as a year of revolutions when such efforts are measured by their impact rather than by the violence of their birth.

On the other hand, the contemporary use of the term 'revolution' still connotes transformation through violence, a change in meaning which reflects the experience of the modern world. After the seminal French Revolution of 1789, the world needed a special term to capture dramatic, seismic shifts in the social and political order; and 'revolution' in the modern sense was born (Lachmann, 1997).

BOX 9.4

A century of revolutions

	Year	Outcome
Mexico	1910	A populist revolution leading to rule by the Institutional Revolutionary Party (PRI) which continued until 2000.
Russia	1917	The world's first communist state, lasting until 1990.
Turkey	1922	A secular nation state built amidst the ruins of the Ottoman Empire.
China	1949	The People's Republic of China, led by a party which is now communist only in name.
Iran	1979	An Islamic theocracy originally led by Ayatollah Khomeini. The current religious leaders lack Khomeini's authority, especially among the young.

Social psychological and structural theories

The twentieth century vastly increased the world's stock of revolutions (Box 9.4), stimulating a search for general theories of these events. Here we will consider two such accounts: first, the social psychological account associated with Gurr; and, second, Skocpol's structural interpretation.

The social psychological theory focuses on individual motivations rather than social groups. It seeks to answer such questions as: What inspires people to participate in revolutionary activity? Why do some people sometimes feel so strongly about politics that they are willing to give time, energy and ultimately their lives to achieve change?

In his study of the French Revolution, de Tocqueville (1856) noted that grievances patiently endured become intolerable once a brighter future seems possible. Gurr (1980) sought to develop de Tocqueville's insight, suggesting that political instability only results from deprivation when combined with a belief that conditions are worse than they could and should be. What matters is not absolute deprivation, a condition associated with a struggle for survival and therefore political passivity. As the Russian revolutionary Leon Trotsky wrote, 'the mere existence of privations is not enough to cause an insurrection; if it were, the masses would always be in revolt' (1932/3, p. 103). More important is **relative deprivation**.

When relative deprivation is widespread, Gurr suggests, instability may result. Specifically, the most explosive situation arises when a period of improvement is followed by a decline in the ability of the regime to meet rising demands. Such a situation creates a dangerous gap between expectations of continued improvement and the reality of decline. These conditions produce a revolutionary gap between expectations and achievement (Figure 9.3).

Relative deprivation arises when people believe they are receiving less (value capability) than they feel they are entitled to (value expectations). This perceived deficit may be relative to past times, to an abstract standard of justice, or to the rewards accruing to other groups. Comparison of some kind is integral to the idea and breeds a sense of resentment which contributes to political discontent.

Figure 9.3 The J-curve theory of revolutions

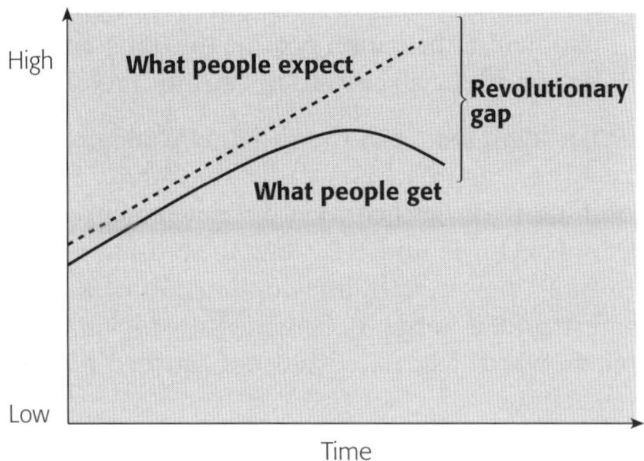

Note: 'What people expect' and 'What people get' refers to government.

Davies (1962) sums up the implications of this psychological approach: 'Revolutions are most likely to occur when a prolonged period of economic and social development is followed by a short period of sharp reversal'. This hypothesis is known as the J-curve theory, with the top of the 'J' indicating an abrupt halt to a previous period of rapid growth.

The contribution of this social psychological approach lies in demonstrating that how people perceive their condition is more important than their actual situation. Relative deprivation is certainly a background factor in many revolutions. Peasant frustrations, in particular, were involved in the French, Russian and Chinese examples. Note, however, that by citing actual revolutions, we are restricting our attention to positive cases. Relative deprivation may often be extensive without signalling uprisings of any kind. Its status is more likely to be that of a necessary rather than a sufficient condition of revolution.

Although the social psychological account provides some insight into the conditions of political instability and violence, it seems incapable of explaining revolutionary progress and outcomes. Whose discontent matters? How and why do uprisings turn into revolutions? How is discontent channelled into organized opposition movements? Why is such opposition usually suppressed but sometimes not? Because relative deprivation has no answer to these important questions, it is better regarded as a theory of political violence in general rather than of revolutions in particular.

Given the limitations of the psychological approach, in the 1970s the study of revolutions turned away from broad psychological theories and returned to a more fine-grained historical examination. Skocpol's (1979) influential discussion of the French, Russian and Chinese revolutions represented a culmination of this more political and structural approach.

For Skocpol, the causes of revolutions cannot be found in the motives of the participants. What matters are the structural conditions: that is, the relationships between groups within a state and, equally important, between states. The background to revolution, suggests Skocpol, is provided by a regime that is weak internationally and ineffective domestically. The classic revolutions occurred when well-organized agitators succeeded in exploiting peasant frustration with an old order which had lost its capacity to compete with more developed international competitors. With the landed aristocracy resisting economic modernization, and offering only limited support to the imperial ambitions of the regime, the old order becomes vulnerable to insurrection:

> Caught in cross-pressures between domestic class structures and international exigencies, the autocracies and their centralized administrations and armies broke apart, opening the way for revolutionary transformations spearheaded by revolts from below (Skocpol, 1979, p. 47).

Seizing power from a failing regime can be quite straightforward. The real revolution begins as the new rulers develop and impose their vision on society and, in particular, on opposition groups. Revolutions do not stop with the taking of power, as the social psychological theory seemed to imply, but only start at this point. Skocpol tells us much about how discontent is mobilized into political activity and how that activity is turned into a revolutionary transformation. In this way, she returns political, and especially state-centred, analysis to the fore.

The French Revolution

We conclude by considering the French and Russian revolutions in the context of the social psychological and structural theories we have introduced. Our scrutiny must certainly begin with France in 1789, as this was the defining revolution of modern times. Indeed, it is no exaggeration to say that both the modern concept of revolution and modernity itself were born in France.

What, then, were the contours of this landmark episode? Before the Revolution, France still combined an absolute monarchy with feudalism. Governance was a confused patchwork of local, provincial and royal institutions. However, in the 1780s the storm-clouds gathered: the old regime came under pressure as the monarchy became virtually bankrupt. Then, in 1788, a poor grain harvest triggered both peasant revolts and urban discontent. The Revolution itself was initiated after the Third Estate of the Estates General, convened in May 1789 for the first time in over 150 years, declared itself to be France's National Assembly.

There followed a half-decade of radical reform in which, amid the enormous violence of the Terror, the old institutions (including the monarchy) were torn down and the foundations of a modern state constructed. After a further period of instability, Napoleon instituted a period of authoritarian rule lasting from 1799 to 1814. Universal male suffrage was not adopted until 1848 and the conflict between radicals and conservatives embedded in the Revolution remained important to French political debate for the next 200 years.

Marx described the Revolution as a 'gigantic broom' sweeping away 'all manner of medieval rubbish'. The shockwaves of the events in France certainly reverberated throughout Europe as ruling classes in other countries saw their very existence imperilled. The Revolution's mixed outcomes notwithstanding, its progressive character is indisputable:

- Politically, the Revolution destroyed absolute monarchy based on divine right. It established the future shape of liberal democracy: popular sovereignty, a professional bureaucracy and a liberal philosophy;
- Economically, the Revolution weakened aristocratic control over the peasantry, helping to create the conditions under which market relations could spread and capitalism would eventually emerge;
- Ideologically, the Revolution was strongly secular, fathering individual rights enforceable through codified law. It was also powerfully nationalist: the nation became the transcendent bond, uniting all citizens in patriotic fervour.

What light, then, can the social psychological and structural approaches cast on the French Revolution? Davies's concept of relative deprivation certainly helps in understanding the peasant revolts, driven as they were by the conjunction of a failed harvest and a series of unsuccessful government policies which had raised but not satisfied popular expectations.

But there seems little doubt that Skocpol's perspective offers deeper insight. The international dimension behind 1789 can be seen in France's generally unsuccessful competition with England in the eighteenth century. The limited domestic effectiveness of the monarchy was then demonstrated by its inability to pay for foreign adventures, resulting in a fiscal crisis that came to a head in the late 1780s. Further, Skocpol's emphasis on the complex dynamics and long-term effects of revolution certainly fits the French experience. The French Revolution became far more than a peasant revolt.

The Russian Revolution

Just as the French Revolution mapped the contours of liberal democracy, so the Russian Revolution of October 1917 established the world's first communist state. It signalled the advent of a regime, an ideology and a revolutionary movement which sought to overthrow Western democracy. The Russian Revolution was a pivotal event of the twentieth century.

The Russian Revolution swept away the ramshackle and decaying empire of the tsar, just as its French counterpart had destroyed medieval remnants in that country over a century earlier. Although Russia underwent significant state-sponsored industrialization towards the end of the nineteenth century, the political framework remained conservative and autocratic. Under the tsarist bureaucracy, Russian society had remained inert. In particular, the mass of poorly educated peasants remained locked in serfdom, dependent on the landowning nobility. Russia was an important imperial power but, domestically, its political, economic and social structures were falling behind its Western competitors.

The country was ripe for revolution, a fact widely recognized at the time. But in Russia, unlike France, a dress rehearsal occurred before the Revolution proper got under way. An unsuccessful war with Japan stimulated a naval mutiny in 1905, leading to a failed insurrection. The government quickly concluded the war with Japan, freeing loyal troops to suppress what the regime claimed was a 'passing squall' of domestic rebellion.

A decade later, the military disasters of the First World War, and the resulting economic and administrative chaos within Russia, could not be dismissed so easily. By 1917, the capacity of the central government to rule Russia had virtually disintegrated. The tsarist regime collapsed in March, to be replaced by a weak provisional government. Reflecting Lenin's decisive leadership, the Bolsheviks succeeded in November in replacing this administration ('Bolshevik', meaning majority, was the name of a radical faction in the broad Marxist movement).

In Russia, as in France, the Revolution was made not by an insurrection but by the transformation of the political order which followed. Even before Lenin ended Russia's involvement in world war in 1918, the country was consumed by a civil war which lasted until 1921. The decisive outcome was the re-establishment of central authority in the form of a communist dictatorship. Despite their democratic and anarchist origins, the Bolsheviks developed into a communist party wielding a monopoly of power. In this fateful transition, Lenin's notion of the vanguard party – an elite body of revolutionaries which claimed to understand the long-term interests of the working class better than that class itself – provided the crucial rationale.

Why did the first major communist revolution of the twentieth century occur in one of the less-developed links in the capitalist chain? After all, Marx himself had predicted that such events would occur in advanced capitalist countries with an industrial working class, not in largely unmodernized agrarian societies such as Russia. Here, Davies's theory of relative deprivation provides useful service. Although nineteenth-century Russia remained a poor country with a serf economy, the tsar did institute important reforms between 1860 and 1904, including notional freedom for the serfs, the introduction of a modern legal system, state-sponsored industrialization and general liberalization.

But these reforms served only to induce relative deprivation. Although the peasants were theoretically free, most remained burdened by debt. Many flocked to the expanding cities in fruitless search of a better life. Rapid economic expansion in the final decade of the 1890s, stimulated by industrial development, turned into recession in the first decade of the twentieth century. Expectations raised by political reforms were dashed by the tsar's inability to push ahead with further, more radical changes. In these ways, reform oscillated with repression in a perfect formula for fostering relative deprivation.

Where Davies is less successful, however, is in explaining why one attempted revolution failed in Russia in 1905 but another succeeded just 12 years later. At this point, Skocpol's emphasis on regime collapse amid international failure comes back into play. With Russia's armies outclassed by the superior equipment and support available to Germany's forces, the tsar's regime disintegrated, leading to a power vacuum which Lenin's Bolsheviks exploited during the summer and autumn of 1917.

Learning Resources for Chapter 9

Next step

Putnam (2000) is an interesting assessment of the decline of social participation in the USA, with an eye to its political impact.

Further reading

Verba *et al.* (1995) examine the United States in their major study of participation. For a comparable British investigation see Parry *et al.* (1992). On social movements, see Tarrow (1998) for a general account, Tilly (2004) for a history, Zirakzadeh (1997) for a comparative study, della Porta *et al.* (1999) for the global context, and Ibarra (2003) and Norris (2002) for the uncertain relationship between the movements and orthodox democracy. The literature on participation in post-communist societies is now expanding; on Russia, see Eckstein (1998b). For participation in African transitions, see Bratton and van de Walle (1997, ch. 4). Hatzfeld (2005) reports important interviews with perpetrators of the Rwandan genocide while Gambetta (2005a) makes sense of suicide missions; both books are strongly recommended. On revolutions, see Skocpol (1979) for a classic analysis and Foran (1997) for a theoretical account.

Internet sources

American Sociological Association
Section on Collective Behavior and Social Movements
http://www2.asanet.org/sectioncbsm/

CIVNET, Civitas International
An online resource for civic education practitioners
http://www.civnet.org

The Communitarian Network
For individual rights and social responsibility
http://www.gwu.edu/~ccps/index.html

International Institute for Democracy and Electoral Assistance (IDEA)
Includes valuable publications on political participation
http://www.idea.int/

Chapter 10

Elections and voters

'Elections are the defining institution of modern democracy', writes Katz (1997, p. 3). For the brief moment of an election campaign, voters are the masters and are seen to be so. As liberal and indeed illiberal democracies grow in number, so elections become a more widespread instrument, with the total number of voters in 2004 exceeding one billion (Muñoz, 2006, p. 1).

Clearly, one function of elections is to provide a competition for office and a means of holding the government to account. But that is not their only role. An election campaign also permits a dialogue between voters and parties, and so between society and state: 'no part of the education of a politician is more indispensable than the fighting of elections', claimed Winston Churchill. Like coronations of old, competitive elections also endow the new office-holders with authority, contributing thereby to the effectiveness with which leaders can perform their duties (Ginsberg, 1982). In short, competitive elections facilitate choice, accountability, dialogue and legitimacy – a rich bounty for what is, after all, only an occasional event.

Yet even today, not all elections are competitive. Most authoritarian rulers maintain an assembly and employ controlled elections as the means of legislative recruitment. Even these non-competitive elections can provide a measure of legitimacy with the international community, as well as a panel of docile representatives who can safely be permitted to raise harmless grievances emanating from their local area. In illiberal democracies, elections are manipulated but not fraudulent; the election is made rather than stolen (Mackenzie, 1958).

But it is competitive elections in a democratic setting that provide the heart of this chapter. We begin with the neglected issues of the scope and franchise of elections. We then turn to electoral systems, referendums, turnout and voting behaviour. The final sections discuss elections in authoritarian states and illiberal democracies.

Scope and franchise

An important question to raise about elections in liberal democracies is their scope. Which offices are subject to election varies considerably between, say, the United States and Europe. The USA possesses more than 500,000 elected offices, a figure reflecting a strong tradition of local self-government. By comparison, many democracies in Europe have traditionally confined voting to national assemblies and local governments, with regional and European elections recently added. To illustrate the contrast, Dalton and Gray (2003, p. 38) point out that 'between 1995 and 2000 a resident of Oxford, England, could have voted four times; a resident of Irvine, California, could have cast more than 50 votes in just the single year of 2000'. Similarly, Australia has many more elected posts than does New Zealand, even when Australia's larger population is taken into account.

Other things being equal, the greater the number of offices subject to competitive election, the more democratic a political system becomes. However, there are dangers in electionitis. One is voter fatigue, leading to a fall in interest, turnout and quality of choice. American estimates suggests that five additional trips to the polls over a five-year period are likely to depress turnout by around 4 per cent over that same period (Dalton and Gray, 2003, p. 39).

In particular, the least important contests tend to become **second-order elections**: that is, their outcomes reflect the popularity of national parties even though they do not install a national government. The difficulty with such second-order contests is that they weaken the link between the office-holder's performance and the voters' response (Anderson and Ward, 1996).

Votes in a **second-order election** are heavily influenced by support at first-order contests, often occurring at the same time. For example, a party's votes at local contests may reflect its popularity at national level, thus degrading the link between local governance and local elections.

Many American electors, for example, still vote a straight party ticket for all the offices included on a single ballot. This easy option is encouraged by the use in most states of the party-column or Indiana ballot, which arranges all of a party's candidates in a single column. To vote for the party's entire ticket, the elector can just place one cross or pull a single lever, a process that can lead to a party winning extra posts on the **coat-tails** of a popular candidate for the White House. Similar, if less direct, processes operate in Europe. For instance, elections to the European Parliament become referendums on *national* governments, although their supposed purpose is to elect a member for the *European* Parliament.

The franchise (who can vote) is another underemphasized aspect of contemporary elections. Following a reduction in the voting age in the 1960s and 1970s, the franchise in most democracies now extends to nearly all citizens aged at least 18. This extensive franchise is fairly recent, particularly for women. Few countries can match Australia and New Zealand where women have been electors since the start of the twentieth century. In some countries, women did not gain the vote on the same terms as men until after 1945, reflecting male recognition of women's contribution to the war effort (Table 9.1).

The American notion of **coat-tails** refers to the electoral bonus accruing to lesser candidates from the strength of the candidate heading the party's ticket.

The main remaining exclusions from suffrage are criminals, the insane and non-citizen residents such as temporary workers. Yet in each of these areas there may still be room for progress. Should the electoral process adopt techniques enabling people with even severe learning difficulties to express preferences? Is denial of the vote really an appropriate response to citizens convicted of a criminal offence? Should non-citizen residents be granted the vote in the country where they live, work and pay taxes alongside citizens? If so, should they also retain the vote in their home country? (Day and Shaw, 2002).

Electoral systems: legislatures

Most discussion of electoral systems centres on the rules for converting votes into seats. Such rules are as important as they are technical. They form the inner workings of democracy, often little understood by voters but essential to the system's operation. In this section, we examine the rules for translating votes into seats in parliamentary elections, leaving presidential elections to the next section (Box 10.1).

The main feature of an electoral system is whether the parliamentary seats obtained by a party are directly proportional to the votes it receives. Proportional representation (PR) simply means that a mechanism to achieve this goal is built into the allocation of seats. In non-proportional systems, parties are not rewarded in proportion to the share of the vote they obtain; instead, 'the winner takes all' within each district, whether a Canadian riding, an American district or a British constituency. These non-proportional systems take one of two forms: plurality or majority. We examine these older non-proportional formats before turning to the more common system of PR.

BOX 10.1

Electoral systems: legislatures

PLURALITY AND MAJORITY SYSTEMS

1. Single-member plurality: ' first past the post'

Procedure	The candidate securing most votes (not necessarily a majority) is elected on the first and only ballot within each single-member district (SMD).
Where used	Forty-seven countries, including Bangladesh, Canada, India, UK, USA.

2. Absolute majority: 'alternative vote' (AV)

Procedure	Voters rank candidates. If no candidate wins a majority of first preferences, the bottom candidate is eliminated and his or her votes are redistributed by second preferences.
Where used	Australia, Fiji, Papua New Guinea.

3. Two-round system

Procedure	If no candidate wins a majority on the first ballot, the leading candidates (usually the top two) face a second, run-off election.
Where used	Twenty-two countries including Egypt, Iran, Mali, Vietnam.

PROPORTIONAL SYSTEMS

4. List system

Procedure	Votes are cast for a party's list of candidates, though in some countries the elector can also express support for individual candidates on the list.
Where used	Seventy countries including Brazil, Czech Republic, Israel and the Netherlands.

5. Single transferable vote (STV)

Procedure	Voters rank candidates in order of preference. Any successful candidate needs a set number of votes – the quota. All candidates are elected who exceed this quota on first preferences. Their 'surplus' votes are then distributed to the second preferences shown on these ballot papers. When no candidate has reached the quota, the bottom candidate is eliminated and these votes are also transferred. Continue until all seats are filled.
Where used	Ireland, Malta.

6. Mixed member proportional (MMP)

Procedure	Electors normally have two votes. One is for the district election (which usually uses the plurality method) and the other for a PR contest (usually party list). The two tiers are linked so as to deliver a proportional outcome overall. The party vote determines the number of seats to be won by each party. Elected candidates are drawn first from the party's winners in the district contests, topped up as required by candidates from the party list.
Where used	Nine countries, including Germany and New Zealand.

PARALLEL SYSTEM

7. Mixed member majoritarian (MMM)

Procedure	As for MMP, except that these two tiers are separate, with no mechanism to achieve a proportional result overall.
Where used	Twenty-one countries, including Japan, Russia, South Korea, Thailand.

Note: Based on elections to lower chambers. Figures based on the 199 countries and territories examined in Reynolds, Reilly and Ellis (2005).

We also discuss the recent trend to mixed systems, in which electors cast two ballots: one for a district representative and the other for a party. These systems, too, can take either a proportional or non-proportional form, depending on whether a mechanism is incorporated to achieve proportionality between the party vote and seats in the assembly.

Plurality system

In the single-member plurality (also called 'first past the post') format, the winning candidate is simply the one receiving most votes in a particular electoral district. A party's representation in the legislature then consists of those of its candidates who win these constituency contests.

Despite its antiquity and simplicity, the plurality system is becoming less common. It survives principally in Britain and British-influenced states such as Canada, various Caribbean islands, India and the United States. However, because India and the USA are so populous, the largest share of the world's people living under democratic rule still vote by the plurality method.

The crucial point about the plurality method is the bonus in seats it offers to the party leading in votes. To see how this bias operates, consider an example in which just two parties, the Reds and the Blues, compete in every constituency. Suppose the Reds win by one vote in each district. There could hardly be a closer contest yet the Reds sweep the board in seats. One approximation to this theoretical example is Lesotho in 1998, when the Lesotho Congress for Democracy won 79 of 80 seats with 61 per cent of the vote. The winner took nearly everything and the losers secured practically nothing; riots followed.

The political significance of this amplifying effect lies in its ability to deliver government by a single majority party. In parliamentary systems with dominant national parties, the plurality method is a giant conjuring trick, pulling the rabbit of majority government out of a hat containing only minority parties. This amplifying characteristic is crucial for those who consider that the function of an electoral system is to deliver decisive majority government by a single party.

For example, all but one of the 17 general elections in Britain between 1945 and 2005 yielded a majority in the House of Commons for a single party, even though no party secured a majority of votes in any of these contests. A similar pattern holds for most federal elections in Canada. In 1993, for instance, the Liberals won 60 per cent of the seats on 42 per cent of the vote; their Conservative opponents gained a mere two seats despite winning 16 per cent of the vote (Table 10.1).

It is, however, important to note that this amplifier works best when two dominant parties (or in Lesotho just one) compete throughout the country. The British contest between Labour and the Conservatives still fits this bill, enabling the swing of the pendulum to deliver a parliamentary majority first for one party, then for the other.

But where parties are more fragmented, majority government is less likely. The weak performance of Canada's two main parties in 2006, with neither the Liberals and the Conservatives gaining much more than a third of the vote, meant that no majority government ensued (Table 10.1). Regional parties also limit the capacity of the plurality method to deliver majority government. Such parties win in their own strongholds but lack the national appeal needed for overall victory. In India's increasingly regional party system, plurality elections have not delivered majority government since 1989.

So a failure to consider how the system works beyond its British homeland leads to an exaggerated

Table 10.1 The Canadian federal elections of 1993 and 2006

Party	1993		2006	
	Votes (%)	Number of seats	Votes (%)	Number of seats
Liberal	**42**	**177**	30	103
Conservative	**16**	**2**	36	124
New Democratic Party	7	9	**17**	**29**
Reform/Alliance	19	52		
Bloc Québécois	14	54	**10**	**51**
Other			6	1
Total	98	294	99	308

Note: **Bold** entries illustrate disproportional results between the major parties in 1993 and between the minor parties in 2006.

view of the ability of the plurality method to produce majority government. Weakening party loyalties, furthermore, mean that a national competition between just two strong parties is becoming less prevalent.

Because the plurality system is based on the representation of districts, it offers no guarantee that the party which leads in votes nationally will secure most seats in the legislature. Another party may achieve such an **efficient** distribution of votes that it wins a majority of seats with fewer votes.

Again, consider an example. Suppose the Blues pile up massive majorities in their own geographical stronghold while the Reds scrape home with narrow wins throughout the rest of the country. The Reds could well win more seats despite obtaining fewer votes, reflecting the greater efficiency of their vote distribution. This possibility arises because the average number of votes required to win a seat is not constant but varies between parties according to how their votes are distributed across constituencies.

This bizarre situation has arisen twice in post-war British general elections. In 1951, the Conservatives won 26 more seats than Labour, and formed a majority government, even though Labour won 231,000 more votes. In February 1974, the anomaly was reversed. Labour won four more seats than the Conservatives and formed a minority administration, even though the Conservatives won 226,000 more votes (Kavanagh and Butler, 2005, p. 203).

For Lijphart (1999, p. 134), this possibility of 'seat victories for parties that are mere runners-up in vote totals is probably the plurality method's gravest democratic deficit'. In a democratic era, the expectation is that votes rather than seats should count. Thus, an election resulting in a government formed by the party coming second in votes is regarded as yielding the wrong winner. Certainly, if we were designing an electoral system from scratch, we would surely reject a method in which the party with most votes can come second in seats.

> The **efficiency** of a party's vote is its ratio of seats to votes. Under plurality elections, a perfectly efficient distribution consists in never winning a seat by more than one vote and securing no votes at all elsewhere.

Three other weaknesses of the plurality method deserve mention:

- It encourages **tactical voting** because electors may feel their favoured party stands no chance of victory in their particular district. Tactical voting at district level exaggerates the regional basis of party support, reducing the extent to which parties integrate different regions within a national party system.
- The plurality method treats minority parties inconsistently, according to the geographical concentration of their support. Small parties with even support are hit badly (the Liberal Democrats in the UK, the New Democrats in Canada). But parties with a concentrated vote can secure a nice bonus (the Bloc Québécois in Canada) (Table 10.1).
- The importance of constituency boundaries gives incentives for **gerrymandering**. In the United States, partisan districting has become a fine art in elections to the House of Representatives and state legislatures, enabling incumbents to choose their voters, rather than the other way round. The solution to this problem is to cede control of districting to an independent agency (Mann and Cain, 2005).

> **Tactical voting** occurs when electors vote instrumentally for a party or candidate other than their preferred choice. In plurality electoral systems, voters sometimes desert their favoured party when it has no chance of winning in their local district. A good electoral system will offer few incentives for voters to misrepresent their preferences.

> **Gerrymandering** is the art of drawing seat boundaries to maximize the efficiency of a party's support. The term comes from a constituency designed by Governor Gerry of Massachusetts in 1812. It was so long, narrow and wiggly that it reminded one observer of a salamander – hence gerrymander.

Majority systems

The plurality system is not the only form of non-proportional representation. There is also a less common but perhaps more democratic version: the majority method. As its name implies, this formula requires a majority of votes for the winning candidate, an outcome normally achieved through a second round. If no candidate wins a majority on the first round, an additional ballot is held, usually a run-off between the top two candidates.

Many countries in Western Europe used majority voting before switching to PR early in the twentieth century. The system remains significant in France and its ex-colonies. The democratic argument for a majority system is intuitively quite strong: namely, that no candidate should be elected without being shown to be acceptable to a majority of voters.

Within the majority category, the alternative vote (AV) is a rather efficient way of achieving a majority outcome in a single round within single-member seats. This system was devised by W. J. Ware, an American academic, in 1873. Voters rank candidates in order of preference but lower preferences only come into play if no candidate gains a majority of first preferences on the first count. Compared to simple plurality voting, AV takes into account more information about voters' preferences but is not necessarily more proportional. AV is used for Australia's lower chamber, the House of Representatives.

AV encourages candidates to reach out beyond their natural supporters to secure the second preferences of voters in other social groups. For this reason, AV deserves particular consideration when tensions between races, religions and ethnicities run high. This virtue explains why ethnically diverse Papua New Guinea returned to AV in 2002, following a failed flirtation with the plurality method.

Proportional representation

We move now from non-proportional systems to proportional representation. PR is more recent than non-proportional systems: it emerged in continental Europe towards the end of the nineteenth century, stimulated by the founding of associations dedicated to electoral reform. Even so, PR is now more common than plurality and majority systems; it has been the method of choice for most democratic countries since the early 1920s. PR is the norm in Europe, both West and East, and in Latin America.

The underlying principle of PR is to achieve representation for a range of parties rather than just to elect representatives for a given territory. Given that parties rather than electoral districts form the centrepiece of modern politics, this principle is certainly plausible. In a perfectly proportional system, every party would receive the same share of seats as of votes; 40 per cent of the votes would mean 40 per cent of the seats. Although the mechanics of PR are designed with this principle in mind, most 'PR' systems are not perfectly proportional. They usually offer at least some bonus to the largest party, though less than most non-proportional methods, and they also discriminate by design or practice against the smallest parties. For these reasons, it would be wrong to assume that any system labelled 'proportional' must be completely so.

A single party rarely wins a majority of seats under PR. Hence majority governments are unusual and coalitions become standard. Because PR usually leads to post-election negotiations in parliament about which parties will form the next government, it is best interpreted as a method of selecting parliaments rather than governments.

How does PR achieve its goal? The most common method is the list system. In a pure list system, an elector votes for a slate of the party's candidates rather than for a single person. The number of votes won by a party determines how many candidates are elected from that party's list while the order in which candidates appear on the list (decided by the party itself) governs which people are elected as the party's representatives. A simple example will clarify the procedure. Suppose a party wins 10 per cent of the vote in an election to a 150-seat assembly. Assuming perfect proportionality, that party will be entitled to 15 members and these will be the first 15 candidates on its list. The next few can be kept in reserve as alternates.

List systems vary in how much choice they give voters between candidates on a party's list. Many employ closed-party lists; as in our example above, voters have no choice over candidates but can only vote for a party. Portugal, South Africa and Spain are examples. In this format, party officials exert enormous control over political recruitment, including the ability to include women and minorities near the top of the list. Closed party lists undoubtedly benefit female representation in parliament (Table 9.1).

However, most European list systems give voters at least some choice between candidates. This option, known as preference voting in Europe, allows or requires voters to select one or more candidates from the party list. The total of votes cast for a given list still determines the party's overall number of representatives but a candidate's preference votes influence (to varying degrees) the order of appointment. Switzerland and Luxembourg operate exceptionally free lists in which electors are given the opportunity to vote either for a party's list or for as many candidates as there are seats to be filled in the district (Villordes, 2003).

Potentially, preference voting sets candidates from the same party in competition with each other. In practice, however, most voters still spurn the choices offered by this possibility. They adopt the simple procedure of voting for a party's entire slate, just as American electors vote for 'their' party's entire ticket when multiple offices are included on a single ballot. When voters in party list PR are required by the rules to vote for a specific candidate rather than a party, they usually simply select the one at the top. The candidate in number one spot is informally known as the list-puller or locomotive (Millard and Popescu, 2005).

List systems require multimember constituencies. Normally, the country is divided into a set of multimember districts and seats are allocated separately within each district. Employing constituencies in this way preserves some territorial basis to representation but reduces the proportionality of the outcome. Many countries have therefore introduced a compensating mechanism by which some seats are held back from the district allocation to be reallocated at regional and/or national level. These seats go to parties with votes left over after the initial lower-level distribution. These additional tiers increase both the proportionality and the complexity of the system.

The number of members returned per district is known as its **district magnitude**. This figure – which varies within countries as well as between them – is a critical influence on how proportional PR systems are in practice. As Farrell (2001, p. 79) observes, 'The basic relationship for all proportional systems is: the larger the constituency size, and hence the larger the district magnitude, the more proportional the result'.

District magnitude refers to the number of representatives chosen for each electoral district (not to its number of electors). The more representatives to be elected for a district, the more proportional the electoral system can be and the smaller the discrimination against minor parties.

For example, Spain is divided into 52 districts, returning an average of just seven members each. This small magnitude means that minor parties may be denied seats and that large parties receive an artificial boost. In four of the first eight elections in Spain's democratic era, a single party received a majority of seats in the Congress of Deputies with a vote share of between 39 and 44 per cent (Colomer, 2004, p. 262). The Spanish case shows that party list PR is consistent with majority government when the district magnitude is small.

However, in the Netherlands, Israel and Slovakia, the whole country serves as a single large constituency, extending proportionality even to small parties. The Israeli election of 2006, for example, saw a total of 12 parties winning seats in the 120-member Knesset. The smallest party won three seats with just 2.3 per cent of the vote.

Most PR systems add an explicit threshold of representation. If a party's vote share falls below the threshold, it receives no seats, whatever its entitlement under the list formula (Figure 10.1). Thresholds, operating at district or national level, help to protect the legislature from extremes. As Kostadinova (2002) observes, 'The threshold is a powerful mechanism for reducing fragmentation in the assembly. It can be and is manipulated by elites to cut off access to parliament for smaller parties'.

Turkey is an extreme case. Its demanding threshold of 10 per cent of votes cast was designed by the country's secular rulers to exclude small Islamic parties. However, such a high hurdle can have capricious results comparable to those that can arise under simple plurality. In the Turkish election of 2002, won ironically by a party with Islamic origins, over 40 per cent of voters cast their ballots for parties which won no seats in parliament. Here is a striking case of 'PR' delivering a most unproportional, and seemingly unfair, outcome.

Mixed systems

Plurality and PR systems are usually considered alternatives yet a hybrid form has emerged which combines the two. This mixed method combines geographical representation with party representation (Shugart and Wattenberg, 2000). The best known blend, often known as mixed member proportional (MMP), retains a mechanism for achieving overall proportionality and is indeed a form of PR.

Figure 10.1 Explicit thresholds of representation in some PR systems (per cent of total votes cast)

Note: Hungary and Germany use mixed electoral systems. German parties winning three district contests achieve representation in the Bundestag even if they fall below the 5 per cent threshold on the party vote.

Sources: Colomer (2004b), Jasiewicz (2003), LeDuc *et al.* (2002a).

Germany has been the inspiration for MMP. Here, electors have two votes: one for a district candidate and the other for a regional party list. Half the seats in the Bundestag are filled by candidates elected by plurality voting within single member districts. However, the party list vote is more important because it determines the total number of seats to be awarded to each party. Candidates from the party's list are used to top up its directly elected candidates until proportionality is achieved. Should a party win more district seats than its entitlement under the party vote, it retains the extra seats and the Bundestag expands in size (Kreuzer, 2004).

Table 10.2 shows how the German electoral system operated in 2005. Comparing columns A and D reveals that the system did its job of delivering a proportional result overall. Note that none of the minor parties won a significant number of district seats (column B). Without the compensation of the list element (column C), the Bundestag would have been completely dominated, British style, by the Christian Democrats and the Social Democrats.

The compromise character of MMP has encouraged other countries, such as New Zealand, to experiment with similar methods, though sometimes varying the balance between district and list members. The system has also been adopted for the Scottish and Welsh assemblies within the UK.

Other countries have introduced the idea of parallel district and party list votes but without any top-up device to achieve a proportional outcome overall. This non-proportional mixed member majority (MMM) system can result in what amounts to two separate campaigns. In Russia, for instance, 'the two contests may be separately organized, with different headquarters and campaign headquarters and campaign staff even in the case of candidates from the same party' (White, 2005b, p. 324). Many independent candidates, often drawn from local elites or reflecting local concerns, have been elected through the district contests. Despite this feature, however, MMM is more popular than the German format, and is expanding more rapidly (Reynolds, Reilly and Ellis, 2005).

Electoral systems and party systems

The relationship between electoral systems and party systems remains a matter of controversy. In a classic work, Duverger (1954, p. 217) argued that 'an almost complete correlation is observable' between the plurality method and a two-party system; he suggested that this relationship, based on **mechanical** and **psychological** effects, approached that of 'a true sociological law'.

But in the 1960s a reaction set in against attributing weight to political institutions such as electoral systems. Writers such as Rokkan (1970) adopted a more sociological approach, pointing out that social cleavages had produced multiparty systems in Europe long before PR was adopted early in the twentieth century. Jasiewicz (2003, p. 182) makes exactly the same point about post-communist Europe: 'Political fragmentation usually preceded the adoption of a PR-based voting system, not vice versa'. Miller (2005, p. 13) adopts a similar position in discussing New Zealand's move away from

> Duverger (1954) distinguished two effects of electoral systems. The **mechanical** effect arises directly from the rules converting votes into seats. Example: the threshold for representation used in many proportional systems. The **psychological** effect is the impact of the rules on how electors cast their votes. Example: tactical voting in plurality systems when the first choice party has no prospect of winning in the elector's own district.

Table 10.2 How the mixed member proportional system works: the German federal election, 2005

	A Party list vote (%)	B Number of district seats won	C Number of list seats awarded (to bring D closer to A)	D Seats won in the Bundestag (%)
Christian Democrats/ Christian Social Union	35.2	150	76	36.8
Social Democrats	34.2	145	77	36.1
Free Democrats	9.8	0	61	9.9
Left Party	8.7	3	51	8.8
Green Party	8.1	1	50	8.3
Others	4.0	0	0	0

Note: Total number of seats is 614.

Source: Álvarez-Rivera (2006).

the plurality method in 1996: 'The fracturing of the two-party system occurred long before the advent of PR'. Electoral systems result from a party system as much as they influence it.

Design and reform of electoral systems

Questions of electoral system design have come to the fore as new democratic institutions have been built in the transition from communist and military rule. So what advice can we give those charged with designing a new electoral system, particularly for countries with a legacy of instability and division?

It is worth bearing in mind that the history of electoral reform is, in the main, a story of the expansion of PR. Table 10.3 shows the direction of changes in 94 countries over the course of the nineteenth and twentieth centuries. By far the most common switch has been from a majority or plurality system to PR. This shift outnumbered moves in the reverse direction by almost four to one.

Because PR is not a winner-takes-all system, it is always a safe option for parties negotiating electoral reform. In the discussions preceding the introduction of an extended suffrage in Europe early in the twentieth century, conservative and liberal parties felt that a shift from a majority system to PR would at least guarantee their survival into the new era of mass suffrage. Socialist parties, still uncertain of their electoral potential, also judged that PR would at least remove the bias of the majority system against them. So for all the major players, PR was the least bad option (Lewin, 2004). Proportional representation has also predominated in the more recent wave of democratic transitions. With memories of communist and military dictatorships still fresh, democratic reformers were keen to see a range of interests represented in the assembly.

PR is also a safe choice for those designing an electoral system for a new regime. PR will usually provide at least some representation for parties based on minority groups, typically leading to coalition governments which offer further protection for the parties in office. Explicit thresholds and small district magnitudes can limit fragmentation and discord by excluding small anti-system parties from the legislature. Because there are no wasted votes, PR also leads to higher turnout than the plurality system (IDEA, 2006).

The list system is inherently party-based, encouraging the strong parties which are an important component of a stable democracy. The candidate list offers parties the opportunity to construct an order balanced by gender and ethnicity without requiring the government to impose quotas. When the whole country serves as a single electoral district, PR also avoids the complexity and expense of constructing, policing and revising constituency boundaries.

Table 10.3 Major changes to the electoral systems used in legislative elections, 1800–2002

From	To	Number of changes	Example (year)
Majority or plurality	Proportional representation	27	Belgium (1900)
Majority or plurality	Mixed	6	New Zealand (1996)
Proportional representation	Majority or plurality	7	France (1988)
Proportional representation	Mixed	6	Italy (1993)

Note: Based on 94 countries with some democratic experience. Records are incomplete for the earlier years. Some countries have experienced multiple changes (e.g. Italy returned to PR, albeit with a winner's bonus, in 2006).

Source: Adapted from Colomer (2004a), Table 1.3, p. 55.

Yet an electoral system cannot, by itself, be expected to resolve underlying social conflicts. In general, a method of election is performing its function if it proves to be widely acceptable and therefore stable over time. Its purpose is to deliver an equilibrium point such that no party with the power to change the rules feels it will obtain a long-run benefit from doing so. If the winners do not seek to modify the system to their own advantage, and the losers do not blame the election rules for their own defeat, then the electoral system has done its job. It has become, as it should be, taken for granted.

More refined electoral engineering is of course possible but can be counter-productive, yielding unforeseen side-effects and further reforms. Typically, frequent change reflects partisan manoeuvring, as in Greece, Italy and Portugal. In France, where the parliamentary electoral system changed 12 times between 1870 and 1988, Alexander (2005, p. 209) notes that this French 'reform-mongering' shows that 'parties in a position to design the rules were unembarrassed to change if other rules better served their purposes'. Rejigging the electoral system became a victor's perk.

Electoral systems: presidents

Electoral systems for choosing presidents receive less attention than those for electing legislatures. Yet the presidential office is invariably elected in countries with presidential or semi-presidential government. The president is sometimes elected even when the post is mainly honorary; Ireland is an example. So this neglected subject certainly merits attention.

In one sense, the rules for electing presidents are straightforward. Unlike seats in parliament, a one-person presidency cannot be shared between parties; the office is indivisible. So PR is impossible and the main choice is between the plurality and the majority method. However, in another sense, presidential electoral systems are more complicated since many, including the USA, are still based on indirect election through a special college.

We begin with directly elected presidents. As Figure 10.2 shows, 61 of the 91 directly elected presidents in the world are chosen by a majority system. This number is increasing as countries dispense not only with indirect election but also move away from the plurality method (Colomer, 2004, p. 59). The reason for the pre-eminence of the majority system in presidential elections is that it is more important to confirm majority backing for a single president than for every single member of a legislature. Plurality contests, in which the candidate with most votes wins on the first and only round, can lead to victory with a small share of the vote. For example, Fidel Ramos became president of the Philippines in 1992 with only 24 per cent support in a plurality election.

Most majority elections for presidents use a run-off ballot of the top two candidates, assuming neither wins a majority on the first round. France is a leading case. But there are variations. In Costa Rica, a first-round share of at least 40 per cent suffices for victory; Ecuador also uses this threshold

Figure 10.2 Methods for selecting presidents

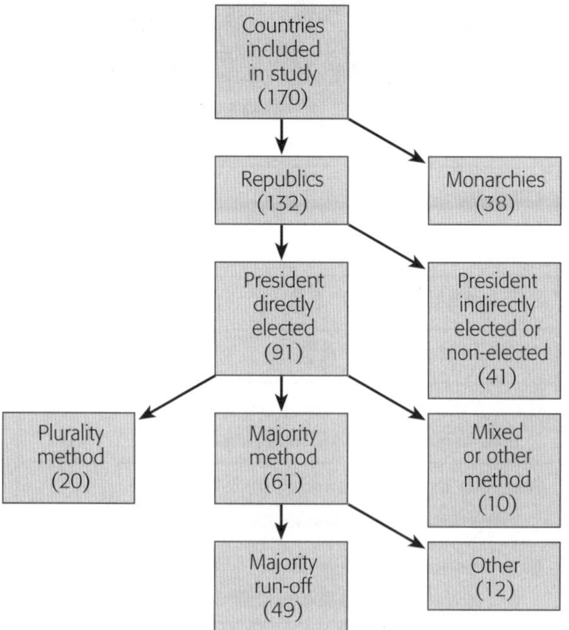

Source: Blais, Massicotte and Dobrzynska (1997).

but adds an additional first-round requirement of a 10-point margin over the second-placed candidate.

Given that most presidential elections are by national ballot, it is possible to require the winning candidate to obtain a certain level of support in the regions as well as nationally. Such **distribution requirements** are still uncommon but they do encourage candidates to broaden their support. This virtue is important in regionally divided societies. In Indonesia, for instance, a first-round victory requires at least 20 per cent of the vote in a majority of provinces. In Nigeria, the requirement is for a third of the vote in at least two thirds of the provinces. However, distribution rules create the possibility of a **failed election**.

Distribution requirements set out how a winning candidate's votes must be arranged across different sections of the electorate. The most common (but still unusual) requirement is that of a minimum level of support in a certain number of provinces. Such requirements can lead to **failed elections** in which no candidate jumps through all the hoops.

A further requirement, encountered only occasionally, is to impose a turnout threshold of 50 per cent. If turnout falls below that level, the contest begins anew. Such conditions were common in communist states, where the party could dragoon electors to the polls, but are dangerous in free elections. In the winter of 2002/03, Serbia and Montenegro each experienced two failed presidential elections for this reason.

As Figure 10.2 shows, almost a third of presidents still manage to avoid the perils of direct election altogether. Many of these are chosen via **indirect election** in which a special body (which may itself be elected) supposedly acts as a buffer against the whims of the people. In the United States, for example, the Electoral College is still technically used to elect an incoming president. Today, the college survives only as a procedural and pre-democratic relic mandated by the constitution. Delegates still assemble but, with the odd exception, they conscientiously follow the verdict of the state they represent.

Indirect election occurs when office-holders are elected by a body which has itself been chosen by a wider constituency. The device is employed in many presidential elections and for upper houses of parliament.

Three other features of presidential elections are worthy of note: the length of term, the possibility of re-election and the link with other elections. On the first point, the presidential term is sometimes longer, and is normally no shorter, than that served by members of the legislature. The longer the term, the easier it is for presidents to adopt a broad perspective free from the immediate burden of re-election. At just four years, the term of office of American presidents is unusually short. The danger is that year one is spent acquiring experience and year four campaigning, leaving only the middle years as a phase of accomplishment.

Second, term limits are often imposed, restricting the incumbent to just one or two periods in office (Box 10.2 on p. 198). The fear is that without such constraints presidents will be able to exploit their unique position in order to try to remain in office too long. Thus, the USA introduced a two-term limit after Franklin Roosevelt won four elections in

COUNTRY PROFILE

UNITED STATES

Form of government ■ a presidential republic comprising a federation of 50 states.

Legislature ■ the 435-member House of Representatives is the lower house. The 100-member Senate contains two directly elected senators from each state. The two chambers form the Congress – the world's most powerful legislature.

Executive ■ the president (who can serve a maximum of two four-year terms) is supported by a massive apparatus, including the Executive Office of the President and the White House Office. However, the Cabinet is far less significant than in parliamentary systems. Despite administrative support, presidents experience difficulty in getting their way on domestic issues, with federal agencies and Congress offering resistance.

Judiciary ■ the Supreme Court heads a dual system of federal and state courts. This nine-member body can nullify laws and actions running counter to the constitution. Many political issues are resolved through the courts.

Electoral system ■ the USA is one of the few large countries still employing the plurality method. The president is elected indirectly through an electoral college. As in 2000, a candidate who wins the key states may be elected through this college even though he comes second in the popular vote. Reelection rates in Congress are exceptionally high.

Party system ■ the Democratic and Republican parties show great resilience, despite periodic threats from third parties. The survival of the major parties reflects ideological flexibility, an entrenched position in law and the bias of plurality elections against minor parties.

Population (annual growth rate): 298.4m (+0.9%)
World Bank income group: high income
Political Rights score: 1
Civil Liberties score: 1
Human development index (rank/out of): 8/177
Freedom of the press index (rank/out of): 24/194
Ease of doing business index (rank/out of): 3/175

Note: For meaning and sources of scales and indexes, see p. xvi. In all cases a score and rank of 1 is 'best'.

With the end of the Cold War, the **UNITED STATES** became the world's one remaining superpower. This unique status is based partly on the country's hard power: a large population, the ability to project military force anywhere and a dynamic economy. Yet America's soft power is also significant. Its leading position in the media, medical, technology and telecommunications sectors is underpinned by a strong base in science and university education while its culture, brand names and language have universal appeal.

Yet hardly had commentators begun to refer to the emergence of an American 'empire' than the global reputation of the United States underwent a massive decline (Pew Global Attitudes Project, 2006):

- The assault on Iraq in 2003 was widely condemned even before it became bogged down in confrontations with insurgents
- The country's continuing failure to lead on environmental issues represented dereliction of its global duty
- Images of the initial reaction to Hurricane Katrina in 2005 reminded the world not just of poverty within the USA but also of its racial base

For the foreseeable future, though, the internal politics of the United States will remain of vital interest. Domestically, the world's No.1 operates a political system intended to frustrate decisive policy-making. By constitutional design, power is divided between federal and state governments. The centre is itself fragmented between the executive, legislature and judiciary. American politics is extraordinarily pluralistic; reforms are more easily blocked by interest groups than carried through by the executive.

The president, the only official elected by a national constituency, finds his plans obstructed by a legislature which is the most powerful, and among the most decentralized, in the world. In normal times, Washington politics is a ceaseless quest for that small amount of common ground on which all interests can agree. The president may lead the world but the separation of powers mean that in domestic politics even the country's chief executive is a supplicant before Congress.

Further reading: Bardes, Shelley and Schmidt (2006), McKay (2005), Peele *et al.* (2006).

SPOTLIGHT

Elections in the United States

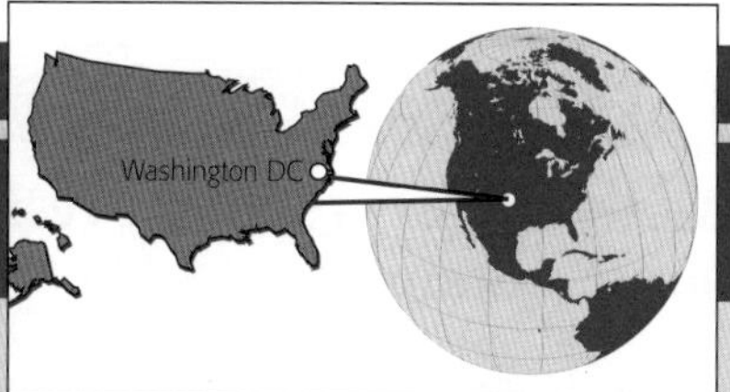

The United States is unique in its massive range of elected offices. At federal level, Americans can vote for the president and vice president, two senators per state and their member of the House of Representatives. But a much larger range is subject to election at state and local level. These posts include auditors, judges, members of school boards, sheriffs, treasurers and, in North Dakota, the soil conservation supervisor. So why does the USA possess so many elected officers? And how successful has its national experiment with appointment through election proved to be?

The exceptional array of elected posts in the USA reflects not just the practical requirements of governing a large, frontier society but also a culture that emphasizes equality, competence and a belief that administration is a practical matter. The task of those elected was, and is, to get the job done.

America also played a pioneering role in extending the franchise for white men. As early as 1830, just 40 years after ratification of the constitution, property qualifications for voting had been withdrawn and nearly all states selected members of the Electoral College by direct popular ballot. In addition, traditions of direct democracy live on. Images of town meetings in New England form part of the political culture while most western states still employ some direct democratic devices such as the referendum, initiative and recall. Further, reforms to the distinctly American institution of primary elections have opened up the selection of a party's candidates to a remarkably wide proportion of the population.

Yet American experience with elections is far from an unconditional celebration of democracy. Southern blacks were effectively denied the vote until the Voting Rights Act of 1965. The log cabin to White House ideal is widely accepted but money is increasingly necessary, though insufficient, for electoral success. The constitution does not allow national referendums. In many elections, advertising by interest groups overwhelms the candidates' voices.

The many confusions of the 2000 presidential election (including the fact that more electors voted for Al Gore than for George W. Bush) hardly contributed to the authority with which the eventual winner entered the White House. This election also drew attention once more to the fact that under the cumbersome Electoral College procedure, American presidents are still not elected by a direct national ballot.

In addition, turnout remains low. In 1992 and 1996, Bill Clinton was supported by under a quarter of the adult population. Not since Richard Nixon in 1972 has any president been elected with the support of more than a third of the population.

However, a technical comment is needed here. American turnout figures are based on the adult population rather than the registered voters. In 2004, for example, about 20 million prisoners and immigrants were ineligible to vote. If those exclusions (and the partial offset provided by three million overseas voters) are taken into account, estimated turnout in the presidential election goes up by five points to a more respectable 60 per cent.

Figure 10.3 Turnout at American presidential elections, 1948–2004

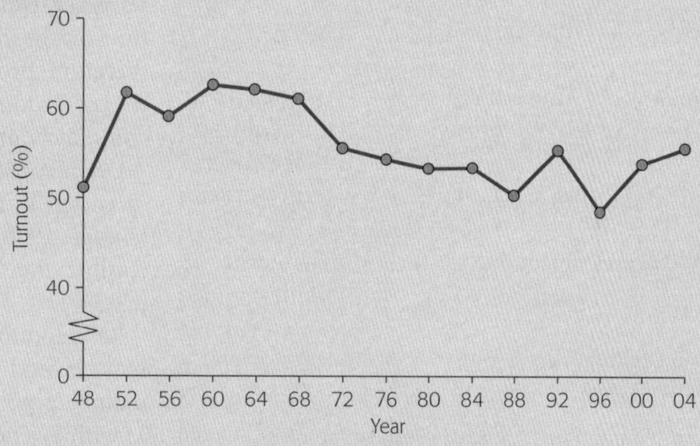

Note: Base is population of voting age.

Source: Adapted from McKay (2005), table 6.2.

Sources and further reading: Bardes, Shelley and Schmidt (2006), Flanigan and Zingale (2005), Wood (1993).

BOX 10.2

Methods for electing presidents: some examples

	Method of election	Term (years)	Re-election permitted?
Argentina	Electoral college	6	After one term out
Brazil	Run-off	5	After one term out
Finland	Plurality	6	Yes
France	Run-off	5*	Yes
Mexico	Plurality	6	No
Russia	Run-off	5	One term out required after two terms served
United States	Electoral college	4	Two-term limit

* Reduced from seven years by constitutional amendment in 2000.

Source: Adapted from Jones (1995b). *See also*: Nurmi and Nurmi (2002).

a row between 1932 and 1944. Mexican presidents (like the deputies in the country's parliament) cannot stand for re-election.

As with many institutional fixes, term limits solve one problem at the cost of creating others. Clearly, a president who cannot be re-elected is no longer directly accountable to the voters. Also, lame-duck presidents lose clout as their term nears its end. And popular presidents, replete with confidence and experience, may be debarred from office at the peak of their careers.

Third, the timing of presidential elections is also important. When these contests occur alongside elections to the assembly, the successful candidate is more likely to be drawn from the same party as dominates the legislature. Without threatening the separation of powers, concurrent elections limit fragmentation, increasing the chance that congress will support the president's plans (Jones, 1995a). This thinking lay behind the reduction of the French president's term to five years in 2000, the same tenure as the assembly.

Referendums

Elections are instruments of representative democracy; the role of the people is only to decide who will decide. By contrast, referendums, and similar devices such as the initiative and the recall, are devices of direct democracy, enabling voters to decide issues themselves. A *refer*endum involves a *refer*ence from another body, normally the legislature or the government, to the people. The device therefore provides a practical counter-example to the common argument that direct democracy is completely impossible in large states.

Further, technology has opened up the possibility of voting in referendums through electronic means (Budge, 1996). E-democracy has become technically feasible; the question now is whether it is politically prudent.

Referendums vary in their status. Their outcome may be binding, as with constitutional amendments requiring popular approval, or merely consultative, as with Sweden's vote in 1994 on membership of the European Union. A binding referendum will normally be triggered automatically under the constitution whereas a consultative referendum is typically an option for a hesitant government.

In a few countries (now including New Zealand), referendums can also be initiated by citizen petition, a device extending popular influence to the political agenda itself. The initiative, as such citizen-initiated ballots are known, is used widely in Switzerland where 100,000 electors can propose a new law or an amendment to the constitution. The initiative has also been adopted by many western states in the USA, notably California. For instance, Proposition 13 in 1978 limited property taxes in the state, launching a sequence of taxpayers' revolts.

We should note two unusual forms of the initiative. First, Italy uses what has become known as the abrogative referendum. Five regional councils or 500,000 electors can initiate a popular vote but only on whether to repeal an existing law. So, unlike normal initiatives, the abrogative referendum does not permit the people to raise fresh issues but it does provide a check on unpopular laws, thus discouraging governments from passing them in the first place (Qvortrup, 2005, p. 136).

Second, some 15 American states make provision for recall elections. These are ballots held on whether an elected official should be removed from office during normal tenure. A vote is initiated by a petition signed by a minimum proportion (typically, 25 per cent) of the votes cast for that office at the previous election. Originally designed as a weapon against corrupt politicians, the recall has rarely been used.

However, a ballot to recall Democratic Governor Gray Davis did take place in California in 2003, following a petition by more than one million registered voters. This recall election allowed numerous Republican candidates (including Arnold Schwarzenegger, the eventual victor) to stand as a potential replacement for Davis without going through the extensive vetting needed to win a party nomination for an ordinary gubernatorial election.

Referendums are growing in frequency. Most referendums held in the twentieth century occurred after 1960 and most liberal democracies held at least one referendum in the final quarter of the century (LeDuc, 2002). Switzerland headed the list, holding referendums on such issues as:

- Abandoning nuclear power;
- Constructing new Alpine railways;
- Joining the United Nations;
- Registering same-sex partnerships;
- Limiting immigration;
- Reducing working hours;
- Restricting car use on Sundays.

However, few countries have made more than occasional use of the device and the American federal constitution makes no provision for national referendums.

What is the contribution of referendums to democracy and governance? How desirable is it to transform citizens into legislators? On the plus side, referendums do seem to increase voters' understanding of the issue, their confidence in their own political abilities and their faith in government responsiveness (Bowler and Donovan, 2002). Like elections themselves, referendums help to educate the participants.

Referendums can also inform the politicians. For instance, the rejection of the proposed European constitutional treaty by French and Dutch voters in referendums held in 2005 informed the pro-European elements within the political elite that national electorates had grown weary of grand European projects.

But there are also reasons for caution. A surfeit of referendums can tire the voters, depressing turnout. By its nature, the referendum treats an issue in an isolated way, ignoring the implications for other areas. What would happen, for instance, if the electorate decided both to raise teachers' salaries and to lower taxes? At the same time, voters' judgements are often informed by wider considerations than the specific proposition on the ballot. 'The answer was "Non" but what was the question?' asked one analyst after the French rejection of the European treaty in

BOX 10.3

The referendum, initiative and recall

Referendum	a vote of the electorate on an issue of public policy such as a constitutional amendment. The vote may be binding or consultative.
Initiative	a procedure which allows a certain number of citizens (typically around 10 per cent in American states) to initiate a referendum on a given topic.
Recall	allows a certain number of voters to demand a referendum on whether an elected official should be removed from office.

Sources: Bowler *et al.* (1998), Cronin (1989).

2005 (Ivaldi, 2006). Further, voters are often reluctant to embrace change, turning referendums into instruments of conservatism as much as democracy (Kobach, 1997).

Despite their democratic credentials, the outcome of consultative referendums can be influenced by government control of timing. In 1997 the British government only held a referendum in Wales on its devolution proposals after a similar vote in Scotland, where support for devolution was known to be firmer. In 2003, Eastern European countries began a sequence of referendums on joining the EU in Hungary, judging that a positive result there would influence the outcome in other candidate states where public opinion was more sceptical. The plan worked: all the accession countries holding referendums voted in favour.

More crudely, rulers can simply ignore the result of a referendum. In 1955, Swedes voted decisively to continue driving on the left; the country now drives on the right. A quarter of a century later, Swedes voted to decommission their nuclear power stations; almost twenty years passed before the first reactor closed. Alternatively, a referendum can be repeated until the desired outcome is obtained. Ireland, for instance, only ratified the Nice Treaty on the European Union in 2002, at the second time of asking.

In addition to these difficulties, referendums can easily be hijacked by:

- Wealthy companies waging expensive referendum campaigns on issues in which they have an economic interest;
- Government control over wording as well as timing;
- Intense minorities seeking reforms to which the majority is indifferent.

The main benefit of referendums is to provide a double safety valve. First, a referendum allows governments to put an issue to the people when for some reason it is incapable of reaching a decision itself. Like a plumber's drain-rods, referendums resolve blockages. Second, where the initiative and the recall are permitted, aggrieved citizens can use these devices to raise issues and criticisms that might otherwise go unheard. In these ways, referendums supplement rather than supplant representative democracy (Qvortrup, 2005).

Turnout

Despite rising education, turnout is falling throughout most of the democratic world. In 19 liberal democracies, turnout declined on average by 10 per cent between the 1950s and the 1990s (Wattenberg, 2000). Figure 10.4 shows the trend for one high-turnout country (Sweden), one traditionally middle-turnout country (United Kingdom), and one low-turnout country (Switzerland). The pattern is clear, with the fall concentrated in the 1990s. In many countries, abstainers are now the majority at regional and local contests.

It is possible that the main fall in turnout has already taken place, at least for national contests. As the figure shows, participation increased modestly at recent elections in Switzerland and the United Kingdom. In the USA, too, turnout among the adult population recovered in the closer elections of 2000 and 2004. But for now, prudence suggests that we should regard low turnout as a continuing issue.

Why the fall? Precisely because the phenomenon is so widespread, it is difficult to pinpoint exact causes. However, the decline surely forms part of a wider trend in the democratic world: namely, a growing distance between voters, on the one hand, and parties and government, on the other. It is surely no coincidence that turnout has reduced as **partisan dealignment** has gathered pace, as party member-

Figure 10.4 Turnout at parliamentary elections, 1970–2005

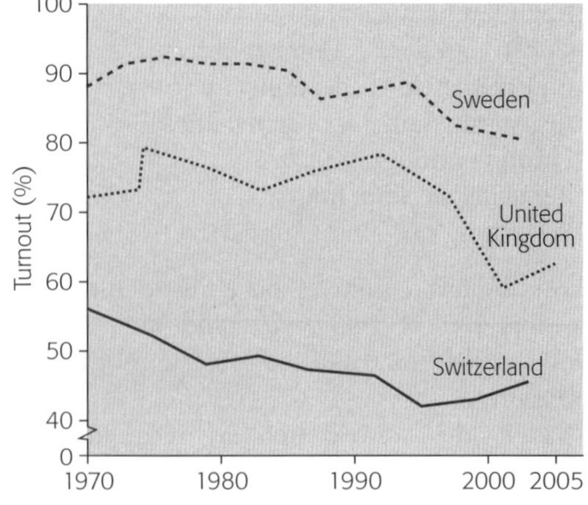

Source: IDEA (2004).

> **Partisan dealignment** refers to the weakening of bonds between (a) electors and parties, and (b) social groups and parties.

ship has fallen and as the class and religious cleavages which sustained party loyalties in the early post-war decades have decayed.

Franklin (2002, p. 174) links the decline of turnout to the diminishing significance of elections. He suggests that the success of many democracies in establishing welfare states and achieving full employment in the post-war era resolved long-standing conflicts between capital and labour. With class conflict disarmed, electors possessed fewer incentives to come out and vote on election day. As Franklin writes, 'Elections in recent years may show lower turnout for the simple reason that these elections decide issues of lesser importance than elections did in the late 1950s'.

Declining satisfaction with the performance of democratic governments has also played its part (Norris, 1999a). Especially in the 1980s, popular trust in government and parties fell in many democracies, reflecting the growing complexity, internationalization and perhaps corruption of governance. Even though mass support for democratic principles remains strong, rising cynicism about government performance has probably encouraged more people to stay away from the polls (Putnam *et al.*, 2000).

Turnout varies not just over time but also between countries. How then can we explain these cross-national difference in turnout? Here a cost-benefit analysis is useful (Downs, 1957). Turnout tends to be higher in those countries where the costs or effort of voting are low and the perceived benefits high (Box 10.4). On the cost side, turnout is reduced when the citizen is required to take the initiative in registering as an elector, as in the USA. It is also lower when electors must vote in person and during a weekday. So voting can be encouraged by allowing voting at the weekend, in advance, by proxy and by mail (Blais, Dobrzynska and Massicotte, 2003). By contrast, experiments at reducing the effort involved in casting a ballot – and attempting to refresh the image of elections – by allowing e-voting over the internet and through mobile communications have not so far met with great success. Along with mail and proxy voting, these solutions also raise security concerns (Norris, 2004b).

BOX 10.4

Features of the political system and of individuals which increase turnout

Features of the political system

- Compulsory voting
- Automatic registration
- Voting by post and by proxy permitted
- Advance voting permitted
- Weekend polling
- Election decides who governs*
- Cohesive parties
- Proportional representation
- Close result anticipated

Features of individuals

- Middle aged
- Strong party loyalty
- Extensive education
- Attends church
- Belongs to a union
- Higher income
- Voted in previous elections

* Examples of elections which do *not* decide who governs are those to the American Congress and the European parliament.

Sources: Blais, Dobrzynska and Massicotte (2003), Endersby, Petrocik and Shaw (2006), Franklin (2002, 2004), IDEA (2006).

On the benefit side, both election significance and vote significance contribute to higher turnout (Horiuchi, 2004). On the former, the more important the election, and the more cohesive the parties, the greater the turnout. On the latter, the greater the impact of a single vote, the more willing voters are to incur the costs of voting. Thus, proportional representation enhances participation because each ballot affects the outcome. A comparative study of turnout between 1945 and 2000 found that participation was, on average, six points higher among countries employing party list PR than in those states using the plurality method (IDEA, 2006).

DEBATE

SHOULD VOTING BE COMPULSORY?

As turnout declines across most of the democratic world, so attention focuses on potential solutions. Technical fixes, such as locating polling stations in supermarkets and permitting voting by e-mail, may have some role to play. Countries using plurality or majority voting could also boost turnout by introducing proportional representation, in which every vote counts. But has the time come to consider the most effective solution of all: compulsory voting?

YES

Most citizens acknowledge obligations to the state such as paying taxes, serving on juries and even fighting in war. So why should they reject what Hill (2002) calls the 'light obligation and undemanding duty' of voting at national elections? Currently, abstainers take a free ride on the efforts of the conscientious.

By definition, an election based on a full turnout would be representative of the whole population, creating greater political equality. It would enhance the authority of the government, a collective benefit.

If required to vote, disengaged groups such as the young and ethnic minorities would be drawn into the political process, strengthening knowledge, citizenship and community.

As with military service, people who object on principle to participating could be exempted. Also, the requirement could just be to cast a ballot, not necessarily to fill it out. Alternatively, the ballot could include an 'against all' option, as in Russia.

Further, the mere existence of compulsory voting would provide sufficient incentive to participate without any great need to punish non-voters. Compulsory voting brings a high turnout in Australia, even though the fine is a mere $20 if the abstainer fails to provide a satisfactory explanation for absence.

Finally, mandatory voting is neither rare nor new. It is practised in over 20 states and has existed in Belgium from 1892, Argentina from 1914 and Australia from 1924. Few problems are reported; compulsory voting works.

NO

Mandatory voting denies the liberty which is an essential part of liberal democracy. Requiring people to participate is a sign of an authoritarian regime, not a democracy. Paying taxes and fighting in battle are duties where every little helps, and where numbers matter. However, elections in all democracies still attract more than enough votes on which to base a decision.

Requiring a vote from those with least knowledge and interest would lower the quality of choice, as shown by the high number of invalid ballots when voting is required. Further, the law should be enforced, otherwise the reputation of the entire legal system would suffer.

Turnout in some countries with compulsory voting

Country	Turnout (%)	Invalid votes (%)
Australia	94.6	5.8
Belgium	91.6	5.5
Turkey	79.4	3.9
Brazil	68.9	8.3
Greece	76.4	2.2

Note: Year of election is 2002–04. For comparison, invalid votes were 1.6 per cent in the German election of 2005, at which voting was optional.
Source: ARC (2006).

The real task is to attract people back to the polls of their own volition. In any case, why worry? Perhaps non-voting just reflects contentment. Krauthammer (1990) claims that 'low voter turnout means that people see politics as quite marginal to their lives, as neither salvation nor ruin. That is healthy'.

ASSESSMENT

Compulsory voting does make a difference: when the Netherlands made voting optional in 1970, turnout fell considerably (Andeweg and Irwin, 2002, p. 74). However, introducing mandatory voting where it does not previously exist has rarely been tried in recent times. The danger is that the reform would backfire, increasing political distrust between government and governed. When a Swedish minister floated the possibility in 1999, the reaction was negative. There is surely a case for testing other turnout-enhancing reforms first.

Further reading
Franklin (2004), Gratschew (2004), Hill (2002), van Deth (2000).

However, a closely fought contest at national and even local level will stimulate people to turn out even in a plurality system. In the British election of 2005, the average turnout in marginal seats was 67 per cent, compared to just 57 per cent in safe seats (Curtice, Fisher and Steed, 2005, p. 249). When electors feel their vote is wasted, they are more likely to stay at home.

Explicit get out the vote (GOTV) campaigns can make a difference but the key finding here is that 'a personal approach to mobilizing voters is generally more effective than an impersonal approach' (Green and Gerber, 2004, p. 9). We should also mention the unconventional lottery experiment conducted in Bulgaria in 2005. Fearing that low turnout among young voters might damage its prospects, the governing party arranged for electors who cast their ballot to be able to send in a text message and be entered into an official raffle. The prizes on offer, valued at more than a million dollars in total, included a car, holidays and televisions. Turnout improved but the ruling party still lost.

At the level of the individual, variations in turnout reflect the pattern found with other forms of political participation. Specifically, high turnout reflects political resources and political interest. Thus, educated, affluent, married, middle-aged citizens with a job and a strong party identification, who belong to a church or a trade union, and are long-term residents of a neighbourhood, are particularly prone to vote. By contrast, abstention is most frequent among poorly educated, unemployed young single men belonging to no organizations, lacking party ties and newly moved to their current address (Box 10.4).

Turnout decline tends to be led by the youngest cohort; lowering the voting age to 18 has reduced the turnout rate even as it has increased the absolute number of voters (Franklin, 2004). Minorities are also particularly likely to abstain. Hispanics formed ten per cent of the American population but provided only four per cent of the voters in the American presidential election of 2000 (Conway, 2001, p. 81).

Attempts to boost turnout must therefore be sensitive to political realities. Conservative parties have reason to be cautious about such schemes, given their assumption (which is plausible if rarely directly substantiated) that abstainers would vote disproportionately for the left. Increased participation may benefit the system as a whole but impact unequally on the players within it, thus delaying or preventing reform.

Voting behaviour

Given that voters have a choice, how do they decide who to vote for? Although this is the most intensively studied question in all political science, there is no single answer. As a summary, however, we can suggest that since the 1960s electors in the established liberal democracies have moved away from group and party voting towards voting on issues, the economy, leaders and party competence. Franklin (1992) describes this process as 'the decline of cleavage politics and the rise of issue voting'.

For two decades after the Second World War, most studies of electoral behaviour disputed the intuitive proposition that voters do 'choose' which party to support. An influential theory of electoral choice, originally developed in the United States in the 1950s, argued that voting was an act of affirmation rather than choice (Campbell *et al.*, 1960). Voting was seen as an expression of loyalty to a party, a commitment which was both deep-seated and long-lasting.

In the USA, **party identification** was confirmed by the traditional requirement to register as a party's supporter in order to be eligible to vote in its primaries. In this way, American electors learned to think of themselves as Democrats, Republicans or, in a minority of cases, as Independents. This view of American voters as habitual supporters of a particular party is called the socialization or party-identification model.

The pattern in Europe was slightly different. Here voting expressed loyalty to a social group and only indirectly to the party representing it. The act of voting flowed from identification with a particular religion, class or ethnic group. Thus electors thought

Party identification is a long-term attachment to a particular party which anchors voters' interpretations of the remote world of politics. Party identification is often inherited through the family and reinforced by the elector's social milieu (for example, colleagues at work).

of themselves as Catholic or Protestant, middle class or working class; and they voted for parties which explicitly stood for these interests. In short, party choice was anchored in social identity.

But whether the emphasis was placed on identification with the party (as in the USA) or with the social group (as in Europe), voting was viewed as a reflex, not a choice. The electoral 'decision' was an ingrained habit which, once acquired, was unlikely to change over a voter's lifetime. These loyalties helped to account for the stability of parties in the early post-war decades.

However, models of party and group voting had become less useful by the 1970s. The 1960s and 1970s were decades of partisan dealignment. The ties which once bound voters, social groups and political parties together began to loosen. By the 1990s, the proportion of party identifiers had declined still further (Box 10.5). However, party loyalties have reduced in strength but they have not disappeared; electorates are dealigning rather than dealigned (indeed, as Stonecash (2005) argues, partisan conflict in the United States has recently intensified, stimulating a modest recovery of partisanship).

BOX 10.5

Decline in party identification, 1970s–1990s

Decline over 10%	Decline of 1–10%	No decline
Austria	Australia	Belgium
Canada	Finland	Denmark
France	Japan	
Germany	Netherlands	
Ireland	New Zealand	
Italy	Norway	
Sweden	United Kingdom	
USA		

Note: Figures are based on a standard survey question asking people whether they 'think of themselves' as, for example, a Democrat or a Republican. Decline is measured between an initial survey (1967–78, depending on country) and a later survey (1991–98).
Sources: Bentley *et al.*, (2000), Dalton and Wattenberg (2000).

What caused this general weakening in party loyalties? One factor was political: the decay was not uniform but tended to be focused on periods of disillusionment with governing parties. In the USA, for instance, the fall of party identification was sharpest during the period of the Vietnam War and the associated student protests.

A broader factor precipitating party dealignment was the diminishing capacity of social cleavages to fashion electoral choice. In Europe, class and religious identities became less relevant to young, well-educated people living in urban, mobile and more secular societies. Class voting, in particular, declined throughout the democratic world, allowing Dalton (2002b, p. 193) to conclude that 'class-based voting . . . currently has limited influence in structuring voting choices'. New divisions, such as that between employees in the public and private sectors, cut across rather than reinforced the traditional class cleavage (Knutsen, 2001). Television – more neutral and leader-centred than the press – also weakened old commitments.

The consequences of dealignment have proved to be substantial. Much of the democratic world has witnessed the emergence of new parties such as the Greens. Turnout, and active participation in campaigns, has fallen. Electoral volatility has expanded, split-ticket voting has increased and more electors are deciding how to vote closer to election day. Also, candidates and leaders seem to have grown in electoral importance somewhat relative to the parties they represent (Dalton *et al.*, 2000).

However, in none of these areas have we witnessed a complete transformation. In most democracies, most of the time, most electors still go to the polls to support the same party for which they have always voted. Most campaigns still witness only modest changes in party support. Dealignment, we should remind ourselves, refers to the weakening of existing patterns but not to their disappearance (non-alignment) or replacement (realignment).

The decay of group and party voting has led political scientists to focus on the question of how voters do now decide. The contemporary emphasis is on four factors: political issues, the economy, party leaders and party image. Fiorina's account (1981) of **retrospective voting** captures many of these themes. From Fiorina's perspective, a vote is no longer an expression of a lifelong commitment. Rather it is a piece of business like any other. The elector asks of the government, 'what have you done for me (and the country) lately?'. Party identification is no longer a lens through which to view the political world but just a running tally of how well different parties are judged to have performed in office. The electoral decision becomes an act of calculation rather than affirmation.

Retrospective voting helps to explain why economic conditions, particularly disposable income, unemployment and inflation, seem to have such a consistent impact on the popularity of governments (Hibbs, 2006). More voters now proceed on the brutal assumption that governments should be punished for bad times and perhaps also rewarded for economic advance. Especially where a single party forms the government, more voters are happy to judge by results; they are now fairweather supporters. The feel-good factor, however, is not just a matter of objective economic performance; voters' perceptions of the economy are the key battleground and here politicians have some room for manoeuvre.

In the current era of pragmatism, electors assess the general competence of parties. Increasingly, they ask not just what a party proposes to do but also how well it will do it. Given that parties are less rooted in ideology and social groups than in the past, their reputation for competence in meeting the unpredictable demands of office becomes a crucial marketing asset. So party image becomes vital, especially for opposition parties which do not have a record in government to brandish. The skill is to generate trust in one's own side and to cast doubt on the opposition's capacity to govern. Given volatile and sceptical voters, gaining credibility – or at least more than one's opponents – is the cardinal objective (Bowler and Farrell, 1992).

Retrospective voting means casting one's ballot in response to government performance. The phrase was introduced by Fiorina (1981); it tells us much about electoral choice in an age of dealignment.

Elections in authoritarian states

A few authoritarian regimes, including several ruling families in the Middle East, dispense with elections altogether, either because they do not have assemblies or because members are appointed by the king. However, most non-democratic rulers recognize that elections can be a useful fiction (Liddle, 1996). Elections satisfy international donors who are often happy enough if just the façade is democratic. We begin this section by looking at elections in totalitarian states before turning to their somewhat more subtle role in authoritarian regimes.

Elections in totalitarian regimes did not make much pretence of offering choice. There was no possibility that the ruling party could be defeated or even opposed through elections. In the Soviet Union, for instance, the official candidate was simply presented to the electorate for ritual endorsement, just as God presented Eve to Adam and said, 'now choose your wife'. In the Soviet case, any competition was for the nomination, not the election. Campaigns themselves were grim, ritualistic events, irrelevant to the real politics taking place within the party. They were little more than an opportunity for the party's agitators to lecture the population on the party's achievements (Zaslavsky and Brym, 1978).

The voting act itself discouraged dissent. In Mao's China, voting took place in public. In some other communist states, voters who wanted to accept the party's choice could just place their ballot in the box whereas those who wanted to mark their ballot had to move, under the watchful eye of an official, to a special area. In such biased conditions, most votes really did go to the communist candidate even if the margin of victory was sometimes exaggerated when the results were announced.

Some communist states did introduce a measure of choice to their elections by allowing a choice of candidates from within the ruling party. These controlled candidate-choice contests were characteristic of Eastern Europe in communism's later phase of the 1970s and 1980s. Central rulers found candidate-choice elections useful in testing whether local party officials retained the confidence of their communities.

This is one reason for the gradual introduction of such elections to many of China's 930,000 villages since 1987 and, more recently and tentatively, to some townships. Elected village committees help to build state capacity in a country where power has traditionally operated on a personal basis. However, even in contemporary China no explicit opposition to the party's policy platform is permitted. In many villages, real authority still resides with the local party official, who may in any case also serve as chair of the village committee. A revision to the election law in 1997 explicitly affirmed the supervisory role of the party. Neither in the countryside nor the towns are there signs of elections threatening the party's control.

Elections in authoritarian rather than totalitarian regimes exhibit a different character. Here, competition is constrained rather than eliminated. Some opposition victories may be permitted but too few to affect the overall result. Independent candidates find themselves operating in a threatening environment. The secret police follow them around, breaking up some of their meetings. Independent politicians may be banned from standing or subject to harassment if elected. Control over the media, the electoral system and the government is exploited to favour the ruling party. Through its conduct of campaigns, the regime projects both the illusion of choice and the realities of power, securing its victory without needing to falsify the count (though this option remains if all else fails).

Egypt provides an example of such processes. Since 1976, numerous parties have competed for seats in the People's Assembly, offering the appearance of a vigorous multi-party system. But the National Democratic Party (NPD), led by President Gamal Mubarak, has retained its dominant position throughout. Lesch (2004, p. 605) outlines the mechanisms employed:

- The Law of Political Parties (1977) requires new parties to be approved by the regime, which is dominated by the NPD itself;
- The Public Prosecutor must approve all candidates standing for election;
- Opposition poll watchers are often refused entry to polling places or arrested beforehand;
- The security forces sometimes bar electors lacking NDP-issued voting cards from entering the polling station;
- The assembly rejects challenges to the fairness of the election.

Elections in illiberal democracies

In an illiberal democracy, elections play a more important part in confirming the legitimacy of the ruler. The election outcome is more than just a routine acceptance by the people of the realities of power. Explicit vote-rigging is avoided, some candidates from non-governing parties are elected and the possibility of defeat cannot be entirely ruled out. Even so, elections do not operate on as free and fair a playing field as in a liberal democracy. In particular, the leading figure dominates media coverage, using television to trumpet his often real achievements in office. The emphasis is as much on the carrot (providing reasons for voting for the dominant figure) as on the stick (threatening opposition supporters).

Incumbents seeking re-election can exploit unique resources. These include unparalleled visibility built over time and easy access to television. In addition, they can draw on the state's coffers for their campaign, implement a favourable electoral system, and call in political credits carefully acquired while in office. Anticipating the president's re-election, underlings will seek to help the campaign along while credible opponents are deterred from embarking on a hopeless cause.

In lower-income countries, patronage networks based on the leader's control of government provide a vote-gathering resource unavailable to the opposition. These networks are often supported by a culture which is sympathetic to rewarding the 'big man' with another term in office. As Bratton (1998, p. 65) notes, 'In a "big man" political culture, it is unclear whether the re-election of an incumbent constitutes the extension of a leader's legitimacy or the resignation of the electorate to his inevitable dominance'. Africa still provides several examples where former dictators and military leaders have made the transition to an illiberal democracy, quickly mastering the arts of winning elections using patrimonial techniques similar to those employed in the pre-democratic era. Through such devices, a favourable result is manufactured before election day, so that the growing army of independent monitors may not detect many if any irregularities during the ballot itself (Santa-Cruz, 2005).

Vladimir Putin proved to be a skilled exponent of these techniques in ensuring victory in both the parliamentary elections in Russia in 2003 and his own re-election in the presidential contest the following year. McFaul (2005) describes how Putin moved early to neutralize potential threats in three main areas: the media, the regions and business. In each sector, a few opponents were despatched, yielding the desired servility among the remainder. McFaul's summary of the Russian president's strategy could be applied to election management in many other illiberal democracies:

> The effect of these reforms occurred well before the votes were actually cast. The absence of independence within media, regional elite and oligarchic ranks reduced the freedom to manoeuvre for opposition political parties and candidates. At the same time, the state's larger role gave incumbents enormous advantages, be it national television coverage, massive administrative support from regional executives or enormous financial resources from companies like Gazprom (McFaul, 2005, p. 77).

Such techniques presuppose weaknesses in the rule of law, the market economy and civil society in general. These deficits are not easy to measure: 'in an age of images and symbols', writes Zakaria (2003, p. 156), 'elections are easy to capture on film. But how do you televise the rule of law?'. But it is precisely such constraints on candidates that justify the distinction between elections in illiberal democracies such as Russia and those in liberal democracies such as the USA, even though American incumbents – like Russian presidents – also secure more media attention, political backing, financial support and electoral success than their challengers.

Learning Resources for Chapter 10

Next step

LeDuc, Niemi and Norris (2002b) provide an excellent comparative study of elections and voting, reviewing a wide literature.

Further reading

On electoral systems, Farrell (2001) provides a clear introduction. Colomer (2004a) and Gallagher and Mitchell (2005) offer comparative collections. Shugart and Wattenberg (2000) look at mixed systems specifically and Norris (2004a) examines the impact of electoral systems on party systems. Dalton and Wattenberg (2000) is a comparative study of voting trends; Franklin (2004) performs the same task for turnout; IDEA (2006) adds practical suggestions. For the impact of campaigns, see Brady and Johnston (2006) and Farrell and Schmitt-Beck (2002). King (2002) examines the influence of leaders' personalities specifically. On referendums, consider Mendelsohn and Parkin (2001) and Qvortrup (2005).

Internet sources

Inter-Parliamentary Union
The PARLINE database provides election results.
http://www.ipu.org

IFES
Supports the building of democratic societies.
http://www.ifes.org/

Center for Voting and Democracy
'Promotes voter turnout, fair representation, inclusive policy and meaningful electoral choices in the USA.'
http://www.fairvote.org/

International Institute for Democracy and Electoral Assistance (IDEA)
Supports sustainable democracy worldwide. An informative site with a practical focus.
http://www.idea.int/

Chapter 11
Interest groups

Interest groups, like political parties, are a major channel of communication between society and government, espaecially in liberal democracies. Both groups and parties represent their concerns upwards, though many groups pursue more specialized interests than the broad agendas followed by the major parties. Interest groups are distinguished from political parties by their narrower goal of seeking only to influence, without becoming, the government. Interest groups are not election-fighting organizations; instead, they typically adopt a pragmatic and often low-key approach in dealing with whatever power structure confronts them.

Although many interest groups go about their work quietly, their activity is pervasive in liberal democracies. Their staff are to be found negotiating with bureaucrats over the details of proposed regulations, pressing their case in legislative committee hearings and seeking to influence media coverage. In authoritarian regimes, however, interests are articulated in a less public, more spasmodic and sometimes more corrupt fashion. Interests are still expressed to government but often through individual firms or powerful individuals rather than through pressure groups.

From the perspective of narrow self-interest, people have no reason to join interest groups when the fruits of the group's efforts are equally available to non-members (Olson, 1968). Yet the fact is that new groups do emerge and grow. The environmental lobby, for instance, has expanded enormously in recent decades, along with many other groups pursuing their interpretation of the general interest. Agreement with the groups' goals is certainly one reason for joining a group but this reason is often combined with material or even social incentives (Box 11.1). Many an organizer comments wryly that people join as singles but leave as couples.

From a historical perspective, interest groups developed in a rather predictable way. In the West, they emerged in a series of waves formed by social change (e.g. industrialization) and the expansion of state activity (e.g. public welfare). Periods of social change raise new problems while an active government gives people more hope of gains from influencing public policy. Like many other aspects of modern politics, interest group activity is a response to the growth of public regulation.

Box 11.2 summarizes the development of interest groups in the United States. Most Western nations have followed a similar if somewhat less vigorous course, resulting in the mosaic of independent group activity found in nearly all contemporary liberal democracies.

Interest groups (also called pressure groups) are 'organizations which have some autonomy from government or political parties and which try to influence public policy' (Wilson, 1990). Examples include employers' organizations, trade unions, consumer groups, bodies representing specific industries and professions, and broader campaigning organizations seeking to promote their particular cause.

BOX 11.1

Motives for joining interest groups

	Definition	Example
Material	Tangible economic benefits	Joining a union because it offers discounted services (e.g. insurance, legal advice)
Social	Intangible benefits from joining with others	Wanting to meet like-minded people
Purposive	Agreement with the group's goals	Joining Amnesty International to further the cause of human rights

Source: Adapted from Clark and Wilson (1961), with 'social' substituted for 'solidary'.

Classifying interest groups

When we think of 'interest groups', the bodies which first come to mind are protective groups articulating the material interests of their members: for instance, trade unions, employers' organizations and professional associations (Box 11.3). Sometimes called sectional or functional groups, these protective bodies give priority to influencing government and can invoke sanctions to help them achieve their goals. Workers can go on strike; medical practitioners can refuse to cooperate with a new prescription policy. Protective groups seek selective benefits for their members and insider status with relevant government departments. Because they represent clear occupational interests, protective associations are often the most influential of all groups. They are well-established, well-connected and well-resourced.

But protective groups can also be based on local, rather than functional, interests. Geographic groups arise when the shared interests of people living in the same location are threatened by plans for, say, a new highway or a hostel for ex-convicts. Because of their negative stance – 'build it anywhere but here' – these geographical bodies are known as NIMBY groups (not in my back yard) and are often accused of following a BANANA strategy: 'build absolutely nothing anywhere near anyone'. Unlike functional organizations, NIMBY groups come and go in response to specific threats to a locality.

Protective groups are not the only type of organized interest. Indeed, many associations founded since the 1960s are promotional rather than protective. Promotional bodies advocate ideas, identities, policies and values. Also called advocacy, attitude, campaign and cause groups, promotional organizations focus on such issues as abortion, pornography and the environment. In liberal democracies, promotional groups have undoubtedly grown in number, significance and recognition by government. The increasing influence of such groups since the 1960s, especially in the United States, constitutes a major trend in interest politics. For example, Common Cause (2006) describes itself as 'a nonprofit, non-partisan citizen's lobbying organization promoting open, honest and accountable government'. Its 300,000 members and 38 state organizations are a tribute to the willingness of people to join organizations committed to the public interest.

The boundary separating protective and promotional groups is poorly defined. For example, bodies such as the women's movement and the gay lobby seek to influence public opinion and are often classified as promotional. However, their prime purpose is to promote the interests of specific groups: they are, perhaps, best viewed as protective interests employing promotional means.

BOX 11.2

Waves of interest group formation in the United States

	Description	Examples
1830–60	Founding of first national organizations	YMCA and many anti-slavery groups
1880–1900	Creation of many business and labour associations, stimulated by industrialization	National Association of Manufacturers; American Federation of Labor
1900–20	Peak period of interest group formation	Chamber of Commerce; American Medical Association
1960–80	Founding of many environmental and public interest groups	National Organization for Women; Common Cause

Source: Adapted from Hrebenar (1997), pp. 13–15.

Interest groups do not always lobby government directly. Often, protective groups join with other organizations to increase their effectiveness, forming a **peak association.** Examples include the Association of Dutch Companies-Dutch Association of Christian Employers in the Netherlands, the National Association of Manufacturers in the USA and the Confederation of British Industry in the UK (Figure 11.1). Unlike conventional groups, the members of these peaks are not individuals but firms or interest groups representing specific industries.

A **peak association** is an organization representing the broad interests of capital or labour to government. The members of peak associations are not individuals but other organizations such as firms, trade associations or labour unions.

Trade unions respond similarly: Britain's Trades Union Congress (TUC) consists of 70 affiliated unions with about 6.5 million individual members who do not themselves belong directly to the TUC. America's AFL-CIO is arranged in a similar way, with 53 affiliated unions containing nearly 9 million members.

Peak organizations seek to influence public policy and often succeed. They are attuned to national government, possess a strong research capacity and talk the language of policy. In some states, the peaks play an integral role linking government with their own members and, through them, with society.

When business and labour peak associations become centrally involved in negotiating broad policy packages (including such issues as price controls, wage increases and welfare benefits), the system is known as **corporatism** (Berger and Compston, 2002). Under corporatism, capital and labour become full social partners, working alongside government and playing a full role in implementing agreements reached. For the peaks to acquire such a position, however, they must achieve some autonomy from, as well as control over, their members. The frequency with which peak associa-

In a democratic context, **corporatism** (often called social partnership in Europe) is a relationship between the state and interest groups in which major decisions on domestic matters emerge from discussion between the government and peak associations representing the major social partners: capital and labour.

BOX 11.3

Protective and promotional groups

	Protective groups	Promotional groups
Aims	A group *of* – defends an interest	A group *for* – promotes a cause
Membership	Closed – membership is restricted	Open – anybody can join
Status	Insider – frequently consulted by government and actively seeks this role	Outsider – consulted less often by government. Emphasizes public opinion and the media
Benefits	Selective – only group members benefit	Collective – benefits go to both members and non-members
Focus	Group aims to influence national government on specific issues affecting members	Group also seeks to influence national and global bodies on broad policy matters

tions label themselves 'federations' or 'confederations', suggests such centralization is frequently lacking, especially in the English-speaking world.

With the decline of trade-union membership and large manufacturing companies, as well as the rise of pro-market thinking, traditional corporate arrangements have decayed even in those European countries such as Austria where they were once entrenched (Tálos and Kittel, 2002). However, extensive consultation – if no longer joint decision-making – continues between the peaks and government, not least in Scandinavia (Blom-Hansen, 2000). And some countries, including Ireland and the Netherlands, have even developed or revived social partnerships as a route to improved efficiency. Certainly, the political significance of peak associations continues to vary across the liberal democratic world, precluding any simple assumption of decline.

Figure 11.1 A peak association: Britain's CBI

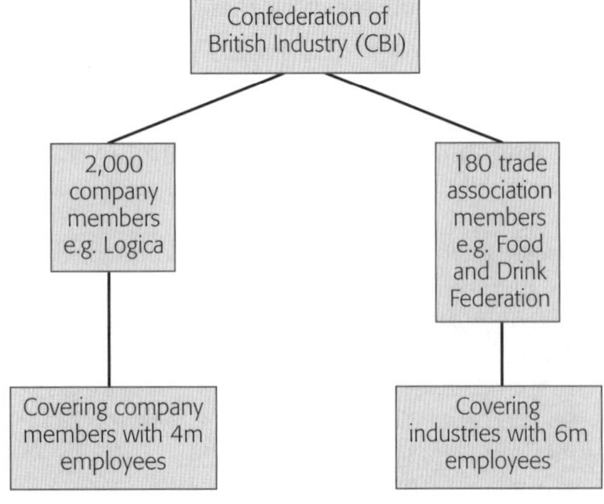

Interest groups in liberal democracies

The range and influence of modern interest groups raises awkward questions about the distribution of power in liberal democracies. Despite only representing small minorities, interest groups are deeply entrenched in policy-making, certainly more so than many supposedly 'sovereign' parliaments. Interest group activity creates a system of functional representation operating alongside electoral representation. To what extent, then, do interest groups possess power without accountability? Are interest groups, as Lowi (1969) contended, 'a corruption of democratic government'? Or does group access to policy-making simply express the right to organize in defence of specific objectives? In short, do interest groups help or hinder democracy?

Pluralism

Pluralism provides an important perspective on the role played by interest groups in liberal democracy. This American-inspired view regards competition between freely organized interest groups as a form rather than a denial of democracy. In this way, pluralism offers not merely a claim about how interest groups operate but also, and significantly, a perspective on liberal democracy itself.

In a pluralist system, the state becomes largely an arena for competition between interest groups. The groups compete for influence over a government that is willing to listen to all the voices it can hear in the political debate. The government is an arbiter, not an initiator. For Bentley (1908), an American pioneer of this approach, 'when the groups are adequately stated, everything is stated. When I say everything, I mean everything'.

> Literally 'rule by the many', **pluralism** refers to a political system in which numerous competing interest groups exert strong influence over a responsive government. The state is more umpire than player. Each group concentrates on its own area (for example education or health care) so that no single elite dominates all sectors.

All kinds of interest have their say before the court of government. Groups compete on a level playing field, with the state showing little bias either towards interests of a particular type or towards specific groups within that type. As new interests and identities emerge, groups form to represent them, quickly finding a voice in the halls of power. In a pluralist system, politics forms an open, competitive market with few barriers to entry.

Pluralism brings healthy fragmentation across the range of government activity since most interests are restricted to a single policy sector; in other words, power is non-cumulative. The influence of physicians is confined to health care; that of teachers, to education policy. Indeed the central tenet of pluralism is that no single elite dominates the entire sphere of government. Rather, different interest groups lead the way in each area of policy. Overall, pluralism depicts a wholesome process of dispersed decision-making in which the variety of groups allows government policies to reflect not just economic interests but also professional expertise.

The significance of pluralism lies in its implications for our understanding of contemporary democracy. Pluralists accept that majority rule is an insufficient (but not necessarily incorrect) account of how democracies work in practice. Rather, pluralists judge that democracy must, in reality, include a strong element of rule by minorities, each operating in a particular policy area but subject to the checks and balances of other groups operating in the same sector, with the government as broker.

Pluralists invite us to consider the proposition that for all the froth of party competition, most policy decisions emerge from discussion between government departments and interest groups, creating a system of interest representation parallel to political representation through parties and elections. At the level of detailed decisions reached by executive departments, governing parties experience mandate uncertainty; their manifesto and ideology provide little guidance. Interest groups fill the gaps.

Pluralism weighs interests rather than votes, taking account of intensity of preferences by assuming, perhaps complacently, that organized opinion will in the main be strongly held opinion. In these ways, competing interest groups become a key instrument of democracy as rule by minorities, complementing the role played by parties in a traditional reading of democracy as majority rule. The strengths of pluralistic governance are substantial. Dahl suggests that

> groups have served to educate citizens in political life, strengthened them in their relations with the state, helped to ensure that no single interest would regularly prevail on all important decisions, and, by providing information, discussion, negotiation and compromise, even helped to make public decisions more rational and more acceptable (1993, p. 706).

In addition, interest groups help to scrutinize government activity, for example by monitoring whether governments do what they say. Gordon (2005, p. 5) notes that 'because their interests are focused on the policy effects of legislative outcomes and not just the political benefits of legislation, groups have significant incentives to make sure that the policies they support are duly instituted by the executive branch'.

Pluralism remains an important perspective but many political scientists now accept that its portrayal of the relationship between groups and government is one-sided; some also claim that the pluralist portrait is superficial (Smith, 1995). Criticism focuses on four areas:

- Interest groups do not compete on an equal playing field. Some interests, such as business, are inherently more powerful than others. Others, such as professional groups, are central to policy implementation. In reality, groups form a stable hierarchy of influence, with their ranking reflecting their usefulness to government.
- Pluralism neglects the bias of the political culture and political system in favour of some interests and against others. Groups advocating modest reforms within the established order are heard more sympathetically than those seeking radical change (Walker, 1991). Regulation is achievable; redistribution less so. Some groups, such as migrants, patients, the elderly and the low-paid, experience difficulty in organizing at all.
- The state is far more than a neutral umpire. In addition to deciding which groups to heed, it may regulate their operation and even encourage their formation in favoured areas, thus shaping the interest group landscape itself. In some democracies, notably France, the state is expected to embody and define the public interest, standing above more partial concerns.
- Pluralist conflict disguises interests shared by leaders of all the mainstream groups, such as their common membership of the same class and ethnic group. Mills (1956) argued that in the USA the leaders of industry, the military and government formed an interlocking power elite rather than separate, competing centres of power. All parts of this elite shared a commitment to the system which they commanded; disputes were restricted to detail.

From iron triangles to issue networks

While the debate about pluralism provides a general perspective on the position of interest groups in liberal democracies, we must also examine how the role of groups has changed over time. In the United States, certainly, this pattern can be described as a transition from **iron triangles** to **issue networks**. Elements of this trend, involving a shift from secretive back-scratching to more transparent and pluralist problem-solving, can also be found in other liberal democracies.

> **Iron triangles**, subgovernments and policy communities are terms used to refer to inward-looking coalitions of interests, based on senior bureaucrats, interest group leaders and sometimes relevant legislators, that dominate policy-making in particular sectors (e.g. agriculture). In many liberal democracies, these secretive cartels have given way to looser **issue networks** which are more open to outside organizations and pluralistic debate.

American political scientists used the term iron triangle to describe the traditional relationship between groups and government in many (but not all) policy sectors in the USA. The three points on the triangle were government departments (or agencies within them), interest groups and congressional committees (Figure 11.2). Such triangles became an exercise in mutual exchange and support: the committee appropriated funds which were spent by the department for the benefit of interest group members. Thus, the Department of Agriculture, the relevant committees in Congress and farmers' groups would collude on larger food subsidies. Each

Figure 11.2 Iron triangles: how subgovernments operated in the USA

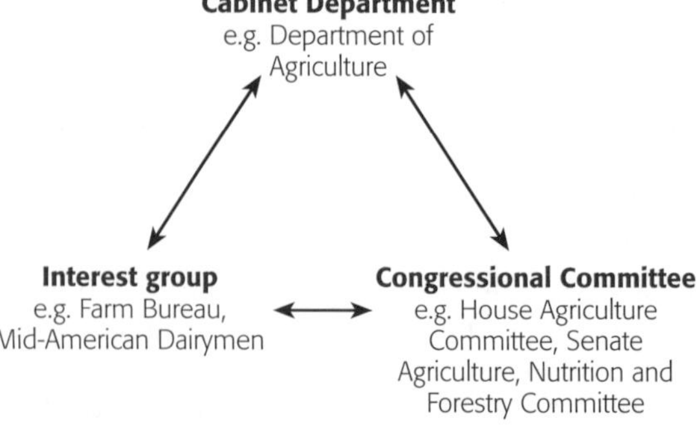

DEBATE

IS THE AMERICAN POLITICAL SYSTEM PLURALIST?

Both as an ideal and as a description of how politics works, pluralism draws on American experience. But can American politics really be presented as an open competition between freely organized interests? Or is the entire decision-making process in the hands of an elite which, in effect, excludes consideration of any policies which would threaten its own values? Is the American political system really the pluralist archetype?

YES

In the USA, interest group patterns come closer to the pluralist model than anywhere else. As de Tocqueville (1856) wrote, 'in no country in the world has the principle of association been more successfully used, or applied to a greater multitude of objects, than in America'. Petracca (1992, p. 3) makes the point succinctly: 'American politics is the politics of interests.'

Nowhere else are interest groups so numerous, visible, organized, competitive or successful. Tens of thousands of groups, ranging from Happiness of Motherhood Eternal to the United Autoworkers of America, seek to influence policy at federal, state and local levels. Nor are such groups confined to protective economic interests. Promotional groups are uniquely prominent in the USA, with over 500 groups focusing on environmental protection alone.

Washington politics reflects the competitive spirit that is pluralism's hallmark. Members of Congress realize they are under constant public scrutiny. In the House, a two-year election cycle means that politicians must be constantly aware of their ratings by interest groups.

If one interest group seems to be gaining the upper hand, others will form to counter its influence. Vigorous, independent and competitive media are always willing to listen to new groups with a story to tell. The separation of powers gives interest groups many points of leverage: congressional committees, executive agencies and the courts. By design, American government is too fragmented to be anything more than an umpire of group demands.

NO

All political systems generate myths and America's is pluralism. In reality, pluralist 'competition' operates within an unquestioned acceptance of broad American values favouring the free market and the pursuit of individual self-interest.

Policy debate works within a narrow ideological range, shaping the demands expressed so as to benefit, in particular, corporate USA. Even more than in other countries, foreign policy is framed by short-term national interests, producing a bias against groups with a wider perspective.

Washington's intricate political games are dominated by middle-aged, middle-class English-speaking graduates, a group which forms only a small minority of an ethnically and linguistically diverse population.

While Washington politics is certainly competitive, the outcome is normally a decision not to decide. The constitution deliberately fragments government authority, thus entrenching the interests of the wealthy and powerful. The voice of the *status quo* speaks louder than that of reform.

In any case, some interest groups are wealthier and better organized than others so that the pluralist ideal of equal representation for all groups is a myth.

And some interests are left out of the debate altogether. As Schattschneider (1942) claimed, 'the system is skewed, loaded and unbalanced in favour of a fraction of a minority'. Some interests are organized into American politics but others are organized out.

ASSESSMENT

Those who favour the American way discern pluralism; those who are more critical see a hidden elite. But one point is clear. While overseas observers may interpret American politics as much ado about nothing, that view is not shared by the players themselves. To understand what happens in American politics (as opposed to what radical observers might like to happen), we must appreciate the vigorous competition between interest groups, even if the battle is fought over a narrow terrain.

Further reading

Cigler and Loomis (2006), Dahl (1961), Mills (1956), Schattschneider (1942).

point on the triangle benefited considerably, even though the drain on the public purse as a whole was only small. This was a game without losers – except for the taxpayer who rarely knew what was going on.

Iron triangles were also called subgovernments, implying that each triangle formed a mini-government of its own, largely independent of policy-making in other sectors. Within each of these islands, a policy cartel presided. The effect was to reinforce the very fragmentation of the executive which made such triangles possible in the first place. The system could deflect the political aims of the majority party in Congress or even of the president himself, providing a further example of the tension between interest groups and democracy (Ripley and Franklin, 1991). In contrast to the open and competitive debates assumed by pluralism, the idea of iron triangles suggests that a decentralized political system can sometimes just lead to closed, secretive policy-making.

Beyond the United States, the term **policy community** was sometimes used to describe a similar pattern of inward-looking policy-making (Marsh and Rhodes, 1992). Within a particular sector, it was alleged, interest group leaders and senior civil servants formed their own small communities. All the members in the policy village knew each other well, used given names and tried not to upset each other. The participants developed shared working habits and common assumptions about what could be achieved. They learned to trust each other and to respect each other's goals and confidences.

Shared interests predominated. For instance, the road builders and bureaucrats in the transport ministry would seek ever larger highway budgets, fully aware that similar coalitions in other sectors – defence, say, or education – would be seeking to maximize their own funding and autonomy. Business was done behind closed doors to prevent political posturing and to allow a quiet life for all. Insiders were sharply distinguished from outsiders. The golden rule was never to upset the apple cart.

Fortunately, perhaps, these cosy iron triangles and policy communities have decayed in many liberal democracies. Today, policies are subject to closer scrutiny by the media; new public interest groups protest loudly when they spot the public being taken for a ride; and some legislators are less willing to keep quiet when they see public money being wasted. As issues become more complex, so more groups are drawn into the policy process, making it harder to stitch together insider deals. In the United States, where this trend has gone furthest, the committee barons who used to dominate Congress have lost much of their power. The iron has gone out of the triangle; now influence over decisions depends on what you know as much as who you know.

Reflecting these trends, the talk now is of **issue networks**. These refer to the familiar set of organizations involved in policy-making: government departments, interest groups and legislative committees plus expert outsiders. However, the structure of an issue network is much looser than that of an iron triangle; the impact of a particular interest group varies from one topic within the field to the next, depending on its expertise. As Heclo (1978, p. 102) pointed out,

> the notions of iron triangles and subgovernments presume small circles of participants who have succeeded in becoming largely autonomous. Issue networks, on the other hand, comprise a large number of participants with quite variable degrees of mutual commitment . . . it is almost impossible to say where a network leaves off and its environment begins.

Clearly, the idea of issue networks enables us to portray policy-making in liberal democracies more positively. A wider range of interests participate in decisions, the bias towards protective groups is reduced, new groups enter the debate and a sound argument carries greater weight. Because networks operate in a non-hierarchical way, we can portray their participants as engaged in a constructive exchange of their resources such as knowledge (e.g. academic specialists), legitimacy (elected politicians), engagement in implementation (interest groups) and the capacity to draft bills and regulations (bureaucrats). An issue network remains more structured than the pluralist model of open competition would want; but it is certainly more pluralist than an iron triangle.

Channels of influence

We turn now to the detailed channels of communication between interest groups and the government. How do interest groups communicate with decision-makers? What are the channels through which this process takes place? Figure 11.3 sets out three mechanisms characteristic of liberal democracies: direct dealings with policy-makers, indirect influence through political parties and indirect influence through public opinion. In this section, we will also look at specialist lobbying companies which help to pilot their interest group clients through these channels.

Direct discussion with policy-makers

The core business of most interest groups, especially protective ones, is influencing public policy. Those who shape and apply policy are the ultimate target. So direct conversations with the ministers who form the political *executive* are ideal if access is available. Talking with ministers before specific policies have crystallized enables a group to enter the policy process at an early, formative stage. But in many large political systems, such privileges are confined to a few well-connected individuals: the heads of the major peak associations, perhaps, or the chief executives of the country's largest corporations.

In practice, most interest group activity focuses on the bureaucracy, the legislature and the courts. Of these, the *bureaucracy* is undoubtedly the main pressure point. Interest groups follow power and it is in civil servants' offices that detailed decisions are formed. As Matthews (1989, p. 217) comments,

Figure 11.3 Channels of interest group influence

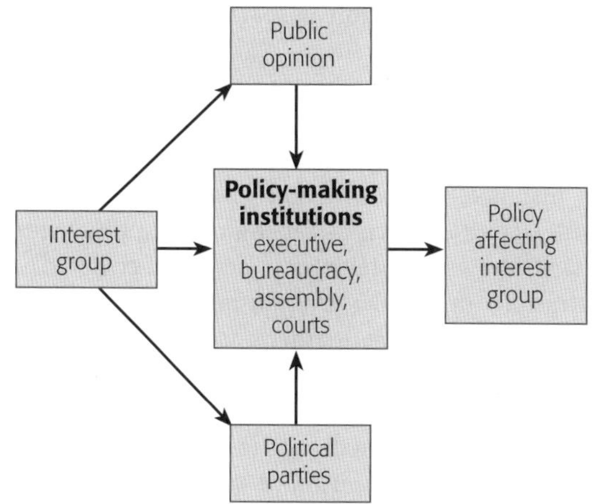

> the bureaucracy's significance is reinforced by its policy-making and policy-implementing roles. Many routine, technical and 'less important' decisions, which are nonetheless of vital concern to interest groups, are actually made by public servants.

Shrewd protective groups focus on the small print because details are easier to modify. While access to ministers is difficult, most democracies follow a convention of discussion over detail with organized opinion through consultative councils or committees. Often the law requires such consultation. In any case, the real expertise frequently lies in the interest group rather than the bureaucracy and, from the government's viewpoint, a policy acceptable to all is politically safe.

While the bureaucracy is invariably a crucial arena for groups, the significance of the *assembly* depends on its political weight. A comparison between the United States and Canada makes the point. The American Congress (and especially its committees) forms a vital part of the policy process. A range of factors combine to create an ideal habitat for lobby operations: the separation of powers, the constitutional right 'to petition the government for a redress of grievances', weak party discipline and independent-minded committees within the legislature. Many interest groups have access to individual members of Congress and can arrange to contribute to committee deliberations. The ability of interest groups to endorse particular candidates, and to indirectly support their re-election campaigns, means legislators are sensitive to group demands (Cigler and Loomis, 2006).

But the USA is a unique case. In most democracies, parliaments are more reactive than proactive; as a result, interest groups treat members of parliament as opinion-leaders rather than decision-makers. Where party voting is entrenched, lobbyists concentrate their strongest fire on the bureaucracy. As Landes (1995, p. 488) comments on Canada,

> interest groups have an acute sense of smell when tracking the scent of power. Interaction with the bureaucracy and not with MPs is the goal of most groups and one reason why interest group activity is not highly visible to the untrained eye.

If interest groups feel ignored in the policy-making process, they may still be able to seek redress through the *courts*. In the European Union, an interest group that is unsuccessful at home can take its case to the European Court of Justice. In the United States, business corporations routinely subject government statutes and regulatory decisions to legal challenge. **Class action** suits are particularly common there.

> A **class action** is a legal device initiated by complainants on their behalf and 'for all others so situated'. This mechanism enables legal costs and gains to be shared among a large group and provides a lever by which interest groups can pursue their goals through the courts.

But just as the USA is exceptional in the powers of its legislature, so too does it rely heavily on the courts to resolve disputes. Elsewhere, the courts are growing in importance but remain a remedy of last resort. In Australia, for instance, the requirement for litigants to prove their personal interest in the case hinders class actions. When the outcome of a legal case affects only the person initiating it, the policy and financial implications are more limited than in a class action covering all those in the same position.

Indirect influence through political parties

Interest groups overlap with both political parties and social movements; all are devices through which social interests seek to influence government. Britain's labour movement historically regarded its industrial wing (the trade unions) and political wing (the Labour Party) as part of a single movement promoting broad working-class interests. In a similar way, the environmental movement has spawned both promotional interest groups and green political parties.

But intimate relationships between interest groups and political parties are the exception. Most interest groups seek to hedge their bets rather than to develop close links with a political party. Loose, pragmatic links between interests and parties are the norm. In the United States, business and organized labour gravitate towards the Republican and Democratic parties respectively but these are partnerships of convenience, not indissoluble marriages.

The traditional maxim of the American trade union movement has been to reward its friends and punish its enemies, wherever these are to be found. American business is equally pragmatic. Despite an ideological affinity with the Republican Party, business groups still contribute to the election campaigns of many Democratic members of Congress. Whether representing capital, labour or neither, most interest groups give more to incumbents. They want access to legislators, whatever their ideological colours. They do not waste money on no-hopers.

The theme of pragmatic links with any party close to power is similar, if less explicit, in other countries. In Germany, for instance, the powerful Federation of German Industry (BDI) certainly enjoys close links with the conservative Christian Democratic Union. However, it wisely remains on speaking terms with the more left-wing Social Democrats. The rule is that protective interests follow power, not parties.

Political parties, too, have weakened their links with the interests from which they originally emerged. The religious and class parties of Western Europe have broadened their appeal in the post-war era, seeking to be viewed not as representatives of a particular group but rather as national custodians. The distinction between parties bent on power and interest groups focused on influence has sharpened as marriages of the heart have given way to alliances of convenience.

Indirect influence through public opinion

Press, radio and television provide an additional resource for interest groups. By definition, messages through the media address a popular audience rather than specific decision-makers. Thus the media are a central focus for promotional groups seeking to steer public opinion, especially when such groups compete for members (Binderkrantz, 2005). Their field of operation is society as much as government.

Because promotional groups usually lack both the resources and the access available to protective groups, free publicity becomes their stock-in-trade. For instance, environmental groups mount high-profile activities, such as seizing oil rigs, to generate footage shown on television across the world. In contrast to protective groups, promotional groups view the media as sympathetic to their cause – and they may indeed be justified in their assumption (Dalton, 1994).

Traditionally, the media are less important to protective groups with their more specialized and secretive demands. What food manufacturer would go public with a campaign opposing nutritional labels on foods? The confidentiality of the government meeting room is a quieter arena for fighting rear-guard actions of this kind; going public is a last resort. Keen to protect their reputation in government, protective groups steer away from disruptive tactics in particular.

But even protective groups are now seeking to influence the climate of public opinion, especially in political systems where legislatures are important political actors. In the United States, most protective groups have learned that to impress Congress they must first influence the public. Therefore groups follow a dual strategy, going public and going Washington. In Denmark, too, 'decision makers seem to accept that groups seek attention from the media and the general public without excluding them from access to making their standpoint heard in decision-making' (Binderkrantz, 2005, p. 703). Slowly and uncertainly, protective groups are emerging from the bureaucratic undergrowth into the glare of media publicity.

Lobbyists

Although interest groups are often their own best **lobbyists**, our focus here is on specialist companies whose job it is to open the doors of government to their interest group clients. These lobbying firms, sometimes known as contract lobbyists, are technicians of influence: hired guns in the business of interest group communication. And they are growing in number though not necessarily in influence.

> A **lobbyist** is defined by the United States Legislative Reorganization Act (1946) as any person or organization that receives money to be used principally to influence legislation before Congress. The term is derived from the hall or lobby of Britain's House of Commons where people can and do approach members of parliament to plead their case.

Why is lobbying an expanding profession? Three reasons suggest themselves. First, government regulation continues to grow, often impinging directly on companies, interest groups and trade unions. For instance, a decision to permit the sale of a new medicine can be a matter of life and death for the drug company as well as for potential patients. One prosaic task of lobbying firms is just to keep a close eye on proposed regulations under consideration by legislative committees. A specialist firm working for a number of interest groups can often monitor parliamentary developments more efficiently than would be the case if each interest group undertook the task itself.

Second, public relations campaigns are becoming increasingly sophisticated, often seeking to influence both the grass roots and the government in one integrated project. Professional advisers come into their own in planning and delivering multifaceted campaigns, which can be too complex for an interest group client to manage directly.

Third, many firms now approach government directly, rather than working through their trade association. Many large companies have established what amounts to corporate embassies in the national capital; smaller companies engage in political diplomacy as the need arises. Companies both large and small find that using a lobbying company to help them contact a government agency or a sympathetic legislator can yield quicker results than working through an industry body which has to address the concerns of all its members. McKay (2005, p. 250) reports that in the United States

> since the 1960s there is overwhelming evidence that individual firms have taken a more active part in public policy-making. Most major corporations now have Washington offices and employ professional lobbyists to advance and protect their interests.

At the level of access and potential influence, the central feature of the lobbying business is its intensely personal character. A legislator is most likely to return a call from a lobbyist if the caller is a former colleague. For this reason, lobbying firms are always on the look-out for former legislators or bureaucrats with a warm contact book. More than in most professions, lobbying is about who you know.

What then is the political impact of lobbying companies? Is it now possible for wealthy interest groups and corporations simply to pay a fee to a lobbying firm to ensure that a bill is defeated or a regulation deferred? On the whole, the answer is no. Lobbyists are inclined to exaggerate their own impact for commercial reasons but in reality most

PROFILE

EUROPEAN UNION

Form of government ■ a unique hybrid body in which policy is made partly by European Union institutions and partly through negotiations among the 27 member states.

Executive

- The powerful *European Commission*, arranged into directorates general and specialized service units, initiates many proposals and oversees their implementation by the member states; it is a cross between an executive and a bureaucracy, representing the EU itself.
- The *Council of the European Union* ('Council of Ministers') is the meeting place for ministers from national governments; it must approve all Commission proposals before they become law.
- The separate *European Council* is the EU forum for meetings of heads of government from the member states (the *Council of Europe* is a separate body again, unconnected with the EU).

Population of member states: 457m
Gross domestic product per head: $28,100 (+1.7%)

Assembly ■ the members of the large, unicameral multi-site *European Parliament* are directly elected from each country for a five-year term. The number of MEPs from each country reflects its population but with over-representation for small states. Though still lacking full legislative authority, the parliament has acquired greater powers of consultation and approval since the 1970s.

Judicial branch ■ the influential *European Court of Justice*, composed of one judge from each member country, has developed the EU's strong legal foundations, supporting the drive for European integration in the final decades of the twentieth century.

The **EU**'s emergence owes much to Europe's history of conflict. After the 1939–45 war, many European leaders set out to create a unified continent within which war would no longer be feasible: a United States of Europe. However, economic factors were also fundamental. European economies needed to be rebuilt after the war and then, to achieve benefits of scale, integrated into a large, single market.

Later members, notably Britain, emphasized the economic basis of the Union while rejecting the federal vision. Margaret Thatcher said in 1988 that 'willing and active cooperation between independent sovereign states is the best way to build a successful European Community'. In developing this line, Britain has exploited the continental notion of subsidiarity to argue that decisions should be taken at the lower, national level whenever possible. While remaining sceptical about further efforts at deepening integration, Britain has supported the admission of new members.

Even on the continent, some publics have grown sceptical of deepening. Proposals for a European constitutional treaty, expressing a commitment 'to forge a common destiny', were defeated in French and Dutch referendums in 2005. This rejection signalled the public's uncertainty about grand projects and deeper integration at a time of low growth and high unemployment. So the EU's basis still lies in treaties rather than a constitution. In addition the euro currency is currently confined to 13 countries, reflecting a 'variable geometry' in which integration proceeds at a different pace among particular groups of members.

Future developments in the EU remain uncertain. On the one hand, pressures to complete the single market, to provide an effective response to environmental and terrorist threats, and to counter American and Asian influence in the world, will continue, providing strong ammunition to those with a political or institutional commitment to further deepening. On the other hand, more sceptical leaders and members (mindful of their often cynical electorates) will continue to suggest that such matters can be adequately addressed through intergovernmental means. What does seem likely, though, is that the pace of expansion will slow, with Croatia better positioned than the other candidate countries (Macedonia and Turkey) to achieve membership in the medium term.

Further reading: Hix (2005), Hosli *et al.* (2002), Nugent (2006).

SPOTLIGHT

Interest groups and the EU

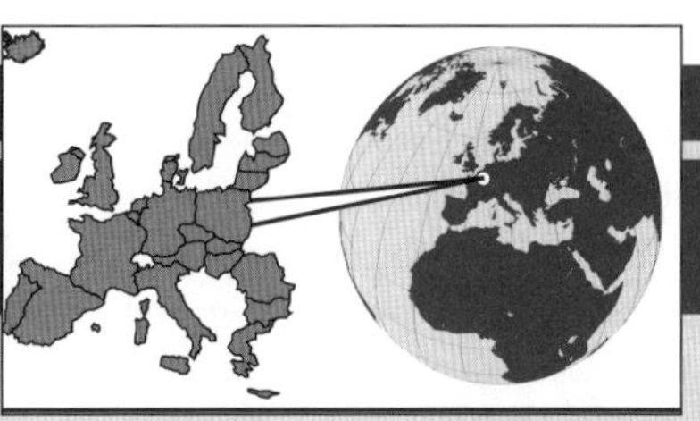

One European Commission official said, 'My division is responsible for 44 directives and 89 regulations. And I have about nine staff to deal with all of this. The corresponding administration in the US has 600 people' (Greenwood, 2007, p. 6). It is no surprise therefore that the Commission has encouraged relevant interest groups to develop and has remained accessible to them. How then do interest groups operate in the unique hybrid that is the European Union?

Reflecting the European tradition of social partnership, the EU has encouraged interest groups. Over 900 are listed in the Commission's directory; most are small, policy-focused entities. The main peak associations are the Union of Industrial and Employers' Confederation of Europe (UNICE), with 40 employees, and the European Trade Union Federation (ETUC), with 45 staff. The European Round Table of Industrialists – a forum of European industrial leaders – offered substantial support to the single-market project, with Jacques Delors (Commission President, 1985–95) commenting that 'these men are very powerful and dynamic . . . when necessary they can ring up their own prime ministers and make their case' (Mattli, 1999, p. 78).

Although the emergence of the parliament has extended the field for lobbyists, most work is still focused on the Commission, which has pursued not only the creation of a single market but also the protection of consumer interests (where it has fostered influential public interest groups). There are probably more lobbyists working in Brussels than there are policy-makers employed by the European Commission. So even more than national governments, the Commission depends on interest groups not just for information but also for intelligence and advice.

Originally, the Commission preferred to deal with groups organized on a Europe-wide basis. However, many of these federations possess few resources and experience difficulty in taking prompt positions acceptable to members drawn from a range of countries. Increasingly, therefore, the Commission has turned not just to national peak associations but also to individual companies capable of offering greater insight into current market developments (however, national and functional divisions within a multinational corporation may themselves articulate varying positions). Many individual companies have also become more willing to lobby the Commission directly, reflecting the trend also found at national level.

Compared to the lobbying of member governments, interest representation in the European Union differs in three main respects:

- Policy is more frequently revised or dropped as it passes through the complex filters of the Union's institutions. For this reason, any initial agreements reached with the Commission retain a conditional quality.
- Brussels remains at one remove from the glare of national politics. The focus is organizations rather than individuals, interest groups rather than social movements and reasoned arguments rather than political grandstanding. Effective lobbying depends on developing relationships of trust, built up over time, together with sensitivity to the Commission's agenda.
- Because the European Union operates in the context of states, groups retain the option of seeking influence though their national government. Similarly, the Commission must depend on national governments for implementation – and on its interest group partners to monitor whether member states are, in fact, complying with EU policies and regulations. Here, then, we see the reality of multilevel governance (Chapter 14).

How the ETUC views the European social model

'In the ETUC's view, social dialogue, collective bargaining and workers' protection are crucial factors in promoting innovation, productivity and competitiveness. This is what distinguishes Europe, where post-war social progress has matched economic growth, from the US model, where small numbers of individuals have benefited at the expense of the majority. Europe must continue to sustain this social model as an example for other countries around the world.'

Source: ETUC (2006).

Further reading: Eising (2003), Greenwood (2007), Hosli *et al.* (2002), Mazey and Richardson (2001).

can achieve little more than access to relevant politicians and, perhaps, bureaucrats. Often, the lobbyist's role is merely to hold the client's hand, helping an inexperienced company to find its way around the corridors of power when its executives come to town.

However, shaping the policy-maker's response to the message is a far greater challenge. Allegations of sleaze notwithstanding, influence can rarely be purchased through a lobbyist but must come, if at all, from the petitioning group itself. And impact depends first and foremost on the intrinsic strength of the case. To the experienced politician, a convincing case direct from the petitioner sings louder than yet another rehearsed presentation from a lobbying firm. In general, lobbyists – like the interest groups they represent – tend to cancel each other out.

Rather than viewing professional lobbying in a negative light, we should recognize its contribution to effective political communication. It can focus the client's message on relevant decision-makers, ensuring that the client's voice is heard by those who need to hear it. Of course, not everything in the lobby is rosy. Even if a company achieves no more for its lobbyist's fee than access to a decision-maker, perhaps that exchange in itself compromises the principle of equality which underpins democracy. In the public's mind, buying access and buying influence are rarely distinguished, damaging the legitimacy of the political process.

Conditions of influence

There is no doubt that some interest groups exert more influence over government than others. So what is it that gives particular groups the ability to persuade? Much of the answer is to be found in four attributes, ranging from the general to the specific: legitimacy, sanctions, membership and resources. The more general factors in this funnel (e.g. legitimacy) also influence the more specific ones (e.g. resources) (Figure 11.4)

First, the degree of *legitimacy* achieved by a particular group is clearly important. The aphorism 'what is good for General Motors is good for America' still expresses the point, even if that particular corporation has fallen on hard times. Interests enjoying high prestige are most likely to prevail on particular issues. For example, professional groups whose members stand for social respectability can be as militant on occasion, and as restrictive in their practices, as blue-collar trade unions once were. But lawyers and doctors escape the public hostility that unions attract.

Figure 11.4 Conditions of interest group influence

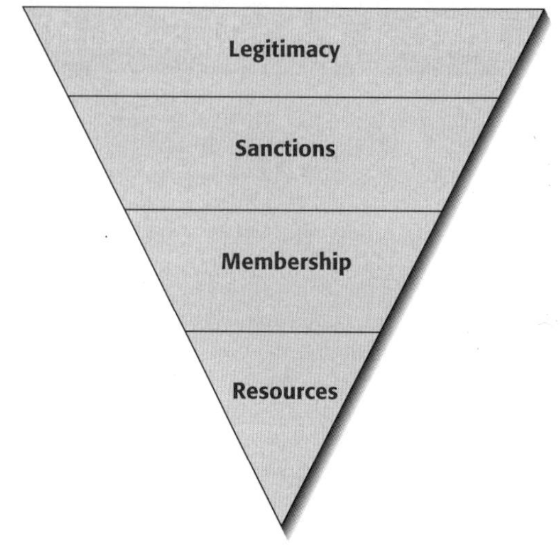

Second, the ability of a group to invoke *sanctions* is clearly important. A labour union can go on strike, a multinational corporation can take its investments elsewhere, a peak association can withdraw its cooperation in forming policy. As a rule, promotional groups (such as environmental movements) have fewer sanctions available to use as a bargaining chip.

Third, a group's influence depends on its *membership*. This is a matter of **density** and commitment as well as sheer numbers. The highest penetrations are usually achieved when, as with many professional bodies such as physicians and lawyers, membership is a condition of practice. By contrast, the declining density of trade-union membership in the final quarter of the twentieth century undoubtedly

Density of membership refers to those who actually join a group as a proportion of all those who are eligible to do so so. An encompassing membership gives more authority and, in turn, a stronger bargaining position with government.

weakened labour's bargaining power throughout the democratic world.

Influence is further reduced when membership is spread among several interest groups operating in the same sector. American farmers are divided between three major organizations with lower total coverage than Britain's National Farmers Union. To be sure, the larger American food producers are politically well-connected but the interests of agriculture as a whole would be better served if all farmers belonged to a single national association.

The commitment of the membership is also important. For instance, the four million members of America's National Rifle Association (NRA) include many who are prepared to contact their congressional representatives in pursuit of the group's goal of 'preserving the right of all law-abiding individuals to purchase, possess and use firearms for legitimate purposes'. This well-schooled activism led George Stephanopoulos, former spokesman for President Clinton, to this assessment: 'Let me make one small vote for the NRA. They're good citizens. They call their Congressmen. They write. They vote. They contribute. And they get what they want over time' (NRA, 2006).

Fourth, the organizational *resources* available to an interest group affect influence. Here, money talks but not always loudly. Take the NRA once more. With an annual budget of $40 million, the NRA can afford to employ 275 full-time staff. The coalition of gun control groups cannot match the NRA's fire power. Yet it would be naïve to suppose that the cause of gun control in the USA is held back solely by the NRA. Two other factors are equally important: (1) the difficulty of passing any legislation opposed by a significant minority within Congress and (2) an ambiguous constitutional reference to the 'right of the people to keep and bear arms'. The NRA has exploited both features but created neither.

Just as the impact of lobbying firms is often exaggerated, so too is the significance of the money available to an interest group. As a rule, finance is rarely decisive. In general, interest groups inherit an endowment of political resources which substantially determines the influence they can exert. The size of this stock reflects the group's position in society and politics. Skilful lobbying can exploit such resources but cannot, in itself, create them.

Interest groups in authoritarian states

The role played by interest groups in non-democratic states provides a sharp contrast to their position in liberal democracies. Authoritarian rulers see freely organized groups as a potential threat to their own power; hence, they seek either to repress such groups or to incorporate them within their power structure. In this section, we will examine the workings of these strategies in authoritarian regimes before turning to the special case of totalitarian states.

In the latter half of the twentieth century, many authoritarian rulers had to confront the challenge posed by the new groups unleashed by economic development. These included labour unions, peasant leagues and educated radicals. How did rulers respond to these new conditions? One strategy was to suppress such groups completely. Where civil liberties were weak and many groups were new, this approach was feasible. For example, a strategy of repression was adopted by many military regimes. Military leaders often had their own fingers in the economic pie, sometimes in collaboration with overseas corporations; the rulers' goal was to maintain a workforce that was both compliant and poorly paid. Troublemakers seeking to establish labour unions were quickly removed.

This syndrome of forced exploitation continues in Burma. There, the military junta has outlawed independent trade unions, collective bargaining and strikes; imprisoned labour activists; and maintained strict control of the media. This repressive environment enables the regime to use forced labour, particularly from ethnic minorities, to extract goods such as timber which are exported through the black market for the financial benefit of army officers.

On the other hand, authoritarian rulers could seek to manage the expression of new interests. That is, they could allow interests to organize but seek to control them, a policy of incorporation rather than exclusion. By enlisting part of the population, particularly its more modern sectors, into officially sponsored associations, rulers hoped to accelerate the push towards modernization. This approach was common in Latin America, where the state licensed, funded and granted a monopoly of representation

Figure 11.5 Incorporating interests: Mexico under the PRI

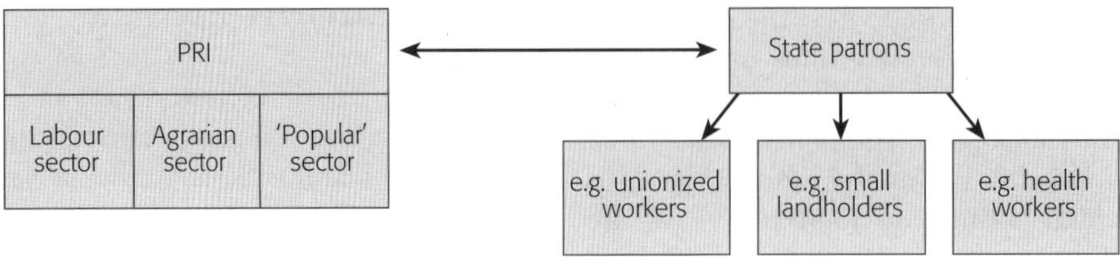

to favoured groups, reflecting a Catholic, corporate tradition established in colonial times (Wiarda, 2004a).

Before the democratic and economic reforms of the 1980s and 1990s, Mexico offered a particular working of this format. Its governing system was founded on a strong ruling party (the Institutional Revolutionary Party, PRI) which was itself a coalition of labour, agrarian and 'popular' sectors (the latter consisting mainly of public employees). Favoured unions and peasant associations gained access to the PRI. Party leaders provided resources such as subsidies and control over jobs to these groups, in exchange for their political support. In addition, officials in the state apparatus served as patrons to other organized groups such as health workers and teachers (Figure 11.5).

In effect, Mexico became a giant patron–client network: a form of corporatism for a developing country. In both the PRI and the state apparatus, groups at the same social level were divided against each other, discouraging wider, class-based organizations that might have threatened the regime itself. For the many people left out of the network, however, life could be hard indeed. Further, powerful groups such as the church, the army and large companies retained their direct access to the governing elite.

Just as corporatism is decaying in liberal democracies, so Mexico's system – and many others like it – is also in decline. It was over-regulated, giving so much power to civil servants and PRI-affiliated unions as to deter business investment, especially from overseas. As the market sector expanded, so the patronage available to the PRI diminished. In 1997, an independent National Workers Union emerged to claim that the old mechanisms of state control were exhausted, a point which was confirmed by the PRI's defeat in a presidential election three years later.

The position of interest groups in communist states was even more marginal than in other nondemocratic regimes, providing a complete contrast to pluralism. For most of the communist era, independent interest groups did not exist. Their absence was a deliberate result of communist ideology. Communist states were led by the party, not by society. Groups served the party, not the other way round. Interest articulation by freely organized groups was inconceivable. Communist rulers sought to harness all organizations into transmission belts for party policy. Trade unions, the media, youth groups, professional associations were little more than branches of the party, serving the cause of communist construction through social transformation.

The capacity to articulate interests did increase as communist economies matured. The use of coercion and terror declined and conflicts over policy became more visible. Institutional groups such as the military and heavy industry became more important as decisions became more technical. In the 1970s and 1980s, sectional interests began to be openly expressed, particularly in Poland, Hungary and Yugoslavia.

However, one sharp contrast with Western pluralism remained: ruling communist parties restricted interest articulation to safe technical matters. The party continued to crack down vigorously on dissent going beyond these confines. The objectives of the communist state remained beyond criticism. Thus 'socialist pluralism', to the extent that it existed, remained far more limited than its Western counterpart.

Even in reforming China, the Western notion of an 'interest group' still carries little meaning. China's

Map 11.1 The European Union

- Founding members (1952 ECSC; 1958 EEC and Euratom): Belgium, France, (West) Germany, Italy, Luxembourg, Netherlands. The territory of the German Democratic Republic (East Germany) was incorporated into a united Germany in 1990.
- First enlargement (1973): Denmark, Ireland, United Kingdom.
- Mediterranean enlargement: Greece (1981); Portugal, Spain (1986).
- EFTA enlargement (1995): Austria, Finland, Sweden.
- 2004 enlargement: Cyprus, Czech Republic, Estonia, Hungary, Latvia, Lithuania, Malta, Poland, Slovakia, Slovenia.
- 2007: Bulgaria, Romania.

Key

1 Croatia
2 Bosnia and Herzegovina
3 Serbia-Montenegro
4 Former Yugoslav Republic of Macedonia
5 Albania
6 Switzerland
7 Moldova
8 Slovenia

Note: See also, timeline of the European Union, p. 39.

Source: Adapted from Nugent (2006), p. xxiv.

BOX 11.4

Examples of social organizations in contemporary China

	Type	Comment
All-China Federation of Trade Unions	Mass organization	A traditional transmission belt for the party
All-China Women's Federation	Mass organization	Traditionally a party-led body, this federation has created some space for autonomous action
China Family Planning Association	Non-governmental organization	Sponsored by the State Family Planning Commission, this association operates at international and local level
Friends of Nature	Non-governmental organization	Led by a well-connected and charismatic figure, Friends of Nature has mobilized student support in defence of habitats threatened by illegal logging

Source: Adapted from Saich (2004), pp. 186–92.

Communist Party continues to provide the framework for most formal political activity. 'Mass organizations' such as the All-China Federation of Trade Unions and the Women's Federation are led by party officials and continue to transmit policy downwards rather than popular concerns upwards.

However, a new breed of non-governmental organizations did emerge in the 1980s, strengthening the links between state and society. Examples include the China Family Planning Association, Friends of Nature, the Private Enterprises Association and the Federation of Industry and Commerce (Box 11.4). Typically, only one body is officially recognized in each sector, indicating the state's continuing control. From the party's viewpoint, this corporatist arrangement reduces the threat of wider links developing across sectors. The limited status of these new entities is shown by the use of the Chinese phrase: government-organized non-governmental organization (GONGO).

Private business is intertwined with the state sector through personal and often corrupt links. This network of contacts operating through the back door leaves little space for policy-orientated interest groups. 'Rightful resistance' enables citizens to protest to higher authority about lower officials exceeding their legal powers but again such appeals operate on an individual rather than a group basis. As Manion (2004, p. 448) concludes, 'for the most part, the function of interest aggregation is monopolized by the communist party'.

In fascist theory, as under communism, the state dominated partial interests. Indeed, the central premise of fascist thought was that the state must lead. But unlike communism, the fascist state sought to mobilize, rather than to destroy, group activity. In particular, it wanted to exploit, rather than take over, private industry. Fascism advocated a corporate relationship between state and industry (Brooker, 2000, p. 156).

The theory was that the economy would be arranged by industrial sector. Within each industry, special corporations (committees or chambers) composed of employers, employees and party and government officials would plan production, set wages, control prices and resolve disputes. In this vertical arrangement, horizontal conflicts between business groups and labour unions would be overcome as both sides learned to serve national goals as defined by the supreme leader. Thus fascist corporatism would secure the national interest by overriding class conflict.

Such a system was formally implemented in Italy in the mid 1930s but in practice the 22 corporations established there were given only token powers. Their impact was minimal. Corporatism was even less significant in Nazi Germany. Indeed, the man charged by Hitler with implementing the format claimed that after learning of his assignment, 'I did not sleep for several nights on account of the corporate system because I could not make head or tail of it' (O'Sullivan, 1986, p. 133). In practice, industrial policy took the practical form of ensuring that large manufacturers in the private sector met the demands of an expansionist regime. Corporate institutions took second place to the task of serving the Nazi war machine.

Interest groups in illiberal democracies

By the nature of illiberal democracy, the borders between the public and private sectors are poorly policed, allowing the president and his allies to intervene in the economy so as to reward friends and punish enemies. But this involvement is selective rather than comprehensive, operating to override normal business practices and not (in contrast to a communist state) to replace them. At least in the more developed illiberal democracies, the result can be a dual system of representation, combining some role for interest groups on routine matters, with more personal relationships, nurtured by patronage, regarding matters that are key to the president and his ruling group. In these sensitive areas, employer is set against employer in a competition for political influence, leaving little room for the development of influential business associations. The general point is that even though illiberal democracies allow some expression of interests, interest groups are less significant than in a liberal democracy.

Russia is, as always, an interesting case. Certainly, the separation between public and private sectors, so central to the organization of interests in the West, has not fully emerged there. Particularly in the early post-communist years, ruthless business executives, corrupt public officials and jumped-up gangsters made deals in a virtually unregulated free-for-all. Individual financiers pulled the strings of their puppets in government but the politics were personal rather than institutional. In such an environment interests were everywhere but interest groups were nowhere. 'Comrade Criminal' was disinclined to join trade associations.

However, as Russian politics stabilized and its economy recovered, so some business associations of a Western kind emerged, even if they have not yet secured extensive political influence. Peregudov (2001, p. 268) claims that 'in Russia a network of business organizations has been created and is up and running'. He suggests that this network is capable of adequately representing business interests to the state. However, it received limited attention from President Putin, who continued to reward his business friends and, on occasion, to imprison his enemies.

We must be wary here of assuming that Russia will eventually develop a Western system of interest representation. Pluralism is not currently on the agenda. Evans (2005, p. 112) suggests that Putin 'has sought to decrease the degree of pluralism in the Russian political system; it has become increasingly apparent that he wants civil society to be an adjunct to a strong state that will be dedicated to his version of the Russian national ideal'. In a manner similar to China's GONGOs, the state has sought to collaborate with favoured groups while condemning the remainder to irrelevance. The government's strong nationalist tone has led to particular criticism of those groups (such as women's associations) which depend on overseas support to survive in a hostile domestic environment. Few promotional groups in Russia have a significant mass membership and most groups operate solely at grassroots level, working on local projects such as education or the environment in conjunction with the public sector. Russia's combination of an assertive state and a weak society is not conducive to interest group development.

Illiberal democracy often arises in polarized and relatively poor societies. This environment is again a difficult one in which to strengthen interest groups pursuing specialized and technical concerns. In many of the illiberal democracies of Latin America, for example, fundamental issues of poverty, inequality, crime and drugs remain unresolved. These are political problems requiring political solutions. Certainly, social movements emerged to address such concerns but these groups were typically local groups founded on opposition to the state.

At national level, the leaders of illiberal democracies – such as Hugo Chávez in Venezuela – have often governed in a personal and populist way, seeking support through the media rather than through institutions such as interest groups (Crisp, 2000). Indeed, Chávez's political appeal rests partly on his rejection of the carefully crafted links between the oil industry, political parties and the government which characterized the preceding regime. Rather, Chávez has used oil revenues for a highly political form of redistribution to his predominantly poor supporters.

This personalist style of rule is long familiar to Latin America and has been further encouraged as privatization and market mechanisms have undercut the old corporatist channels. Also, the emergence of powerful indigenous movements in countries such as Bolivia raises political challenges which go beyond the technical, detailed concerns of protective interest groups. The relationship between state and society in much of Latin America remains one of mutual suspicion, providing difficult ground for strengthening interest groups.

In much of Africa, too, group politics in an era of post-military government continues to be based on ethnicity rather than interests generated through the workplace. Many poorer countries lack the complex economy needed to develop interest group patterns found in affluent liberal democracies. In Botswana, for example, only two organizations – a business association and a conservation group – employ staff to lobby the government (Herbst, 2001).

When such economic resources as are available are parcelled out on ethnic lines, or in any other personal or unregulated way, incentives for orthodox interest groups to develop are limited. 'In this respect', suggests Rothchild (1997, p. 75), 'ethnic groups can be likened to the interest-defined groups that they compete with for state-controlled resources'. In addition, the space between state and society can be colonized by foreign non-governmental organizations, often providing needed services in collapsed states but also, by their presence and resources, inhibiting the development of domestic interest groups.

Learning Resources for Chapter 11

Next step

Many of the best studies of interest groups continue to be about the United States; Cigler and Loomis (2006) is an excellent collection.

Further reading

Wilson (1990) remains a clear and straightforward introduction to interest groups. Hrebenar (1997) is a good text on the USA, Eising and Cini (2002) cover Western Europe while M. Smith (1995) is a brief but helpful introduction to Britain. On European corporatism, Berger and Compston (2002) is a useful collection while Arter (1999) and Blom-Hansen (2000) review the relevance of the concept to the Nordic states. Two useful comparative studies are Wilson (2003) on the relationship between business and politics and Thomas (2001) on the links between parties and interest groups. Evans (2005) covers civil society in post-communist Russia.

Internet sources

Influence
Chronicles the relationship between lobbyists and their clients in the United States
http://www.influence.biz/

opensecrets.org
A guide to money in American elections
http://www.opensecrets.org/

National Rifle Association
'Seeks to preserve the right of all law-abiding Americans to purchase, possess and use firearms'
http://www.mynra.org/
http://www.nraila.org/About/

Brady Campaign
'Leading the fight to prevent gun violence'
http://www.bradycampaign.org/

Chapter 12
Political parties

'In this book I investigate the workings of democratic government. But it is not institutions which are the object of my research: it is not on political forms, it is on political forces I dwell.' So Ostrogorski (1902) began his pioneering comparison of party organization in Britain and the United States. Ostrogorski was one of the first students of politics to recognize that **political parties** were becoming vital in the new era of democratic politics: 'wherever this life of parties is developed, it focuses the political feelings and the active wills of its citizens'.

Ostrogorski's supposition that parties were growing in importance proved to be fully justified in the twentieth century. In Western Europe, mass parties battled for the votes of enlarged electorates. In communist and fascist states, ruling parties monopolized power in an attempt to reconstruct society. In the developing world, nationalist parties became the vehicle for driving colonial rulers back to their imperial homeland.

In all these ways, parties proved to be a key mobilizing device, drawing millions of people into the national political process for the first time. Parties jettisoned their original image as private factions engaged in capturing and even perverting the public interest. Instead, they became accepted as a necessary instrument in shaping the collective interest. In the second half of the twentieth century, parties began to receive explicit mention in newly written constitutions. By the century's end, most liberal democracies offered some public funding to support party work. Parties had become part of the system.

Major parties continue to perform four main functions:

- Ruling parties offer direction to government, performing the vital task of steering the ship of state.
- Parties function as agents of political recruitment. They serve as the major mechanism for preparing and recruiting candidates for the legislature and the executive.
- Parties serve as devices of interest aggregation, filtering a multitude of specific demands into more manageable packages of proposals. Parties select, reduce and combine policies.
- To a declining extent, political parties also serve as a brand for their supporters and voters, giving people a lens through which to interpret a complicated political world.

Sartori (1976, p. 63) defines a **political party** as 'any political group identified by an official label that presents at elections, and is capable of placing through elections candidates for public office'. Unlike interest groups, serious parties aim to obtain the keys to government; in Weber's phrase, they live 'in a house of power'.

Political parties are complex multilevel organizations, with their varied elements united by a common identity and, sometimes, shared objectives. 'A party', wrote Duverger (1954, p. 17), 'is not a community but a collection of communities, a union of small groups dispersed throughout the country and linked by co-ordinating institutions'. It is a political system in miniature. Box 12.1 sets out the elements of a typical major party in Western

BOX 12.1

Typical elements of party organization in Western Europe

	Comment	Level
Party leadership	The leaders typically include government ministers when the party is in office	National
The party in parliament	Members of the parliamentary party, including backbenchers	National
The party's central organization	Officials at party headquarters	National
The party at regional and local levels	Party members elected to regional and local assemblies; local officials and ordinary party members	Subnational
The party in the European Union	Members of the European Parliament, where representatives of a national party join broader, transnational party groups	Supranational

Source: Adapted from Cotta (2000). *See also*: Katz and Crotty (2006).

Europe (Deschouwer, 2006). These elements typically come together at an annual conference which is often nominally supreme, at least in parties with origins outside parliament.

At national level, the main distinction is between the party in parliament and the officials in party headquarters. But the top leaders often span and integrate these arenas, spearheading the parliamentary party as well as heading the party organization. Beneath the national level, parties are also represented in both regional and local government. This superstructure is supported at the base by ordinary members, usually organized by area in branches. This array tends to become more complex as parties respond to decentralization within the state itself.

In Western Europe, parties typically possess a large if declining subscription-based membership, a coherent ideology and strong discipline among their members of parliament. Reflecting this importance, much of the most authoritative writing about parties in liberal democracies is based on this region. However, we should recognize that Western Europe is in some ways untypical. In federal North America, party organization is weaker and even more decentralized. Apart from the legislature (where party organization is strong), American and Canadian parties are largely devices for organizing elections; they often seem to hibernate between campaigns. Volunteer helpers with campaigns often have no formal links with their party. Most new democracies, in Eastern Europe and beyond, also lack the West European tradition of a large, dues-paying national membership.

The question for the twenty-first century is whether we are witnessing a crisis of parties or merely a change in their role. No longer do parties seem to be energetic agents of society, seeking to bend the state towards their supporters' interests. Rather, they seem to be at risk of capture by the state itself. No longer do parties provide a home for the politically engaged; instead, we witness the export to the rest of the democratic world of the North

BOX 12.2

Types of party organization

	Cadre party	Mass party	Catch-all party
Emergence	19th century	1880–1960	After 1945
Origins	Inside the assembly ('internally created')	Outside the assembly ('externally created')	Developed from existing cadre or mass parties
Claim to support	Traditional status of leaders	Represents a social group	Competence at governing
Membership	Small, elitist	Large card-carrying membership in local branches	Leaders become dominant
Source of income	Personal contacts	Membership dues	Many sources, including state subsidy
Examples	19th-century conservative and liberal parties, many post-communist parties	Socialist parties	Many modern Christian and Social Democratic parties in Western Europe

American (and East European) format of weak, leader-dominated organizations. If Ostrogorski were writing today, would he still interpret parties as a 'focus for the active wills' of the citizens?

Party organization

As Panebianco (1988) reminds us, internal organization is a key issue in the study of parties. How is power distributed within the party? What is the relationship between leaders, members and parliamentarians? The answer to these questions, Panebianco claims, must be historical. He stresses the importance of the party's founding moment in dealing out the power cards between the elements of party organization. These 'continue in many ways to condition the life of the organization even decades afterwards'. In this section, we will examine a classification of parties based on their origins before turning to their internal distribution of power.

Types of party organization

Adopting Panebianco's historical approach leads to a threefold distinction between cadre, mass and catch-all parties (Box 12.2). Cadre (or elite) parties are internally created. They are formed by groups of members within an assembly – the cadres – joining together to reflect common concerns and then to fight effective campaigns in an enlarged electorate. The earliest nineteenth-century parties were of this elite type: for example, the conservative parties of Britain, Canada and Scandinavia. The first American parties, the Federalists and the Jeffersonians, were also loose elite factions, based in Congress and state legislatures. Cadre parties are sometimes called caucus parties, the 'caucus' denoting a closed meeting of the party's members in the legislature. Such parties remain heavily committed to their leader's authority, with the ordinary members playing a supporting but not a sovereign role.

Mass parties are a later innovation. These originate outside the assembly, in groups seeking representation in the legislature as a way of achieving their goals. The working-class socialist parties that spread across Europe around the turn of the twentieth century epitomized these externally created parties. The German Social Democratic Party (SPD), founded in 1875, is a classic example. Such socialist parties exerted tremendous influence on European party systems in the twentieth century, stimulating many cadre parties to copy their extra-parliamentary organization. Mass parties acquired an enormous membership organized in local branches. Unlike cadre parties, they aimed to keep their representatives in parliament on a tight rein. They also sought influence over their members through affiliated organizations such as trade unions and sports clubs. Becoming a party member represented a distinct commitment, not least a formal statement of support for the party's ideological goals, but in exchange the organization would treat its members as part of the family.

The catch-all party is a more recent form. Kirchheimer (1966) used this phrase to describe the outcome of an evolutionary path followed by many parties, both cadre and mass, in post-1945 conditions. The catch-all party responds to a mobilized political system in which governing has become more technical and in which electoral communication takes place through the mass media. Leaders communicate with the voters through television, bypassing the membership. Such parties seek to govern in the national interest rather than as representatives of a social group: 'a party large enough to get a majority has to be so catch-all that it cannot have a unique ideological program' (Kirchheimer, quoted in Krouwel, 2003, p. 29). Catch-all parties seek electoral support wherever they can find it; their purpose is to govern rather than to represent. The broadening of Christian Democratic parties (such as the CDU in Germany) from religious defence organizations to broader parties of the centre-right is the classic case of the transition to catch-all status. The subsequent transformation of several radical socialist parties into leader-dominated social democratic parties, as in Spain and the United Kingdom, is another example.

Power within the party

Given the complex nature of modern parties, it is natural to ask where authority within them really resides. Of all the elements in Box 12.1, which truly commands the party? The answer is far from clear, reflecting the blunt nature of the question. American parties, in particular, are sometimes seen as empty vessels waiting to be filled by fresh ideas and ambitious office-seekers. The American party is not controlled from any single point; no one pulls the levers, no one rules the party.

Yet much European research on parties does suggest that authority within the party flows from the top down, with the leaders who represent the party to the public playing a key role. In 1911, the German scholar Robert Michels (1875–1936) published *Political Parties,* perhaps the most influential work on the distribution of power within parties. Michels argued that even organizations with democratic pretensions become dominated by a ruling clique of leaders and officials. Using Germany's Social Democratic Party (SPD) as a critical case, Michels suggested that leaders develop organizational skills, expert knowledge and an interest in their own continuation in power. The ordinary members, aware of their inferior knowledge and amateur status, accept their own subordination as natural, even in a mass party such as the SPD with origins outside the assembly. Michels's pessimism about the possibility of democracy within organizations such as political parties was expressed in his famous **iron law of oligarchy**.

Certainly, the party leaders in the legislature are normally the key actors within the parliamentary systems of Europe. When their party is in power, these leaders typically become the ministers of the government, with all the publicity which flows from such positions. It is difficult for ordinary members to make a stand if their leader is also prime minister. But even in opposition, the leaders are often the party's public face, defining its strengths (and weaknesses) on the national stage.

We should, however, note that the party organization outside the assembly retains some useful power cards. Most state financial aid normally goes to the

> Michels's **iron law of oligarchy** states that 'to say organization is to say a tendency to oligarchy' (often reproduced as, 'who says organization, says oligarchy'). Michels argued that even parties formally committed to democracy become dominated by a ruling elite (**oligarchy** is rule by and for the few).

party bureaucracy, not to the party in parliament. And only experts, working in or for the party, can cope with increasingly technical tasks such as raising funds through mail-shots, and arranging for advertising, briefings and press conferences during election campaigns. The contemporary importance of these tasks is captured in Panebianco's concept (1988) of an electoral–professional party centred on fighting elections through the mass media.

Selecting candidates and leaders

Elite recruitment is a vital and continuing function of parties. Even as parties decline in other ways, they continue to dominate elections to the national legislature from which, in most parliamentary systems, the nation's leaders are drawn. Given that candidates who are nominated for safe districts or who appear near the top of their party's list are virtually guaranteed a place in parliament, it is the **selectorate**, not the electorate, which opens the door to the house of power.

> The **selectorate** consists of those who nominate a party's candidates for an election. This group often plays a more critical role than the electorate in determining who will represent the party in office.

Schattschneider (1942, p. 46) famously wrote that 'the nature of the nominating convention determines the nature of the party; he who can make the nominations is the owner of the party'. In similar vein, Duverger (1954, p. 353) commented that

> the representative receives a double mandate: from the party and from his electors. The importance of each varies according to the country and the parties: on the whole the party mandate seems to carry more weight than that of the electors.

How, then, do major parties select their candidates and leaders? In answering this question, we will observe an increasing role for ordinary members, a finding suggesting that Michels's iron law is showing signs of corrosion.

Candidates

The nomination process is surprisingly decentralized. In Western Europe, a few parties do give control to the national leadership, though even here the leaders usually select from a list generated at lower levels. More often, local parties are the active force, either acting autonomously or with nominations ratified at national level. Small and extreme parties, and those in Scandinavia, are the most decentralized in their selection procedures (Lundell, 2004).

The nomination task is constrained by three wider features of the political system:

- Nearly all countries impose conditions such as citizenship on members of the legislature while a few – including several in Latin America – also impose gender quotas on party candidates.
- Incumbents (current members of parliament) possess an advantage almost everywhere, usually achieving reselection without much ado. Often, candidates are only 'chosen' when the incumbent stands down.
- The electoral system is a crucial influence on the nomination process. Choosing a series of candidates for individual constituencies is naturally a more decentralized task than preparing a single national list.

Consider the impact of the electoral system in more detail (Box 12.3). Under the list form of proportional representation, parties must develop a ranked list of candidates to present to the electorate. In the Netherlands, for example, each party needs to present a single list of candidates for the whole country. The major parties use a nominating committee to examine applications received either from local branches or directly from individuals. A senior party board then produces the final ordering, with the party leader serving as list-puller – that is, occupying number one position.

In a few countries, the candidate lists are prepared though a ballot of party members. This procedure is more democratic but, as Michels would have predicted, it causes difficulties of its own. Ballots advantage celebrity over competence, and wealth over party experience. Significantly, most of the Israeli parties that introduced ballots of members early in the 1990s soon withdrew the procedure.

In the few countries using plurality elections based on local electoral districts, the nomination procedure is more decentralized. Candidates must win selection by local parties keen to guard their autonomy against encroachment from headquarters.

BOX 12.3

Selecting candidates for legislative elections

Electoral system used for national elections	How parties typically select candidates for these elections	Example
Proportional representation (party list)	Party officials (or special party conventions) draw up a ranked list of candidates	Netherlands
Plurality system	Local parties select the candidate, sometimes drawing from a list prepared by head office*	Canada, United Kingdom
Mixed system	The party draws up a list for the PR element and local parties select a candidate for the district contest	Germany

* In the USA, primary elections are held among a party's registered supporters in the area.

In Canada, for instance, constituency parties seek candidates with an attractive local profile, showing little concern for national needs (Carty, 2002). In Britain, selection is also through local associations, drawing on lists of potential candidates approved by party headquarters.

Decentralization does not necessarily imply broad participation. The nomination meeting may be the exclusive preserve of the local party's management committee, the traditional practice in Britain. However, in Britain and elsewhere, the selection meeting is increasingly open to all members. Some parties in some countries now even choose their candidates through a postal ballot of all members in the locality.

The USA developed the unusual device of **primary elections**, enabling a party's supporters to choose its candidates for a particular office. In the absence of a tradition of direct party membership, a 'supporter', in most states, is defined simply and generously as anyone who declares, in advance, an affiliation to that party. An **open primary** extends the choice still further, to any registered elector. Originally introduced to formalize selection procedures and to weaken the control of corrupt party bosses, primaries are now well-entrenched. Most delegates to the presidential nominating conventions of the Democratic and Republican parties have been chosen by primary since 1976. Yet as with membership ballots, primaries seem to be a mixed blessing. They take control over selection away from the party itself, reducing its cohesion and giving an advantage to better-known, well-financed candidates.

An increasing number of countries operate a mixed electoral system, in which electors vote for both a party list and a district candidate. These circumstances complicate the party's task of selecting candidates, requiring both a national or regional list and local constituency nominees. In this situation, individual politicians also face a choice: should they seek election via the party list or through a constituency? Many senior figures ensure they appear on both ballots, using a high position on the party's

A **primary election** is a contest in which a party's supporters select its candidate for a subsequent general election (a direct primary) or choose delegates to the presidential nominating convention (a presidential primary). A closed primary is limited to a party's registered supporters but any registered elector can participate in an **open primary** though only for one party. Primaries are rarely encountered outside the United States.

list as insurance against restlessness in their home district.

Leaders

The method of selecting the party leader and presidential candidate merits special attention. Just as many parties now afford their ordinary members a greater voice in candidate selection, so too has the procedure for selecting the party leader become broader. As Mair (1994) notes, 'more and more parties now seem willing to allow the ordinary members a voice in the selection of party leaders', perhaps to compensate members for their declining role in media-driven election campaigns. Yet whether this wider selection process yields improved results is debatable.

The most common way to choose the leader is still by a special party congress or convention (Box 12.4). American parties have long selected their presidential candidates through such conventions but these meetings are no longer the effective site of decision. The real choice is made by voters in the primaries, with the convention itself transformed since the 1970s into a media event for the party and its anointed nominee.

A ballot of party members is an increasingly popular method of selecting leaders. Such elections are usually described as OMOV (one member, one vote) contests. They provide an incentive for people to join and can also be used to limit the power of entrenched factions within the party. In Belgium, for example, all the major parties have adopted this approach to choosing their party president. Britain's Liberal party introduced an OMOV vote even earlier, in 1975. Moving away from its traditional conventions, the new Conservative Party of Canada also adopted a membership election for its initial leadership contest in 2004, albeit with equal weight for each riding above a certain size.

Election by the parliamentary party, the remaining widely used technique of selecting (and removing) the leader, involves a much narrower constituency. This format is of course the traditional method, especially for cadre parties with their assembly origins. The device is still used in several countries, including Australia, Denmark and New Zealand. Britain's Conservative party adopts a two-stage process, giving ordinary members a choice between two candidates selected by the parliamentary party.

BOX 12.4

Selection of party leaders in liberal democracies

	Countries in which most major parties use this method	Total number of parties using this method
Party congress or convention	Finland, Norway, Sweden	37
Rank-and-file members	Belgium	19
Members of the parliamentary party	The Netherlands, New Zealand	17
Party committee	Italy	8

Source: Adapted from Hazan (2002, p.124). Analysis based on 16 democracies.

Of course, the ability of potential leaders to instil confidence in their parliamentary peers may say little about their capacity to win a general election fought on television. Even so, colleagues in the assembly will have a close knowledge of the candidates' abilities; they provide an expert constituency for judging the capacity to lead not only the party but also, and more importantly, the country.

Membership and finance

In the first decade of the twenty-first century, many parties in liberal democracies have more money but fewer members than at any time in living memory. This combination tells us much about the changing character of parties and their evolving relationship with society and state.

Table 12.1 Falling party membership in selected democracies, 1960–99

	Total party membership as a percentage of the electorate			
	Beginning of 1960s	**Beginning of 1980s**	**End of 1990s**	**Decline 1960s–1990s**
Austria	26	22	18	−8
Finland	19	13	10	−9
Belgium	8	9	7	−1
Norway	16	14	7	−9
Denmark	21	8	5	−16
Italy	13	10	4	−9
Germany	3	4	3	0
Netherlands	9	3	3	−6
New Zealand	23	9	3	−20
UK	9	3	2	−7

Note: The New Zealand denominator is votes cast, not the whole electorate.

Sources: Adapted from Mair (1994), Table 1.1; Mair and van Biezen (2001), Table 1; Sundberg (2002), Table 7.10; Miller (2005), Table 1.1.

Membership

The marked and often dramatic decline in party membership between the 1960s and the 1990s is shown in Table 12.1. In Scandinavia, 'since the 1970s and 1980s, membership decline has set in at an unprecedented rate' (Sundberg, 2002, p. 196). Denmark is a particularly extreme case, with membership falling from one in every five people in the 1960s to one in twenty by the 1990s. Across the democratic world, millions of party foot soldiers have simply given up.

Many new members do not engage with their party beyond paying an annual subscription; these member-donors are especially likely to leave the party, resulting in increased turnover. Seyd and Whiteley's assessment (2002, p. 169) of trends in Britain's Labour Party is widely applicable:

> Whatever activity one focuses on, participation has been declining over the past 10 years. The extent of the commitment of the average member is increasingly merely one of paying a yearly subscription and occasionally donating money to the party when asked to do so.

Lacking a steady flow of young members, the average age of members has increased. Nearly everywhere, those who belong to a party are older than those who vote for it. By the late 1990s, the average age of members of Canada's main parties was 59 (Cross and Young, 2004). Fewer than one in twenty members of Germany's Christian Democratic Union (CDU) is under 30. The older age profile of members may partly reflect the life-cycle (with younger people joining as they age) but a permanent generational shift is surely also at work. If so, membership is likely to continue to fall as the oldest cohort of members goes unreplenished.

However, we must locate this recent decline in a longer perspective. If statistics were available for the entire twentieth century, they would probably show a rise in membership over much of the century followed by a fall in the final third. The recent decline is from a peak only reached, in many countries, in the 1970s. In other words, it is perhaps the bulge in party membership after the Second World War, rather than the later decline, which requires explanation. Certainly, Putnam's comment (2000, p. 24) about civic engagement in the USA applies equally to party membership throughout the democratic world:

BOX 12.5

Public funding of political parties: for and against

FOR	AGAINST
Parties perform a public function, supplying policies and leaders to the state.	Public funding is creeping nationalization, creating parties that serve the state, not society. A new regulatory body is required to monitor party spending.
Parties should be funded to a professional level and not appear cheap.	Public funding favours established and large parties, encouraging a cartel.
Public funding creates a level playing field between parties.	To maintain a level playing field, cap spending rather than subsidize it.
Without public support, pro-business parties gain access to more funds.	Why should taxpayers fund parties against their wishes? A tax credit for voluntary donations is a preferable compromise.
Relying on private donations encourages corruption.	Corruption can be reduced by banning anonymous donations.

It is emphatically not my view that community bonds in the United States have weakened throughout our history – or even throughout the last hundred years. On the contrary, American history is a story of ups and downs in civic engagement, not just downs.

The reduction in membership has occurred in tandem with dealignment among electors and surely reflects similar causes. These include the weakening of social cleavages, the loosening of the bond linking trade unions and socialist parties, the decay of local party organization in an era of media-based election campaigns, and the appeal of social movements rather than parties to younger generations.

Finance

Falling membership implies a smaller subscription income for parties in an era when party expenses (not least for election campaigns) continue to rise. The problem of funding political parties has therefore become highly significant (Box 12.5). Should members, donors or the state pay for the party's work? Should donations be encouraged (to increase funds and encourage participation) or restricted (to maintain fairness and reduce scandals)? Do limits on contributions and spending interfere with free speech? Underlying these questions is another, perhaps deeper, one: are parties private or public entities?

In the main, the battle for public funding has been won. State support for national parties is now virtually universal in liberal democracies, providing the main source of party revenue in such countries as Austria, Denmark and Sweden. As Fisher and Eisenstadt (2004, p. 621) comment, 'public subsidies have replaced private sponsorship as the norm in political finance'. In Germany, where the constitution requires parties to participate in forming the democratic will, 'parties are the self-appointed beneficiaries of extraordinarily generous public subsidies which in recent years have provided on average 20–40 per cent of total party revenues' (Scarrow, 2002a, p. 86). State subsidies have also developed quickly in the new democracies of Eastern Europe, where party memberships are far smaller than in the West.

What forms does public funding take? Typically, support is provided for parliamentary groups, election campaigns or both. Campaign support, in turn, may be offered to parties, candidates or both. In an effort to limit state dependence, public funding may be restricted to matching the funds raised by the party from other means, including its members. In any case, most funding regimes only reimburse a specified proportion of party spending.

Indirect subsidies are also on offer, usually in the form of free access to the mass media. Historically, this subsidy took the form of free political broadcasts on state-owned television and radio. Some countries also require commercial broadcasters to make free time available as a condition of their licence. This subsidy in kind is extremely valuable and certainly wasteful. A more efficient use of resources would ensue if parties were given the cash equivalent, thus freeing them to decide for themselves on the best use of the money.

Altering the way in which any organization obtains its funds is always consequential; parties are no exception. Three points are significant here. First, public financing reduces a party's incentive to attract members. Party leaders know that their funding comes from the state and that they can appeal to the electorate directly through the mass media, limiting the political value of a membership army. Thus, the evolution of party funding contributes to a move away from mass parties and to a partial recovery of the old format of cadre parties.

Second, public funding tends to reinforce the status quo. Subsidies are normally proportional to party size: the more seats in the assembly, and the more votes won in the previous election, the greater the payout. Thus large established parties have an advantage over new ones. Some authors have developed this point by suggesting that the transition to public funding has led to a convergence of the state and the top levels of major parties on a single system of rule, sometimes called a party state. Governing parties in effect authorize subsidies for themselves, a process captured by Katz and Mair's idea (1995) of **cartel parties**: 'Colluding parties become agents of the state and employ its resources to ensure their own survival.' The danger here is that the largest parties are viewed as part of the political establishment, further weakening their historic role as agents of particular social groups. Seen as 'them' rather than 'us', cartel parties find their popular appeal diminishing still further.

Cartel parties are leading parties that exploit their dominance of the political market to establish rules of the game, such as public funding, which reinforce their own strong position. In politics, as in business, the danger of cartels is that they damage the standing of the colluders over the longer term.

Third, those who pay the piper can influence the tune. Public funding gives governments a device for influencing parties which they may wish to use in future to promote democracy within parties, to encourage particular types of candidate, or to discourage platforms judged unacceptable. To a degree, public funding is bound to turn parties into public utilities.

Issues of party finance extend beyond the provision of subsidies. What of donations: who can give how much and with what reporting requirements? This topic has also become more newsworthy, with increasing restrictions on **hard money** donations as a result of scandals in which cash-hungry parties have raised funds from private sources perceived by the public, rightly or wrongly, to be in search of a payback. But as hard money is regulated more tightly, so **soft money** expands, reducing the coherence of campaigns. In the United States, the perverse result can be that candidates avoid any contact with supporters running 'independent' campaigns (Cain and Goux, 2006).

Just as most democracies have introduced public funding, so too have most now banned anonymous contributions. A financial donation is treated as a public act, even though a vote is cast in secret (Nassmacher, 2006). Such transparency limits the freedom of citizens to use their money as they see fit

Hard money consists of campaign expenditure which is offically regulated. **Soft money** consists of campaign spending which is free of such regulation, often because it is made by organizations claiming to be independent of a party. The terms are American but there is a universal tendency for soft money to expand as hard money is regulated.

and must surely scare off publicity-shy donors. Several countries also outlaw foreign contributions, even though international organizations have played a major role in funding campaigns and elections in many new democracies. A few countries, including several new democracies, ban or limit contributions from public organizations, private companies and trade unions.

The issues involved in limiting donations emerge from considering the main outlier: the United States. American campaigns involve a relatively high proportion of private funding. The point here is not the high cost of American campaigns (expensive though they are) but the philosophical priority accorded to free speech. The judiciary has been especially concerned to enforce the first amendment: 'Congress shall make no law . . . abridging the freedom of speech'. Alexander (2005, p. 7) contrasts the United States with the more representative case of Canada:

> The United States follows a more libertarian or free-speech approach, with more dependence upon private financing through more generous contribution limits from individual, political action committee and political party sources. Spending limits are provided only in presidential campaigns and according to a Supreme Court decision, *Buckley* v. *Valeo* (1976), are acceptable only when candidates voluntarily agree to them as a condition of their acceptance of public funding.

Whether regulation concerns public or private funding, a regulator is required to ensure compliance. Often, responsibility for implementing party finance laws lies with an independent electoral commission. Like other regulators, these agencies engage in a never-ending game with parties that show endless ingenuity in circumventing the rules: 'The more perfect the regulation', it is said, 'the more perfect the loophole'. As in many areas or regulation, those subject to the rules – political parties – tend to be one step ahead of their regulator.

The waning social base

Most modern parties in Western Europe emerged from outside the assembly to express group interests, naturally developing a specific social base which continues to influence their policies and outlook. Although these foundations have weakened significantly since the 1960s, West European parties retain a bedrock of electoral support in the social structure. In the post-communist systems of Eastern Europe, by contrast, most contemporary parties lack secure anchors in society.

Western Europe

In a renowned analysis focused on Western Europe, Lipset and Rokkan (1967) showed how critical moments on the journey to a modern, developed state created **cleavages** which provided a long-term foundation for political parties.

Thus, the decisive moment in the development of the state in Western Europe – the penetration of state authority throughout its territory – encouraged the formation of conservative parties representing the centralizing elite and, by reaction, regional parties representing the threatened periphery. Often, too, state-building led to the founding of Catholic parties seeking to defend the traditional autonomy of the church against state encroachment, particularly in education.

> A **cleavage** is a social division creating a collective identity among those on each side of the divide. These interests are expressed in such organizations as trade unions, churches and parties. In Western Europe, class and religion have proved to be the widest and deepest cleavages (Mair, 2006).

At a later stage, beginning in the nineteenth century, the industrial revolution created further cleavages. The agricultural sector found itself threatened by the rise of industry, encouraging both farmers' parties and liberal parties representing the rising class of entrepreneurs. At a later stage, class conflict intensified between industrial workers and employers, leading almost everywhere to socialist parties representing the new industrial working class.

Lipset and Rokkan claimed that in the 1960s West European parties still remained largely frozen in the framework established by the way these historic cleavages developed in particular countries. Even though the underlying cleavages had begun to fade, the parties based on them remained secure. However, considerable thawing has taken place since the 1960s. For instance:

- Many Catholic parties have repositioned themselves on the centre-right;
- Most agrarian parties have moved to the centre;
- Working-class socialist and communist parties have adopted a milder social democratic flavour.

These more open conditions have permitted the emergence in many West European countries of right-wing **protest parties** such as France's National Front, Austria's Freedom Party and Switzerland's People's Party. By the mid 1990s, 15 far right parties had gained seats in national legislatures or the European parliament; a few had acquired power at local level or even, as with Austria's Freedom Party, participated in governing coalitions (Ignazi, 2006). Even where power has not been achieved, the extreme right has often succeeded in influencing the agenda of mainstream conservative parties.

These protest parties are an exception to the thesis that parties emerge to represent well-defined social interests. Such parties draw heavily on the often transient support of uneducated and unemployed young men. Disillusioned with orthodox democracy, this constituency is attracted to parties that blame immigrants, asylum seekers and other minorities for its own insecurity in a changing world (Lubbers *et al.*, 2002). However, many right-wing movements have proved to be **flash parties** whose prospects are held back by inexperienced leaders with a violent or even criminal background. Were the more extreme of these parties to expand to a point where they threatened the existing order, many protest voters would cease to vote for them, thus creating a natural ceiling to their support.

Although no one today would describe party systems as frozen, the plain fact is that in the political market (as in many others) the major players have retained their leading position. Decline does not imply disintegration. In New Zealand, for instance, 'despite the array of parties represented in parliament, the two major parties have continued to attract the lion's share of the vote' (Miller 2005, p. 5). Sundberg (2002, p. 210) offers a similar appraisal of Northern Europe:

> Parties in Scandinavia remain the primary actors in the political arena. To be old does not automatically imply that the party as a form of political organization is obsolete. The oldest car makers in the world are more or less the same age as the oldest parties in Scandinavia, yet nobody has questioned the capacity of these companies to renew their models. The same is true for political parties. They have developed their organizations and adapted their policies to a changing environment.

Protest parties exploit popular resentment against the government or the political system, usually by highlighting specific issues such as high taxes or a permissive immigration or asylum policy. They are often short-lived **flash parties** which fall as quickly as they rise. Their leaders are typically populist but inexperienced, with activists operating on the margins of the law.

Eastern Europe

In Eastern Europe, post-communist parties have failed to develop the large memberships, strong extra-parliamentary organizations and tangible links with social groups that still characterize many of their equivalents in the West. Often, the successor to the old communist party remains the best-organized entity, with a loyal if ageing membership. The weakness of new parties in Eastern Europe is important because it suggests that strong membership organizations are no longer necessary in contemporary conditions. The mass parties of Western Europe may be an increasingly unreliable guide to party developments elsewhere.

As the national movements which initially seized power from the communists began to split, many new parties certainly appeared in the East, representing groups such as peasants or ethnic minorities and embracing positions ranging from liberalism to nationalism. However, most of these East European parties are of the cadre type. Their base is in parliament or even the government itself. Steen's comment (1995, p. 13) about the Baltic countries – Estonia, Latvia and Lithuania – applies more generally to the post-communist world: 'The parties are more like campaigning institutions before elections than permanent institutions propagating ideology'. In that respect, post-communist parties follow the American rather than the Western European model.

The failure of parties to penetrate post-communist societies reflected continuing suspicion of politics among the population. Even after communism fell, it remained difficult to enthuse electors who had been denied a political voice during, and often before, the communist era. In addition, parties lacked the incen-

DEBATE

ARE PARTIES IN CRISIS?

Parties were major players in twentieth-century politics, drawing millions of people into politics for the first time and enabling emerging social groups to be represented in national debates. The question for the new century is whether this work is largely complete, leading to a crisis of parties and their decline into weak, decentralized organizations (on the North American model) or their reversion to leader-dominated cartel parties (as in Eastern Europe).

YES

The mounting evidence for a crisis of parties can be summarized in ten cumulative statements:

- Major parties no longer offer radically different visions of the good society;
- Electors' party loyalties are weakening as traditional social divisions decay;
- Party links with organizations such as trade unions and churches have eroded;
- Party members are older than the average person and becoming less active;
- Party membership is falling and will continue to do so as older members leave the electorate;
- Young people are more likely to join single-issue groups than parties;
- Parties have become charity cases, relying for funding on state handouts;
- Parties are subject to increasing regulation by the state;
- Trust in parties is lower than for other political institutions, and is declining;
- Parties remain state-based even though politics itself has become more international.

NO

Our friend on the left makes a familiar error in political analysis, mistaking change for decline and evolution for crisis. Rather, let Crotty (2006, p. 499) be our guide: 'The demands of society change, and parties change to meet them'.

Too often, models of what parties 'ought' to be like are drawn from the narrow experience of Western Europe in the twentieth century.

Today, it is unrealistic to expect the rebirth of mass membership parties with their millions of working-class members and their supporting pillars of trade unions.

In an era of mass media and electronic communciation, such an organizational format has gone for good.

In its stead, comes the new format of parties found in the new democracies: lean and flexible, with communication from leaders through the broadcast media and the internet.

Rather than relying on outdated notions of a permanent army of members, new-format parties mobilize volunteers for specific, short-term tasks, such as election campaigns.

The form of parties will continue to evolve but their purpose of giving direction to government continues unchanged.

ASSESSMENT

Parties may well be shifting their base from society to state but it is difficult to see how any democracy, liberal or illiberal, could survive without them altogether. As banks are to the financial system, so parties are to democracy: too important to fail. Just as many people retain an interest in politics, even if they no longer vote, so parties continue to perform essential political functions, even if their membership has fallen. Besides, few major parties in the democratic world have disappeared; decline does not equal crisis and even a crisis would not equal collapse.

Further reading

Bartolini and Mair (2001), Crotty (2006), Mair, Müller and Plasser (2004).

BOX 12.6

Party systems in liberal democracies

	Definition	Examples
Dominant party system	One party is constantly in office, either governing alone or in coalition with other parties	Japan (Liberal Democrats), South Africa (African National Congress)
Two-party system	Two major parties compete to form single-party governments	Great Britain (Conservative and Labour), United States* (Democratic and Republican)
Multiparty system	The assembly is composed of several minority parties, leading to government by coalition or a minority party	Belgium, Netherlands, Scandinavia

* However, divided government means one party can control the presidency while the other has a majority in either or both houses of Congress.

tives to build a mass organization that had stimulated socialist parties a century earlier. Since voting had already extended to virtually the whole population, there was no need for socialist parties to emerge to demand the suffrage for an excluded working class. Also, parties in the Czech Republic, Poland, Hungary and Slovakia soon obtained state subsidies, eliminating the financial need to build a dues-paying membership. And the existence of television provided a channel of communication from the leaders to the electorate, reducing the value of local activists. Kitschelt *et al.* (1999, p. 396) even suggest these soft party structures may be advantageous:

> The absence of sunk costs in large membership organizations enables Eastern European democracies to enjoy the 'advantages of backwardness' and frees its politicians from devoting their energies to fighting armies of party functionaries.

Party systems

To understand the political significance of parties, we must move beyond an examination of them individually. Just as a football game consists of two teams, so a **party system** consists of interaction between several parties. Even more than countries, parties copy, learn from and compete with each other, with innovations in organization, fund-raising and election campaigning spreading across the party system. Similarly, the rules affecting all parties, such as legal regulations and the electoral system, exert an influence across the board. They shape the party system as a whole.

Like parties themselves, patterns of party competition persist over time, forming part of the operating procedures of democratic politics. We can distinguish three overlapping formats: **dominant**, **two-party** and **multiparty systems** (Box 12.6). Before we discuss each type, we should note that both dominant and two-party systems are now in decline.

A **party system** denotes the number of significant parties and the patterns of interaction between them. In a democracy, parties respond to each other's initiatives in competitive interplay. The United States shows that a party system can be strong even when the parties themselves are weak.

Multiparty systems, lacking a single dominant party, have become the most common configuration in liberal democracies.

Dominant party systems

Sartori (1976, p. 193) offers a straightforward definition of this format: 'Whenever we find a party that outdistances all the others, this party is dominant in that it is significantly stronger than all the others'. Sustaining a predominant position is a difficult assignment for any party in a liberal democracy. In practice, such parties use their control of the state to reward their supporters, thus building a more secure support base but also rendering themselves vulnerable to corruption and decline.

One of the few contemporary examples of a dominant party is the African National Congress (ANC) in South Africa. This party has multiple strengths, benefiting not just from memories of its opposition to apartheid and from its strong position among the black majority but also from its use of office to reward its own supporters. In the 2004 assembly elections, the party secured 70 per cent of both votes and seats, a remarkable achievement. The opposition parties, in contrast, are weak and divided, with a smaller social base.

Sweden provides an additional case of a party that continues to dominate despite operating in what is clearly a competitive and well-regulated multiparty system. The oddity of the Swedish case is that, in contrast to South Africa, its leading party does not usually possess a parliamentary majority but typically governs in a minority administration with parliamentary support from minor parties of the left.

Even so, the Social Democratic Workers' Party (Socialdemokraterna, SAP) has formed all but a handful of governments since the war. It is the country's oldest party, gaining support from both the working class and the large public sector, and occupies a pivotal ideological position on the centre-left. More than most dominant parties, SAP has combined stable leadership with competent governance, enabling it to maintain its leading position in a genuinely competitive party system. Even though the Social Democrats suffered a loss of power in 2006, they remained the largest party in both votes and seats.

In the long run, dominant parties have tended to fall victim to their own success. The very strength of a dominant party's position means that factions tend to develop within it, leading to an inward-looking perspective, a lack of concern with policy and increasing corruption.

India provides us with a diminished 'dominant' party. From independence in 1947, Indian politics was led by the Congress Party, an organization which under Mahatma Gandhi had provided the focus of resistance to British colonial rule. To maintain its leading position, the party relied on a patronage pyramid of class and caste alliances to sustain a national organization in a fragmented and religiously divided country. For two decades, Congress proved to be a successful and resilient catch-all party, drawing support from all social groups. Lacking access to the perks of office, no other party could mount a challenge to Congress's hegemony. But authoritarian rule during Indira Gandhi's State of Emergency (1975–77) cost Congress dear. The party suffered its first defeat at a national election in 1977 and in the 2004 election it secured just 27 per cent of the vote. It remains the largest party, and the lead party in a minority coalition government, but its glory days are gone.

Two-party systems

In a two-party system, two major parties of comparable size compete for electoral support, providing the framework for political competition. The remaining parties exert little if any influence on the formation and policies of governments. Neither major party dominates by itself but in combination they provide the pillars of a strong party system.

Today, the United States is the surest example. Although American parties may lack the sociological foundations of their West European counterparts, a two-party system has been a constant feature of American history. The Republicans and Democrats have dominated electoral politics since 1860, assisted by the high hurdle that plurality elections set for minor parties. In particular, winning a presidential election is a political mountain which can only be climbed by major parties capable of assembling a broad national coalition.

Legal regulation has reinforced America's two-party system. From the 1880s, state legislatures and then the courts imposed a burden of regulation on America's parties, initially to root out corruption. These regulators have traditionally viewed parties as

COUNTRY PROFILE

ITALY

Form of government ■ parliamentary, with an indirectly elected president who can play a role in government formation.

Legislature ■ the Chamber of Deputies (630 members) and the Senate (315) are elected simultaneously by popular vote for a maximum of five years. A bill must receive the positive assent of both houses and (as in Australia) the Cabinet is equally responsible to both chambers.

Executive ■ the prime minister formally appoints, but cannot dismiss, the members of the large Cabinet. Coalition requirements limit the PM's choice.

Judiciary ■ based on the civil law tradition, Italy has both ordinary and administrative judicial systems. A 15-member Constitutional Court has powers of judicial review.

Electoral system (Chamber of Deputies, 2006) ■ party list 'proportional' representation with the winning coalition guaranteed at least 340 seats.

Population (annual growth rate): 58.1m (+0.04%)
World Bank income group: high income
Political Rights score: 1
Civil Liberties score: 1
Human development index (rank/out of): 27/177
Freedom of the press index (rank/out of): 77/194
Ease of doing business index (rank/out of): 82/175

Note: For meaning and sources of scales and indexes, see p. xvi. In all cases a score and rank of 1 is 'best'.

ITALY was late to join the club of states, uniting only in 1861. As in many countries, unification preceded rather than followed the emergence of a common national identity. The powerful Catholic Church organized itself outside, and to an extent against, the new state. Acute regional contrasts, particularly between the more modern North and the underdeveloped South, remain important.

Since unification, Italy has experienced three different systems of rule:

- A constitutional monarchy which continued until 1922
- The fascist regime of Benito Mussolini, overthrown by an Allied invasion in 1943
- A parliamentary and republican democracy established in 1946

The constitution taking effect in 1948 established a liberal democracy with a strong emphasis on checks and balances: two legislative chambers of equal status; a constitutional court; an independent judiciary; proportional representation; and provisions for referendums and regional government. As a concession to the left, the constitution also emphasized social and economic rights and placed the state under an obligation to address inequality.

The most obvious feature of government in the new republic was its instability, with over 50 governments in as many years. Coalitions emerged and fell, limiting the authority of the prime minister and the standing of government as a whole. Yet after a government fell, the same ministers would often return under a new administration (Giulio Andreotti was prime minister seven times) and public policy was rather more stable than government turnover might imply.

Government instability proved compatible with social modernization. Like other European countries, Italy underwent enormous development in the post-war decades. Although the economy became more industrial and open, contrasts persisted between a few large industrial companies (often politically well-connected) and a throng of smaller, family firms operating independently of the state.

The overall environment for business remains difficult by the standards of high income countries. Regulation is extensive, the non-wage costs of employment are high and the legal system remains extremely slow-moving.

The disparity between an increasingly sophisticated private sector and a spendthrift state with an inefficient bureaucracy provided part of the backdrop to the 1990s' transformation.

Further reading: Ginsborg (2003), Hine (1993).

SPOTLIGHT

Parties in Italy

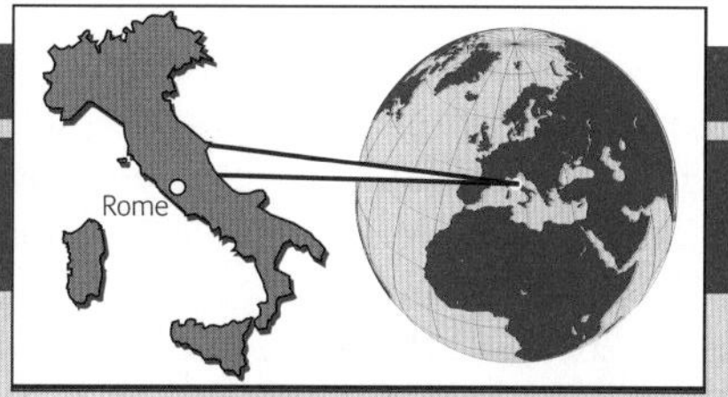

The story of Italian politics is, first and foremost, a story about parties. In the 1990s, a dominant party system collapsed with astonishing speed, to be replaced after an interregnum by a more bipolar, but still not completely stable, system. Changes of this magnitude and speed are rarely encountered in liberal democracies.

Until 1992, Italy was a leading example of a dominant party system. The Christian Democrats (DC) were a leading player in all post-war governments until 1992. A patronage-based, Catholic catch-all party that derived its political strength from serving as a bulwark against Italy's strong communist party, the DC slowly colonized the state, with particular ministries becoming the property of specific factions. The party used its control of the state to reward its supporters with jobs and contracts, creating a patronage network that spun across the country.

Between 1992 and 1994, this party system disintegrated. Still the largest party in 1992, the Christian Democrats had ceased to exist two years later. Its old sparring partner, the communists, had already given up the ghost, largely reforming as the Democratic Party of the Left (PDS) in 1991. Why then did this party-based system collapse? Catalysts included the collapse of communism; referendums on electoral reform in the early 1990s which revealed public hostility to the existing order; vivid attacks by Francesco Cossiga (President, 1985–92) on the patronage power of the leading parties; and the success of a newly assertive judiciary in exposing corruption. Like many other dominant parties, the DC's reliance on patronage also came under global and EU pressures for a genuinely open market.

Although the collapse of the old system was decisive, Italy's new order is only now beginning to deliver more stable government. The election of 1994, the first fought under a new electoral system designed to reduce fragmentation, fell apart after seven months. It was replaced by an astonishing crisis government of technocrats containing no parliamentary representatives at all. The next election, in 1996, did produce signs of consolidation. Two major alliances emerged: the centre-left Olive Tree Alliance and the more right-wing Liberty Pole.

But it was not until 2001, when Berlusconi's House of Freedom coalition won a majority in both legislative chambers, that stable government seemed to become a serious possibility. However, consolidation remained insecure partly as a result of Berlusconi's own volatile temperament. Berlusconi's miscalculations permitted a narrow victory in 2006 for Romano Prodi's coalition of the centre-left, now renamed The Union. Prodi's new administration still faced the problem of all post-war Italian governments: many difficulties to resolve (including its own survival) but insufficient means to do so.

Whatever the future may bring, Italy's old mass parties have disappeared, replaced by the looser, leader-dominated parties which are characteristic of the new democracies founded in the 1990s. The rapid decline of the DC showed just how vulnerable and outdated its form of dominant party rule had become.

Election to the Chamber of Deputies, 2006

Party group	*Leader*	*Votes (%)*	*Seats*
The Union	Romano Prodi	49.8	348
House of Freedom	Silvio Berlusconi	49.7	281
Turnout: 83.6% (+2.4)			

Source: IPU (2006b).

Further reading: Bull and Newell (2005).

semi-official utilities performing the collective service of selecting candidates for public office. This perspective encourages sympathetic oversight of the major parties; minor parties, unable to present winning candidates, meet with indifference (Lowenstein, 2006). So the position of the Republicans and Democrats is heavily entrenched. In the country of the free market, they form a powerful cartel.

Although Britain is often presented as emblematic of the two-party pattern, its contemporary politics barely passes the two-party test. Certainly, the Conservative and Labour parties regularly alternate in office, offering clear accountability to the electorate. However third parties have gained ground; far more so, indeed, than in the United States. In 2005, the centre Liberal Democrats won 62 seats in a parliament of 646 members, the highest proportion for a third party in over 50 years. With six million votes, compared to 9.5 million for Labour and 8.8 million for the Conservatives, the Liberal Democrats can hardly be dismissed as also-rans. The Liberal Democrats have also progressed in local government and the new assemblies in Scotland and Wales. Today, Britain is best conceived as a two-and-a-half or even a multiparty system (Blondel, 1995, p. 165).

Like dominant parties, the two-party format now appears to be in decline, kept alive only by the ventilator of the plurality electoral method and sometimes not even then. The long-term shift away from first-past-the-post elections has damaged the prospects of two-party systems. Even where a favourable electoral regime continues, as in Canada, the two-party system has buckled. Canada's Conservatives and Liberals no longer dominate the political landscape to the exclusion of other parties.

Multiparty systems

In multiparty systems, several parties – typically, at least five or six – achieve significant representation in parliament, becoming serious contenders for a place in a governing coalition. The underlying philosophy is that political parties represent specific social groups (or, increasingly, opinion constituencies such as environmentalists) in historically divided societies. Parliament then serves as an arena of conciliation, with coalition governments forming and falling in response to often minor changes in the political balance. This emphasis on the representative and consensus-seeking function of parties contrasts sharply with the American notion of parties as post-fillers. The smaller European democracies, such as the Benelux countries and Scandinavia, exemplify the multiparty pattern.

The exact configuration of parties in a multiparty system varies by country. Typically, parties will be drawn from some but not all of the families identified in Box 12.7. In the left bloc are far left parties (usually with a communist origin), the greens and the social democrats. The centre and right bloc contains what are sometimes called bourgeois parties: Christian Democratic, conservative, centre and liberal, plus the far right. In multiparty systems, the familiar competition between a social democratic party of the left and either a Christian Democratic or a conservative party of the right is supplemented by parties drawn from other families. These additional parties are rarely large but their combined representation in parliament, facilitated by proportional representation, suffices to yield a multiparty system.

Denmark provides a clear example. Here, no party has held a majority in the unicameral Folketing (People's Diet) since 1909. The country's complex party system has been managed through careful consensus-seeking but this practice has come under some pressure from the rise of new parties. Traditionally, the Danish party system was composed of four main parties: the Social Democratic Party, the Social Liberal Party, the liberal Venstre Party and the Conservative People's Party. After 1945, the typical coalition produced by this stable four-party system was between the Social Democrats and the pivotal Social Liberals. However, in an explosive election in 1973 three new parties achieved representation and since then a minimum of seven parties has been represented in parliament. The coalition that emerged in 2005 was between the liberal Venstre party and the Conservative People's Party, with support in parliament from the far right Danish People's Party.

Clearly, multiparty systems such as Denmark's are far removed from the concentration of power in Britain or even the focus of responsibility in the United States on the president in the White House. To evaluate multiparty systems, we must therefore take a view on the nature of coalitions. How effective are they in delivering sound governance? Should we agree with Herbert Asquith, British prime

BOX 12.7

Major party families in Western Europe

	Level of support	Trend in electoral support	Examples	Comment
LEFT				
Far Left	Low	⇩	Communist Party (France). Left Party (Sweden).	Once a strong force in Finland, France and Italy, most communist parties have now reformed or decayed.
Green	Low	⇧	Alliance '90/The Greens (Germany). Green League (Finland).	Ecology parties emerged from the late 1970s and have participated in coalition governments in several countries.
Social Democrat	High	⇧	Social Democratic Workers' Party (Sweden). Social Democrats (Finland).	Originally created to advance working-class and trade union interests, as well as socialist values, most such parties no longer challenge the capitalist order.
CENTRE AND RIGHT				
Christian Democrat	High	⇩	Christian Democratic Appeal (Netherlands). Christian Democratic Union (Germany).	Mainly Catholic in origin but with some Protestant cases, Christian Democratic parties now mainly represent the centre-right.
Conservative	High	⇔	Conservative Party (Britain, Norway).	These parties emphasize shared national loyalties and class unity, advocating a strong state and a market economy.
Centre	Medium	⇔	Centre Party (Finland, Norway, Sweden).	Farmers' parties by origin, these parties have moved to the centre while often retaining traditional moral values.
Liberal	Medium	⇔	Liberal Party (Netherlands). Venstre, Denmark's Liberal Party.	Early advocates of universal suffrage, liberal parties favour individual rights and decentralization.
Far Right	Low	⇧	Flemish Block (Belgium). National Front (France).	These racist and anti-immigration parties possess a strong nationalist and anti-establishment flavour.

Note: Level of support is assessed for countries in which a relevant party exists. Trend in support is from 1950 or foundation. Regional and New Left parties are also significant in some states.

Source: Adapted from Gallagher, Laver and Mair (2006), Chapter 8.

minister 1908–16, when he wrote, 'Nothing is so belittling to the stature of public men, as the atmosphere of a coalition'?

Answers to this question have evolved over time, largely in response to economic performance. As the quotation from Asquith suggests, the English-speaking world has long treated coalitions with suspicion, regarding them as weak in operation and confused in their accountability. If things went wrong, which parties should be blamed? But opinions of coalitions became more positive as post-war recovery took hold. In practice, coalitions seemed to produce policy continuity while two-party systems such as Britain's now stood accused of an outdated adversarial approach.

However, the link between coalitions and weak government resurfaced in the 1990s. This reinterpretation reflected the tough 1990s agenda: welfare cuts, privatization and tax reductions. It was the traditional two-party systems, notably in Britain and New Zealand, that pursued the new policies with most energy. Continental Europe lagged behind, leading to doubts about whether multiparty systems were sufficiently flexible to produce the rapid policy changes needed to adapt to a global economy. Blondel (1993), for one, argued that

> the consensus mode of politics is not well-equipped to lead to long-term strategic action ... its value appears to lie primarily in its ability to handle deep social cleavages rather than policy development.

A balanced conclusion is perhaps that coalitions produce continuity of policy which is helpful when the economy is growing naturally, but are slower, though not necessarily less successful in the long run, at reviving economies which have fallen on hard times.

Parties in authoritarian states

'Yes, we have lots of parties here', says President Nazarbaev of post-communist Kazakhstan. 'I created them all' (Cummings, 2005, p. 104). This quotation indicates the secondary character of parties in most non-democratic settings. As Lawson (2001, p. 673) says of parties in dictatorships, 'the party is a shield and instrument of power. Its function is to carry out the work of government as directed by other agents with greater power (the military or the demagogue and his entourage)'.

However, the position of parties in totalitarian regimes is an exception to this rule about the inferior position of parties in non-democracies. Under communism, of course, the party directed the work of government rather than the other way round. In this section, we examine the role of parties in non-totalitarian authoritarian regimes before turning to the distinctive and contrasting experience of parties under communism and fascism.

Authoritarian regimes

Some authoritarian regimes still survive with no parties at all. These are either **pre-party** or **anti-party** states. Pre-party states are most commonly found in the Middle East: for example, Saudi Arabia, Jordan and Kuwait. In these traditional monarchies, a ruling family dominates and parties are considered incompatible with its esteemed position. In the more common anti-party state, existing parties were banned when a new regime took over. For example, newly installed military rulers quickly moved to abolish parties, claiming that the nation could no longer afford the bickering and corruption associated with them.

> No-party systems are **pre-party** or **anti-party**. In the former, parties have yet to emerge or be permitted by authoritarian rulers. In the latter, parties are banned following a change of regime.

However, most civilian authoritarian rulers have found a single party useful as a disguise for personal rule and as a technique for distributing patronage. In post-independence Africa, for example, the heroes of the nationalist struggle soon put a stop to party competition. With independence achieved, one-party systems were established, with the official party serving as the leader's personal vehicle. The tradition of the chief was skilfully exploited by dictators such as President Mobutu of the Congo (later Zaire):

> In our African tradition, there are never two chiefs; there is sometimes a natural heir to the chief, but can anyone tell me that he has known a village that

has two chiefs? That is why we Congolese, in the desire to conform to the traditions of our continent, have resolved to group all the energies of the citizens of our country under the banner of a single national party (quoted in Meredith, 2006, p. 295).

But even these single parties proved to be weak. Like government itself, they lacked presence in the countryside, were riven by ethnic and regional divisions and showed little concern with policy. True, the party was one of the few national organizations, and proved useful in recruiting supporters to public office, but these functions could not disguise a lack of cohesion, direction and organization. Indeed, when the founder–leader eventually departed, his party would sometimes disappear with him. When a coup overthrew Kwame Nkrumah in Ghana in 1966, his Convention People's Party also collapsed.

Cases of authoritarian rule where the political party, rather than a dominant individual, is the true source of power are few and far between. One example is Singapore. Here the People's Action Party (PAP) maintains a close grip despite permitting a modest degree of opposition. Thus Lee Kuan Yew, the island's Prime Minister from 1959 to 1990, acknowledged that his party post rather than his executive office was the real source of authority: 'all I have to do is to stay Secretary-General of the PAP. I don't have to be president'. Tremewan (1994, p. 184) refers to the 'PAP-state' in which the party uses its control of public resources to ensure the quiesence of the citizens:

It is the party-state with its secretive, unaccountable party core under a dominating, often threatening personality which administers Singaporeans' housing, property values, pensions, breeding, health, media, schooling and also the electoral process itself.

Communist states

Communist states provide the limiting case of control by a single ruling party. If the mass party was the key political innovation of the twentieth century, the device reached its zenith in the dominance of ruling communist parties over state and society, notably in the Soviet Union (1917–91). Here we will outline the role of the party in traditional communist states before turning to its changing functions in contemporary China.

The monopoly position of ruling communist parties was justified by Lenin's notion of the vanguard party: the idea that only the party could fully understood the long-term interests of the working class. Armed with this doctrine, the Communist Party of the Soviet Union sought to implement its vision of a total transformation of society following the 1917 revolution.

In the USSR, the party's control was pervasive. It acted as a watchdog over society, vetted appointments to all positions of responsibility, controlled the media and carried out agitation and propaganda. Initially, few independent groups were permitted, leading to an absence of virtually any associations standing between the family and the state.

As with all totalitarian regimes, coercion (and even more its threat) helped communist parties to maintain their control. The secret police were the main instrument of repression, as with the feared NKVD (later KGB) in the Soviet Union. The KGB used a vast network of informers to identify, and then eliminate, 'class enemies' and 'poisonous weeds'. Where this system of social control operated fully, it provided the most systematic penetration of society that any political party anywhere has ever achieved.

Reforms notwithstanding, the Chinese Communist Party (CCP) still illustrates the elaborate internal hierarchy of ruling communist parties (Figure 12.1). At the party's base stand 3.3 million primary party organizations, found not just in local areas such as villages but also in factories and military units. At the top, at least in theory, is the sovereign National Party Congress, a body of around 2,000 people which meets infrequently and for short periods. In practice, the Congress delegates authority: to its 300-member Central Committee

Democratic centralism was a key feature of communist party organization. It was based on two principles: lower levels must accept decisions made by higher levels (the centralism dimension) and each level is to be elected by the one immediately beneath, forming a pyramid of indirect election (the democratic dimension). But only one person was nominated for each election and this candidate was chosen from above. In reality, democratic centralism was centralism without democracy.

Figure 12.1 Organization of the Chinese Communist Party

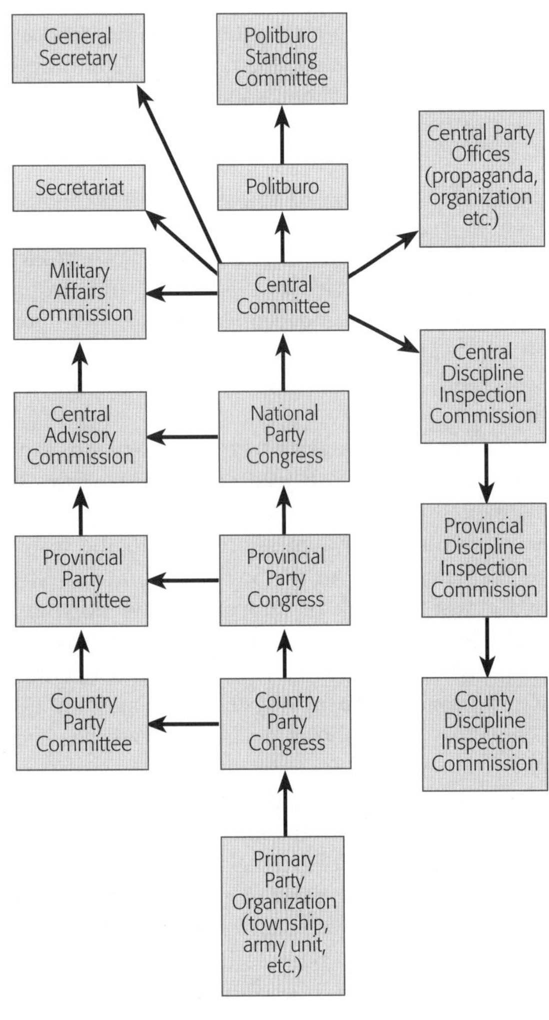

and, through that body, to the 22-strong Politburo ('political bureau') and its Standing Committee. This intricate pyramid allows the nine men on the Standing Committee to exert enormous influence over the political direction of the most populous country on earth – in itself, an astonishing political achievement.

The party is massive. In 2005, its membership reached 71 million, equivalent to the entire population of Turkey. And unlike most parties in the democratic world, the CCP's membership is still growing, increasing by five million between 2000 and 2005. Even in 2005, the membership was still only an elite 5 per cent of the total population; women, in particular, remain heavily under-represented (ChinaToday.com, 2006).

What accounts for the party's continuing appeal? The answer can hardly be ideology for the CCP's communist commitment is now nominal. Indeed, Saich (2004, p. 95) reports that on his travels he has met 'party members who are Maoists, Stalinists, Friedmanites, Shamans, underground Christians, anarchists, and social and liberal democrats'. At local level, many contemporary members of the Communist Party are now successful capitalists with businesses to run.

Party members are united by ambition rather than ideology. The CCP remains an important academy for go-getters. A business route to worldly success has now emerged but even the most apolitical entrepreneur still finds value in close party links. Members are prepared to undergo a searching entry procedure, and the continuing obligation to participate in dull party tasks, to secure privileged access to education, travel, information, contacts and above all opportunities to acquire wealth. Those who are particularly determined will seek out a patron to help them ascend the party hierarchy. Within the party's formal structure, it is personal patron–client networks, not political ideologies or policy differences, that provide the guiding force.

Unlike many authoritarian parties, the CCP has sought since the 1990s to strengthen its control over its own members, the government and even public debate. Tighter political control is a response to economic liberalization. Although reform has created sustained growth, its side effects have included massive unemployment, rural depopulation and increased corruption. Party leaders fear a reduction in the party's standing and eventually a threat to its political monopoly. Experience elsewhere in the communist world suggests they may well be right to do so.

Fascist parties

Unlike some communist parties, fascist parties never achieved comprehensive control over either state or society. The limited command of the fascist party reflected its commitment to the cult of the leader (**führerprinzip**). Where communist ideology venerated the party as the foundation of progress, fascist

The **Führerprinzip**, associated with the German philosopher Hermann Keyserling (1880–1946), views an organization as a quasi-military hierarchy of meritocratic leaders. Each leader possesses unqualified authority and answers only to those above. As applied by Hitler to the Nazi Party the *Führerprinzip* left little room for coherent, stable organization.

thinking was orientated to the leader as the living law and the personification of state and people. The fascist party served its leader, not the other way round. The party could not become a site of debate because policy was the leader's preserve.

The German experience confirms the tangential role of the party in fascist governance. The rise to power of the Nationalsozialistiche Deutsche Arbeiterpartei (NSDAP, Nazi Party) owed much to Hitler's opportunistic skills. Yet once power was achieved in 1933, the party became increasingly marginal. The regime focused more on personal loyalty to Hitler, downgrading the party. Soldiers, for instance, were prohibited from joining the party; they were servants of the state – and its leader. State officials were made to swear an oath of loyalty to the Führer rather than the party. The feared SS (*Schutzstaffel*, protection units) began as the Nazi Party's security force but developed into Hitler's own agency. The NSDAP became primarily a propaganda organization and even this function was eventually taken over by the government's own ministry. As Mommsen (1997, p. 170) writes:

> Many foreign observers, impressed by well-organized mass rallies, took it for granted that the NSDAP exerted an authoritative influence on decision-making; yet, in fact, it was increasingly condemned to political sterility.

Thus the significance of political parties in totalitarian states is not an issue which can be addressed without acknowledging the fundamental contrasts between communist and fascist regimes. Under communism, the political party reached its twentieth-century apogee, with Lenin's notion of the vanguard party rationalizing communist command of both state and society. By contrast, the ruling fascist party occupied a marginal position, becoming the vehicle of a supreme leader in a system that was simultaneously personal, state-centred and unstable.

Parties in illiberal democracies

The role of parties provides us with a fundamental contrast between liberal and illiberal democracies. In liberal democracies, a choice between coherent parties is the crucial instrument of representation, allowing voters to influence the direction of government. In an illiberal democracy, however, the choice becomes muddled. Either parties are not the true source of power or the selection on offer does not present alternative programmes to the electorate. To return to Ostrogorski's distinction, parties in an illiberal democracy are often as much a political form as a political force. They are shells for ambitious politicians (and powerful presidents) rather than disciplined actors in their own right. The result is the appearance of democracy but only, and to a varying degree, an approximation to its reality.

Post-communist Russia provides an example of ineffectual parties in an illiberal democracy. The party system is unstructured and free-floating, with parties playing second or even third fiddle in the president's orchestra (Rose, 2000). At national level, power is focused on the Kremlin and at most confirmed by the Duma (lower chamber). The party composition of the Duma is therefore only of secondary political interest. For example, Boris Yeltsin's dismissal of three governments in 1998–99 had no connection with the party balance in the Duma (White, 2005a).

In any case, the choice on offer in Duma elections is limited by the rapid turnover and limited coherence of parties. Where major Western parties have developed a recognized brand over the course of 100 or so years, Russian parties come and go with astonishing rapidity. Even a decade after the end of communist rule, most parties competing in the 2003 parliamentary elections were fighting their first campaign. What is more, these new parties succeeded in winning a majority of the list vote, showing the lack of entrenched party loyalties in the electorate. Only the dwindling communist successor party offered continuity and organization. Clearly, when parties cease to exist from one election to the next, it is impossible for them to be held to account.

Far more than in the United States, voters in Russia's presidential elections are choosing between candidates, not parties. The party is the vehicle but not the driver. President Putin did not even deign to belong to United Russia, an organization that had no clear vision other than to support him. Its guiding principle is 'common sense': the 'government should do what is best for the majority of citizens' (White, 2005a, p. 85). United Russia is what Russians term the 'party of power', meaning that the Kremlin uses threats and bribes to ensure it is supported by powerful ministers, regional governors and large companies. The equivalent in the USA would occur if the president were to start a new party just before his re-election campaign, dragooning state governors and the CEOs of well-known corporations into supporting his new entity.

Given their weak position, it is not surprising that Russian parties are poorly organized, with a small membership and minimal capacity to integrate a large and diverse country. In a manner typical of illiberal democracies, the rules concerning the registration of parties, the nomination of candidates and the receipt of state funding operate in favour of larger parties. Of course, the notion of cartel parties shows that similar processes are at work in liberal democracies too but usually to the benefit of at least two major parties. In post-communist Russia (as in the communist era), there is only one party of power.

Although the Russian story is distinctive in its details, the narrative is fundamentally similar in other illiberal democracies. In Latin American and African cases, too, the leading personality tends either to stand above the parties or to create a distinctly uneven playing field for the competition between them.

Venezuela under President Hugo Chávez is an example. From 1958, this oil-rich country was governed through the Pact of Punto Fijo – an agreement between the two major parties to marginalize other parties and to keep divisive issues off the agenda. This cartel gradually became corrupt and inefficient, allowing Chávez to promise in his 1998 presidential campaign that he would break the ossified puntofijismo system, thus empowering ordinary people. In reality, though, Venezuela has witnessed a transition from a system in which two parties were over-powerful to a populist regime in which parties are, by conventional democratic standards, insufficiently central to the political process.

Learning Resources for Chapter 12

Next step

Katz and Crotty (2006) is a comprehensive handbook on party politics.

Further reading

Webb *et al.* (2002) examine the condition of parties in a range of liberal democracies; Gunther *et al.* (2002) is a more thematic collection; Mair, Müller and Plasser (2004) focus on parties and dealignment while Luther and Müller-Rommel (2005) is thematic within Europe. In an interesting collection, Scarrow (2002c) gathers historic writings on parties from Bolingbroke to Ostrogorski. Ignazi (2006) considers extreme right parties in Western Europe. Kitschelt *et al.* (1999) and Lewis (2003) cover post-communist parties, van Biezen (2003) looks at new democracies in Europe and Brooker (2000) surveys parties in non-democratic regimes. Nassmacher (2001, 2006) discusses party finance.

Internet sources

ECPR Standing Group on Political Parties
Facilitates communication among political scientists studying parties
http://www.keele.ac.uk/depts/spire/sgpp/index.html

Parties and Elections in Europe
Database on European elections, parties and leaders
http://www.parties-and-elections.de/

Political Organizations and Parties Section, American Political Science Association
Furthers scholarship on American and comparative political parties
http://www.apsanet.org/~pop/

Part IV
GOVERNMENT AND POLICY

In this part we reach the heart of the subject, examining the major institutions of government and the policies crafted through them.

We begin with a chapter on constitutions and the legal framework (Chapter 13). Essential foundations of a liberal democracy, constitutions and the judiciary are growing in political significance as more governments come to operate under the rule of law. We then analyse multilevel governance, reviewing the relationships between central, provincial and local governments in the context of federal and unitary systems (Chapter 14).

Our focus next moves to the core institutions of national government, starting with the legislatures or parliaments which still serve as the key symbol of popular representation in national politics (Chapter 15). We then turn to what many people would naturally think of as 'the government': namely, the top political tier of leadership within the administration (Chapter 16).

Chapter 17 examines the supporting tier of departments and agencies which gives effect to, and also helps to shape, political decisions. There we seek to map the complex terrain of contemporary public administration. Chapter 18, finally, switches the focus from institutions to policy, aiming to understand its origins, implementation, evaluation and instruments.

Chapter 13
Constitutions and the legal framework

The academic study of politics began as a branch of law and belatedly these friends are now renewing old acquaintance. Four factors seem to be involved in this rebirth of interest in the legal dimension of politics:

- The late twentieth century witnessed an explosion of constitution-making among post-authoritarian states, with 85 constitutions introduced between 1989 and 1999 (Derbyshire and Derbyshire, 1999);
- Stimulated by the legal character of the European Union and by judicial activism in the USA, judges have become more willing to step into the political arena, not least in investigating corrupt politicians;
- Policy-makers have become more aware of the potential for a clear and consistent legal framework, expeditiously applied, to stimulate investment and economic growth;
- The expanding body of international law increasingly impinges on domestic politics, with judges called on to arbitrate between the conflicting claims of supranational and national law.

In connecting law and government, the idea of the **rule of law** offers a useful entry point. In liberal democracies, the rule of law has succeeded in ensnaring absolute rulers in the threads of legal restraint. In the words of A. V. Dicey (1885, p. 27), the nineteenth-century English jurist, the purpose of the rule of law is to substitute 'a government of laws' for a 'government of men'. Where law rules, governors cannot exercise arbitrary power and the powerful are subject to the same laws as everyone else. More specifically, the rule of law implies that laws are general, public, prospective, clear, consistent, practical and stable (Fuller, 1969).

The gradual implementation of the rule of law and **due process** is an accomplishment of liberal politics, providing a basis for distinguishing liberal from illiberal democracies, and both from authoritarian regimes. That success, however, is never completely secure. The American constitution did not alter on 11 September 2001 but the rights of immigrants who found themselves imprisoned for several months without charge suddenly became less certain. As with all countries facing external threats, the rule of law took second place to national security and needed to be rebuilt subsequently through the courts (Dempsey, 2002).

The **rule of law** is a Western and primarily Anglo-American term. Its varied dimensions include consistent application of the law; the same law for all; and **due process** (respect for an individual's legal rights) in implementation (Kleinfeld, 2006).

Within Western democracies, the two fundamental systems of law are **common law** and **civil law**. The common law is used mainly in the United Kingdom and its former colonies, including the USA. Originally based on custom and tradition, the common law consists of judges' decisions on specific cases. These decisions were first published as a way of standardizing legal decisions across a state's territory. Because judges abide by *stare decisis* (stand on decided cases), their decisions create precedents and form a predictable legal framework, contributing thereby to nation-building.

Common law, then, is judge-made law. Of course, explicit statutes (laws) are also passed by the legislature in specific areas but these statutes usually build on the common law and are themselves refined through judicial interpretation. So judges in common-law systems constitute an independent source of authority which is to some degree separate from the government itself.

Civil law, by contrast, is founded on written legal codes which seek to provide an overarching framework for the conduct of public affairs, including public administration and business contracts. The original codes were developed under Justinian, Roman Emperor between 527 and 565. **Roman law** has evolved into distinct civil codes, as for example in France and Germany, with the codes elaborated through laws passed by parliament. Civil law has shaped the legal character of the European Union, continental Europe and Latin America.

The **common law**, found in England and many of its former colonies, consists of judicial rulings on matters not explicitly treated in legislation. Common law is based on precedents created by decisions in specific cases. In the more widespread **civil law** system, judges reach decisions by applying extensive written codes rather than by comparing cases. Civil law derives from the original **Roman law** codes (civil law is unconnected with a 'civil case', a term used to indicate a non-criminal action).

In civil law, judges rather than juries identify the facts of the case (often indeed directing the investigation) before applying the relevant section of the code. Judges are viewed as impartial officers of the state, engaged in an administrative task; they are merely *la bouche de la loi* (the mouth of the law). The underlying codes often emphasize social stability as well as individual rights, although the more recent introduction of constitutions (which have established a strong position in relation to the codes) has strengthened the liberal theme in many civil law countries.

Constitutions

We can look at **constitutions** in two ways. The first reflects their historic role as regulator of the state's power over its citizens. For the Austrian philosopher Friedrich Hayek (1960), a constitution was nothing but a device for limiting the power of government. In similar vein, Friedrich (1937) defined a constitution as 'a system of effective, regularized restraints upon government action'. From this perspective, the key feature of a constitution is its statement of individual rights and its expression of the rule of law.

Certainly a bill of rights now forms part of nearly all written constitutions (Box 13.1). Although America's Bill of Rights confined itself to such traditional liberties as freedom of religion, speech and assembly, more recent constitutions are more ambitious, often imposing duties on rulers such as fulfilling citizens' social rights to employment and medical care. The Mexican constitution of 1917 was the first to introduce such provisions. Several post-communist constitutions have extended the list further, to include the right to childcare and a healthy environment.

The second and somewhat neglected role of constitutions is to specify a power map. Constitutions define the structure of government, articulating the pathways of power and the procedures for law-making. As Sartori (1994, p. 198) observes, the defining feature of a constitution lies in this provision of a frame of government. A constitution without a declaration of rights is still a constitution, whereas a document without a power map is no constitution at all. A constitution is therefore a form of political engineering, to be judged like any other construction by how well it survives the test of time. From this perspective, the American version, still standing after more than 200 years, is a triumph.

A traditional distinction contrasts written and unwritten constitutions. Yet no constitution is wholly unwritten; even the 'unwritten' British and New Zealand constitutions contain much relevant statute and common law. A contrast between **codified** and

A **constitution** sets out the formal structure of the state, specifying the powers and institutions of central government, and its relationship with other levels. In addition, constitutions express the rights of citizens and in so doing create limits on government. A **codified** constitution is set out in a single document; an **uncodified** constitution is spread among a range of documents and is influenced by tradition and practice.

BOX 13.1

The arrangement of constitutions

- A *preamble* seeks popular support for the document with a stirring declaration of principle and, sometimes, a definition of the state's purposes;
- An *organizational section* sets out the powers of government institutions;
- A *bill of rights* covers individual and perhaps group rights, including access to legal redress, and thereby sets limits on government;
- *Procedures for amendment* define the rules for revising the constitution.

Further reading: Duchacek (1991), Maddex (2000).

uncodified systems is perhaps more useful. Most constitutions are set out in detail within a single document, rather like a civil law code. By contrast, the uncodified constitutions of Britain and New Zealand come closer to the common law tradition. Sweden falls in between: its constitution comprises four separate acts passed at different times.

Amendment

Procedures for amendment are an important building block of the constitutional structure. Most constitutions are rigid (or 'entrenched'), thus rendering them more acceptable to the various interests involved in their construction. An entrenched constitution offers the general benefit, much prized by liberals, of predictability for those subject to it. A rigid framework also limits the damage should political opponents obtain power, for unless they can clear the amendment hurdle they too must abide by the values embedded in the settlement.

Uncodified constitutions, though rare, do offer the advantage of ready adaptability. In New Zealand, this flexibility permitted a recasting of the country's electoral system and government administration in the 1980s and 1990s. Similarly, the United Kingdom was able to devolve significant powers to Scotland and Wales without much constitutional ado. In most other countries such radical changes would have required constitutional amendment.

Constitutions are entrenched by setting a higher level and wider spread of support for constitutional amendments than for ordinary bills. Typically, amendment requires both a two-thirds majority in each house of parliament and additional endorsement from a broader constituency. In a federation, this extra ratification is from the component states; unitary countries usually employ a referendum (Box 13.2).

The amendment procedure offers clues as to the status of the constitution in relation to the legislature. When modifications cannot be approved by the legislature alone, the constitution stands supreme over parliament. In Australia, for example, amendments must be endorsed not just by the national parliament but also by a referendum achieving a concurrent majority: in most states and also in the country as a whole.

In a few countries, however, special majorities within the legislature alone are authorized to amend the constitution. In such a situation, the status of the constitution is somewhat reduced and that of the assembly increased. Germany is a partial example: amendments simply require a two-thirds majority in both houses. At the same time, the nucleus of Germany's Basic Law – which sets out core rights – is accorded the ultimate entrenchment. It cannot be amended at all.

Flexible constitutions can be amended in the same way that ordinary legislation is passed; Britain is the major example. **Rigid constitutions** are entrenched, containing a more demanding amendment procedure.

Although rigid constitutions may appear to be incapable of coping with change, in practice they are adapted through judicial interpretation. As we will see, the American Supreme Court has shown particular skill at adjusting an old document to fit new times. It has reinterpreted a constitution designed in the eighteenth century for the fresh challenges of later eras. Thus one contrast between rigid and flexible constitutions is that in the former the judiciary manages evolution while in the latter politicians take the lead.

BOX 13.2

Entrenching the constitution: some examples

	Amendments require the approval of
Australia	both houses of parliament, then a referendum achieving majority support (a) overall and (b) in a majority of states
Canada	both houses of parliament and two-thirds of the states containing at least half the population
Germany	a two-thirds majority in both houses of parliament[1]
Spain	a two-thirds majority in both houses of parliament and, if demanded by a tenth of either house, a referendum achieving majority support[2]
Sweden	majority vote by two successive sessions of parliament with an intervening election[3]
USA	a two-thirds majority in both houses of Congress and approval by three-quarters of the states[4]

Notes:

1 The federal, social and democratic character of the German state, and the rights of individuals within it, cannot be amended.

2 'Fundamental' amendments to the Spanish constitution must be followed by an election, ratification by the new parliament and a referendum.

3 Sweden has four fundamental laws which comprise its 'constitution'. These include the Instrument of Government and Freedom of the Press Act.

4 An alternative method, based on a special convention called by the states and by Congress, has not been used.

Origins

Constitutions are a deliberate creation, designed and built by the politicians of the day. As the English political theorist John Stuart Mill (1861) wrote, constitutions 'are the work of men . . . Men did not wake up on a summer morning and find them sprung up'. How then do constitutions come into being? What conditions create the founding moment in which societies set about reconstructing their political order?

New constitutions typically form part of a fresh start after a period of disruption. Such circumstances include:

- Regime change: for example, the collapse of communist rule;
- Reconstruction after defeat in war: for example, Japan after 1945;
- The achievement of independence: for example, much of Africa in the 1950s and 1960s.

Most constitutions experience a difficult birth. Often, they are compromises between political actors who have merely substituted distrust for conflict. In Horowitz's terms (2002), constitutions are built from the bottom up rather than designed from the top down. For instance, South Africa's post-apartheid settlement of 1996 achieved an accommodation between leaders of the white and black communities against a backdrop of near slavery and continuing racial hostility. Acceptability was everything; elegance was nothing.

As vehicles of compromise, most constitutions are vague, contradictory and ambiguous. They are fudges and truces, wrapped in fine words (Weaver and Rockman, 1993). As a rule, drafters are more concerned with a short-term political fix than with establishing a resilient structure for the long run. In principle, everyone agrees with Alexander Hamilton (1788b, p. 439) that constitutions should 'seek merely to regulate the general political interests of the nation'; in practice, they are lengthy documents reflecting an incomplete settlement between suspicious partners. Some topics are over-elaborated but other issues are left unresolved.

The lauded American constitution of 1787, although shorter than most, is no exception to this general picture. Finer's description (1997, p. 1495) makes the point: 'The constitution was a thing of wrangles and compromises. In its completed state, it was a set of incongruous proposals cobbled together. And furthermore, that is what many of its framers thought.'

The main danger of a new constitution is that it fails to endow the new rulers with sufficient authority. Too often, political distrust means the new government is hemmed in with restrictions, limiting its effectiveness. The American constitution, for instance, divides power to the point where its critics allege that the 'government', and specifically the president, can hardly govern at all.

The Italian constitution of 1948 is a further illustration of the tendency to under-power new constitutions. Its hallmark is *garantismo,* meaning that all political forces are guaranteed a stake in the political system. Thus the document establishes a strong bicameral assembly and provides for regional autonomy. These checks on power were intended to prevent a recurrence of fascist dictatorship and to accommodate the radical aspirations of the political left. In practice *garantismo* led to ineffective governance, contributing to the transformation of the parties (not the constitution) in the 1990s.

Judicial review and constitutional courts

Constitutions are no more self-implementing than they are self-made. Some institution must be found to enforce the constitution, striking down laws and practices that offend its principles. This review power has fallen to the judiciary. With a capacity to override the decisions and laws produced by democratic governments, unelected judges occupy a unique position both in and above politics. India's Supreme Court is even empowered to override constitutional amendments themselves. Through their power of review, constitutional courts express a liberal conception of politics, restricting the power of even elected rulers. In this way, **judicial review** both stabilizes and limits democracy.

Judicial power, furthermore, is only partly limited by the constitution. Inevitably, judicial interpretation varies with the temper of the times, creating a living constitution. Justice Thurgood Marshall (1987, p. 181) gives the example of the Supreme Court's evolving treatment of black Americans: they 'were enslaved by law, emancipated by law, disenfranchised by law; and, finally they have begun to win equality by law'. So, as another justice pointed out, 'we live under a constitution. But the constitution is what the judges say it is' (Hughes, 1916, pp. 185–6).

In reality, judicial power is far from unqualified. For one thing, constitutions do restrict what judges can plausibly say about them. Justices are only unfree masters of the document whose values they defend; like the hole in a doughnut, judicial discretion only exists as an area left open by a surrounding belt of restriction (Dworkin, 1977). Judges are aware of the danger of converting their court into a continuous constitutional convention and will normally seek to decide a case on narrow grounds (or assert that the issue should be resolved in the political arena). Like good generals, they prefer to keep their powder dry for the big occasion.

In any event, the impact of a court's judgements depends on its status among those who carry them out. As the American President Andrew Jackson said of his Chief Justice, 'John Marshall has made his decision, now let him enforce it'. Courts seeking to protect their own standing must therefore follow a delicate course, paying heed to the climate of opinion without being seen to pander to it. Ruth Ginsburg, an American Supreme Court justice, expressed her approach thus: 'an effective judge strives to persuade, not to pontificate' (1992, p. 194).

The function of judicial review can be allocated in two ways (Box 13.3). The first and more traditional

COUNTRY PROFILE

SOUTH AFRICA

Form of government ■ a liberal democracy with an executive president and entrenched provinces.

Legislature ■ the National Assembly, the lower house, consists of 400 members elected for a five-year term. The president cannot dissolve the assembly. The weaker upper house, the National Council of Provinces, contains ten delegates from each of the nine provinces.

Executive ■ a president heads both the state and the government, ruling with a cabinet. The National Assembly elects the president after each election.

Judiciary ■ the legal system mixes common and civil law. The Constitutional Court decides constitutional matters and can strike down legislation.

Electoral system ■ the National Assembly is elected by proportional representation using closed party lists. Provincial legislatures appoint the members of the National Council of Provinces.

Party system ■ the African National Congress (ANC; 279 seats and 70 per cent of the vote in 2004) has dominated the post-apartheid republic. The more liberal Democratic Alliance (50 seats), based largely on white support, forms the official opposition.

Population (annual growth rate): 44.2m (+0.4%)

World Bank income group: upper middle

Political Rights score: ❶

Civil Liberties score: 

Human development index (rank/out of): 119/177

Freedom of the press index (rank/out of): 58/194

Ease of doing business index (rank/out of): 29/175

Note: For meaning and sources of scales and indexes, see p. xvi. In all cases a score and rank of 1 is 'best'.

South Africa was shaped by two groups of settlers: the Boers (farmers), descended from Dutch-speaking colonists of the seventeenth century, and a smaller group of British colonists. The discovery of diamonds and gold in the late nineteenth century consolidated a reliance on migrant labour, providing the economic foundations for the system of apartheid (apartness) which was institutionalized after 1945.

Apartheid defined three races – white, coloured and black – and outlawed inter-racial marriage. Apartheid's survival into the 1990s showed that governments based on brute power can last a long time. Yet change was eventually induced by three main factors:

- The collapse of communism which destroyed the regime's bogeyman
- The imposition of sanctions by the EU and the United States
- Black opposition which began to encompass armed resistance

As so often, initial reforms merely stimulated demands for more and faster change. In 1990, ANC leader Nelson Mandela was released from prison after 26 years, symbolizing recognition by the white rulers that the time had come to negotiate their own downfall. Four years later, Mandela became president of a government of national unity, including the white-led National Party, after the ANC won the first multiracial elections with 63 per cent of the vote.

The ANC has subsequently confirmed its position as a dominant party. It remains the natural party of the black majority and has proved adept at incorporating a range of other organizations, including trade unions, into its framework. Unlike many other liberation movements, the cohesiveness of the party survived the transition from opposition to government and the retirement of its hero-leader. With a majority in the National Assembly and a leading position in every provincial assembly, the party remains in an exceptionally strong position.

Like many dominant parties, the ANC provides order in a country beset with social problems. These difficulties include not only the sensitive legacy of apartheid but also crime, inequality, poverty, unemployment, corruption, HIV/Aids and inadequate infrastructure and education. Average life expectancy is a mere 43 years and, unusually, is lower among women than among men.

Further reading: Buhlungu *et al.* (2006), Glaser (2001), Worger and Clark (2003).

SPOTLIGHT

The constitution and the legal framework in South Africa

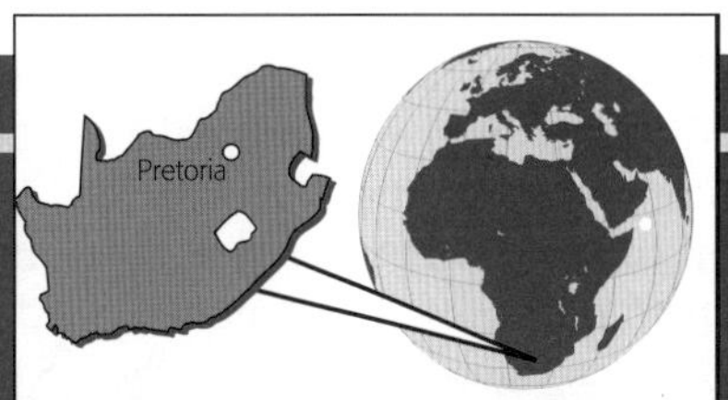

South Africa's transformation from a militarized state based on apartheid to a more constitutional order based on democracy was one of the most remarkable political transitions of the late twentieth century. The fact that the transition was largely peaceful, defying numerous predictions of an inevitable bloodbath, was the most astonishing fact of all.

In 1996, after two years of hard bargaining between the ANC and the white National Party (NP), agreement was reached on a new 109-page constitution to take full effect in 1999. The NP expressed general support despite reservations that led to its withdrawal from government.

In a phrase reminiscent of the American constitution, South Africa's constitution declares that 'the Executive power of the Republic vests in the President'. As in the USA, the president is also head of state. Unlike the United States, though, the president is elected by the National Assembly after each general election. He can be removed through an assembly vote of no confidence (though this event would trigger a general election) or by impeachment. The system is therefore fundamentally parliamentary in character. The president governs in conjunction with a large cabinet.

Each of the country's nine provinces elects its own legislature and forms its own executive headed by a premier. But far more than in the USA, authority and funds flow from the top down. In any case, the ANC provides a glue linking not just executive and parliament but also national, provincial and municipal levels of government. So far, at least, the ruling party has dominated the governing institutions whereas in the USA the institutions have dominated the parties.

It remains to be seen how South Africa's rainbow nation will be able to reconcile constitutional liberal democracy with the political dominance of the ANC. The ANC's strength in parliament is such that it could by itself virtually achieve the two-thirds majority required to amend the constitution, thus providing an exception to the generalization that fresh constitutions normally deny sufficient authority to a new government. Yet the country's politics, more than most, should be judged by what preceded it. By that test the achievements of the new South Africa are remarkable indeed.

Further reading: Butler (2004), Deegan (2001).

Preamble to the South African constitution, 1999

We, the people of South Africa,
Recognise the injustices of our past;
Honour those who suffered for justice and freedom in our land;
Respect those who have worked to build and develop our country; and
Believe that South Africa belongs to all who live in it, united in our diversity.

We therefore, through our freely elected representatives, adopt this Constitution as the supreme law of the Republic so as to

- Heal the divisions of the past and establish a society based on democratic values, social justice and fundamental human rights;
- Lay the foundations for a democratic and open society in which government is based on the will of the people and every citizen is equally protected by law;
- Improve the quality of life of all citizens and free the potential of each person; and
- Build a united and democratic South Africa able to take its rightful place as a sovereign state in the family of nations.

May God protect our people.

Source: South African Government Information (2006).

method is for the highest or supreme court in the ordinary judicial system to take on the task of constitutional protection. A supreme court rules on constitutional matters just as it has the final say on other questions of common and statute law. Australia, Canada, India and the USA are examples of this approach. Because a supreme court heads the judicial system, its currency is legal cases which bubble up from lower courts.

Judicial review empowers ordinary or special courts to nullify both legislation and executive acts that contravene the constitution. **Abstract review**, practised by constitutional courts only, is an advisory but binding opinion on a proposed law. **Concrete review**, practised by both types of court, arises in the context of a specific case.

A second and more recent method is to create a special constitutional court, standing apart from the ordinary judicial system. This approach originated with the Austrian constitution of 1920 and is now used in about 30 countries. It is much favoured in both Western and Eastern Europe. Spain, typically, has both a Constitutional Tribunal to arbitrate on constitutional matters and a separate Supreme Court to oversee national criminal law. The relationship between constitutional and ordinary courts is not always easy but most constitutional courts have established the priority of the constitution over the civil law codes.

Supreme courts

We will first examine the supreme court approach, using the United States as the original and most renowned example. The constitution vests judicial power 'in one Supreme Court, and in such inferior Courts as the Congress may from time to time ordain'. Although the Court possesses **original jurisdiction** over cases to which an American state or a representative of another country is a party, its main role is **appellate**; constitutional issues can be raised at any point in the ordinary judicial system, with the Supreme Court selecting for **concrete review** those cases that it regards as possessing broad significance. Most petitions to review a case are turned down.

The constitution does not itself specify the Court's role in adjudicating constitutional disputes. Rather, this function was gradually acquired by the justices themselves, with *Marbury* v. *Madison* (1803) proving decisive. In this case, Chief Justice Marshall struck down part of the Judiciary Act (1789) as unconstitutional, thereby establishing the principle of judicial review. At the same time, he skilfully avoided offending the administration on the specific issue, which involved the administration's disputed appointment of Marbury to a lower-level judgeship.

BOX 13.3

Judicial review: supreme courts vs. constitutional courts

	Supreme court	Constitutional court
Form of review	Concrete	More abstract
Relationship to other courts	Highest court of appeal	A separate body dealing with constitutional issues only
Recruitment	Legal expertise plus political approval	Political criteria more important
Normal tenure	Until retirement	Typically one non-renewable term (six to nine years)
Examples	Australia, United States	Austria, Germany, Russia

Original jurisdiction entitles a court to try a case at its first instance. **Appellate jurisdiction** authorizes a court to review decisions reached by lower courts.

The Court established its principle while avoiding an immediate controversy; honour was satisfied.

Stare decisis notwithstanding, the Supreme Court does occasionally strike out in new directions. This 'inconsistency' has proved to be a source of strength, enabling the Court to adapt the constitution to changes in national mood. For example, after its rearguard struggle against the New Deal in the 1930s, the Court conceded the right of the national government to regulate the economy.

At other times the Court has sought to lead rather than follow. The most important of these initiatives, under the leadership of Chief Justice Warren in the 1950s and 1960s, concerned black civil rights. In its unanimous decision in *Brown* v. *Topeka* (1954), the Court outlawed racial segregation in schools, dramatically reversing its previous policy that 'separate but equal' facilities for blacks fell within the constitution. The decision was path-breaking but its implementation was tortuous (Riches, 2004).

Constitutional courts

Continental Europe, both West and East, favours constitutional rather than supreme courts. In Western Europe, such courts were adopted after 1945 in, for instance, West Germany and France (Figure 13.1). They represented a general attempt to prevent a revival of dictatorship, whether of the left or the right, and in post-fascist states in particular a distrust of ordinary judges who had remained in place throughout the era of dictatorship. Half a century later, the successful German example in its turn provided an influential model for all post-communist countries in Eastern Europe (Kühn, 2006).

Where a supreme court is a judicial body making the final ruling on all appeals (not all of which involve the constitution), a constitutional court is more akin to an additional parliamentary chamber. The Austrian inventor of constitutional courts, Hans Kelsen (1881–1973), argued that these courts should function as a negative legislator, striking down unconstitutional bills but leaving positive legislation to parliament (Kelsen, 1942). Certainly, their approach is more political and less legal than that of supreme courts. Constitutional courts practice **abstract review**, judging the validity of a law or issuing advisory judgements on a bill without the stimulus of a specific case. Compared to the American Supreme Court, judgements are shorter and usually unsigned.

Just as the USA illustrates the supreme court tradition, so Germany has become an exemplar of the newer constitutional court approach. Its Constitutional Court consists of 16 members, divided into two specialized chambers of which one focuses on the core liberties defined in the constitution. Because political power was still under a cloud after the Second World War, the Federal Constitutional Court was charged not just with constitutional review but also with maintaining the constitutional order against groups seeking its overthrow. It has done just that, banning both communist and neo-Nazi parties in the 1950s. Its success is shown by its impact on the thinking of judges in ordinary courts, despite the formal separation of the constitutional court from the rest of the judicial hierarchy.

The Court's decisions have impinged on topics such as abortion, immigration, party funding, reli-

Figure 13.1 Establishing constitutional courts in Europe

* These countries also possessed similar, but somewhat ineffective, courts in the interwar period.

Source: Adapted from Stone Sweet (2000, p. 31).

gion in schools and university reform. Between 1951 and 1990, the Court ruled that 198 federal laws (nearly five per cent of the total) contravened the constitution. Its reputation has been enhanced by the unusual provision of constitutional complaint, a device permitting citizens to petition the Court directly once all other judicial remedies are exhausted. Conradt (2005, pp. 253–4) offers a useful assessment of the Court's achievements:

> More than any other postwar institution, the Constitutional Court has enunciated the view that the Federal Republic is a militant democracy whose democratic political parties are the chief instrument for the translation of public opinion into public policy. The court has become a legitimate component of the political system, and its decisions have been accepted and complied with by both winners and losers.

It would be remiss to conclude this section without considering the Court of Justice of the European Communities. Just as the Federal Constitutional Court in Germany helped to shape the development of a new republic, so too has the Court of Justice contributed to building the European Union. Especially between the 1960s and the 1980s, it was the decisive actor in expanding the EU's legal order. The cumulative impact of its decisions amounted to what Weiler (1994) terms a 'quiet revolution' in developing the founding treaties into something closer to a European constitution.

The Court's formal purpose is to ensure that the Union's treaties, and the provisions of its institutions, are correctly interpreted and applied. Cases can be brought by member states or by other institutions of the Union. As the final arbiter of European Union law, the Court of Justice also responds to requests from national courts for preliminary rulings on European law. It is unconnected with the European Court of Human Rights in Strasbourg.

The Court of Justice consists of one judge appointed from each member state for a renewable six-year term, with broad experience more important than judicial expertise. Many cases are dealt with by small chambers of three to five judges; further support is provided by eight advocates-general whose function is to make an initial recommendation on most cases before the Court. Even though a Court of First Instance was established in 1988 to share the workload, the time between lodging a case and final decision still averages almost two years (Nugent, 2006, p. 296).

In its early decades, the Court's decisions consistently and creatively strengthened the authority of central institutions (see Timeline). It achieved this goal in three ways, insisting that European law:

- Applies directly within member states (direct applicability);
- Must be enforced by national courts (direct effect);
- Takes precedence over national law (primacy).

In the 1990s, however, some member states began to question both the Court's procedures and further expansion of its authority. Some slippage occurred in implementing the Court's decisions and a few national courts grew restive. In particular, Germany's Federal Constitutional Court was keen to retain jurisdiction over whether European treaties violated Germany's own constitution.

Even so, the Court of Justice of the European Communities remains the pre-eminent example of a judicial contribution to the emergence of a new political order, justifying Shapiro's comment (1987, p. 1007) that 'no other court has ever played so prominent a role in the creation of the basic governmental and political process of which it is a part'. Other courts, including America's, have strengthened the central authority; the European Court helped to create one.

Judicial activism

Perhaps with the exception of Scandinavia, judicial intervention in public policy has grown throughout the liberal democratic world since 1945, marking a transition from **judicial restraint** to **judicial activism**. Judges have become more willing to enter political arenas that would have once been left to

> **Judicial activism** refers to the willingness of judges to venture beyond narrow legal decisions so as to influence public policy. **Judicial restraint**, a more conservative philosophy, maintains that judges should simply apply the letter of the law, leaving politics to elected bodies.

TIMELINE

THE COURT OF JUSTICE OF THE EUROPEAN COMMUNITIES (ECJ)

1952	*Court of Justice of the European Communities* established as part of the European Coal and Steel Community.
1957	*Treaty of Rome*: the Court's jurisdiction extends to the new European Economic Community and Euratom treaties.
1963	*Van Gend en Loos*: European laws apply directly to individuals, creating rights and obligations that national courts must implement.
1964	*Costa* v. *Enel*: European law takes priority over national law.
1979	*Cassis de Dijon*: a product sold lawfully in one member state must be accepted for sale in other member states ('mutual recognition').
1987	*Foto-Frost*: national courts cannot invalidate EU measures but must refer their doubts to the ECJ for resolution.
1988	*Court of First Instance* established to reduce the ECJ's workload and to improve its scrutiny of factual matters.
1992	*Francovich and Bonifaci* v. *Italy*: when member states breach EU law, they must compensate those affected. *Maastricht Treaty* clarifies the ECJ's jurisdiction, e.g. to include treaty provisions for closer cooperation between member states but to exclude the Common Foreign and Security Policy.
2003	*Constitutional Treaty* for Europe published in draft.
2005	*Commission* v. *Council*: the Community can require member states to adopt criminal legislation. *Constitutional Treaty* rejected in referendums in France and the Netherlands.

Further reading: Dehousse (1998), de Burea and Weiler (2002).

elected politicians and national parliaments. For instance:

- The Australian High Court under Sir Anthony Mason (Chief Justice, 1987–95) boldly uncovered implied rights in the constitution which had remained undetected by its predecessors (Mason, 1993);
- Even though the Dutch constitution explicitly excludes judicial review, its Supreme Court has produced important case law on issues where parliament was unable to legislate, notably in authorizing euthanasia (Van Geffen, 2001);
- The Israeli Supreme Court has addressed conflicts been secular and orthodox Jews left unresolved by mainstream politics (Hirschl, 2002).

What explanation can we offer for this significant judicialization of politics? Four reasons suggest themselves. First, the increasing reliance on regulation as a mode of governing has encouraged court intervention. A government decision to deny gay partners the same rights as married couples is open to judicial challenge in a way that a decision to go to war or raise taxes is not.

Second, the decay of left-wing ideology enlarged the judiciary's scope. Socialists were suspicious of judges, believing them to be unelected defenders of property specifically and the status quo as a whole. Now, the left has discovered that the courtroom can be a venue for harassing authoritarian rulers of the right.

Third, international conventions have given judges an extra lever they can use to break free from their traditional shackles. Documents such as the United Nations Universal Declaration of Human Rights (1948) and the European Convention on Human Rights (1950) have given judges a foundation on which to construct what would once have been viewed as excessively political statements.

Fourth, the continuing prestige of the judiciary has encouraged some transfer of authority to its domain. The judicial process has in most liberal democracies retained at least some reputation for integrity and impartiality, a status reinforced when, as in Italy in the 1990s, civil law judges were seen to be investigating corrupt politicians (Inoguchi, 2002).

The expansion of judicial authority has become self-reinforcing. Stone Sweet (2000, p. 55) makes the point: 'As constitutional law expands to more and more policy areas, and as it becomes "thicker" in each domain, so do the grounds for judicialized debate. The process tends to reinforce itself'. Sensing the growing confidence of judges in addressing broader political issues, interest groups, rights-conscious citizens and even political parties have also become more willing to continue their struggles in the judicial arena.

Of course, judicial activism has proceeded further in some democracies than in others. In comparative rankings of judicial activism, the United States invariably comes top (Figure 13.2). America is founded on a constitutional contract and an army of lawyers will forever quibble over the terms. The USA exhibits all the features contributing to judicial activism. These include a written constitution, federalism, judicial independence, no separate administrative courts, easy access to the courts, a legal system based on judge-made case law and high esteem for judges.

Figure 13.2 Levels of judicial activism in selected democracies

Source: Adapted from Holland (1991, p. 21).

Fewer of these conditions are met in Britain, a country in which parliamentary sovereignty has traditionally reigned supreme. Lacking the authority to annul legislation, judicial review in the British context normally refers to the capacity of judges to review executive decisions against the template provided by administrative law. Even in Britain, however, judicial activism has increased, reflecting European influence. British judges were willing accomplices of the European Court as it established a legal order applying to all member states. The country's adoption of the European Convention on Human Rights (ECHR) in 1998, and the decay of the royal prerogative which once allowed the state to stand above the law, also encouraged judicial assertiveness. The establishment of a Supreme Court in 2009, albeit without the authority to veto legislation, is likely to continue this process.

Formal statements of rights have also encouraged judicial expansion in other English-speaking countries. In Canada, a Charter of Rights and Freedoms was appended to the constitution in 1982, giving judges a more prominent role in defending individual rights.. Similarly, New Zealand introduced a bill of rights in 1990, protecting 'the life and security of the person' and also establishing traditional but previously uncodified democratic and civil rights.

These charters pose a difficulty in countries with a tradition of parliamentary sovereignty, such as New

DEBATE

SHOULD THE JUDICIARY PLAY A POLITICAL ROLE?

More than ever before, judges participate in politics, striking down policies and laws deemed to contravene the constitution. But why should the judiciary be permitted to encroach on the authority traditionally accorded to the elected branches of government? Why should 'they, the judges' supplant 'we, the people'?

YES

The fundamental argument for judicial authority is a liberal one: that tyranny of the majority is tyranny nonetheless. 'The courts correct the aberrations of democracy', wrote de Tocqueville (1856, p. 287). Subjecting government to the rule of law is a core achievement of Western politics. This is an accomplishment to be cherished rather than criticized, not least in an era when governments impinge on liberty in pursuit of national security. Dividing power between the legislature, the executive and the judiciary is in practice the only way of containing it.

Of course, interpreting the constitution is bound to cause controversy but an independent judiciary is well-suited to the job of arbiter. Judges are held in higher esteem than politicians and judicial interpretation is likely to be more stable and disinterested than political decision-making, thus providing more continuity to citizens and businesses alike.

In any case, judicial authority is often exaggerated. Judges review after the event; political initiative remains with the executive. The justices wisely keep away from sensitive areas such as war and taxation. They know that even judges are assessed in the court of public opinion.

Even an independent judiciary does not escape political influence. Politicians have a say in the appointment of senior justices, the government can always seek to change the constitution if it disagrees with judicial interpretation and in practice the executive retains responsibility for crisis management.

NO

In a democracy, the people must be sovereign. If a government behaves poorly, the solution lies in the polling booth rather than the courtroom. In the European tradition stimulated by the French Revolution of the eighteenth century, the legislature expresses the national will and the role of the judges is simply to execute it.

As Bork (2003) argues, societies must be responsible for their own moral judgements and should avoid simply delegating difficult decisions to judges.

Historically, judicial authority developed as a device enabling the wealthy to protect their property in a democratic era and even today the judiciary shows a bias towards established interests. This conservative disposition is strengthened by the narrow social and educational background of judges, most of whom are middle-aged to elderly middle-class white men.

Further, the modern judiciary places increasing reliance on international conventions, a form of imperialism that enables judges to escape democratic control exercized through national elections. From this perspective, judicial power is a mechanism through which global forces override elected governments.

Even if a mechanism of constitutional arbitration is needed (and Britain has got by well enough by relying on informal conventions), why should judges, with their narrow legal training, be given the job? Why not call upon an upper chamber to perform the task?

ASSESSMENT

This debate would benefit from fuller appreciation of the constitutional courts that have emerged in many European countries. In the political basis of their appointments, relatively rapid turnover of members and reliance on a political style of operation, constitutional courts have already become the third chamber of politics. Those who want the judiciary to be kept out of politics are fighting not a losing battle but one that is already lost.

Further reading

Bork (2003), Ferejohn and Pasquino (2003), Stone Sweet (2002), Sunstein *et al.* (2006).

Zealand and the UK. Ingenuity is needed to integrate a bill of rights with the supposed sovereignty of the legislature. Fortunately, New Zealand has delivered a clever solution. There, the Attorney General (a cabinet minister who bridges the political and judicial worlds) advises MPs on whether legislative proposals are consistent with basic rights. Technically, at least, parliament retains sole responsibility for adjusting its bills accordingly. Britain has adopted a similar halfway house. In theory, the legislature remains supreme but in practice MPs are unlikely to override a judicial opinion that a bill contradicts protected rights. In this way, sovereignty can be simultaneously defended and diluted.

Judicial independence and recruitment

Given the growing political authority of the judiciary, the question of maintaining its independence gains in importance. Liberal democracies accept judicial autonomy as fundamental to the rule of law but how is this independence to be achieved?

Security of tenure is of course important. In Britain, as in the American federal judiciary, judges hold office for life during 'good behaviour'. America's constitution even stipulates that judges' pay 'shall not be diminished during their Continuance in Office'. Although the constitutional courts of Europe usually limit their judges to one term of seven to nine years, the position of the judge remains secure during this period.

But judicial autonomy depends not only on security of tenure. It also raises the question of recruitment. If the selection of judges is controlled by politicians who appoint their own placemen, the judiciary may just reinforce partisan authority, providing an integration rather than a separation of powers. This problem is particularly important when judicial tenure is short. Political systems have developed varying solutions to judicial selection; the main methods are shown in Figure 13.3.

At one extreme, co-option by judges already in post offers the surest guarantee of independence but can lead to a self-perpetuating elite if the existing judges seek new recruits with an outlook resembling their own. At the other extreme, democratic election, as practised in some American states, is more (perhaps excessively?) responsive to popular concerns. In between lie appointment by the assembly, the executive and independent panels. The British government, for example, has recently ceded power of appointment to an independent commission, a decision justified by the relevant minister in the following way:

> In a modern democratic society, it is no longer acceptable for judicial appointments to be entirely in the hands of a government minister. For example the judiciary is often involved in adjudicating on the lawfulness of actions of the executive. And so the appointments system must be, and must be seen to be, independent of government (Falconer, 2003).

In practice, many countries now combine these pure methods, with the government choosing from a pool of candidates prepared by a professional body. In South Africa, for instance, the President of the Republic appoints senior judges after consulting a Judicial Services Commission which includes representatives from the legal profession as well as the legislature. Alternatively, and more traditionally, some judges on the senior court can be selected by one method while others are chosen by a different method. Thus, a third of the members of Italy's Constitutional Court are appointed by parliament in joint sitting, a third are nominated by

Figure 13.3 Methods of appointing judges

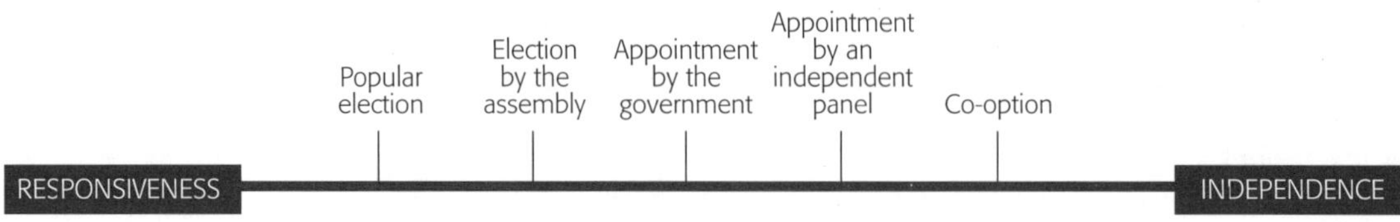

the president and a third are selected by the judiciary itself.

For most courts charged with judicial review, selection still involves a clear political dimension. In the USA, the stature of the Supreme Court is such that appointments to it (nominated by the president but subject to Senate approval) are key decisions. Senate ratification can involve a set-piece battle between presidential friends and foes (Davis, 2005). In these contests, the judicial experience and legal ability of the nominee may matter less than ideology, partisanship and a clean personal history. Even so, Walter Dellinger, former acting US Solicitor-General, argues that 'the political appointment of judges is an appropriate "democratic moment" before the independence of life tenure sets in' (Peretti, 2001). Life tenure, of course, insulates the Court from excessive influence by the incumbent president.

A political dimension is also apparent in selection to constitutional courts. Typically, members are selected by the assembly in a procedure that can involve party horse-trading. For instance, eight out of the twelve members of Spain's Constitutional Court are appointed by the party-dominated parliament. In both America and Europe, political factors influence court appointments.

Below the level of the highest court, there remains the issue of **internal independence**. Noting that 'judicial organizations in continental Europe traditionally operate within a pyramid-like organizational structure', Guarnieri (2003, p. 225) argues that 'the role played by organizational hierarchies is crucial in order to highlight the actual dynamics of the judicial corps'. This issue arose in acute form in some continental European countries after 1945, when judges appointed under right-wing regimes continued in post, discouraging initiative by new recruits lower in the pyramid. Guarnieri concludes that promotion and salary progression within the judiciary should depend solely on seniority, noting that such reforms were needed in Italy before younger judges – informally called assault judges – became willing to launch investigations into corruption in government.

The **internal independence** of the judiciary refers to the autonomy of junior judges from their senior colleagues who often determine career advancement. Where autonomy is limited, judicial initiative is stifled.

Administrative law

Where constitutional law sets out the fundamental principles governing the relationship between citizen and state, administrative law covers the rules governing this interaction in detailed settings. If a citizen (or other affected body) is in dispute with a public agency over a specific issue such as immigration, military service, a passport, treatment of a prisoner or eligibility for a welfare benefit, some procedures and standards must be developed enabling allegations of maladministration to be resolved. This task too has fallen to the judiciary; it is a role that grew in importance with the expansion of government activity in the twentieth century.

Administrative regulation may lack the high-profile political activity of constitutional courts but subjecting the work of public officials to law is a function essential to a liberal society. Clear and enforceable regulations help to secure a balanced relationship between state and citizen.

Administrative law sets out the principles governing decision-making by public bodies, mainly the bureaucracy, and the remedies for breaching such rules. For example, America's Administrative Procedure Act (1946) requires courts to hold unlawful any agency action that is 'arbitrary, capricious, an abuse of discretion, or otherwise not in accordance with law'.

The issues involved here concern public law and have no clear analogy in the private sector. Typical questions asked in administrative law are:

- *Competence*: was an official authorized to make a particular decision?
- *Procedure*: was the decision made in the correct way (e.g. with adequate consultation)?
- *Fairness*: does the decision accord with natural justice?
- *Liability*: what should be done if a decision was incorrectly made or led to undesirable results?

How can administrative justice be realized? Liberal democracies handle the problem of legal regulation of the administration through a separatist or integrationist approach, with the chosen method reflecting and reinforcing conceptions of the state.

The first solution, common in codified legal systems, is to establish a separate system of administrative courts concerned exclusively with legal oversight of the bureaucracy. This **separatist approach** marks out a strong public sphere operating within a codified legal framework. Often, the work of civil servants is seen as legal in character, based on the uniform application of codes, leading naturally to judicial oversight.

The **separatist approach** to administrative justice (as in France) is to establish special courts and laws to review the interaction between citizen and state. By contrast, the **integrationist approach** (as traditionally favoured in the United Kingdom) sought to control the bureaucracy by reviewing disputes in ordinary courts, relying in large part on the ordinary law of the land.

France is the most influential example of this separatist model. It has developed an elaborate structure of administrative courts, headed by the *Conseil d'Etat*, founded in 1799 (Figure 13.4). All administrative decisions taken by ministers and their officials are subject to review by the Council, a wide remit which can lead to slow decisions. Nonetheless, by developing its own case law, the Council has established general principles regulating administrative power. The Council's prestige expresses the autonomy of the public realm while also enabling it to check executive power.

This separatist solution speaks directly to the specific problems arising in public administration but runs the risk of boundary disputes over whether a case should be processed through administrative or ordinary courts. Such disputes can be especially awkward when, as is increasingly the case, a public task has been outsourced to a private contractor. In addition, special administrative courts reinforce a legalistic interpretation of public service which can lead to inflexible and unresponsive decision-making by officials (as those with experience of the French bureaucracy will testify).

The second solution, favoured in Anglo-American countries with a common law tradition, seeks to deny the distinction between public and private. This **integrationist approach** asserts that the one set of courts should address both public and private

Figure 13.4 Administrative courts in France

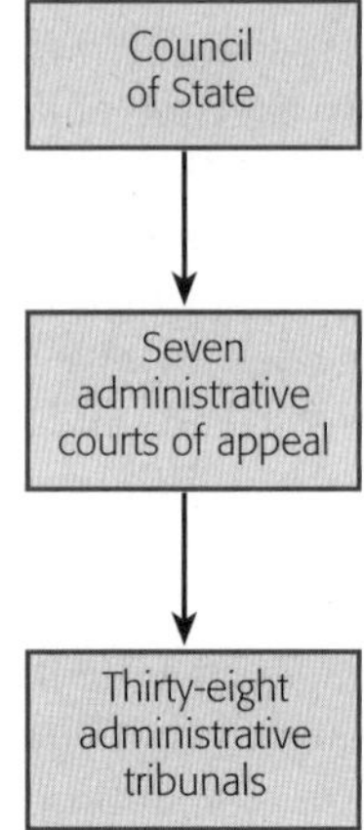

Note: Separate courts exist for constitutional cases and for civil and criminal law.

Source: Adapted from Elgie (2003).

law. The same principles should span both sectors: for instance, employment in the public sector should be regulated by the same rules as apply to private firms. Ordinary courts should be able to arbitrate disputes between bureaucrats and citizens; no *Conseil d'Etat* is required.

One strength of this integrationist philosophy is that it prevents boundary disputes and simplifies the judicial system. Above all, the integrationist philosophy affirms a modest aspiration for the public sphere; the state must abide by the same laws as its citizens. A. V. Dicey (1885) was the strongest exponent of this approach; his thinking was that special laws and courts for public business would in practice serve to advantage the government against the citizen.

In reality, special courts are rarely avoided entirely, even in the English-speaking world. The United States has administrative courts dedicated to taxation, military, bankruptcy and patent issues. Influenced by the strong public law tradition in the European Union, the United Kingdom introduced an Administrative Court in 2001 to provide judicial review of 'the decisions of inferior courts and tribunals, public bodies and persons exercising a public function' (Her Majesty's Court Service, 2005). Dicey seems to have lost this particular battle.

Judicial review is the final court of appeal for citizens protesting against an administrative decision. The earlier stages are rightly less legal in character. Often, the first level of complaint is to an appeals panel operating within the department making the original decision. This can be followed by appeal to an external tribunal. These tribunals review the substantive decision reached by the official; by contrast, judicial review will normally focus solely on procedural issues.

Tribunals do have their strengths: they are quicker, cheaper, more flexible and substantive and less formal than the courts. They can also focus more on mediation and can redress the imbalance of legal expertise between a government agency and a citizen. So, in theory at least, the work of tribunals and courts should be complementary, with judicial intervention serving as a final court of appeal, especially on matters of procedure. However, tribunals themselves need to be seen to operate in a fair and consistent way, so just like the courts they tend to develop their own standards and rules. In effect, they too become a source of administrative law and a form of court, sometimes leading to complaints that they have become too formal and expensive to serve the practical purpose for which they were originally designed.

In some countries, citizens also have access to an ombudsman, a public official who can investigate a complaint about inadequate, if not illegal, behaviour by public authorities (see p. 366).

The twentieth-century expansion of government created not only new rights for citizens but also fresh opportunities for public agencies to evade those rights. In a liberal state, administrative courts and tribunals make by their mere existence a worthwhile statement that public servants are expected to behave in a fair and reasonable way to the public. It is for such reasons that in 1982 Lord Diplock, a senior British judge, said that he regarded the development of administrative law 'as the greatest achievement of the English courts in my lifetime' (McEldowney, 2003, p. 3).

Law in authoritarian states

In authoritarian regimes, constitutions are feeble. The nature of such states is that any restraints on rule go unacknowledged; power, not law, is the political currency. As guardian of the law, the status of the judiciary is similarly diminished.

Non-democratic rulers follow two broad strategies in limiting judicial authority. One tactic is to retain a framework of law but to influence the judges indirectly. In Indonesia, for example, the Ministry of Justice still administers the courts and pays judges' salaries; the justices understand the implications. More crudely, unsatisfactory judges can simply be dismissed. Egypt's President Nasser adopted this strategy with vigour in 1969. He got rid of 200 in one go: the 'massacre of the judges'. In Uganda, an extreme case, the killing was real rather than metaphorical; President Amin had his Chief Justice shot dead.

A second strategy is to bypass the judicial process altogether. For instance, many non-democratic regimes use Declarations of Emergency as a cover to make decisions which are exempt from judicial scrutiny. Once introduced, such 'temporary' emergencies can drag on for decades. Alternatively, rulers can make use of special courts that do the regime's bidding without much pretence of judicial independence; Egypt's State Security Courts are an example. Military rulers frequently extend the scope of secret military courts to include civilian troublemakers. Ordinary courts can then continue to deal with non-political cases, offering an image of legal integrity to the world.

Communist states offered a more sophisticated downgrade of constitutions and the judiciary. Marxist theory explicitly rejected the Western idea of constitutional rule with its emphasis on limited government, individual rights and private property. What does the Western tradition amount to, asked the communists, other than an affirmation of the status quo? Rather, the aim of a communist constitution – and of **socialist law** as a whole – should be to support the development of socialism, with new constitutions introduced as societies reached

Socialist law was a term used to describe the legal system of communist states. Strongly influenced by the codes used in the Soviet Union, socialist law was a version of civil law which rejected the Western notion of private property. The purpose of law was to contribute to socialist development as defined by the ruling party.

particular milestones in the transition. The Soviet Union, for example, introduced new constitutions in 1918, 1924, 1936 and 1977. In allowing for constitutional change, the communist philosophy resembled the British emphasis on a flexible rather than a fixed constitution.

Judges in communist states also had to play their part in building socialism and therefore in protecting the party. Throughout the communist world, judges were selected for their party-mindedness and were expected to put this virtue to good effect in court. Although routine cases proceeded without interference, 'telephone law' was employed in sensitive cases; a party official would discreetly order a particular verdict.

China provides a contemporary example of the evolution of communist thinking about constitutions and law. Like the Soviet Union, China has had four constitutions: 1954, 1975, 1978 and 1982. Even though the current version still begins by affirming the country's socialist status (Box 13.4), it is much the least radical of the four. It seeks to establish a more predictable environment for economic development and downgrades the historic emphasis on class conflict, national self-reliance and revolutionary struggle. The leading role of the party is now mentioned only in the preamble, with the main text even declaring that 'all political parties ... must abide by the Constitution'. In the context of communist states, such a liberal statement is remarkable, even if a poor guide to reality. Amendments in 2004 gave further support to private property and human rights.

BOX 13.4

Article I of the Chinese constitution, 1982

1 The People's Republic of China is a socialist state under the people's democratic dictatorship led by the working class and based on the alliance of workers and peasants.

2 The socialist system is the basic system of the People's Republic of China. Sabotage of the socialist system by any organization or individual is prohibited.

Source: Tschentscher (2004).

In addition to moderating its constitution, contemporary China also gives greater emphasis to law in general. In the early decades of the People's Republic, legal perspectives were dismissed as 'bourgeois rightist' thinking. There were very few laws at all, reflecting a national tradition of unregulated power; the judiciary was largely a branch of the police force. However, laws did become more numerous, precise and significant after the hiatus of the Cultural Revolution in the 1960s. In 1979, the country passed its first criminal laws; later revisions abolished the vague crime of counter-revolution and established the right of defendants to seek counsel. Law could prevail to the benefit of economic development.

Reform notwithstanding, Chinese politics remains authoritarian. 'Rule by law' means exerting political control through law rather than limiting the exercise of power. The courts are regarded as just one bureaucratic agency among others; legal judgements are not tested against the constitution and many decisions are simply ignored. The police remain largely unaccountable. Legal institutions remain less specialized, and legal personnel less professional, than in liberal democracies. Trial procedures, while improving, still offer only limited protection for the innocent. The death penalty is still used, supposedly to strike hard against crime. Political opponents are still imprisoned without trial. Above all, party officials continue to occupy a protected position above the law. Politics still comes first and power still trumps the constitution (Peerenboom, 2002).

With the virtual demise of communism, **Islamic law** is the main form of law found in contemporary authoritarian states. As with all aspects of Islam, we should resist viewing Muslim legal thinking as a single, unchanging system. Some Muslim societies, such as Turkey and Uzbekistan, possess intensely secular governments; others, such as Saudi Arabia, regard Islamic texts as their main source of law. Most Muslim countries fall in between, with religious law coexisting alongside secular laws introduced by the state. Like the justices of America's Supreme Court, Islamic legal scholars possess considerable flexibility to adapt and revise. In many ways, Islamic law is more 'an endless discussion on

Islamic law is based on the Sharia, which is in turn derived from the Koran (Mohammad's revelations) and the ***hadith*** (reports of what the prophet said and did). The ***Sharia*** sets out the path for Muslims to follow. However, most Muslim countries do not possess ***Sharia*** courts; in some states, they are banned.

the duties of a Muslim' rather than a precise code implemented through the judicial system (Rahman, 1982, p. 32).

Sharia is a code for life, not a constitution: 'liquor and gambling, idols and diving arrows are only a flighty work of Satan; give them up so that you may prosper'. Severe punishments, pragmatically applied, are specified for those judged guilty against demanding standards of evidence. The *Sharia* and ***hadith*** are refined and adapted in Islamic jurisprudence, known as the *fiqh* (understanding of details). It is the *fiqh* that classifies all actions into the five categories of obligatory, recommended, neutral, discouraged or forbidden.

Even when *Sharia* courts do exist, they are often confined to specific areas such as marriage and inheritance; secular courts cover a wider sphere of justice. In any case, the *Sharia* itself requires Muslims to obey secular laws, except when they require sinful acts. It is clear, nonetheless, that Islam's comprehensive religious code, even if unenforced through the courts, is difficult to reconcile with the liberal traditions of individual rights and the separation of public and private realms.

Law in illiberal democracies

By definition, constitutions and the law play second fiddle to elected authority in illiberal democracies. The leader is elected within a constitutional framework but that environment has usually itself been shaped by the leader. More important, the exercise of power is rarely constrained by an independent judiciary. Rather it is the president who stands on high, defining the national interest under the broad authority granted to him by the voters:

> How could it be otherwise for somebody who claims to embody the nation? In this view other institutions – such as congress and the judiciary – are nuisances that come attached to the domestic and international advantages of being a democratically elected president. Accountability to these institutions appears as an unnecessary impediment to the full authority that the president has been delegated to exercise (O'Donnell, 1994, p. 63).

Put differently, presidential accountability in an illiberal democracy is vertical (to the voters) rather than horizontal (to congress and the judiciary) (O'Donnell, 2003). In contrast to a liberal democracy, where the main parties have concluded that being ruled by law is preferable to being ruled by opponents, in an illiberal democracy the commanding figure still sees the constitution, the law and the courts as a source of political advantage.

In Latin America, where illiberal democracy is common, several elected presidents have treated the constitution as a flexible document to be adapted to suit their own political needs. For example, some have sought to abolish term limits so that they can stand for re-election. Other South American constitutions have retained privileges for departing generals, thus perpetuating a sense of an additional institution remaining above the law. For instance, Chile's armed forces were initially granted immunity from prosecution in civilian courts, a tactic that effectively enabled former generals to escape justice for political murders committed during their tenure. In Argentina, similar legal exemptions dating from the 1980s still formed a running political sore 20 years later.

In addition to the difficulties of establishing the constitution as an effective political framework, the rule of law is held back throughout Latin America by the low standing and standards of the judiciary. Prillaman (2000) chronicles the problems: chronic inefficiency within the judicial system, the vulnerability of judges to political pressure, outdated laws, insufficient resources and the public's lack of trust in legal remedies. Judgements are slow to emerge and, even when made, are often ignored. The problem is circular: politicians are unwilling to grant real autonomy to an ineffective legal system but until the judiciary acquires more responsibilities, its professionalism is unlikely to rise.

In many low-income countries with marked inequalities of wealth, status and power, the rule of law remains a distant idea. In some Latin America cities, the police probably commit almost as many crimes as they solve. Coordination between the police and judges is poor; sometimes both are bribed and threatened by drug barons. In Colombia, one in three judges received a death threat in the 1980s. Judges in Guatemala stand so directly in the firing line that they cannot obtain insurance (Dodson and Jackson, 2003, p. 248). In these conditions, informal arbitration, indigenous justice and lynchings may provide cheaper and faster remedies than appealing to a remote legal system.

However, the Russian experience shows that the law can gain ground in at least some illiberal democracies. The post-communist constitution of 1993 sets out an array of individual rights (including that of owning property), proclaims that 'the individual and his rights and freedoms are the supreme value' and establishes a tripartite system of general, commercial and constitutional courts. The Constitutional Court, in particular, represented a major innovation in Russian legal thinking. Since 1993, the government has established detailed and lengthy codes appropriate for a civil law system. From 1998, criminal defendants who have exhausted all domestic remedies have even been able to appeal to the European Court of Human Rights (Sharlet, 2005, p. 147).

In contrast to many Latin America presidents, Vladmir Putin supported the strengthening of law. He is certainly not above selective use of the law for political ends but, as a law graduate once charged with promoting foreign investment in St Petersburg, he may have recognized the contribution that a legal framework can make to economic revival. More to the point, he may have calculated that uniform legal codes could help him to re-establish control over his country's corrupt bureaucrats and fragmenting republics while simultaneously strengthening Russia's international reputation.

Even in Russia, 'there has been and remains a considerable gap between individual rights on paper and their realization in practice. The further one goes beyond Moscow and St Petersburg into the provinces, the enforcement gap tends to grow greater' (Sharlet, 1997, p. 134). For instance:

- The conviction rate in criminal cases remains suspiciously high;
- Expertise and pay within the legal system are low, creating a vulnerability to corruption;
- The police behave violently towards suspects;
- Conditions in prison are degrading;
- The state's responses to political violence, as in Chechnya, is brutal.

But we should beware of judging the constitutional quality of post-communist Russia, and similar illiberal democracies, against contemporary Western standards. As Sharlet (1997, p. 134) reminds us:

> while the Founding Fathers of the American republic quickly added the Bill of Rights to their newly ratified Constitution in the late eighteenth century, a number of these rights remained essentially 'parchment rights' and did not garner nationwide respect and judicial enforcement until well into the twentieth century. Is it surprising that Russia with its thousand-year authoritarian past and long tradition of legal nihilism should be proceeding slowly in Rule of Law development? Surely it is more remarkable that Russia has made the progress it has, including in the uncharted territory of civil rights.

The impact of international law

We conclude this chapter with a discussion of the impact of international law on the state. For three reasons, international law must now receive attention from students of comparative politics:

- International law helped to define the division of the world into the states which provide the unit of comparative politics. States were the only, and remain the major, subjects of international law. Through international law, states reinforced their dominant political position and it is through participation in an international legal community that statehood is formally acquired.
- International law forms part of national law, often without any special mechanism of incorporation. Many constitutions are explicit on this point. Germany's constitution, for instance, states that 'the general rules of public international law are an integral part of federal law. They shall take precedence over the laws and shall create rights and duties for the inhabitants of the federal territory'.

- National sovereignty notwithstanding, international laws can apply directly to individuals, thus qualifying state sovereignty. The famous example here is the Nuremberg Charter used to try Nazi war leaders (Box 13.5). Held (2004, p. 125) claims that such changes in international law have 'reshaped the powers and the constraints on, and the rights and duties of, states'.

International agreements constrain national policy-makers. Such accords set out objectives (for example reducing carbon dioxide emissions) which national governments must, or at least should, put into effect. When states fail to abide by conventions they themselves have signed, affected individuals can in principle seek a remedy through the courts, both national and international.

International agreements can also intrude on the balance between different levels of government within a state. An example from Australia illustrates this point. After the national government ratified a protocol to the International Covenant on Civil and Political Rights in 1991, Nick Toonen, a gay-rights activist, lodged a complaint against Tasmania's prohibition of sexual relations between men. Tasmania remained resolute but the federal government in Canberra passed a liberalizing law, overriding provincial legislation. Critics allege that Australia's federal government could in theory use its expanding treaty commitments to interfere in virtually any area of activity which, under the national constitution, is supposedly reserved to the states (Scott, 1997).

A further bypass around the tradition of state sovereignty has been achieved by setting up international courts to try individuals directly for their alleged crimes, even if these were committed in the name of the state. Of course, the Nuremberg trials after the Second World War had established that individuals are responsible for their own acts in war. That view itself departed from the notion of treating states as the only subjects of international law. However, in the 1990s, the International Court of Justice set up new tribunals, the first since Nuremberg, to try war crimes suspects from Rwanda and former Yugoslavia. In 1998, the Rwanda Tribunal became the first to convict a former head of state, Jean Kambanda, of crimes against humanity. He was sentenced to life imprisonment.

In general, though, these special tribunals proved to be expensive and slow-moving. In the long run, the establishment of the International Criminal Court (ICC) in The Hague in 2003 to deal with allegations of genocide, war crimes and crimes against humanity may prove to be more significant. Importantly, however, the United States is not a party to the Court.

International law is the system of rules which states (and other actors) regard as binding in their mutual relations. It derives from treaties, custom, accepted principles and the views of legal authorities. The term 'international law' was coined by the English philosopher Jeremy Bentham (1748–1832).

BOX 13.5

Principles 1–4 of the Nuremberg Charter, 1945

1 Any person who commits an act which constitutes a crime under international law is responsible therefore and liable to punishment.

2 The fact that internal law does not impose a penalty for an act which constitutes a crime under international law does not relieve the person who committed the act from responsibility under international law.

3 The fact that a person who committed an act which constitutes a crime under international law acted as Head of State or responsible government official does not relieve him from responsibility under international law.

4 The fact that a person acted pursuant to order of his Government or of a superior does not relieve him from responsibility under international law, provided a moral choice was in fact possible to him.

Note: 'crimes under international law' are defined as crimes against peace, war crimes and crimes against humanity.

Source: Nuclear Age Peace Foundation (2006).

Learning Resources for Chapter 13

Next step

Stone Sweet (2000) examines constitutional politics in five European political systems.

Further reading

Shapiro and Stone Sweet (2002) is a collection on political jurisprudence, including the United States. Von Beyme (2003) covers constitution-making in Eastern Europe. On the judiciary, Guarnieri and Perderzoli (2002) is a cross-national study. For the USA, Baum (2003) and O'Brien (2005) examine the American Supreme Court; O'Brien (2004) also usefully collates the views of American judges on judging. For the post-communist world, see Solomon and Foglesong (2000) for Russia, and Sadurski (2005) for constitutional courts in Eastern Europe. Lubman (1999) and Peerenboom (2002) review China's long march towards the rule of law. Prillaman (2000) assesses the judiciary in Latin America. Two books with a political perspective on administrative law are Hall (2005) for the USA and Loveland (2004) for the UK. On international law, Bull (1977) remains a good starting point while Carothers (2006) is an interesting study of American efforts to promote the rule of law abroad.

Internet sources

Constitution Finder
Constitutions and charters
http://confinder.richmond.edu/

European Court of Justice
The official site and links to national sites
http://curia.europa.eu/en/index.htm

International Criminal Court
The official site
http://www.icc-cpi.int/home.html&l=en

Political Database of the Americas
Constitutions and much more in the Americas, North and South
http://pdba.georgetown.edu/Constitutions/constudies.html

Researching Constitutional Law on the Internet
Numerous links
http://www.lib.uchicago.edu/~llou/conlaw.html

Universal Declaration of Human Rights
The 1948 Declaration in over 300 translations
http://www.unhchr.ch/udhr/

Chapter 14
Multilevel governance

Governing always has a territorial dimension. Rulers need to extract resources from their territory while also retaining the willingness of the population to remain within the state's orbit. To achieve these ends, the modern state consists of an intricate network of organizations, typically consisting of the central government, its offices and representatives in the field, regional governments and local authorities. For member states the European Union provides an additional tier.

In this chapter, we begin by introducing the idea of multilevel governance, a term which seeks to capture the complexities of relationships across government levels. We then examine the two formal solutions to the territorial organization of power, federal and unitary, before turning to the lowest level of authority within the state, local government. We then discuss the rather less intricate patterns of central–local relations found in authoritarian states and illiberal democracies.

What is multilevel governance?

Multilevel governance is the term used to describe how policy-makers and interest groups in liberal democracies find themselves discussing, persuading and negotiating across multiple levels, seeking to deliver coherent policy in specific functional areas such as transport or education. In practice, a policy-maker in a department of education will spend more time on vertical relationships, talking to people from different tiers within the same field, than on horizontal coordination, involving people at the same level but working in a different policy area (Figure 14.1).

In multilevel governance, furthermore, communication is not nested, such that people at one level communicate only with the adjacent level. Rather, national, regional and local officials in a given sector will form their own policy community, with interaction across all tiers. For example, regional administrations within EU countries will negotiate directly with the European Commission as well as with and through their national government. The use of the term 'governance' rather than 'government' directs our attention to these extensive relationships across levels, rather than to the institutions themselves.

In addition, the term 'multilevel governance' is used to acknowledge the wide range of actors involved in regulating contemporary societies. In education, for example, the central department will want to improve educational attainment in schools but to achieve its target it will need not only to consult lower tiers within the public sector (such as education boards) but also wider interests such as parents' associations, teachers' unions and educational researchers. In fact, the multiple tiers of government involved in

Multilevel governance emerges when experts from several tiers of government share the task of making regulations and forming policy, usually in conjunction with relevant interest groups (Hooghe and Marks, 2001). The term is commonly used in the European Union, whose presence adds a supranational tier to national, regional and local levels.

policy-making give more points of access and influence for these private groups. So even more than similar terms such as intergovernmental relations and executive federalism, the concept of multilevel governance denotes a pluralistic pattern of policy-making whose participants include relevant interest groups. The resulting networks resist hierarchical political control.

Clearly, the balance between these assorted tiers raises important questions of democratic governance. Who initiates policy? Who funds it? Who executes it? Who is accountable for it? What are the costs of transacting business in this complicated way? And, in view of 9/11, how well can such intricate networks respond to national emergencies?

Understanding multilevel governance requires an appreciation of the resources which each tier brings to the table. Typically, the representatives from the centre will have more money, strong political backing on high profile issues and the authority that flows from a national perspective. But, just like interest groups, officials from lower levels will possess their own cards: detailed knowledge of the problem and the ability to judge the efficacy of the remedies proposed. If lower tiers are both resourced and enthused, they are in a position to make a difference; if not, they may lose focus.

Figure 14.1 Coordination within and across tiers of government

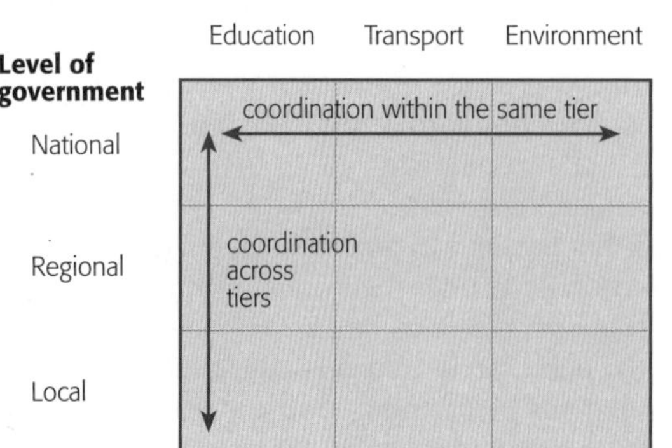

It would be wrong to infer that power in multilevel governance is just the ability to persuade. Communication still operates in a constitutional framework that provides both limits and opportunities for representatives from each tier. If the constitution allocates responsibility for education to central government, local authorities are unlikely to build new schools until the Ministry of Education signs a cheque. Thus the formal allocation of responsibilities remains the rock on which multilevel governance is constructed.

Federalism

Federalism is a form of multilevel governance which shares sovereignty, and not just power, between governments within a single state. It is a constitutional device, presupposing a formal political agreement establishing both the levels of government and their spheres of authority. So, like the constitutions within which they are embedded, **federations** are always a deliberate creation. In such a system, legal sovereignty is shared between the federal (or national) government and the constituent subunits (called states in this context). Neither tier can abolish the other. It is this protected position of the states, not the extent of their powers, which distinguishes federations (such as the USA and Canada) from unitary governments (such as the UK and France). Multiple levels of governance are integral to a federation whereas in a unitary system sovereignty resides solely with the centre, with lower levels existing at its pleasure.

A federal constitution allocates specific functions to each tier. The centre takes charge of external relations – defence, foreign affairs and immigration – and some common domestic functions such as the currency. The functions of the states are more variable but typically include education, law enforcement and local government. Residual powers may also lie with the states, not the centre (Box 14.1). In nearly all federations, the states have a guaranteed voice in national policy-making through an upper chamber of the assembly. In that chamber each state normally receives equal, or nearly equal, representa-

Federalism is the principle of sharing sovereignty between central and state (or provincial) governments; a **federation** is any political system that puts this idea into practice. A **confederation** is a looser link between participating countries, with the members retaining their separate statehood.

tion. The American Senate, with two senators per state, is the prototype.

The natural federal structure is for all the states within the union to possess identical powers under the constitution. However, reflecting national circumstances, some federations are less balanced. Asymmetric federalism arises when some states within a federation are given more autonomy than others. In Canada, for example, Quebec nationalists have long argued for special recognition for their French-speaking province; they view Canada as a compact between two equal communities (English- and French-speaking) rather than a contract between ten equal provinces. Although asymmetric federalism is an understandable response to differences in power and culture between regions, the solution carries its own dangers. The risk is that a spiral of instability will develop as the less favoured states seek the status granted to more privileged provinces.

Federations must be distinguished not just from unitary states but also from **confederations**. In the latter, the central authority remains the junior partner, acting merely as an agent of the component states. Thus, a confederation is more than an

BOX 14.1

The allocation of functions in the Canadian and German federations

	Canada	Germany
Exclusive jurisdiction (federal level)	The federal government exclusively controls 29 functions, including criminal law, the currency and defence.	The federal government's responsibilities include defence, citizenship and immigration.
Exclusive jurisdiction (provincial level)	The provinces control 'all matters of a merely local or private nature' in the province, including local government.	Few specific powers are explicitly granted to the *Länder* (states) which nonetheless implement federal laws 'in their own right'.
Concurrent jurisdiction (functions shared between levels)	Both the national and provincial governments can pass laws dealing with agriculture and immigration.	Concurrent powers include criminal law and employment. A constitutional amendment in 1969/70 created a new category of joint tasks, including agriculture.
Residual powers (the level responsible for functions not specifically allocated by the constitution)	The national parliament can make laws for the 'peace, order and good government of Canada'.	Any task not otherwise allocated remains with the *Länder*.

Note: Extensive reforms to the German constitution in 2006 sought to reduce the overlap in responsibilities between federal and *Länder* governments.

Map 14.1 Belgium

alliance but less than a federation. The classic case is the short-lived system adopted in 1781 in what is now the United States. The weak centre, embodied in the Continental Congress, could neither tax nor regulate commerce. It also lacked direct authority over the people. It was the feebleness of the Articles of Confederation that led to the drafting of a federal constitution, and to the creation of the United States proper, in 1787.

Federalism is a recognized solution to the problem of organizing the territorial distribution of power. Elazar (1996, p. 426) counts 22 federations in the world, containing some two billion people or 40 per cent of the world's population (for some examples see Table 14.1). Federalism is particularly common in large countries, whether size is measured by area or by population. Four of the world's largest states by area are federal: Australia, Brazil, Canada and the United States. In India, 10 out of 25 provinces each contain more than 40 million people, providing the only realistic framework for holding together a large and diverse democracy. Germany, the largest European country by population, exemplifies federalism on that continent.

As Bryce (1919, p. 350) wrote, 'Federalism is an equally legitimate resource whether it is adopted for the sake of tightening or for loosening a pre-existing bond'. So there are two routes to a federation: first, by creating a new central authority ('coming together') or, second, by transferring sovereignty from an existing national government to lower levels ('holding together'). In practice, the bond is more often tightened than loosened; federalism is almost always a compact between separate units pursuing a common interest. The United States, for instance, emerged from a meeting of representatives of 13 American states in 1787. Similar conventions, strongly influenced by the American experience, took place in Switzerland in 1848, Canada in 1867 and Australia in 1897/98.

So far, restructuring as a federation to hold a divided country together is a rare occurrence. Belgium is the main example. First established in 1830, Belgium has been beset by divisions between its French- and Dutch-speaking regions. Constitutional revisions in 1970 and 1980 devolved

Table 14.1 Some federations in liberal democracies

	Year established as a federation	Area, thousand sq. km (rank in world)	Population, million (rank in world)	Number of states in federation
United States	1776	9,373 (3)	298 (3)	50
Canada	1867	9,976 (2)	33 (36)	10
Switzerland	1874	41 (137)	8 (94)	26
Brazil	1891	8,512 (5)	188 (5)	27
Australia	1901	7,687 (6)	20 (52)	6
Germany	1949	357 (62)	82 (14)	16
India	1950	3,288 (7)	1,095 (2)	25
Belgium	1983	30 (141)	10 (76)	3

Source: CIA (2006) for area and population.

more power to these separate groups. In 1983, the country finally proclaimed itself a federation comprising three main parts: French-speaking Wallonia; Dutch-speaking Flanders; and the Brussels region, centred on the predominantly French-speaking capital city (Map 14.1). The Belgian experience does suggest that federation can be an alternative to disintegration, a lesson of value to other states confronting internal divisions with a spatial dimension.

What, then, provokes distinct peoples to set out on the journey to a federation? Motives are more often negative than positive; fear of the consequences of remaining separate must overcome the natural desire to preserve independence. Historically, the most common aspiration has been to secure the military and economic bonus of size.

Riker (1975, 1996) emphasized this military factor, arguing that federations emerge in response to an external threat. The American states, for instance, joined together in 1789 partly because they felt themselves to be vulnerable in a predatory world. When large beasts are lurking in the jungle, smaller creatures must gather together for safety. Or, as the American statesman Benjamin Franklin (1706–90) put it, 'we must indeed all hang together or, most assuredly, we shall all hang separately' (Jay, 1996, p. 142).

However, the federal bargain has also been based on the economic advantages of scale. Even the Australian and American federalists felt that a common market would promote economic activity. But just as the military case for forming new federations is currently rather weak, given the paucity of orthodox wars, so federation is also a convoluted way of securing gains from trade. Straightforward free trade areas (FTAs) between neighbouring countries are proving to be a more popular way forward. Unlike federations, FTAs such as the North American Free Trade Agreement entail no loss of sovereignty.

Military and economic arguments for forming new federations may have weakened but interest in ethnic federalism has grown. The Belgian experience shows that federations are useful for bridging ethnic diversity within a divided society; they are a device for incorporating such differences within a single political community. People who differ by descent, language and culture can nevertheless seek the advantages of membership in a shared enterprise. Thus, the Swiss federation integrates 23 cantons, two and a half languages (German and French, plus Italian) and two religions (Catholic and Protestant).

The danger of ethnic federations is that they merely reinforce the divisions they were designed to accommodate. This risk is particularly acute when only two communities are involved. In these conditions, the gains of one group are the visible losses of another and the majority community may still be able to impose its will, defeating the original object of diffusing power. Citing Pakistan and Czechoslovakia as examples, Watts (2005, p. 234) suggests that 'bipolar federations have invariably experienced serious tensions, instability and a high failure rate'. Even in Belgium, usually judged to be a federal success story, 'the granting of autonomy to the language groups . . . has increased and deepened the differences between both communities and regional entities' (Deschouwer, 2005, p. 105). Federation may be more effective when it cuts across, rather than entrenches, ethnic divisions.

Dual and cooperative federalism

It is helpful to distinguish between dual and cooperative federalism. The former represents the federal spirit and remains a significant theme in American culture; the latter is an important ideal within European thinking and moves us closer to the realities of multilevel governance.

Reflecting the original federal principle as conceived in the United States, **dual federalism** implies that the national and state governments operate independently, each tier acting autonomously in its own sphere, and linked only through the constitutional compact. Bryce (1919 p. 425) offered the image of two sets of machinery working well precisely because they avoid contact – the very opposite of multilevel governance. In the circumstances of eighteenth-century America, such separation was a plausible objective; extensive coordination between federal and state administrations was judged to be neither necessary nor feasible.

In particular, the federal government was required to confine its activities to functions explicitly allocated to it, such as the power 'to lay and collect taxes, to pay the debts and provide for the common defence and welfare of the United States'. In the world after 9/11, 'providing for the common defence' has of course again become a pivotal and complex task, calling for cross-level collaboration.

COUNTRY PROFILE

CANADA

Form of government ■ a federal parliamentary democracy with ten provinces. Most Canadians live in Ontario or Quebec.

Legislature ■ the 308-seat House of Commons is the lower chamber. Unusually for a federation, the 105 members of the Senate, the upper chamber, are appointed by the prime minister. However, plans to fill Senate vacancies in the light of advisory votes in the provinces were announced in 2006.

Executive ■ the prime minister leads a cabinet whose members he selects with due regard for provincial representation. A governor-general serves as ceremonial figurehead.

Judiciary ■ Canada employs a dual (federal and provincial) court system, headed by a traditionally restrained Supreme Court. In 1982 the country introduced the Canadian Charter of Rights and Freedoms.

Electoral system ■ a plurality system with single-member districts. This produces large swings and distortions. Interest in electoral reform has developed in the provinces but not yet at national level.

Party system ■ the major parties are the Conservative Party of Canada and the Liberals. The Conservatives reunited in 2003 after a period of division between the Progressive Conservatives and the Western-based Alliance. The other significant parties are the Bloc Québécois (BQ) and the left-wing New Democratic Party (NDP) (see Table 10.1).

Population (annual growth rate):	33.1m (+0.8%)
World Bank income group:	high income
Political Rights score:	1
Civil Liberties score:	1
Human development index (rank/out of):	4/177
Freedom of the press index (rank/out of):	24/194
Ease of doing business index (rank/out of):	4/175

Note: For meaning and sources of scales and indexes, see p. xvi. In all cases a score and rank of 1 is 'best'.

CANADA is a large country with a relatively small population. Its land mass is the second largest in the world but its population is little more than a tenth of its powerful American neighbour. Most Canadians live in urban settlements in a 100-mile strip bordering the United States. Its economy depends heavily on the USA, a relationship reinforced by the formation of the North American Free Trade Agreement in 1994.

The United States therefore provides a natural contrast. Although both countries are settler societies, Canada never experienced America's radical break with the colonial power. The basis of its constitution remains the British North America Act (1867), now redesignated the Constitution Act. Not until the more recent Constitution Act (1982) was authority to amend the constitution returned to Canada; indeed, the Governor General is still formally appointed by the British monarch.

Where the American constitution is based on a philosophy of limiting government to protect the liberty of states and individuals, Canada's federation is more centralized and, unusually, combined with a parliamentary system. The country has experienced neither slavery nor civil war; it has also followed a more orthodox path in policy development, with extensive public services premised on the principle of equality.

In common with both the USA and Britain, Canada uses a plurality electoral system which has sustained a two-party system. The major parties (Liberal and Conservative) are more American than British in organization and philosophy: they are election-fighting entities lacking a mass membership and strong central organization. Canada's major parties never acquired the sharp ideological differences which once characterized Britain's Conservative and Labour parties; as in the USA, the spoils of office were a major incentive.

However, Canada's major parties receive less legal protection than their American equivalents and the Conservatives were reduced to a low ebb in the 1990s as the regional dimension intruded, with the Alliance gaining support from dissatisfied voters in the resource-rich west. After reunification in 2003, the retitled Conservative Party of Canada was able to form a minority government in 2006.

Further reading: Bickerton and Gagnon (2004), Brooks (2004).

SPOTLIGHT

Federalism in Canada

The constitution of 1867 gave priority to the national government; at least some of its authors thought of the provinces as little more than glorified municipalities. Since then, however, 'Canada has moved from a highly centralized political situation to one of the most decentralized federal systems in the world' (Landes, 1995, p.101). What accounts for this transformation?

This evolution, perhaps unique among federations, reflects the central issue of Canadian politics: the place of French-speaking Quebec. From the sixteenth century, France and then Britain colonized the territories of Canada, inhabited at that time by around ten million indigenous people. Britain finally defeated the French in 1759.

In contrast to the racial division in the USA, where blacks do not comprise a majority in any state, about 90 per cent of Canada's francophones live in Quebec and about 85 per cent of Quebec's population speaks French (Brooks, 2004, p. 196). Canada therefore provides a test case of federalism's ability to integrate a geographically concentrated minority.

For many Francophones, Canada consists of two founding peoples – the British and French – whose status should be equal. The assumption is that the country is a compact between two cultures, implying that Quebec should receive special recognition within the federation, rather than a contract between ten provinces.

Since the 1960s a revived nationalist party in Quebec has sought to implement this vision. However the federal response has been to decentralize power to all provinces, not Quebec only. In Quebec itself, the Parti Québécois (PQ), elected to power in 1994, held a provincial referendum in 1995 on 'sovereignty association' for Quebec. This scheme would have combined political sovereignty for Quebec with continued economic association with Canada. The proposal lost by the narrowest of margins. Subsequently, the issue of constitutional reform declined in intensity, with the PQ voted out of provincial office in 2003, replaced by the Québec Liberal Party (no longer affiliated with the Liberal Party of Canada).

Self-reported ethnic origin of the population (six largest groups), 2001

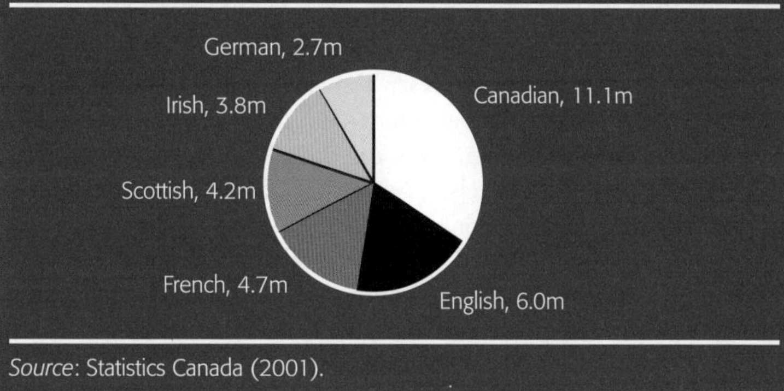

Source: Statistics Canada (2001).

Multilevel governance, known in Canada as executive federalism, continues to operate even during phases of intense debate over the position of French-speaking Canada. As Brooks (2004, p. 204) puts it, 'divided jurisdiction has given rise to a sprawling and complicated network of relations linking the federal and provincial governments. This network is often compared to an iceberg, only a small part of which is visible to the eye'.

The secrecy and unclear accountability of this intergovernmental network has come in for significant criticism in Canada, not least because it lacks any explicit base in law and the constitution. Even so, the practices of multilevel governance are surely an inherent feature of all liberal democracies, federal or otherwise.

Further reading: Bakvis and Skogstad (2002), Burgess (2001), Simeon (2002).

Perhaps always a myth, dual federalism has long since disappeared, overwhelmed long before the arrival of terrorist threats by the demands of an integrated economy and world war. Even so, it expresses an implicit if unrealizable strand in federal thinking. Just as democracies are often judged against an unrealistic model of direct self-government, so contemporary federations are often found wanting against an unattainable ideal of independent tiers.

Dual federalism, as originally envisaged in the USA, meant that national and state governments retained separate spheres of action. Each level independently performed the tasks allocated to it by the constitution. **Cooperative federalism**, as practised in Germany, is based on collaboration between levels. National and state governments are expected to act as partners in following the interests of the whole.

The second approach is **cooperative federalism**. This interpretation is favoured in the main by European federations, especially Germany and German-influenced Austria. While federalism in the USA is based on a contract in which the states join together to form a central government with limited functions, the European form rests on the idea of cooperation between levels. Such solidarity expresses a shared commitment to a united society, binding the participants together. The moral norm is solidarity and the operating principle is **subsidiarity**: the idea that decisions should be taken at the lowest feasible level. The central government offers overall leadership but implementation is the duty of lower levels: a division rather than a separation of tasks.

Cooperative federalism lacks the theoretical simplicity of the dual model but, as a more recent form, it provides a realistic account of how federal governance proceeds in practice. In a sense, it provides a theoretical justification for the realities of multilevel governance found in all federal democracies. Consider, for example, the German federation. Imposed by the Allies in 1949 as a constitutionally entrenched barrier against dictatorship, federalism represented a return to the country's strong regional roots (Gunlicks, 2003). Federalism is reflected in the country's official title, the Federal Republic of Germany: under the Basic Law Germany's federal character cannot be amended. Federalism quickly became an accepted part of the postwar republic (Umbach, 2002).

The principle of **subsidiarity** is that no task should be performed by a larger and more complex organization if that task can be executed as well by a smaller and simpler body. The tenet emerges from Catholic social thought, where it was invoked to defend the role of the Church and voluntary associations against the encroachments of the welfare state. Today, the term is often applied to federations and especially the European Union.

From its inception, German federalism has been based on interdependence, not independence. All the *Länder* (states) are expected to contribute to the success of the whole; in exchange, they are entitled to respect from the centre. The federal government makes policy but the *Länder* implement it, a division of labour expressed in the constitutional requirement that 'the *Länder* shall execute federal laws as matters of their own concern'. Because the states are the implementing agent, they must first approve bills affecting them through parliament's upper chamber, the Bundesrat, where provincial governments are directly represented. Further, the constitution now explicitly defines some 'joint tasks', such as higher education, where responsibility is shared (Box 14.1). These mechanisms of interdependence have been reinforced by the Constitutional Court, which implements the detailed specification laid out in the Basic Law. Reflecting the ethos of collaboration, the Court has required the participants to show due sensitivity to the interests of the other actors in the federation.

Although German federalism remains far more organic than its American equivalent, its cooperative ethos has come under pressure from a growing perception that decision-making has become cumbersome and opaque. In particular, agreement between the government and the upper house was often stymied because the ruling parties lacked a majority in the *Länder*-based Bundesrat. Accordingly, constitutional reforms finalized in 2006 sought to establish clearer lines of responsibility between Berlin and the *Länder*, for example by giving the states more autonomy in education and environmental protection. The main aim was to reduce the proportion of bills requiring Bundesrat approval from around 60 per cent to 40 per cent. Although this package repre-

DEBATE

IS THE EUROPEAN UNION A FEDERATION?

Our understanding of federalism can be usefully tested against the challenging case of the European Union (EU). Leaving aside opinion on whether the EU ought to develop as a federation, to what extent can this singular entity already be regarded as a federation? Have those sceptics, particularly in Britain, who would prefer the EU to be merely an intergovernmental organization already been left behind?

YES

Shared sovereignty is the core feature of federalism and by this test the Union already possesses a broadly federal character.

Like the United States, the European Union has a strong legal basis in the treaties on which it is founded. The influential European Court of Justice, just like America's Supreme Court, adjudicates disputes between levels of government. In both cases, court decisions apply directly to citizens and must be implemented by member governments.

In neither the European Union nor the USA is there any provision for member states to withdraw. The citizens of member state are also citizens of the Union. Even British passports are adorned with 'European Union' as well as 'United Kingdom'. Externally, the EU is represented in international bodies such as the United Nations and it maintains over 130 diplomatic missions.

As with the American national government, the Union has specific policy responsibilities, notably for the single market. There is no reason why all federations should share the same division of functions between levels.

In short, in Europe – as in America – sovereignty is already pooled. It is only British intransigence that insisted on the name 'European Union' rather than 'European Federation'. McKay's judgement from 1999 (p. 220) is even more justified today: 'We can conclude that although, after the implementation of Maastricht (1992), the EU remains an unusual and still evolving political entity, it also qualifies as a species of federal state.'

NO

To describe the EU as a federation would be to exaggerate its cohesion. Again, comparisons with the American exemplar are helpful:

- The USA possesses a single currency and freedom of movement but these goals have only been partly achieved within the EU.
- The EU is still governed by treaties between states whereas the United States was founded on a constitution.
- Where the USA was designed as a federation from the start, the EU was built on agreeing concrete policies, particularly for a single market, with federation only as an aspiration.
- Where the USA fought a civil war to preserve its union, the EU has not faced this vital test nor, without its own military force, is it in any position to do so.

In addition:

- The EU does not tax its citizens directly. Its main revenue source is a levy on the gross national income of member states.
- Member states have retained national control of foreign and defence policy, including the use of armed force.
- Member states retain individual membership of intergovernmental bodies such as the United Nations.

If the EU were a true federation with a coherent central government, Henry Kissinger would not need to have asked, 'When I want to speak to Europe, who do I telephone?'.

ASSESSMENT

Originally, the USA was still described in the plural – these United States – yet no one would question that those same states had formed a federation (Forsyth, 1996). In a similar way, the EU represents a pooling of some of its members' sovereignty and consists of institutions through which sovereignty is exercised. In these respects, the Union is more than a confederation yet, as in the early decades of the United States, its members retain much of their traditional autonomy. If the EU is to be seen as a federation, it is certainly a unique one.

Further reading

Burgess (2000, 2003), McKay (2001), Menon and Schain (2006), Nugent (2006, pp. 550–3), Wiener and Diez (2004).

sents a move away from cooperative federalism towards greater subsidiarity, consultation remains embedded in German political practice. Multilevel governance cannot be legislated away.

An evolving balance

In the game of multilevel governance, the central government tended to gain influence for much of the twentieth century. Partly, this trend reflected the centre's financial muscle. The flow of money became more favourable to the centre as income tax revenues grew with the expansion of both the economy and the workforce. Income is mainly taxed at national level because otherwise people and corporations could move to low-tax states. By contrast, the states had to depend for their own independently raised revenue on sales and property taxes, a smaller and less dynamic revenue base. In most federations, the central government now receives the lion's share of total public revenue, redistributing some of this money to the provinces through grants of various kinds (Box 14.2). In the USA, for instance, the federal share of total government spending grew from 17 per cent in 1929, before the depression, to an estimated 66 per cent in 2006 (Bardes, Shelley and Schmidt, 2006, p. 98).

But the enhanced authority of the centre in federal systems was more than a financial matter. It also reflected the emergence of a national economy demanding overall planning. Clearly, coordination is needed to forestall the absurdity of highways ending at a state's borders or of villains expelled from one state to the next but arrested in neither. Such planning needs continue. When California experienced an electricity shortage in 2000, the federal government inevitably became involved as the state began to draw in power from surrounding areas. Similarly, power cuts on the Eastern seaboard three years later exposed the weaknesses of an electricity grid partly controlled by 50 separate states.

The broader expansion of public functions also worked to the centre's advantage over the twentieth century. Wars and depressions invariably empowered the national government. Such additional powers, once acquired, tended to be retained. The post-1945 drive to complete a welfare state enhanced the central power still further.

This changing balance between tiers of government was reflected in decisions by constitutional courts. Generally, the courts acceded to central initiatives, particularly when justified by national emergencies. In the rulings of the US Supreme Court, federal law prevailed over state law for most of the twentieth century. In Australia, decisions of the High Court favoured the centre to the point where some commentators came to regard federalism as little more than a constitutional fiction.

Since the 1980s, however, the trends have become more ambivalent. On the one hand, big projects run by the centre went out of fashion, partly because national governments found themselves financially stretched in an era of lower taxation. The states discovered they had more of their own money to spend and hence more control over how to spend it. Reflecting this trend, a number of courts also made some effort to encourage state autonomy. In the USA, a more conservative Supreme Court used states' rights to strike down a number of congressional laws. For instance, in *United States* v. *Lopez*

BOX 14.2

Financial transfers from the federal government to states

Categorical grant	For specific projects (e.g. a new hospital)
Block grant	For particular programmes (e.g. medical care)
Revenue-sharing	General funding which places few limits on the recipient's use of funds
Equalization grant	Used in some federations (e.g. Canada and Germany) in an effort to harmonize financial conditions between the states. Can create resentment in the wealthier states.

(1995) the justices declared unconstitutional a federal law banning possession of a gun within 1,000 feet of a school. Such matters were judged to be a state preserve.

On the other hand, the centre still sought to provide overall direction. Most obviously, national governments led the response to the terrorist threat. In the USA, 'national control of domestic security eliminates a great deal of the discretion available to state and local government in areas that have previously been left free of federal interference' (Albritton, 2006, p. 14). In this and other areas, the American government continued to issue **unfunded mandates**, even though the Unfunded Mandates Reform Act (1995) sought to reduce their introduction. Talk of the renaissance of the states faded as phrases such as coercive cooperation resurfaced (Elazar, 1990).

An **unfunded mandate** is an American term with general relevance. It indicates a federal requirement for state or local governments to perform an action in the absence of specific resources from the centre.

Any review of the changing balance between the tiers of a federation will show an evolution over time, reflecting both financial and political developments. Such changes indicate flexibility rather than instability; indeed, they are a means of adjustment which enhances the stability of the core federal bargain. Like constitutions, federations are reinterpreted for each generation. But where constitutions are adapted through the courts, federations also evolve through the murkier and more political means of multilevel governance. This manner of evolution may lack legitimacy but still enhances underlying stability.

Assessing federalism

What conclusions can we reach about the federal experiment (Box 14.3)? The case for federalism is that it offers a natural and practical arrangement for organizing large states. It provides checks and balances on a territorial basis, keeps some government functions closer to the people and allows for the representation of ethnic differences. Federalism reduces overload in the national executive while the existence of multiple provinces produces healthy competition and opportunities for experiment. The

BOX 14.3

Federalism: strengths and weaknesses

Strength	Weakness
A practical arrangement for large countries	May be less effective in responding to security threats (e.g. terrorism)
Provides additional checks and balances	Decision-making is slow and complicated: 'trouble, expense and delay', claimed Bryce (1919, p. 341).
Allows for the recognition of diversity	Can entrench divisions between provinces
Reduces overload at the centre	The centre experiences greater difficulty in launching national initiatives
Provides competition between provinces and allows citizens to move between them	How citizens are treated depends on where they live
Offers opportunities for policy experiments	Unclear accountability to the public
Allows small units to cooperate in achieving the economic and military advantages of size	May permit majorities within a province to exploit a minority
Brings government closer to the people	Basing representation on provinces violates the principle of one person, one vote

BOX 14.4

Methods for distributing power away from the centre

	Definition	Example
Deconcentration	Central government functions are executed by staff in the field	Almost 90 per cent of US federal civilian employees work away from Washington, DC
Decentralization	Central government functions are executed by subnational authorities	Local governments administer national welfare programmes in Scandinavia
Devolution	Central government grants some decision-making autonomy to lower levels	Regional governments in France, Italy and Spain

Note: Deconcentration and decentralization occur in federal as well as unitary states.

states can move ahead even when the federal level languishes: for example, California and some other American states have recently shown more concern with climate change than has the federal government. Citizens and firms also have the luxury of choice: if they dislike governance in one state, they can always move to another. Above all, federalism reconciles two modern imperatives: it secures the economic and military advantages of scale while retaining, indeed encouraging, cultural diversity.

But a case can also be mounted against federalism. Compared to unitary government, decision-making in a federation is complicated, slow-moving and indecisive. When a gunman ran amok in Tasmania in 1996, killing 35 people, federal Australia experienced some political problems before it tightened gun control uniformly across the country. By contrast, unitary Britain acted speedily when a comparable incident occurred in the same year at a primary school in Dunblane, Scotland. When the American president moved quickly to set up a new Department of Homeland Security after 11 September 2001, one of his motives was precisely to improve coordination between tiers of government. Significantly, federalism often receives short shift in wartime.

Federalism can place the political interests of rival governments above the resolution of problems. Fiscal discipline becomes harder to enforce; several Latin American governments have struggled to control their free-spending (and free-riding) provinces, denting the fiscal strength of the state as a whole (Braun *et al.*, 2003).

Any final judgement on federalism must take a view on the proper balance between the concentration and diffusion of political power. Should power rest with one body to allow decisive action?

Table 14.2 Subnational government in unitary states: some European examples

	France	Italy	The Netherlands	Norway	Poland	Sweden
Highest tier ('regions')	22	20	12	19	16	18
Middle tier ('provinces')	96	94			308	
Lowest tier ('communes')	36,565	8,074	1496	434	2500	289

Note: Figures are from the late 1990s to the early 2000s. Labels used for a given tier vary by country.

If so, federalism is likely to be seen as an obstacle and impediment, as an anti-democratic device. Alternatively, should power be dispersed so as to reduce the danger of majority dictatorship? Through this lens, federalism will appear as an indispensable aid to liberty.

Unitary states

Most states are unitary, meaning that sovereignty lies exclusively with the central government. In this hierarchical arrangement, the national government possesses the theoretical authority to abolish lower levels. Subnational administrations, whether regional or local, may make policy as well as implement it but they do so by leave of the centre. In most unitary states, the national legislature has only one chamber since there is no need for a second house to represent the provinces.

Unlike federations, a unitary framework is not always a deliberate creation; rather, such systems emerge naturally in societies with a history of rule by sovereign monarchs and emperors, such as Britain, France and Japan. Unitary structures are also the norm in smaller democracies, particularly those without strong ethnic divisions. The countries of Eastern Europe have also chosen a unitary structure for their post-communist constitutions, viewing federalism as a device through which Russia dominated the old Soviet Union. In Latin America, nearly all the smaller countries (but none of the larger ones) are unitary.

After the complexities of federalism, a unitary structure may seem straightforward and efficient. However, the location of sovereignty is rarely an adequate guide to political realities; unitary government is often decentralized in its operation. Indeed in the 1990s many unitary states attempted to push responsibility for more functions on to lower levels. In practice, unitary states, just like federations, involve the detailed bargaining found in all multilevel governance.

We can distinguish three broad ways in which unitary states can disperse power from the centre: **deconcentration**, **decentralization** and **devolution** (Box 14.4, p. 292). The first of these, deconcentration, is purely an administrative matter, denoting the movement of central government employees away from the capital. The case for a deconcentrated structure is that it spreads the work around, reduces costs by allowing activities to move to cheaper areas and frees central departments to focus on policy-making. There is, after all, no reason in principle why such functions as driving licences and passports should be administered from the capital.

The second, and politically more significant, way of dispersing power is through **decentralization**. Here, policy execution is delegated to subnational bodies such as local authorities. In Scandinavia, for instance, local governments have put into effect many welfare programmes agreed at national level. In a similar way, local government in the UK serves as the workhorse of central authority.

The third and most radical form of power dispersal is **devolution**. This occurs when the centre grants decision-making autonomy (including some legislative powers) to lower levels. In the United Kingdom, devolved assemblies were introduced in Scotland and Wales in 1999. But the contrast with federations remains. Britain remains a unitary state because these new assemblies could be abolished by Westminster through normal legislation. As the English politician Enoch Powell (1912–98) observed, 'power devolved is power retained'. Spain is another example of a unitary state with extensive devolution. Its regions were strengthened in the transition to democracy following General Franco's death in 1975 and devolution has continued apace since, with Catalonia's status as a distinct nationality recognized in 2006. At least in theory, though, the framework is still unitary.

With the widespread introduction of elected regional councils, many unitary states such as France and Italy now possess three levels of subnational government: regional, provincial and local (Table 14.2). Also, some have or are considering special arrangements for large cities. The result is a multilevel system that is even more intricate than the two levels of subnational authority – state and local – within a federation. Whether federal or unitary, multilevel governance has become a refrain repeated in all liberal democracies.

Although regional governments can pass laws in their designated areas of competence, their main contribution has been in economic planning and infrastructure development. Such tasks are beyond the scope of small local authorities but beneath the national vision of the centre. The Spanish region of Valencia, for example, has sought to improve telecommunications, roads, railways, ports and airports. In Italy, too, regional authorities outside the south have made a notable contribution, with some left-wing parties determined to display their competence through showpiece governance.

So the evolution of regional government is a significant development in unitary states. The original demand for greater self-government has given way towards a more administrative role in which regions stand between other levels of government. In a system of multilevel governance, regions are indeed finding their level. As Balme (1998, p. 182) concludes of France, regional governments in Europe are becoming arenas in which policies are formed, even if they seem unlikely to become decisive actors in their own right.

The European Union has encouraged the development of a regional level within its member states, thereby stimulating the emergence of the concept of multilevel governance itself. The European Regional Development Fund, established in 1975, distributed aid directly to regions, rather than through central governments. The notion, somewhat exaggerated but significant in itself, was that the European Union and the regions would gradually become the leading policy-makers, outflanking central governments which would be left with less to do in this multilevel arena.

In 1988, the EU furthered such aspirations by introducing a Committee of the Regions and Local Communities, a body composed of subnational authorities. However, the Committee has proved to be merely consultative. National executives remain more central to the policy process than some of the more committed proponents of multilevel governance had originally envisaged (Bourne, 2003).

Local government

Local government is universal, found in federal and unitary states alike. It is the lowest level of elected territorial organization within the state. Variously called communes, municipalities or parishes, local governments are 'where the day-to-day activity of politics and government gets done' (Teune, 1995b, p. 16). For example, 9/11 was certainly a global event but it was New York City officials who faced the immediate task of providing emergency services.

At their best, local governments express the virtues of limited scale. They can represent natural communities, remain accessible to their citizens, reinforce local identities, offer a practical education in politics, provide a recruiting ground to higher posts, serve as a first port of call for citizens and distribute resources in the light of specialist knowledge. Yet local governments also have characteristic weaknesses. They are often too small to deliver services efficiently, lack financial autonomy and are easily dominated by traditional elites.

The balance struck between intimacy and efficiency varies over time. In the second half of the twentieth century, local authorities were encouraged to become more efficient and customer-led, leading to larger units. For example, the number of Swedish municipalities fell from 2,500 in 1951 to 274 in 1974 (Rose, 2004, p. 168).

But around the turn of the century signs began to emerge of a rebirth of interest in citizen involvement, stimulated by declining turnout at local elections. In New Zealand, for instance, successful managerial reforms introduced in 1989 were followed by the Local Government Act (2002). This law outlined a more expansive – and possibly expensive – participatory vision for the country's territorial local authorities. Similarly, 'in the early 1990s, Dutch local government was preoccupied with a concern for effectiveness and efficiency. During the 1990s, however, the emphasis switched to the issue of public responsiveness' (Denters and Klok, 2005, p. 65). Norway resolved in 1995 that 'no further amalgamations should be imposed against the wishes of a majority of residents in the municipalities concerned' (Rose, 2004, p. 168).

The status of local government varies across countries (Box 14.5). Consider, first, the contrast between European and New World democracies. In most of Europe, local authorities represent historic communities that pre-date the emergence of strong national governments. Many Italian communes, for instance, can be dated to the twelfth century. Reflecting this status, European constitutions normally mandate some form of local self-government. Sweden's Instrument of Government roundly declares that Swedish democracy 'shall be realized through a rep-

BOX 14.5

Exploring the status of local government

Higher	Lower	Comment
In European democracies	In New World democracies (e.g. Australia, USA)	In Europe, local governments often represent historic communities but in the New World, local government is more utilitarian in character
In Northern Europe (e.g. Scandinavia)	In Southern Europe (e.g. France, Italy)	Local governments administer the extensive welfare states found in Northern Europe but perform fewer functions in Southern Europe
When local governments possess general competence to represent their community	When local governments cannot act *ultra vires* ('beyond the powers')	General competence allows local authorities to take the initiative whereas *ultra vires* restricts them to designated functions
In unitary states	In federations	In federations, local government is the preserve of the states, creating diversity in organization and reducing coherence

Sources: Adapted from Goldsmith (1996), John (2001) and Page and Goldsmith (1987).

resentative and parliamentary polity and through local self-government'.

In the New World, by contrast, local government reveals a more pragmatic, utilitarian character. Local authorities were set up as needed to deal with 'roads, rates and rubbish'. Special boards (appointed or elected) were added to deal with specific problems such as mosquito control, harbours and land drainage. The policy style was apolitical: 'there is no Democratic or Republican way to collect garbage'. Indeed special boards were often set up precisely to be independent of party politics.

Second, the standing of local government varies within Europe, on a broad north–south axis. In the Northern countries, local authorities became important delivery vehicles for the extensive welfare states that matured after 1945. Services such as social assistance, unemployment benefit, childcare and education were funded by the state but provided locally, giving rise to such phrases as the welfare municipality and the local welfare state. In effect, local authorities became the government's front office, employing about one in four of the total workforce in the Nordic countries (Rose, 2004, p. 169). In some countries, including Denmark, local authorities also act as tax collectors for the centre.

In Southern Europe, by contrast, welfare states are less extensive, with the Catholic Church playing a greater role in providing care, while public services such as education remain under the direct control of the centre. In Italy, for instance, teachers are civil servants rather than employees of local councils. Also, communes in Southern Europe have remained small, especially in France (Figure 14.2). Limited scale precludes an extensive administrative role except when neighbouring areas form collaborative syndicates to supply utilities such as water and energy.

Third, **general competence** enhances both the powers and the standing of local authorities. Germany's Basic Law, for instance, gives local communities 'the right to regulate [all local matters] under their own responsibility and within the limits of the law' while the Dutch constitution states that local communities have 'autonomous' powers to regulate their own affairs.

General competence is the authority of a local government to make regulations in any matter of concern to its area. Where general competence is lacking, local authorities are restricted to those tasks expressly delegated by higher authority.

But in other countries, including the United Kingdom, councils could traditionally only perform those tasks expressly designated by the centre; any other act would be *ultra vires* (beyond the powers). In the United States, Dillon's Rule similarly restricts local governments to tasks delegated by their particular state. Some countries where *ultra vires* applies, including the United Kingdom and New Zealand, did establish a more liberal legal framework at the start of the twenty-first century but without granting the full power of general competence to local areas (Bush, 2005).

Fourth, local government tends to enjoy higher status in unitary states than in federations. For instance, the unitary nature of most European states allows direct links to form between powerful local administrations (especially in large cities) and the centre. By contrast, even in an era of multilevel governance, local authorities in federations tend to be creatures of the states, creating diversity but also reducing coherence. In these conditions local government tends to be the forgotten level.

Structure

The structure of local government has recently attracted attention, largely in an attempt to make decision-making clearer to local electorates in an era of falling turnout. In particular, efforts have been made to represent the mayor as the leading personification of the area. Just as political parties have sought to reverse a decline in membership by giving their supporters more say in the selection of candidates and leaders, so local governments in such countries as Italy, the Netherlands and the United Kingdom have encouraged turnout by experimenting with direct election of the mayor. A high profile mayor can enhance the area's visibility not just within the district itself but also, and equally importantly, among potential visitors and investors from outside. We see here a growing relationship between political institutions and place marketing.

There are, in fact, three broad ways of organizing local government: the council, mayor–council and council–manager formats (Box 14.6). The first and most traditional method concentrates authority in a college of elected councillors rather than a single individual. This council is formally responsible for overseeing the organization's work but more detailed supervision is normally delegated. In Sweden and traditionally in England, the full council operates through powerful committees covering the main local services – housing and education, for example – with professional appointees (such as architects and educational administrators) also playing a significant role. Alternatively, the mayor and selected councillors ('aldermen') may form a working body, as for example in Belgium and the Netherlands. In either case, the mayor is appointed

Figure 14.2 Average population of elected local authorities (lowest tier) in selected European democracies

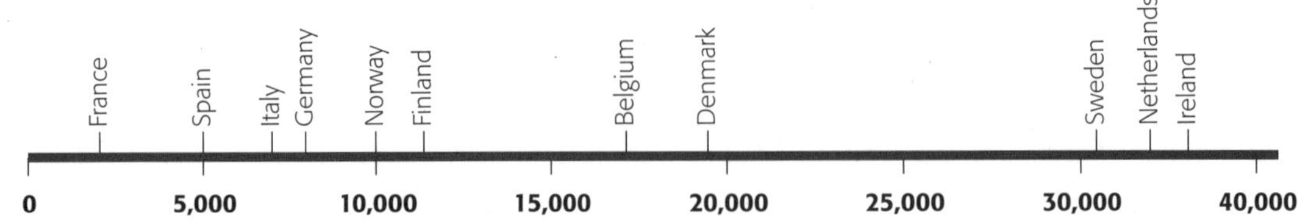

Note: Figures are from the late 1990s to 2003. Not shown: UK (137,000).

Sources: Adapted from John (2001), Denters and Rose (2005), Rose (2004).

BOX 14.6

Structures for local government

	Description	Examples
Council	Elected councillors form a council which operates through a smaller subgroup or through functional committees. The unelected mayor is appointed by the council or by central government.	Belgium, Netherlands, Sweden
Mayor–council	An elected mayor serves as chief executive. Councillors elected from local wards form a council with legislative and financial authority. This format is often subdivided into strong mayor and weak mayor systems.	About half the 7,000 cities in the USA, including Chicago and New York
Council–manager	The elected mayor and council appoint a professional manager to run executive departments.	About 3,000 American cities, including Dallas and Phoenix

Sources: Bowles (1998), Denters and Rose (2005), Mouritzen and Svara (2002).

by the council itself or by central government. Whatever virtues this format may have, its collegiate character presents a rather opaque picture to the electorate; it is this structure which has come under most scrutiny from reformers.

Accordingly, a second method of organization known as the mayor–council system has attracted attention. This model is based on a separation of powers between a mayor, who is the chief executive, and an elected council with legislative and budget-approving powers. This elaborate and highly political structure, used in many large American cities such as New York, permits a range of urban interests to be represented within the framework. The mayor and council often disagree, just as at national level the president is frequently in conflict with Congress. Again as at national level, the mayor is usually elected at large (from the entire area) while councillors represent a specific neighbourhood.

The powers awarded to the mayor and council vary considerably, defining 'strong mayor' and 'weak mayor' variants. In the strong mayor format, the mayor is the focus of authority and accountability, with the power to appoint and dismiss department heads without council approval. New York City is an example. In the weak mayor format, by contrast, the council retains both legislative and executive authority, keeping the mayor on a closer leash. London's new mayor (directly elected since 2000) is a classic weak mayor, lacking the strong powers of his NYC equivalent (Sweating, 2003).

The third structure for local government, again originating in the United States, is the council–manager system. Unlike the mayor–council format, this arrangement seeks to depoliticize and simplify local government by separating politics from administration. This distinction is achieved by appointing a professional city manager, operating under the elected council and mayor, to administer the authority's work. This council–manager format emerged early in the twentieth century in an attempt to curb corruption; it has been widely adopted in western and south-western states in the USA. The model has corporate overtones, with the voters (shareholders) electing councillors (board of directors) to oversee the city manager (chief executive) who is responsible for cost-effective service delivery. However, the distinction between politics and administration is difficult to maintain in practice.

Functions

What is it that local governments do? Broadly, their tasks are two-fold: to provide local public services (such as refuse collection) and to implement national welfare policies (Box 14.7). However, a static description of functions fails to reveal how the role of local government has evolved since the 1980s.

The major trend, especially prominent in the English-speaking world and Scandinavia, has been for municipal authorities to reduce their direct provision of services by delegating tasks to private organizations, both profit-making and voluntary. This transition from local government towards local governance reflects the emergence of new public management at national level (see p. 366). In Denmark, for example, many local governments have set up user boards in primary schools. These boards are given block budgets and the authority to hire and fire staff (Bogason, 1996). In a similar way, private firms located in the commercial district of some American cities have taken over much of the responsibility for funding and organizing improvements to local services such as street-cleaning.

This transition is often presented as an evolution from providing to enabling. The **enabling authority** does not so much provide services as ensure that they are supplied. In theory, the authority can become a smaller, coordinating body, more concerned with governance than government. More organizations become involved in local policy-making, many of them functional (e.g. school boards) rather than territorial (e.g. county councils). An increased concern with economic development, especially by attracting inward investment, often forms part of this more coordinating and strategic approach.

BOX 14.7

Typical powers of local authorities

Cemeteries
Economic development
Environmental protection
Fire service
Homes for the elderly
Libraries
Local planning
Primary education
Recreation
Refuse disposal
Roads
Social housing
Tourism
Water supply
Welfare provision

Source: Adapted from Norton (1991), Table 2.2.

Relationships with the centre

How is local government integrated into the national structure of power? This question is key to appreciating how multilevel governance operates in practice within unitary states. The answer reveals contrasting notions of state authority. The relationship between centre and locality usually takes one of two forms: dual or fused. Broadly, this distinction matches that between dual and cooperative federalism.

The **enabling authority** is a term used to summarize one vision of local governance. Such an authority does not provide many services itself. Rather, its concerns are to coordinate the provision of services and to represent the community both within and beyond its territory. An enabling authority is strategic, contracting out service provision to private agencies, whether voluntary or profit-making.

In a **dual** approach, local government is seen as an organization separate from the centre: public authority is separated rather than integrated. It is as if there were two spheres of authority, connected for practical reasons only. Local governments retain free-standing status, setting their own internal organization and employing staff on their own conditions of service. Employees tend to move horizontally – from one local authority to another – rather than vertically, between central and local government. Ultimate authority rests with the centre but local government employees do not regard themselves as working for the same employer as central civil servants. National politicians rarely emerge from local politics.

Traditionally, Britain was regarded as the best example of a dual system. Even though the country is unitary, with sovereignty focused on the centre, local

A **dual** system of local government (as in Britain) maintains a formal separation of central and local government. Although the centre is sovereign, local authorities are not seen as part of a single state apparatus. In a **fused** system (as in France), municipalities form part of a uniform system of administration applying across the country.

government is regarded as more than a sub-branch of national authority. This separation reflects history. Even before the rise of the modern state, local magistrates administered their local communities. The spirit of self-government survives in a perception that central and local government are distinct, if intensely interdependent, spheres. In the Nordic countries, too, local authorities are still viewed as self-governing units operating with discretionary authority within a unitary framework, even though much of their detailed work involves implementing national welfare programmes (Rose, 2004, p. 180).

Under a **fused** system, by contrast, central and local government combine to form a single sphere of public authority. Both levels express the leading position of the state. In some European countries, such as Belgium and the Netherlands, the local mayor is appointed by central government and is responsible to the centre for maintaining local law and order. In addition, central and local authority are fused in the office of the prefect, a central appointee who oversees the administration of a particular community and reports to the Ministry of the Interior. In theory, a prefectoral system signals central dominance by establishing a clear hierarchy running from national government through the prefect to local authorities.

France is the classic example of this fused approach. The system was established by Napoleon early in the nineteenth century and consists of 96 *départements* in France, each with its own prefect and elected assembly. The framework is uniform and rational but in practice the prefect must cooperate with local councils rather than simply oversee them. In fact, the prefect is now as much an agent of the *département* as of the centre, representing interests upwards as much as transmitting commands downwards. Although the powers of the prefect have declined, the French model remains influential. Many other countries have adopted it, including all France's ex-colonies and several post-communist states.

One effect of a fused system is the ease with which politicians can move between, or even straddle, the national and the local. In Belgium, two out of three MPs also hold local political office (Winter and Brans, 2003, p. 51). In France, too, national politicians often become or remain mayor of their home town: the *cumul des mandats* (accumulation of offices). Even after a tightening of the rules in 1985 and 2000, the most popular *cumul* – combining the office of local mayor with membership of the National Assembly – is still permitted (Stevens, 2003, p. 170).

Central–local relations in authoritarian states

Studying the relationship between centre and periphery in authoritarian states confirms the relative insignificance of institutions in non-democracies. In these regimes, the distinction between local government and local power is fundamental. The former is weak: authority flows from the top down and bottom-up institutions of representation are subordinate. Where national power is exercised by the military or a ruling party, these bodies typically establish a parallel presence in the provinces, where their authority overrides that of formal state officials. For a humble mayor in such a situation, the main skill required is to lie low and avoid offending the real power-holders. Little of the sophisticated policy-making suggested by the notion of multilevel governance takes place and the more neutral term 'central–local relations' is more accurate.

But it would be wrong to conclude that authoritarian regimes are highly centralized. Rather, central rulers – just like medieval monarchs – often depend on established provincial leaders to sustain their own, sometimes tenuous, grip on power. Central–local relations therefore tend to be more personal and less structured than in a liberal democracy. The hold of regional strongmen on power is not embedded in local institutions; such rulers command their fiefdoms in a personal fashion, replicating the authoritarian pattern found at national level. Central and local rulers are integrated by patronage: the national ruler effectively buys the support of local bigwigs who in turn maintain their position by selectively distributing resources to their own supporters. Patronage, not institutions, is the rope that binds.

As always, totalitarian regimes offered more sophisticated excuses for their centralized order. Fascism, for example, sought unqualified obedience to the state and its supreme leader. Unity in the state implied a unitary state; multilevel governance would have been dismissed as liberal idiocy. In Italy, Mussolini relied on centrally appointed prefects to run local areas, decreeing that the prefect represented the 'entire, undiminished power of the state'. Spain under Franco proceeded similarly, with a civil governor in each province overseeing an elaborate structure of government outposts. These were fused systems *par excellence*.

Given that the supreme leader could not in fact take all decisions, in practice the local representatives of the state exerted considerable influence over their own areas. They sought to become their own little dictators and they often succeeded. So in fascist regimes, as in authoritarian ones, the doctrine of central power resulted in a system where its local exercise went unchecked.

It was perhaps only some communist regimes, most notably the Soviet Union, which achieved real political centralization. In communist states, the leading role of the party always took precedence over local concerns. As long as the party itself remained highly centralized, national leaders could command outlying areas through the party hierarchy. Technically, the 'Union of Soviet Socialist Republics' was a federation but in reality any attempt by a republic to apply its constitutional right to 'freely secede from the USSR' would have been crushed by force.

Central–local relations in China, the principal remaining communist state, take a rather different form. Despite its vast scale and multinational population, China never adopted a federal solution. It remains a unitary state governed, in theory, from Beijing. Certainly, the structure is far from uniform. It includes two *Special Administrative Regions* (Hong Kong and Macao) which are ex-colonial regions returned to Beijing's control in the 1990s. These regions are ruled under a formula of 'one country, two systems'. There are also five *administrative regions* (including Tibet and Inner Mongolia) which encompass national minorities and are ruled from Beijing in an imperial fashion, with garrisons to protect against national uprisings. In addition, four large *municipalities*, (including Shanghai) come under Beijing's direct control.

With those exceptions, though, subnational government takes the form of 22 provinces (the largest containing over 80 million people), with further subdivisions into either a) counties and townships or b) cities and districts. Provinces have gained substantial practical autonomy as the moral authority of, and funding from, the centre has declined. Provincial and city governments have spearheaded local economic development, stimulated by the desire of local political elites not just to achieve personal wealth but also to improve the resource base of their administrations.

As in the Soviet Union, the party itself provides a method of integrating centre and periphery. In particular, the circulation of party leaders between national and provincial posts helps to connect the two tiers. Several provincial leaders serve on the party's politburo; most politburo members have worked in top provincial posts in their career. As Saich (2004, p.160) comments, 'ultimately, Beijing has the power of control over 7,000 appointments and this makes it difficult for any provincial leader to defy the centre for too long'. Central–local relations may not deliver the intricate policies generated by multilevel governance in liberal democracies but 'when the centre really wishes to implement a policy and moves coherently, local officials will comply even at significant cost to their own economic interests' (Saich, 2004, p. 161). Successes such as the one-child policy and economic reform demonstrate the capacity of party leaders in Beijing to make a difference throughout this large and populous land.

Central–local relations in illiberal democracies

An illiberal democracy provides a difficult environment within which to foster central–local relations. The personal relationship between leader and people lends itself to an intermittent and unstructured engagement by the president in local affairs: indifference combined with the occasional intervention. The focus is on the national level. In Venezuela, for instance, critics allege that 'the paternalist mentality created by easy oil money induces Venezuelans to look to the central government, which administers the revenue, for quick solutions to their problems' (Ellner, 2004, p. 15). This orientation is of course encouraged by the populist style of President Hugo Chávez. For such reasons, Romero (1997, p. 32) regards centralism – along with paternalism and populism – as a core feature of what he calls 'degraded democracy' in Venezuela.

At the same time, many illiberal democracies are located in poor countries where subnational administrations in remote districts simply lack the resources to offer effective governance. As in many authoritarian regimes, powerful landowners and businessmen may run the local show, often with tacit or explicit support from the central elite. Thus a nominally centralized system may coexist with a practical decentralization of power. The connections between centre and periphery, and therefore the capital and the countryside, operate on a personal basis rather than through either institutions such as federalism or the broader policy-making regimes of multilevel governance.

The astonishing trajectory of federalism in Russia illustrates some of these themes. The post-communist era experienced the most remarkable decentralization of power under Boris Yeltsin followed by considerable recentralization under Vladimir Putin. As Hahn (2006, p. 148) writes, this is a game played for high stakes: 'the success or failure of Russia's transformation into a stable state with a viable market democracy will depend much on the creation of an effective and balanced federal system'. The challenge is to integrate a country of massive size containing numerous religions and national minorities.

Unlike China, post-communist Russia inherited a tradition of at least formal federalism from the old Soviet Union. Communist theory and practice had also encouraged the development of national groups within the USSR. These traditions were amplified by Boris Yeltsin. 'Take as much sovereignty as you can swallow', he told the regions in 1990, as part of his tactical campaign to undermine Mikhail Gorbachev's authority in Moscow. A 'parade of sovereignties' then marched across Russia, as republics declared their autonomy in what they hoped would be a Russian confederation. In the eyes of republican leaders, Russia was to be constructed *snizu vverkh*: from the bottom up.

Yeltsin continued on a confederal path after becoming president in 1991, even though the 1993 constitution gave priority to the centre. Ignoring the federal principle of symmetry, Yeltsin signed bilateral treaties between 1994 and 1998 with about half of the 89 geographical units in the federation. These short-term agreements, probably inconsistent with the constitution of the time, included specific and highly variable deals on how taxation and spending were to be shared with the centre. Many republics launched their own constitutions, again often contradicting federal law. Some districts within republics themselves became federal subjects, rather as if Seattle were able to elect its own senators in addition to those chosen to represent Washington state. All this amounted to asymmetric federalism on a grand scale.

There may have been sound political reasons for this cavalier approach. Hahn (2006, p. 152) judges that Yeltsin's 'compromise with regional native elites prevented or at least forestalled separatism (except in Chechnya), civil war and even the dissolution of Russia'. Certainly, these agreements represented a unique moment in federalism's history. However, it was difficult to see how the patchwork resulting from the 'parade of treaties' could provide a stable foundation for a federal state.

That, at any rate, was the view of Vladimir Putin. He gave high priority to consolidating the **power vertical**. This goal was achieved in three ways:

- President Putin ended nearly all of the bilateral treaties struck by his predecessor, seeking to replace them with a more uniform system of revenue-sharing between federal and lower-level units.
- The president passed a law requiring any future treaties to be approved by both houses of the legislature.
- In 2000, the president created seven extra-constitutional federal *okrugs* (districts) to oversee lower-level units. Each *okrug* is responsible for between 6 and 15 regions. These overlords

The **power vertical** is a Russian phrase denoting central control over lower levels of government within the federation.

> ensure that branches of the federal government in the regions remain loyal to Moscow and that regional laws are rendered consistent with national ones.

As is often the case with illiberal democracies, these reforms can be read in various ways. First, President Putin created a more symmetrical federation and enhanced the authority of central authority throughout the land. In essence, he created a federation from what had become a confederation. By strengthening the state, Putin surely enhanced the potential for a fully democratic state in Russia.

Second, the reforms also strengthened Putin's own political position. He staffed the *okrugs* with his own trusted appointees, often drawn from military or police backgrounds, and used them to mobilize support for his own re-election.

Third, he increased the capacity of the state to govern over, more than with, the Russian people. In that sense, the reforms contributed to Putin's project to create what he calls a 'sovereign democracy' in Russia. In Putin's eyes, a sovereign democracy is not built on the uncertain pluralistic foundations of multilevel governance. Rather, a sovereign democracy gives priority to the interests of Russia herself, interests which include an effective central state capable of controlling its population and on that foundation, strengthening Russia's position in the world.

Learning Resources for Chapter 14

Next step

Karmis and Norman (2005) bring together the classic texts on federalism.

Further reading

Comparative studies of federalism include Burgess (2006), Galligan (2006), McKay (2001) and Stepan (2001). Elazar (1996) provides an enthusiast's overview. Menon and Schain (2006) compare the EU and the USA, Bakvis and Skotsgad (2002) examine Canada, Gunlicks (2003) considers Germany, Gibson (2004) surveys Latin America while Kahn (2002) looks at Russia. Gagnon and Tully (2001) is a comparative study of multinational democracies, focusing on federalism. Loughlin (2001) reviews subnational democracy in the European Union. Denters and Rose (2005), John (2001) and Mouritzen and Svara (2002) survey local governance.

Internet sources

Forum on Federations
Seeks to enhance federalism's contribution to maintaining and constructing democracy
http://www.forumfed.org/

Institute of Intergovernmental Relations, Queen's University
Research on federalism and intergovernmental relations in Canada and beyond
http://www.iigr.ca/iigr.php/index.html

International Association of Centers for Federal Studies
An association of centers for federal studies
http://www.iacfs.org/index.php?page=1&lang=0

Centre for Studies on Federalism
Promotes research, documentation and exchange of information in federal studies
http://www.csfederalismo.it/User/index_en.html

Committee of the Regions, European Union
Provides local and regional authorities with a voice in the European Union. Includes online studies
http://www.cor.europa.eu/

Chapter 15
Legislatures

Legislatures are symbols of popular representation in politics. They are not governing bodies, they do not take major decisions and usually they do not even initiate proposals for laws. Yet they are still the foundation of both liberal and democratic politics. This significance arises from their representative role: 'Legislatures join society to the legal structure of authority in the state. Legislatures are representative bodies: they reflect the sentiments and opinions of the citizens' (Olson, 1994, p. 1).

In potential and often in reality, legislatures are the authentic representative of the people's will. For this reason they help to mobilize consent for the system of rule. As liberal democracy spreads throughout the world, so more legislatures are gaining the political weight which comes from performing this function of standing for the people.

How did legislatures acquire this significance? The origin of parliaments lies in ancient royal courts in Europe. There, monarchs would judge important legal cases and meet with noblemen of the realm. Gradually these assemblies became more settled, coming to represent the various estates – the clergy, the nobility and the towns – into which society was then divided. In the thirteenth and fourteenth centuries, kings began to consult estate leaders more consistently on issues of war, administration, commerce and taxation.

Although the initiative for calling these colloquia lay with the king, a principle of Roman law was sometimes invoked in justification. This notion was *quod omnes similter tangit, ab omnibus comprobetur* (what concerns all, should be approved by all). So these early European assemblies were viewed as possessing a right to be consulted long before they became modern legislatures with the sovereign authority to pass laws.

Where European parliaments accumulated powers gradually and with difficulty, most modern constitutions celebrate the importance of the legislature. In the debates surrounding the American constitution, for instance, James Madison declared that 'in republican government, the legislative power necessarily predominates' (Hamilton, 1788d, p. 265). A leading role for the legislature was judged an essential defence against executive tyranny; in consequence, the list of powers awarded to Congress was longer and more detailed than that given to the president. Few other parliaments are as important as the American Congress but the principle of expressing the popular will through a legislature has become a fundamental tenet of liberal democracy.

A **legislature** is a multi-member representative body which considers public issues and 'gives assent, on behalf of a political community that extends beyond the executive authority, to binding measures of public policy' (Norton, 1990, p. 1). The words used to denote these bodies reflect their origins: assemblies gather, congresses congregate, diets meet, dumas deliberate, legislatures legislate and parliaments talk. The term 'legislature' is most often used in presidential systems.

Structure

Only two things, writes Blondel (1973), can be said with certainty about every assembly in the world: how many members and chambers it has. Both are important aspects of parliamentary structure. But a third factor, the committee system, is an increasingly significant influence on the operation and effectiveness of modern parliaments. In this section, we examine all three aspects of assembly structure.

Although some European assemblies originally contained multiple chambers, one for each of the feudal estates, most parliaments today are either **unicameral** (one chamber) or bicameral (two chambers). In **bicameral** legislatures, the first or lower chamber is typically called the chamber of deputies, national assembly or house of representatives. The second or upper chamber is usually known as the senate.

Size

The size of an assembly, as indicated by the number of members in the more important lower chamber, reflects a country's population (Figure 15.1). In China, the world's most populous country, the cumbersome National People's Congress has almost 3,000 members. By contrast, the assembly in the South Pacific island of Tuvalu (population 11,810) contains just 15 representatives.

Size rarely indicates strength. Rather, the opposite applies: giant assemblies are rendered impotent by their inability to act cohesively. They are in constant danger of being taken over by more coherent actors such as political parties or even by their own committees. Ruling communist parties, as in China, preferred a large legislature precisely because it was easier to control.

By contrast, a very small chamber – say, under 100 – offers opportunities for all deputies to have their say in a collegial environment. A small chamber may be entirely appropriate for small island communities such as Tuvalu. In practice, as Figure 15.1 shows, few lower houses possess more than 500–600 members, and this is probably a fair estimate of the maximum size for an effective body.

Number of chambers

Should a legislature have one chamber or two? If the latter, what role should the second chamber play and how should its members be selected? These old questions acquired practical significance in the 1990s as a new wave of democratic constitutions moved parliaments closer to the centre of the political stage.

Unicameral legislatures are the norm today. By 2006, 114 of the world's 189 parliaments possessed only one chamber (IPU, 2006). This number rose in the second half of the twentieth century as several smaller democracies abolished their second chamber, notably New Zealand in 1950, Denmark in 1954, Sweden in 1970 and Iceland in 1991. Many smaller post-colonial and post-communist states have also embraced a single chamber. **Bicameral** legislatures are most often found in larger countries and in democracies; they are universal in federations where the second chamber expresses the voice of the component states (Uhr, 2006).

The choice between one and two chambers is not just a technical matter of institutional design. Fundamentally, the decision reflects contrasting visions of democracy. Unicameral parliaments are justified by a majoritarian reading of popular control. The proposition is that an assembly based on direct popular election reflects the popular will and should not be obstructed. The radical French cleric Abbé Sièyes (1748–1836) put the point well: 'if a second chamber dissents from the first, it is mischievous; and if it agrees, it is superfluous' (Lively, 1991). Also, a single chamber is more accountable, economical and decisive, lacking the petty politicking and point-scoring which becomes possible as soon as two houses with separate interests are created (Tsebelis and Money, 1997).

Figure 15.1 Population and assembly size, 2005

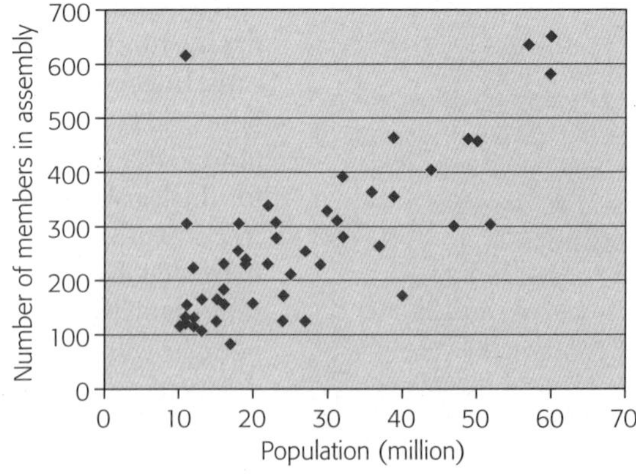

Note: For bicameral assemblies, the size of the lower chamber is used. Analysis is confined to countries with populations in the range 10–60 million.

Source: CIA (2006).

But the defenders of bicameral parliaments reject both the majoritarian logic of Abbé Sièyes and the penny-pinching of accountants. Bicameralists stress the liberal element of democracy, arguing that the upper chamber offers checks and balances. It can defend individual and group interests against a potentially oppressive majority in the lower house. The second chamber can also serve as a house of review, revising bills (proposed laws), scrutinizing constitutional amendments and eliminating intemperate legislation: a second chamber for second thoughts. From this perspective, the power to delay is a positive virtue; for example, James Madison (1751–1836) suggested that an upper house afforded protection against 'an excess of law-making' (Hamilton, 1788e).

In addition, a second house can share the workload of the lower chamber, conduct detailed committee work and assist with appointments (e.g. to the judiciary). An upper chamber provides a modern approximation to the traditional idea of a council of elders, often debating in a less partisan style than the lower house. Reflecting these points, Robert Cecil, thrice British prime minister in the nineteenth century, declared that the House of Lords 'represents the permanent, as opposed to the passing, feelings of the nation' (Russell, 2001).

Where legislatures do consist of two chambers, the question arises of the relationship between them. Usually, the lower chamber dominates. This format of **weak bicameralism** is typical of parliamentary government where the government's survival depends on maintaining the assembly's support and one chamber becomes the focus of such accountability. Where a government is equally accountable to two houses, as in Australia, it can be caught in the grip of contradictory pressures, unable to command the confidence of one or other chamber.

This task of sustaining or voting down the government falls naturally to the lower house, with its popular mandate. The dominance of the first chamber can also be seen in other ways. It often has special responsibility for money bills, is the forum where major proposals are introduced and is entitled to override vetoes or amendments proffered by the second chamber.

In presidential systems, by contrast, the president is directly elected and his continuation in office does not depend on the legislature's confidence. This independent survival means that there is no need for accountability to focus on a single chamber. **Strong bicameralism** can emerge in these conditions, especially when combined with federalism. The American Congress is the best illustration. With its constitutional position as representative of the states, the Senate plays a full part in the country's legislative and budget-making processes.

A bicameral structure raises the question of how the members of the second chamber should be chosen (Russell, 2001). Some divergence with the lower house is needed if the upper chamber is not simply to mirror the party balance in the first chamber. The three main methods are:

- Direct election (used by 27 of 66 upper houses);
- Indirect election through regional or local governments (21);
- Appointment, usually by the government (16).

Even when members of the upper chamber are elected, a contrast with the lower house is still normally achieved. The upper house is normally given a longer tenure: typically six years compared to three to five in the lower chamber (Table 15.1). The election cycle can also be varied and staggered. For instance, American Senators have a six-year term, with a third of the seats up for election every two years. By contrast, the entire membership of the House of Representatives must stand for re-election on an unusually short two-year cycle.

A federal structure also produces a natural divergence between chambers. In federations, Canada excepted, elections to the upper chamber are organized by state, with the number of senators per state varying far less than population figures would imply. The American Senate contains two members for each of 50 states, meaning that California (population 36.1 million) has the same representation as Nevada (2.4 million). In more recent federations, membership is also weighted towards the smaller states but to a lesser extent.

Weak bicameralism arises when the lower chamber dominates the upper house, providing the primary focus for government accountability in parliamentary systems. In **strong bicameralism**, found in a few federations, the two chambers are more balanced (Lijphart, 1999).

Table 15.1 Selection to the upper chamber in some liberal democracies

	Chamber	Members	Term (years)	Method of selection
Australia	Senate	76	6	Direct election by the single transferable vote in each state
Germany	Bundesrat	69		Appointed by state governments
Ireland	Senate	60	5	Appointed by the PM (11), elected from vocational panels (43) and from two universities (6)
Japan	House of Councillors	242	6	Direct election by a mixed-member majoritarian system
Netherlands	'First chamber' (Senate)	75	4	Elected by and from provincial councils
USA	Senate	100	6	Direct election by plurality voting in each state

Source: IPU (2006a).

Committees

Committees have grown in number and significance, becoming the workhorses of effective legislatures. Yet their operations lack the profile accorded to meetings of the whole chamber. So what purposes do committees serve? And what makes them effective?

Committees are small workgroups of members, created to cope with the volume of parliamentary business, particularly in the larger and busier lower chamber. These workgroups traditionally took the form of standing committees to consider bills and financial proposals together with conference or mediation committees to reconcile differences in bills passed by the two houses of a bicameral assembly. However, the more recent development has been the creation and strengthening of select committees which scrutinize government administration and investigate matters of concern, drawing on external witnesses (Box 15.1). The growing status of select committees reflects the increasing importance of the scrutiny function in contemporary legislatures. Members are usually allocated to a committee in proportion to overall party strength but partisanship is often held in check, yielding a more cooperative outlook.

The American Congress is unique in the impact of its committees. Although unmentioned in the constitution, committees rapidly became vital to Congress's work. 'Congress in session is Congress on public exhibition, whilst Congress in its committee rooms is Congress at work', wrote Woodrow Wilson (1885, p. 79). Bryce (1921, p. 68), a nineteenth-century British observer of American politics, described the House of Representatives as 'a huge panel from which committees are selected'. Despite a resurgence of partisanship since the mid 1990s, Bryce's comment still applies. Congressional committees are uniquely well-supported, employing over 3,000 policy specialists. Committees decide the fate and shape of most legislation. Further, each committee creates its own subcommittees: in the 108th Congress, there were 86 subcommittees in the Senate and 88 in the House.

So autonomous did committees become that they reduced the overall coherence of Congress. Their chairs became congressional lions, powerful and protective of their own territory. By the 1990s, however, party leaders were ready to fight back. They sought to rein in the committees. In the House, Republican Newt Gingrich, elected Speaker in 1995, asserted party control over appointments to committee chairs and used party task forces to drive legislation forward. But congressional committees are immensely resilient. They largely reasserted their control over bills once Gingrich's star began to wane. However, one legacy of the Republican revolution – a six-year term limit on committee chairs – may prove to be long-lasting.

Committees have less influence on legislation in party-dominated legislatures. In Britain's House of

Commons, government bills are examined by standing committees which largely replicate party combat on the floor of the chamber. These committees, unlike those of Congress, do not challenge executive dominance in framing legislation. They are unpopular, unspecialized and under-resourced. However, like many other legislatures, the Commons has expanded its system of select committees of scrutiny. Since 1979, select committees have shadowed all the main government departments, probing government policy and monitoring its implementation. Norton (1997, p. 166) suggests that Britain's select committees 'mark a remarkable advance in terms of parliamentary scrutiny'.

But it is Scandinavia that provides the best example of influential committees operating in the context of strong parties and parliamentary government. Scandinavia's main governing style, sometimes called 'committee parliamentarianism', is one in which influential standing committees negotiate the policies and bills on which the whole parliament later votes. In Sweden, for instance, committees modify about one in three government proposals and have the right, sometimes exercised, to put their own proposals (including bills) to the *Riksdag* as a whole (Arter, 2003).

The key to the influence of committees lies in the three factors of expertise, intimacy and support:

- *Expertise* emerges over time from committees with specialized responsibilities and a clear field of operation. Expertise is most likely to develop in permanent committees with continuity of operation and membership. Detailed knowledge is further encouraged if members are restricted to serving on a small number of committees.
- *Intimacy* emerges from small size (perhaps no more than a dozen members) and is again reinforced by stable membership. Particularly when meetings take place in private, a small group can encourage cooperation and consensus, overcoming hostility between the parties.
- *Support* refers to the use of qualified staff to advise committees. Expert researchers can help busy politicians produce credible recommendations, countering the wall of knowledge available to the executive.

Significantly, all three factors are present in the American Congress.

BOX 15.1

Parliamentary committees

Standing ('permanent') committee	Considers bills in detail.
Select committee	Scrutinizes the executive, often with one committee for each main government department. *Ad hoc* temporary committees investigate particular matters of public interest.
Conference or mediation committee	In bicameral legislatures, a joint committee usually reconciles differences in the versions of a bill passed by each chamber.

Functions

Representation, we have suggested, is the key function of legislatures. But deliberation and legislation follow close behind. Other functions, crucial to some but not all assemblies, are authorizing expenditure, making governments and scrutinizing the executive (Box 15.2). In discussing each of these roles, we will see how the significance of parliaments in liberal democracies extends well beyond the narrow task of simply converting bills into laws.

Representation

If the essence of assemblies is that they represent society to government, how can we judge whether, and how well, that function is fulfilled? What features would a fully representative assembly exhibit?

One interpretation of representation, plausible at first sight, is that an assembly should be a **microcosm** of society. The idea here is that a legislature should be society in miniature, literally 're-presenting' society in all its diversity. Such a parliament would balance men and women, rich and poor, black and white, even educated and uneducated, in the same mix as in society. How, after all, could a parliament composed entirely of middle-aged white men go about representing young black women (or *vice versa*)? To retain society's confidence, the argument continues, an assembly should reflect social diversity, standing in for society and not just acting on its behalf (Phillips, 1995).

A legislature would be a **microcosm** if it formed a miniature version of society, precisely reflecting its social diversity. An exact microcosm is impractical but there may still be value in ensuring that all major social groups achieve some parliamentary presence.

The notion that an assembly should mirror society was popular in some states in eighteenth-century America, where it was held to provide an approximation to the assemblies of ancient Athens. In 1778, for instance, the citizens of Essex County, Massachusetts, issued this comment on their state's proposed constitution:

> Representatives should have the same views and interests with the people at large. They should think, feel, and act like them and in fine, should be an exact miniature of their constituents. They should be (if we may use the expression) the whole body politic, with all its property, rights and privileges reduced to a smaller scale, every part being diminished in just proportion (Kramnick, 1987, p. 44).

But there is a considerable difficulty here. An exact transcript of society could only be achieved by quota or random selection, dispensing with election altogether (as with juries). If such a practice were implemented, we would have to accept that parliaments, like juries, would contain their fair share of the addicted, the corrupt and the ignorant. Even the well-intentioned citizens of Essex County baulked at including women (due to their 'lack of promiscuous intercourse with the world') and slaves (who 'have no will').

Whether elected or not, representatives would need to be replaced regularly lest they become tainted by the very experience of office, a point that led the American politician John Adams (1735–1826) to proclaim that 'where annual election ends, there slavery begins'. In reality, the assembly as microcosm is an impractical and probably undesirable goal.

Today, representation operates through party. Victorious candidates owe their election to their party and they vote in parliament largely according to its commands. In New Zealand, Labour members must agree to abide by the decisions of the party caucus. In India, an extreme case, members lose their seat if they vote against their party, the theory being that they are deceiving the voters if they

BOX 15.2

Functions of legislatures

Representation	Most members articulate the goals of the party under whose label they were elected
Deliberation	Debating matters of moment is the classic function of Britain's House of Commons
Legislation	Most bills come from the government but the legislature still approves them and may make amendments in committee
Authorizing expenditure	Parliament's role is normally reactive, approving or rejecting a budget prepared by the government
Making governments (pp. 336–40)	In most parliamentary systems, the government emerges from the assembly and must retain its confidence
Scrutiny	Oversight of government activity and policy is growing in importance and is a task well-suited to committees

switch parties after their election. Party is the vehicle of representation.

Elsewhere, party discipline is combined with at least some independence for members. In France and Germany, for instance, party obligations must be reconciled with the constitutional requirement that members of the legislature owe allegiance to the nation and not to any group within it. Even in these democracies, party voting remains the norm, though it is not enforced with the eagerness found in New Zealand and India.

Deliberation

An important function of many legislatures is to serve as a deliberative body, considering public matters of national importance. This function contrasts sharply with the microcosm and party views of representation and gives an additional perspective on what parliaments are for.

In the eighteenth and nineteenth centuries, before the rise of disciplined parties, deliberation was regarded as parliament's core activity. Politicians were expected to serve as trustees of the nation, applying exceptional knowledge and intelligence to the matters before them. Clearly, this philosophy of deliberation stands in complete opposition to the idea of the microcosm.

The British statesman Edmund Burke (1729–97) offered the classic account of deliberation. Elected member of parliament for Bristol in 1774, Burke admitted in his victory speech that he knew nothing about his constituency and had played little part in the campaign. But, he continued,

> Parliament is not a congress of ambassadors from different and hostile interests; which interests each must maintain, as an agent and advocate against other agents and advocates; but Parliament is a deliberative assembly of one nation, with one interest, that of the whole; where, not local purposes, not local prejudices, ought to guide, but the general good, resulting from the general reason of the whole. You choose a member indeed; but when you have chosen him, he is not a member for Bristol, but he is a member of Parliament (Burke, 1774).

Deliberation of course continues today even if its status is no longer as exalted as in Burke's time. However, the deliberative style varies across countries in a manner captured in a contrast between **debating** and **committee-based legislatures**.

> In a **debating legislature**, such as the British House of Commons, floor debate is the central activity; it is here that major issues are addressed and parties gain or lose ground. In a **committee-based legislature**, such as the American Congress, most work takes place in committees. There, members transform bills into laws, conduct hearings and scrutinize the executive.

In a debating legislature such as Britain's, deliberation takes the form of debate in the chamber. Key issues eventually make their way to the floor of the House of Commons where they are discussed with passion and often with flair. Floor debate is the arena for national political discussion, forming part of a continuous election campaign. One of the achievements of the Commons is precisely its ability to combine effective deliberation, at least on vital issues, with strong partisanship.

Appropriately, it was the English political philosopher John Stuart Mill (1806–73) who made the case for a debating assembly:

> I know not how a representative assembly can more usefully employ itself than in talk, when the subject of talk is the great public interests of the country, and every sentence of it represents the opinion either of some important body of persons in the nation, or of an individual in whom such bodies have reposed their confidence (Mill, 1861, p. 353).

By contrast, in committee-based assemblies such as the American Congress and the Scandinavian parliaments, deliberation is less theatrical, taking the form of policy discussion in committees. The task is to improve the government's bills through the process of transforming them into laws while also providing measured scrutiny of the executive. This deliberative style makes its own contribution to governance, less dramatic than a set-piece debate but no less important.

Legislation

Most constitutions explicitly assert the legislative function of parliaments. The end of absolute executive power is affirmed by giving to parliament, and to it alone, the right to make laws. Arbitrary government is replaced by a formal procedure for law-

TIMELINE

THE EUROPEAN PARLIAMENT

Although this timeline demonstrates the widening competence of the European Parliament (EP), the assembly's legislative authority remains limited. However, as the EU itself has deepened, so the parliament has become more willing to assert its expanding rights to at least be consulted on legislation, the budget and appointments.

1952	Assembly of the European Coal and Steel Community established as an instrument of scrutiny, with the right to dismiss the Commission in some circumstances. Assembly members are drawn from national legislatures.
1962	The Assembly is renamed the European Parliament.
1970	The Treaty Amending Certain Budgetary Provisions of the Treaties gives the EP more influence over the budget.
1975	The Treaty Amending Certain Financial Provisions of the Treaties gives the EP the right to propose modifications in areas where expenditure is not mandated by previous agreements.
1979	First direct elections. Average turnout 62 per cent.
1980	Isoglucose judgment by the European Court requires the EP to be consulted on proposed laws.
1986	The Single European Act initiates cooperation and assent procedures which give the EP more influence over legislation.
1992	The Maastricht Treaty requires members of the Commission to be approved by the EP. A new co-decision procedure gives the EP some veto authority over legislation.
1997	The Treaty of Amsterdam extends the co-decision procedure and formalizes the EP's right to veto the nominee for Commission president.
1999	All 20 commissioners (the Santer Commission) resign rather than face dismissal by the EP for mismanagement. Fifth direct elections. Average turnout 50 per cent.
2004	Sixth direct elections. Average turnout 46 per cent (including 27 per cent in the ten countries joining the Union in 2004).

Further reading: Corbett, Jacobs and Shackleton (2005), Judge and Earnshaw (2003), Nugent (2006).

making. The painstaking process for passing bills into law signals the importance attached to government by rules rather than individuals. Authoritarian rulers govern by decree but in a democracy bills are scrutinized and authorized by a national congress.

But we must be careful here. Legislation is rarely the function in which 'legislatures' exert most influence. Indeed, after 50 years the European Parliament – admittedly a special case – does not even control the formal law-making process in the European Union (*see* Timeline). In most liberal democracies, effective control over legislation rests with the government. Bills pass through the assembly without being designed or even transformed there.

In party-dominated Australia, for instance, the government treats the legislative function with virtual contempt. On a single night in 1991 it sought to put 26 bills through the Senate in three hours flat. In the era before New Zealand adopted proportional representation, a prime minister boasted that if an idea came to him while shaving, he could have it on the statute book by the evening, truly a case of slot-machine law.

In Britain, similarly, the governing party dominates law-making. Ninety-seven per cent of bills proposed by government between 1945 and 1987 became law. As Rose (1989, p. 173) said of Britain, 'Laws are described as Acts of Parliament but it would be more accurate if they were stamped "Made in Whitehall"'. In the party-dominated parliaments of Britain and some of its ex-colonies, the legislative function is reduced to quality control: patching up errors in bills prepared in haste by ministers and civil servants. In legislation, at least, these assemblies are reactive rather than active.

By contrast, many parliaments in continental Europe do play a more positive role. Coalition governments, influential committees and an elite commitment to compromise combine to deliver laws acceptable to all sides. In a few European countries, indeed, this more flexible approach is reflected not just in substantive discussion of bills but also in their initiation. In Switzerland, for instance, a bill may originate not just from the executive but also from members of either house of the federal assembly or from any canton.

But it is in presidential systems, including the United States, that the assembly achieves most autonomy in making laws. The separation of powers and personnel inherent in a presidential regime limits executive influence over the legislature. This institutional separation is often reinforced by divided government. In the United States, the party that does not occupy the White House may still possess a majority in either or both houses of Congress. In Latin America, where parties are weaker and proportional representation is the norm for congressional elections, the president's party may be no more than a minor player in the legislature.

Yet even in presidential systems the initiative in framing bills usually lies with the executive. Certainly, in the American Congress only members of the House of Representatives can formally introduce bills. But the executive can easily find a friendly representative to initiate a bill on its behalf. The political reality is that bills are developed by the administration and then transformed in Congress if indeed they do not expire in its maze of committees. 'You supply the bills and we work them over', one member of Congress said to an administration official. The executive proposes, as in most political systems, but Congress disposes, usually by saying no.

Figure 15.2 Typical steps in making a law

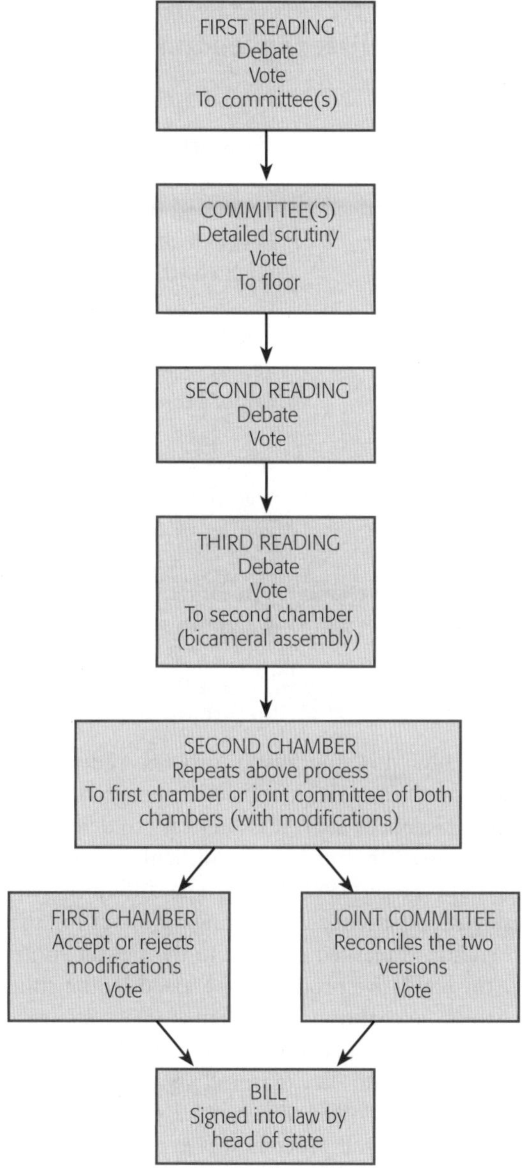

Source: Adapted from Mahler (2003), table 4.9.

BOX 15.3

Resolving differences in the versions of a bill passed by each chamber

	Comment	Example
Indefinite shuttle	Amended versions continue to shuttle between chambers until agreement is reached (if ever)	Italy is the main example of this rare procedure
Lower house is decisive	The lower house decides whether to accept or reject amendments from the upper house	Czech Republic, Spain, United Kingdom
Conference or mediation committee	A joint committee of both chambers negotiates a compromise version which is then voted on by each house	Many countries, including France, Germany, Switzerland and the USA
Vote of a joint session of both chambers	The larger lower chamber exerts more weight in a joint vote	Australia, Brazil, India, Norway

Source: Adapted from Tsebelis and Money (1997), Table 2.2a.

Inevitably, this pluralistic process reduces the coherence of America's legislative programme. As President Kennedy said, 'It is very easy to defeat a bill in Congress. It is much more difficult to pass one' (Eigen and Siegel, 1993, p. 82). The difficulty which presidents experience in securing approval for their bills stands in marked contrast to the tighter control over the legislative programme exerted by the ruling party or even coalitions in parliamentary systems.

Although the process by which a legislature transforms a bill into law naturally varies from one democracy to another, Figure 15.2 offers a general outline. The overall procedure is explicitly deliberative, involving several readings (debates) as the bill moves from the floor to committee and back again (Döring and Hallerberg, 2004).

Bicameral legislatures face an additional hurdle in realizing the legislative function. What happens if the second chamber amends a bill passed by the lower house? There must be some means of resolving such discrepancies. In almost all countries, the initial step is for the amended bill to return to the lower chamber for further discussion. But if the bill continues to shuttle between houses in this way until an agreed version emerges, as in Italy's strongly bicameral legislature, the danger is that it will be delayed or never become law at all. In Italy, for instance, a bill on rape introduced in 1977 did not become law until 1995.

To resolve this problem, most legislatures develop a procedure for short-circuiting the shuttle (Box 15.3). The most common arrangement is to employ a special conference committee, containing an equal number of members from each chamber, to produce an agreed bill. This compromise version must then be approved or rejected by the main chambers without further modification. The American, French and German legislatures are among those employing this device. Conference committees are sometimes described as third chambers for it is here that the final deals are struck and the decisive compromises made. They can be a vital arena in which to resolve political issues and deserve closer study than they receive.

Authorizing expenditure

This is one of the oldest functions of parliament and of the lower house in particular. The origin of European assemblies, after all, lay in the monarch's requirement for money. Since, as Spencer Walpole (1881, p. 4) wrote, 'the necessities of kings are the opportunities of peoples', assemblies were able to establish the right to raise grievances before granting supply (revenue). In Britain, this tradition continued until 1982 in the form of 'supply days' during which the opposition could raise any issues it wished.

The power to authorize spending may be one of parliament's oldest functions but in many democracies it has become nominal. Even more than the law-making function, it forms part of the myth rather than the reality of parliamentary authority. Lack of real financial control is a major weakness of the modern assembly. Typically, the executive prepares the budget which is then reported to parliament but rarely modified there.

For the legislature to possess the power of the purse, suggests Wehner (2006), a large number of conditions must be fulfilled. These include an effective committee system, sufficient time to consider the budget (say, three months) and access to underpinning information on revenue and spending. In addition, the assembly must be able to amend the budget (as opposed to, say, just being allowed to reallocate the total sum or to make cuts only). Finally, the executive must be limited in its ability to alter budget allocations during implementation and the **reversionary budget** must differ from the government's own proposals.

A **reversionary budget** is the default (typically, last year's) budget which takes effect should the legislature fail to approve a new one in time.

Inevitably, few countries meet all these conditions. Among liberal democracies, the United States and Scandinavian countries come closest. At the other extreme, states in which the legislatures possess least control include Australia, France, South Africa and the United Kingdom. In general, parliamentary approval is after the fact, serving to confirm budget compromises worked out between government departments. In many democracies, once the budget reaches the assembly, it is a done deal. If the assembly began to unpick any part of the budget, the whole package would fall apart.

Australia is an extreme case of government control over the budget. Emy and Hughes (1991, p. 361) described the political realities:

> There is no suggestion of the House of Representatives ever 'refusing supply' since control over the whole process of financial appropriations is firmly in the hands of the executive. Only they may propose to spend money . . . Moreover, it seems members of the House themselves lack both the knowledge of, and an interest in, the financial procedures which are, ultimately, crucial to the concept of parliamentary control.

The United States is once more the great exception to the thesis of executive control of the purse. Congress remains central to the confused tangle that is American budget-making. The sums involved here are huge: the budget proposed for fiscal year 2006 amounted to $2.57 trillion – about ten times Sweden's gross domestic product. Under America's constitution, all money spent by executive departments must be allocated under specific spending headings approved by members of Congress. No appropriations by Congress means no government programme. As Flammang *et al.* (1990, p. 422) write, 'without the agreement of members of Congress, no money can be doled out for foreign aid, salaries for army generals or paper clips for bureaucrats'.

The result is that the annual American budget has become an elaborate game of chicken. The executive and the legislature each hopes the other side will accede to its own proposals before the money runs out. Each year between 1978 and 1996, Congress failed to pass a complete budget by its own deadline, forcing agencies to operate under a reversionary budget. This rather alarming method of allocating $2.57 trillion supports the proposition that financing the modern state is, like the law-making function, too important to be left to the assembly's many hands.

Scrutiny

The final function of legislatures is scrutiny (oversight) of the executive. Mill emphasized this role as early as 1861:

> The proper office of a representative assembly is to watch and control the government: to throw the light of publicity on its acts, to compel a full exposition and justification of all of them which any one considers questionable; [and] to censure them if found condemnable (1861, p. 258).

DEBATE

ARE LEGISLATURES IN DECLINE?

> 'If a general survey is made of the position and working of legislatures in the present [twentieth] century, it is apparent that, with a few important and striking exceptions, legislatures have declined in certain important respects and particularly in powers in relation to the existing government' (Wheare, 1963b, p. 148).

Wheare's argument is familiar: 'every description of the form of government of the modern state seems to end up with a discouraging conclusion about the actual role of parliament' (Petersson, 1989, p. 96). Since legislatures express popular sovereignty, the implication is that democracy itself is in retreat. But is it the case that legislatures are in decline?

YES

As early as 1921, the British historian Lord Bryce (p. 370) referred to the growth of disciplined parties and to the increased complexity of policy-making, both of which have strengthened the executive against the assembly. In essence, the parliamentary agenda has been captured by the governing party or coalition.

In particular, assemblies have lost control of the legislative process. Bills pass through the assembly on their way to the statute book but their origins lie elsewhere: in the executive, the bureaucracy and interest groups.

That crucial statement of political priorities, the budget, is also in the hands of the executive. And with good reason: who would really want the size and composition of the government's spending to be determined by a free vote of members of parliament?

Since Bryce's day, growing interdependence between countries has posed insuperable problems for assemblies. Parliaments are creatures of the nation; they are poorly adapted to a global era. How can national parliaments grapple with a world of international trade, intergovernmental deals, complex treaties and war?

To be sure, a European Parliament now exists but it remains the runt in the litter of EU institutions, lacking conventional legislative powers.

Today, the executive takes the decisions and the judiciary reviews them when necessary. Parliaments have become political museum-pieces.

NO

To speak of the decline of legislatures in a global era is too simple, for three reasons:

- Even if parliaments no longer initiate many bills, they continue to perform such functions as casework, representation, scrutiny and, in parliamentary systems, recruitment to government office.
- The decline thesis is a generalization from parliamentary regimes to all liberal democracies. But the argument is less relevant to presidential systems, where congress benefits from the separation of powers.
- Assemblies are growing in importance as arenas of debate, as raisers of grievances and especially as agencies of oversight.

Moreover, where the American Congress led the way in equipping assembly members with the resources to do their jobs professionally, other legislatures are following suit. Throughout the democratic world, backbench members have become more assertive and independent: party leaders can no longer expect educated politicians to be totally deferential.

Specialized committees, and members with a driving interest in policy, are increasingly successful in contributing to political debate. Televising proceedings has strengthened the profile of assemblies among voters.

The worldwide transition to democracy has raised the standing of parliaments in post-authoritarian regimes, giving many legislatures fresh impetus.

ASSESSMENT

The role of parliaments is changing rather than declining. Legislatures do not initiate many laws but what they can do, and what many are now better equipped than ever to do, is to oversee the executive. Parliaments possess a unique authority to force politicians and civil servants to account for their actions before a body which still represents the nation.

Further reading

Carey (2006), Loewenberg, Squire and Kiewiet (2002), Norton (1998), Sjolin (1993).

However, in many countries such activity has only been growing in significance and value in recent decades.

To emphasize the scrutiny function is to accept that the executive, not the legislature, must govern. But the assembly can restate its key role as representative of the people by acting as a watchdog over the administration. Effective monitoring can compensate for the downgrading of the assembly's legislative and expenditure functions, providing a new direction to parliament's work.

A modern assembly possesses three main instruments with which to monitor the executive: first, questions and interpellations; second, emergency debates and confidence votes; and, third, committee investigations. As Box 15.4 indicates, the availability of these devices varies between parliamentary and presidential systems. The box may appear to suggest more opportunities for scrutiny in parliamentary systems but such a conclusion would be misleading. In a parliamentary system, the members of the ruling party or parties will normally see their task as that of sustaining the government, thus limiting their room for manoeuvre. By contrast, legislators in a presidential system can be freer with criticism precisely because they know the survival of the executive is not at stake.

Questions refer to direct queries of ministers. In many parliamentary systems, oral and written questions are mainstays of oversight. In Britain, for example, members of the House of Commons ask a total of over 70,000 questions a year, keeping many civil servants busy as they prepare answers for their political masters. Prime Minister's Question Time, though now reduced from twice to once a week, remains a theatrical joust between the PM and the leader of the opposition. In other parliaments, questions have lower status; French ministers often fail to answer them at all (Hayward, 2004).

But in some assemblies in continental Europe, including Finland, France and Germany, the **interpellation** provides an alternative form of interrogation. An interpellation is a substantial form of question demanding a prompt response which is followed by a short debate and a vote on whether the government's response is deemed acceptable. This technique, often linked to a vote of no confidence or censure motion, brought down several governments in the French Third and Fourth Republics.

An **interpellation** is an enquiry of the government, interrupting normal business, which is followed by a debate and usually a vote on the assembly's satisfaction with the answers given.

BOX 15.4

Techniques for scrutinizing the executive

	Parliamentary government	Presidential government
Questions and interpellations on the floor	✔	✘
Emergency debates and votes of confidence	✔	✘
Committee investigations	✔	✔

Emergency debates are a further, and higher-profile, way in which parliament can call the government to account. Normally a minimum number of members, and the Presiding Officer (Speaker), must approve a proposal for an emergency debate. Although the event usually ends with a government win, the significance lies in the debate itself and the fact of its calling. An emergency debate creates publicity and demands a careful response from the government's spokesperson.

Votes of confidence or censure motions are the ultimate test which a legislature can pose to the executive in a parliamentary system. Such motions are not so much a form of detailed scrutiny as a decision on whether the government can continue at all. Again, special rules may apply: in France and Sweden, a majority of all members (not just those voting) is required to demonstrate the legislature's loss of confidence. In other cases, a confidence motion is not specifically designated but is simply any vote on which the government would feel obliged to resign if defeated. In some countries, again including Sweden, votes of confidence can be directed against individual ministers as well as the government as a whole.

The final and most detailed way in which legislatures can exercise oversight is through **committee investigations**. Because the floor of the house is an inappropriate venue for detailed scrutiny, committees are the key to oversight. The American Congress is the classic case here. Exceptionally, the constitution gives Congress, rather than the executive, responsibility for such important matters as commerce, the currency, defence and taxation. Of course, Congress does not carry out these functions itself; it delegates the tasks to the bureaucracy. But because of its constitutional position, and the budgetary authority flowing from it, Congress possesses inherent powers of oversight. A British civil servant can afford to treat a parliamentary question as a minor distraction but the head of a government agency in the United States knows that next year's budget may depend on maintaining good relations with the relevant members of Congress.

The sheer extent of committee engagement in the activity of American government is remarkable, providing more detailed scrutiny than is possible through the floor-based questions, interpellations, emergency debates and confidence votes found in parliamentary systems. With more than 3,000 committee staffers offering support, Congress achieves a unique level of involvement with government. Although much committee work is as a partner rather than an overseer of the executive, a few investigative committees have achieved national status: for instance, the House Committee on Un-American Activities in the 1940s and 1950s and the Senate Watergate Committee in the 1970s.

Even in the USA, committee oversight is limited. It can only cast light on a few corners of a vast bureaucracy; Congress sometimes seeks to micro-manage departments rather than setting broad targets; and reports can quickly be forgotten as the political spotlight changes its focus. In the United States, and even more elsewhere, the government's battalions outnumber the forces available to the legislature.

Recruitment

Legislative recruitment is the process by which the huge pool of potential members of parliament is reduced to the small number who achieve election. How does this process operate? Within liberal democracies, the significance of the process does of course depend on the form of government. In parliamentary systems, government ministers are usually selected from the assembly. In such cases, the legislature becomes the key channel of recruitment to political office and its members constitute the shortlist from which national leaders are drawn. A local party selecting a parliamentary candidate for its own district is therefore also engaged in the more important task of choosing a potential national leader.

In presidential systems, the separation of executive and legislature means that people cannot belong to both at the same time. Although members of the legislature can resign to join the government, and even stand for president, the assembly is generally less important as a recruiting agent to high office. In the USA, for instance, recent presidents such as Bill Clinton (Arkansas) and George W. Bush (Texas) have been drawn from state governorships rather than Congress. In these circumstances, legislative and executive recruitment are distinct processes.

Box 15.5 outlines a four-stage model of legislative recruitment comprising legal, social, party and electoral filters.

At the first stage, legal considerations reduce the entire population to those who are technically **eligible** to join the legislature. Many countries apply more stringent age limits for legislators than for voters. In the United States, for instance, the minimum age is 25 for the lower house and 30 for the Senate; in Italy, the minima are 25 and 40 respectively. Some countries also impose citizenship and residence requirements. In the USA, again, the constitution stipulates that members of Congress must be American citizens residing in the state they represent. By excluding what is often a significant number of illegal immigrants and other non-citizen residents from the assembly, such legal requirements render the legislature inherently less representative.

At the second stage, a powerful social filter reduces those who are eligible to stand to those who **aspire** to do so. Here, social influences on political interest and ambition, such as being brought up in a political family or even being the off spring of a legislator, come into play. It is this social filter which does the most work in reducing the size of the field and in biasing it to advantaged social groups. As Borchert and Copeland (2003, p. 404) comment on the United States, 'The most significant factor in the link between voters and office-holders is the choice of individuals to make themselves available for office'.

At the third stage, a party filter reduces the aspirants to the small subset of **candidates** – those who succeed in convincing the gatekeepers that they should be nominated for an electoral district or granted a place on a party list. Party rules on such issues as gender quotas are important here as are such personal skills as the ability to present well to the gatekeepers, whether officials, members or supporters.

The fourth electoral filter reduces those who stand as candidates to those who win the contest and become **members** of the national parliament. The candidate's goal here is to be nominated for a safe seat or to obtain a high position on the party's list. If this objective is achieved, election is virtually automatic. But previous and often lengthy political experience – in local government, say, or in the party itself – is likely to be essential to the award of such a plum posting. 'The door is wide but the corridor is long', says Hagevi (2003, p. 354).

This four-stage model, taking us from the eligibles to the elected, reveals that political recruitment is a far broader process than election alone. Indeed, the voters join the game only at the end, when most winnowing out has already taken place. By the time the voters come to pass judgement, the die of recruitment has already been cast.

BOX 15.5

Stages of recruitment to the legislature

Segment	Main influence	Example
Population		
↓	Legal rules	Age and residence requirements
Eligibles		
↓	Socialization	Growing up in a political family
Aspirants		
↓	Party gatekeepers	Gender quotas
Candidates		
↓	Elections	
Members of the legislature		

Source: Adapted from Norris (1996), Figure 7.1.

Membership

Who then are the members who populate the legislature? And how do they go about their work? The central theme here is the rise of the professional politician: the degree-educated legislator with limited experience outside politics who expects politics to provide a full-time and fulfilling career. Local landowners representing 'their' territory, ageing trade unionists rewarded with a seat in the assembly for their final years, business executives seeking some short-term political experience – all have lost ground to career politicians who know no other job.

Particularly in Europe, the rise of the professional has led to speculation about the growth of a **political class** with a background and interests removed from the people it represents. Like any other occupational group, legislators from all parties share a concern with improving their conditions such as hours of work, research support, pay and pension. But parliamentarians are in a unique position to act on their common interests by simply voting themselves an enhancement.

In addition, incumbent members from all parties usually seek their own re-election. They can and do supply themselves with campaign resources unavailable to their challengers (e.g. free mail), thus creating a powerful cartel against newcomers. Viewing politics purely as a clash *between* parties often leads to inadequate emphasis on this distinction *within* parties between incumbents and challengers. Like any other established class, politicians in post – of whatever party – are reluctant to upset the apple cart that has served them so well.

COUNTRY PROFILE

UNITED KINGDOM

Form of Government ■ a parliamentary liberal democracy, with an heriditary monarch playing a largely ceremonial role.

Legislature ■ the House of Commons (646 members) is the dominant chamber. The House of Lords, the composition of which has been under review since 1997, acts in a revising and restraining capacity.

Executive ■ the cabinet is the top decision-ratifying body; the prime minister selects and dismisses its members. The balance between prime minister and cabinet depends on the PM's political strength. Meetings of full cabinet are largely formal; its effective work is conducted in committee.

Judiciary ■ based on the common law tradition. In 2003, the government published proposals to introduce a supreme court albeit without the authority traditionally associated with such a body.

Electoral systems ■ The House of Commons is still elected by the single-member plurality method. A range of systems are used for elections to other bodies such as the Scottish Parliament, the Welsh Assembly and the European Parliament. The Labour government elected in 1997 expressed sympathy for electoral reform in Commons elections but soon lost interest once in power.

Population (annual growth rate):	60.6m (+0.3%)
World Bank income group:	high income
Political Rights score:	1
Civil Liberties score:	1
Human development index (rank/out of):	12/177
Freedom of the press index (rank/out of):	30/194
Ease of doing business index (rank/out of):	6/175

Note: For meaning and sources of scales and indexes, see p. xvi. In all cases a score and rank of 1 is 'best'.

The **UNITED KINGDOM** is a liberal democracy whose political system has nonetheless been in transition. Traditional models portrayed Britain as a centralized, unitary state; as a two-party system; as an exemplar of parliamentary sovereignty in which ministers were held to account by the assembly; and as a political system whose uncodified constitution offered little formal protection of individual rights. Yet the accuracy of all these images came under review, particularly after the election in 1997 of a reforming Labour administration.

The centralized and even the unitary character of the United Kingdom was put in question by the creation in 1999 of new assemblies for Scotland and Wales. The reform was asymmetric, with the Scottish *parliament* receiving more devolved powers than the Welsh *assembly*. Labour has proved to be the leading player in both countries, governing Scotland in coalition with the Liberal Democrats. Devolution to Northern Ireland was suspended in 2002 but reinstated five years later, reflecting the ending of armed conflict between Catholic and Protestant groups and the UK government..

The two-party system has been challenged by the rise of the centre-left Liberal Democrats. In the 2005 election, the Liberal Democrats won six million votes and 62 seats; the share of the vote accruing to the two major parties fell to 68 per cent.

Parliamentary sovereignty has been dented by British membership of the European Union and a more assertive judiciary (which may yet be called on to adjudicate conflicts between Westminster and the devolved regions). Individual rights now receive clearer protection, exerted through the judiciary, from the incorporation into British law of the European Convention on Human Rights. The rebranding of the highest judicial body as a Supreme Court may enhance the judiciary's visibility.

Ministerial accountability has been complicated by the delegation of government tasks to semi-independent agencies. In a particularly significant reform, the 1997 Labour government immediately took steps to delegate monetary policy to the Monetary Policy Committee of the Bank of England.

The cumulative impact of these developments remains to be established. What is clear is that many of the old assumptions about British politics have ceased to apply; in a more complicated and fragmented polity, replacement clichés may be harder to find.

Further reading: Dunleavy *et al.* (2006), Kavanagh and Butler (2005).

SPOTLIGHT

The British parliament

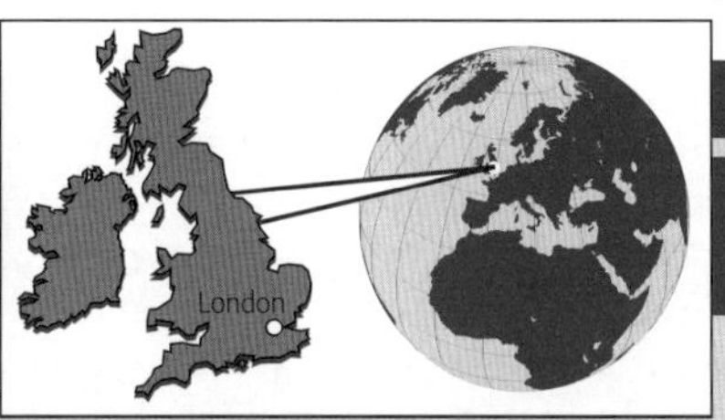

The new era of transition in British politics has impinged on its assembly. Traditionally, Britain's parliament (one of the world's oldest) mixed omnipotence and impotence in a seemingly impossible combination. Omnipotence, because parliamentary sovereignty, allied to an uncodified constitution, meant there could be no higher authority in the land. Impotence, because the governing party exercised tight control over its own backbenchers, turning parliament into an instrument rather than a wielder of power. How then has the mother of parliaments adapted to this time of change?

In the twenty-first century, parliament's position has become less certain. The tired rituals of adversary politics in the Commons have become less convincing, not least for the 260 new MPs elected in 1997 and the 99 who followed in 2001. The notion that parliament still possesses some abstract quality called 'sovereignty' still carries weight but, like many assemblies, Britain's legislature runs the risk of being left behind by international integration, by competition from the media as an arena of debate and by the indifference of prime ministers who choose to spend less time in the House.

But not all developments are negative. MPs themselves have become more professional and committed; the era of the amateur is over. Members devote more time to an increasing volume of constituency casework and receive more back-office support. The number of late sittings has been cut. Select committees have established themselves in the debate over policy and contribute to scrutinizing the executive. The prime minister now appears twice a year before a select committee for a more detailed discussion than is possible in Question Time in the chamber. Overall, Cowley (2006, p. 49) judges that 'the Commons has become more efficient in what it does, but it has not necessarily become much stronger or more effective as a result'.

As an upper chamber in what remains a unitary state, the House of Lords occupies an uncertain position. Historically, its base consisted of hereditary peers but the introduction of life peerages in 1958 led to some recovery in the chamber's standing. The abolition of all but 92 hereditary peers in 1999 served to increase the chamber's confidence. Since no single party possesses a majority in the Lords, it can offer some significant tests to the government. When finally agreed, reform is likely to involve a substantial measure of election to the chamber, a development which may well make the Lords even more assertive in challenging the executive.

Yet even as Britain's parliament updates its skills, it will surely continue to do what it has always done best: acting as an arena for debating issues of central significance to the nation, its government and its leaders. Even in an era of reform, the House of Commons has retained its position as a classic debating assembly, reinforced by the less partisan style in the Lords.

The Vote Bundle

The daily papers of the House of Commons are known as the Vote Bundle. Its contents are:

- Summary agenda
- Order of business
- Standing committee notices
- Future business
- Order of business in Westminster Hall
- 'The vote' (*record of proceedings*)
- Notices of questions
- Private business
- Notices of motions
- Notices of amendments
- Other documents

Source: adapted from House of Commons Information Office (2003).

Further reading: Cowley (2006), Norton (2005), Rush (2005).

In Weber's renowned distinction (1918), **professional politicians** live *off*, and not merely *for*, politics. They are full-timers requiring an appropriate income, support, career development and pension. Professional politicians are sometimes said to form a **political class**, implying the existence of a group that possesses, and can potentially act on, its shared interests.

Politics as profession implies a distinct view not just of representation but also of politics. It rejects the notion that governance is a task which ordinary citizens can and should undertake. It implies dissatisfaction with the idea that an assembly should draw together a representative sample of citizens 'different in nature, different in interests, different in looks, different in language' (Bagehot, 1867, p. 155). Rather, politics as profession implies an emphasis on training, knowledge, experience and skill. Politics is a job, just like law or medicine.

Within the category of professional politician, the main contrast is between the American political entrepreneur and the more party-based careerist found in the parliaments of other liberal democracies. In the United States, candidates must compete against opponents from their own party in a primary; in office, they must build a personal profile and record of achievement which protects them from challenge and offers insurance should their party fall on hard times. And they must raise money for their campaign. In most other liberal democracies, strong parties at both parliamentary and electoral level leave less room for independent action, resulting in loyal backbenchers rather than political entrepreneurs.

Of course, career politicians can only flourish in parliament when re-election prospects are good. Generally, re-election is the norm in liberal democracies. Typically, most sitting legislators return for a new term following a general election (Figure 15.3; Best and Cotta, 2000). The return rate is high enough to sustain professional members but not so high as to create the three As which Jackson (1994) associates with a surfeit of incumbency: arrogance, apathy and atrophy. Generally, turnover is greater in countries employing proportional representation. Under party list PR, of course, party leaders can manipulate the list to ensure some fresh blood.

In countries employing plurality elections, the extent of turnover is less predictable and return rates can become indefensibly high. For instance, in the United States congressional elections of 2004, only seven of 404 incumbent candidates in the House, and one of 26 Senators, were defeated. This **incumbency effect** arises because existing members can exploit such resources as public recognition, government subsidies, financial backing, their own experience and even (in the House) the ability to manipulate the boundaries of their electoral districts. They can also cultivate their constituency so that it becomes their own political territory. For these reasons, fresh candidates are most likely to win when an existing representative stands down, creating an **open seat**.

The **incumbency effect** refers to the electoral bonus accruing to sitting members in securing re-election. In the United States, where the effect is large, an **open seat** is defined as one in which the existing representative has stood down, creating a more even contest.

Term limits provide one solution, but a blunt one, to this incumbency effect. When members are automatically removed after each election, no parliamentary career is possible. In Mexico, for example, members of the Chamber of Deputies are restricted to a single three-year tenure. Term limits are also now employed widely in states of the USA although the Supreme Court declared in *U.S. Term Limits, Inc.* v. *Thornton* (1995) that states cannot impose term limits on their federal representatives.

Term limits restrict elected politicians to a maximum number of periods in office, or ban re-election without a break. They enforce turnover at the price of reducing professionalism (Carey, 1998).

The danger of term limits is that they create more problems than they solve. The outcome is lame duck legislators lacking electoral accountability and concerned mainly to secure their next job. Carey *et al.* (2006) find that term-limited legislators in American states are, in fact, less responsive to their constituents. Ideally, turnover of legislators should be enforced by levelling the playing field, not by banning all experienced players.

Professional politicians are the leading category in most contemporary legislatures but they do not

Figure 15.3 Incumbent return rates to the national legislature, 1979–94

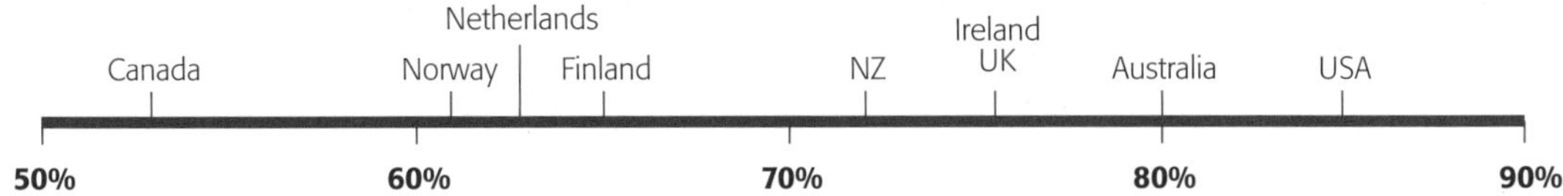

Note: based on at least four elections to the lower or only chamber of the national parliament. Except where indicated, the figure for bicameral assemblies refers to the lower house.

Source: adapted from Matland and Studlar (2004).

have it entirely their own way. One group, in particular, stands out in contrast to the now traditional political professional. **Celebrities-turned-politicians** leverage fame acquired in other fields to leapfrog into the legislature or (as with Governor Arnold Schwarzenegger of California) direct to executive office (Box 15.6).

It is tempting to regard celebrities-turned-politicians as an emerging group of post-professional politicians who exploit both their media-generated fame and their status as political outsiders to achieve quick political success. Certainly, their presence in the assembly seems to convey a message that voters want to judge politicians by what they stand for, not just by their technical competence. In an era when electors have become less partisan and are less exposed to news coverage, politicians as a class may find themselves driven to compete in the celebrity space, rather than for the diminishing media coverage set aside for politics. If so, those politicians who have already acquired public recognition in other fields will have a head start.

But we should avoid easy generalization here. The celebrity-turned-politician is far from new. For example, American actress and singer Helen Gahagan Douglas was elected to the House of Representatives as early as 1944. India's Lok Sabha may contain more Bollywood stars than ever before but it is not self-evident that the liberal democratic world (including India itself) is experiencing a mass migration from film studio to parliament. Rather, the appeal of celebrities-turned-politicians seems to lie partly in their outsider status and their very rarity,

Celebrities-turned-politicians exploit the fame they have acquired in non-political arenas to ease their entry into political office, including the legislature. Such characters are distinct from **politicians-as-celebrities** whose style is to present themselves to the electors as if they are famous stars of stage and screen.

BOX 15.6

Actresses, athletes and astronauts: celebrities in national legislatures

	Year of birth	Country	Source of celebrity
Helen Gahagan Douglas	1900	USA	Actress
John Glenn	1921	USA	Astronaut
Melina Mercouri	1925	Greece	Actress
Sonny Bono	1935	USA	Singer
Glenda Jackson	1936	UK	Actress
Bill Bradley	1943	USA	Basketball player
Imran Khan	1952	Pakistan	Cricketer
Sebastian Coe	1956	UK	Athlete
Govinda Arun Ahuja	1963	India	Actor
Tony Halme	1963	Finland	Pugilist
Tanja Saarela	1970	Finland	Beauty queen

Further reading: Canon (1990), Corner and Pels (2003), Jones (2005), West and Orman (2003).

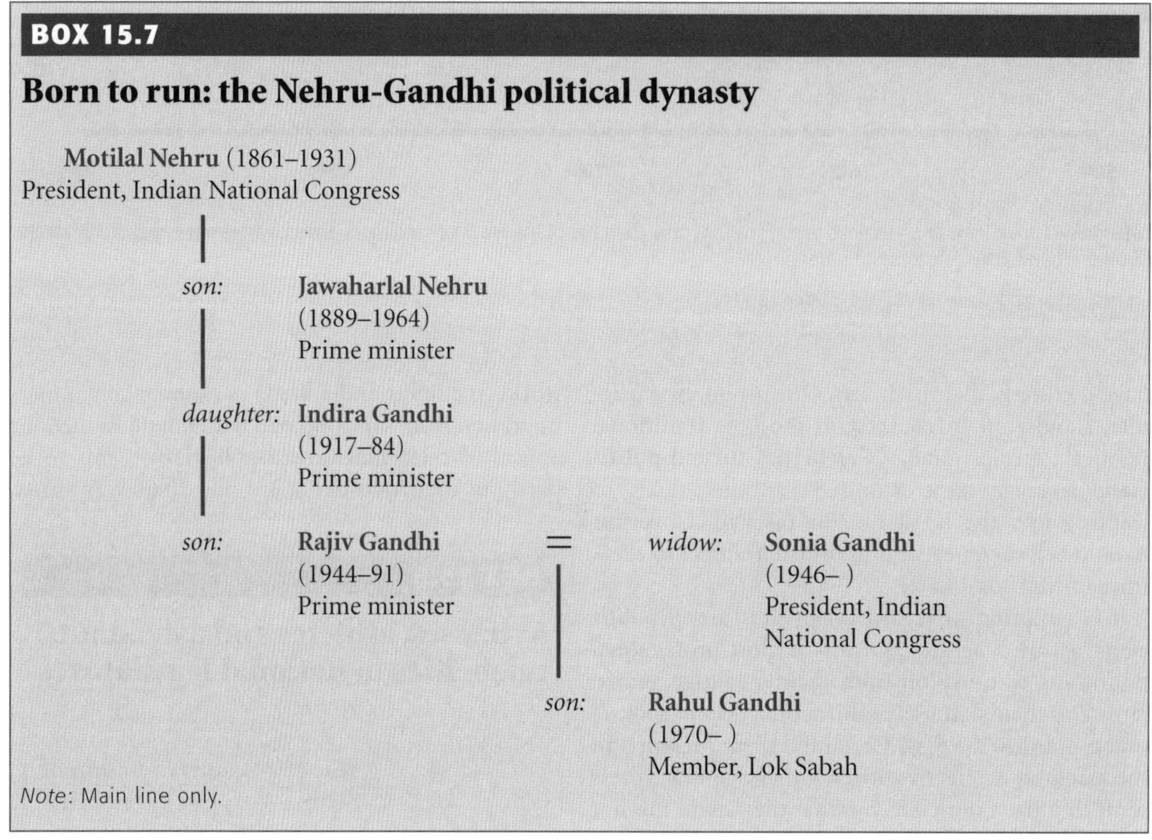

suggesting a natural limit to their ability to colonize the legislature. In all likelihood, Hollywoodization is a continuing but not a transformative process. The era of the professional legislator is far from over.

One final group of representatives is worthy of note: offspring who follow a parent into the legislature. In Asia, political families often represent lineages with an established national reputation, or at least tight control over a particular electoral district. The Gandhis are far from the only example in India (Box 15.7). More than a third of the members of the Japanese Diet are second-generation lawmakers, often inheriting the same seat as the first-generation member (Derichs and Kerbo, 2003). Where the notion of the professional politician gives rise to the concept of a political class, the idea of a political dynasty encourages us to think of a political caste. Neither of these ideas is easily reconciled with the traditional interpretation of democracy as government by the people.

Beyond Asia, the phenomenon of second-generation legislators may simply reflect socialization: growing up in a family where politics is viewed not just as an interest but as an occupation. This effect surely helps to explain why as many as a quarter of the candidates standing in the Australian election of 2001 had a close family member who had also stood for elective office (McAllister, 2003). From this perspective, political families may be no more disturbing than family lines of physicians and accountants.

Legislatures in authoritarian states

Since assemblies are symbols of popular representation in politics, their significance in authoritarian regimes is inherently limited. Such assemblies generally function only as shadow institutions. Sessions are short and some members are often appointed by the government. Members concentrate on raising grievances, pressing constituency interests and sometimes lining their own pockets. The rulers regard these activities as non-threatening because the real issues of national politics are left untouched.

Yet legislatures are difficult to extinguish completely. Most authoritarian regimes possess an assembly of some description. So why do non-democratic rulers bother with them at all? Their value is fourfold:

- A parliament provides a fig leaf of *legitimacy*, both domestic and international, for the regime. The ruler can say to visiting dignitaries, 'Look! We too have an assembly, just like the British House of Commons and America's Congress!'
- The legislature can be used to *incorporate moderate opponents* into the regime, providing a forum for negotiating matters that do not threaten rulers' key interests.
- *Raising constituents' grievances* and *lobbying for local interests* provide a measure of integration between centre and periphery and between state and society. Such activity oils the political wheels without threatening those who control the machine.
- Assemblies provide a convenient *pool of potential recruits* to the elite. Behaviour in parliament provides a useful initial test of reliability.

In totalitarian systems, assemblies were even more marginal than in authoritarian regimes. Fascist states, in particular, had no time for parliamentary debate or indeed for parliaments. The vital juices of national revival could not be thinned by the party divisions apparent within parliament. Power was to be concentrated in a single leader, not diluted through a liberal separation of powers. For such reasons, Mussolini abolished the remnants of the Italian parliament in 1938, introducing a new if even more subservient corporate institution in its place.

In communist states, legislatures were not treated with quite the same contempt. Indeed, communist regimes often went to considerable lengths to produce statistically representative assemblies. Women and favoured groups such as industrial workers achieved greater representation than in Western legislatures. However, this feature reflected tight party control of the nomination process and the limited political significance of the parliamentary body. In practice, a socially representative assembly has more often indicated impotence than authority; for this reason, the fall in female representation after the end of communism should be interpreted sympathetically. The short sessions of communist assemblies (typically around ten days a year) were dominated by the party, which used them to outline past successes and future targets. Standing ovations were written into the script; free debate was written out.

As communist regimes became somewhat more pluralistic in their later decades, so legislatures acquired a measure of autonomy. China illustrates this trend. In the 12 years before Mao Zedong's death in 1976, the National People's Congress (NPC) did not meet at all. However, in the subsequent era of economic reform, the NPC began to emerge. A growing emphasis on the rule of law raised the status of the legislature which has now also begun to express popular hostility to corruption. Many votes are no longer unanimous, proceedings are less easily choreographed and some professional support is available to support its work. Senior figures drafted into the assembly skilfully strengthened the NPC's position in Chinese governance, not by confrontation with the ruling party but by assisting the growth of the private sector and by making efforts to encourage national integration through links with subnational congresses (O'Brien, 1990).

However the NPC, still the world's largest legislature, remains strongly hierarchical in its internal functioning. Plenary sessions remain formal and infrequent. More than in any democracy, legislative influence operates through smaller subgroups. The most important of these is the Standing Committee, a group of about 150 members which meets regularly throughout the year. These subgroups remain sensitive to the party's interests; most members of the Standing Committee – as of the NPC – also belong to the party, giving the leadership an additional mechanism of control. Of course, party domination of legislative proceedings is also found in parliamentary systems in liberal democracies but there the party in command varies with election results. Although the NPC and its subgroups have become part of the Chinese power network, they still cannot be understood through Western notions of the separation of powers and parliamentary sovereignty.

BOX 15.8

Comparing Russia's State Duma and America's House of Representatives

	State Duma	House of Representatives
Members enjoy immunity from arrest	Yes	Yes
Consents to president's appointment of prime minister	Yes	No post of prime minister
Government depends on chamber's confidence	Yes	No
President can dissolve chamber	Yes	No
Initiates impeachment of president	Yes	Yes
External bodies can introduce bills	Yes	No
Members can introduce money bills	No	Yes
Can override presidential veto of legislation	Yes	Yes

Note: 'Yes' may only apply in specific circumstances. Russia's system of government is formally semi-presidential, with the president sitting above the government.

Legislatures in illiberal democracies

The presence of an assembly is a defining feature of a democracy of any kind, liberal or illiberal. So legislatures certainly form part of the furniture of an illiberal democracy. Furthermore, their political position can be significant in areas that do not threaten the realities of presidential leadership: for instance, in representing local districts and in passing routine legislation. However, such assemblies operate in the shadow of executive authority. A nose for power will lead us away from the parliament and to the presidential office. There, we may discover an incumbent who governs by decree as well as by law and who may, *in extremis*, simply dissolve a recalcitrant legislature in search of more congenial arrangements.

The political environment of an illiberal democracy is particularly hostile to the notion that assemblies can hold the government to account through detailed scrutiny. Rather, the national leader considers himself responsible to the whole nation, not to what he sees as corrupt, partisan and parochial representatives in the assembly. In addition, many illiberal democracies are either new regimes or located in relatively poor countries; both factors militate against the development of a professional congress with a stable membership, extensive research support and a well-developed committee system. Diamond's observation about new democracies applies also to many illiberal democracies: 'These legislatures lack the organisation, financial resources, information service, experienced members and staff to serve as a mature and autonomous point of deliberation in the policy process' (1999, p. 98).

For instance, the position of legislatures in Latin America has undoubtedly strengthened in the post-military era of illiberal, and sometimes even liberal, democracy. As presidents have become more accountable, at least in the larger and more democratic countries, so assemblies have asserted the authority which flows from the separation of powers in a presidential executive. But it would be wrong to conclude that legislatures in these democracies have achieved, or will achieve, the exalted position of Congress in the United States. They still have considerable distance to travel before they can be said to 'restrain the prince and discipline the powerful' (Chalmers, 1990).

In the main, Latin American constitutions do not separate powers as completely as in the USA, giving presidents greater control over the budget and some latitude to govern through decrees. After Hugo Chávez assumed the Venezuelan presidency in 1998, he virtually dismantled Congress as part of his planning for a new constitution. In 2007, the National Assembly (stripped of opposition by an anti-Chávez boycott of an earlier election) meekly passed a law allowing the President to govern by decree for 18 months. While resources and professionalism have increased in many Latin American legislatures, their expertise and influence still lag far behind the American Congress. For such reasons, electorates still prefer to take their chance with a strong-man president rather than an ill-disciplined assembly.

In Russia's illiberal democracy, too, parliament (known as the Federal Assembly) occupies a secondary position. Certainly, the communist era of mute and meek assemblies has withered. The post-communist constitution (1993) created a significant bicameral legislature which is now well-established. The State Duma (lower house) contains 450 members elected for a four-year term. The Federation Council (upper house) has 178 members – two selected by each of the 89 units of the federation. Laws take precedence over presidential decrees.

The weaknesses of the Federal Assembly lie more in its relationship with the executive. In the United States, the relationship between congress and president is one of mutual checks and balances; in Russia, the balance is tilted to the presidency. Where America sought to limit presidential authority, the Russian tradition – characteristic of illiberal democracies – emphasizes strong government. Thus, the 1993 constitution states that Russia's president is not only 'guarantor of the constitution' but is also required to 'ensure the coordinated functioning and collaboration of bodies of state power'. President Putin performed this latter duty with particular skill and no great regard for the legislature.

In addition, the limited autonomy of the Duma, at least compared to America's House of Representatives, is reflected in a generally inferior constitutional position. For instance, other actors (including the president) can introduce bills for its consideration and only the government can initiate money bills (Box 15.8).

As in other illiberal democracies, the exact political weight of Russia's parliament is difficult to judge and remains subject to change. Donaldson (2004, p. 230) suggested 'that the Russian parliament has become an important counter-weight to its presidency'. Writing just two years later, with Putin's party in the ascendancy within the Duma, Remington (2006, p. 58) judged that 'in the Putin era, parliament's independence has been reduced to virtually nil'. Perhaps so but even President Putin himself claimed to find value in legislative institutions: 'today, we can justifiably call this period a time of strengthening the country's parliamentary and legal culture. One can speak about a modern State Duma as a working instrument of power' (quoted in Donaldson, 2004, p. 249).

Learning Resources for Chapter 15

Next step

Borchert and Zeiss (2003) is an excellent comparative study of the political class as represented in the legislatures of liberal democracies.

Further reading

Olson (1994) offers a useful comparative treatment of parliaments. Bicameralism and second chambers have attracted a flurry of interest: see Patterson and Mughan (1999), Russell (2000a), Uhr (2006) and Tsebelis and Money (1997). Committees are examined comparatively in Longley and Davidson (1998); see also Carey (2006). Best and Cotta (2000) provide a comparative treatment of long-term changes in parliamentary careers. Corbett, Jacobs and Shackleton (2005) survey the European Parliament. The most intensively studied legislature remains the American Congress: Davidson (2003) and Dodd and Oppenheimer (2004) are standard texts. West and Orman (2003) review celebrity politicians in the USA.

Internet sources

Centre for Legislative Studies, University of Hull
Research, publication and education about legislatures
http://www.hull.ac.uk/cls/

Commonwealth Parliamentary Association
The parliaments of the Commonwealth
http://www.cpahq.org/

Inter-Parliamentary Union
The leading information source on, and links to, national parliaments
http://www.ipu.org/english/home.htm

Legislative Studies Quarterly
Includes titles and abstracts of articles in the journal
http://www.uiowa.edu/~lsq/

Chapter 16

The political executive

The **political executive** is the core of government, consisting of political leaders who form the top slice of the administration: presidents and ministers, prime ministers and cabinets. The executive is the regime's energizing force, setting priorities, resolving crises, making decisions and supervising their implementation. Governing without an assembly or judiciary is perfectly feasible but ruling without an executive is impossible.

The political executive, which makes policy, must be distinguished from the bureaucracy, which puts policy into effect. Unlike appointed officials, the members of the executive are chosen by political means, most often by election, and can be removed by the same method. The executive is accountable for the activities of government; it is where the buck stops.

Democratic and authoritarian regimes are defined by the operation of their executive. Liberal democracies have succeeded in the delicate task of subjecting executive power to constitutional limits. The government is not only elected but remains subject to rules which limit its power; it must also face regular re-election. In an authoritarian regime, by contrast, constitutional and electoral controls either do not exist or are completely ineffective. The scope of the executive is limited not by the constitution but by political realities.

The executives of liberal democracies fall into three main groups: presidential, parliamentary and semi-presidential. We examine each in turn before considering the executive in authoritarian states and illiberal democracies.

The **political executive** forms the top tier of government. It directs the nation's affairs, supervises the execution of policy, mobilizes support for its goals and offers crisis leadership

Presidential government

The world contains many presidents but few examples of **presidential government**. Any tin-pot dictator can style himself 'president' and many do so. Also, many presidents are elected in parliamentary systems to serve as ceremonial head of state. However, the existence of a president is an inadequate sign of a presidential system.

Presidential government consists of four features:

- Direct election of the president who steers the government and makes appointments to it;
- Fixed terms of offices for the president and the assembly, neither of which can bring down the other;
- No overlap in membership between the executive and the legislature;
- The president serves as head of state.

Presidentialism proper is a form of constitutional rule in which a single chief executive governs using the authority derived from popular election, with an independent legislature (Figure 16.1). Almost always, this election takes the form of a direct vote. The president directs the government and, unlike most prime ministers, also serves as ceremonial head of state. Because both president and legislature are elected for a fixed term, neither can bring down the other, giving each institution some autonomy. This separation of powers is the hallmark of the presidential system and is typically reinforced by a separation of personnel. Members of the executive cannot sit in the assembly, creating further distance between the two institutions. Similarly, legislators must resign their seats if they wish to serve in the government, limiting the president's ability to buy congressional votes with the promise of posts.

Contrasting methods of election yield a further divergence in interests: legislators depend only on the support of voters in their home district or state while the president (and the president only) is elected by a broader constituency, typically a national ballot.

So despite the focus on a single office, presidential government divides power against itself. The system sets up a requirement for the executive to negotiate with the legislature and, by this mechanism, seeks to ensure that deliberation triumphs over dictatorship. Defenders of the format argue that it captures the essence of democracy, setting constitutional limits on executive pretension. However, detractors suggest that presidentialism is a conspiracy against government. The dangers are that deliberation turns into stalemate, that the democratic will is thwarted by excessive fragmentation and that the system itself becomes unstable.

Presidential government predominates in the Americas. It is entrenched not just in the United States but also throughout Latin America. We must begin with the USA, where the format emerged, but we will then turn to Brazil as a more typical example of the system.

Figure 16.1 Presidential government

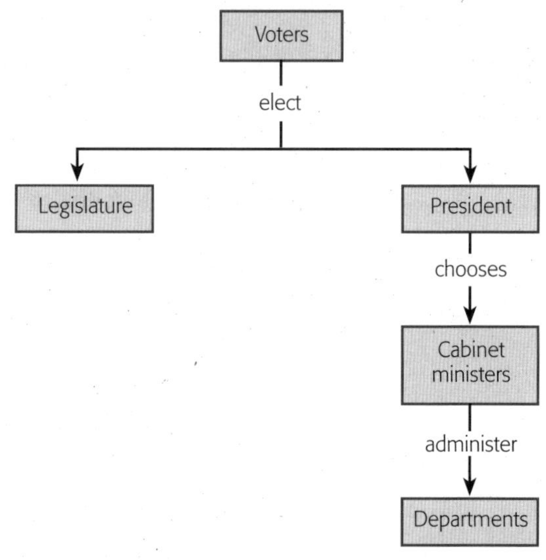

United States

When the framers of the American constitution met in Philadelphia in 1787, the issue of the executive created a dilemma. On the one hand, the Founding Fathers wanted to avoid anything that might prove to be a 'foetus of monarchy'. After all, the American revolution had just rid the new nation of England's George III. On the other hand, many delegates agreed with Alexander Hamilton that a single executive was needed for 'decision, activity, secrecy and dispatch'. Eventually, the founders settled on the presidency, an office that could provide prompt action for a republic in which Congress was nonetheless expected to play the leading role.

But how could a non-monarchical president be selected? Here the delegates were less clear. One possibility was to allow the national legislature to choose the chief executive. A subcommittee of the constitutional convention did canvass this possibility, which would have led to a form of parliamentary government. But the idea that the executive should be beholden to the assembly was not yet established, even in Britain. Instead, rather late in the proceedings, the delegates agreed to select the president through an electoral college whose members would be appointed by state legislatures. The framers had stumbled across an essential feature of presidential government: separate election of executive and legislature (Dahl, 2001).

The case for separate selection was well-made by James Madison (1788) in *Federalist Paper* No. 51:

> In order to lay a due foundation for that separate and distinct exercise of the different powers of government, which to a certain extent is admitted on all hands to be essential to the preservation of all liberty, it is evident that each department should have a will of its own; and consequently should be so constituted that the members of each should have as little agency as possible in the appointment of the member of the others.

The founders were not, however, prepared to embrace direct election of the chief executive. On the contrary, the original purpose of the Electoral College was to insulate the choice of president from

BOX 16.1

The American presidency: a classification of powers

	Definition	Example
Express powers	Powers explicitly listed in the constitution	'The President shall be Commander-in-Chief of the Army and Navy of the United States'
Implied (inherent) powers	Powers held to derive from the president's explicit constitutional obligations	The president's obligation 'to preserve, protect and defend the Constitution' is taken to contain within it the notion of emergency powers
Statutory powers	Additional powers explicitly granted by Congress	Many highly specific grants by legislation, such as the authority to restrict imports from China

influence by the 'excitable masses'. It is somewhat ironic, therefore, that today the president is effectively chosen by precisely the national vote that the delegates so feared. Each state is given a certain number of votes in the College, determined by its number of senators (two) plus its number of representatives in the House (which reflects its population). The leading presidential candidate in each state then receives all its votes in the College. The College itself is now a mechanical device.

The constitution also ensures that a president, once selected, remains secure in office, establishing the separate survival of executive and legislature which is another hallmark of presidential government. The president can only be dismissed by Congress through 'Impeachment for, and on Conviction of, Treason, Bribery, or other high Crimes and Misdemeanors'. So far, just two – including Bill Clinton in 1998 – have been impeached though neither was convicted (Richard Nixon, however, resigned in 1974, anticipating conviction.) Just as Congress cannot normally remove the president, neither can the president dissolve Congress and call new elections. Again, Madison made the case in No. 51:

> But the great security against a gradual concentration of the several powers in the same department consists in giving to those who administer each department the necessary constitutional means and personal motives to resist encroachments of the others. The provision for defense must in this, as in all other cases, be made commensurate to the danger of attack. Ambition must be made to counteract ambition.

The constitution states that 'The executive Power shall be vested in a President of the United States of America'. In addition to a general obligation to 'take Care that the Laws be faithfully executed', the president is given explicit roles such as commander-in-chief. These express powers have been interpreted over time as giving the president additional implied powers: those without which he could not fulfil his constitutional duties. In addition, the President has further specific powers granted, and revocable, by Congressional statute (Box 16.1).

Although the American presidency is often seen as a symbol of power, the institution was designed as part of a concerted attempt to control executive pretension. As President Kennedy commented, 'The president is rightly described as a man of extraordinary powers. Yet it is also true that he must wield those powers under extraordinary limitations'. Thus, many of the president's powers are shared with Congress:

- The president is commander-in-chief but Congress retains the power to declare war;
- The president can make government appoint-

ments and sign treaties but only with 'the advice and consent' of the Senate;

- The president 'recommends to Congress such measures as he shall judge necessary and expedient' but is offered no means to ensure his proposals are accepted;
- The president can veto legislation but Congress can override his objections;
- Congress, not the president, controls the purse strings.

Certainly, the president also possesses implied powers which derive from his role as chief executive and which are independent of Congress. These include the ability to issue executive orders and national security directives (Warber, 2006). President George W. Bush made strong use of these executive tools in waging his self-proclaimed war on terror (Howell, 2005). Even in these areas, however, any administrative act which [illegible] public expenditure [illegible] authorized by Congress and any executive act which offends the constitution [illegible]. A wise president [illegible] the political consequences of [illegible] unilateral powers.

Two points flow from the president's constitutional position. First, to describe the relationship between the president and Congress as a 'separation of powers' is misleading. In reality there is a separation of institutions rather than of legislative and executive powers. President and Congress share power: each seeks to influence the other but neither is in any position to dictate. This separated system, as C. Jones (1994) calls it, is subtle, intricate and balanced. It reflects a successful attempt by the founders to build checks and balances into American government.

This tension within the system, it is important to note, continues even when the same party controls both the White House and Congress. As Mayhew observes in *Divided We Govern* (1991, p. 135), 'to suppose that an American party winning Congress and the presidency thereby wins the leeway of a British governing party is to be deluded by the election returns'. Whatever their party, members of Congress have different electoral interests from the president. They are elected without term limits from local areas for distinct terms of two years in the House and six years in the Senate (Box 16.2). These particular interests mean that presidential government is inherently less party-based than its parliamentary cousin (Milkis, 2005).

Second, in a system of shared control presidential power becomes the power to persuade (Neustadt, 1991). As President Truman said, 'The principal power that the president has is to bring people in and try to persuade them to do what they ought to do without persuasion'. In this task of persuasion, the contemporary president can follow two strategies: **going Washington** and **going public** (Kernell, 1997).

> **Going Washington** involves the American president in wheeling and dealing with Congress and its members, assembling majorities for his legislative proposals. **Going public** occurs when the president [illegible] unrivalled access to the mass media to [illegible] public opinion and so persuade [illegible] indirectly.

Lyndon Johnson, a former leader of the Senate Democrats who succeeded to the presidency following President Kennedy's assassination in 1963, [illegible] of the Washington strategy. To secure his [illegible] domestic reforms, he leant heavily on members of Congress, using a potent combination of bullying, flattery, persuasion and bribery. He was, however, less successful with the wider public, lacking sparkle in front of a television camera. By contrast, 'the great communicator' Ronald Reagan adopted the wider approach, seeking to communicate his agenda to the public and, indirectly, to influence Congress by his domination of the agenda. (Wisely, Reagan also employed experienced aides to keep the pressure on key legislators.)

The paradox of the American presidency – a weak governing position amid the trappings of omnipotence – is reflected in the president's support network. To meet presidential needs for information and advice, a conglomeration of supporting bodies has evolved. Collectively known as the Executive Office of the President, these bodies provide far more direct support than is available to the prime minister in any parliamentary system, forming what is often called the institutional presidency (Burke, 2005). The days have passed when presidents asked family members to provide secretarial support at no cost to the public purse.

BOX 16.2

Separate elections in the United States

	Electoral unit	Length of term	Limit on re-election
Presidency	A national vote, aggregated by state in an electoral college	4 years	Maximum of two terms
Senate	Direct popular vote in each of 50 states	6 years	No limit
House of Representatives	Direct popular vote in each of 435 districts	2 years	No limit

Yet the massive apparatus of advice available to today's president has often proved to be a weakness. Many advisers are political outsiders, appointed by the president at the start of his tenure before his eye for Washington's politics is in. Far from helping the president, advisers sometimes end up undermining his position. The Watergate scandal in the 1970s destroyed the presidency of Richard Nixon; the Iran–Contra scandal in the 1980s lay siege to the reputation of Ronald Reagan. Presidents such as George W. Bush who adopt a hierarchical management style are particularly at risk from hearing only a limited range of opinions.

One problem is that the presidential system lacks a strong cabinet to offer a counterbalance to personal advisers. In the USA, the cabinet goes unmentioned in the constitution; its meetings are little more than a presidential photo-opportunity. Cabinet members often experience difficulty in gaining access to the president through his thicket of advisers.

Brazil

With democracy now established in parts of Latin America, students of presidential government can broaden their horizons beyond the USA. The United States remains the prototype of the system but most working examples are now found to the south. The Latin America experience with presidentialism is generally less positive than that north of the border, reflecting the difficulties of integrating a presidential system with proportional representation and a multiparty system.

A comparison between the USA and Brazil is particularly useful, demonstrating the value of distinguishing between presidentialism in two-party and multiparty conditions. Brazil and the USA are two large and populous former colonies now governed as federations, each with a strongly bicameral legislature. As the poorer and more unequal society, in which the military only withdrew from rule in 1985, Brazil is of course a far less easy country to govern. We must therefore express some caution in attributing its political style solely to its institutional architecture.

Where the American president is hemmed in with restrictions, the Brazilian constitution appears to offer the country's president an arsenal of weapons (Box 16.3). First, the Brazilian president can issue decrees – provisional regulations with the force of law – in specified areas. These decrees stay in effect for 60 days without parliamentary approval and can be renewed once. Second, he can declare bills to be urgent, forcing Congress to make a prompt decision on these proposals. Third, he (and in some areas he alone) can initiate bills in Congress. Fourth, he proposes a budget which goes into effect, month by month, if Congress does not itself pass a budget. The combined effect of these entitlements would

BOX 16.3

Comparing presidential powers in Brazil and the USA

	Brazil	USA
Can the president issue decrees?	Yes, in many areas. Valid for 60 days, renewable once	No
Can the president initiate bills?	Yes, exclusively so in some areas	No
Can the president declare bills urgent?	Yes	No
Can the president veto legislation?	Yes, in whole and part	Yes
How can Congress override a veto?	Absolute majority in joint meeting of both houses	Two-thirds majority in each house
President's control over the budget	Stronger	Weaker
Party system	Multiparty	Two-party
Does the president's party possess a majority in Congress?	No	Sometimes
Party discipline in Congress	Weak	Stronger

Sources for Brazil: Ames (2002), Cox and Morgenstern (2002), Neto (2002).

appear to give Brazil's president the means to govern.

Yet despite their panoply of formal powers, Brazilian presidents face the same problem as their North American colleagues: legislators who know their own interests. Indeed, Brazilian leaders experience even greater difficulty in bending Congress to their will. The explanation for this contrast lies in Brazil's fragmented multiparty system. In 2006, 20 parties were represented in the Chamber of Deputies and 12 in the Senate; as usual, the president's party was in the minority in each chamber.

Furthermore, party discipline within Brazil's Congress is exceptionally weak, reflecting the use of preference votes in the party list electoral system. Deputies often switch party in midterm; unlike the country's soccer players, they do not even wait until the end of the season before transferring. Members are more concerned to obtain resources for their district than to show loyalty to their party. In Brazil, parties are not only more numerous but also less cohesive than in the USA, a contrast which complicates the president's task.

Reflecting partisan fragmentation, Brazil's presidents must attempt to build informal coalitions. This requirement takes the form of appointing ministers from a range of parties to the executive in an attempt to extract loyalty from these parties' deputies. It is as though a Republican president in the United States, confronting a hostile Congress, were able to bolster his support by appointing a few Democratic congressmen to his cabinet.

In making coalitions, Brazilian presidents are assisted by a more flexible interpretation of the separation of institutions than is found in the USA. The United States is, in fact, exceptional within presidential systems in insisting on a strict separation of personnel between government and assembly. For instance, we certainly could not substitute 'the United States' for 'Brazil' in this quotation:

> In Brazil, ministers will occasionally resign their government positions just before an important vote in the assembly, resume their legislative seats, vote and then resign their legislative seats and resume their ministerial posts again (Cox and Morgenstern, 2002, p. 459).

Thus Brazil shows that presidential government does not need to be single-party government. Like

DEBATE

SHOULD A NEW DEMOCRACY ADOPT PRESIDENTIAL GOVERNMENT?

In the final decades of the twentieth century, many countries emerged from military or communist rule to embrace democracy. Constitution-writers faced the question of whether to adopt a presidential or parliamentary form of government for the new democratic order. The drafters frequently sought advice from political scientists in established democracies. Had we been asked, should we have argued for presidential government for these new democracies?

YES

A presidential system offers the stability which is the first requirement for a new regime. The president's fixed term provides continuity in the executive, avoiding the collapse of governing coalitions to which parliamentary governments are prone. Presidents who prove to be wholly unsuitable can always be impeached.

Furthermore, winning a presidential election requires candidates to develop broad support across the country. Elected by the country at large, the president can take a national view, rising above the squabbles between minority parties in the assembly.

A president provides a natural symbol for a new order, offering a familiar face for domestic and international audiences alike. The leader can pursue a steady course in foreign policy, free from the volatility which would arise if the executive were directly accountable to a fractious assembly.

Since a presidential system necessarily involves a separation of powers, it should also encourage limited government and thereby protect liberty.

Remember, finally, that the USA is the world's dominant power and has sustained presidential government for over 200 years. Not only is there pragmatic good sense in following No. 1 but the American experience demonstrates that presidential government can be stable when combined with the rule of law.

NO

Presidential government is inappropriate for a new democracy because only one party can win the presidency; everyone else loses. All-or-nothing politics is unsuited to a new regime where political trust is still developing. In addition, fixed terms of office are too inelastic; 'everything is rigid, specified, dated,' wrote Bagehot (1867). The deadlock arising when executive and legislature disagree means that the new political system may be unable to address pressing problems.

There is a danger, too, that presidents will grow too big for their boots: Latin American experience shows presidents amending the constitution so as to continue in office beyond their one- or two-term limit. Even worse, a frustrated or ambitious president may turn into a dictator; presidential democracies are more likely than parliamentary democracies to disintegrate (Cheibub, 2002). The USA remains the world's only case of stable presidential government over the long term – an exception to admire but not, it seems, a model that can be replicated elsewhere.

Presidential government involves betting the country on one person, thus inhibiting the development of the rule of law in new democracies. The risks are altogether too great, leading Lijphart (2000, p. 267) to regard presidentialism 'as a strongly negative feature for the future of democracy'. Prudence mandates a parliamentary system governed by a broad coalition cabinet.

ASSESSMENT

In practice, the choices made by new democracies seemed to reflect history and geography more than the wisdom of politics professors. Central European countries such as the Czech Republic and Hungary adopted the parliamentary form which dominates Western Europe, mindful no doubt of their decision to join the European Union. By contrast, post-military regimes in Latin American countries drew on their own political histories, and the presence of the USA to the north, to embrace a presidential system. Only time will tell if Latin America made the right choice.

Further reading

Andrews and Montinola (2004), Cameron, Blanaru and Burns (2004), Linz (1990), Lijphart (2000), Stepan and Skatch (1993).

some other chief executives in the region, Brazilian presidents rely on a multiparty governing coalition as a technique for influencing the legislature. These coalitions are, however, more informal and unstable than the carefully crafted interparty coalitions which characterize parliamentary government in Western Europe.

So although Latin American constitutions appear to give the chief executive a more important political role, appearances are deceptive. The Latin American experience confirms that presidents operating in a democratic setting confront inherent difficulties in securing their programmes. Mainwaring's assessment (1992, p. 112) remains valid:

> My own view is that under democratic conditions, most Latin American presidents have had trouble accomplishing their agendas. They have held most of the power for initiating policy but have found it hard to get support for implementing policy. If my analysis is correct, it points to a significant weakness in democratic presidencies.

Figure 16.2 Parliamentary government

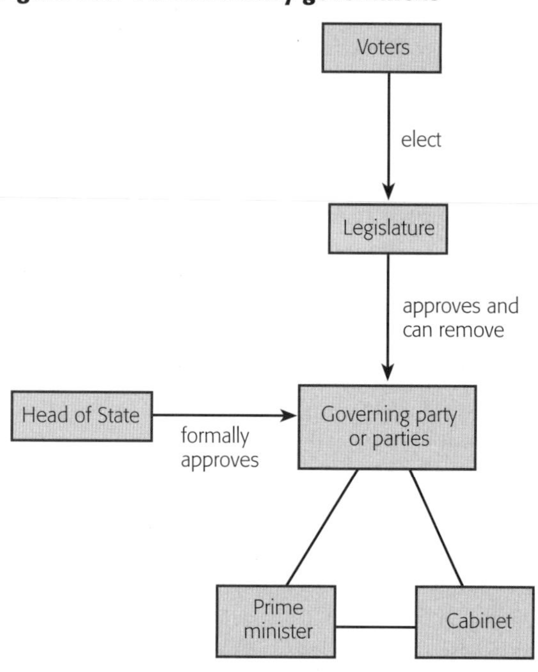

Parliamentary government

Unlike presidential systems, in which the chief executive is separate from the legislature and independently elected, the executive in **parliamentary government** is organically linked to the assembly (Figure 16.2). The government emerges from parliament and can be brought down by a vote of no confidence. By the same token the government can, in nearly all cases, dissolve parliament and call fresh elections. If the paradox of presidentialism is executive weakness amid the appearance of strength, the puzzle of parliamentary government is to explain why effective government can still emerge from this mutual vulnerability of assembly and executive. The solution is clear: party provides the necessary unifying device, bridging government and legislature in a manner that presidential systems are designed to prevent.

> **Parliamentary government** has three main features:
>
> - The governing parties emerge from the assembly and can be dismissed from office by a vote of no confidence. In many but not all countries, government ministers are drawn from, and remain members of, the legislature.
> - The executive is collegial, taking the form of a cabinet (council of ministers) in which the prime minister (premier, chancellor) was traditionally just first among equals. This plural executive contrasts with the single chief executive in presidential government.
> - A ceremonial head of state is normally separate from the post of prime minister.

The crucial influence on the operation of parliamentary government is the party balance in the legislature. Where a single party wields a majority (as normally in Britain), government can be stable and decisive, perhaps even excessively so. But the British model of single-party majority government, facilitated as it is by a plurality electoral system, is exceptional. In many parliamentary systems, the assembly is elected by proportional representation, a system which rarely results in a majority of seats for one party. The normal outcome is government by coalition.

So parliamentary government is as variable in operation as the presidential form. Just as the working of presidential government depends on whether the legislature is based on a two-party system (USA) or a multiparty system (Brazil), so too does the parliamentary system have two variants, one based on majority government (UK) and the other on minority (Denmark) and coalition (Finland) government.

We examine these forms separately before turning to two broader questions. First, how is power in parliamentary government distributed between prime minister, cabinet and ministers? Second, where does the head of state fit in?

Majority government

Britain is the classic example of parliamentary government based on a single ruling party with a secure majority. The plurality method of election customarily delivers a working majority in the House of Commons to a single party. The leader of this party becomes prime minister (PM), selecting twenty or so parliamentary colleagues from the same party to form the cabinet. This ministerial council remains the formal lynchpin of the system; it is the focus of accountability to parliament and even the strongest PM cannot govern without its support. The cabinet meets most weeks, chaired by the PM. The monarch now sits above the entire political process, meeting regularly with the PM but rarely if ever intervening in political decisions.

Government accountability to the House of Commons is tight. All ministers, including the PM, must regularly defend their policies in the chamber; further, the opposition will demand a vote of no confidence whenever it senses an advantage from launching an attack. Should the government lose such a vote, it would be expected to resign, leading either to the opposition taking power or to fresh elections.

However, party discipline turns the cabinet into the master of the Commons rather than its servant. The governing party spans the cabinet and the assembly, securing its domination of the parliamentary agenda and timetable. The cabinet is officially the top committee of state but it is also an unofficial meeting of the party's leaders. As long as senior party figures remain sensitive to the views of their backbenchers (and often even if they do not), they can control the Commons. The government does indeed emerge from its parliamentary womb but it dominates its parent from the moment of its birth.

How does the ruling party achieve this level of control? Each party has a Whip's Office to ensure that backbenchers (ordinary MPs) vote as its leaders require. Even without the attention of the whips, MPs will generally toe the party line if they want to become ministers themselves. In a strong party system such as Britain's, a member who shows too much independence is unlikely to win promotion. In extreme cases, MPs who are thrown out of their party for dissent are unlikely to be re-elected by constituents for whom a party label is still key. Whatever their private views, it is in members' own interests to demonstrate public loyalty to their party.

Minority and coalition government

Many countries using parliamentary government elect their legislature by proportional representation, resulting in a situation where no single party gains a majority of seats. Here the tight link between the election result and government formation weakens. In this more fragmented situation, government takes one of three forms (Müller and Strøm, 2000a):

- A *majority coalition* in which two or more parties with a majority of seats join together in government. This is the most common form of government across continental Europe; it characterizes Belgium, Finland, Germany and the Netherlands in particular.
- A *minority coalition* or alliance. These are formal coalitions or informal alliances between parties which, even together, still lack a parliamentary majority. Minority coalitions have predominated in Denmark since the 1980s. They were also found in Italy, especially before the transformation of the party system in the 1990s.
- A *single-party minority government* formed by the largest party. Single-party cabinets comprised about 30 per cent of continental European governments between 1945 and 1999 and were the most frequent form in Norway over the twentieth century (Rasch, 2004, p. 130).

Through both its statements and its silences, the constitution helps to account for these contrasts. The constitution lays out the hurdles a new government must clear before taking office. As Box 16.4 shows, some constitutions (and most recent ones) demand that the legislature demonstrates majority support for the new government through a formal vote of investiture. Spain and most post-communist countries of Eastern Europe are examples. Clearly, this requirement for a positive investiture vote by the assembly encourages a majority coalition with an overall programme.

Since 1975, Sweden has adopted a less stringent test: a vote is held but the test is negative. That is, the proposed prime minister can form a government as long as no more than half the members of the Riksdag object (Bergman, 2000). In other countries, however, the constitution is entirely silent on the procedure for approving a new government. In these circumstances, the new government takes office, and continues in power, until it is voted down by the assembly. Denmark and Norway are examples here.

These less demanding conventions – a negative investiture vote or none at all – facilitate the formation and survival of minority governments. Such administrations often receive the tacit support of other parties which even outside government can continue to influence legislation through their presence on parliamentary committees. Gallagher, Laver and Mair (2006, p. 418) suggest that such a situation should be understood as a parliamentary coalition without a government coalition.

On occasion, parties state their preferred coalition partners (or those parties with which they refuse to entertain an agreement) before the election, thus allowing voters to make a more informed judgement of the likely consequences of their own decisions. More often, though, the party composition of government is decided after the election, through intricate negotiations between the leaders of the relevant parties. While this activity is underway, the outgoing government remains as a caretaker administration for an average of 30 days.

Some constitutions specify a procedure which the parties follow in forming, and not merely installing, a government. This usually involves the head of state appointing the largest party, or its leader, as ***formateur***. The *formateur*'s task is to form an administration through negotiation; this work helps not only to form but also to legitimize the new administration (Figure 16.3).

The parties agreeing to go into coalition will detail a joint programme in a lengthy public statement. These package deals cover the policies to be pursued and the coalition's rules of conduct: for instance, how it proposes to resolve disputes. Questions of office – which party obtains which ministry and whether that party alone determines the appoint-

A ***formateur*** is a person or party charged by the head of state with initiating negotiations for a coalition. The *formateur* is usually the leader of the party with most seats in parliament.

BOX 16.4

Procedure for installing a government in parliamentary systems when no party possesses a majority of seats

	Description	Example
Positive investiture vote	To take office, a new government must obtain majority support in parliament	Spain
Negative investiture vote	A new government takes office unless voted down by a majority in parliament	Sweden
No investiture vote	No formal parliamentary vote is required before a new government takes office	Denmark

ment – are also negotiated, with a party's bounty tightly reflecting its representation in parliament, plus a bonus for the smallest parties.

So much for the formalities of coalition formation. What though are the political realities? In particular, why do some parties end up in a governing coalition while others – with an equal or even larger number of seats – remain on the sidelines? Political scientists have devoted considerable effort to answering this question. The most common type of coalition, it turns out, contains the smallest number of parties (typically two to four) needed to make a viable government. Party interest favours **minimum winning coalitions** because including additional parties in a coalition which already possesses a majority would simply dilute the number of posts obtained by each participant. The rule of political meanness applies: only share when you have to and then no more than necessary.

A **minimum winning coalition (MWC)** is a government formed by the smallest number of parties which together can secure a parliamentary majority. MWCs are the most common form of party government in post-war Europe (Gallagher, Laver and Mair, 2006, p. 401).

In addition, coalitions are also usually based on parties with adjacent positions on the ideological spectrum. This test shapes which of many possible MWCs are chosen. In most Scandinavian countries, for example, coalitions have usually only drawn on parties from within either the left-wing bloc or the right-wing bloc. Even where such clearly defined blocs are lacking, the preference is still for coalitions formed from parties lying next to each on a left–right scale. The rule of political meanness needs qualification: if you have to share, do so with friends.

This tendency for neighbours to cooperate benefits central pivot or swing parties which can jump either way. In Germany, for instance, the small liberal Free Democrat Party participated in most coalition governments between 1949 and 1998, sometimes with the more conservative Christian Democrats and sometimes with the more left-wing Social Democrats. Either coalition could be presented as ideologically coherent.

Occasionally, rainbow coalitions emerge which span the ideological spectrum. An influential example is the five-party coalition, ranging from the conservative National Coalition to the Left Alliance, which governed Finland between 1995 and 2003 (Jungar, 2002). One reason why rainbow coalitions are unusual is that they are oversized: they exceed the minimum number of participants needed for a majority.

We must address one final issue about coalitions. Such governments are frequently condemned as unstable, not least by English-speaking critics of proportional representation. How valid is this charge? In a few countries, certainly, government duration has been measured in months rather than years: an average of five months for the French Fourth Republic (1945–58) and eight months for Italian governments between 1948 and 1989. In these over-cited examples, chronic political instability certainly contributed to poor governance.

But in most of contemporary Europe, coalition governments last a good deal longer, typically for around two years (Müller and Strøm, 2000b). Some

Figure 16.3 *Formateurs* and coalition governments

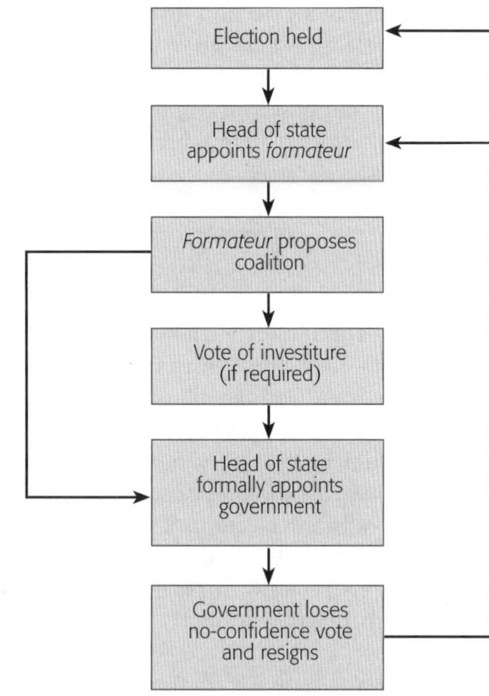

Source: Adapted from Laver and Schofield (1998), p. 63.

coalition agreements in the Netherlands (and most in Austria and France) include a clause stating that the partners will call an election if they dissolve the coalition. This **election rule** gives the partners an incentive to soldier on. Coalitions require compromise over policy and posts but compromise can be a route to stability rather than instability.

An **election rule** is an agreement among coalition partners that they will call an election if the coalition ends.

Just as formal rules influence government formation, so too can they affect government survival. Two procedures from Germany illustrate this point. First, the **constructive vote of no confidence** enhances government durability. Second, the chancellor can only request the president to dissolve the Bundestag and call fresh elections if he has first lost a vote of confidence. As a result of these rules, German coalitions typically survive the four years until the next scheduled election.

The **constructive vote of no confidence** requires an assembly to select a new prime minister before it can dispose of the incumbent. The purpose is to prevent legislatures from acting destructively by bringing down a government without any thought to its successor. The device comes from Germany but has also been adopted in Hungary, Israel and Spain.

In any case, a slight modification of the parties in a governing coalition does not constitute a political earthquake in European countries. When a government resigns after (or more often before) a vote of no confidence, normally as a result of defection by a coalition partner, the procedure for forming governments begins anew. Often there is no need to trouble the voters. Many of the same characters will frequently return to power, often to the same ministries, so that continuity is maintained. In Italy, for instance, one government was defeated only for the exact same parties to resume office when no other combination proved to be feasible.

Who governs?

Parliamentary government lacks the clear focus of the presidential system on a single chief executive. Rather, it involves a subtle and variable relationship between prime minister, cabinet and government ministers (Box 16.5).

For advocates of parliamentary government, collective leadership is its key strength, encouraging more deliberation and so resulting in fewer mistakes than occur under a presidential format. When Olsen (1980, p. 203) wrote that 'a Norwegian prime minister is unlikely to achieve a position as superstar', many advocates of parliamentary government would have regarded the comment as praise. By contrast, Tony Blair's cavalier attitude to consulting his cabinet may have been one factor contributing to his widely-criticized decision to participate in the invasion of Iraq in 2003.

Finland still provides a clear case of *cabinet government*. By law, the Finnish State Council is granted extensive decision-making authority. Both the prime minister and individual ministers are subject to constraints arising from Finland's complex multiparty coalitions. Prime ministers are primarily chairs of Council meetings; individual ministers also find their hands tied by their party and its coalition agreements.

Germany, by contrast, gives us an example of *prime ministerial government*, called chancellor democracy in the country itself. The guiding prin-

BOX 16.5

Location of decision-making in parliamentary government

	Description	Example
Cabinet	Discussion in cabinet determines overall policy	Finland
Prime minister	The PM is the dominant figure, dealing directly with individual ministers	Germany
Individual ministries	Ministers operate with little direction from the PM or the cabinet	Italy

ciple here is hierarchy rather than collegiality. The Bundestag (lower house) appoints a chancellor, not a party, and accountability to the Bundestag is mainly through her. She answers to parliament; ministers answer to her. The strong position of Germany's chief executive derives from the Basic Law (constitution) which states that the 'chancellor shall determine, and be responsible for, the general policy guidelines'. But the constitution is an imprecise guide to the political realities of coalitions. Angela Merkel, appointed Chancellor of Germany in 2005 in a grand coalition between her Christian Democratic party and the more left-wing Social Democrats, had to tread with particular care.

Ministerial government arises when ministers operate without extensive direction from either prime minister or cabinet. This decentralized pattern can emerge either from respect for expertise or from the realities of coalition. Germany, again, is an example of the importance attached to specialization. Although the chancellor sets the overall guidelines, the constitution goes on to say that 'each Federal Minister shall conduct the affairs of his department autonomously and on his own responsibility'. So Germany operates ministerial government within the framework of chancellor democracy. Ministers are appointed for their knowledge of the field and are expected to use their professional experience to shape their ministry's policy under the chancellor's guidance.

In many coalitions, parties appoint their own leading figures to head particular ministries, again giving rise to ministerial government. In the Netherlands, for instance, the prime minister neither appoints, dismisses nor reshuffles ministers. Cabinet members serve with but certainly not under the government's formal leader. In these conditions the premier's status is diminished, with ministers owing more loyalty to party than to the prime minister. The chief executive is neither a chief nor an executive but rather a skilled conciliator.

Similarly, the Italian constitution enjoins collective responsibility of the Council of Ministers to parliament but this has been notably lacking. Not least before the transformation of the party system in the 1990s, interdepartmental coordination of policy was notoriously weak. Factions within parties, and not just parties themselves, came to own particular ministries. Imagine how the authority of British prime ministers would decline if the cabinet contained members appointed by factions from other parties.

Trends in parliamentary government

In assessing the balance of power within the parliamentary executive, we must address trends in the relationship between prime minister and cabinet and in the workings of cabinet itself. The broad tendency here is summarized in the **presidentialization** thesis: the idea that prime ministers, especially but not only in single-party administrations, are acquiring greater prominence in relation to the cabinet and the government as a whole. The proposition is that prime ministers have ceased to be first among equals and instead have become president–ministers. Fiers and Krouwel (2005, p. 128), for example, tell us that

> within the last two decades, party leaders and prime ministers alike, both in Belgium and the Netherlands, acquired more prominent and powerful positions, transforming these consensus democracies into a kind of 'presidentialized' parliamentary system.

More generally, Poguntke and Webb (2005, p. 340) conclude from a comparative study that 'leaders' power resources and autonomy within national political executives have increased and/or were already at a high level (compared to the type of collegial government that one associates with parliamentarism).'

> **Presidentialization** (strictly, prime ministerialization) is the process by which prime ministers in parliamentary systems have, over the last few decades, strengthened their position in relation to their cabinet and government. The term is metaphorical, implying neither a formal transition from a parliamentary to a presidential regime, nor that presidents are dominant within their own political systems.

Like many propositions about political change, the presidentialization thesis is distinctly imprecise (Helms, 2005). It is often left unclear whether the starting point for the comparison is an earlier historical period or a theoretical model of parliamentary government that may never have existed. Thus, analysts who claim that cabinet government no longer exists in Britain rarely pause to tell us when it did. If we were to adopt a specific starting-point, we might well discover that prime ministers were strong even then – as with Disraeli and Gladstone in nineteenth-century Britain.

In any case, the decline of cabinet government does not itself make the case for prime ministerial government; there is also the category of ministerial government and of *ad hoc* groups of ministers which form to address relevant issues. Also, of course, there is a wider governance literature which suggests that power is leaking from central political authority altogether to more specialized expert networks (Bevir and Rhodes, 2006).

Furthermore, the presidentialization thesis has been advanced for so long that, if the trend really were continuous, most prime ministers would by now have become not merely presidents but absolute dictators. Selection bias is a problem here: strong prime ministers in the current era receive disproportionate attention, and even the weaker phases of their own tenure are neglected. Rhodes (2006b, p. 328) wisely observes that

> Of the twelve postwar British prime ministers, only three have attracted the epithet 'presidential' – Harold Wilson, Margaret Thatcher and Tony Blair. And of these three, judgements about their presidentialism varied while they were in office.

If there is some broad if irregular tendency to presidentialism, what might be its causes? King (1994) identifies three factors: increasing media focus on the premier, the growing international role of the chief executive and the emerging need for policy coordination as governance becomes more complex. Someone needs to bring government policy together and commit the country to international agreements with domestic consequences; that person is usually the prime minister. In addition, the prime minister is usually leader of a party – and party leaders may also be growing in importance as their party's public face in the broadcast media.

Presidentialization aside, two less publicized but more certain changes have taken place in the operation of the cabinet system. First, the expansion of the cabinet has been contained at around two dozen by introducing the category of non-cabinet or junior ministers. To belong to 'the ministry', to use a New Zealand phrase, no longer guarantees a seat round the cabinet table. In Canada, the same device of non-cabinet ministers has been used to contain a cabinet which had reached the unwieldy size of 40 by 1987. At least in larger countries, to be a member of the government is not necessarily to share in the deliberations of the cabinet.

Second, **cabinet committees** have emerged as important decision arenas in larger countries. These committees developed during and after wars, reflecting the volume and urgency of business, and then obtained more formal status in peacetime. New Zealand has around 12 such committees, including an influential one that addresses overall strategy; Canada has six (Box 16.6). The United Kingdom, as at 2006, had no less than 32, covering a range of issues such as Animal Rights Extremism and Welfare Reform.

> **Cabinet committees** are small workgroups of full cabinet, established to focus on specific areas such as the budget, legislation or overall strategy. In addition to these standing committees, prime ministers also set up ad hoc committees of ministers to respond to specific issues such as labour disputes and terrorist acts.

The functions of these committees are set out in Britain's Ministerial Code:

> First, they relieve the pressure on the Cabinet itself by settling as much business as possible at a lower level or, failing that, by clarifying the issues and defining the points of disagreement. Second, they support the principle of collective responsibility by ensuring that, even though an important question may never reach the Cabinet itself, the decision will be fully considered and the final judgement will be sufficiently authoritative to ensure that the Government as a whole can be properly expected to accept responsibility for it (Cabinet Office, 2006).

So cabinet government has become government by the cabinet network, with the real decisions merely confirmed in the full meetings. In Australia, decisions reached in committee can only be reopened in full cabinet with the approval of the prime minister. Even committees largely ratify decisions fixed up before the meeting through informal consultations usually led by the minister most directly concerned.

BOX 16.6

Cabinet committees in Canada, 2006

Economic Affairs	Growth, trade and development
Foreign Affairs and National Security	Foreign affairs, international development, security and defence
Operations	Coordination of the agenda, issues management
Priorities and Planning	Strategic direction
Social Affairs	Aboriginal affairs, culture, health, immigration, justice, training
Treasury Board	Administrative management

Source: Canada's New Government (2006).

Thus, the governing capacity of prime ministers now depends on their ability to manipulate this entire network rather than the increasingly formal meetings of the full cabinet. Hefferman (2006, p. 25), for instance, finds that since Tony Blair became British prime minister in 1997, 'it is impossible to cite a meaningful collective decision that has been taken by the full cabinet by truly collegial means. The exception may be the decision in 2003 to embrace the London Olympic bid'.

Heads of state and parliamentary government

One hallmark of a parliamentary system is, in Bagehot's classic analysis (1867), the distinction between the **dignified** and **efficient** aspects of government. Unlike presidential systems, which combine the offices of head of state and head of government, parliamentary rule separates the two roles. Dignified or ceremonial leadership lies with the head of state; efficient leadership rests with the premier, cabinet and ministers. Such a division creates more time for prime ministers to concentrate on running the country.

> 'In such constitutions there are two parts: . . . first, those which excite and preserve the reverence of the population – the **dignified** parts, if I may so call them; and next the **efficient** parts – those by which it, in fact, works and rules. . . . Every constitution must first gain authority and then use authority; it must first win the loyalty and confidence of mankind, and then employ that homage in the work of government' (Bagehot, 1867, p. 6).

How then are heads of state selected? The position is either inherited (a monarchy) or elected (a presidency) (Box 16.7). At least in Europe and Asia, royal heads of state remain surprisingly numerous. Half the countries of Western Europe are constitutional monarchies, including Belgium, Denmark, the Netherlands, Spain and the United Kingdom. In some former British colonies such as Canada, a governor general acts as a stand-in for the monarch.

In a democratic era, monarchs reign but they do not rule. They are reluctant to enter the political arena but royal influence can occasionally be significant, especially in times of crisis or transition. In the 1970s, for instance, King Juan Carlos helped to steer Spain's transition to democracy. The King of Belgium also played a conciliatory role in his country's long march to federal status, leading Senelle (1996, p. 281) to claim that 'were it not for the monarchy as symbol of the cohesion of the kingdom and therefore the visible incarnation of federal loyalty, the Belgian experiment would be doomed to failure.'

Monarchies aside, most heads of state in parliamentary systems are elected, either by popular vote (e.g. Ireland) or by parliament (e.g. Israel). Alternatively, a special electoral college is used, often comprising the national legislature plus representatives from regional or local government (e.g. Germany).

Elected presidents in a parliamentary regime have more latitude than monarchs in addressing national issues though far less, of course, than chief executives in presidential government. Many presidents in parliamentary systems do occasionally use their public position to nudge the political agenda in a particular direction, especially when the national

BOX 16.7

Selecting the head of state in some parliamentary democracies

	Head of state	Method of selection	Tenure
Austria	President	Direct popular election by a two-round system	6 years
Canada	British monarch*	Heredity (eldest male)	Life
Germany	President	Election by a joint Bundestag and *Land* convention	5 years
India	President	Election by a college of federal and state assemblies	5 years
Spain	Monarch	Heredity (eldest male)	Life
United Kingdom	Monarch	Heredity (eldest male)	Life

* Represented in Canada by a governor general appointed for five years by the monarch on recommendation from Canada's prime minister.

interest and issues of integrity are involved. For example, in 2003 the Italian President Carlo Ciampi refused to sign into law a media bill which would have strengthened the commercial interests of the country's Prime Minister, Silvio Berlusconi. Such presidential interventions can earn respect as long as they are rare and based on an assessment of the national interest. But the situation is inherently delicate since the possibility of political influence itself depends on the perception that the president is above politics.

Semi-presidential government

Presidential and parliamentary government provide the pure models of the political executive. By contrast, the semi-presidential executive mixes both formats to produce a new system with its own characteristics. Specifically, **semi-presidential government** combines an elected president with a prime minister and cabinet accountable to parliament (Figure 16.4). Unlike the head of state in parliamentary systems, the president in a semi-presidential executive is *in* rather than *above* politics. As a two-headed system, the semi-presidential executive creates a division of authority within the executive itself and, for that reason, an invitation to struggle between president and prime minister.

Semi-presidential government, sometimes called the dual executive, combines an elected president performing political tasks with a prime minister who heads a cabinet accountable to parliament. The prime minister, usually appointed by the president, is responsible for day-to-day domestic government but the president retains an oversight role, responsibility for foreign affairs and can usually take emergency powers.

The French political scientist Maurice Duverger (1980) provided the original definition of semi-presidentialism. He defined the system thus:

> A political regime is considered semi-presidential if the constitution which established it combines three elements: (1) the president of the republic is elected by universal suffrage; (2) he possesses quite considerable powers; (3) he has opposite him, however, a prime minister and ministers who possess executive and governmental power and can stay in office only if the parliament does not show its opposition to them.

The 'quite considerable powers' of the president are variable but often include special responsibility for foreign affairs, appointing the prime minister, initiating referendums, vetoing legislation and dissolving the assembly. In theory, the president can offer leadership on foreign affairs while the prime minister addresses the intricacies of domestic politics through parliament.

Figure 16.4 Semi-presidential government

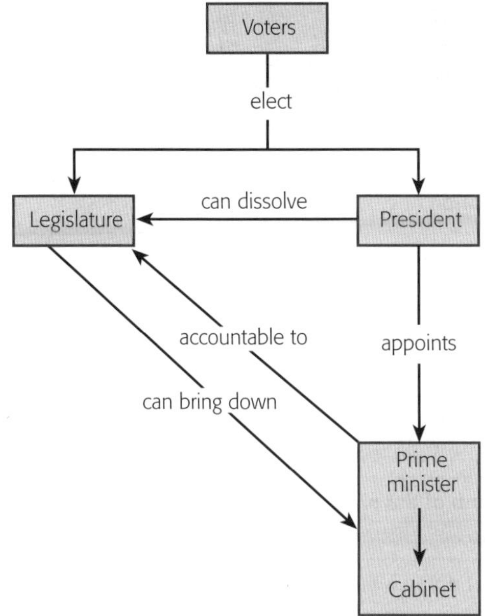

Note: Within semi-presidential government, Shugart and Carey (1992) distinguish between premier–presidential and president–parliamentary regimes. In the former, the cabinet is responsible to parliament; the president cannot dismiss ministers unilaterally. In the latter, the president as well as t he assembly exert authority over the cabinet's composition; and the president's position is therefore strengthened.

If the United States exemplifies the presidential system, the French Fifth Republic provides the model for the semi-presidential executive. The 1958 constitution establishing the new regime was designed to provide stable governance in the context of a political crisis caused by a divisive colonial war in Algeria and a rebellious army. In addition, the unstable Fourth Republic, which had experienced 23 prime ministers in its short 12-year life, provided a model to avoid.

The new constitution created a presidency fit for the dominating presence of its first occupant, General Charles de Gaulle (1890–1970). Regarding himself as national saviour, de Gaulle argued that 'power emanates directly from the people, which implies that the head of state, elected by the nation, is the source and holder of that power' (Knapp and Wright, 2006, p. 53). In office, de Gaulle's imperious style developed the office to, and perhaps even beyond, its constitutional limits.

Since a constitutional amendment of 1962, the president has been directly elected, thus fully establishing the semi-presidential form. The effect of this amendment, it is argued, was to create a powerful presidency where previously there had just been a powerful president. In a further amendment in 2000, the presidential term was reduced from seven years to five years. There are no limits on re-election.

The constitution certainly grants the French president extensive powers. The president:

- Is guarantor of national independence and the constitution;
- Takes emergency powers (not invoked since 1961);
- Heads the armed forces and chairs the main defence committee;
- Negotiates treaties;
- Calls referendums;
- Appoints some senior judges and civil servants;
- Presides over the Council of Ministers;
- Dissolves the National Assembly (but cannot veto legislation);
- Formally appoints (but cannot dismiss) the prime minister, in practice from the party winning assembly elections.

In pursuing these roles, the president is supported by an influential personal staff in the Élysée Palace. So far, all five presidents have sought to govern in expansive style, seeking to steer the ship of state rather than just to arbitrate conflicts emerging among the crew.

What of prime ministers in France's semi-presidential executive? Their main concern is domestic affairs, casually dismissed by de Gaulle as 'the price of milk'. Appointed by the president but accountable to parliament, the prime minister's task is rarely straightforward. He or she (Edith Cresson was PM 1991–92) directs the day-to-day work of the government, operating within the president's style and tone. Since the government remains accountable to parliament, much of the prime minister's work focuses on managing the National Assembly. The ability of the assembly to force the prime minister and the Council of Ministers to resign after a vote of censure provides the parliamentary component of the semi-presidential executive.

COUNTRY PROFILE

FRANCE

Form of government ■ a liberal democratic republic, headed by an elected president. The current republic, established in 1958, is the fifth republican regime since the revolution.

Legislature ■ weaker than in many liberal democracies. The lower chamber, the National Assembly, contains 577 directly elected members. The 331 members of the Senate are indirectly elected, a third at a time, through local government for a nine-year term (from 2010, to be reduced to six years with a half renewed every three years).

Executive ■ the semi-presidential executive combines a strong president, directly elected for a renewable five-year term, with a prime minister who leads a Council of Ministers accountable to the assembly.

Judiciary ■ French law is still based on the Napoleonic Codes (1804–11). The Constitutional Court has grown in significance during the Fifth Republic.

Electoral system ■ a two-round system is used for both presidential and assembly elections, with a majority vote needed for victory on the first round.

Party system ■ In the 2007 presidential election, Nicolas Sarkozy of the centre right was elected in a run-off with the socialist candidate, Ségolène Royal. Sarkozy, the son of a Hungarian immigrant father, became the first French president to be born after the second world war.

Population (annual growth rate): 60.9m (+0.3%)

World Bank income group: high income

Political Rights score: 

Civil Liberties score: 1

Human development index (rank/out of): 16/177

Freedom of the press index (rank/out of): 37/194

Ease of doing business index (rank/out of): 35/175

Note: For meaning and sources of scales and indexes, see p. xvi. In all cases a score and rank of 1 is 'best'.

Just how different is modern France? The case for French exceptionalism can be stated in three words: the French Revolution. The revolution created a distinctive ethos within the country, centred on the idea of the nation. Expressed through a distinct language and culture, the nation is the fundamental source of political authority.

The state stands above mere partial interests, defining the long-term national will. Like other states built on revolution, notably the United States, France is an ideal as well as a country. But whereas American ideals led to pluralism, the French state is expected to be the leading player, uniformly implementing the secular ideals of liberty, equality and fraternity. All citizens possess the same rights and obligations and it is the state's task both to secure the rights and to extract the obligations.

The country became more modern, urban and industrial after 1945, as French uniqueness declined. Retreat from empire left France, like Britain, as a middle-ranking power – albeit with a new base in the European Union. The creation of a new regional level of governance within France reduced the state's traditional centralization. Immigration from North Africa moderated the country's homogeneity, leading some to favour a more relaxed interpretation of citizenship. 'The revolutionary impulse is exhausted,' concluded Hayward (1994, p. 32).

Yet to portray France as just another democracy is to go too far. Inherited traditions still condition the way the country approaches its cosseted workforce, subsidized farmers and considerable but unequal affluence. Public discourse still assumes that the state must be capable of creating new jobs while simultaneously protecting existing workers. Sovereignty is still presented as a cardinal virtue, with the result that globalization (and the USA specifically) is seen more as threat than opportunity. *Dirigisme* (state direction), suggests Wright (1997), has evolved rather than disappeared. Even if *l'exception française* is a myth, the legend itself still gives French politics its distinctive flavour.

Further reading: Cole, Le Galès and Levy (2005), Knapp and Wright (2006), Stevens (2003).

SPOTLIGHT

The political executive in France

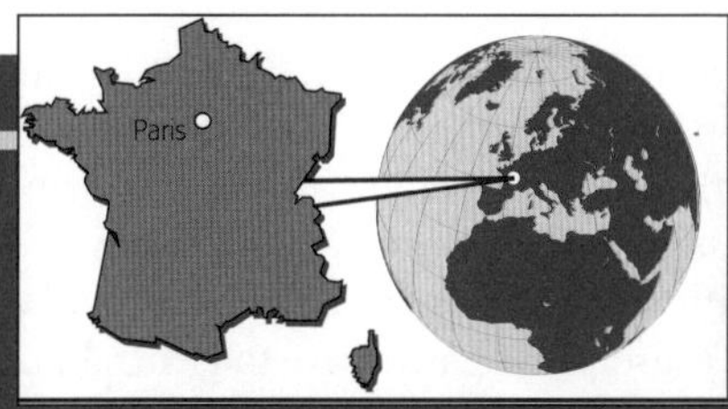

In France's semi-presidential executive, the crucial relationship is between the president, on the one hand, and prime minister and assembly, on the other. While the constitution may give control of foreign affairs to the president and reserve domestic policy to the prime minister, an interdependent world does not permit such pigeon-holing. France's relationship with the EU, for instance, encompasses both foreign and domestic affairs, complicating the decision-making process. Before one EU summit, Germany's chancellor insisted on meeting the French president and prime minister together, to speed negotiations. How then does France's complex political executive operate?

Presidents and prime ministers need to work in harmony, a task made easier when the party in the Élysée Palace also has a majority in the assembly. This has been the case for most of the Fifth Republic. Indeed, the reduction of the president's term to five years was partly an attempt to coordinate presidential and parliamentary election terms, limiting the likelihood of cohabitation.

When cohabitation does occur, as it has done three times since 1986, presidential power tends to shrink. In these circumstances, prime ministers assert their constitutional duty to 'determine and direct the policy of the nation'. Crucially, though, cohabitation has not led to a crisis of the regime. The Fifth Republic has delivered the stability that its architects intended. Just as the United States copes with power divided between the White House and Congress, so French experience confirms that the semi-presidential executive can provide stable government even when president and prime minister are drawn from different political blocs.

Cohabitation occurs in a semi-presidential executive when president and prime minister are drawn from different political camps. It intensifies competition between the two principals and places the president in the awkward position of leading both the nation and the opposition.

Cohabitation in the Fifth Republic, 1958–2006

	President	*Party*	*Prime minister*	*Party*
1986–1988	François Mitterrand	Socialist	Jacques Chirac	Gaullist
1993–1995	François Mitterrand	Socialist	Edouard Balladur	Gaullist
1997–2002	Jacques Chirac	Gaullist	Lionel Jospin	Socialist

Beneath the president and prime minister, the government's day-to-day political work is carried out by between 40 and 50 ministers. There are four main reasons, however, why this group lacks even the public collegiality displayed by members of the British cabinet:

- Most (though not all) governments in the Fifth Republic have been coalitions, with ministers drawn from more than one party
- the Council of Ministers (the cabinet), chaired by the president, is more ritual than discussion; its functioning resembles the American rather than the British equivalent
- ministers are given a detailed specification of their responsibilities on appointment and often come to the job with a background in its area, thus generating an expectation that they can function autonomously
- interventions by the prime minister and the president are often to resolve disputes rather than to form or impose an overall agenda

Ministerial autonomy is further enhanced by limited accountability to the assembly (ministers cannot be members of parliament though they do speak before it) and by a tradition of deferential treatment by the media, particularly on personal matters. These conditions encourage corruption, leading to Williams's description of France 'as the classic land of political scandal' (1970, p. 3).

Further reading: Elgie (2005), Godin and Chafer (2006), Hayward and Wright (2002).

Semi-presidential government has held particular appeal to European countries facing international difficulties. Finland found a semi-presidential system helpful in managing its sensitive relationship with its large Russian neighbour. And a dual executive also proved attractive to Central European states in the immediate aftermath of communism's collapse. As international pressures recede, however, so the president's star in this format of government tends to wane. In 2000, Finland modified its constitution to strengthen the parliamentary element (Nousiainen, 2001). Further, some post-communist countries, such as Hungary, have moved to a parliamentary form. The semi-presidential executive is more than a transitional device but it has not threatened the pre-eminence of parliamentary government in Europe.

The executive in authoritarian states

In authoritarian states, formal executive structures – the executive, legislature and the judiciary – are less well-developed than in democracies. The top office may consist of a presidency (as in many civilian regimes) or a ruling council (as in many military governments) but the central feature of the authoritarian executive is its lack of institutionalization. The leader seeks to concentrate power on himself and his supporters, not to distribute it among institutions. Jackson and Rosberg's idea of **personal rule** (1982), developed in the context of African politics, travels widely through the nondemocratic world. Politics takes precedence over government and personalities matter more than institutions: a feast of presidents but a famine of presidential systems.

This formula of strong politics amid weak institutions results in characteristic ailments, including struggles over succession, insufficient emphasis on policy, poor governance and even a danger of regime collapse. In particular, the lack of a succession procedure (excepting hereditary monarchies) can create a conflict among potential inheritors not just after the leader's exit but also in the run-up to it. Authoritarian leaders keep their job for just as long as they can ward off their rivals. They must monitor threats and be prepared to neuter those who are becoming too strong. Politics comes before policy.

Jackson and Rosberg (1982, p. 19) define **personal rule** as 'a system of relations linking rulers not with the "public" or even with the ruled but with patrons, associates, clients, supporters and rivals who constitute the "system". The system is "structured" not by institutions but by the politicians themselves. The fact that it is ultimately dependent upon persons rather than institutions is its essential vulnerability.'

The price of defeat, furthermore, is high; politics can be a matter of life and death. When an American president leaves office, he can retire to his library to write his memoirs but ousted dictators risk a harsher fate. By necessity, therefore, the governing style of non-democratic rulers inclines to the ruthless.

We will use post-colonial Africa, the Middle East and post-communist countries in central Asia to illustrate these themes, before turning to the executive under totalitarian rule.

Africa

In the authoritarian era before the 1990s, post-colonial Africa illustrated the importance of personal leadership in non-democratic settings. Leaders were adept at using the coercive and financial resources of the regime to reward their friends and punish their enemies. As Sandbrook (1985) wrote of Mobutu Sese Seko during his dictatorial tenure as President of Zaire (1965–97):

> No potential challenger is permitted to gain a power base. Mobutu's officials know that their jobs depend solely on the president's discretion. Frequently, Mobutu fires cabinet ministers, often without explanation. Everyone is kept off balance. Everyone must vie for his patronage.

In post-colonial Africa, as in most authoritarian regimes, personal rule was far from absolute. Inadequately accountable in a constitutional sense, many personal rulers were highly constrained by other political actors. These included the military, leaders of ethnic groups, landowners, the business class, the bureaucracy, multinational companies and even factions in the leader's own court. To survive, leaders had to distribute the perks of office so as to maintain a viable coalition of support drawn from these groups. Enemies could be bought off by allowing them a share of the pie but their slice must not become so large as to threaten the big man himself. Mobutu himself set out the ground rules: 'If you want to steal, steal a little in a nice way. But if you steal too much to become rich overnight, you'll be caught' (Gould, 1980, p. 485).

These domestic imperatives explain why presidents ignored the advocacy by international agencies of competitive markets. Presidents preferred to invest in their own political future rather than the long-term economic development of their country.

The Middle East

In the Middle East, personal rule remains central to authoritarian rule. Shahs, sheikhs and sultans continue to rule oil-rich kingdoms in traditional patriarchal style. 'Ruling' rather than 'governing' is the appropriate term. In Saudi Arabia, for instance, advancement within the ruling family depends less on merit than on proximity to the family's network of advisers, friends and guards. Public and private are interwoven, each forming part of the ruler's sphere. Government posts are not secure but are occupied on good behaviour, as demonstrated by unswerving loyalty to the ruler's personal interests.

Such systems of personal rule have survived for centuries, limiting the development of strong institutions. Leaving succession difficulties to one side, the paradox of Middle Eastern politics is that personal rule itself constitutes a stable regime, providing an exception to the general theme of instability in the authoritarian executive.

Central Asia

Personal rule also characterizes the post-communist states of central Asia such as Kyrgyzstan and Uzbekistan. While central Europe has moved in a democratic direction, many of the successor republics to the Soviet Union have seen the rise of authoritarian regimes with strong, personalized and non-accountable presidents. In these impoverished and mainly agricultural republics, where democracy has never flourished and experience of independent statehood is limited, rulers are concerned with power and voters with their daily struggle. Neither group cares greatly for structures of government.

In the central Asian republic of Uzbekistan, for example, the presidency is strongly personalized:

> Power resides as much in the person of the president as in the office. The Uzbek presidency is not just a formal power position; it is also the center of an extensive informal network of regionally based, patron–client ties. The president is, in effect, the chief patron (Easter, 1997).

The totalitarian executive

We might expect the institutions of government to have played a more central role in the totalitarian systems of fascism and communism. After all, these were political regimes par excellence, seeking to lead and transform society. But under fascism, at least, personal rule dominated.

In fascist thinking, the personal authority of the ruler rather than the institutions of state provided the driving force. The purpose of the executive was to realize the leader's vision. Once Hitler and Mussolini achieved power, state and party merged as personal vehicles of the supreme ruler. The leader defined the interests of the regime; duties owed to the dictator took priority over any obligations to state or party. In Nazi Germany, for example, the notorious SS (*Schutzstaffel*, protection units) began as a party security force but underwent a huge expansion after Hitler came to power, becoming the personal instrument of the Führer (Brooker, 2000, p. 136).

Nazi Germany, less so Mussolini's Italy, was a political regime in which power bases were established informally with Hitler acting as an arbiter of conflict among the barons beneath. Power was neither contained in institutions nor exercised through bureaucratic rules; had it been, the Führer's personal ascendancy would have been threatened.

The situation differed substantially in communist states. Most communist states did have a clear structure of government, resembling the parliamentary form (Figure 16.5). A presidium (equivalent to a cabinet) was headed by a chairperson (prime minister). This presidium was, in turn, an inner steering body of a larger Council of Ministers which was itself formally 'elected' by the Supreme Soviet (parliament). An honorific post of state president also existed.

But in practice the ruling communist party dominated the formal institutions of state; the key post was general secretary of the party, not chairman of the presidium. The party secretary often confirmed his supremacy by taking a state post, whether prime minister or president. However, power remained

Figure 16.5 Typical executive structure in communist states

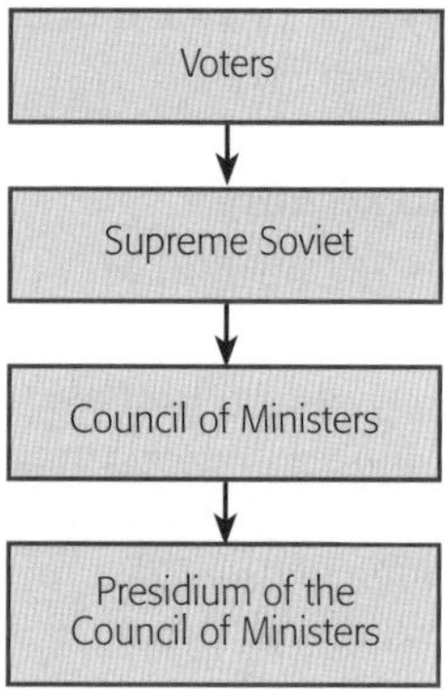

rooted in the party; if the top leader lost his position as party secretary, he was politically doomed.

China offers a partial exception to this picture of a party-dominated executive in communist states. Chinese politics has always been more fluid and personal than in other communist states; some past leaders have not occupied any formal positions at all, whether in the party or the government. As is customary in communist countries, the state is led by the party. But the party itself is divided into factions based on personality and patronage. It is these factions within the party which provide political glue, binding the actors together in a predictable but non-institutionalized way.

Thus the Chinese case returns us to the theme of personal rule in authoritarian regimes. In China's factional environment, the top figures require cunning and patronage to prosper. Indeed, the evidence from China confirms that even this massive communist state can be ruled in a highly personal way. As Saich (2004, p. 83) observes:

> Personal power and relations with powerful individuals are decisive throughout the Chinese political system. While this may decline as reforms become more institutionalized, most Chinese recognize that the best way to survive and flourish is to develop personal relationships (*guanxi*) with a powerful political patron.

Authoritarian rule and despotism

The personal basis of rule in most non-democratic regimes leads to an important question: are such states always likely to degenerate into despotism and even barbarism? Are the murderous excesses of twentieth-century dictators an inherent risk of failing to subject power to constitutional limits?

Certainly, some communist states fell victim to brutal tyranny, despite – or because of? – the strong organization provided by the communist party. The Soviet Union under Joseph Stalin was an extreme but important example. After Lenin's death in 1924, Stalin slowly acquired ascendancy over the party. He methodically picked off the other party leaders, becoming undisputed ruler of the Soviet Union by 1929 and remaining so until his death in 1953. Having risen to power through the party, he eventually reshaped it into one of his personal instruments, alongside the political police and the state bureaucracy. Stalin's method of rule was fierce indeed:

> In the Great Terror of 1937–38, the political police arrested some five million people, executed over 800,000 of them and incarcerated most of the remainder in prisons or labour camps. Among the victims were a large majority of the party's Central Committee and more than half the delegates to the most recent Party Congress. The Terror destroyed the party as an independent political entity; it was now officially described as a party of Lenin–Stalin followers (Brooker, 2000, p. 138).

One-man rule and extreme leadership cults were features of many other communist states, including Mao Zedong in China, Castro in Cuba, Ho Chi Minh in Vietnam, Tito in Yugoslavia, Ceauçescu in Romania and Kim Il Sung in North Korea. And such cults of personality were often linked to extreme brutality, albeit rarely on the scale of Stalin's Russia.

But not all totalitarian, and still less all authoritarian, regimes descended into barbarity. After all, Stalin drew not just on communist ideology and party organization but also on Russia's highly autocratic history. Elsewhere, communist rule was less severe. In Eastern Europe, rulers in the late communist period sought to soften the harshness of Soviet domination. Some national leaders were anonymous party functionaries. János Kádár, General Secretary of the Hungarian Communist Party from 1956 to 1988, rode the tramcar to work each day, unrecognized by his people. Overall, the communist experience suggests that personal despotism is far from an inevitable consequence of authoritarian rule.

In any case, many non-communist authoritarian rulers have lacked the means of social control needed to indulge in Stalinist terror. The experience of the Middle East suggests that personal rule is not usually despotic. There, at least, it has delivered an often balanced, if rarely progressive, form of governance.

The executive in illiberal democracies

The characteristic form of the executive in illiberal democracies is presidential rather than parliamentary. Whereas a prime minister in a parliamentary regime is traditionally first among equals, a presidential regime provides a natural platform for a leader who seeks to set himself apart from – and above – all others. In an illiberal democracy, the president operates without the full set of constitutional restraints which contain the chief executive of a liberal democracy. Instead, the president uses his direct mandate from the people and his claim to act in their long-term interests to cast a shadow over competing institutions such as the courts and the legislature without, however, reducing these bodies to token status.

Post-communist Russia provides an example of strong executive power in an illiberal democracy, with the increasing concentration of authority under President Putin leading some observers to question whether Russia should still be considered a democracy of any sort. Formally, Russia is a semi-presidential regime arranged along French lines, with a directly-elected president coexisting with a chairman of the government (that is, prime minister) who is nominated by the president and approved by the Duma (lower house).

In some minor respects, the Russian president's position is only slightly stronger than that of an American president. Both are limited to two four-year terms in office but the Russian leader can stand again after a term out. Both are subject to impeachment but the threshold is more demanding in Russia: a two-thirds majority in both parliamentary chambers and confirmation by the courts. President Yeltsin narrowly avoided impeachment in 1999.

In reality, though, the Russian president can grasp the levers of power more easily than either an American or a French president. Under the 1993 constitution, the president acts as head of state, commander-in-chief and guarantor of the constitution. In the latter capacity, he can suspend the decisions of other state bodies. He can also issue decrees, though these can be overridden by legislation. In contrast to most semi-presidential systems, the president is empowered to remove ministers without parliamentary consent; and does so.

Russia's president is also charged with 'defining the basic directions of the domestic and foreign policy of the state' and with 'ensuring the coordinated functioning and collaboration of bodies of state power'. These broad duties affirm Russia's long tradition of executive power, a norm which both predates and was reinforced by the communist era. Strong government is regarded as a necessary source of effective leadership for a large and sometimes lawless country.

Administrative means give effect to this cultural emphasis. Political power is exercised through state institutions which, unlike federal agencies in the USA, do not regard themselves as beholden to the legislature. The president is directly supported by numerous agencies, including directorates covering such areas as constitutional affairs, domestic policy and control. About 2,000 staff in the Presidential Executive Office provide immediate support, offering a resource that is comparable in scope and effectiveness to that available to an American president through his Executive Office. These organizations can be restructured at the president's discretion. In addition, representatives of the Russian president sit on many state and parliamentary bodies while the president himself plays a leading role in federal–provincial relations, not least through the State Council (Box 16.8).

'The federal presidency is hegemonic', says Willerton (2005, p. 23), 'not only because its position is legally superior to that of other institutions, but because it possesses considerable independence and freedom of manoeuvre'. If there is any comparison at all with French semi-presidentialism, it is with the early days of the Fifth Republic, when de Gaulle was seen (and saw himself) as the guarantor

BOX 16.8

Institutional support for the Russian president

Presidential Executive Office	Supports the president in the execution of his duties. Drafts laws and decrees and oversees their implementation.
Security Council	Oversees the defence of the country against internal and external threats.
State Council	A forum for discussion with regional leaders.
Presidential Commissions	Six, covering such topics as cooperation with other states.
Presidential Councils	Ten, covering such topics as enhancing the judiciary and combating corruption.

Source: President of Russia (2006).

of political order. But where the French president has since lost some ground as the country's politics has become more conventional, Vladimir Putin's tenure of Russia's presidency saw a deliberate strengthening of executive power in the Kremlin. It remains to be discovered whether this strategy served the interests of a 'dictatorship of law' or of dictatorship pure and simple.

With its heavy artillery of supporting institutions, Russia's presidency is untypical of executive rule in illiberal democracies. Most often, illiberal democracy is found in smaller countries in Africa and Latin America, where the formal structure is presidential rather than semi-presidential but where presidential authority operates in a more personal way, often linked to effective use of patronage and a populist style. For instance, many African countries continue to find themselves locked into a situation where even elected presidents rule through personal relationships, preventing the growth of strong institutions that might encourage a transition from an illiberal to a liberal democracy. As Hyden (2006, p. 114) writes:

> African rulers continue to see their interests as tied to local communities rather than to systems of abstract rule. They act at the level of the state as they do in their community. They rely on investments in personal reciprocity that are self-enforcing and hence not a matter for a court or any other third party to judge. They act in ways that go contrary to the principles of transparency and accountability.

In the illiberal democracies of Latin America, too, accountability tends to be **vertical** (between the president and the voters) rather than **horizontal** (between the president and other political institutions such as the courts and congress). The concentration of authority in the presidency is both justified and reinforced by the weakness of other institutions. However, vertical accountability provides a broad and blunt device for holding the executive to account; it is horizontal accountability that can pin down a president in specific areas, thus moving democracy in a liberal direction (Mainwaring and Welna, 2003).

Vertical accountability exists when an actor at one level is overseen or is subject to sanction by an actor at another level. An example is a president subject to periodic re-election. **Horizontal accountability** exists when oversight or superintendence operates at the same level. An example is a president whose actions are subject to judicial review.

'US presidentialism', writes Philip (2003, p. 24), 'has been historically based on ideas of checks and balances, while Latin American presidentalism was often based on a search for leadership'. Philip cites the campaign slogan of a Brazilian politician from the 1940s: 'I steal but I get things done'. Even in recent times, many presidents have stolen from their own constitution, modifying its content to permit both their own re-election and government by decree. The leader still stands at the top of the tree, preventing both regression to dictatorship and progression to liberal democracy.

Learning Resources for Chapter 16

Next step

Lijphart (1992) remains an excellent collection on parliamentary and presidential government.

Further reading

Much work on the executive has focused on presidential government (including Latin America): for instance, Linz and Valenzuela (1994), Mainwaring and Shugart (1997) and Shugart and Carey (1992). On semi-presidential government, the original source is Duverger (1980). Elgie (1999, 2001) and Moestrup and Elgie (2005) offer comparative perspectives. On the American presidency, see Neustadt (1991), Rose (2000) and helpful collections by Nelson (2005) and Ellis and Nelson (2006). Comparative but contrasting studies of parliamentary government include Müller and Strøm (2000a), Rhodes (2006b) and, on presidentialization, Poguntke and Webb (2005). Helms (2005) compares the United States, Britain and Germany, thus providing a contrast between presidential and parliamentary systems. The executive in post-communist Europe is covered in White *et al.* (2003); see Willerton (2005) for Russia. On personal rule, Jackson and Rosberg (1982) is the classic analysis, using African examples; Bill and Springborg (1999) examine the Middle East. Brooker (1995) assesses twentieth-century dictatorships.

Internet sources

AmericanPresident.org
Covers the history and functions of the American presidency
http://www.americanpresident.org/

Cabinet Office, UK
An informative site, not least on cabinet committees
http://www.cabinetoffice.gov.uk/

Center on Institutions and Governance, University of Berkeley
Research and education on the origins, effects, and evolution of institutions
http://igov.berkeley.edu/about.html

President of Russia
An informative site
http://www.kremlin.ru/eng/

Chapter 17
Public management and administration

The study of public administration and management is concerned with the networks of central departments and public agencies that underpin the political executive. These networks provide advice to ruling politicians before policy is made and help to implement decisions once reached. The department secretary offering advice to the minister, the inspector checking tax returns, the regulator monitoring food safety, the official making judgements on patent applications, the health officer trying to implement a national anti-obesity strategy – all are part of the complex operation that is modern government.

Traditionally, the study of public administration and management focused on the central **bureaucracy**: the permanent salaried officials employed in central government departments to advise on, and administer, government policy. These elite officials, and the ministries they occupy, remain of obvious importance but attention increasingly focuses on the wider networks beyond: in semi-independent agencies, local governments and even the non-governmental organizations to which the delivery of public programmes is increasingly subcontracted. For the time being, at least, the emphasis is as much on managing networks as on advising ministers.

A chapter on public management and administration must therefore address both the old and the new agendas. We begin by examining the evolution of the public sector, reviewing the forces shaping its development, before turning to the intricate organization of the contemporary public sector and the resulting issues of accountability raised by this complexity. We then discuss new public management, a philosophy which seeks to escape from traditional notions of bureaucracy, and we conclude by examining public management in authoritarian states and illiberal democracies.

Bureaucracy is, literally, rule by officials. The word 'bureau' comes from the Old French term *la bure*, meaning the brown woollen cloth on which the king's administrators laid out their accounts. The second half of the word comes from the Greek *kratos*, meaning rule, just as in demo*cracy*. Today, the bureaucracy refers to the salaried officials who conduct the detailed business of public administration, advising on and applying policy decisions.

Evolution of the public sector

To appreciate modern bureaucracy, we must consider what preceded it. As with other aspects of government, the precursors varied between Europe and the New World. In Europe, clerical servants were originally agents of the royal household, serving under the personal instruction of the ruling monarch (Raadschelders and Rutgers, 1996). Many features of modern bureaucracies – regular salaries, pensions, open recruitment – arose from a successful attempt to overcome this idea of public employment as personal service to the monarch.

Indeed, the evolution of royal households into twentieth-century bureaucracies was a massive transformation, intimately linked to the rise of the

BOX 17.1

Max Weber on bureaucracy

The German sociologist Max Weber (1864–1920) conceived of bureaucracy as a structured hierarchy in which salaried officials reach rational decisions by applying explicit rules to the facts before them. His model contains five features:

- Bureaucracy involves a carefully defined division of tasks.
- Authority is impersonal, vested in the rules that govern official business. Decisions are reached by methodically applying rules to particular cases; private motives are irrelevant.
- People are recruited to serve in the bureaucracy based on proven or at least potential competence.
- Officials who perform their duties competently have secure jobs and salaries. Competent officials can expect promotion according to seniority or merit.
- The bureaucracy is a disciplined hierarchy in which lower officials are subject to the authority of their superior.

modern state (Hyden, 1997). Today, we take the features of bureaucratic organization for granted, and even react against them, but in the early twentieth century, the form was strikingly new: a phenomenon to be both admired and feared. The analysis presented by Max Weber exemplified this perspective, providing the traditional hierarchical view of public administration against which the newer ideas of networks and governance have been formed (Box 17.1)

Weber's central claim was that bureaucracy made administration more efficient; he believed that it was the means by which the techniques of modern industry could be brought to bear on civil affairs:

> The fully developed bureaucratic apparatus compares with other organizations exactly as does the machine with non-mechanical modes of production. Precision, speed, clarity, knowledge of files, continuity, discretion, unity, strict subordination, reduction of friction and of material and personal costs – these are raised to the optimum point in the strictly bureaucratic administration (quoted in Kahlberg, 2005, p. 199).

Like many modern devices, bureaucracy brought the risk of dominating its supposed masters. Weber's contribution was to pose the question of the relationship between bureaucracy and democracy, a concern that inspired much twentieth-century discussion.

In the New World, however, civil service development was more pragmatic. Lacking the European state tradition, public administration was initially considered to be a routine application of political directives. In the United States, the original philosophy was that of governance by the common man; almost every citizen, it was assumed, was qualified for almost every public job. The notion of a professional civil service was considered somewhat elitist and undemocratic (Christensen and Peters, 1999, p. 100).

This populist theory of public administration conveniently underpinned the **spoils system**, a term deriving from the phrase 'to the victor, the spoils'. The spoils system continued at least until 1883 when the Pendleton Act created a Civil Service Commission to recruit and regulate federal employees. So where a **merit system** had emerged in Europe in reaction to monarchy, in the USA it supplanted spoils.

In a **spoils system**, successful candidates distribute government jobs to those with the foresight to support the winning candidate. In nineteenth-century America, the election of a new president led to a virtually complete turnover of employees in what was then a much smaller federal government. In a **merit system**, public employees are recruited by competitive examination.

In the twentieth century, Western bureaucracies reached their zenith. The depression and two world wars vastly increased government intervention in society. The welfare state, completed in Western and especially Northern Europe in the decades following the Second World War, required a massive bureaucratic apparatus to distribute grants, allowances and pensions in accordance with complex eligibility conditions set by politicians. By 1980, public employment accounted for almost a third of the total workforce in Britain and

Scandinavia, though much of this expansion occurred at local level.

However, the final quarter of the twentieth century witnessed declining faith in government and bureaucracy. Where Weber had lauded the efficiency of the administrative machine, critics now judged that civil servants engaged in unproductive games to increase the budgets and staffing of their particular sections (Niskanen, 1971). More to the point, public finances deteriorated in the 1970s. Seizing on this fiscal crisis, right-wing politicians such as Margaret Thatcher called for, and to an extent delivered, not just a reduced role for the state but also a change in the style of bureaucratic operation away from strict Weberian guidelines. Mrs Thatcher knew what she wanted to achieve and sought to refocus the bureaucracy on execution rather than advice (Page and Wright, 2006).

More generally, the policy-forming community in many liberal democracies has widened, diminishing any monopoly which civil servants once exerted over policy advice and encouraging them to focus rather more on delivery – and specifically on the three Es of economy, efficiency and effectiveness (Box 17.2).

In the twenty-first century, therefore, senior civil servants must be skilled in the arts of both government and governance. Facing conflicting expectations derived from management philosophies old and new, they must aim to

- Show flexibility while abiding by rules;
- Deliver results while working within set procedures;
- Distil policy advice for ministers while managing complex networks;
- Act decisively while consulting widely;
- Help ministers realize political goals while also remaining neutral.

BOX 17.2

The three Es: economy, efficiency and effectiveness

	Definition	Objective
Economy	Minimize inputs	Spend less
Efficiency	Achieve maximum output of goods and services for a given input	Spend well
Effectiveness	Ensure that policy achieves its goals	Spend wisely

Source: National Audit Office (2006)

Recruitment to the public sector

Recruitment to bureaucracies has evolved in tandem with the development of the civil service itself. The shift from patrimonial to Weberian bureaucracies was a transition from recruitment by personal links with the ruler to open selection on merit. At least in theory, jobs became available to the whole population. Even though these reforms occurred in most democracies as long ago as the late nineteenth century, recruitment to the civil service remains an important theme. Selection methods and employee profiles are scrutinized more carefully than in the private sector. Further, what counts as 'merit' still varies between countries, revealing contrasting ideas of a civil servant's role.

Britain exemplifies a **unified** (or generalist) tradition. Indeed, it pushes the cult of the amateur to extremes. Administration is seen as the art of judgement, born of intelligence and honed by experience. Specialist knowledge should be sought by bureaucrats but then treated with scepticism; experts should be on tap but not on top. Recruiters look for general ability, not technical expertise. All-round ability should enable successful candidates to acquire or at least interpret whatever technical knowledge is needed; the key requirement is not knowledge but the ability to learn. For the same reason, a good administrator is expected to be able to serve in a variety of departments and will be the more rounded for having doing so.

An alternative method of pursuing the unified approach is to recruit to a *corps* (body) of civil servants rather than to a specific job in a ministry. The French civil service, for example, recruits civil ser-

In a **unified** bureaucracy, recruitment is to the civil service as a whole, not to a specific job within it. Administrative work is conceived as requiring intelligence and education but not technical knowledge. By contrast, a **departmental** approach recruits people with technical backgrounds to a specific department or job.

vants through competitive examinations to such bodies as the Diplomatic Corps and the Finance Inspectorate. Although recruitment is to a specific *corps*, it is in reality as much to an elite which encompasses both public and private realms. Even within the civil service, more than a third of *corps* members are working away from their home *corps* at any one time. At its highest levels, the French bureaucracy is clearly generalist albeit within a *corps* framework that provides more of a bow to specialized training than is offered in Britain.

Some unified civil services stress one particular form of technical expertise: law. In many European countries with a codified law tradition, a legal training remains common among higher bureaucrats. Germany is a good illustration. Over 60 per cent of top German civil servants are lawyers, compared to just 20 per cent in the United States. The German emphasis on law has influenced several other countries, including Denmark and Japan.

In a **departmental** (or specialist) system, recruiters follow a different philosophy from Britain's generalist approach or the French *corps*. Rather than seeking generalists, they look for specialist experts for individual departments, with more movement in and out of the civil service at a variety of levels. The Finance Ministry will recruit economists and the Department of Health will employ staff with medical training. Recruitment is to particular posts, not to an elite civil service or a *corps*.

This emphasis on a specific job is common in countries with a weak state in which the administration lacks the status produced by centuries of service to pre-democratic rulers. The United States, New Zealand and the Netherlands are examples. In the Netherlands, each department sets its own recruitment standards, normally requiring prior training and expertise in its own area. Once appointed, mobility within the civil service itself is limited; staff who remain in public service usually stay in the same department for their entire career (Andeweg and Irwin, 2002, p. 176). The notion of recruiting talented young graduates to an elite, unified civil service, or even to a *corps*, is weak or non-existent.

Organization of the public sector

Here we examine the detailed organization of central government activity, looking at how the cogs of the administrative machine are arranged. Although structures – and labels – vary by country, we can distinguish between three main kinds of organization (Box 17.3).

The first and most important unit is the department (or ministry) where policy is made. In nearly all countries, a dozen or so established departments form the stable core of central government, covering such areas as finance, defence and foreign affairs.

A second unit comprises the divisions (or sections, bureaus) into which departments are divided. These are the government's operating units, acting at the level where expertise resides and in which detailed policy is both formed and applied. To complicate matters, these divisions are sometimes called 'departments' in countries where the larger unit is termed a 'ministry'.

The third unit is the non-departmental body operating at one or more removes from departments. These semi-detached organizations combine public funding with operational autonomy; they are growing in number and significance.

Departments

Government departments (or ministries) form the centrepiece of modern bureaucracies. Here we find the bodies pursuing the traditional tasks of government. Their number varies but is typically between 12 and 24. The United States has 15 departments, each headed by a Secretary of State appointed by the president. The Netherlands has 13, the United Kingdom 20, Canada over 20 and New Zealand more than 30.

Most countries followed a similar sequence in introducing departments (Figure 17.1). The first to be established were those performing core state functions such as finance, law and order, defence and foreign affairs. These ministries are often as ancient as the state itself. In the United States, for instance, the Department of State and the Treasury each date from 1789. Later, countries added extra ministries to deal with new functions. Initially these were usually agriculture, and commerce and labour. Later in the twentieth century came welfare departments dealing with social security, education, health and housing. More recent additions include the environment and, in a few countries, security.

Reflecting Weber's principles, departments are usually organized in a clear hierarchy (Figure 17.2). A single minister sits at the pinnacle albeit often supported in large departments by junior ministers with divisional responsibilities. A senior civil servant, often known as the secretary or vice min-

BOX 17.3

The organization of government: departments, divisions and agencies

Government department
An administrative unit over which a minister exercises direct management control. Usually structured as a formal hierarchy and often established by statute.

Division
An operating unit of a department, responsible to the minister but often with considerable independence in practice, especially in the USA.

Non-departmental public body
Operates at one or more removes from the government, in an attempt to provide management flexibility and political independence. Sometimes called quangos – a term of American origin that originally meant a quasi non-governmental organization but which is often now taken to mean a quasi-governmental organization.

Figure 17.1 Founding of federal departments in Canada and the USA

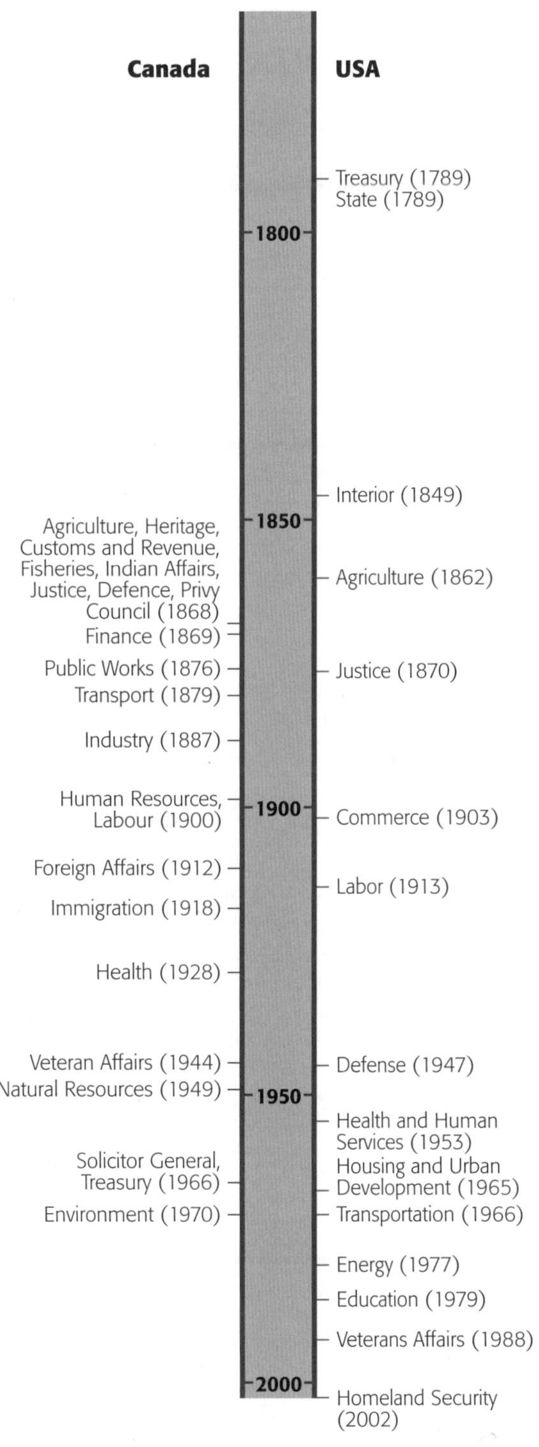

Sources: Rockman (2000); Tardi (2002), pp. 302–3.

DEBATE

SHOULD AFFIRMATIVE ACTION BE USED TO OBTAIN A REPRESENTATIVE BUREAUCRACY?

> You do not take a person who, for years, has been hobbled by chains and liberate him, bring him up to the starting line of a race and then say, 'you are free to compete with all the others', and still justly believe that you have been completely fair. Thus it is not enough just to open the gates of opportunity. All our citizens must have the ability to walk through those gates (President Lyndon Johnson, 1965).

In liberal democracies, a top civil servant is typically a white male graduate from a middle- or upper-class family that was itself active in public affairs (Aberbach *et al.*, 1981, p. 80). These findings have disturbed advocates of a representative bureaucracy such as Kingsley (1944). So should recruitment on merit be modified by affirmative action in favour of under-represented groups such as ethnic minorities and women?

YES

Three arguments support the thesis that a bureaucracy should reflect the social profile of the population:

- Civil servants whose work involves direct contact with specific groups will perform better at the job if they also belong to that category. A shared language is the most obvious example (e.g. Spanish-speakers in the USA).
- A civil service balanced between particular religions and regions may encourage stability in divided societies such as Iraq.
- A diverse and representative civil service, involving participation by all major social groups, should enhance the acceptability of decisions.

Affirmative action, in the sense of giving preference to the members of under-represented groups, is the only effective solution to the problem. Such a policy is justified because it counters the legacy of past discrimination.

Visible employment of minorities in the public sector will have a positive demonstration effect across the labour market, including private companies.

Positive discrimination will only be needed for a transitional period because, once a representative bureaucracy is established, it will maintain itself naturally as minorities emulate existing role models.

NO

The principle of recruitment on merit is fundamental to public administration and should not be abandoned in favour of social engineering. The public interest is best served by selecting the best people for the job, irrespective of their background.

The correct solution to under-representation is not affirmative action but improving the qualifications of the excluded groups. Affirmative action in the weaker sense of additional encouragement for minorities to apply for jobs can be adopted without embracing positive discrimination (i.e. lowering entry standards for particular groups).

Positive discrimination creates two additional problems. First, those denied jobs because they belong to a majority group are naturally resentful, especially if they are themselves drawn from the less advantaged section of their group. Second, those who are accepted just because they come from a minority background are placed in an awkward position which saps rather than builds confidence.

In practice, the main beneficiaries of affirmative action are the better-resourced members of minority groups who may not need an artificial lift anyway. In other words, the policy does not reach those who need it most.

ASSESSMENT

In the 1970s and 1980s, considerable efforts were made in the United States to ensure that staff profiles matched those of the wider population. Canadian governments, concerned since the 1960s to improve recruitment from French-speakers, also extended their recruitment efforts. However, such schemes never achieved the same popularity in Europe, perhaps because they would have involved accepting the inadequacy of the constitutional requirement of neutrality imposed on some civil services there.

Further reading

Curry and West (1996), Kennedy-Dubourdieu (2006), van der Meer and Roborgh (1996), Wise (2003).

Figure 17.2 The structure of a typical government department

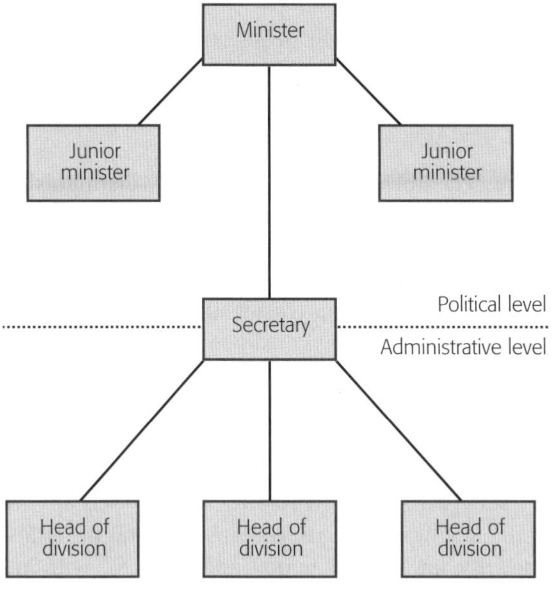

ister, is responsible for administration and providing the crucial bridge between political and bureaucratic levels.

Divisions

Departments are typically arranged into several divisions or sections, each responsible for an aspect of the organization's work. Thus an Education Department might have separate divisions for primary, secondary and higher education – and, in practice, for many other aspects of its work. Divisions are the operating units of departments, the sections within which the work gets done. They are the workhorses of government, the store of its experience and, in practice, the site where many important decisions are reached. Divisions are the state's engine room.

In some democracies, divisions acquire added importance because they are partially autonomous from their parent department. The extreme case is the USA, whose bureaucracy is the great exception to Weber's principle of hierarchy in departments. Even in their formal structure, American departments are more like multinational corporations, containing many divisions jostling within a single shell. The departments are merely the wrapping round a collection of disparate divisions and it is these bureaus which form the main operating units of the federal government (Box 17.4).

Reporting formally to the president, bureau chiefs spend much of their time ensuring their operational independence from the White House. Congress, not the president, creates and funds bureaus. And what Congress gives it can (and occasionally does) take away. The autonomy of bureaus within American departments is a major and often underestimated reason why American presidents experience such difficulty in imposing their will on Washington's complex political process.

Even in governments with more hierarchical departments, it would be naïve to suppose that working practices correspond exactly to organization charts. Rarely does information move smoothly up and down the administrative pyramid. For instance, the 2,000 divisions of the German federal ministries possess a concentration of expertise that enables them to block or at least circumvent reforms proposed from on high. A monopoly of knowledge and control over implementation combine to deliver the potential to neutralize change. In most liberal democracies, divisions

BOX 17.4

Agencies within the Department of Health and Human Services, USA

Administration for Children and Families
Administration on Aging
Agency for Healthcare Research and Quality
Agency for Toxic Substances and Disease Registry
Centers for Disease Control and Prevention
Centers for Medicare & Medicaid Services
Food and Drug Administration
Health Resources and Services Administration
Indian Health Service
National Institutes of Health
Substance Abuse and Mental Health Services

Source: Department of Health and Human Services (2006).

within departments also possess their own ethos derived from long experience with their area. This in-house view breeds a natural cynicism towards the latest political initiative and the top minister may need to circumvent divisional resistance by seeking support from political advisers.

Non-departmental public bodies

So far, we have considered government ministries and the divisions nested within them. But there is another type of public organization which is growing in importance: the non-departmental public body. The essential feature of these entities is that they operate at one remove from government departments, with a formal relationship of at least semi-independence. Such bodies occupy an ambivalent position, created and funded by the government, but in contrast to divisions within a department they are free from day-to-day ministerial control. Once appointed by the government, the members of such boards are expected to operate with considerable autonomy.

Throughout the democratic world, non-departmental bodies are expanding in number, complicating not just the academic task of mapping government but also the practical job of ensuring that the government as a whole acts coherently. Modern governance cannot be understood without delving deeper into the ecology of these organizations.

Non-departmental bodies have long been prominent in the United States where 56 'independent establishments and government corporations' range alphabetically from the Africa Development Foundation to the US Postal Service. Scandinavian countries, notably Sweden, also rely on non-departmental bodies to implement policy set by the ministry. In Sweden, government departments are small in size and ministers exercise little practical authority over the implementation of policy. Rather, a network of independent and relatively autonomous central boards – such as the Social Welfare Board, the National Labour Market Board and the National Pensions Board – executes policy (Arter, 1999, p. 154).

Non-departmental public bodies are established for a range of reasons including:

- To provide protection from political interference in day-to-day operations;
- To operate with more flexibility (and at lower cost) than would be acceptable for a division of a ministry;
- To acknowledge the professional status and autonomy of their staff;
- As a response to short-term pressure to do something about a problem.

The classification in Box 17.5 distinguishes between four kinds of non-departmental body: state-owned enterprises, service delivery agencies, regulatory agencies and advisory bodies. In many English-speaking democracies, the balance between these formats changed considerably in and after the 1980s. Specifically, privatization eliminated many state-owned enterprises while demand for regulatory agencies increased. As a result, the shape of the public sector underwent considerable alteration.

A **state-owned enterprise** (SOE) is – perhaps we should say 'was' – a government corporation established by law to sell goods and services, with no private shareholders. Examples include Canada's Crown Corporations, Britain's nationalized industries and New Zealand's SOEs such as Mighty River Power Limited. Although these public corporations were supposed to operate at arm's length from government, political interference often led to overstaffing and under-investment. In Britain, most government corporations were sold back to the private sector by Conservative governments between 1979 and 1997, a policy that has now been emulated elsewhere.

Yet the privatization earthquake has certainly not destroyed the role of the state in society; rather, it has reshaped the landscape of regulation. Ownership and control have given way to supervision. Today, the most important non-departmental bodies are not government corporations but agencies: public organizations operating separately from departments but charged (normally by statute) either with delivering public services or with regulating an aspect of social life in which a public interest is at stake.

Service delivery agencies cover such activities as gathering intelligence, managing public buildings and providing driving licences. According to the school of new public management (p. 366), specialist agencies, operating in a businesslike manner free from detailed political interference, should be more efficient at supplying services than a division of a government department.

BOX 17.5

Types of non-departmental public body

	Definition	Comment
State-owned enterprise (SOE)	A government corporation established by statute to trade goods or services	The mail service is still state-owned in many countries
Service delivery agency	Provides a specific service, usually to end-users	Many welfare programmes are delivered in this way
Regulatory agency	Oversees a specific sector by establishing standards and monitoring compliance	Consumer safety; regulation of the nuclear power industry; election commissions
Advisory body	Provides expertise and recommendations to government departments	Scientific research councils; advisory bodies on the arts; ad hoc groups advising on specific issues

Regulatory agencies supervise natural monopolies (e.g. water supply) and such activities as adoption, broadcasting, elections, food standards and nuclear energy. Regulatory agencies are increasing in nearly all liberal democracies, partly to balance risks which cannot be well-judged by the private sector. For example, weighing the benefits of introducing a new drug against the danger of side effects is a task for public-minded experts rather than for self-interested drug companies or even busy politicians. Britain now has well over 100 regulatory bodies, employing over 20,000 people and costing around £1 billion per year. The hope, at least partly reflected in reality, is that regulatory agencies will act as a buffer between the government and the regulated bodies, reducing the excessive intervention which held back many state-owned enterprises.

The media entrepreneur Rupert Murdoch (1997) claimed in a lively speech that regulation represents socialism's comeback trail: 'socialism is alive and well, and living in regulatory agencies'. Murdoch alleges that this policing is performed by a 'new class' of professional regulators (compare Djilas, 1955):

> It is the self-interest of this bureaucratic class that drives neosocialism. These are the people who benefit from proliferating regulations because they administer them. They want to see the nanny state, because they are the nannies. They want to see 'politics in command,' because they are the commanders – elected and unelected.

Unsurprisingly, Murdoch omitted to mention the danger of agencies coming to serve the interests of those they supervise. **Regulatory capture** has been widely observed, not least with state-level utility commissions in the United States (Wilson, 1989).

Reflecting their importance, government corporations and agencies are usually established by a specific statute (i.e. law). However, ministers also set up (and occasionally dissolve) external **advisory bodies** to provide additional expertise to that available in a department. Even if many of these councils do outlast their usefulness, ministers seem to find them indispensable in providing information on specialized topics. In general terms, then, charting the non-departmental public bodies in any liberal democracy

Regulatory capture arises when public agencies created to regulate a particular industry come to serve the interests of those they supervise.

confirms the complexity of contemporary governance and gives the lie to any simplistic claims of a diminished role for the state.

Control and accountability

The relationship between politicians and senior administrators has always been sensitive. Traditionally, the problem was posed as one of ensuring political control over non-elected officials: how could civil servants be prevented from obstructing the goals of legitimate and often radical governments? The problem of controlling bureaucratic power in a democracy was a particular concern of Max Weber. He identified the danger of public servants coming to dominate their elected masters, suggesting that

> under normal conditions, the power position of a fully developed bureaucracy is always overwhelming. The 'political master' finds himself in the position of the 'dilettante' who stands opposite the 'expert', facing the trained official who stands within the management of administration (quoted in Kahlberg, 2005, p. 211).

Today, Weber's insight is widely accepted. Commentators recognize that the bureaucracy's expertise, permanence, scale and control of implementation mean that it is bound to be more than a mechanical conduit for political directives. Senior public employees – department secretaries, heads of divisions, chairs of non-departmental public bodies – are invariably in a position to influence and elaborate policy. The contemporary response to this reality has been to reframe the issue as one of **accountability** rather than control (Mulgan, 2003). Increasingly, the philosophy is to encourage civil servants to defend their actions after the fact rather than to seek pre-emptive control over the actions themselves. In this way, accountability both acknowledges and potentially defuses Weber's fear of bureaucratic power – a neat move all round (Bovens, 2006).

> **Accountability** can be used narrowly, to refer to a reporting requirement ('to be called to account') or more broadly as a synonym for responsibility ('to be held to account'). In the latter sense, to be accountable is to be held responsible for one's actions by and often before another body. Accountability is a recent form of delegated authority which seeks to reconcile bureaucratic authority with political oversight.

BOX 17.6

Multiple accountabilities: deputy ministers (DMs) in Canada*

Accountable to	Why?
Prime Minister	The PM appoints the DM
Minister	The DM is required to assist and serve the minister
Clerk of the Privy Council	The Clerk heads the Public Service and acts as the PM's DM
Treasury Board	DMs report to the Treasury Board on resource management
Public Services Commission	DMs report to the Public Services Commission on staffing issues
House of Commons committees	DMs give evidence to parliamentary committees
Committee of Senior Officials (COSO)	COSO oversees performance appraisal of DMs

* In Canada, 'deputy minister' denotes the senior public official in a department.

Source: Bourgault (2002), p. 438.

For example, Polidano (1998, p. 35) argues that in a complex environment, where most policy-making involves coordination between several organizations, straight-line accountability to a minister no longer suffices. He suggests that 'bureaucrats can be prevented from complying with ministerial directions, however legitimate those directions may be. Multiple accountabilities are an inescapable part of

BOX 17.7

Overseeing the bureaucracy

Internal controls
- Ministerial direction
- Regulators
- Professional standards

External scrutiny
- Legislature and judiciary
- Ombudsmen
- Interest groups and the mass media

the reality of government'. Today, senior officials are accountable not just to ministers in their own department but also to the prime minister, the finance ministry and to the obligations inherent in agreements with other national and even international organizations. To take a specific example, 'the accountability system for deputy ministers [top civil servants] in Canada has been described as multiple, complex and at times contradictory' (Bourgault, 2002, p. 446). As in other countries, the highest officials in Canada march to many drums (Box 17.6).

In setting out detailed methods of overseeing the bureaucracy, we distinguish between internal controls and external scrutiny, examining each category in turn (Box 17.7).

Internal controls

The traditional form of internal control is, of course, *ministerial direction*. Ministers direct; public servants execute. Although no longer sufficient, hierarchical control by a minister remains an essential component of oversight. However, in practice, the capacity of ministers to exert such control is conditioned by two other factors: the reach of political appointments into the bureaucracy and the use ministers make of personal advisers.

In theory, the greater the number of political appointments in a department, the easier it is to impose a specific direction. Recognizing that senior bureaucrats should possess political craft, many liberal democracies now tend to staff important ministries with politically loyal and sympathetic civil servants. This practice, long familiar in Germany and Finland, is spreading to other Western democracies. Increasingly, politicians want civil servants who are, in Mrs Thatcher's famous phrase, 'one of us'.

Political accountability of the bureaucracy can also be aided by providing ministers with personal advisory staff. Because such advisers are not part of the department's permanent staff, they can act as their minister's eyes and ears, reporting back on issues which might otherwise be lost in the official hierarchy. In France, for example, a minister is aided by a *cabinet*: a group of about 15 to 20 people who form the minister's personal advisory staff and work directly under his or her control. French-style *cabinets* provide the minister with ideas and help in liaising with the department, other ministries, the party and the constituency. The danger, however, is that such personal advisers are too dependent on their patron, preferring to offer blandishments and flattery rather than home truths.

In addition to formal control by the minister, public officials are overseen by an army of *regulators* within government: the 'waste watchers, quality police and sleaze busters' as Hood *et al.* (1999) term them. Auditors inspect the books, standard-setters check performance, funding bodies assess outcomes and inspectors monitor everything from fire escapes to recycling rates. Contemporary ideology may preach a bonfire of regulations but modern practice is an overdose of inspection, resulting in cynicism among officials and occasionally distracting from the main business at hand. To prevent the overdose from proving fatal, inspection is now beginning to operate with what is claimed to be a lighter touch, including a greater focus on key objectives – smart tape rather than red tape, allegedly (Hood, Rothstein and Baldwin, 2004).

Even amid the regulatory avalanche, liberal democracies continued to rely on the *professional standards* of civil servants, particularly in bureaucracies with a strong technical emphasis. In Norway and Sweden, for instance, many civil servants work in specialist directorates covering functions such as engineering, medicine and the railways. These directorates give expression to professional expertise and are at least partially independent of ministries. In these small Scandinavian countries, trust between politicians and bureaucrats remains high and the system usually functions smoothly. In the main, senior civil servants respond to political signals without explicit direction – a good result but not easily replicated elsewhere (Christensen and Peters, 1999).

External scrutiny

External scrutiny is an expanding form of accountability for public servants. Departments and agencies find themselves issuing extensive reports to outside bodies. However, these reports are often largely ignored by a focus on the most political corner of the organization's work. In reality, external scrutiny tends to be episodic and politically driven. The result, suggest Hogwood, Judge and McVicar (2000, p. 221), is that accountability gaps and accountability overload can coexist within the same agency.

In the United States, bureaucrats have always been forthcoming in their appearances before the *legislature*; it is Congress, after all, that grants the appropriations. But even in Britain, where ministers alone were considered responsible to parliament for the actions of their officials, civil servants now appear before select committees. Slowly and shyly, and still with a concern to avoid embarrassing their minister, British public officials are becoming willing to report in public on their work.

As with other areas of politics, the *judiciary* is also growing in importance as an arena in which the bureaucracy can be called to account. Administrative law gives the judiciary a tool for checking bureaucratic decision-making, allowing judges to overrule decisions that, for example, result from faulty procedures or which violate natural justice (p. 273).

A more recent addition to the mechanisms of external scrutiny is the **ombudsman**. This watchdog was first introduced in Sweden in 1809, followed by Finland in 1919 and then other liberal democracies after 1945. In 1995, a European Ombudsman was appointed to investigate complaints about 'instances of maladministration in the activities of the Community institutions' (Diamandouros, 2005, p. 10). A single advocate may cover the entire public sector or, at the risk of reduced visibility and uncertain jurisdictions, separate commissioners may be appointed for specific areas. Ombudsmen must have strong powers of investigation if they are to succeed. In addition, the public must be aware of their existence and be prepared to complain to them. So far, these conditions have rarely been fully met beyond Scandinavia (Ansell and Gingrich, 2003). In the United Kingdom, for instance, many citizens still prefer to approach their member of parliament rather than an ombudsman.

> An **ombudsman** (grievance officer) is a public official appointed by the legislature to investigate allegations of maladministration in the public sector. These watchdogs originated in Scandinavia but have been emulated elsewhere though often with more restricted jurisdiction and resources.

Finally, *interest groups* and the *mass media* provide some external checks on bureaucratic bungling. Interest groups have an obvious vested interest in monitoring the detailed implementation of policy by public officials. A vigorous mass media can also act as a selective check on the bureaucracy: regular television programmes, for example, now specialize in exposing public scandal and bureaucratic ineptitude. However, oversight tends to be selective and, in the case of the media, short-term. Exposés may encourage competence but rarely lead to structural reform; the specific case is resolved but bureaucratic complacency often remains.

New public management

'Government is not the solution to the problem; government is the problem.' This famous declaration by Ronald Reagan was one inspiration behind the new public management (NPM), a creed which swept through the Anglo-American world of public administration in the final decades of the twentieth century. NPM represented a powerful critique of Weber's ideas about bureaucracy. It attracted many specialists who did not share the ideological perspective of Ronald Reagan, it was spoken of warmly by international bodies such as the Organisation for Economic Co-operation and Development and it led to radical change in the public sectors of Australia, Canada, the United Kingdom and especially New Zealand.

The best way to approach NPM is to consider Osborne and Gaebler's *Reinventing Government* (1992), an exuberant statement of the new

BOX 17.8

Steer, don't row! Osborne and Gaebler's ten principles for improving the effectiveness of government agencies

- Promote competition between service providers;
- Empower citizens by pushing control out of the bureaucracy into the community;
- Measure performance, focusing not on inputs but on outcomes;
- Be driven by goals, not rules and regulations;
- Redefine clients as customers and offer them choices – between schools, between training programmes, between housing options;
- Prevent problems before they emerge, rather than offering services afterwards;
- Earn money rather than simply spend it;
- Decentralize authority and embrace participatory management;
- Prefer market mechanisms to bureaucratic ones;
- Catalyse all sectors – public, private and voluntary – into solving community problems.

Source: Adapted from Osborne and Gaebler (1992).

approach. Subtitled *How the Entrepreneurial Spirit is Transforming the Public Sector*, this American best-seller outlined ten principles which government agencies should adopt to enhance their effectiveness (Box 17.8). Whereas Weber's model of bureaucracy was based on ideas of efficiency drawn from the Prussian army, Osborne and Gaebler were inspired by the freewheeling world of American business.

The authors cited with enthusiasm several examples of public sector organizations which followed their tips. One was the California parks department that allowed managers to spend their budget on whatever they needed, without seeking approval for individual items of expenditure. Another was the public convention centre which formed a joint venture with private firms to bring in well-known entertainment acts, with each side sharing both the risk and the profit. The underlying theme was the gains achievable by giving public servants the flexibility to manage by results (that is, managerialism). And the significance of this empowerment, in turn, was the break it represented with Weber's view that the job of a bureaucrat was simply to apply fixed rules to cases. For its supporters, NPM was public administration for a new century; Weber's model was dismissed as history. Public administration, it was alleged, had been displaced by public management.

While Osborne and Gaebler provided a convert's handbook, Hood (1996) offered a more dispassionate and comparative perspective (Box 17.9). Hood showed that NPM penetrated furthest in Anglo-American countries and Scandinavia, where the public sector was most amenable to political control. By contrast, countries with a strong state and a high-prestige bureaucracy, for example Germany, Japan and Spain, made little progress in implementing the new philosophy. In these states, where administration is conceived as a branch of law, civil servants guard the public interest by applying legal codes to specific cases.

This approach leads to a sharp distinction between the style of public and private authority, including in particular a reluctance to apply the techniques of the latter to the former (Ziller, 2003). A particular problem is that the duties of civil servants are entrenched in extensive civil law codes, making radical change impossible without legislation. Such reforms as occurred have concentrated more on improving existing operations (e.g. improved budgeting) rather than radical restructuring.

Within the Anglo-American countries, New Zealand 'achieved what was probably the most comprehensive and radical set of public management reforms of any Western democracy' (Pollitt and Bouckaert, 2004, p. 280). In the 1980s and 1990s, successive governments – first Labour and then National – revolutionized the structure, management and role of the public sector. A remarkable coalition of economic theorists in the Treasury, senior politicians from both major parties and business leaders came together to ram through unpopular but far from ineffective reforms.

One particular feature of the New Zealand model was its massive use of contracts (Boston *et al.*, 1995). This technique went far beyond the standard fare of using private firms to supply local services such as garbage collection. It extended to engaging private suppliers in sensitive areas such as debt collection. By such means, the Department of Transport reduced its direct employees from around 5,000 in 1986 to fewer than 50 in the mid 1990s, an astonishing transformation. In addition, contracts were introduced within New Zealand's public sector to govern the relationships between purchasers (e.g. the Transport Department) and providers (e.g. Transit New Zealand, responsible for roads, and the Civil Aviation Authority, charged with air safety and security). Contractual arrangements within the public sector were an additional step, and a more direct challenge to Weber's model, than simply contracting out services to the private sector.

What lessons can be learned from New Zealand's ambitious innovations in public administration? Mulgan (1997, p. 146) offered a balanced assessment, concluding that

> The recent reorganization of the public service has led to greater clarity of government functions and to increased efficiencies in the provision of certain services to the public. At the same time, it has been expensive in the amount of resources consumed by the reform process itself and also in the added problems of coordination caused by the greatly increased number of individual public agencies.

BOX 17.9

Components of new public management

- Managers given more discretion but held responsible for results;
- Performance assessed against explicit targets;
- Resources allocated according to results;
- Departments unbundled into more independent operating units;
- More work contracted out to the private sector;
- More flexibility allowed in recruiting and retaining staff;
- Costs cut in an effort to achieve more with less.

Source: Adapted from Hood (1996).

The rise of NPM and the contract culture was one reason why the accountability of public officials became more complex. When something goes wrong with a service provided by an agency operating under contract to government, who should take the blame: the supplier or the department? In Britain, parliament has traditionally held ministers to account for all the actions carried out in their name. As *The Times* wrote in 1977, 'the constitutional position is both crystal clear and entirely sufficient. Officials propose. Ministers dispose. Officials execute.'

Yet as early as 1994 most British civil servants were working in one of about 100 semi-independent agencies. In theory, the minister sets the policy and the agency carries it out. But when a political storm blows up – when convicts escape from prison or a National Health Service hospital fails to clean its wards properly – it is still ministers who are hauled before parliament. Knowing this, ministers are inclined to interfere selectively with operational matters, contradicting the original purpose. Agency managers discover that they are not free to manage after all, reducing morale and increasing turnover in the top posts (Pollitt and Bouckaert, 2004).

The complexities of accountability in a reformed civil service led some critics to suggest that 'a huge hole now exists in the operation of British democracy' (Campbell and Wilson, 1995, p. 287). Public servants became a shade more responsive downwards, to their users, and also more open to scrutiny from alternative political authorities, such as parliamentary committees. Probably these developments represented a change in accountability rather than a decline. Control melted away from the minister's office to a more diffuse set of agencies and their clients. Weber's hierarchy of control based on direct provision by departments gave way to a looser network based on persuasion rather than order-giving. Governance supplemented government.

Public management in authoritarian states

Like the military, the bureaucracy is usually a more powerful force in non-democratic regimes than it is in democracies. By definition, institutions of representation – elections, competitive parties and freely organized interest groups – are weak under authoritarian rule, leaving more room for agencies of the state to prosper. A dictator can dispense with elections or even with legislatures but he cannot rule without bureaucrats to give effect to his will.

But the bureaucracy can be more than a dictator's service agency, not least in developing countries. Often in conjunction with the military, it can itself become a leading political force, claiming that its technical expertise and ability to resist popular pressures is the only route to long-term economic development. This assertion may have initial merit but eventually bureaucracies in non-democratic regimes are prone to become bloated, over-politicized and inefficient, acting as a drag on rather than a stimulus to further progress. In the long run, bureaucratic regimes, like military governments, become part of the problem rather than the solution.

The bureaucracy has undoubtedly played a positive role in most authoritarian regimes that have experienced rapid economic growth. In the 1950s and 1960s, for instance, it helped to foster economic modernization in several regimes in the Middle East and North Africa. In conjunction with the military and a strong national leader such as Abdul Nasser (President of Egypt, 1956–70), modernizing bureaucracies were able to initiate state-sponsored development even against the opposition of conservative landowners.

O'Donnell (1973) introduced the term **bureaucratic authoritarianism** to describe Latin American countries which followed a similar course, under repressive military leadership, in the 1960s and 1970s. The high-performing economies of East Asia, such as Indonesia and Malaysia, provide more recent examples of the contribution that the bureaucracy can make to development in largely authoritarian settings.

But instances of the bureaucracy instigating successful modernization are the exception. More often, the bureaucracy has inhibited rather than encouraged economic development. The experience of sub-Saharan Africa following independence provides a more sobering and representative assessment of the role of bureaucracy in a non-democratic environment. After colonial rulers departed, authoritarian leaders used their control over public appointments as a political reward, overwhelming the delicate distinction between politics and administration. This cavalier approach to public appointments was compounded by chronic unemployment which led to excess labour, especially among new graduates, being absorbed into the administration as a way of buying support or at least preventing opposition.

Bureaucratic authoritarianism was a term coined by O'Donnell (1973) to describe regimes in which technocrats in the bureaucracy imposed economic stability under the protection of a military government. Such regimes repressed popular movements. The concept emerged in the context of Latin American countries such as Argentina and Brazil in the 1960s and 1970s.

The outcome was uncontrolled expansion of the civil service. By the early 1990s, public employment accounted for most non-agricultural employment in Africa (B. Smith, 1996, p. 221). Once appointed, public employees found that ties of kinship meant that they were duty-bound to use their privileged positions to reward their families and ethnic group, producing further expansion of the civil service.

The outcome was a fat bureaucracy incapable of acting as an effective instrument for development. Rather, the expanding administrative 'class' extracted resources from society for its own benefit, in that sense continuing rather than replacing the colonial model. With the main source of national wealth (e.g. commodity exports) under state control, public employment became the highway to riches, creating a bureaucratic bourgeoisie. Only towards the end of the twentieth century, under pressure from international agencies, were attempts made to rein in the public sector through an emphasis on building **administrative capacity** (Turner and Hulme, 1997, p. 90).

Even where bureaucracy-led development has succeeded, the formula often outlasts its usefulness. Several East Asian states discovered at the end of the twentieth century that public administrators are more effective at building an industrial economy than at continuing to manage it once it becomes mature and open to international competition. In Indonesia, for example, the Asian financial crisis of

Administrative capacity refers to the bureaucracy's ability to address social problems through effective management and implementation of public policy.

COUNTRY PROFILE

JAPAN

Form of government ■ a parliamentary liberal democracy with a ceremonial emperor.

Legislature ('Diet') ■ the 480 members of the House of Representatives are elected for a four-year term. The smaller upper house, the House of Councillors, is less significant.

Executive ■ an orthodox parliamentary executive, with a cabinet and prime minister accountable to the Diet.

Judiciary ■ the 15-member Supreme Court possesses the power of judicial review under the 1946 constitution but has proved unassertive in the face of LDP dominance.

Electoral system ■ under the mixed member majoritarian system introduced in 1996, 300 members of the lower house are elected in single-member constituencies while the remainder are elected by proportional representation.

Party system ■ In 2005, the dominant LDP gained a resounding victory, winning 296 seats. The main opposition comes from the reformist Democratic Party of Japan (113 seats).

Population (annual growth rate): 127.4m (+0.02%)
World Bank income group: high income
Political Rights score: 1
Civil Liberties score: 
Human development index (rank/out of): 9/177
Freedom of the press index (rank/out of): 37/194
Ease of doing business index (rank/out of): 11/175

Note: For meaning and sources of scales and indexes, see p. xvi. In all cases a score and rank of 1 is 'best'.

JAPAN offers one of the few surviving cases of a dominant party system in a liberal democracy. Either alone or in coalition, the LDP has governed Japan for all but 11 months since 1955. As Scheiner (2006, p. 1) points out, the opposition has been unable to mount an effective challenge even though the LDP is unpopular with many voters. The key to the party's success lies in its willingness to use its control of an interventionist state to offer financial support and subsidies to those local areas which consistently elect the party's candidates. Because Japan's local governments depend heavily on central funding, their voters possess a strong incentive to support the party that serves their local interests. This network works especially well in rural areas, which are over-represented in parliament.

The system is economically inefficient, generating unnecessary bridges, roads and dams throughout the land – and a large budget deficit for the state. The LDP's requirement for a steady flow of funds from the private sector also encourages corruption. So far, however, the formula has proved to be a political success.

Japan's interest is not confined to its party system. In addition, its political economy has attracted considerable attention. Contained in a series of islands the size of Montana, and lacking all major natural resources, Japan's 127 million people have built the second largest economy in the world. After the Second World War, Japan took remarkable advantage of favourable circumstances for recovery, eventually becoming the world's leading producer and exporter of sophisticated industrial and consumer goods. Although the country's post-war constitution was an American-imposed liberal democracy, in practice the political system was led by business interests. The government succeeded in dampening popular demands for rapid increases in domestic consumption, thereby facilitating long-term investment but also creating the paradox of a rich country with poor people.

In the 1990s, however, the Japanese economy fell on hard times. A collapse in land prices precipitated a banking crisis which in turn led to deflation and rising unemployment. A growth rate of 10 per cent in the 1960s declined to just 1.7 per cent in the 1990s. More consistent policy choices might have alleviated some problems but the government continued to run a large budget deficit and proved reluctant to deregulate the economy. It was not until the new century that the economy began to shake off these difficulties.

Further reading: Johnson (2003), Matsuura *et al.* (2004).

SPOTLIGHT

Public management in Japan

The Japanese bureaucracy is probably more bally-hooed than any other bureaucracy in the world', write Rosenbluth and Theis (2004, p. 327). In particular, the civil service is usually accorded an important place in histories of the country's rapid growth phase.

Certainly, the bureaucracy as a whole remains relatively small, employing a lower proportion of the workforce than even the United States. In 1994, there were only 40 government workers for every 1,000 people in Japan, compared to 86 in the USA (Neary, 2002, p. 113). One reason why expansion was contained was the 'scrap and build' law (1964) which required an existing division within a ministry to be abolished if a new one was to be created.

However, the Japanese civil service possesses high status and motivates its recruits with the thought of good post-retirement jobs in the private sector and local government. The bureaucracy attracts able (albeit overwhelmingly male) recruits through open competition. Typically, only about 2,000 of the 30,000 applicants who take the higher civil service examination (the 'dragon gate' test) are recruited. Many of these are graduates from just one department: Tokyo University's Law School.

The philosophy of the bureaucracy is unified rather than departmental but mobility is rare. Each group of recruits forms a distinct cohort within a ministry, progressing through the hierarchy but with a smaller proportion achieving promotion to the next level; the convention is that staff should not have to serve under anyone recruited later than them. The system is competitive and demanding but, at the highest levels only, rewarding.

As Johnson (1995, p. 68) writes, senior bureaucrats form part of 'the economic general staff, which is itself legitimated by its meritocratic character'. The bureaucracy undoubtedly played a substantial role in post-war reconstruction. It was intertwined with the Liberal Democratic Party – conservative in all but name – and big business. The professional economic bureaucracy, and in particular the Ministry of International Trade and Industry (MITI), was a significant factor in Japan's success. As post-war reconstruction began, MITI targeted specific growth industries such as cameras which were shielded from overseas competition until they became competitive. MITI operated mainly through discussion and persuasion, thus reducing the risk of major mistakes, but could rely on the authority inherent in a highly regulated society when necessary. In the decades of high growth, Japan provided the preeminent example of how a small, merit-based bureaucracy, operating largely on the basis of persuasion, could guide economic development within a predominantly market framework.

Ministries and agencies of the Japanese government, following the 2001 reforms

Cabinet Office
National Police Agency
Defence Agency
Ministry of Public Management, Home Affairs, Posts and Telecommunications
Ministry of Justice
Ministry of Foreign Affairs
Ministry of Finance
Ministry of Education, Culture, Sports, Science and Technology
Ministry of Health, Labour and Welfare
Ministry of Agriculture, Forestry and Fisheries
Ministry of Economy, Trade and Industry
Ministry of Land, Infrastructure and Transport
Ministry of Environment

Source: Web Japan (2006).

In the 1990s, state-led deflation painted the bureaucracy in a harsher light. A few civil servants were caught up in bribery cases; these scandals made some large companies more wary of hiring retired bureaucrats. More fundamentally, in a global economy civil servants can no longer offer the same strategic direction to industry, given that the largest companies now operate on a world scale and that some overseas corporations are established within Japan. Reflecting these developments, as well as a desire to improve coordination, the central bureaucracy was reorganized in 2001, with the number of departments reduced from 20 to 10 and the once-mighty MITI becoming part of a new ministry. The Japan Fair Trade Commission acquired a more extensive role in enforcing competition, signalling greater emphasis on consumer interests.

Further reading: Neary (2002), Scheiner (2006).

the late 1990s exposed the extent to which investment patterns had been distorted by crony capitalism, with access to capital depending on official contacts rather than the anticipated rate of return.

The position of the bureaucracy in totalitarian systems in some ways echoes its role in authoritarian regimes. But one key difference marks out administration in the communist form of totalitarian rule: its sheer scale. The size of the bureaucracy under communism flowed from the totalitarian character of its guiding ideology. To achieve its theoretical mission of building a new society, the party had to control all aspects of development, both economic and social, through the state. Most obviously, the private sector disappeared and the economy became an aspect of state administration. In the extreme case of the Soviet Union virtually every farm, factory and shop formed part of the bureaucracy. The shop assistant, the butcher, the electrician – all were employees of the Union of Soviet Socialist Republics. This required one army of administrators to do the work and another to provide coordination. The Soviet Union became the most bureaucratic state the world had ever seen.

In addition, communist bureaucracies were intensely political, with the ruling party penetrating deeply into the administration. Indeed, the essence of communist rule lay in combining bureaucratic and political rule in one gigantic system. Reflecting Weber's concerns in the democratic world, the ruling party regarded the bureaucracy as both indispensable and potentially unreliable – as a force which through its control of implementation might one day come to dominate its political masters (Lewin, 1997). Hence, the party sought to pacify the bureaucracy in the same way that it controlled the armed forces: by controlling all major appointments. This goal was achieved through the **nomenklatura**, a mechanism that provided a powerful incentive for the ambitious to gain and retain a sound reputation within the party. The *nomenklatura* system continues to this day in China, where the list is now said to contain over eight million names (Manion, 2004, p. 435).

The **nomenklatura** (list of names) was a large panel of trusted individuals from which ruling communist parties appointed people to posts in the bureaucracy.

Fascist regimes provided both similarities and contrasts to the communist approach. Like communist states, fascism was an ideology of mobilization, seeking to place the entire resources of the society at the service of an expansionist state; 'war in peacetime' was Hitler's phrase. However, unlike communist leaders Hitler was uninterested in how the administration achieved his demanding objectives. Instead, the leadership of men was regarded as superior to sterile rules and bureaucratic procedures. Hitler applauded the personal form of rule practised in Germany's annexed territories, where local commanders wielded complete power. As Mommsen (1997, p. 75) writes, 'The Nazi dictatorship did not so much expand governmental prerogatives through bureaucratic means as progressively undermine hitherto effective public institutions through arbitrary use of power'. Caplan (1988, pp. 322–3) argues that under Hitler the 'subversion of the civil service was piecemeal and ad hoc, the effect of incompetence, impatience and neglect rather than the pursuit of a clear alternative'. The profoundly non-bureaucratic character of Nazi rule – described by Caplan as 'government without administration' – contrasts deeply with communist practice.

Public management in illiberal democracies

The bureaucracy generally receives little attention in discussion of illiberal democracies. The reason is understandable: illiberal democracies are typically founded on a personal relationship between president and people. This implicit contract works against the strengthening of rule-governed institutions, including a Weberian bureaucracy. Illiberal democracies are political, not bureaucratic, regimes.

Further, the rulers of illiberal democracies often present themselves in opposition to institutions such as the bureaucracy. In Latin America, particularly, administrators frequently imitate the haughty remoteness of their long-gone colonial predecessors, producing a corrupt and unresponsive bureaucracy which provides a convenient target for a populist politician (Nef, 2003). When the political leader of an illiberal democracy can secure the financial benefits from natural resources such as oil, he can spend these resources on maintaining a viable political coalition through patronage, thus further weakening formal institutions such as the civil service.

In Venezuela, for instance, Hugo Chávez introduced a new constitution in 1999 which defined the country's political system as 'democratic, participatory, elective, decentralized, responsible to the people, pluralist, based on term limits for elected officials and revocable mandates' (Alvarez, 2004, p. 152). This new order was born out of a discredited regime dominated by two strong parties. However, the radical pretensions and inherent uncertainties of the new constitution contributed nothing to building an effective bureaucracy. Rather, the effect was to concentrate attention on the political realm – and on Chávez himself.

In many illiberal democracies, therefore, public management operates in a somewhat uncoordinated way, with separate bureaucratic islands serving the interests of their local managers rather than those of the public they ostensibly serve. Corruption inherited from the authoritarian order may continue unabated and jobs may be allocated on the basis of political rewards and ethnic ties. Much routine work may continue to be conducted; illiberal democracies, after all, are far from failed states. Indeed, Nef (2003, p. 531) points out that the onset of illiberal democracy in Latin American has led not just to privatization and fiscal prudence but also to some improvements 'in the quality and time of service rendered to customers in many of the countries'. But the real action lies in the political realm and the bureaucracy as a whole often lacks the administrative capacity which international agencies – and sometimes even the political leadership itself – would like to see.

BOX 17.10

The organization of central government in Russia

	Number	Examples
Federal ministries under the president	12	Internal Affairs, Foreign Affairs, Defence, Justice
Federal ministries under the government	11	Education and Science, Finance, Natural Resources, Transport
Other executive bodies under the government	12	Space Agency, Sport and Physical Culture, Tourist Agency

Source: President of Russia (2006).

Russia's illiberal democracy illustrates but also qualifies these themes. More than in most illiberal democracies, Russia's presidents have drawn on – rather than defined themselves in opposition to – the country's long tradition of state power. As Willerton (1997, p. 39) points out, 'All past Russian political systems were characterised by a strong executive, with power concentrated on a small governing elite. An administrative bureaucracy supporting the political executive emerged under the Tatars [Turkic-speaking overlords of Russia, 1236–1452]. By the early eighteenth century Peter the Great had rationalised and professionalised that bureaucracy'.

In the post-communist era, securing control over these bureaucratic agencies required significant attention even from such a skilled political mechanic as Vladimir Putin. In contrast to most liberal democracies, Russia never developed an integrated public bureaucracy with standard rules and merit-based appointments. Under communism, party and state became so intertwined that the collapse of the former came close to bringing down the latter. In the chaotic early years of post-communism, provision of public services inevitably devolved to local level, fragmenting the administration in what is in any case a large, diverse country. The Civil Service Act (1995) did introduce more uniform provisions across the public sector, including for example a rigid grading structure, but the operation of Russia's bureaucracy still falls well short of Weber's standards. Even today, the legacy of inefficiency and corruption renders most of Russia's bureaucracy far less professional and responsive than, say, its American equivalent (Ágh, 2003, p. 545).

The result is problems of bureaucratic control in Russia which exceed those found in the United States, whose constitution at least vests sole executive power in the president. The Russian president also faces an additional issue: under the semi-presidential constitution of 1993, some key functions fall under direct presidential supervision but others are the responsibility of a government with its own head (Box 17.10). Where the American president heads the executive branch, Russia's president, like his French counterpart, stands above the government.

In an attempt to resolve these problems, Russia's post-communist presidents have developed a massive constellation of supervisory agencies, based in or reporting to the Kremlin. By 2006, President Putin's Executive Office contained 19 separate units, staffed in the main by loyal, competent and reliable supporters. These offices include the Presidential Control Directorate which 'is responsible for ensuring and verifying that the federal and regional executive authorities and also other organisations properly execute federal laws, in particular as concerns the President's powers' (President of Russia, 2006). Frequent reorganization of the Executive Office suggests that its success remains incomplete and that Russia's president is not yet, if he is ever to become, an elected dictator.

Learning Resources for Chapter 17

Next step

Peters (2006) is a clear and comparative introduction to bureaucracy.

Further reading

Heady (2001) is an alternative to Peters while Bekke *et al.* (1996) is a lively edited collection. Osborne and Gaebler (1992) is an enthusiast's account of new public management while Pollitt and Bouckaert (2004) offer a balanced comparative review. Page and Wright (2006) and Peters and Pierre (2004) provide collections on the changing role of senior civil servants in liberal democracies. Mulgan (2003) is a thoughtful review of the concept of accountability. Shafritz, Hyde and Parkes (2003) provide a chronological selection of classics on American public administration. For Japan, Johnson (1995) remains an influential starting point; see also Neary (2002). Kershaw and Lewin (1997) contains useful chapters on bureaucracy in the contrasting dictatorships of Stalin and Hitler. With an emphasis on the relationship between administration and development, Turner and Hulme (1997) portray the role of bureaucracy in authoritarian regimes. For the enthusiast, Peters and Pierre (2003) offer a 49-chapter handbook of public administration.

Internet sources

Administrative and Civil Service Reform, World Bank
Reviews the main debates on civil service management and reform
http://www.worldbank.org

AEI-Brookings Joint Center for Regulatory Studies
Analyses regulatory programmes and new proposals
http://www.aei-brookings.org/

Sigma Programme
A joint initative of the OECD and EU, this programme supports improvements in governance and public management
http://www.sigmaweb.org/

United Nations Online Network in Public Administration and Finance
Promotes effective public administration and efficient civil services
http://www.unpan.org/

Verstehen: Max Weber's home page
A site for undergraduates, by Frank Elwell
http://www.faculty.rsu.edu/~felwell/Theorists/Weber/Whome.htm#words

Chapter 18
Public policy

The task of policy analysis is to understand what governments do, how they do it and what difference it makes (Dye, 2004). Where political science examines the organization of the political factory, policy analysis examines the products emerging from it. So the focus is on the content, instruments, impact and evaluation of public policy. The particular emphasis is downstream, on the implementation and results of policy, as much as upstream, on the origins of policy in its institutional sources.

Policy analysis is concerned with improving the quality and efficacy of public policy, giving the subject a distinctly practical air. Policy analysts want to know whether and why a policy is working and how else its objectives might be pursued. Reflecting this interest, policy analysis is a subject that connects academic studies with political practice. For example, the chapter on political economy in this book is an exercise in policy analysis because its underlying concern is to discover the policies that will strengthen economic performance.

As a plan of action, a **policy** covers both an aim or goal (say, to discourage obesity) and a series of decisions, past or future, designed to achieve the objective (for example, by reducing advertising of fast food). Policy can also take the form of explicit non-decisions: 'our policy is that nutritional choices should be left to the individual'. According to Colebatch (1998), policies are expected to show coherence (policy as strategy), hierarchy (policy as instructions) and instrumentality (policy as purpose).

In understanding the policy process, it is important to avoid imposing rationality on what is often a deeply non-rational process. Three points are relevant here. First, public policies are often contradictory. There is nothing to prevent governments from subsidizing tobacco growers while simultaneously running anti-smoking campaigns. Second, policies can be nothing more than window-dressing – an attempt to be seen to be doing something but without any realistic expectation that the notional objective will be achieved. Third, statements of policy can be a disguise for doing nothing whatsoever. A leader of a low-income country who dutifully informs international agencies that his policy is to privatize state-owned industries may have no intention whatever of reducing his control of his honey pot. In short, public policy is a part as much as a product of politics. 'Policy' and 'politics', we should remember, are words with the same root.

It is helpful to distinguish the five stages of the policy process shown in Figure 18.1: initiation, formulation, implementation, evaluation and review. Of course, these divisions are more analytical than chronological, meaning that in the real world they often overlap. Nonetheless, a review of these stages will provide a way to explore the distinct focus of policy analysis.

A **policy** is a broader notion than a decision (or non-decision). At a minimum, a policy covers a bundle of decisions (or non-decisions). More generally, it reflects an intention to make future decisions in accordance with an overall objective.

Initiation and formulation

Why did governments expand welfare for the first three decades after 1945 and then reduce it thereafter? Why did many Western governments take companies into public ownership after the war and then start selling them back to the private sector in the 1980s and 1990s? These are questions about policy initiation and formulation – about the decision to make (and reverse) policy in a particular area and the development of specific proposals.

Figure 18.1 Stages of the policy process

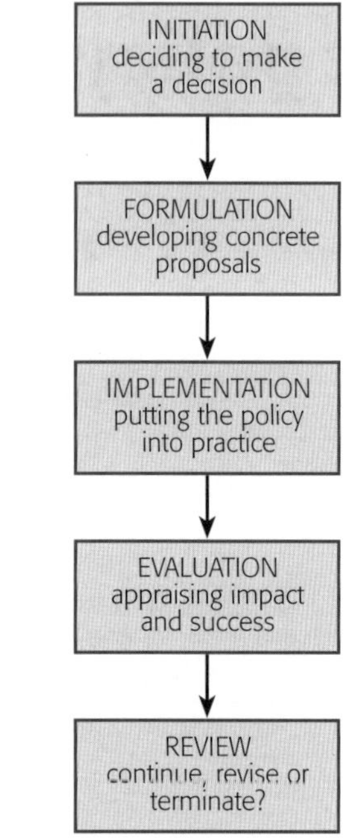

Initiation

In grappling with policy initiation, it is helpful to distinguish between the systemic and institutional agendas. The **systemic agenda** refers to the wide range of potential problems for which public action is considered appropriate within the political system as a whole (the boundaries of this agenda are of course disputed and variable, as with sexual behaviour and abortion). The **institutional agenda** denotes the much smaller number of policy proposals under consideration by policy-makers at any given time.

In all democracies, much of the institutional agenda bubbles up from below, delivered to agenda-setters by bureaucrats in the form of issues requiring immediate attention. These requirements include the need to fix the unforeseen impacts of earlier decisions, leading to the notion of 'policy as its own cause' (Wildavsky, 1979, p. 62). For example, once a highway is opened, additional action will be needed to combat the spillover effects of congestion, accidents and pollution. Rather like legal decisions, public policy naturally tends to thicken over time; cases of withdrawal, such as the ending of prohibition in the United States, are unusual. In addition, much political business, including the annual budget, occurs on a regular cycle. Unpredictable crises also demand attention, dominating the to-do list.

The broad **systemic agenda** contains 'all issues that are commonly perceived by members of the political community as meriting public attention and as involving matters within the legitimate jurisdiction of existing governmental authority'. The narrower **institutional agenda** is 'that set of items explicitly up for active and serious consideration of authoritative decision-makers' (Cobb and Elder, 1983, p. 85).

Policy proposals mover from the systemic to the institutional agenda in uncertain and unpredictable ways (Kingdon, 1984). In the pluralistic world of American politics, the transfer depends on the opening of policy windows (such as the opportunities for innovation created by the election of a new government). These openings soon close: the cycle of attention to a particular issue is short, and both political debate and the public mood continue to evolve. Thus, Kingdon suggests that policy entrepreneurs are needed to seize the moment. Like surfers, these initiators must 'ride the big wave' by convincing the political elite not only of the scale of the problem but also of the timeliness of a policy aimed at its resolution.

From this perspective, interest group leaders succeed by linking their own agenda to a wider narrative: save the whale and you may be able to defuse criticism that you are failing to rescue the planet. Adopt our proposals for skills training and you will be seen to be addressing the bigger question of international competitiveness. More prosaically, a new government will want to distinguish itself from its predecessor by addressing a fresh agenda or by adopting a new approach to existing problems. It will be open to offers.

The concepts of policy entrepreneur and policy window offer insight into the pluralistic style of American politics. However, they carry less resonance in the more structured democracies of Western Europe. Here the barriers between the systemic and the institutional agendas are firmer. In the extreme case of the European Union, the policy agenda is formally the preserve of the supranational, non-party European Commission. This body is granted the sole right of initiation, enabling it to fulfil its commitment to integration:

> The European Commission plays a very important role because of its monopoly of policy initiation. This monopoly has been granted by the founding Treaty and is carefully protected by the European Court of Justice. Hence, no national government can induce the Commission to make a specific proposal changing the status quo, unless that proposal also makes the Commission better off. Such tight control of the policy agenda has no analogue either in parliamentary or presidential democracies (Majone, 2006, p. 231).

At national level, too, party manifestos and coalition agreements in Western Europe set out an agenda for government in more explicit and even ideological form than in the USA.

In more general terms, we can identify three external influences on policy initiation: science, technology and the media. These factors identify both problems and solutions. *Science* is clearly one driver of policy agendas. The current concern with climate change, for instance, began primarily with scientific assessments of its future implications. Rather unusually, the science forewarned us that a problem was on its way.

Second, the application of science – that is, *technology* – also influences policy initiation. Many new technologies involve regulation. Designs for nuclear power stations must be assessed for safety; frequencies for mobile telephones must be allocated; new drugs must be examined for side effects; and the effects of allowing genetically altered plants, fish and animals into the environment must be considered. In all these cases technological innovation forces policy initiation from government.

Third, the ability of the *media* to highlight issues means they are also a significant, if sometimes overstated, influence on policy initiation. A single and perhaps unusual incident is often taken up by one media outlet and then, through pack journalism, amplified by other channels. Common topics of such media-induced moral panics include asylum seekers, crime waves, drug crazes, food scares, gang wars, infectious diseases, mad dogs, teenage hooligans and welfare scroungers (Henshel, 1990). These balloons of concern often collapse as quickly as they are inflated; only in a few cases are the media turning their searchlight on a problem where public policy does indeed need to be initiated.

Formulation

Once a decision has been taken to address a specific problem, policy must be formed. Deciding *to* decide is one thing; deciding *what* to decide is much more difficult. The coalition which formed behind the vague idea that something must be done soon dissolves when it comes to concrete proposals producing losers as well as winners. Formulating precise legislative and administrative proposals in response to diffuse support for action is a task requiring good political craft and one normally conducted by an inner circle of politicians and bureaucrats, often supported by the leaders of the best-connected interest groups.

Generally, policy-formers will share a common discourse about the problem, for example viewing poverty as a soluble problem rather than an unavoidable condition, and will seek solutions which are consistent with broader currents of opinion and previous policies within the sector. Compare American and British attitudes to medical care. In the United States, the Clinton administration soon learned that there is little to be gained (and much to be lost) by proposing health-care reforms which depart from the American preference for private, non-bureaucratic provision. In Britain, by contrast, 60 years of the National Health Service have entrenched an expectation that medical care will be provided free at the point of care, and on a non-profit basis.

In analysing policy formulation, scholars have developed two models: the rational or synoptic model associated with Simon (1983) and the incre-

BOX 18.1

Rational and incremental models of policy-making

Rational model	Incremental model
Goals are set before means are considered	Goals and means are considered together
A good policy is the most appropriate to achieve explicit goals	A good policy is one on which all main actors can agree
Analysis is comprehensive; all effects of all options are addressed	Analysis is selective; the object is acceptable policy, not the best policy
Theory is heavily used	Comparison with similar problems is heavily used

Sources: Adapted from Lindblom (1959), p. 81 and Parsons (1995), p. 285.

mental model developed by Lindblom (1979). These accounts form an important part of the policy analysis tradition and we will consider them in more detail (Box 18.1).

The key contrast between the two models is this. The rational model views policy formulation as emerging from a systematic search for the most efficient means of achieving defined goals. By contrast, the incremental model sees policy as emerging from a compromise between actors who have goals which are ill-defined or even contradictory. Where the rational model seeks the best policy in theory, an incremental framework seeks out a practical policy acceptable to all the interests involved.

An example will clarify this contrast. Suppose we are in charge of secondary education and we have decided to initiate a policy to improve students' performance. If we were to adopt a rational approach, we would first specify the outcomes sought, such as the proportion of students achieving a given level of qualifications. Then we would consider the most efficient means of maximizing that goal: should we invest in new schools, improved facilities, more teachers or some combination thereof?

An incremental approach, however, starts from a different point. Here we would begin with regular consultation with all the organized interests: teacher unions, parents' associations, educational researchers. We would hope that from these discussions a consensus might emerge on how extra resources should be spent. The long-term goals of this expenditure might not be measured or even specified but we would assume that a policy acceptable to all is unlikely to be disastrous. Such an approach is policy-making by evolution, not revolution; an 'increment' is literally a small change to an existing sequence.

Of these two approaches, the rational model is clearly more demanding, requiring detailed analysis rather than careful politics. Specifically, it requires policy-makers to:

- Rank all their values;
- Formulate specific options;
- Check all the results of choosing each option against each value;
- Select the alternative that achieves most values.

This is an unrealistic counsel of perfection. It requires policy-makers to foresee the unforeseeable and measure the immeasurable. Even so, techniques such as **cost-benefit analysis** have developed in an attempt to implement aspects of the rational model (Boardman *et al.*, 2000).

Cost-benefit analysis (CBA) involves giving a monetary value (positive or negative) to every consequence of choosing each option and then selecting the option with the highest net benefit. Thus, the efficiency gain from adding a new runway to an airport can be netted off against the additional noise pollution for local residents.

Seeking to analyse the costs and benefits associated with each possible decision does have strengths, particularly when one from a small set of options needs to be chosen. Specifically, CBA brings submerged assumptions to the surface, benefiting those interests that would otherwise lack political clout. It discourages symbolic policy-making which addresses a concern but is unlikely to achieve anything more specific. It requires explicit consideration of a **discount rate**. It contributes to transparent policy-

The **discount rate** is the factor by which the expected future benefits of a policy are reduced to estimate their present value. In general, a high discount rate based on market levels of interest will sharply reduce the current value of projects with long-term benefits, such as schemes to contain global warming (Stern, 2007).

making by forcing decision-makers to account for policies whose costs exceed benefits. In short, CBA can help to keep policy-makers honest.

For such reasons, CBA has been formally applied to every regulatory proposal in the USA expected to have an impact on the economy exceeding $100m. It has also played its part in the development of risk-based regulation in the United Kingdom, under which many regulators seek to focus their efforts on the main dangers, in preference to mechanically applying the same rules to all (Hutter, 2005).

However, CBA, and with it the rational model of policy formulation, also has weaknesses. It underplays soft factors such as fairness and the quality of life. It ignores the distribution of costs and benefits. It is cumbersome, expensive and time-consuming. It does not automatically incorporate estimates of the likelihood that benefits will, in fact, be achieved. In the real political world, the conclusions from CBA are often sidestepped. Just as the 'rational' model is not always more rational in application than an incremental approach, so too a CBA of CBA would not always yield positive results.

The incremental model was developed by Lindblom (1959) as part of a reaction against the rational model. Lindblom's starting point is that policy is continually remade in a series of minor adjustments, rather than as a result of a single, comprehensive plan. In reality, policy formulation rarely sails out on an open sea; mostly, it is a process of making small adjustments to modify the existing direction. Incrementalism represents what Lindblom calls the science of muddling through. This approach may not lead to achieving grand objectives but, by taking one step at a time, it does at least avoid making huge mistakes. In incremental policy-making, what matters is not that those involved should agree on objectives but that agreement should be reached on the desirability of following a particular policy, even when objectives differ. Hence policy emerges from, rather than precedes, negotiation with interested groups.

As Lindblom (1977, 1990) himself came to recognize, incremental policy formulation deals with existing problems rather than with avoiding future ones. It is politically safe but unadventurous; public policy becomes remedial rather than innovative. But the threat of ecological disaster, for instance, has arisen precisely from human failure to consider our long-term, cumulative impact on the environment,

A rather more alarming view of policy-making emerges from the **garbage-can model** of decision-making. This model imagines that issues and policy-makers mix at random within an organization, just as different forms of trash blend haphazardly in a garbage can. In a university, for instance, a committee containing one group of staff may happen to address one aspect of a particular problem, with some implications possibly picked up later by a completely separate group. Policy-making is partial, fluid, chaotic and incomplete, exhibiting no more rationality than is found in the arrangement of waste in a dustbin (Cohen, March and Olson, 1972).

The **garbage-can model** of policy formulation sees problems and solutions mixing at random within an organization, rather as the garbage in a waste container depends on what garbage is produced at a given time and how often the bin is emptied. If problems are resolved at all, it is in an ad hoc, piecemeal fashion.

Although this model was mainly concerned with decision-making within organizations, its perspective also has relevance to the political system as a whole. For example, several government departments may deal with different aspects of pollution, with none having an overall perspective. Or one department may be charged with reducing pollution while another works to attract investments in new factories which will increase it. Clearly, the garbage-can model suggests that real policy-making is far removed from the rigours of rationality. At best, some problems will be partly addressed some of the time; Tony Blair's 'joined-up government' is nowhere to be found (Bendor *et al.*, 2001).

Implementation

After a policy has been set, it must be put into effect. An obvious point, of course, except that much traditional political science stopped at the point where government reached a decision, ignoring the myriad difficulties which arise in policy execution. Probably the main achievement of policy analysis has been to direct attention to these problems of implementation. No longer can execution be dismissed with Woodrow Wilson (1887) as 'mere administration'.

Turning a blind eye to implementation issues can still be politically convenient for ministers but is always dangerous and can be damaging. For example, the British government's failure to prevent mad cow disease from crossing the species barrier to humans in the late 1980s was a classic instance of implementation failure. Official committees instructed abattoirs to remove infective material (such as the spinal cord) from slaughtered cows but initially took no special steps to ensure these plans were carried out carefully. As a result of incompetence in slaughterhouses, the disease agent continued to enter the human food chain.

Again reflecting the standard conventions of political science, the **top-down** approach represents the traditional view of implementation. Within this perspective, the question posed was the classical problem of bureaucracy: how to ensure political direction of unruly public servants. Elected ministers had to be able to secure compliance from departments and agencies already committed to pet projects of their own. Without vigilance from on high, sound policies would be hijacked by lower-level officials obsessed with existing procedures, thus diluting the impact of new initiatives.

This top-down approach focuses excessively on control and compliance. Like the rational model of policy-making from which it springs, it may be unrealistic and even counterproductive. The plausible suggestion emerging from the contrasting **bottom-up** perspective is that policy-makers should seek to engage rather than control those who translate policy into practice. Writers in this tradition, such as Hill and Hupe (2002), ask: what if circumstances have changed since the policy was formulated? And what if the policy itself is poorly designed? Much legislation, after all, is based on uncertain information and is highly general in content. Often, it cannot be followed to the letter because there is no letter to follow.

> A **top-down** approach conceives the task of policy implementation as ensuring that policy execution delivers the outputs and outcomes specified by the policy-makers. By contrast, a **bottom-up** approach considers that the role of those who execute policy in reshaping broad objectives to fit local and changing circumstances should be both recognized and welcomed.

Many policy analysts now suggest that objectives are more likely to be met if those who execute policy are given not just encouragement and resources but also flexibility. At street level (the point where policy is delivered), policy emerges from interaction between local bureaucrats and affected groups. Here at the sharp end, goals can often be best achieved by adapting them to local conditions. For instance, education, health care and policing must surely differ between the rural countryside and multicultural areas in the inner city. If the policy is left unmodified, its fate will be that of the mighty dragon in the Chinese proverb: no match for the neighbourhood snake.

Further, local implementers will often be the only people with full knowledge of how policies interact, and sometimes contradict each other. They will also know the significant actors in the locality, including the growing number of for-profit and voluntary sector agencies involved in policy execution. Implementation is often a matter of building relationships between organizations operating in the field, an art which is rarely covered in central manuals. When the American politician Tip O'Neill said, 'all politics is local', he could well have had policy implementation in mind.

So a bottom-up approach reflects an incremental view of policy-making in which implementation is seen as policy-making by other means. This approach reflects the contemporary emphasis on governance, with its stress on the many stakeholders involved in the policy process. The trick is to ensure that local coalitions work for the policy rather than forming a conspiracy against it.

Evaluation and review

Just as policy analysis has increased awareness of the importance of policy implementation, so too has it sharpened our focus on evaluation and review. The job of policy evaluation is to work out whether a policy has achieved its goals and if so how cost-effectively. The task of policy review is to decide whether to continue, modify or end a particular programme.

Evaluation

Public programmes, and the organizations created to put them into practice, lack the clear yardstick of profitability used in the private sector. How do we appraise a defence department if there are no wars and no win–loss record? Is the office of crisis management doing its job if there were no crises last year? Which is the more successful police force: the one that solves most crimes or the one that has the fewest crimes to solve?

Evaluation is further complicated because goal-shift often occurs during implementation, transforming a failing policy into a different but more successful one. This 'mushiness of goals', to use Fesler and Kettl's phrase (2005, p. 287), means that policy-makers' intent is often a poor benchmark for evaluation. Few programmes have such a specific objective as President Kennedy's commitment in 1961 to land a man on the moon and return him safely to earth 'before the decade is out' (mission accomplished, five months spare).

The question of evaluation has often been ignored, not just in traditional political analysis but also by governments themselves. Sweden is a typical example. In the post-war decades, a succession of Social Democratic governments concentrated on building a universal welfare state without even conceiving of a need to evaluate the quality and cost-effectiveness with which services were delivered by an expanding bureaucracy. In France and Germany, and other continental countries where bureaucratic tasks are interpreted as the legalistic application of rules to cases, the issue of policy evaluation still barely surfaces.

Yet without some evaluation of policy, governments will fail to learn the lessons of experience. In the United States, Jimmy Carter (President, 1977–81) did insist that at least 1 per cent of the funds allocated to any project should be devoted to evaluation. President Carter was concerned with what policies achieved and not just with the policies themselves. In the 1990s evaluation began to return to the fore. To take the USA again, the Government Performance and Results Act (1993) now requires each agency to perform an annual programme evaluation which is then intended to be used to revise plans and budgets.

Similarly, the Labour government elected in Britain in 1997 claimed a new pragmatic concern with evidence-based policy: what matters is what works (Sanderson, 2002). In some other democracies, too, public officials began to think, often for the first time, about whether policies were achieving their goals and at what cost.

Evaluation studies distinguish between **policy outputs** and **policy outcomes**. Outputs are easily measured by quantitative measures of activities (visits, trips, treatments, beneficiaries) which frequently become targets in their own right. But outcomes are more important and more resistant – which is one reason why they are highlighted less often than outputs. Even when outcomes are affected, the cost per unit of impact can be extraordinarily high, with gains sometimes proving to be temporary. With social programmes, a creaming process often dilutes the impact: the people who gain the most are those within the target group least in need of the support. For example, addiction treatment centres find it easiest to reach those users who would have been most likely to resolve their addiction anyway.

Certainly, the link between outputs and outcomes is often tenuous. In 1966, for example, the US government published the results of the Coleman Report, a massive sociological study of American secondary schools. This renowned study found that outputs such as teachers' salaries and educational expenditure had little effect on the ultimate outcome of education: namely, children's learning. The main influence on pupils' educational success was the family background of the child and its peers, not public spending. Children from a lower-class background were likely to underperform even if they were placed in a well-resourced school.

Policy outputs are what government does; **policy outcomes** are what government achieves. Outputs are the activity; outcomes are the effects, both intended and unforeseen. Outputs are measured easily enough: so many new prisons built or a specified increase in the state pension. Outcomes are harder to ascertain: a reduction in recidivism or in the number of elderly people living in poverty.

The Coleman Report illustrates a point familiar to most policy-makers: outcomes resist change, even when resources are devoted to altering them. The stickiness of social reality means that attempts to 'remedy the deficiencies in the quality of human life' can never be a complete success but can be, and sometimes are, a total failure (Rossi, Freeman and Lipsey, 1999, p. 6).

Just as policy implementation in accordance with the top-down model is an unrealistic goal, so judging policy effectiveness against specific objectives is often an implausibly scientific approach to evaluation. A more bottom-up, incremental approach to evaluation has therefore emerged. Here, the goals are more modest: an evaluation should simply gather in the opinions of all the stakeholders affected by the policy, yielding a qualitative narrative rather than a barrage of implausibly precise statistics. As Parsons (1995, p. 567) describes this approach, 'Evaluation has to be predicated on wide and full collaboration of all programme stakeholders: agents (funders, implementers); beneficiaries (target groups, potential adopters); and those who are excluded ('victims')'.

In such a naturalistic evaluation, the varying objectives of different interests are welcomed. They are not dismissed as a barrier to objective scrutiny of policy. Unintended effects can be written back into the script. This is a more pragmatic, indeed incremental, approach because the stakeholders might agree on the success of a policy even though they judge it against different standards. The object can simply be to learn from the project rather than to make uncertain judgements of success.

The danger of these naturalistic evaluations is that they become games of framing, blaming and claiming: politics all over again, with the most powerful stakeholder securing the most favourable write-up. To prevent the evaluation of a project from turning into nothing more than an application for continued funding, evaluation studies should always include some external perspectives.

Review

Once a policy has been evaluated, or even if it has not, the three possibilities are: to continue, to revise or to terminate. Most policies, or at least the functions associated with them, continue with only minor revisions. Once a role for government is established, it tends to continue. But the agency charged with performing the function does change over time. In the United States, for instance, 426 separate agencies were established between 1946 and 1997 but a majority of these had been terminated by the end of the period. The mechanism of change was usually an alteration in the partisan colour of the administration (D. Lewis, 2002). So the observation that there is nothing so permanent as a temporary government organization appears to be wide of the mark. Functions continue but the agencies performing them can evolve, either by splitting a task between two or more agencies or by consolidating previously separate functions into a single organization.

Yet even if agency termination is surprisingly common, the intriguing question remains: why is policy termination so rare? Why does government as a whole seemingly prefer to adopt new functions than to drop old ones? Bardach (1976) suggests five reasons for the difficulties of policy termination:

- Policies are designed to last a long time, creating expectations of future benefits;
- Policy termination brings conflicts which leave too much blood on the floor;
- No one wants to admit the policy was a bad idea;
- Policy termination may affect other programmes and interests;
- Politics rewards innovation rather than tidy housekeeping.

Policy instruments

So far, we have treated policy in a general way: goals are (sometimes) set; outputs are (usually) achieved; outcomes are (occasionally) affected. But what are the instruments which give effect to policy? To put the question in a broader way, how exactly do governments govern? The question is simple but useful, not least because a consideration of policy tools demonstrates the complexity of contemporary governance.

In thinking about the tools used to translate policy into practice, it is easy to overstate the importance of legislation and direct public provision. To be sure, parliament can establish a legal entitlement to a welfare benefit and then arrange for local governments to pay out the relevant sum to those who

BOX 18.2

A selection of policy instruments

	Type	Example: reducing tobacco consumption[1]
Primary legislation	Stick	Authorizing the health department to take measures to limit passive smoking
Delegated legislation	Stick	Banning tobacco consumption in restaurants
Permits	Stick	Requiring retailers to obtain or buy a permit before they can sell tobacco products
Tradable permits	Stick	Capping the number of permits but allowing them to be bought and sold on the market
Auctions	Stick	Capping the number of permits but auctioning them to the highest bidder
Labelling	Stick	Requiring health warnings on cigarette packets
Self-regulation agreements	Threat of stick	The industry agrees to phase out advertising in media heavily used by children
Fees and charges	Stick	Taxing tobacco products
Contracting out	Carrot	Paying a non-governmental organization to set up smoking cessation clinics
Tax expenditures[2]	Carrot	Removing sales tax on nicotine replacement products
Loan guarantees	Carrot	Guaranteeing repayment of loans to companies researching more effective nicotine replacement products
Vouchers	Carrot	Providing subsidies to cover all or part of the cost of attending smoking cessation clinics
Grants	Carrot	Funding anti-smoking groups and research on the effectiveness of anti-smoking strategies
Information	Sermon	Launching a publicity campaign about the harmful effects of smoking
Suasion	Sermon	Launching a publicity campaign to persuade people to stop smoking

Notes:

1 Some categories overlap; some examples are hypothetical.

2 The tax 'spent' is that which would have been raised without the exemption: in this case, the sales tax revenue from nicotine replacement products. A tax exemption can be viewed as a form of public spending.

meet specified eligibility requirements. The welfare states of Northern European states developed in precisely this way and these state-administered mechanisms have generally proved to be popular with their electorates.

In reality, however, legislation and direct provision are just two of many policy instruments; what is more, these devices are becoming less prominent in an era of limited public resources and increased social complexity. Even when legislation provides a framework, it is increasingly fleshed out in lengthy and detailed **delegated legislation** issued by the sponsoring department.

A government's repertoire is remarkably wide-ranging. A selection of policy instruments is listed in Box 18.2, using the example of a policy to restrict tobacco use. The items in this lengthy list overlap but are by no means comprehensive; more detailed catalogues extend to over 30 tools (Osborne and Gaebler, 1992).

Delegated legislation (also known as secondary or subordinate legislation) consists of detailed regulations issued by a relevant department to give effect to primary legislation. In the USA, the national government publishes about 70,000 pages of regulations in the Federal Register each year; the British government also publishes thousands of Statutory Instruments every year.

The box classifies tools as sticks (sanctions), carrots (rewards) and sermons (information and suasion) (Vedung, 1998). Sticks include traditional command-and-control functions: banning this, requiring that. Carrots include positive financial incentives such as subsidies and tax rebates. Sermons include that stalwart of administrations seeking to demonstrate their concern to all and sundry: the public information campaign.

More esoteric devices include tradable permits and auctions. Although rarely used in the tobacco field, such mechanisms are increasingly used in environmental policy as a way of ensuring that any pollution rights available within a government-set ceiling reach those producers who generate most economic value from their pollution-creating activity. These producers will be the ones willing to pay the highest price for their licence. Permit trading and auctions are ingenious methods of integrating public policy with market allocations (Cordes, 2002).

Policy instruments can be grouped in various ways. In addition to the distinction between sticks, carrots and sermons, Hood (1983) divides policy tools into four categories according to the government resource on which they are based:

- Communication, exploiting government's knowledge and credibility;
- Financial resources, exploiting government's ability to write cheques;
- Authority, exploiting government's official status;
- Organization, exploiting government's ability to act directly and powerfully.

Given a classification of tools, it is tempting to imagine a policymaker dialling up instruments as we might call out for a pizza, perhaps selecting a new combination for added zest. However, such an image would be a caricature of how policy is and should be formed. In practice, instrument selection is strongly influenced by past practice in the sector and by national policy styles.

More explicit criteria for choosing between tools include effectiveness (will it work?), efficiency (at what cost?), equity (is it fair?), appropriateness (does the instrument fit the problem?) and simplicity (is it manageable?). Rather than thinking of a policymaker drawing from an instrument menu, we should think of agents in the field asking, why should we bother with this? What's in it for us? Policy selection must remain sensitive to implementation issues since, as Pressman and Wildavsky (1973) taught us, great expectations in Washington are always at risk of being dashed in Oakland.

Public policy in liberal democracies

While policy can be usefully analysed into its component parts, it is also helpful to take a broader view. In this section, we seek to chart the major shifts in the policy agenda of Western states, transformations which reflect evolving conceptions of the state itself yet which, like other aspects of policy analysis, remain understated in descriptions of government institutions.

Broadly, we can divide the history of public policy in what are now established liberal democracies into three phases: the nightwatchman or liberal state of the nineteenth century and earlier; the welfare state of the later twentieth century; and the emerging regulatory state of the twenty-first century (Box 18.3). This scheme fits the experience of Northern European states, including the UK, with fair accuracy. However, the history of the USA, which never developed a welfare state but which was one of the first democracies to introduce independent regulatory agencies, is exceptional once more.

The nightwatchman state

The nightwatchman state was a minimal operation, concentrating on maintaining law and order, protecting private property and extracting sufficient resources to allow rulers to pursue their foreign policy. The state apparatus remained poorly developed, with a limited bureaucracy. Local administration was largely the responsibility of provincial notables. The nightwatchman role was an early form taken by the post-feudal but pre-democratic state in much of Europe, notably the United Kingdom, up to the nineteenth century; it reflected a liberal philosophy of non-intervention.

BOX 18.3

The changing agenda of the Western state

	Domestic agenda	Period
Nightwatchman state	Maintains law and order and protects private property	Nineteenth century and earlier
Welfare state	Provides minimum welfare to all citizens	Second half of twentieth century, particularly in Western Europe
Regulatory state	Sets rules and standards	Final decades of the twentieth century and later

The nightwatchman metaphor comes from John Locke (1632–1704), the English philosopher who laid the early foundations of liberal thinking. Locke considered the sole function of government to be that of protecting natural, God-given rights to life, liberty and property. In Locke's view, citizens should merely be provided with order, protection and the means of enforcing contracts.

In the United States, a country built to a liberal design, Thomas Jefferson (1743–1826) expressed the nightwatchman conception when he wrote: 'that government is best which governs least'. The nightwatchman state had no interest in public welfare: 'the drunkard in the gutter is just where he ought to be', commented the American sociologist William Sumner (1840–1910).

This liberal philosophy of clear but limited individual rights reflected the struggle for religious toleration. However, limiting the state to a nightwatchman role also proved highly congenial to the emerging business class. Indeed, the free-market doctrine of laissez-faire ('to allow to do') was perhaps the most significant element in the nightwatchman construct. As Opello and Rosow (2004, p. 97) comment,

> The liberal state, then, is in one respect a minimal state; that is, it is deliberately structured not to be itself a threat to the 'natural right' of property ownership, which is the ultimate justification for the dominant position of the bourgeoisie within the state.

The welfare state

The welfare state, which reached its zenith in Western and especially Northern Europe in the 1960s and 1970s, was clearly based on a more expansive and positive view of the state's role. However, the culmination of the welfare state in the post-war decades reflected a long evolution. Even as industrialization proceeded in the nineteenth century, the nightwatchman state had been drawn into a measure of economic and environmental regulation. In Britain, for example, the Factory Act (1833) had created a framework for inspecting factories while its successor of 1847 limited the working day to a maximum of ten hours.

Table 18.1 Introduction of social insurance to some liberal democracies

	Industrial accident	Health	Pensions	Unemployment benefit	Family allowances
Australia	1902	1945	1909	1945	1941
Austria	1887	1888	1927	1920	**1921**
Canada	1930	1971	1927	1940	1944
Denmark	1898	1892	1891	1907	1952
Finland	1895	1963	1937	1917	1948
France	1898	1898	1895	**1905**	1932
Germany	**1871**	**1883**	**1889**	1927	1954
Netherlands	1901	1929	1913	1916	1940
New Zealand	1900	1938	1898	1938	1926
Norway	1894	1909	1936	1906	1946
Sweden	1901	1891	1913	1934	1947

Note: Innovator in red.

Source: Adapted from Pierson (1998), table 4.1.

However, the real origins of collective welfare provision lay in Germany before the First World War. Under the rule of Otto von Bismarck (Chancellor, 1871–90), Germany had pioneered social insurance schemes which shared risks such as accident and illness, at least for industrial workers. Building on this innovative German model, the period from the 1920s saw the gradual extension of collective welfare in most liberal democracies to more areas of life (e.g. pensions and family allowances) and to more groups in the population (e.g. rural people and dependants of industrial workers). By the 1970s, coverage for the main aspects of welfare extended to virtually the entire population (Table 18.1).

By then, European democracies had become 'welfare states' in a triple sense. First, the state took a prime role in ensuring the provision of a minimum standard of welfare to all its citizens, supplanting ad hoc provision through churches and charities in the nightwatchman state. Second, providing welfare became the main function of public administration, consuming the lion's share of both taxpayers' revenue and officials' time. Third, welfare rights became an expression of social citizenship, a notion which sought to extend the scope of democracy itself.

The concept of social citizenship was developed by the British sociologist T. H. Marshall (1893–1981). In an influential account written in the aftermath of war, Marshall (1950, pp. 16–19) defined social citizenship as covering 'the whole range from the right to a modicum of economic welfare and security to the right to share to the full in the social heritage and to live the life of a civilized being according to the standards prevailing in society'. Influenced by such considerations, several democracies – for instance, France – began to embed a statement of welfare rights in their constitutions.

This development of social citizenship contrasts sharply with the nightwatchman state in which those who received public welfare through the poor laws were denied the vote. Where the nightwatchman state gave priority to liberty, the welfare state was premised on equality.

Of course, democracies continued to vary both in their welfare effort and in their attitude to its ideological underpinnings. To help grasp these variations, Esping-Andersen (1990, 1999) famously distinguished between three types of welfare regime: liberal, conservative and social democratic (Box 18.4). His terms clearly reflect political influences on welfare but, in this context, denote national configurations of welfare provision which go beyond the programmes of specific parties.

In the liberal constellation, as exemplified by the USA, welfare benefits are limited, means-tested and stigmatized: state welfare rather than a welfare state. In the conservative form, as illustrated by Germany,

BOX 18.4

Welfare state regimes

	Definition	Example
Liberal	Low, means-tested benefits provide residual support. High labour market participation expected.	United States
Conservative	Occupational insurance schemes, to which employers and employees contribute, provide salary-linked benefits. This regime traditionally conceives of the family, headed by a full-time male breadwinner and supported as needed by the church, as the main source of care.	Germany
Social democratic	Universal welfare provision is provided by the state and funded by high taxation. State-supplied child care encourages women to work.	Sweden

Note: Liberal and conservative welfare regimes can be linked to the liberal and coordinated market economies discussed in Chapter 8.

Sources: Adapted from Esping-Andersen (1990, 1999) and Ellison (2006).

benefits are based more on occupational insurance schemes and are intended to support family care. This format reflects the importance of the workplace to social functioning, and the influence of powerful employers, as well as church resistance to direct provision of welfare by the state. In the social democratic version, exemplified by Sweden, benefits are universal, provided to all citizens by the state and funded through taxation rather than insurance. This social democratic regime is the classic welfare state, seeking to protect citizens from market risk as well as reducing income inequality.

The 1980s witnessed the first real setbacks for welfare regimes. The underlying problem was financial: as the average age of the population increased, so the total cost of pensions, medical care and support services went up – and was projected to continue growing well into the twenty-first century. At the same time the working population, which shoulders the burden of support for the elderly, declined in number. The overall effect was a marked worsening of the **dependency ratio**. Even in the USA's liberal regime, projections of future welfare spending were daunting. Given the expanding cost of its Social Security and Medicare schemes, one journalist was even moved to describe the American government as 'a giant insurance company with a small defence affiliate' (i.e. its military forces) (Plender, 2003).

International economic pressures also impinged on thinking about welfare. If the cost of one country's welfare system was higher than all the rest, the international competitiveness of its economy might be endangered. Pierson (1998) suggested that the move to a more open international economy at least 'curtailed opportunities for the further development of national welfare states'. Certainly the oil crises of the 1970s, marking a transition to slower growth in the liberal democracies, were a catalyst to rethinking first the feasibility and then the desir-

The **dependency ratio** is the ratio of the economically dependent part of the population to the employed part. Dependents are those who are too young or old to work, the latter group being more significant in most developed states. Other things being equal, the higher the ratio, the greater the cost of welfare provision.

Table 18.2 Social expenditure in major Nordic states as a percentage of gross domestic product, 1981–2004

	1981	1987	1990	1995	2001	2004
Sweden	34	35	33	35	31	33
Denmark	30	28	29	32	30	30
Finland	22	26	25	32	26	26
Norway	22	26	26	27	26	26

Sources: Adapted from Nordic Social-Statistical Committee (2004), Table 10.6a and Steen (2004), Table 12.2.

ability of state-provided welfare from cradle to grave.

Such problems led to some retrenchment of welfare provision in the 1980s and 1990s, led by the liberal regimes such as the United States where benefits were in any case least generous. Benefits were marginally reduced, eligibility rules were tightened, charges were introduced for services such as medical treatment, few new commitments were taken on and the state made an effort to revive older caring agencies such as charities and churches. In particular, many states began to put more emphasis on individual responsibility, pressing the unemployed in particular to find work.

But the welfare state experienced a correction rather than a crisis. Fears of a race to the bottom in an era of globalization proved to be wide of the mark. Reflecting a worsening dependency ratio, overall spending stayed up even as some services were reduced (Table 18.2):

> Over nearly two decades, in which welfare state reform has been an ostensibly major concern, many Western governments, welfare state structures and priorities, at least in so far as these may be revealed by spending patterns, have remained much as they were in the early 1980s (Castles, 2004, p. 15).

The regulatory state

Although the crisis of the welfare state may have been overplayed, the final decades of the twentieth century did witness a fundamental shift in the agenda and focus of public policy in many liberal democracies, especially in Europe. In social welfare, service delivery was increasingly contracted out to private agencies; in the economy, public industries were privatized. Since one motive here was to render economies more competitive, this transition is sometimes discussed as a move from a welfare state to a competition state (Cerny, 1990).

But it is not clear that the frontiers of the state have been decisively modified; on the contrary, newly privatized monopolies must be regulated and public oversight has become more intense in such sectors as education, the environment, employment, scientific research and consumer protection. Indeed, smart regulation – allocating radio frequencies to mobile telephony, encouraging broadband internet use, moving to high definition television – may be capable of enhancing growth in advanced economies.

For want of a happier term, we will describe this shift in the policy approach as a transition to a regulatory state (Box 18.3, p. 387). Such a state uses rules, standards and other public statements as major policy instruments, rather than relying on direct provision of goods and services. Regulation has always been a leading mode of governance in the USA; its philosophy is now diffusing to other liberal democracies in Europe and elsewhere.

The most striking evidence for the retreat of the state from direct provision comes from the influential policy of privatization followed by Britain's Conservative government under Mrs Thatcher in the 1980s. The speed and thoroughness with which the United Kingdom government 'sold off the family silver' (to quote the words of former Conservative prime minister Harold Macmillan) attracted international interest (Table 18.3). Just as nationalization had been seen by the post-war Labour government as a way of introducing public control and rational planning to key industrial sectors, so privatization reflected an ideologically charged desire to 'roll back the frontiers of the state'.

The key point, though, was that creating private monopolies – as with telephones, gas and electricity – required the creation of new offices of regulation at least until competition became established. As Majone (1996, p. 2) notes, 'In Britain and elsewhere, the privatization of the public utilities has been followed by price regulation . . . the last fifteen years have been a period less of deregulation than of intense regulatory reform'. The outcome is as much a regulatory state as a rolled-back state.

In analysing the rise of the regulatory state in Britain, Moran (2003) identifies three major dimensions. These are:

- Regulation of privatized industries where competition remains weak (e.g. water supply);
- External supervision of previously self-regulating institutions such as universities and financial markets;
- Social regulation in such areas as equal opportunities, health and safety, and food standards.

This new style of governance through regulation has, however, brought forth some fresh problems. Perhaps the most important of these is the issue of democratic legitimacy. Most new regulatory bodies operate not as divisions of ministries but as agencies operating at one remove from the centres of political – and therefore democratic – power. Similar attempts to depoliticize regulation can be observed in the independence given to central banks to set interest rates, as now applies in both Britain and the eurozone. In the USA, regulatory independence is accepted, and was indeed deliberately instituted as a reaction against political corruption, but elsewhere it represents a newer and less welcome phenomenon.

Table 18.3 Case-by-case privatization in the United Kingdom, 1980s

Year	Company privatized	Proceeds (£ million)
1981	British Aerospace	149
1981	Cable & Wireless	224
1982	Britoil	549
1983	BP	565
1984	Enterprise Oil	392
1984	Jaguar Cars	294
1984	British Telecom	3,916
1985	British Aerospace	551
1986	British Gas	5,434
1987	British Airways	900
1987	Rolls Royce	1,362
1987	British Airports Authority	1,281
1988	British Steel Corporation	2,482
1989	Water Authorities	5,240

Note: Only privatizations yielding over £100m are shown.

Source: Adapted from Prosser and Moran (1994), Table 3.2.

Majone (1996) suggests two defences of this trend away from political control, even though it runs counter to orthodox democratic thinking. First, autonomous agencies can adopt more consistent, credible and long-term policies than are feasible for elected politicians who remain subject to short-term pressures from the voters. If an unelected central bank can control inflation more effectively than an elected government, the argument goes, then surely the bank should be given the job (Bernhard, 2002)?

Second, delegating political authority to specialized professional regulators is particularly appropriate for issues that are technical (e.g. telecommunications) rather than redistributive (e.g. taxation) in nature. The level of taxation is a political question for which there is no technical answer but there may well be a single best way of regulating mobile telephony. As the regulatory state matures, so we may expect the rebalancing it represents between political and professional authority to become taken for granted.

Public policy in authoritarian states

If there is a general theme to the policy process in non-democracies, it is the subservience of policy to politics. Often, the key task for non-elected rulers is to play off domestic political forces against each other so as to ensure the ruler's own continuation in office, an art developed to its highest level by the cautious ruling families of the Middle East. Alternatively, the ruler may want to enrich himself, his family and his ethnic group, a task hardly conducive to orderly policy development. As Hershberg (2006, p. 151) says,

> To be successful, policies must reflect the capabilities – encompassing expertise, resources and authority – of the institutions and individuals charged with their implementation. Those capabilities are more likely to be translated into effective performance in environments characterized by predictable, transparent and efficient procedures for reaching decisions and for adjudicating differences of interest.

But it is precisely this predictable and efficient environment which non-democracies find difficulty in supplying. Often, opaque patronage is the main political currency; the age-old game of building up and paying down political debts works against 'transparent procedures' of any kind. As Chazan *et al.* (1999, p. 171) note in their discussion of Africa, 'patriarchal rule has tended to be conservative: it propped up the existing order and did little to promote change. It required the exertion of a great deal of energy just to maintain control'.

In addition, rulers may simply lack the ability to make coherent policy. This weakness was especially common among military governments. The generals sometimes seized power in an honest attempt to eliminate corruption and improve policy-making but then discovered that governance was more complicated than they had imagined. Eventually, they slunk back to their lair, with little achieved.

Policy inertia is therefore a familiar pattern under authoritarian rule. Stagnation is reinforced when, as in many of the largest non-democracies, the rulers rely on rents from natural commodities such as oil as their main source of revenue. In these circumstances, the government need not achieve the penetration of society required to collect taxes, nor need it concern itself with the development of human capital. Rather, a stand-off of mutual distrust develops between rulers and ruled, a context which is incompatible with the sophisticated and complex policy initiatives and instruments found in the most developed liberal democracies. In the absence of effective social policy at national level, problems of poverty, welfare and medical care are addressed locally, and occasionally not at all.

The absence of an extensive network of voluntary associations and interest groups prevents the close coordination between state and society needed for effective policy-making and implementation. The blocking mechanism here is fear. As Saich (2004, p. 223) writes of China,

> While it is true that public discourse is breaking free of the codes and linguistic phrases established by the party-state, it is also clear that no coherent alternative vision has emerged that would fashion a civil society. From the party's point of view, what is lurking in the shadows waiting to pounce on any opening that would allow freedom of expression is revivalism, religion, linguistic division, regional and non-Han ethnic loyalties.

As always, however, it is important to distinguish between different types of authoritarian government. At one extreme, many military and personal rulers show immense concern about their own prosperity but none at all for their country's, leading to a policy shortage. At the other extreme, many modernizing communist states attempted, and for a while achieved, a type of planning virtually without precedent in history; every communist state formulated clearer national goals and targets than any democracy. The result was a decisive, ruthless and often successful commitment to a single goal, notably industrialization. Yet planning eventually yielded economic stagnation and thus contributed to the collapse of communism in Eastern Europe and the Soviet Union. The formula delivered production rather than productivity and emphasized quantity over quality.

Public policy in illiberal democracies

The policy process in illiberal democracies falls between that found in liberal democracies and in authoritarian regimes. On the one hand, illiberal democracies inherently lack the strong institutions, legal framework and detailed connections with society that permit the sophisticated policy processes found in liberal democracies. On the other hand, these democracies cannot simply retreat from policy in the manner of, say, many military governments. There are elections to be won and popular dreams to be fed, often in the unpromising context of a poor country.

The response of the rulers of illiberal democracies to these dilemmas is by no means uniform. However, one syndrome is to combine strong political control of key economic resources, particularly commodities, with a freer market in less sensitive sectors of the economy. In most cases, social and economic inequality is pronounced, with considerable wealth for a small group of well-connected business owners coexisting alongside unremitting poverty for a large sector of the population.

Whether living in urban ghettos or remote rural areas, the poor must rely largely on self-help, with the government lacking the organization and resources needed to deliver an effective and uniform social policy. The populist leader both draws on, and claims he is the only means of overcoming, the glaring gap between the poverty of the many and the wealth of the few.

It is important to bear in mind that many illiberal democracies have emerged from an authoritarian past, creating major problems of transition. Post-communist states provide the most dramatic examples of the policy transformation required of new democracies. When the communist order collapsed, an entire method of organizing society went with it; far from springing a leak, the communist boat sank. The task facing new leaders was to transform societies fuelled by power into societies based on rules, a project of enormous scale.

Under communism, large state-owned enterprises not only dominated the economy but also served as welfare providers, producing what Elster *et al.* (1998, p. 204) describe as a 'tight coupling' between the workplace and social policy:

> Firms provided crèches, holiday homes, housing, health services, training and other welfare facilities for their staff. Continuous and lifelong participation in the production process was the proviso of collectivist protection.

This elaborate, inefficient but functioning network could not be quickly replaced by market mechanisms in the economy or by social policy delivered through central or local governments. In particular, a successful *private* economy, as in liberal democracies, is in fact an intricate *public* and even political achievement. It requires entrepreneurs to show initiative, capital markets to provide resources for investment, consumers to spend money, courts to resolve disputes, bureaucrats to keep their fingers out of the pie and a government to act as an umpire rather than a player. The legal challenge of establishing property rights, as well as tax, competition and bankruptcy laws, is considerable.

For example, after its exceptionally chaotic transition from communism, Russia's state has begun to rebuild its capacity to govern an unequal and diverse society. A body of law has been established which provides a more predictable environment for business investment, although political risks remain far higher than in liberal democracies. A recentralization of power has encouraged the more uniform application of the newly codified legal system. The tax-take has improved, offering an improvement in public revenues with the prospect of further gains as the economy itself continues to grow. The philosophy of social policy has become more coherent, with a 'controversial 2005 reform that replaces the bulk of Soviet-era privileges (free or subsidised housing, transportation, medicine and the like for pensioners, students and others) with supposedly equivalent cash payments' (Twigg, 2005, p. 219).

Such reforms notwithstanding, the notion that Russia, and other illiberal democracies, are simply in transition to a liberal democracy remains fanciful. The business environment has improved but industrialists who pose a political threat to the president soon find that numerous rules and regulations are still invoked selectively against them. The state has disposed of many enterprises but has tightened its control over the key resources of oil and gas. In 2006, for example, Russia's government simply rewrote a contract with Royal Dutch Shell so as to provide state-owned companies with a greater share of the Sakhalin-2 oil field in Siberia.

As in other rentier states, state control of export commodities will enable the Russin state to sustain its own position even if it neglects the development of closer connections with, and support for, the Russian population. Social problems such as poverty, alchoholism, violent crime and rural depopulation remain deep-rooted. Despite the attempt to modernize social policy, for many improverished Russians the transition from communism must appear as a move from a crude welfare state to an even cruder nightwatchman state.

Many public officials are so poorly paid that corruption remains an essential tool for making ends meet, meaning that even-handed policy implementation is impossible. An escape from this position cannot be achieved just by improved policy-making but will require, in addition, the continuation of consistent, broad-based economic development.

When we turn to illiberal democracies in the smaller states of Africa and Latin America, we find that the problems of capacity-building are even greater. The policy agenda here is about strengthening the capacity of *both* the public sector and the private sector; the emphasis in post-communist democracies on rebalancing the relationship between public and private is a dubious prescription for illiberal democracies in poor countries where capacity of any kind is limited.

It is certainly true that the state has been an important economic and political force in these smaller low-income countries, sometimes crowding out the private sector. But the solution is not so much less government but a different government, embedded in rule-following institutions rather than personal rule. Similarly, there is little point in adopting Western ideas of new public management within the bureaucracy; rather, the purpose should be to build up an orthodox civil service that applies rules consistently and economically. As Adam Smith (1776) well understood, developing the market also requires enhancing the public infrastructure of transport, communication and education.

In Africa, however, fragmentary attempts at capacity-building have so far produced only meagre results. Governments often lack the ability to implement their policies throughout the territory. They lack numbers on the ground and must often rely on traditional local leaders who are therefore able to veto the implementation of the reform agenda. Whether its government is elected or not, a state that barely exists cannot be expected to engage in serious and effective policy-making and implementation.

Similarly, the smaller and more fragile illiberal democracies in Latin America find themselves immersed in a sea of difficulties which inhibit institutional development and the policy-implementing capacity flowing from it. The imposition of market economics has failed to accelerate growth rates or reduce fundamental inequalities in society. States find themselves sharing power with regional leaders and drug barons. As in Russia, corruption breeds distrust in public services.

Writing of the Andean states of Bolivia, Colombia, Ecuador, Peru and Venezuela, where democracy has retained a toe-hold, Drake and Hershberg (2006, p. 20) note that

> reforms intended to increase the effectiveness or legitimacy of the state have sometimes sapped rather than strengthened state capacity . . . Never very strong, the central government has been challenged by international and transnational actors; by domestic regional and local competitors; by purveyors of violence among criminals, guerrillas and paramilitaries; and by drug growers and traffickers.

In these circumstances, the task is to build the capacity of the state to implement policies of any kind.

Learning Resources for Chapter 18

Next step

Birkland (2005) is a clear and accessible introduction to theories and concepts in public policy.

Further reading

Stone (2001) and Fischer (2003) adopt critical but accessible approaches to public policy. Colebatch (1998) discusses the policy concept while Sabatier (1999) reviews theories of the policy process. On implementation, the classic American study by Pressman and Wildavsky (1973) can be supplemented by Hill and Hupe (2002). For policy instruments, see the classic work by Hood (1983) and more recent Canadian work such as Salamon (2002) and Eliadis, Hill and Howlett (2005). Peters (2004) covers both the policy process and specific policy sectors in the USA. Rose (2004) is a comparative study of lesson-drawing in public policy. Pierson (1998, 2000) and Esping-Andersen (2002) are excellent sources on the welfare state; Ellison (2006) is a more recent review. Majone (1996) is outstanding on regulation. Moran, Rein and Goodin (2006) provide a 44-chapter handbook on public policy.

Internet sources

National Institute for Research Advancement
Includes a directory of public policy institutes and a searchable bibliography of their publications
http://www.nira.go.jp/

Economics and Cost Analysis Support, Environment Protection Agency, USA
Analytical guidance on estimating the costs and benefits of environmental policy
http://www.epa.gov/ttn/ecas/about.html

The Brookings Insitution
An American private non-profit organization devoted to independent research and innovative policy solutions
http://www.brookings.org

Independent Evaluation Group, World Bank
An evaluation of the World Bank's support for capacity building in six African states
http://www.worldbank.org/ieg/africa_capacity_building/?goog=3208

References

These references are listed by chapter at http://www.palgrave.com/politics/hague

A

Aberbach, J. *et al.* (1981) *Bureaucrats and Politicians* (Cambridge, MA: Harvard University Press).

Adams, F. (2003) *Deepening Democracy: Global Governance and Political Reform in Latin America* (New York: Praeger).

Ágh, A. (2003) 'Public Administration in Central and Eastern Europe', in *Handbook of Public Administration,* ed. B. Guy Peters and J. Pierre (London and Thousand Oaks, CA: Sage) pp. 536–48.

Agüero, F. (2004) 'Authoritarian Legacies: The Military's Role', in *Authoritarian Legacies and Democracies in Latin America and Southern Europe*, ed. K. Hite and P. Cesarini (Notre Dame, IN: University of Notre Dame Press) pp. 233–62.

Albritton, R. (2006) 'American Federalism and Intergovernmental Relations', in *Developments in American Politics 5*, ed. G. Peele *et al.* (New York and Basingstoke: Palgrave Macmillan) pp. 124–45.

Alexander, G. (2005) 'France: Reform-mongering between Majority Runoff and Proportionality', in *Handbook of Electoral System Choice*, ed. J. Colomer (Basingstoke and New York: Palgrave Macmillan) pp. 209–21.

Alexander, H. (2005) 'Comparative Analysis of Political Party and Campaign Financing in the United States and Canada', in *The Delicate Balance between Political Equity and Freedom of Expression: Political Party and Campaign Financing in Canada and the United States*, ed. S. Griner and D. Zovatto (Washington, DC: International IDEA) http://www.idea.int/publications/pp_can_usa/upload/Freedom_Full1.pdf, accessed 28 July, 2006.

Allen, M. (2006) *The Varieties of Capitalism Paradigm: Explaining Germany's Comparative Advantage* (Basingstoke and New York: Palgrave Macmillan).

Almond, G. (1983) 'Communism and Political Culture Theory', *Comparative Politics* (15) 127–38.

Almond, G. (1993) 'The Study of Political Culture', in *Political Culture in Germany,* ed. D. Berg-Schlosser and R. Rytlewski (New York: St. Martin's Press) pp. 13–26.

Almond, G. and Verba, S. (1963) *The Civic Culture* (Princeton, NJ: Princeton University Press).

Almond, G. and Verba, S. (eds) (1980) *The Civic Culture Revisited* (Princeton, NJ: Princeton University Press).

Althaus, S. (2003) *Collective Preferences in Democratic Politics: Opinion Surveys and the Will of the People* (Cambridge and New York: Cambridge University Press).

Alvarez, A. (2004) 'State Reform Before and After Chávez's Election' in *Venezuelan Politics in the Chávez Era: Class, Polarization and Conflict*, ed. S. Ellner and D. Hellinger (Boulder, CO and London: Lynne Rienner) pp. 147–60.

Álavrez-Rivera, M. (2006) 'Elections to the German Bundestag, September 18, 2005', *Election Resources on the Internet*, http://electionresources.org/de/bundestag.php?election=2005, accessed 9 June, 2006.

Ames, B. (2002) 'Party Discipline in the Chamber of Deputies', in *Legislative Politics in Latin America,* ed. S. Morgenstern and B. Nacif (Cambridge and New York: Cambridge University Press) pp. 185–221.

Anderson, B. (1998) *The Spectre of Comparisons: Nationalism, South-East Asia and the World* (London and New York: Verso).

Anderson, C. and Ward, D. (1996) 'Barometer Elections in Comparative Perspective', *European Journal of Political Research* (15) 447–60.

Andeweg, R. and Irwin, G. (1993) *Dutch Government and Politics* (Basingstoke: Macmillan).

Andeweg, R. and Irwin, G. (2002) *Governance and Politics of the Netherlands* (Basingstoke and New York: Palgrave Macmillan).

Andrews, J. and Montinola, G. (2004) 'Veto Players and the Rule of Law in Emerging Democracies', *Comparative Political Studies* (37) 55–87.

Ansell, C. and Gingrich, J. (2003) 'Reforming the Administrative State', in *Democracy Transformed? Expanding Political Opportunities in Advanced Industrial Democracies,* ed. B. Cain, R. Dalton and S. Scarrow (Oxford and New York: Oxford University Press) pp. 164–91.

Arblaster, A. (2002) *Democracy,* 3rd edn (Buckingham and Philadelphia, PA: Open University Press).

ARC (F. Clifton White Applied Research Center for Democracy and Elections) (2006) *Election Guide* (Washington, DC: IFES) http://www.electionguide.org/about.php, accessed 13 June, 2006.

Aristotle (1962 edn) *The Politics,* trans. T. Sinclair (Harmondsworth and Baltimore, MD: Penguin).

Arter, D. (1999) *Scandinavian Politics Today* (Manchester: Manchester University Press, and New York: St Martin's Press).

Arter, D. (2003) 'Committee Cohesion and the "Corporate Dimension" of Parliamentary Committees: A Comparative Analysis', *Journal of Legislative Studies* (9) 73–87.

Atton, C. (2004) *An Alternative Internet: Radical Media, Politics and Creativity* (Edinburgh: Edinburgh University Press).

Avdagić, S. and Crouch, C. (2006) 'Organized Economic Interests: Diversity and Change in an Enlarged Europe' in *Developments in European Politics*, ed. P. Heywood *et al.* (Basingstoke and New York: Palgrave Macmillan) pp. 196–216.

Aznar, J. (2005) 'It Is Not Too Late to Cast off Europe's Pessimism', *Financial Times,* 17 October, p. 21.

B

Baer, M. (1993) 'Mexico's Second Revolution: Pathways to Liberalization', in *Political and Economic Liberalization in*

Mexico: At a Critical Juncture?, ed. R. Roett (Boulder, CO and London: Lynne Rienner) pp. 51–68.

Bagehot, W. (1867) [1963 edn] *The English Constitution* (London: Fontana).

Bakvis, H. and Skogstad, G. (eds) (2002) *Canadian Federalism: Performance, Effectiveness and Legitimacy* (Don Mills, Ontario and Oxford: Oxford University Press).

Balfour, S. (2005) *The Politics of Contemporary Spain* (London and New York: Routledge).

Balme, R. (1998) 'The French Region as a Space for Public Policy', in *Regions in Europe*, ed. P. Le Galès and C. Lequesne (London and New York: Routledge) pp. 181–98.

Banks, A. and Textor, R. (1963) *A Cross-Polity Survey* (Cambridge, MA: MIT Press).

Barber, B. (1995) *Jihad vs McWorld* (New York: Ballantine Books).

Barber, J. (1992) *The Pulse of Politics: Electing Presidents in the Media Age* (New Brunswick, NY and London: Transaction Books).

Bardach, E. (1976) 'Policy Termination as a Political Process', *Policy Sciences* (7) 123–31.

Bardes, B., Shelley, M. and Schmidt, S. (2006) *American Government and Politics: The Essentials*, 2006/7 edn (Belmont, CA: Thomson Wadsworth).

Barry, B. (1988) *Sociologists, Economists, and Democracy* (Chicago, IL: University of Chicago Press).

Bartolini, S. and Mair, P. (2001) 'Challenges to Contemporary Political Parties', in *Political Parties and Democracy*, ed. L. Diamond and R. Gunther (Baltimore, MD: Johns Hopkins University Press) pp. 327–44.

Batt, J. (2003) 'Defining Central and Eastern Europe' in *Developments in Central and East European Politics 3*, ed. S. White, J. Batt and P. Lewis (Basingstoke: Palgrave Macmillan) pp. 3–22.

Baum, L. (2003) *The Supreme Court*, 7th edn (Washington, DC: CQ Press).

Beetham, D. (2004) 'Freedom as the Foundation', *Journal of Democracy* (15) 61–75.

Bekke, H., Perry, J. and Toonen, T. (1996) *Civil Service Systems in Comparative Perspective* (Bloomington, IN: Indiana University Press).

Bellin, E. (2005) 'Coercive Institutions and Coercive Leaders', in *Authoritarianism in the Middle East*, ed. M. Posuney and M. Angrsit (Boulder, CO and London: Lynne Rienner) pp. 21–42.

Bendor, J., Moe, T. and Shorts, K. (2001) 'Recycling the Garbage Can: An Assessment of the Research Program', *American Political Science Review* (95) 169–90.

Bennett, W. Lance (2005) 'Social Movements beyond Borders: Understanding Two Eras of Transnational Activism', in *Transnational Protest and Global Activism*, ed. D. della Porta and S. Tarrow (Lanham, MD: Rowman & Littlefield) pp. 203–26.

Bennett, W. Lance and Entman, R. (eds) (2001) *Mediated Politics: Communication in the Future of Democracy* (Cambridge and New York: Cambridge University Press).

Bentley, A. (1908) *The Process of Government* (Chicago, IL: University of Chicago Press).

Bentley, T., Jupp, B. and Stedman Jones, D. (2000) *Getting to Grips with Depoliticization* (London: Demos) http://www.demos.co.uk, accessed 6 June, 2006.

Berg-Schlosser, D. and Rytlewski, R. (eds) (1993) *Political Culture in Germany* (New York: St. Martin's Press).

Berger, S. and Compston, H. (eds) (2002) *Policy Concertation and Social Partnership in Western Europe: Lessons for the 21st Century* (New York and Oxford: Berghahn).

Bergman, T. (2000) 'Sweden: When Minority Cabinets Are the Rule and Majority Coalitions the Exception', in *Coalition Governments in Western Europe*, ed. W. Müller and K. Strøm (Oxford and New York: Oxford University Press) pp. 192–230.

Bernhard, W. (2002) *Banking on Reform: Political Parties and Central Bank Independence in the Industrial Democracies* (Ann Arbor, MI: University of Michigan Press).

Best, H. and Cotta, M. (2000) *Parliamentary Representatives in Europe, 1848–2000* (Oxford and New York: Oxford University Press).

Bevir, M. and Rhodes, R. (2002) 'Interpretive Theory', in *Theory and Methods in Political Science*, 2nd edn, ed. D. Marsh and G. Stoker (Basingstoke and New York: Palgrave Macmillan) pp. 131–52.

Bevir, M. and Rhodes, R. (2006) 'Prime Ministers, Presidentialism and Westminster Smokescreens', *Political Studies* (54) 671–90.

Bickerton, J. and Gagnon, A.-G. (eds) (2004) *Canadian Politics*, 4th edn (Peterborough, ON: Broadview Press).

Bill, J. and Springborg, R. (1999) *Politics in the Middle East*, 5th edn (New York: Longman).

Binderkrantz, A. (2005) 'Interest Group Strategies: Navigating Between Privileged Access and Strategies of Pressure', *Political Studies* (53) 694–715.

Birkland, T. (2005) *An Introduction to the Policy Process: Theories, Concepts and Models of Public Policy Making*, 2nd edn (Armonk, NY and London: M. E. Sharpe).

Bishop, G. (2004) *The Illusion of Public Opinion: Fact and Artifact in American Public Opinion Polls* (Lanham, MD and Oxford: Rowman & Littlefield).

Blais, A., Dobrzynska, A. and Massicotte, L. (2003) *Why is Turnout Higher in Some Countries than in Others?* (Ottawa, Ontario: Elections Canada) http://www.elections.ca/content.asp?section=loi&document=summary&dir=tur/tuh&lang=e&textonly=false, accessed 14 June, 2006.

Blais, A. and Massicote, L. (2002) 'Electoral Systems', in *Comparing Democracies 2: New Challenges in the Study of Elections and Voting*, ed. L. LeDuc, R. Niemi and P. Norris (Thousand Oaks, CA and London: Sage) pp. 40–69.

Blais, A., Massicotte, L. and Dobrzynska, A. (1997) 'Direct Presidential Elections: A World Summary', *Electoral Studies* (16) 441–55.

Blom-Hansen, J. (2000) 'Still Corporatism in Scandinavia: A Survey of Recent Empirical Findings', *Scandinavian Political Studies* (23) 157–81.

Blondel, J. (1973) *Comparative Legislatures* (Englewood Cliffs, NJ: Prentice Hall).

Blondel, J. (1993) 'Consensus Politics and Multiparty Systems', paper presented at the Conference on Consensual Policymaking and Multiparty Politics, Australian National University, 1993.

Blondel, J. (1995) *Comparative Government: An Introduction*, 2nd edn (Harlow and New York: Longman).

Boardman, A. *et al.* (2000) *Cost-Benefit Analysis: Concepts and Practice*, 2nd edn (Englewood Cliffs, NJ: Prentice Hall).

Bodin, J. (1576) [1962 edn] *The Six Books of a Commonwealth*, ed. K. McRae (Cambridge, MA: Harvard University Press).

Bogason, P. (1996) 'The Fragmentation of Local Government in Scandinavia', *European Journal of Political Research* (30) 65–86.

Borchert, J. and Copeland, G. (2003) 'United States: A Political Class of Entrepreneurs', in *The Political Class in Advanced Democracies*, ed. J. Borchert and J. Zeiss (Oxford and New York: Oxford University Press) pp. 393–415.

Borchert, J. and Zeiss, J. (eds) (2003) *The Political Class in Advanced Democracies* (Oxford and New York: Oxford University Press).

Bork, R. (2003) *Coercing Virtue: The Worldwide Rule of Judges* (Washington, DC: American Enterprise Institute).

Borón, A. (1998) 'Faulty Democracies? A Reflection on the Capitalist "Fault Lines"', in *Fault Lines of Democracy in Post-Transition Latin America*, ed. F. Agüero and J. Stark (Coral Gables, FL: University of Miami) pp. 41–66.

Börzel, T. and Sedelmeieir, U. (2006) 'The EU Dimension in European Politics' in *Developments in European Politics*, ed. P. Heywood *et al.* (Basingstoke and New York: Palgrave Macmillan), pp. 54–70.

Boston, J. *et al.* (eds) (1995) *Reshaping the State: New Zealand's Bureaucratic Revolution* (Oxford and New York: Oxford University Press).

Bourchier, D. (2006) *Illiberal Democracy in Indonesia* (London and New York: Routledge).

Bourgault, J. (2002) 'The Role of Deputy Ministers in Canadian Government', in *The Handbook of Canadian Public Administration*, ed. C. Dunn (Don Mills, Ontario: Oxford University Press) pp. 430–49.

Bourgault, L. (1995) *Mass Media in Sub-Saharan Africa* (Bloomington, IN: Indiana University Press).

Bourne, A. (2003) 'Regional Europe', in *European Union Politics*, ed. M. Cini (Oxford and New York: Oxford University Press) pp. 278–93.

Bovens, M. (2006) 'Analysing and Assessing Public Accountability: A Conceptual Framework', *European Governance Papers*, http://www.connex-network.org/eurogov/pdf/egp-connex-c-06–01.pdf, accessed 22 December, 2006.

Bowler, S. and Donovan, T. (2002) 'Democracy, Institutions and Attitudes about Citizen Influence on Government', *British Journal of Political Science* (32) 371–90.

Bowler, S. and Farrell, D. (eds) (1992) *Electoral Strategies and Political Marketing* (London: Macmillan).

Bowler, S., Donovan, T. and Tolbert, C. (eds) (1998) *Citizens as Legislators: Direct Democracy in the United States* (Columbus, OH: Ohio State University Press).

Bowles, N. (1998) *Government and Politics of the United States*, 2nd edn (Basingstoke: Macmillan).

Boyer, R. (1997) 'French Statism at the Crossroads', in *Political Economy of Modern Capitalism: Mapping Convergence and Diversity*, ed. C. Crouch and W. Streeck (London and Thousand Oaks, CA: Sage) pp. 71–101.

Brady, H. and Johnston, R. (eds) (2006) *Capturing Campaign Effects* (Ann Arbor: University of Michigan Press).

Brams, S. (2004) *Game Theory and Politics* (Mineola, NY: Dover).

Bratton, M. (1998) 'Second Elections in Africa', *Journal of Democracy* (9) 51–66.

Bratton, M. and van de Walle, N. (1997) *Democratic Experiments in Africa: Regime Transitions in Comparative Perspective* (Cambridge and New York: Cambridge University Press).

Braun, D. *et al.* (2003) *Fiscal Policies in Federal States* (Aldershot and Burlington, VT: Ashgate).

Breslin, S. (2004) 'Capitalism with Chinese Characteristics: The Public, the Private and the International', *Working Paper No. 104*, Asia Research Centre (Perth: Murdoch University), http://wwwarc.murdoch.edu.au/wp/wp104.pdf, accessed 20 March, 2006.

Brewer, P., Aday, S. and Gross, K. (2003) 'Rallies All Round: The Dynamics of System Support', in *Framing Terrorism: The News Media, the Government and the Public*, ed. P. Norris, M. Kern and M. Just (London and NY: Routledge) pp. 229–54.

Brodsgaard, K. and Yongnian, Z. (eds) (2006) *The Chinese Communist Party in Reform* (London and New York: Routledge).

Brooker, P. (1995) *Twentieth-Century Dictatorships: The Ideological One-Party States* (Basingstoke: Macmillan).

Brooker, P. (2000) *Non-Democratic Regimes: Theory, Government and Politics* (Basingstoke: Macmillan, and New York: St Martin's Press).

Brooks, S. (2004) *Canadian Democracy: An Introduction*, 4th edn (Don Mills, Ontario and Oxford: Oxford University Press).

Brown, A. (ed.) (2004) *The Demise of Marxism–Leninism in Russia* (London and New York: Palgrave).

Bryce, J. (1919) *The American Commonwealth*, Vol. 1 (London: Macmillan).

Bryce, J. (1921) *Modern Democracies*, Vol. 2 (New York: Macmillan).

Brzezinski, Z. (2002) 'Confronting Anti-American Grievances', *New York Times*, 1 September.

BSA (British Social Attitudes) (2006) *Contents List*, http://www.britsocat.com/Body.aspx?control=BritsocatHome, accessed 15 April, 2006.

Budge, I. (1996) *The New Challenge of Direct Democracy* (Cambridge: Polity).

Buhlungu, S. *et al.* (eds) (2006) *State of the Nation: South Africa, 2005–06* (East Lansing, MI: Michigan State University Press).

Bull, H. (1977) *The Anarchical Society: A Study of Order in World Politics* (Basingstoke: Macmillan).

Bull, M. and Newell, J. (2005) *Italian Politics: Adjustment under Duress* (Cambridge and Malden, MA: Polity).

Burgess, M. (2000) *Federalism and European Union: The Building of Europe, 1950–2000* (London and New York: Routledge).

Burgess, M. (2001) 'Competing National Visions: Canada-Quebec Relations in a Comparative Perspective', in *Multinational Democracies*, ed. A.-G. Gagnon and J. Tully (Cambridge and New York: Cambridge University Press) pp. 257–74.

Burgess, M. (2003) 'Federalism and Federation', in *European Union Politics*, ed. M. Cini (Oxford and New York: Oxford University Press) pp. 65–79.

Burgess, M. (2006) *Comparative Federalism: Theory and Practice* (London and New York: Routledge).

Burke, E. (1774) [1975 edn] 'Speech to the Electors of Bristol', in *Edmund Burke on Government, Politics and Society*, ed. B. Hill (London: Fontana) pp. 156–8.

Burke, J. (2005) 'The Institutional Presidency', in *The Presidency and the Political System*, 8th edn, ed. M. Nelson (Washington DC: CQ Press) pp. 399–424.

Burnham, W. (1982) 'The Constitution, Capitalism and the Need for Rationalized Regulation', in *How Capitalistic Is the Constitution?* ed. R. Goldwyn and W. Schambra (Washington, DC: American Enterprise Institute) pp. 72–87.

Bush, G. (2005) 'New Zealand: A Quantum Leap Forward?', in *Comparing Local Governance: Trends and Developments,* ed. B. Denters and L. Rose (Basingstoke and New York: Palgrave Macmillan) pp. 174–92.

Butler, A. (2004) *Contemporary South Africa* (Basingstoke and New York: Palgrave).

Buxton, J. (2001) *The Failure of Political Reform in Venezuela* (Aldershot and Burlington, VT: Ashgate).

Bytwerk, R. (2004) *Bending Spines: The Propagandas of Nazi Germany and the German Democratic Republic* (East Lansing, MI: Michigan State University Press).

C

Cabinet Office (2006) *Ministerial Code*, http://www.cabinetoffice.gov.uk/propriety_and_ethics/ministers/ministerial_code, accessed 23 December, 2006.

Cain, B. and Goux, D. (2006) 'Parties in an Era of Renewed Partisanship', in *Developments in American Politics 5*, ed. G. Peele *et al.* (Basingstoke and New York: Palgrave Macmillan) pp. 37–52.

Calhoun, C. (1997) *Nationalism* (Buckingham: Open University Press).

Cameron, M., Blanaru, A.-M. and Burns, L. (2004) *Constitutional Frameworks and the Rule of Law: Stepan and Skatch on Parliamentarism versus Presidentialism* (University of Pennsylvania: Penn Comparative Politics Workshop), http://www.polisci.upenn.edu//programs/comparative/cameronpaper.pdf, accessed 14 October, 2006.

Campbell, C. and Wilson, G. (1995) *The End of Whitehall: Death of a Paradigm?* (Oxford and Cambridge, MA: Blackwell).

Campbell, A., Converse, P., Miller, A. *et al.* (1960) *The American Voter* (New York: Wiley).

Canada's New Government (2006) *Cabinet Committee Mandates and Membership*, http://www.pm.gc.ca/eng/feature.asp?pageId=53, accessed 9 November, 2006.

Canel, E. (1992) 'Democratization and the Decline of Urban Social Movements in Uruguay: A Political Institutional Account', in *The Making of Social Movements in Latin America: Identity, Strategy and Democracy,* ed. A. Escobar and S. Alvarez (Boulder, CO and Oxford: Westview) pp. 276–90.

Canon, D. (1990) *Actors, Athletes and Astronauts* (Chicago, IL: University of Chicago Press).

Caplan, J. (1988) *Government Without Administration: State and Civil Service in Weimar and Nazi Germany* (Oxford: Clarendon Press).

Carey, J. (1998) *Term Limits and Legislative Representation* (Cambridge and New York: Cambridge University Press).

Carey, J. (2006) 'Legislative Organization', in *The Oxford Handbook of Political Institutions*, ed. R. Rhodes, S. Binder and B. Rockman (Oxford and New York: Oxford University Press) pp. 431–54.

Carey, J. *et al.* (2006) 'The Effects of Term Limits on State Legislatures: A New Survey of the 50 States', *Legislative Studies Quarterly* (31) 105–34.

Carothers, T. (2002) 'The End of the Transition Paradigm', *Journal of Democracy* (13) 5–21.

Carothers, T. (ed.) (2006) *Promoting the Rule of Law Abroad: In Search of Knowledge* (Washington, DC: Carnegie Endowment for International Peace).

Carriûn, J. (ed.) (2006) *The Fujimori Legacy: The Rise of Electoral Authoritarianism in Peru* (University Park, PA: Penn State University Press).

Carty, K. (2002) 'Canada's Nineteenth-Century Cadre Parties at the Millennium' in *Political Parties in Advanced Industrial Democracies*, ed. P. Webb, D. Farrell and I. Holliday (Oxford New York: Oxford University Press) pp. 131–52.

Case, W. (1996) 'Can the "Halfway House" Stand? Semi-democracy and Elite Theory in Three Southeast Asian Countries', *Comparative Politics* (28) 437–64.

Casper, S. (2001) 'The Legal Framework for Corporate Governance: The Influence of Law on Corporate Strategies in Germany and the United States', in *Varieties of Capitalism: The Institutional Foundations of Comparative Advantage,* ed. P. Hall and D. Soskice (Oxford and New York: Oxford University Press) pp. 387–416.

Castells, M. (2003) *The Internet Galaxy: Reflections on the Internet, Business and Society* (Oxford and New York: Oxford University Press).

Castles, F. (2004) *The Future of the Welfare State: Crisis Myths and Crisis Realities* (Oxford and New York: Oxford University Press).

Center for Systemic Peace (2006) *Global and Regional Trends in Conflict and Governance, 1946–2005,* http://members.aol.com/CSPmgm/conflict.htm, accessed 21 April, 2006.

Cerny, P. (1990) *The Changing Architecture of Politics* (Thousand Oaks, CA and London: Sage).

Chabal, P. and Daloz, J. P. (2006) *Culture Troubles: Politics and the Interpretation of Meaning* (London: Hurst).

Chadwick, A. (2006) *Internet Politics: States, Citizens and New Communication Technologies* (Oxford and New York: Oxford University Press).

Chalmers, D. (1990) 'Dilemmas of Latin American Democratization: Dealing with International Forces', *Papers on Latin America, No. 18* (New York: Columbia University Institute of Latin American and Iberian Studies).

Chazan, N. *et al.* (1999) *Politics and Society in Contemporary Africa,* 3rd edn (Boulder, CO: Lynne Rienner).

Chebabi, H. (2001) 'The Political Regime of the Islamic Republic of Iran', *Government and Opposition* (39) 48–70.

Chebabi, H. and Linz, J. (eds) (1998) *Sultanistic Regimes* (Baltimore, MD and London: Johns Hopkins University Press).

Cheibub, J. (2002) 'Minority Governments, Deadlock Situations and the Survival of Presidential Democracies', *Comparative Political Studies* (35) 284–312.

Chesterman, S., Ignatieff, M. and Thakur, R. (eds) (2005) *Making States Work: State Failure and the Crisis of Governance* (Tokyo and New York: United Nations University Press)

Cheung, G. (2005) 'The Chinese Diaspora as a Virtual Nation: Interactive Roles between Economic and Social Capital', *Political Studies* (52) 664–84.

ChinaToday.com (2006) *Communist Party of China*, http://www.chinatoday.com/org/cpc/, accessed 17 July, 2006.

Christensen, T. and Peters, B. Guy (1999) *Structure, Culture and Governance: A Comparison of Norway and the United States* (Lanham, MD and Oxford: Rowman & Littlefield).

Churchill, W. (1943) [2006] 'The Price of Greatness is Responsibility', *The Churchill Centre*, http://www.winstonchurchill.org/i4a/pages/index.cfm?pageid=424, accessed 6 January, 2006.

Churchill, W. (1947) 'Speech in the House of Commons', London, 11 November.

CIA (Central Intelligence Agency (2006) *The World Factbook*, https://www.cia.gov/cia/publications/factbook/index.html, accessed on several dates.

Cigler, C. and Loomis, B. (eds) (2006) *Interest Group Politics*, 7th edn (Washington: Congressional Quarterly Press).

Clapham, C. (2003) 'The Challenge to the State in a Globalized World' in *State Failure, Collapse and Reconstruction*, ed. J. Milliken (Malden, MA and Oxford: Blackwell) pp. 25–44.

Clark, P. and Wilson, J. (1961) 'Incentive System: A Theory of Organization', *Administrative Science Quarterly* (6) 129–66.

Clark S. (1995) *State and Status: The Rise of the State and Aristocratic Power in Western Europe* (Montreal and Kingston: McGill-Queen's University Press).

Clark, W. (2005) *Capitalism, Not Globalism: Capital Mobility, Central Bank Independence, and the Political Control of the Economy* (Ann Arbor, MI: University of Michigan Press).

Cleaver, T. (2002) *Understanding the World Economy*, 2nd edn (London and New York: Routledge).

Coase, R. (1960) 'The Problem of Social Cost', *Journal of Law and Economics* (3) 1–44.

Cobb, R. and Elder, C. (1983) *Participation in American Politics* (Baltimore, MD: Johns Hopkins University Press).

Cohen, J. (1997) 'Deliberation and Democratic Legitimacy', in *Deliberative Democracy: Essays on Reason and Politics*, ed. J. Bohman and W. Rehg (Cambridge, MA: MIT Press) pp. 67–92.

Cohen, M., March, J. and Olsen, J. (1972) 'A Garbage Can Model of Organizational Choice', *Administrative Science Quarterly* (17) 1–25.

Cole, A., Le Galès, P. and Levy, J. (eds) (2005) *Developments in French Politics 3* (Basingstoke and New York: Palgrave Macmillan).

Colebatch, H. (1998) *Policy* (Buckingham: Open University Press).

Collier, D. (1991) 'The Comparative Method: Two Decades of Change', in *Comparative Dynamics: Global Research Perspectives*, ed. D. Rustow and K. Erickson (New York: HarperCollins) pp. 7–31.

Colomer, J. (ed.) (2004a) *Handbook of Electoral System Choice* (Basingstoke and New York: Palgrave Macmillan).

Colomer, J. (2004b) 'The Strategy and History of Electoral System Choice', in *Handbook of Electoral System Choice*, ed. J. Colomer (Basingstoke and New York: Palgrave Macmillan) pp. 3–80.

Colomer, J. (2004c) 'Spain: From Civil War to Proportional Representation' in *Handbook of Electoral System Choice*, ed. J. Colomer (Basingstoke and New York: Palgrave Macmillan) pp. 253–64.

Common Cause (2006) *About Us* (Washington. D.C.: Common Cause), *http://www.commoncause.org/site/pp.asp?c=dkLNK1MQIwG&b=189955*, accessed 28 June, 2006.

Commonwealth Secretariat (1997) *A Future for Small States: Overcoming Vulnerability* (London: Commonwealth Secretariat).

Comscore Networks (2006) *Measuring the Digital Age*, http://www.comscore.com/press/release.asp?press=849, accessed 21 November, 2006.

Conradt, D. (2005) *The German Polity*, 8th edn (New York: Longman).

Conway, M. (2001) 'Political Participation in American Elections: Who Decides What?' in *America's Choice 2000*, ed. W. Crotty (Boulder, CO: Westview) pp. 79–94.

Coppedge, M. (2005) 'Explaining Democratic Deterioration in Venezuela through Nested Inference', in *The Third Wave of Democratization in Latin America*, ed. F. Hagopian and S. Mainwaring (New York and Cambridge: Cambridge University Press) pp. 289–318.

Corbett, R., Jacobs, F. and Shackleton, M. (2005) *The European Parliament*, 6th edn (London: John Harper).

Cordes, J. (2002) 'Corrective Taxes, Charges and Tradable Permits' in *The Tools of Government: A Guide to the New Governance*, ed. L. Salamon (New York: Oxford University Press) pp. 255–81.

Corner, J. and Pels, D. (eds) (2003) *Media and the Restyling of Politics: Consumerism, Celebrity, Cynicism* (London and Thousand Oaks, CA: Sage).

Cotta, M. (2000) 'Defining Party and Government', in *The Nature of Party Government: A Comparative European Perspective*, ed. J. Blondel and M. Cotta (Basingstoke: Macmillan) pp. 56–95.

Cottey, A. *et al.* (eds) (2003) *Democratic Control of the Military in Post-Communist Europe* (Basingstoke: Palgrave).

Cowley, P. (2006) 'Making Parliament Matter?', in *Developments in British Politics 8*, ed. P. Dunleavy *et al.* (Basingstoke: Palgrave Macmillan) pp. 36–55.

Cox, G. and Morgenstern, S. (2002) 'Latin America's Reactive Assemblies and Proactive Presidents', in *Legislative Politics in Latin America*, ed. S. Morgenstern and B. Nacif (Cambridge and New York: Cambridge University Press) pp. 446–68.

Crandall, R., Paz, G. and Roett, R. (eds) (2005) *Mexico's Democracy at Work: Political and Electoral Dynamics* (Boulder, CO and London: Lynne Rienner).

Crick, B. (2000) *In Defence of Politics*, 5th edn (Harmondsworth: Penguin).

Crick, B. (2004) 'Politics as a Form of Rule: Politics, Citizenship and Democracy', in *What Is Politics?*, ed. A. Leftwich (Cambridge and Malden, MA: Polity) pp. 67–85.

Crisp, B. (2000) *Democratic Institutional Design: The Powers and Incentives of Venezuelan Politicians and Interest Groups* (Stanford, CA: Stanford University Press).

Cronin, T. (1989) *Direct Democracy: The Politics of Initiative, Referendum and Recall* (Cambridge, MA and London: Harvard University Press).

Cross, W. and Young, L. (2004) 'The Contours of Political Party Membership in Canada', *Party Politics* (10) 427–44.

Crotty, W. (2006) 'Party Transformations: The United States and Western Europe', in *Handbook of Party Politics*, ed. R. Katz and W. Crotty (London and Thousand Oaks, CA: Sage) pp. 499–514.

Crouch, C. and Streeck, W. (eds) (1997) *Political Economy of Modern Capitalism: Mapping Convergence and Diversity* (London and Thousand Oaks, CA: Sage).

Crouch, H. (1996) *Government and Society in Malaysia* (Ithaca, NY: Cornell University Press).

Cummings, S. (2005) *Kazakhstan: Power and the Elite* (London and New York: I. B. Taurus).

Curran, J. and Seaton, J. (2003) *Power Without Responsibility: The Press and Broadcasting in Britain,* 6th edn (London and New York: Methuen).

Curry, G. and West, C. (eds) (1996) *The Affirmative Action Debate* (Reading, MA: Addison-Wesley).

Curtice, J., Fisher, S. and Steed, M. (2005) 'The Results Analysed', in *The British General Election of 2005*, ed. D. Kavanagh and D. Butler (Basingstoke and New York: Palgrave Macmillan) pp. 235–59.

D

Dahl, R. (1957) 'The Concept of Power', *Behavioral Science* (2) 201–15.

Dahl, R. (1961) *Who Governs? Democracy and Power in an American City* (New Haven, CT and London: Yale University Press).

Dahl, R. (1989) *Democracy and its Critics* (New Haven, CT and London: Yale University Press).

Dahl, R. (1993) 'Pluralism', in *The Oxford Companion to Politics of the World,* ed. J. Krieger (New York and Oxford: Oxford University Press) pp. 704–7.

Dahl, R. (1998) *On Democracy* (New Haven, CT and London: Yale University Press).

Dahl, R. (1999) 'Can International Organizations Be Democratic?', in *Democracy's Edges,* ed. I. Shapiro and C. Hacker-Cordon (New Haven, CT and London: Yale University Press) pp. 19–36.

Dahl, R. (2000) 'A Democratic Paradox?', *Scandinavian Political Studies* (23) 246–51.

Dahl, R. (2001) *How Democratic is the American Constitution?* (New Haven, CT and London: Yale University Press).

Dahl, R., Shapiro, I. and Cheibub, J. (eds) (2003) *The Democracy Sourcebook* (Cambridge, MA: MIT Press).

Dalton, R. (1994) *The Green Rainbow: Environmental Groups in Western Europe* (New Haven, CT and London: Yale University Press).

Dalton, R. (2002a) *Citizen Politics: Public Opinion and Political Parties in Advanced Industrial Democracies,* 3rd edn (New York: Chatham House).

Dalton, R. (2002b) 'Political Cleavages, Issues and Electoral Change', in *Comparing Democracies 2: New Challenges in the Study of Elections and Voting,* ed. L. LeDuc, R. Niemi and P. Norris (London and Thousand Oaks, CA: Sage) pp. 189–209.

Dalton, R. and Gray, M. (2003) 'Expanding the Electoral Marketplace', in *Democracy Transformed? Expanding Political Opportunities in Advanced Industrial Democracies,* ed. B. Cain, R. Dalton and S. Scarrow (Oxford and New York: Oxford University Press) pp. 23–44.

Dalton, R. and Wattenberg, M. (2000) *Politics Without Partisans: Political Change in Advanced Industrial Democracies* (Oxford and New York: Oxford University Press).

Dalton, R., McAllister, I. and Wattenberg, M. (2000) 'The Consequences of Partisan Dealignment', in *Parties Without Partisans,* ed. R. Dalton and M. Wattenberg (Oxford and New York: Oxford University Press) pp. 37–63.

Dalton, R., Scarrow, S. and Cain, B. (2004) 'Advanced Democracies and the New Politics', *Journal of Democracy* (15) 124–38.

Davidson, B. (1992) *The Black Man's Burden: Africa and the Curse of the Nation-State* (Oxford and Harare: James Currey).

Davidson, R. (2003) *Congress and its Members,* 9th edn (Washington, DC: CQ Press).

Davies, J. (1962) 'Toward a Theory of Revolution', *American Sociological Review* (27) 5–18.

Davis, R. (2005) *Electing Justice: Fixing the Supreme Court Nomination Process* (Oxford and New York: Oxford University Press).

Day, S. and Shaw, J. (2002) 'European Union Electoral Rights and the Political Participation of Migrants in Host Polities', *International Journal of Population Geography* (8) 183–99.

de Burea, G. and Wieler, J. (eds) (2002) *The European Court of Justice* (Oxford and New York: Oxford University Press).

de Tocqueville, A. (1835) [1966 edn] *Democracy in America* (New York: Vintage Books). Also available on-line at the American Studies website at the University of Virginia: http://xroads.virginia.edu.

de Tocqueville, A. (1856) [1954 edn] *The Ancien Regime and the Revolution in France* (London: Fontana).

Deane, P. (1989) *The State and the Economic System: An Introduction to the History of Political Economy* (Oxford and New York: Oxford University Press).

Deegan, H. (2001) *The Politics of the New South Africa: Apartheid and After* (Harlow and New York: Longman).

Dehousse, R. (1998) *The European Court of Justice* (London: Macmillan).

Delanty, G. and Kumar, K. (eds) (2006) *The Sage Handbook of Nations and Nationalism* (London and Thousand Oaks, CA: Sage).

della Porta, D. and Diani, M. (1999) *Social Movements: An Introduction* (Malden, MA and Oxford: Blackwell).

della Porta, D. and Tarrow, S. (eds) (2005) *Transnational Protest and Global Activism* (Lanham, MD: Rowman & Littlefield).

della Porta, D., Kriesi, H. and Rucht, D. (eds) (1999) *Social Movements in a Globalizing World* (London: Macmillan and New York: St Martin's Press).

Dempsey, J. (2002) 'Civil Liberties in a Time of Crisis', *Human Rights* (29) 8–10.

Denters, B. and Klok, P.-J. (2005) 'The Netherlands: In Search of Responsiveness', in *Comparing Local Governance: Trends and Developments,* ed. B. Denters and L. Rose (Basingstoke and New York: Palgrave Macmillan) pp. 65–82.

Denters, B. and Rose, L. (eds) (2005) *Comparing Local Governance: Trends and Developments* (Basingstoke and New York: Palgrave Macmillan).

Department of Health and Human Services (2006) *About HHL,* http://www.hhs.gov/about/index.html#agencies, accessed 2 November, 2006.

Derbyshire, J. and Derbyshire, L. (1999) *Political Systems of the World* (Oxford: Helicon).

Derichs, C. and Kerbo, H. (2003) 'Japan: Political Careers between Bureaucracy and Hereditary Constituencies', in *The Political Class in Advanced Democracies*, ed. J. Borchert and J. Zeiss (Oxford and New York: Oxford University Press) pp. 245–58.

Deschouwer, K. (2005) 'The Unintended Consequences of Consociational Federalism: The Case of Belgium', in *Power Sharing: New Challenges for Divided Societies*, ed. I. O'Flynn and D. Russell (London and Ann Arbor, MI: Pluto Press) pp. 92–106.

Deschouwer, K. (2006) 'Political Parties as Multi-level Organizations', in *Handbook of Party Politics*, ed. R. Katz and W. Crotty (London and Thousand Oaks, CA: Sage) pp. 291–300.

Diamandouros, P. (ed.) (2005) 'Introduction', in *The European Ombudsman: Origins, Establishment, Evolution* (Luxembourg: Office for Official Publications of the European Union) pp. 1–23.

Diamond, L. (1999) *Developing Democracy: Toward Consolidation* (Baltimore, MD and London: Johns Hopkins University Press).

Dicey, A. (1885) [1959 edn] *Introduction to the Study of the Law of the Constitution,* 10th edn (London: Macmillan).

Dittmer, L. and Liu, G. (eds) (2006) *China's Deep Reform: Domestic Politics in Transition* (Lanham, MD and Oxford: Rowman & Littlefield).

Djilas, M. (1955) [1983 edn] *The New Class: An Analysis of the Communist System* (New York: Harcourt).

Dodd, L. and Oppenheimer, B. (eds) (2004) *Congress Reconsidered,* 8th edn (Washington, DC: Congressional Quarterly Press).

Dodson, M. and Jackson, D. (2003) 'Horizontal Accountability and the Rule of Law in Central America' in *Democratic Accountability in Latin America*, ed. S. Mainwaring and C. Welna (Oxford and New York) pp. 228–65.

Dogan, M. and Pelassy, G. (1990) *How to Compare Nations* (Chatham, NJ: Chatham House).

Donaldson, R. (2004) 'Russia', *Journal of Legislative Studies* (10) 230–49.

Dooley, B. and Baron, S. (eds) (2001) *The Politics of Information in Early Modern Europe* (London and New York: Longman).

Dore, R. (2000) *Stock Market Capitalism: Japan and Germany versus the Anglo-Saxons* (Oxford and New York: Oxford University Press).

Döring, H. and Hallerberg, M. (eds) (2004) *Patterns of Parliamentary Behaviour* (Aldershot and Burlington, VT: Ashgate).

Downs, A. (1957) *An Economic Theory of Democracy* (New York: Harper).

Drake, P. and Hershberg, E. (2006) 'The Crisis of State-Society Relations in the Post-1980s Andes' in *State and Society in Conflict: Comparative Perspectives on Andean Crises*, ed. P. Drake and E. Hershberg (Pittsburgh, PA: University of Pittsburgh Press) pp. 1–40.

Drummond, A. (2006) 'Electoral Volatility and Party Decline in Western Democracies: 1970–1995', *Political Studies* (54) 628–47.

Duchacek, I. (1991) 'Constitutions/Constitutionalism', in *The Blackwell Encyclopaedia of Political Science,* ed. V. Bogdanor (Oxford and Cambridge, MA: Blackwell) pp. 142–4.

Dunleavy, P. *et al.* (eds) (2003) *Developments in British Politics 7* (Basingstoke and New York: Palgrave Macmillan).

Dunleavy, P. *et al.* (eds) (2006) *Developments in British Politics 8* (Basingstoke and New York: Palgrave Macmillan).

Duverger, M. (1954) [1970 edn] *Political Parties* (London: Methuen).

Duverger, M. (1980) 'A New Political System Model: Semi-Presidential Government', *European Journal of Political Research* (8) 165–87.

Dworkin, R. (1977) *Taking Rights Seriously* (Cambridge, MA and London: Harvard University Press).

Dye, T. (2004) *Understanding Public Policy,* 11th edn (Englewood Cliffs, NJ: Prentice Hall).

Dyson, K. (1980) *The State Tradition in Western Europe: A Study of an Idea and Institution* (Oxford: Martin Robertson).

E

Easter, G. (1997) 'Preference for Presidentialism: Postcommunist Regime Change in Russia and the NIS', *World Politics* (49) 184–211.

Easton, D. (1965a) *A Framework for Political Analysis* (Englewood Cliffs, NJ: Prentice Hall).

Easton, D. (1965b) *A Systems Analysis of Political Life* (New York: Wiley).

Eberle, J. (1990) 'Understanding the Revolutions in Eastern Europe', in *Spring in Winter: The 1989 Revolutions,* ed. G. Prins (Manchester: Manchester University Press) pp. 193–209.

Eckstein, H. (1998b) 'Russia and the Conditions of Democracy', in *Can Democracy Take Root in Post-Soviet Russia? Explorations in State-Society Relations,* ed. H. Eckstein *et al.* (Lanham, MD and Oxford: Rowman & Littlefield) pp. 349–81.

Eigen, L. and Siegel, J. (1993) *The Macmillan Dictionary of Political Quotations* (New York: Macmillan).

Eising, R. (2003) 'Interest Groups and the European Union', in *European Union Politics,* ed. M. Cini (Oxford and New York: Oxford University Press) pp. 192–204.

Eising, R. and Cini, M. (2002) 'Disintegration or Reconfiguration? Organized Interests in Western Europe', in *Developments in West European Politics 2,* ed. P. Heywood, E. Jones and M. Rhodes (Basingstoke and New York: Palgrave) pp. 168–83.

Elazar, D. (1990) 'Opening the Third Century of American Federalism: Issues and Prospects', *The Annals* (509) 11–21.

Elazar, D. (1996) 'From Statism to Federalism: A Paradigm Shift', *International Political Science Review* (17) 417–30.

Eley, G. and Suny, R. (1996) 'From the Moment of Social History to the Work of Cultural Representation', in *Becoming National: A Reader,* ed. G. Eley and R. Suny (Oxford and New York: Oxford University Press) pp. 3–37.

Elgie, R. (2003) *Political Institutions in Contemporary France* (Oxford and New York: Oxford University Press).

Elgie, R. (2005) 'The Political Executive', in *Developments in French Politics 3*, ed. A. Cole, P. le Galès and J. Levy (Basingstoke and New York: Palgrave Macmillan) pp. 70–87.

Elgie, R. (ed.) (1999) *Semi-Presidentialism in Europe* (Oxford and New York: Oxford University Press).

Elgie, R. (ed.) (2001) *Divided Government in Comparative Perspective* (Oxford and New York: Oxford University Press).

Eliadis, P., Hill, M. and Howlett, M. (eds) (2005) *Designing Government: From Instruments to Governance* (Montreal and London: McGill-Queen's University Press).

Elkit, J., Svensson, P. and Togeby, L. (2005) 'Why is Voter Turnout Not Declining in Denmark?', paper prepared for delivery at the *Annual Meeting of the American Political Science Association*, Washington, DC.

Ellis, R. and Nelson, M. (eds) (2006) *Debating the Presidency: Conflicting Perspectives on the American Executive* (Washington, DC: CQ Press).

Ellison, N. (2006) *The Transformation of Welfare States?* (Abingdon and New York: Routledge).

Ellner, S. (2004) 'The Search for Explanations', in *Venezuelan Politics in the Chávez Era: Class, Polarization and Conflict*, ed. S. Ellner and D. Hellinger (Boulder, CO and London: Lynne Rienner) pp. 7–26.

Elster, J., Offe, C. and Preuss, U. (1998) *Institutional Design in Post-Communist Societies: Rebuilding the Ship at Sea* (Cambridge and New York: Cambridge University Press).

Emy, M. and Hughes, O. (1991) *Australian Politics: Realities in Conflict* (South Melbourne: Macmillan).

Endersby, J., Petrocik, J. and Shaw, D. (2006) 'Electoral Mobilization in the United States', in *Handbook of Party Politics*, ed. R. Katz and W. Crotty (London and Thousand Oaks, CA: Sage) pp. 316–36.

Englebert, R. and Ron, J. (2004) 'Primary Commodities and War: Congo-Brazzaville's Ambivalent Resource Curse', *Comparative Politics* (37) 61–81.

Esarey, A. (2006) *Speak No Evil: Mass Media Control in Contemporary China* (New York: Freedom House), http://www.freedomhouse.org/uploads/special_report/33.pdf, accessed 6 March, 2006.

Esman, M. (1996) 'Diasporas and International Relations', in *Ethnicity*, ed. J. Hutchinson and A. Smith (Oxford and New York: Oxford University Press) pp. 316–20.

Esping-Andersen, G. (1990) *The Three Worlds of Welfare Capitalism* (Oxford: Polity).

Esping-Andersen, G. (1996a) 'After the Golden Age? Welfare State Dilemmas in a Global Economy', in *Welfare States in Transition: National Adaptations in Global Economies*, ed. G. Esping-Andersen (Thousand Oaks, CA and London: Sage) pp. 1–31.

Esping-Andersen, G. (ed.) (1996b) *Welfare States in Transition: National Adaptations in Global Economies* (Thousand Oaks, CA and London: Sage).

Esping-Andersen, G. (1999) *The Social Foundations of Post-industrial Economics* (Oxford and New York: Oxford University Press).

Esping-Andersen, G. (ed.) (2002) *Why We Need a Welfare State* (Oxford and New York: Oxford University Press).

Esser, F. and Pfetsch, B. (eds) (2004) *Comparing Political Communication: Theories, Cases and Challenges* (Cambridge and New York: Cambridge University Press).

Eulau, H. (1963) *The Behavioral Persuasion in Politics* (New York: Random House).

European Trade Union Federation (ETUC) (2006) *What is the 'European Social Model' or 'Social Europe'?*, http://www.etuc.org/a/111, accessed 10 December, 2006.

Evans Jr, A. (2005) 'A Russian Civil Society?', in *Developments in Russian Politics 6*, ed. S. White, Z. Gitelman and R. Sakwa (Basingstoke and New York: Palgrave Macmillan) pp. 96–113.

Evans, P., Rueschemeyer, D. and Skocpol, T. (eds) (1985) *Bringing The State Back In* (Cambridge and New York: Cambridge University Press).

F

Falconer, C. (2003) 'History', *Judicial Appointments Commission*, http://www.judicialappointments.gov.uk/about/history.htm, accessed 4 August, 2006.

Farcau, B. (1994) *The Coup: Tactics in the Seizure of Power* (Westport, CT: Praeger).

Farnen, R. and Meloen, J. (eds) (2000) *Democracy, Authoritarianism and Education* (Basingstoke: Palgrave).

Farrell, D. (2001) *Electoral Systems: A Comparative Introduction* (London and New York: Palgrave).

Farrell, D. and Schmitt-Beck, R. (eds) (2002) *Do Political Campaigns Matter? Campaign Effects in Elections and Referendums* (London and New York: Routledge).

Feaver, P. (1999) 'Civil-Military Relations', *Annual Review of Political Science* (2) 211–41.

Feigenbaum, H., Henig, J. and Hamnett, C. (2003) *Shrinking the State: The Political Underpinnings of Privatization* (Cambridge and New York: Cambridge University Press).

Feldman, O. (1993) *Politics and the News Media in Japan* (Ann Arbor, MI: University of Michigan Press).

Ferejohn, J. and Pasquino, P. (2003) 'Rule of Democracy and Rule of Law', in *Democracy and the Rule of Law*, ed. J. Maravall and A. Przeworski (Cambridge and New York: Cambridge University Press) pp. 242–60.

Fernando J. and Heston A. (1997) 'NGOs between States, Markets and Civil Society', *Annals of the American Academy of Political and Social Sciences* (554) 8–19.

Fesler, J. and Kettl, D. (2005) *The Politics of the Administrative Process*, 3rd edn (Washington, DC: CQ Press).

Fiers, S. and Krouwel, A. (2005) 'The Low Countries: From "Prime Minister" to President-Minister', in *The Presidentialization of Politics: A Comparative Study of Modern Democracies*, ed. T. Poguntke and P. Webb (Oxford and New York: Oxford University Press) pp. 128–58.

Financial Times (2005) *Editorial*, 6 November.

Finer, S. (1962) [1988 edn] *The Man on Horseback: The Role of the Military in Politics* (Boulder, CO: Westview).

Finer, S. (1997) *The History of Government from the Earliest Times*, 3 vols (Oxford and New York: Oxford University Press).

Fink, A. (2005) *How To Conduct Surveys: A Step-by-Step Guide*, 3rd edn (Thousand Oaks, CA and London: Sage).

Finley, M. (1985) *Democracy Ancient and Modern* (London: Hogarth Press).

Fiorina, M. (1981) *Retrospective Voting in American National Elections* (New Haven, CT: Yale University Press).

Fischer, F. (2003) *Reframing Public Policy: Discursive Practice and Deliberative Practices* (Oxford and New York: Oxford University Press).

Fish, M. (2005) *Democracy Derailed in Russia: The Failure of Open Politics* (Cambridge and New York: Cambridge University Press).

Fisher, J. and Eisenstadt, T. (2004) 'Comparative Party Finance: What is to be Done?' *Party Politics* (10) 619–26.

Fishkin, J. (1991) *Democracy and Deliberation: New Directions for Democratic Reform* (New Haven, CT and London: Yale University Press).

Fishkin, J. and Laslett, P. (eds) (2003) *Debating Deliberative Democracy* (Oxford and New York: Blackwell).

Flammang, J. *et al.* (1990) *American Politics in a Changing World* (Pacific Grove, CA: Brooks/Cole).

Flanigan, W. and Zingale, N. (2005) *Political Behavior of the American Electorate*, 11th edn (Washington, DC: CQ Press).

Flora, P. and Heidenheimer, A. (eds) (1981) *The Development of Welfare States in Europe and America* (New York: Transaction).

Foley, M. (1999) 'In Kiev They Fine a Journalist $1m and Cut Off All the Phones', *The Times, 2* April, p. 45.

Fontana, B., Nederman, C. and Remer, G. (eds) (2004) *Historical Perspectives on Rhetoric and Democracy* (University Park, PA: Pennsylvania University Press).

Foran, J. (ed.) (1997) *Theorizing Revolutions* (London and New York: Routledge).

Foreign Policy (2006) *Failed States Index*, http://www.foreignpolicy.com/story/cms.php?story_id=3100, accessed 29 January, 2006.

Forsyth, M. (1996) 'The Political Theory of Federalism: The Relevance of Classical Approaches', in *Federalizing Europe: The Costs, Benefits and Preconditions of Federal Political Systems,* ed. J. Hesse and V. Wright (Oxford and New York: Oxford University Press) pp. 47–64.

FDC (Forum for Democratic Change) (2007) *One Uganda, One People*, http://www.fdcganda.org/, accessed 9 January, 2007.

Foweraker, T., Landman, T. and Harvey, N. (2003) *Governing Latin America* (Cambridge and Malden, MA: Polity).

Franklin, M. (1992) 'The Decline of Cleavage Politics', in *Electoral Change: Responses to Evolving Social and Attitudinal Structures in Western Countries,* ed. M. Franklin, T. Mackie and H. Valen (Cambridge and New York: Cambridge University Press) pp. 383–405.

Franklin, M. (2002) 'The Dynamics of Electoral Participation', in *Comparing Democracies 2,* ed. L. LeDuc, R. Niemi and P. Norris (London and Thousand Oaks, CA) pp. 148–68.

Franklin, M. (2004) *Voter Turnout and the Dynamics of Electoral Competition in Established Democracies* (Cambridge and New York: Cambridge University Press).

Freedom House (2006a) *Freedom in the World*, http://www.freedomhouse.org/template.cfm?page=15&year=2006, accessed 19 November, 2006.

Freedom House (2006b) *Map of Press Freedom*, http://www.freedomhouse.org/template.cfm?page=251&year=2006, accessed 19 November, 2006.

Friedman, M. (1962) *Capitalism and Freedom* (Chicago and London: University of Chicago Press).

Friedman, M. with Schwartz, A. (1963) *A Monetary History of the United States, 1867–1960* (Princeton, NJ: Princeton University Press).

Friedman, M. (1970) 'A Theoretical Framework for Monetary Analysis', in *Milton Friedman's Monetary Framework: A Debate with His Critics,* ed. R. Gordon (Chicago and London: University of Chicago Press) pp. 1–62.

Friedman, M. (1991) *Monetarist Economics* (Oxford and Cambridge, MA: Basil Blackwell).

Friedrich, C. (1937) *Constitutional Government and Politics* (New York: Harper).

Friedrich, C. (1970) 'The Failure of a One-Party System: Hitler Germany', in *Authoritarian Politics in Modern Society: The Dynamics of Established One-Party Systems,* ed. S. Huntington and C. Moore (New York and London: Basic Books) pp. 239–60.

Friedrich, C. and Brzezinski, Z. (1965) *Totalitarian Dictatorship and Autocracy* (New York: Praeger).

Fukuyama, F. (2004) *State Building: Governance and World Order in the Twenty-First Century* (Ithaca, NY: Cornell University Press).

Fuller, G. (2002) 'The Future for Political Islam', *Foreign Affairs* (81) 48–60.

Fuller, L. (1969) *The Morality of Law* (New Haven and London: Yale University Press).

Fund for Peace (2006) *Failed States Index*, http://www.fundforpeace.org/programs/fsi/fsindex2006.php, accessed 22 August, 2006.

G

Gagnon, A.-G. and Tully, J. (eds) (2001) *Multinational Democracies* (Cambridge and New York: Cambridge University Press).

Gallagher, M. and Mitchell, P. (eds) (2005) *The Politics of Electoral Systems* (Oxford and New York: Oxford University Press).

Gallagher, M., Laver, M. and Mair, P. (2006) *Representative Government in Modern Europe: Institutions, Parties, and Governments,* 4th edn (New York and London: McGraw-Hill).

Galligan, B. (2006) 'Comparative Federalism', in *The Oxford Handbook of Political Institutions*, ed. R. Rhodes, S. Binder and B. Rockman (Oxford and New York: Oxford University Press) pp. 261–80.

Gambetta, D. (2005a) 'Can We Make Sense of Suicide Missions?' in *Making Sense of Suicide Missions*, ed. D. Gambetta (Oxford and New York: Oxford University Press) pp. 259–300.

Gambetta, D. (ed.) (2005b) *Making Sense of Suicide Missions* (Oxford and New York: Oxford University Press).

Gasster, M. (1976) 'The Rise of Chinese Communism', in *Comparative Communism: The Soviet, Chinese and Yugoslav Models*, ed. G. Bertsch and T. Ganschow (San Francisco: W. H. Freeman) pp. 97–120.

Gavin, N. and Sanders, D. (2003) 'The Press and its Influence on British Political Attitudes under New Labour', *Political Studies* (51) 573–91.

Geddes, B. (2003) *Paradigms and Sand Castles: Theory Building and Research Design in Comparative Politics* (Ann Arbor, MI: University of Michigan Press).

Geertz, C. (1973) [1993 edn] 'Thick Description: Toward an Interpretative Theory of Culture', in *Interpretation of Cultures,* ed. C. Geertz (London: Fontana) pp. 1–33.

Gellner, E. (1983) *Nations and Nationalism* (Oxford and Cambridge, MA: Blackwell).

George, A. (1969) 'The Operational Code: A Neglected Approach to the Study of Political Leaders and Decision-making', *International Studies Quarterly* (13) 190–222.

George, A. and Bennett, A. (2005) *Case Studies and Theory Development in the Social Sciences* (Cambridge, MA: MIT Press).

Gerston, L. and Christensen, T. (2004) *Recall! California's Political Earthquake* (Armonk, NY and London: M. E. Sharpe).

Gerth, H. and Mills, C. Wright (1948) *From Max Weber* (London: Routledge & Kegan Paul).

Gibson, E. (ed.) (2004) *Federalism and Democracy in Latin America* (Baltimore, MD: Johns Hopkins University Press).

Ginsberg, B. (1982) *The Consequences of Consent* (Reading, MA: Addison Wesley).

Ginsborg, P. (2003) *A History of Contemporary Italy: Society and Politics, 1943–1988* (Basingstoke: Palgrave Macmillan).

Ginsburg, R. (1992) [2004 edn] 'Speaking in a Judicial Voice: Reflections on *Roe* v. *Wade*', in *Judges on Judging: Views from the Bench*, ed. D. O'Brien (Washington, DC: CQ Press) pp. 194–200.

Girard, P. (2006) *Paradise Lost: Haiti's Tumultuous Journey from Pearl of the Caribbean to Third World Hotspot* (Basingstoke and New York: Palgrave).

Gitelman, Z. (2005) 'The Democratization of Russia in Comparative Perspective', in *Developments in Russian Politics 6*, ed. S. White, Z. Gitelman and R. Sakwa (Basingstoke and New York: Palgrave Macmillan) pp. 241–56.

Glaser, D. (2001) *Politics and Society in South Africa* (London and Thousand Oaks, CA: Sage).

Gleason, A. (1995) *Totalitarianism: The Inner History of the Cold War* (New York: Oxford University Press).

Glynn, C. *et al.* (1998) *Public Opinion* (Boulder, CO and Oxford: Westview Press).

Goban-Klas, T. and Sasinka-Klas, T. (1992) 'From Closed to Open Communication Systems', in *Democracy and Civil Society in Eastern Europe*, ed. P. Lewis (London: Macmillan and New York: St Martin's Press) pp. 76–90.

Godin, E. and Chafer, T. (eds) (2006) *The French Exception* (Oxford: Berghahn Books).

Goetz, K. (1997) 'Acquiring Political Craft: Training Grounds for Top Officials in the German Core Executive', *Public Administration* (75) 753–75.

Goetz, K. (2003) 'Government at the Centre', in *Developments in German Politics 3*, ed. S. Padgett, W. Paterson and G. Smith (Basingstoke: Palgrave Macmillan) pp. 17–37.

Goetz, K. (2006) 'Power at the Centre: The Organization of Democratic Systems' in *Developments in European Politics*, ed. P. Heywood *et al.* (Basingstoke and New York: Palgrave Macmillan), pp. 73–96.

Goldsmith, J. and Wu, T. (2006) *Who Controls the Internet? Illusions of a Borderless World* (New York and Oxford: Oxford University Press).

Goldsmith, M. (1996) 'Normative Theories of Local Government: A European Comparison', in *Rethinking Local Democracy*, ed. D. King and G. Stoker (Basingstoke and New York: Macmillan) pp. 174–92.

Goldstone, J. (1991) 'An Analytical Framework', in *Revolutions of the Late Twentieth Century*, ed. J. Goldstone, T. Gurr and F. Moshiri (Boulder, CO and Oxford: Westview) pp. 37–51.

Gong, T. (2002) 'Dangerous Collusion: Corruption as a Collective Venture in Contemporary China', *Communist and Postsocialist Studies* (35) 85–103.

Goodwin, J. and Jasper, J. (2003a) 'Editors' Introduction', in *The Social Movements Reader: Cases and Concepts*, ed. J. Goodwin and J. Jaspers (Malden, MA and Oxford: Blackwell) pp. 3–7.

Goodwin, J. and Jasper, J. (eds) (2003b) *The Social Movements Reader: Cases and Concepts* (Malden, MA and Oxford: Blackwell).

Gordon, S. (2005) *Campaign Contributions and Legislative Voting: A New Approach* (London and New York: Routledge).

Gott, R. (2005) *Hugo Chávez and the Bolivarian Revolution* (London and New York: Verso).

Gould, D. (1980) 'Patrons and Clients: The Role of the Military in Zaire Politics', in *The Performance of Soldiers as Governors*, ed. I. Mowoe (Washington, DC: University Press of America) pp. 473–92.

GPO Access (2006) *US Government Manual*, 2006–07 edn, http://www.gpoaccess.gov/gmanual/index.html, accessed 1 November, 2006.

Graber, D. (2005) *Mass Media and American Politics*, 7th edn (Washington, DC: CQ Press).

Gratschew, M. (2004) 'Compulsory Voting', in *Voter Turnout in Western Europe since 1945: A Regional Report* (Stockholm: IDEA) pp. 105–14.

Green, D. (2002a) 'Constructivist Comparative Politics: Foundations and Framework', in *Constructivism and Comparative Politics*, ed. D. Green (Armonk, NY and London: M.E. Sharpe) pp. 3–59.

Green, D. (ed.) (2002b) *Constructivism and Comparative Politics* (Armonk, NY and London: M.E. Sharpe).

Green, J. (1994) *Dictionary of Cynical Quotations* (London: Cassell).

Green, D. and Gerber, A. (2004) *Get Out the Vote! How to Increase Voter Turnout* (Washington, DC: Brookings Institution).

Greenspan, A. (1994) 'Discussion', in *The Future of Central Banking: The Tercentenary Symposium of the Bank of England*, ed. F. Capie *et al.* (Cambridge and New York: Cambridge University Press) pp. 252–61.

Greenwood, J. (2007) *Interest Representation in the European Union*, 2nd edn (Basingstoke and New York: Palgrave Macmillan).

Gregorian, V. (2004) *Islam: A Mosaic, Not a Monolith* (Washington, DC: Brookings Institution Press).

Griffin, R. (ed.) (2004) *Fascism as a Totalitarian Movement* (London: Frank Cass).

Grugel, J. (2002) *Democratization: A Critical Introduction* (Basingstoke: Palgrave Macmillan).

Guarnieri, C. (2003) 'Courts as an Instrument of Horizontal Accountability: The Case of Latin Europe', in *Democracy and the Rule of Law*, ed. J. Maravall and A. Przeworski (Cambridge and New York: Cambridge University Press) pp. 223–41.

Guarnieri, C. and Pederzoli, P. (2002) *The Power of Judges: A Comparative Study of Courts and Democracy*, trans. C. Thomas (Oxford and New York: Oxford University Press).

Guehenno, J.-M. (1995) *The End of the Nation-State* (Minneapolis, MN and London: University of Minnesota Press).

Guevara, A. (2005) *Chávez, Venezuela and the New Latin America: An Interview with Hugo Chávez* (Melbourne and New York: Ocean Press).

Guibernau, M. (1999) *Nations Without States: Political Communities in a Global Age* (Cambridge and Malden, MA: Polity).

Gunlicks, A. (2003) *The Länder and German Federalism* (Manchester and New York: Manchester University Press).

Gunther, P. and Mughan, A. (eds) (2000) *Democracy and the Media: A Comparative Perspective* (Cambridge and New York: Cambridge University Press).

Gunther, R., Montero, J. and Botella, J. (2004) *Democracy in Modern Spain* (New Haven, CT and London: Yale University Press).

Gunther, R., Montero, J. and Linz, J. (eds) (2002) *Political Parties: Old Concepts and New Challenges* (Oxford and New York: Oxford University Press).

Gurr, T. (1980) *Why Men Rebel* (Princeton, NJ: Princeton University Press).

H

Habermas, J. (1975) *Legitimation Crisis* (Boston, MA: Beacon Press).

Habermas, J. (1978) *Knowledge and Human Interests*, 2nd edn, trans. J. Shapiro (London: Heinemann Education).

Hadenius, A. and Teorell, J. (2005) 'Assessing Alternative Indices of Democracy', *Committee on Concepts and Methods, International Political Science Association*, http://www.concepts-methods.org/papers_list.php?id_categoria=1&titulo=Political %20Concepts August 2005, accessed 3 January, 2007.

Hafez, M. (2005) 'A Tragedy of Errors: Thwarted Democratization and Islamist Violence in Algeria', in *Democratic Development and Political Terrorism: The Global Perspective*, ed. W. Crotty (Boston, MA: Northeastern University Press) pp. 301–31.

Hagevi, M. (2003) 'Sweden: Participation Ideal and Professionalism', in *The Political Class in Advanced Democracies*, ed. J. Borchert and J. Zeiss (Oxford and New York: Oxford University Press) pp. 352–73.

Hagopian, F. and Mainwaring, S. (eds) (2005) *The Third Wave of Democratization in Latin America: Advances and Setbacks* (New York and Cambridge: Cambridge University Press).

Hahn, G. (2006) 'Reforming the Federation' in *Developments in Russian Politics*, ed. S White, Z. Gitelman and R. Sakwa (Basingstoke and New York: Palgrave Macmillan) pp. 148–67.

Hall, B. and Biersteker, T. (2002) (eds) *The Emergence of Private Authority in Global Governance* (Cambridge and New York: Cambridge University Press).

Hall, D. (2005) *Administrative Law: Bureaucracy in a Democracy*, 3rd edn (Upper Saddle River, NJ: Prentice Hall).

Hall, P. (ed.) (1989) *The Political Power of Economic Ideas: Keynesianism across Nations* (Princeton, NJ: Princeton University Press).

Hall, P. and Soskice, D. (2001) 'An Introduction to Varieties of Capitalism', in *Varieties of Capitalism: The Institutional Foundations of Comparative Advantage*, ed. P. Hall and D. Soskice (Oxford and New York: Oxford University Press) pp. 11–70.

Hall, P. and Soskice, D. (2003) 'Varieties of Capitalism and Institutional Change', *Comparative European Politics* (1) 241–50.

Halligan, J. (2003) 'Leadership and the Senior Service from a Comparative Perspective', in *Handbook of Public Administration*, ed. B. Guy Peters and J. Pierre (London and Thousand Oaks, CA: Sage) pp. 343–53.

Halperin, M., Siegle, J. and Weinstein, M. (2005) *The Democracy Advantage: How Democracies Promote Prosperity and Peace* (New York and London: Routledge).

Hamilton, A. (1788a) [1970 edn] *The Federalist*, No. 70, intro W. Brock (London: Dent and New York: Dutton) pp. 357–63.

Hamilton, A. (1788b) [1970 edn] *The Federalist*, No. 84, intro W. Brock (London: Dent and New York: Dutton) pp. 436–45.

Hamilton, A. (1788c) [1970 edn] *The Federalist*, No. 45, intro W. Brock (London: Dent and New York: Dutton) pp. 233–8.

Hamilton, A. (1788d) [1970 edn] *The Federalist*, No. 51, intro W. Brock (London: Dent and New York: Dutton) pp. 263–7.

Hamilton, A. (1788e) [1970 edn] *The Federalist*, No. 62, intro W. Brock (London: Dent and New York: Dutton) pp. 314–20.

Hamilton, A. (1788f) [1970 edn] *The Federalist*, No. 69, intro W. Brock (London: Dent and New York: Dutton) pp. 350–6.

Hansen, M. (1991) *The Athenian Democracy in the Age of Demosthenes* (Oxford and Cambridge, MA: Blackwell).

Harding, N. (ed.) (1984) *The State in Socialist Society* (London: Macmillan).

Hare, T. (1873) *The Election of Representatives, Parliamentary and Municipal*, 4th edn (London: Longmans, Green, Reader & Dyer).

Hartlyn, J. (1998) 'The Trujillo Regime in the Dominican Republic', in *Sultanistic Regimes*, ed. H. Chehabi and J. Linz (Baltimore, MD and London: Johns Hopkins University Press) pp. 85–112.

Hartz, L. (1955) *The Liberal Tradition in America* (New York: Harcourt, Brace).

Hatzfeld, J. (2005) *A Time for Machetes: The Rwandan Genocide – The Killers Speak* (London: Serpent's Tail).

Haugaard, M. (ed.) (2002) *Power: A Reader* (Manchester and New York: Manchester University Press).

Hay, C. (2002) *Political Analysis: A Critical Introduction* (Basingstoke and New York: Palgrave).

Hay, C., Lister, M. and Marsh, D. (2005) *The State: Theories and Issues* (Basingstoke and New York: Palgrave Macmillan).

Hayek, F. (ed.) (1935) *Collective Economic Planning* (London: Routledge & Kegan Paul).

Hayek, F. (1960) *The Constitution of Liberty* (Chicago, IL: University of Chicago Press).

Hayward, J. (1994) 'Ideological Change: The Exhaustion of the Revolutionary Impulse', in *Developments in French Politics*, ed. P. Hall, J. Hayward and H. Machin (Basingstoke: Macmillan) pp. 15–32.

Hayward, J. (2004) 'Parliament and the French Government's Domination of the Legislative Process', *Journal of Legislative Studies* (10) 79–97.

Hayward, J. and Wright, V. (2002) *Governing from the Centre: Core Executive Coordination in France* (Oxford and New York: Oxford University Press).

Hazan, R. (2002) 'Candidate Selection', in *Comparing Democracies 2: New Challenges in the Study of Elections and Voting*, ed. L. LeDuc, R. Niemi and P. Norris (London and Thousand Oaks, CA: Sage) pp. 108–26.

Heady, F. (2001) *Public Administration: A Comparative Perspective*, 6th edn (New York: Marcel Dekker).

Heclo, H. (1974) *Modern Social Policies in Britain and Sweden* (New Haven, CT and London: Yale University Press).

Heclo, H. (1978) 'Issue Networks and the Executive Establishment', in *The New American Political System*, ed. A. King (Washington, DC: American Enterprise Institute) pp. 87–124.

Hefferman, R. (2006) 'The Blair Style of Central Government', in *Developments in British Politics 8*, ed. P. Dunleavy *et al.* (Basingstoke and New York: Palgrave Macmillan) pp. 20–35.

Heilbroner, R. (1953) [2000 edn] *The Worldly Philosophers: The Lives, Times and Ideas of the Great Economic Thinkers*, 7th edn (London and New York: Penguin).

Held, D. (2004) *Global Covenant: The Social Democratic Alternative to the Washington Consensus* (Cambridge and Malden, MA: Polity).

Held, D. (2006) *Models of Democracy*, 3rd edn (Cambridge: Polity).

Held, D. *et al.* (2005) *Debating Globalization* (Cambridge and Malden, MA: Polity).

Hellinger, D. (2003) 'Political Overview: The Breakdown of *Puntofijismo* and the Rise of *Chavismo*', in *Venezuelan Politics in the Chávez Era: Class, Polarization and Conflict*, ed. S. Ellner and D. Hellinger (Boulder, CO and London: Lynne Rienner) pp. 27–54.

Helms, D. (ed.) (2000) *Institutions and Institutional Change in the Federal Republic of Germany* (Basingstoke: Palgrave).

Helms, L. (2005) *Presidents, Prime Ministers and Chancellors: Executive Leadership in Western Democracies* (Basingstoke and New York: Palgrave Macmillan).

Henshel, R. (1990) *Thinking About Social Problems* (New York: Harcourt Brace Jovanovich).

Her Majesty's Court Service (2005) *The Administrative Court*, http://www.hmcourtsservice.gov.uk/cms/admin.htm, accessed 5 August, 2006.

Herb, M. (1999) *All in the Family: Absolutism, Revolution and Democracy in the Middle Eastern Monarchies* (Albany, NY: State University of New York Press).

Herb, M. (2005) 'Princes, Parliaments, and the Prospects for Democracy in the Gulf', in *Authoritarianism in the Middle East*, ed. M. Posusney and M. Angrist (Lynne Rienner: Boulder, CO and Oxford) pp. 169–92.

Herbst, J. (2001) 'Political Liberalization in Africa after 10 Years,' *Comparative Politics* (33) 357–75.

Herbst, J. (2004) 'Let Them Fail: State Failure in Theory and Practice' in *When States Fail: Causes and Consequences*, ed. R. Rotberg (Princeton, NJ: Princeton University Press), pp. 302–18.

Herbst, S. (1998) *Reading Public Opinion: How Political Actors View The Political Process* (Chicago and London: University of Chicago Press).

Hershberg, E. (2006) 'Technocrats, Citizens and Second-Generation Reforms: Colombia's Andean Malaise' in *State and Society in Conflict: Comparative Perspectives on the Andean Crisis*, ed. P. Drake and E. Hershberg (Pittsburgh, PA: University of Pittsburgh Press) pp. 134–56.

Hetherington, M. (2004) *Why Trust Matters: Declining Political Trust and the Demise of Political Liberalism* (Princeton, NJ: Princeton University Press).

Heywood, P. (1995) *The Government and Politics of Spain* (Basingstoke: Macmillan).

Heywood, P. and Closa, C. (2004) *Spain and the European Union* (Basingstoke and New York: Palgrave Macmillan).

Hibbs, D. (2006) 'Voting and the Macroeconomy', in *The Oxford Handbook of Political Economy*, ed. B. Weingast and D. Wittman (Oxford and New York: Oxford University Press) pp. 221–35.

Hilderband, M. (2002) 'Capacity Building', in *Handbook on Development Policy and Management,* ed. C. Kirkpatrick, R. Clarke and C. Polidano (Aldershot and Brookfield, VT: Edward Elgar) pp. 323–32.

Hill, L. (2002) 'On the Rightness of Compelling Citizens to "Vote": The Australian Case', *Political Studies* (50) 80–101.

Hill, M. and Hupe, P. (2002) *Implementing Public Policy: Governance in Theory and Practice* (London and Thousand Oaks, CA: Sage).

Hine, D. (1993) *Governing Italy: The Politics of Bargained Pluralism* (Oxford and New York: Clarendon Press).

Hinsley, F. (1986) *Sovereignty* (Cambridge and New York: Cambridge University Press).

Hirschl, R. (2002) 'The Political Origins of Judicial Empowerment through Constitutionalization: Lessons from Israel's Constitutional Review', *Comparative Politics* (33) 315–35.

Hirst, P. and Thompson, G. (1996) *Globalization in Question: The International Economy and the Possibilities of Governance,* 2nd edn (Oxford and Cambridge, MA: Blackwell).

Hite, K. and Cesarini, P. (eds) (2004) *Authoritarian Legacies and Democracies in Latin America and Southern Europe* (Notre Dame, IN: University of Notre Dame Press).

Hix, S. (2005) *The Political System of the European Union,* 2nd edn (Basingstoke: Palgrave Macmillan).

Hobbes, T. (1651) [1968 edn] *Leviathan,* ed. M. Oakeshott (Toronto: Crowell-Collier).

Hoffman, J. (1998) *Sovereignty* (Buckingham: Open University Press).

Hoffman, S. (1995) 'The Politics and Ethics of Military Intervention', *Survival* (37) 29–51.

Hogwood, B. and Gunn, L. (1984) *Policy Analysis for the Real World* (Oxford: Oxford University Press).

Hogwood, B., Judge, D. and McVicar, M. (2000) 'Accountability and Control in Next Steps Agencies' in *Transforming British Government*, Volume 1: Changing Institutions, ed. R. Rhodes (Basingstoke and New York: Macmillan) pp. 195–222.

Holland, K. (1991) 'Introduction' in *Judicial Activism in Comparative Perspective,* ed. K. Holland (Basingstoke: Macmillan) pp. 1–11.

Hollingsworth, J. and Boyer, R. (eds) (1997) *Comparing Capitalist Economies: The Embeddedness of Institutions* (Cambridge and New York: Cambridge University Press).

Hood, C. (1983) *The Tools of Government* (London: Macmillan).

Hood, C. (1996) 'Exploring Variations in Public Management Reform in the 1990s', in *Civil Service Systems in Comparative Perspective,* ed. H. Bekke, J. Perry and T. Toonen (Bloomington, IN: Indiana University Press) pp. 268–87.

Hood, C. *et al.* (1999) *Regulation Inside Government: Waste-Watchers, Quality Police and Sleaze-Busters* (Oxford and New York: Oxford University Press).

Hood, C., Rothstein, H. and Baldwin, R. (2004) *The Government of Risk: Understanding Risk Regulation Regimes* (New York and Oxford: Oxford University Press).

Hooghe, L. and Marks, G. (2001) *Multilevel Governance and European Integration* (Lanham, MD: Rowman & Littlefield).

Horiuchi, Y. (2004) *Institutions, Incentives and Electoral Participation in Japan: Cross-Level and Cross-National Perspectives* (London and New York: Routledge).

Horowitz, D. (2002) 'Constitutional Design: Proposals versus Processes' in *The Architecture of Democracy: Constitutional Design, Conflict Management and Democracy* (Oxford and New York: Oxford University Press) pp. 15–36.

Hosli, M., van Deemen, A. and Widgrén, M. (eds) (2002) *Institutional Challenges in the European Union* (London and New York: Routledge).

House of Commons Information Office (2003) *The Vote Bundle*, http://www.parliament.uk/parliamentary_publications_and_archives/factsheets/p16.cfm, accessed 19 December, 2006.

Howe, H. (2001) *Ambiguous Order: Military Forces in African States* (Boulder, CO and London: Lynne Rienner).

Howell, W. (2005) 'Unilateral Powers: A Brief Overview', *Presidential Studies Quarterly* (35) 417–39.

Hrebenar, R. (1997) *Interest Group Politics in America*, 3rd edn (Englewood Cliffs, NJ: Prentice Hall).

Hughes, C. (1916) *Addresses of Charles Evans Hughes* (New York: Putnam's) pp. 185–6.

Hull, A. (1999) 'Comparative Political Science: An Inventory and Assessment since the 1980s', *Political Science and Politics* (32) 117–24.

Huntington, S. (1968) *Political Order in Changing Societies* (New Haven, CT and London: Yale University Press).

Huntington, S. (1970) 'Social and Institutional Dynamics of One-Party Systems', in *Authoritarian Politics in Modern Society: The Dynamics of Established One-Party Systems*, ed. S. Huntington and C. Moore (New York and London: Basic Books) pp. 3–47.

Huntington, S. (1991) *The Third Wave: Democratization in the Late Twentieth Century* (Norman, OK and London: University of Oklahoma Press).

Huntington, S. (1993) 'Clash of Civilizations', *Foreign Affairs* (72) 22–49.

Huntington, S. (1996) *The Clash of Civilizations and the Making of World Order* (New York: Simon & Schuster).

Huntington, S. (2004) *Who Are We? America's Great Debate* (New York: Free Press).

Huntington, S. and Nelson, J. (1976) *No Easy Choice: Political Participation in Developing Countries* (Cambridge, MA: Harvard University Press).

Hutter, B. (2005) 'Risk Management and Governance' in *Designing Government: From Instruments to Governance*, ed. P. Eliadis, M. Hill and M. Howlett (Montreal and London: McGill-Queen's University Press) pp. 303–21.

Hutton, W. (2006) *The Writing on the Wall: China and the West in the 21st Century* (Boston, MA: Little, Brown).

Hyden, G. (1997) 'Democratization and Administration', in *Democracy's Victory and Crisis*, ed. A. Hadenius (Cambridge and New York: Cambridge University Press) pp. 242–62.

Hyden, G. (2006) *African Politics in Comparative Perspective* (Cambridge and New York: Cambridge University Press).

I

Ibarra, P. (2003) *Social Movements and Democracy* (London: Palgrave Macmillan).

IDEA (International Institute for Democracy and Electoral Assistance) (2006) *Engaging the Electorate: Initiatives to Promote Voter Turnout From Around the World*, http://www.idea.int/publications/vt_ee/index.cfm, accessed 13 June, 2006.

Ignatieff, M. (2002) 'Intervention and State Failure', *Dissent* (49) 114–23.

Ignazi, P. (2006) *Extreme Right Parties in Western Europe* (Oxford and New York: Oxford University Press).

Inglehart, R. (1971) 'The Silent Revolution in Europe: Intergenerational Change in Post-Industrial Societies', *American Political Science Review* (65) 991–1017.

Inglehart, R. (1990) *Culture Shift in Advanced Industrial Society* (Princeton, NJ: Princeton University Press).

Inglehart, R. (1997) *Modernization and Postmodernization: Cultural, Economic and Social Change in 43 Societies* (Princeton, NJ and London: Princeton University Press).

Inglehart, R. (1999) 'Postmodernization Erodes Respect for Authority, but Increases Support for Democracy', in *Critical Citizens: Global Support for Democratic Governance*, ed. P. Norris (Oxford and New York: Oxford University Press) pp. 236–56.

Inglehart, R. (2000) 'Political Culture and Democratic Institutions', paper delivered at the *Annual Conference of the American Political Science Association*, Washington, DC.

Inoguchi, T. (2002) 'Broadening the Basis of Political Capital in Japan', in *Democracies in Flux: The Evolution of Social Capital in Contemporary Society*, ed. R. Putnam (Oxford and New York: Oxford University Press) pp. 359–92.

Institute for Comparative Social Research (2003) *Future of Democracy in Russia in the Hands of Silent Majority*, http://www.ru/print.php?id=541, accessed 13 December, 2006.

Internet Society of China (2002) *Public Pledge of Self-Regulation and Professional Ethics for the Chinese Internet Industry*, http://www.isc.org.cn/20020417/ca102762.htm, accessed 30 April, 2006.

Internet World Stats (2006) *Internet Usage Stats: The Big Picture*, http://www.internetworldstats.com/stats.htm, accessed 24 April, 2006.

IPU (Inter-Parliamentary Union) (2006a) *Women in National Parliaments*, http://www.ipu.org/wmn-e/classif.htm, accessed 7 September, 2006.

IPU (Inter-Parliamentary Union) (2006b) *Italy: Last Elections*, http://www.ipu.org/parline-e/reports/2157_E.htm, accessed 9 December, 2006.

Ivaldi, G. (2006) 'Beyond France's 2005 Referendum on the European Constitutional Treaty', *West European Politics* (29) 47–69.

J

Jackman, R. and Miller, R. (1996) 'A Renaissance of Political Culture?', *American Journal of Political Science* (40) 632–59.

Jackson, K. (1994) 'Stability and Renewal: Incumbency and Parliamentary Composition' in *The Victorious Incumbent: A Threat to Democracy?* ed. A. Somit *et al.* (Aldershot and Brookfield, VT: Dartmouth) pp. 251–77.

Jackson, P. and Nexon, D. (2002) 'Globalization, The Comparative Method, and Comparing Constructions', in *Constructivism and Comparative Politics*, ed. D. Green (Armonk, NY and London: M.E. Sharpe) pp. 88–120.

Jackson, R. (1990) *Quasi-states: Sovereignty, International Relations and the Third World* (Cambridge and New York: Cambridge University Press).

Jackson, R. and Rosberg, C. (1982) *Personal Rule in Black Africa: Prince, Autocrat, Prophet, Tyrant* (Berkeley, CA: University of California Press).

Jacob, H. *et al.* (1996) *Courts, Law and Politics in Comparative Perspective* (New Haven, CT and London: Yale University Press).

Jamieson, K. and Waldman, P. (2003) *The Press Effect: Politicians, Journalists and the Stories that Shape the Political World* (Oxford and New York: Oxford University Press).

Jasiewicz, K. (2003) 'Elections and Voting Behaviour', in *Developments in Central and East European Politics 3*, ed. S. White, J. Batt and P. Lewis (Basingstoke and New York: Palgrave Macmillan) pp. 173–89.

Jay, A. (1996) *The Oxford Dictionary of Political Quotations* (Oxford and New York: Oxford University Press).

Jayanntha, D. (1991) *Electoral Allegiance in Sri Lanka* (Cambridge and New York: Cambridge University Press).

John, P. (1998) *Analysing Public Policy* (London and New York: Continuum).

John, P. (2001) *Local Governance in Western Europe* (London and Thousand Oaks, CA: Sage).

Johnson, C. (1995) *Japan: Who Governs? The Rise of the Developmental State* (New York and London: Norton).

Johnson, D. (2003) 'A Tale of Two Systems: Prosecuting Corruption in Japan and Italy', in *The State of Civil Society in Japan*, ed. F. Schwartz and S. Pharr (Cambridge and New York: Cambridge University Press) pp. 257–80.

Johnson, J. (2001) 'Path Contingency in Postcommunist Transformations', *Comparative Politics* (33) 253–74.

Jones, C. (1994) *The Presidency in a Separated System* (Washington, DC: Brookings Institution).

Jones, J. (2005) *Entertaining Politics: New Political Television and Civic Culture* (Lanham, MD: Rowman & Littlefield).

Jones, M. (1995a) 'A Guide to the Electoral Systems of the Americas', *Electoral Studies* (14) 5–21.

Jones, M. (1995b) *Electoral Laws and the Survival of Presidential Democracies* (Notre Dame, IN: University of Notre Dame Press).

Jordan, A., Wurzel, R. and Zito, A. (2005) 'The Rise of "New" Policy Instruments in Comparative Perspective: Has Governance Eclipsed Government?' *Political Studies* (53) 477–96.

Joyce, P. (2002) *The Politics of Protest: Extra-Parliamentary Politics in Britain since 1970* (London: Palgrave Macmillan).

Juberías, C. (2004) 'Eastern Europe: General Overview', in *Handbook of Electoral System Choice*, ed. J. Colomer (Basingstoke and New York: Palgrave Macmillan) pp. 309–31.

Judge, D. and Earnshaw, D. (2003) *The European Parliament* (Basingstoke and New York: Palgrave Macmillan).

Jungar, A. C. (2002) 'A Case of a Surplus Majority Government: The Finnish Rainbow Coalition', *Scandinavian Political Studies* (25) 57–83.

K

Kahlberg, S. (ed.) (2005) *Max Weber: Readings and Commentary on Modernity* (Malden, MA and Oxford: Blackwell).

Kahn, J. (2002) *Federalism, Democratization and the Rule of Law in Russia* (Oxford and New York: Oxford University Press).

Karatnycky, A. (2002) 'Muslim Countries and the Democracy Gap', *Journal of Democracy* (13) 99–112.

Karatnycky, A. (2006) *Civic Power and Electoral Politics* (Washington, DC: Freedom House), http://www.freedom.house.org/template.cfm?page=130&year=2005, accessed 19 February, 2006.

Karmis, D. and Norman, W. (eds) (2005) *Theories of Federalism: A Reader* (New York and Basingstoke: Palgrave Macmillan).

Katz, R. (1997) *Democracy and Elections* (Oxford and New York: Oxford University Press).

Katz, R. and Crotty, W. (eds) (2006) *Handbook of Party Politics* (London and Thousand Oaks, CA: Sage).

Katz, R. and Mair, P. (1995) 'Changing Models of Party Organization and Party Democracy: The Emergence of the Cartel Party', *Party Politics* (1) 5–28.

Kavanagh, D. and Butler, D. (2005) *The British General Election of 2005* (Basingstoke and New York: Palgrave Macmillan).

Keitetsi, C. (2004) *Child Soldier* (London: Souvenir Press).

Kelsen, H. (1942) 'Judicial Review of Legislation: A Comparative Study of the Austrian and the American Constitution', *Journal of Politics* (4) 183–200.

Kennedy-Dubourdieu, E. (ed.) (2006) *Race and Inequality: World Perspectives on Affirmative Action* (Aldershot: Ashgate).

Kernell, S. (1997) *Going Public: New Strategies of Presidential Leadership*, 3rd edn (Washington, DC: CQ Press).

Kershaw, I. (2000) *The Nazi Dictatorship: Problems and Perspectives of Interpretation*, 4th edn (London: Arnold).

Kershaw, I. (2001) *Hitler, 1936–1945: Nemesis* (London: Penguin).

Kershaw, I. and Lewin, M. (eds) (1997) *Stalinism and Nazism: Dictatorships in Comparison* (Cambridge and New York: Cambridge University Press).

Keshavarzian, A. (2005) 'Contestation Without Democracy: Elite Fragmentation in Iran', in *Authoritarianism in the Middle East: Regimes and Resistance*, ed. M. Posusney and M. Angrist (Boulder, CO and London: Lynne Rienner) pp. 63–90.

Kettl, D. (2006) 'Public Bureaucracies', in *The Oxford Handbook of Political Institutions*, ed. R. Rhodes, S. Binder and B. Rockman (Oxford and New York: Oxford University Press) pp. 366–85.

Keynes, J. (1923) [1971 edn] *Tract on Monetary Reform* (London: Palgrave Macmillan).

Keynes, J. (1936) *The General Theory of Employment, Interest and Money* (London: Macmillan).

Khadiagala, G. (1995) 'State Collapse and Reconstruction in Uganda' in *Collapsed States: The Disintegration and Restoration of Legitimate Authority*, ed. W. Zartman (Boulder, CO and London: Lynne Rienner) pp. 33–47.

Khatchadourian, A. (2004) 'The Terror at Jaslyk', *The Nation* (web only), http://www.thenation.com/doc/20040426/khatchadourian, accessed 1 April, 2006.

Khodorkovsky, M. (2006) *Official Trial Website*, http://www.mbktrial.com, accessed 24 May, 2006.

Khong, Y. (1992) *Analogies at War: Korea, Munich, Dien Bien Phu and the Vietnam Decisions of 1965* (Princeton, NJ: Princeton University Press).

King, A. (1994) 'Ministerial Autonomy in Britain', in *Cabinet Ministers and Parliamentary Government*, ed. M. Laver and K. Shepsle (Cambridge and New York: Cambridge University Press) pp. 203–25.

King, A. (ed.) (2002) *Leaders' Personalities and the Outcomes of Democratic Elections* (Oxford and New York: Oxford University Press).

King, G., Keohane, R. and Verba S. (1994) *Designing Social Inquiry: Scientific Inference in Qualitative Research* (Princeton, NJ: Princeton University Press).

Kingdon, J. (1984) *Agendas, Alternatives and Public Policy* (Boston, MA: Little, Brown).

Kingsley, J. (1944) *Representative Bureaucracy* (Yellow Springs, OH: Antioch).

Kirchheimer, O. (1966) 'The Transformation of the Western European Party Systems', in *Political Parties and Political Development*, ed. J. LaPalombara and M. Weiner (Princeton, NJ: Princeton University Press) pp. 177–200.

Kitschelt, H. *et al.* (1999) *Postcommunist Party Systems: Competition, Representation and Inter-Party Competition* (Cambridge and New York: Cambridge University Press).

Kjær, A. (2004) *Governance* (Cambridge: Polity).

Klapper, J. (1960) *The Effects of Mass Communication* (New York and London: Free Press).

Klein, S. (2002) *The Most Evil Dictators in History* (London: O'Mara Books).

Kleinfeld, R. (2006) 'Competing Definitions of the Rule of Law', in *Promoting the Rule of Law Abroad: In Search of Knowledge*, ed. T. Carothers (Washington, DC: Carnegie Endowment for International Peace) pp. 31–74.

Knapp, A. and Wright, V. (2006) *The Government and Politics of France,* 5th edn (London and New York: Routledge).

Knutsen, O. (1990) 'Materialist and Postmaterialist Values and Structures in the Nordic Countries', *Comparative Politics* (23) 85–101.

Knutsen, O. (1996) 'Value Orientations and Party Choice: A Comparative Study of the Relationship between Five Value Orientations and Voting Intention in Thirteen West European Democracies', in *Wahlen und Politische Einstellungen in Westlichen Demokratien,* ed. O. Gabriel and W. Falter (Frankfurt: Peter Lang) pp. 247–319.

Knutsen, O. (2001) 'Social Class, Sector Employment and Gender as Party Cleavages in the Scandinavian Countries: A Comparative Longitudinal Study, 1970–95', *Scandinavian Political Studies* (24) 311–50.

Kobach, K. (1997) 'Direct Democracy and Swiss Isolationism', *West European Politics* (20) 185–211.

Koeberle, S. *et al.* (eds) *Conditionality Revisited: Concepts, Experiences and Lessons* (Washington, DC: World Bank).

Kolinsky, E. (2002) 'Party Governance, Political Culture and the Transformation of East Germany Since 1990', in *Continuity and Change in German Politics: Beyond the Politics of Centrality? A Festschrift for Gordon Smith*, ed. S. Padgett and T. Poguntke (London and Portland, OR: Cass) pp. 169–83.

Kooiman, J. (2003) *Governing as Governance* (London and Thousand Oaks, CA: Sage).

Kornhauser, W. (1959) *The Politics of Mass Society* (Glencoe, IL: Free Press).

Korosteleva, E. (2004) 'The Quality of Democracy in Belarus and Ukraine', *Journal of Communist and Transition Politics* (20) 122–42.

Kostadinova, T. (2002) 'Do Mixed Electoral Systems Matter? A Cross-National Comparison of Their Effects in Eastern Europe', *Electoral Studies* (21) 23–34.

Kramnick, I. (1987) 'Editor's Introduction' in J. Madison, A. Hamilton and J. Jay, *The Federalist Papers* (London: Penguin) pp. 11–81.

Krasner, S. (1999) *Sovereignty: Organized Hypocrisy* (Princeton, NJ and Chichester: Princeton University Press).

Krastev, I. (2006) *'Sovereign Democracy', Russian Style*, http://www.opendemocracy.net/globalization-institutions_government/sovereign_democracy_4104.jsp, accessed 16 December, 2006.

Krauthammer, C. (1990) 'In Praise of Low Voter Turnout', *Time*, 21 May, p. 88.

Kreuzer, M. (2004) 'Germany: Partisan Engineering of Personalized Proportional Representation', in *Handbook of Electoral System Choice*, ed. J. Colomer (Basingstoke and New York: Palgrave Macmillan) pp. 222–36.

Krouwel, A. (2003) 'Otto Kirchheimer and the Catch-All Party', *West European Politics* (26) 23–40.

Krueger, R. and Casey, M. (2000) *Focus Groups: A Practical Guide for Applied Research*, 3rd edn (Thousand Oaks, CA and London: Sage).

Kudrle, R. and Marmot, T. (1981) 'The Development of Welfare States in North America', in *The Development of Welfare States in Europe and America,* ed. P. Flora and A. Heidenheimer (New Brunswick, NJ and London: Transaction) pp. 187–236.

Kühn, Z. (2006) 'The Judicialization of European Politics' in *Developments in European Politics*, ed. P. Heywood *et al.* (Basingstoke and New York: Palgrave Macmillan) pp. 216–36.

Kuhnle, S. (2000) 'The Scandinavian Welfare State in the 1990s: Challenged but Viable', *West European Politics* (23) 209–28.

Kymlicka, W. (1995) *Multicultural Citizenship: A Liberal Theory of Minority Rights* (Oxford and New York: Oxford University Press).

L

Lachmann, R. (1997) 'Agents of Revolution: Elite Conflicts and Mass Mobilization from the Medici to the Yemen', in *Theorizing Revolutions,* ed. J. Foran (London and New York: Routledge) pp. 73–101.

Laegreid, P. and Olsen, J. (1978) *Byråkrati og Beslutninger* (Bergen: Norwegian University Press).

Landes, R. (1995) *The Canadian Polity: A Comparative Introduction* (Scarborough, Ontario: Prentice Hall Canada).

Langer, A. (2006) 'A Historical Exploration of the Personalisation of Politics in the Media: The British Prime Ministers, 1945–1999', paper delivered to the *56th Annual Conference of the Political Studies Association*, Reading, England.

Langman, L. (2006) 'The Social Psychology of Nationalism', in *The Sage Handbook of Nations and Nationalism*, ed. G. Delanty and K. Kumar (London: Sage) pp. 71–83.

LaPalombara, J. (1974) *Politics Within Nations* (Englewood Cliffs, NJ: Prentice Hall).

Latouche, S. (1996) *The Westernization of the World* (Cambridge and Cambridge, MA: Polity).

Laver, M. (1983) *Invitation to Politics* (Oxford: Martin Robertson).

Laver, M. and Schofield, N. (1998) *Multiparty Government: The Politics of Coalition in Europe* (Ann Arbor, MI: University of Michigan Press).

Lawson, C. (2004) 'Fox's Mexico at Mid-term', *Journal of Democracy* (15) 139–53.

Lawson, K. (2001) 'Political Parties and Party Competition', in *The Oxford Companion to Politics of the World*, 2nd edn, ed. J. Krieger (Oxford and New York: Oxford University Press) pp. 670–3.

Lazarsfeld, P. and Merton, R. (1948) [1996 edn] 'Mass Communication, Popular Taste and Organized Social Action', in *Media Studies: A Reader,* ed. P. Marris and S. Thornham (Edinburgh: Edinburgh University Press) pp. 14–24.

Lechner, F. and Boli, J. (eds) (2003) *The Globalization Reader* (Oxford and Cambridge, MA: Blackwell).

LeDuc, L. (2002) 'Referendums and Initiatives: The Politics of Direct Democracy', in *Comparing Democracies 2: New Challenges in the Study of Elections and Voting*, ed. L. DeDuc, R. Niemi and P. Norris (London and Thousand Oaks, CA: Sage) pp. 70–87.

LeDuc, L., Niemi, R. and Norris, P. (2002a) 'Comparing Democratic Elections', in *Comparing Democracies 2: New*

Challenges in the Study of Elections and Voting, ed. L. LeDuc, R. Niemi and P. Norris (Thousand Oaks, CA and London: Sage) pp. 1–39.

LeDuc, L., Niemi, R. and Norris, P. (eds) (2002b) *Comparing Democracies 2: New Challenges in the Study of Elections and Voting* (Thousand Oaks, CA and London: Sage).

Lee, S. (2000) *European Dictatorships, 1918–45,* 2nd edn (London and New York: Routledge).

Leftwich, A. (ed.) (2004) *What Is Politics?* (Cambridge and Malden, MA: Polity).

Leib, E. (2004) *Deliberative Democracy in America: A Proposal for a Popular Branch of Government* (University Park, PA: Pennsylvania University Press).

Leites, N. (1960) *American Foreign Policy* (London: George Allen).

Lenin, V. (1902) [1963 edn] *What Is To Be Done?* (Oxford: Clarendon Press).

Lenin, V. (1917) *The State and Revolution* (Marxists Internet Archive), http://www.marxists.org/archive/lenin/works/1917/staterev/ch05.htm#s2, accessed 25 March, 2006.

Lesch, A. (2004) 'Politics in Egypt', in *Comparative Politics Today: A World View,* 8th edn, ed. G. Almond *et al.* (New York: Longman) pp. 581–632.

Levada, Y. (2001) 'Homo Praevaricatus: Russian Doublethink', in *Contemporary Russian Politics: A Reader,* ed. A. Brown (Oxford and New York: Oxford University Press) pp. 312–22.

Levene, M. (2005a) *Genocide in the Age of the Nation-State: Volume I, The Meaning of Genocide* (London and New York: I. B. Taurus).

Levene, M. (2005b) *Genocide in the Age of the Nation-State: Volume II, The Rise of the West and the Coming of Genocide* (London and New York: I. B. Taurus).

Lewin, L. (2004) 'Sweden: Introducing Proportional Representation from Above', in *Handbook of Electoral System Choice,* ed. J. Colomer (Basingstoke and New York: Palgrave Macmillan) pp. 265–78.

Lewin, M. (1997) 'Bureaucracy and the Stalinist State', in *Stalinism and Nazism: Dictatorships in Comparison,* ed. I. Kershaw and M. Lewin (Cambridge and New York: Cambridge University Press) pp. 53–74.

Lewis, B. (2002) *What Went Wrong? Western Impact and Middle Eastern Response* (London: Weidenfeld & Nicolson).

Lewis, B. (2003) *The Crisis of Islam: Holy War and Unholy Terror* (London: Weidenfeld & Nicolson).

Lewis, D. (2002) 'The Politics of Agency Termination: Confronting the Myth of Agency Termination', *Journal of Politics* (64) 89–120.

Lewis, P. (2000) *Political Parties in Postcommunist Eastern Europe* (London and New York: Routledge).

Lewis, P. (2003) 'Political Parties', in *Developments in Central and East European Politics 3,* ed. S. White, J. Batt and P. Lewis (Basingstoke and New York: Palgrave Macmillan) pp. 153–72.

Liddle, R. (1996) 'A Useful Fiction: Democratic Legitimation in New Order Indonesia', in *The Politics of Elections in Southeast Asia,* ed. R. Taylor (Cambridge and New York: Cambridge University Press) pp. 34–60.

Lie, J. (2004) *Modern Peoplehood* (Cambridge, MA and London: Harvard University Press).

Lieberman, E. (2005) 'Nested Analysis as Mixed-Method Strategy for Comparative Research', *American Political Science Review* (99) 435–52.

Lieberman, I., Nestor, S. and Desai, R. (eds) (1997) *Between State and Market: Mass Privatization in Transition Economies* (Washington, DC: World Bank).

Lijphart, A. (1967) *The Politics of Accommodation: Pluralism and Democracy in the Netherlands* (Berkeley, CA: Universtiy of California Press).

Lijphart, A. (1971) 'Comparative Politics and the Comparative Method', *American Political Science Review* (65) 682–93.

Lijphart, A. (1977) *Democracy in Plural Societies: A Comparative Exploration* (Berkeley, CA: University of California Press).

Lijphart, A. (1984) *Democracies: Patterns of Majoritarian and Consensual Government in Twenty One Countries* (New Haven, CT and London: Yale University Press).

Lijphart, A. (ed.) (1992) *Parliamentary versus Presidential Government* (Oxford and New York: Oxford University Press).

Lijphart, A. (1994) *Electoral Systems and Party Systems* (New Haven, CT and London: Yale University Press).

Lijphart, A. (1997) 'Unequal Participation: Democracy's Unresolved Dilemma', *American Political Science Review* (91) 1–14.

Lijphart, A. (1999) *Patterns of Democracy: Government Forms and Performance in Thirty Six Countries* (New Haven, CT and London: Yale University Press).

Lijphart, A. (2000) 'The Future of Democracy: Reasons for Pessimism but also Some Optimism', *Scandinavian Political Studies* (23) 265–72.

Lijphart, A. (2002) 'The Evolution of Consociational Theory and Consociational Practices, 1965–2000', *Acta Politica* (37) 11–20.

Lijphart, A. and Crepaz, M. (1991) 'Corporatism and Consensus Democracy in Eighteen Countries: Conceptual and Empirical Linkages', *British Journal of Political Science* (21) 235–46.

Lijphart, A. and Waisman, C. (1996a) 'The Design of Democracies and Markets: Generalizing Across Regions', in *Institutional Design in New Democracies: Eastern Europe and Latin America,* ed. A. Lijphart and C. Waisman (Boulder, CO and Oxford: Westview) pp. 235–48.

Lijphart, A. and Waisman, C. (eds) (1996b) *Institutional Design in New Democracies: Eastern Europe and Latin America* (Boulder, CO and Oxford: Westview).

Lindblom, C. (1959) 'The Science of Muddling Through', *Public Administration* (19) 78–88.

Lindblom, C. (1977) *Politics and Markets* (New York: Basic Books).

Lindblom, C. (1979) 'Still Muddling, Not Yet Through', *Public Administration Review* (39) 517–26.

Lindblom, C. (1990) *Inquiry and Change: The Troubled Attempt to Understand and Shape Society* (New Haven, CT and London: Yale University Press).

Linz, J. (1975) [2000 edn] *Totalitarian and Authoritarian Regimes* (Boulder, CO and London: Lynne Rienner).

Linz, J. (1978) 'Crisis, Breakdown and Re-equilibration', in *The Breakdown of Democratic Regimes,* ed. J. Linz and A. Stepan (Baltimore, MD and London: Johns Hopkins University Press) pp. 1–124.

Linz, J. (1990) 'The Perils of Presidentialism', *Journal of Democracy* (1) 51–69.

Linz, J. and Stepan, A. (eds) (1978) *The Breakdown of Democratic Regimes* (Baltimore, MD and London: Johns Hopkins University Press).

Linz, J. and Valenzuela, A. (eds) (1994) *The Failure of Presidential Democracy* (Baltimore, MD: Johns Hopkins University Press).

Lippman, W. (1922) *Public Opinion* (London: Allen & Unwin).

Lipset, S. (1960) [1983 edn] *Political Man* (New York: Basic Books).

Lipset, S. (1990) *Continental Divide: The Values and Institutions of the United States and Canada* (London and New York: Routledge).

Lipset, S. and Rokkan, S. (1967) 'Cleavage Structures, Party Systems and Voter Alignments', in *Party Systems and Voter Alignments,* ed. S. Lipset and S. Rokkan (New York and London: Free Press) pp. 1–65.

Litvin, A. and Keep, J. (eds) (2005) *Stalinism: Russian and Western Views at the Turn of the Millennium* (London and New York: Routledge).

Lively, J. (1991) 'Sièyes, Emmanuel Joseph', in *The Blackwell Encyclopaedia of Political Thought,* ed. D. Miller (Oxford and Cambridge, MA: Blackwell) pp. 475–6.

Locke, J. (1689) [1970 edn] *Two Treatises of Government*, ed. P. Laslett (Cambridge and New York: Cambridge University Press).

Locke, J. (1690) [1965 edn] *Two Treatises of Government* (New York: New American Library).

Loewenberg, G. Squire, P. and Kiewilt, D. (eds) (2002) *Legislatures: Comparative Perspectives on Representative Assemblies* (Ann Arbor, MI: University of Michigan Press).

Longley, L. and Davidson, R. (eds) (1998) *The New Roles of Parliamentary Committees* (London: Frank Cass).

Loughlin, J. (2001) *Subnational Democracy in the European Union: Challenges and Opportunities* (Oxford and New York: Oxford University Press).

Loveland, I. (2004) *Constitutional Law, Administrative Law and Human Rights: A Critical Introduction*, 3rd edn (Oxford and New York: Oxford University Press).

Lowenstein, D. (2006) 'Legal Regulation and Protection of American Parties', in *Handbook of Party Politics*, ed. R. Katz and W. Crotty (London and Thousand Oaks, CA: Sage) pp. 456–70.

Lowi, T. (1969) *The End of Liberalism* (New York: Norton).

Lubbers, M., Gijsberts, M. and Scheepers, P. (2002) 'Extreme Right-wing Voting in Western Europe', *European Journal of Political Research* (41) 345–78.

Lubman, S. (1999) *Bird in a Cage: Legal Reform in China after Mao* (Princeton, NJ: Princeton University Press).

Lukes, S. (1974) [2005 edn] *Power: A Radical View*, 2nd edn (Basingstoke and New York: Palgrave Macmillan).

Lukes, S. (ed.) (1986) *Power* (Oxford and Cambridge, MA: Basil Blackwell).

Lundell, K. (2004) 'Determinants of Candidate Selection: The Degree of Centralization in Comparative Prespective', *Party Politics* (10) 25–47.

Luong, P. and Weinthal, E. (2001) 'Prelude to the Resource Curse: Explaining Oil and Gas Development Strategies in the Soviet Successor States', *Comparative Political Studies* (34) 367–99.

Luther, K. and Müller-Rommel, F. (eds) (2005) *Political Parties in the New Europe: Political and Analytical Challenges* (Oxford and New York: Oxford University Press).

Lutz, J. and Lutz, B. (2004) *Global Terrorism* (London and New York: Routledge).

Lynd, R. and Lynd, H. (1929) *Middletown: A Study in Modern American Culture* (New York: Harcourt Brace).

Lyon, D. (2003) *Surveillance after September 11* (Cambridge and Malden, MA: Polity).

M

Mackenzie, G. and Labiner, J. (2002) *Opportunity Lost: The Rise and Fall of Trust and Confidence in Government After September 11* (Washington, DC: Center For Public Service, Brookings Institution), http://www.brookings.edu/gs/cps/oppotunityfinal.pdf, accessed 15 April, 2006.

Mackenzie, W. (1958) *Free Elections: An Elementary Textbook* (London: Allen & Unwin).

Macpherson, C. (1977) *The Life and Times of Liberal Democracy* (Oxford and New York: Oxford University Press).

Macqueen, A. (1989) 'The Art of Shopping', in *Soviet Union: The Challenge of Change,* ed. M. Wright (Harlow: Longman) pp. 76–84.

Maddex, R. (2000) *Constitutions of the World*, 2nd edn. (Washington, DC and London: CQ Press).

Madeley, J. (ed.) (2003) *Religion and Politics* (Aldershot and Burlington, VT: Ashgate).

Madison, J. (1781) [1970 edn] 'The Federalist, No. 10' in *The Federalist or, The New Constitution* ed. A. Hamilton, J. Madison and J. Jay (London: Dent and New York: Dutton pp. 41–7). First pub. in the *New-York Packet,* 23 November.

Magone, J. (2004) *Contemporary Spanish Politics* (London and New York: Routledge).

Magyar, K. (1992) 'Military Intervention and Withdrawal in Africa: Problems and Perspectives', in *From Military to Civilian Rule,* ed. C. Danopoulos (London and New York: Routledge) pp. 230–48.

Mahler, G. (2003) *Comparative Politics: An Institutional and Cross-National Approach,* 4th edn (Upper Saddle River, NJ: Pearson).

Mainwaring, S. (1992) 'Presidentialism in Latin America', in *Parliamentary versus Presidential Government,* ed. A. Lijphart (Oxford and New York: Oxford University Press) pp. 111–17.

Mainwaring, S. and Shugart, M. (eds) (1997) *Presidentialism and Democracy in Latin America* (Cambridge and New York: Cambridge University Press).

Mainwaring, S. and Welna, C. (eds) (2003) *Democratic Accountability in Latin America* (Oxford and New York: Oxford University Press).

Mair, P. (1994) 'Party Organizations: From Civil Society to the State', in *How Parties Organize: Change and Adaptation in Party Organizations in Western Democracies,* ed. R. Katz and P. Mair (Thousand Oaks, CA and London: Sage).

Mair, P. (1996) 'Comparative Politics: An Overview', in *A New Handbook of Political Science,* ed. R. Goodin and H. Klingemann (Oxford and New York: Oxford University Press) pp. 309–35.

Mair, P. (2006) 'Cleavages' in *Handbook of Party Politics*, ed. R. Katz and W. Crotty (London and Thousand Oaks, CA: Sage) pp. 371–5.

Mair, P. and van Biezen, I. (2001) 'Party Membership in Europe, 1980–2000', *Party Politics* (7) 5–22.

Mair, P., Müller, W. and Plasser, F. (eds) (2004) *Political Parties and Electoral Change* (London and Thousand Oaks, CA: Sage).

Majone, G. (1996) *Regulating Europe* (London and New York: Routledge).

Majone, G. (2006) 'Agenda Setting' in *The Oxford Handbook of Public Policy*, ed. M. Moran, M. Rein and R. Goodin (Oxford and New York: Oxford University Press) pp. 228–50.

Malovà, D. and Haughton, T. (2002) 'Making Institutions in Central and Eastern Europe, and the Impact of Europe', *West European Politics* (25) 101–20.

Manion, M. (2004) 'Politics in China', in *Comparative Politics Today: A World View,* 8th edn, ed. G. Almond *et al.* (New York and London: Pearson Longman) pp. 418–65.

Mann, M. (1986) *The Sources of Social Power, Volume 1: A History of Power from the Beginning to AD 1780* (Cambridge and New York: Cambridge University Press).

Mann, M. (2005) *The Dark Side of Democracy: Explaining Ethnic Cleansing* (Cambridge and New York: Cambridge University Press).

Mann, T. and Cain, B. (eds) (2005) *Party Lines: Competition, Partisanship and Congressional Redistricting* (Washington, DC: Brookings).

Manor, J. (2006) *World Bank Aid That Works: Successful Development in Fragile States* (Washington, DC: World Bank).

March, D. and Olsen, J. (1984) 'The New Institutionalism: Organizational Factors in Political Life', *American Political Science Review* (78) 734–49.

March, J. and Olsen, J. (1996) 'Institutional Perspectives on Political Institutions', *Governance* (9) 247–64.

Marks, G. and Diamond, L. (eds) (1992) *Reexamining Democracy: Essays in Honor of Seymour Martin Lipset* (Thousand Oaks, CA and London: Sage).

Marsh, D. and Rhodes, R. (eds) (1992) *Policy Networks in British Government* (Oxford and New York: Oxford University Press).

Marshall, M. and Jaggers, J. (2006) 'Political Regime Characteristics and Transitions, 1800–2003', *Polity IV Project*, http://www.cidcm.umd.edu/inscr/polity/dem2003.jpg, accessed 7 February, 2006.

Marshall, T. (1950) [1991 edn] *Citizenship and Social Class and Other Essays* (London: Pluto Press).

Marshall, T. (1987) [2004 edn] 'The Constitution: A Living Document', in *Judges on Judging: Views from the Bench*, ed. D. O'Brien (Washington, DC: CQ Press) pp. 178–82.

Martin, V. (2003) *Creating an Islamic State: Khomeini and the Making of a New Iran* (London: I. B. Taurus).

Marx, K. (1875) *Critique of the Gotha Programme*, Part IV (Marxists Internet Archive), http://www.marxists.org/archive/marx/works/1875/gotha/index.htm, accessed 25 March, 2006.

Marx, K. and Engels, F. (1848) [1967 edn] *The Communist Manifesto,* intro. G. Stedman Jones (Harmondsworth: Penguin).

Mason, A. (1993) 'The Role of the Courts at the Turn of the Century', *Journal of Judicial Administration* (3) 12–18.

Massicotte, L. (2001) 'Legislative Unicameralism: A Global Survey and a Few Case Studies', *Journal of Legislative Studies* (7) 68–83.

Matland, R. and Studlar, D. (2004) 'Determinants of Legislative Turnover: A Cross-National Analysis', *British Journal of Political Science* (34) 87–108.

Matsuura, K. *et al.* (2004) 'Institutional Restructuring in the Japanese Economy since 1985', in *Where Are National Capitalisms Now?* ed. J. Perraton and B. Clift (Basingstoke and New York: Palgrave Macmillan) pp. 133–53.

Matthews, T. (1989) 'Interest Groups', in *Politics in Australia,* ed. R. Smith and L. Watson (Sydney: Allen & Unwin) pp. 211–27.

Mattli, W. (1999) *The Logic of Regional Integration* (Cambridge and New York: Cambridge University Press).

Mayhew, D. (1991) *Divided We Govern: Party Control, Lawmaking and Investigations, 1946–1990* (New Haven, CT and London: Yale University Press).

Mazey, S. and Richardson, J. (2001) 'Interest Groups and EU Policy-Making: Organizational Logic and Venue Shopping', in *European Union: Power and Policy-Making,* 2nd edn, ed. J. Richardson (London and New York) pp. 217–38.

McAllister, I. (2003) 'Australia: Party Politicians as a Political Class', in *The Political Class in Advanced Democracies*, ed. J. Borchert and J. Zeiss (Oxford and New York: Oxford University Press) pp. 26–44.

McAllister, I. and Studlar, D. (2002) 'Electoral Systems and Women's Representation: A Long-Term Perspective', *Representation* (39) 3–14.

McCargo, D. (2002) *Media and Politics in Pacific Asia* (London and New York: Routledge).

McCarthy, J. and Zald, M. (1977) 'Resource Mobilization and Social Movements: A Partial Theory', *American Journal of Sociology* (82) 1212–41.

McCaughan, M. (2004) *The Battle of Venezuela* (London: Latin America Bureau).

McChesney, R. (1999) *Rich Media, Poor Democracies* (Urbana, IL: University of Illinois Press).

McCreery, D. (2002) 'State and Society in Nineteenth Century Goiás', in *Studies in the Formation of the Nation State in Latin America,* ed. J. Dunkerley (London: Institute of Latin American Studies) pp. 133–60.

McDonald, F. and McDonald, E. (1988) 'Federalism in America: An Obituary', in *Requiem: Variations on Eighteenth Century Themes*, ed. E. McDonald and F. MacDonald (University of Kansas Press) pp. 195–206.

McEldowney, J. (2003) 'Administrative Law', in *The Concise Oxford Dictionary of Politics,* 2nd edn, ed. I. McLean and A. Macmillan (Oxford and New York: Oxford University Press) p. 3.

McFaul, M. (2005) 'The Electoral System', in *Developments in Russian Politics 6*, ed. S. White, Z. Gitelman and R. Sakwa (Basingstoke and New York: Palgrave Macmillan) pp. 61–79.

McFaul, M. and Petrov, N. (2004) 'Russian Democracy in Eclipse: What the Elections Tell Us', *Journal of Democracy* (15) 20–31.

McKay, D. (1999) *Federalism and European Union: A Political Economy Perspective* (Oxford and New York: Oxford University Press).

McKay, D. (2001) *Designing Europe: Comparative Lessons From the European Experience* (Oxford and New York: Oxford University Press).

McKay, D. (2005) *American Politics and Society,* 6th edn (Oxford and Cambridge, MA: Blackwell).

McKenzie, R. (1955) *British Political Parties* (London: Heinemann).

McLean, I. (2006) *Adam Smith, Radical and Egalitarian: An Interpretation for the 21st Century* (Edinburgh: Edinburgh University Press).

Meehan, J. (ed.) (1995) *Feminists Read Habermas: Gendering the Subject of Discourse* (London and New York: Routledge).

Meier, K. (1993) 'Representative Bureaucracy: A Theoretical and Empirical Exposition', *Research in Public Administration* (2) 1–35.

Melleuish, G. (2002) 'The State in World History: Perspectives and Problems', *Australian Journal of Politics and History* (48) 322–35.

Melvin, N. (2000) *Uzbekistan: Transition to Authoritarianism on the Silk Road* (Reading: Harwood).

Melvin, N. (2005) 'Putin's Reform of the Russian Federation', in *Leading Russia: Putin in Perspective*, ed. A. Pravda (Oxford and New York: Oxford University Press) pp. 203–28.

Mendelsohn, M. and Parkin, A. (eds) (2001) *Referendum Democracy: Citizens, Elites and Deliberation in Referendum Campaigns* (Basingstoke: Palgrave).

Menon, A. and Schain, M. (eds) (2006) *Comparative Federalism: The European Union and the United States in Comparative Perspective* (Oxford and New York: Oxford University Press).

Meny, Y. and Knapp, A. (1998) *Government and Politics in Western Europe: Britain, France, Italy, West Germany*, 3rd edn (Oxford and New York: Oxford University Press).

Meredith, M. (2006) *The Fate of Africa: From the Hopes of Freedom to the Heart of Despair* (New York: Public Affairs).

Michels, R. (1911) [1962 edn] *Political Parties* (New York: Free Press).

Migdal, J. (2001) *State in Society: Studying how States and Societies Transform and Constitute One Another* (Cambridge and New York: Cambridge University Press).

Milbrath, L. and Goel, M. (1977) *Political Participation: How and Why Do People Get Involved in Politics*, 2nd edn (Chicago, IL: Rand McNally).

Milkis, S. (2005) 'The Presidency and Political Parties', in *The Presidency and the Political System*, 8th edn, ed. M. Nelson (Washington, DC: CQ Press) pp. 355–98.

Mill, J. (1861) [1991 edn] 'Considerations on Representative Government', in *Collected Works of John Stuart Mill*, Vol. 19, ed. J. O'Grady and B. Robson (Toronto: University of Toronto Press and London: Routledge) pp. 371–577.

Millard, F. and Popescu, M. (2005) *Political Parties and Electoral Systems: Preference Voting in New Democracies* (Budapest: Open Society Institute and the Center for Policy Studies of the Central European University), http://www.policy.hu/popescu/partiesandpreferencevoting.pdf, accessed 22 July, 2006.

Miller, D. (1991) 'Politics', in *Blackwell Encyclopaedia of Political Thought*, ed. V. Bogdanor (Oxford and Cambridge, MA: Blackwell) pp. 390–1.

Miller, R. (2005) *Party Politics in New Zealand* (South Melbourne, Victoria: Oxford University Press).

Miller, W. (1995) 'Quantitative Methods', in *Theory and Methods in Political Science*, ed. D. Marsh and G. Stoker (Basingstoke and New York: Macmillan) pp. 154–72.

Milliken, J. (ed.) (2003) *State Failure, Collapse and Reconstruction* (Malden, MA and Oxford: Blackwell).

Mills, C. Wright (1956) *The Power Elite* (New York and Oxford: Oxford University Press).

Milton, A. (2000) *The Rational Politician: Exploiting the Media in New Democracies* (Aldershot: Ashgate).

Mitchell, A. (1982) 'The Local Campaign, 1977–79', in *Political Communications: The General Election Campaign of 1979*, ed. R. Worcester and M. Harrop (London: Allen & Unwin) pp. 36–42.

Moestrup, S. and Elgie, R. (eds) (2005) *Semi-presidentialism outside Europe* (London and New York: Routledge).

Mommsen, H. (1997) 'Cumulative Radicalization and Progressive Self-Destruction as Structural Determinants of the Nazi Dictatorship', in *Stalinism and Nazism: Dictatorships in Comparison*, ed. I. Kershaw and M. Lewin *et al.* (Cambridge and New York: Cambridge University Press) pp. 75–87.

Montesquieu, C.-L. (1748) [1949] *The Spirit of the Laws*, ed. F. Neumann (New York: Hafner).

Moran, M. (2003) *The British Regulatory State: High Modernism and Hyper-Innovation* (Oxford and New York: Oxford University Press).

Moran, M. (2005) *Politics and Governance in the UK* (Basingstoke: Palgrave Macmillan).

Moran, M., Rein, M. and Goodin, R. (eds) (2006) *The Oxford Handbook of Public Policy* (Oxford and New York: Oxford University Press).

Morgenthau, H. (1966) 'The Purpose of Political Science', in *A Design for Political Science: Scope, Objectives and Methods*, ed. J. Charlesworth (Philadelphia, PA: American Academy of Political and Social Science) pp. 63–79.

Morlino, L. (1995) 'Italy's Civic Divide', *Journal of Democracy* (6) 173–7.

Mouritzen, P. and Svara, J. (2002) *Leadership at the Apex: Politicians and Administrators in Western Local Governments* (Pittsburgh, PA: University of Pittsburgh Press).

Mughan, A. (2000) *Media and the Presidentialization of Parliamentary Elections* (Basingstoke: Palgrave).

Mulgan, R. (1997) *Politics in New Zealand*, 2nd edn (Auckland: Auckland University Press).

Mulgan, R. (2003) *Holding Power to Account: Accountability in Modern Democracies* (Basingstoke: Palgrave Macmillan).

Müller, W. and Strøm, K. (1999a) 'Party Behaviour and Representative Democracy', in *Policy, Office or Votes? How Political Parties in Western Europe Make Hard Decisions*, ed. W. Müller and K. Strøm (Cambridge and New York: Cambridge University Press) pp. 279–310.

Müller, W. and Strøm, K. (1999b) *Policy, Office, or Votes? How Political Parties in Western Europe Make Hard Decisions* (Cambridge and New York: Cambridge University Press).

Müller, W. and Strøm, K. (eds) (2000a) *Coalition Governments in Western Europe* (Oxford and New York: Oxford University Press).

Müller, W. and Strøm, K. (2000b) 'Coalition Governance in Western Europe', in *Coalition Governments in Western Europe*, ed. W. Müller and K. Strøm (Oxford and New York: Oxford University Press) pp. 559–92.

Muñoz, H. (2006) 'The Growing Community of Democracies', in *Democracy Rising: Assessing the Global Challenge*, ed. H. Muñoz (Boulder, CO and London: Lynne Rienner) pp. 1–8.

Munro, W. (1925) *The Governments of Europe* (New York: Macmillan).

Murdoch, R. (1997) 'Reinventing Socialism: The Triumph of

Neosocialism is the Defining Characteristic of Politics Today', *National Review*, September 1, 1997.

Murrie, M. (2006) 'Broadcasters Getting Online, Staying On Air', *eJournal USA* (11), http://usinfo.state.gov/journals/itgic/0306/ijge/ijge0306.htm, accessed 28 April, 2006.

Murrin, J. (1987) 'A Roof without Walls: The Dilemma of American National Identity', in *Beyond Confederation: Origins of the Constitution and American National Identity*, ed. R. Beeman, S. Botein and E. Carter II (Chapel Hill, NC: University of North Carolina Press) pp. 333–48.

Musharraf, P. (2004) 'A Plea for Enlightened Moderation', *Washington Post*, June 21, p. A23, http://www.washingtonpost.com/wp-dyn/articles/A5081–2004May31.html, accessed 5 April, 2006.

Mussolini, B. (1932) [1973 edn] 'The Doctrine of Fascism', in *Italian Fascism: From Pareto to Gentile*, ed. A. Lyttleton (London: Cape) pp. 37–67.

Mutz, D. (2006) *Hearing the Other Side: Deliberative Versus Participatory Democracy* (Cambridge and New York: Cambridge University Press).

N

Nassmacher, K. (ed.) (2001) *Foundations of Democracy: Approaches to Comparative Political Finance* (Baden Baden: Nomos Verlag).

Nassmacher, K. (ed.) (2006) 'Regulation of Party Finance', in *Handbook of Party Politics*, ed. R. Katz and W. Crotty (London and Thousand Oaks, CA: Sage) pp. 446–55.

National Audit Office (2006) *The Role of the National Audit Office*, http://www.nao.org.uk/about/role.htm#meeting, accessed 12 November, 2006.

Neary, I. (2002) *The State and Politics in Japan* (Cambridge and Malden, MA: Polity).

Nef, J. (2003) 'Public Administration and Public Sector Reform in Latin America', in *Handbook of Public Administration*, ed. B. Guy Peters and J. Pierre (London and Thousand Oaks, CA: Sage) pp. 523–35.

Nelson, M. (ed.) (2005) *The Presidency and the Political System*, 8th edn (Washington, DC: CQ Press).

Neto, O. (2002) 'Presidential Cabinets, Electoral Cycles and Coalition Discipline in Brazil', in *Legislative Politics in Latin America*, ed. S. Morgenstern and B. Nacif (Cambridge and New York: Cambridge University Press) pp. 48–78.

Neustadt, R. (1991) *Presidential Power and the Modern Presidents* (New York: Free Press).

Nimni, E. (2006) *Multicultural Nationalism* (London and New York: Routledge).

Niskanen, W. (1971) *Bureaucracy and Representative Government* (Chicago: Aldine, Atherton).

Nordic Social-Statistical Committee (2004) *Social Protection in the Nordic Countries 2004*, http://www.nom-nos.dk/nososco.htm, accessed 1 January, 2007.

Norris, P. (1995) *Comparative Models of Political Recruitment* (Bordeaux: ECPR Workshop on Political Recruitment).

Norris, P. (1996) 'Legislative Recruitment', in *Elections and Voting in Global Perspective*, ed. R. Niemi and P. Norris (Thousand Oaks, CA and London: Sage) pp. 184–215.

Norris, P. (1999a) 'The Growth of Critical Citizens and Its Consequences', in *Critical Citizens: Global Support for Democratic Governance*, ed. P. Norris (Oxford and New York: Oxford University Press) pp. 257–72.

Norris, P. (ed.) (1999b) *Critical Citizens: Global Support for Democratic Governance* (Oxford and New York: Oxford University Press).

Norris, P. (2000) *A Virtuous Circle: Political Communication in Postindustrial Societies* (Cambridge and New York: Cambridge University Press).

Norris, P. (2002) *Democratic Phoenix: Reinventing Political Activism* (Cambridge and New York: Cambridge University Press).

Norris, P. (2004a) *Electoral Engineering: Voting Rules and Political Behaviour* (Cambridge and New York: Cambridge University Press).

Norris, P. (2004b) 'Will New Technology Boost Turnout?', in *Voter Turnout in Western Europe since 1945: A Regional Report* (Stockholm: IDEA) pp. 42–50.

Norris, P. (2006) 'Recruitment', in *Handbook of Party Politics*, ed. R. Katz and W. Crotty (London and Thousand Oaks, CA: Sage) pp. 89–108.

Norris, P., Kern, M. and Just, M. (eds) (2003) *Framing Terrorism: The News Media, the Government and the Public* (London and New York: Routledge).

Norris, P. and Inglehart, R. (2004) *Sacred and Secular: Religion and Politics Worldwide* (Cambridge and New York: Cambridge University Press).

North, D. (1981) *Structure and Change in Economic History* (New York: Norton).

Norton, A. (1991) 'Western European Local Government in Comparative Perspective', in *Local Government in Europe: Trends and Developments*, ed. R. Batley and G. Stoker (Basingstoke: Macmillan) pp. 21–40.

Norton, P. (ed.) (1990) *Legislatures* (Oxford and New York: Oxford University Press).

Norton, P. (1997) 'Parliamentary Oversight', in *Developments in British Politics 5*, ed. P. Dunleavy *et al.* (Basingstoke: Macmillan, and New York: St Martin's) pp. 155–76.

Norton, P. (ed.) (1998) *Parliaments and Governments in Western Europe* (London and Portland, OR: Frank Cass).

Norton, P. (2005) *Parliament in Britain* (Basingstoke: Palgrave Macmillan).

Nousiainen, J. (2001) 'From Semi-Presidentialism to Parliamentary Government: Political and Constitutional Developments in Finland', *Scandinavian Political Studies* (24) 95–109.

NRA (National Rifle Association) *A Brief History of the NRA*, http://www.nra.org/aboutus.apx, accessed 9 December, 2006.

Nuclear Age Peace Foundation (2006) *Principles of Nuremberg*, http://www.wagingpeace.org/menu/issues/international-law/start/un-nuremberg-principles.htm, accessed 7 August, 2006.

Nugent, N. (2006) *The Government and Politics of the European Union*, 6th edn (Basingstoke and New York: Palgrave Macmillan).

Nurmi, H. and Nurmi, L. (2002) 'The 2000 Presidential Election in Finland', *Electoral Studies* (21) 473–9.

O

O'Brien, D. (ed.) (2004) *Judges on Judging: Views from the Bench*, 2nd edn (Washington, DC: CQ Press).

O'Brien, D. (2005) *Storm Center: The Supreme Court in American Politics*, 7th edn (New York: Norton).

O'Brien, K. (1990) *Reform Without Liberalization: China's National People's Congress and the Politics of Institutional Change* (Cambridge and New York: Cambridge University Press).

O'Donnell, G. (1973) *Modernization and Bureaucratic Authoritarianism: Studies in South American Politics* (Berkeley, CA: California University Press), http://ark.cdlib.org/ark:/13030/ft4v19n9n2/, accessed 3 November, 2006.

O'Donnell, G. (1994) 'Delegative Democracy', *Journal of Democracy* (5) 55–69.

O'Donnell, G. (1996) 'Delegative Democracy', in *The Global Resurgence of Democracy,* 2nd edn, ed. L. Diamond and M. Plattner (Baltimore, MD and London: Johns Hopkins University Press) pp. 94–110.

O'Donnell, G. (2003) 'Horizontal Accountability: The Legal Institutionalization of Mistrust', in *Democratic Accountability in Latin America,* ed. S. Mainwaring and C. Welna (Oxford and New York: Oxford University Press) pp. 34–54.

O'Donnell, G., Schmitter, P. and Whitehead, L. (eds) (1986) *Transitions from Authoritarian Rule* (Baltimore, MD and London: Johns Hopkins University Press).

O'Flynn, I. (2006) *Deliberative Democracy and Divided Societies* (Edinburgh: Edinburgh University Press).

O'Sullivan, N. (1986) *Fascism* (London: Dent).

O'Toole, B. and Chapman, R. (1995) 'Parliamentary Accountability', in *Next Steps: Improving Management in Government,* ed. B. O'Toole and G. Jordan (Aldershot and Brookfield, VT: Dartmouth) pp. 118–41.

Oakes, L. (1997) *Prophetic Charisma: The Psychology of Revolutionary Religious Personalities* (Syracuse, NY: Syracuse University Press).

Oates, S. (2005) 'Media and Political Communication', in *Developments in Russian Politics 6*, ed. S. White, Z. Gitelman and R. Sakwa (Basingstoke and New York: Palgrave Macmillan) pp. 114–29.

Ocitti, T. (2006) *Press, Politics and Public Policy in Uganda: The Role of Journalism in Democratization* (Lewiston, NY: Edwin Mellen).

OECD (Organisation for Economic Co-operation and Development) (2005) *National Accounts of OECD Countries* (Paris: OECD).

OHCHR (Office of the the High Commissioner for Human Rights) (1951) *Convention on the Prevention and Punishment of the Crime of Genocide,* http://www.unhchr.ch/html/menu3/b/p_genoci.htm, accessed 4 June, 2006.

Ohmae, K. (1995) *The End of the Nation State: The Rise of Regional Economies* (New York: Free Press and London: HarperCollins).

Olesen, T. (2003) *International Zapatismo: The Construction of Solidarity in the Age of Globalization* (London: Zed Books).

Olsen, J. (1980) 'Governing Norway: Segmentation, Anticipation and Consensus Formation', in *Presidents and Prime Ministers,* ed. R. Rose and E. Suleiman (Washington, DC: American Enterprise Institute) pp. 203–55.

Olson, D. (1994) *Legislative Institutions: A Comparative View* (New York: M.E. Sharpe).

Olson, M. (1968) *The Logic of Collective Action: Public Goods and the Theory of Groups* (New York: Schocken Books).

Opello, W. and Rosow, S. (2004) *The Nation-State and Global Order: A Historical Introduction to Contemporary Politics*, 2nd edn (Boulder, CO and London: Lynne Rienner).

Osborne, D. and Gaebler, T. (1992) *Reinventing Government: How the Entrepreneurial Spirit Is Transforming the Public Sector* (New York and London: Penguin).

Osiander, A. (2001) 'Sovereignty, International Relations and the Westphalian Myth', *International Organization* (55) 251–89.

Ostrogorski, M. (1902) *Democracy and the Organisation of Political Parties* (London: Macmillan).

Ottaway, M. (2003) *Democracy Challenged: The Rise of Semi-Authoritarianism* (Washington, DC: Carnegie Endowment for International Peace).

Owen, J. (2002) 'The Foreign Imposition of Domestic Institutions', *International Organization* (50) 375–409.

Owen, R. (1993) 'The Practice of Electoral Democracy in the Arab East and North Africa: Some Lessons from Nearly a Century's Experience' in *Rules and Rights in the Middle East,* ed. E. Goldberg *et al.* (Seattle, WA: University of Washington Press) pp. 17–40.

Owen, R. (2002) *State, Power and Politics in the Middle East,* 2nd edn (London and New York: Routledge).

P

Padgett, S. (2003) 'Political Economy: The German Model under Stress', in *Developments in German Politics 3,* ed. S. Padgett, W. Paterson and G. Smith (Basingstoke and New York: Palgrave Macmillan) pp. 121–42.

Page, E. and Goldsmith, M. (1987) *Central and Local Government Relations* (London and Thousand Oaks, CA: Sage).

Page, E. and Wright, V. (eds) (1999) *Bureaucratic Elites in Western European States: A Comparative Analysis of Top Officials* (Oxford and New York: Oxford University Press).

Page, E. and Wright, V. (eds) (2006) *From the Active to the Enabling State: The Changing Role of Top Officials in European Nations* (Basingstoke: Palgrave Macmillan).

Paine, T. (1791/2) [1984 edn] *Rights of Man* (Harmondsworth: Penguin).

Palmer, M. (2003) *Breaking the Real Axis of Evil: How to Oust the World's Last Dictators by 2025* (Lanham, MD: Rowman & Littlefield).

Panebianco, A. (1988) *Political Parties: Organization and Power* (Cambridge and New York: Cambridge University Press).

Park, H. (1976) 'Changes in Chinese Communist Ideology', in *Comparative Communism: The Soviet, Chinese and Yugoslav Models,* ed. G. Bertsch and T. Ganschow (San Francisco: W. H. Freeman) pp. 144–50.

Parkinson, J. (2006) *Deliberating in the Real World: Problems of Legitimacy in Deliberative Democracy* (Oxford and New York: Oxford University Press).

Parry, G., Moyser, G. and Day, N. (1992) *Political Participation and Democracy in Britain* (Cambridge and New York: Cambridge University Press).

Parsons, T. (1967) 'On the Concept of Political Power', in *Sociological Theory and Modern Society,* ed. T. Parsons (New York and London: Free Press) pp. 286–99.

Parsons, W. (1995) *Public Policy: An Introduction to the Theory and Practice of Policy Analysis* (Brookfield, VT and Aldershot: Edward Elgar).

Patterson, S. and Mughan, A. (eds) (1999) *Senates: Bicameralism in the Contemporary World* (Columbus, OH: Ohio State University Press).

Paul, T. (ed.) (2004) *The Nation-State in Question* (Princeton, NJ: Princeton University Press).

Paxton, R. (2004) *The Anatomy of Fascism* (London and New York: Penguin).

Pearl, S. (2003) 'No Subject' (*Gmane Culture Studies Mailing List Archive*), http://article.gmane.org/gmane.culture.studies.literature.slavic/2220, accessed 5 April, 2006.

Pedahzur, A. (2005) *Suicide Terrorism* (Cambridge and Malden, MA: Polity Press).

Peele, G. *et al.* (eds) (2006) *Developments in American Politics 5* (Basingstoke and New York: Palgrave Macmillan).

Peerenboom, R. (2002) *China's Long March Toward Rule of Law* (Cambridge and New York: Cambridge University Press).

Pehe, J. (2004) 'Consolidating Free Government in the New European Union', *Journal of Democracy* (15) 36–47.

Pennings, P., Keman, H. and Kleinnijenhuis, J. (2005) *Doing Research in Political Science: An Introduction to Comparative Methods and Statistics,* 2nd edn (Thousand Oaks, CA and London: Sage).

Peregudov, S. (2001) 'The Oligarchical Model of Russian Capitalism', in *Contemporary Russian Politics: A Reader,* ed. A. Brown (Oxford and New York: Oxford University Press) pp. 259–68.

Peretti T. (2001) *In Defence of a Political Court* (Princeton, NJ: Princeton University Press).

Perlmutter, A. (1981) *Modern Authoritarianism* (New Haven, CT: Yale University Press).

Perlmutter, A. (1997) *Making the World Safe for Democracy: A Century of Wilsonianism and its Totalitarian Challenges* (Chapel Hill, NC: University of North Carolina Press).

Perraton, J. and Clift, B. (2004a) 'So Where Are National Capitalisms Now?', in *Where Are National Capitalisms Now?*, ed. J. Perraton and B. Clift (Basingstoke and New York: Palgrave Macmillan) pp. 195–261.

Perraton, J. and Clift, B. (eds) (2004b) *Where Are National Capitalisms Now?* (Basingstoke and New York: Palgrave Macmillan).

Peskin, D. and Nachison, A. (2006) 'Emerging Media Reshape Global Society', *eJournal USA* (11), http://usinfo.state.gov/journals/itgic/0306/ijge/ijge0306.htm, accessed 28 April, 2006.

Peters, B. Guy (1998) *Comparative Politics: Theory and Methods* (London: Macmillan and New York: New York University Press).

Peters, B. Guy (1999) *Institutional Theory in Political Science: The 'New Institutionalism'* (London and New York: Pinter).

Peters, B. Guy (2004) *American Public Policy: Promise and Performance*, 6th edn (Washington, DC: CQ Press).

Peters, B. Guy (2006) *The Politics of Bureaucracy,* 6th edn (London and New York: Routledge).

Peters, B. Guy and Pierre, J. (eds) (2003) *Handbook of Public Administration* (London and Thousand Oaks, CA: Sage).

Peters. B. Guy and Pierre, J. (eds) (2004) *The Politicization of the Civil Service in Comparative Perspective* (London and New York: Routledge).

Petersson, O. (1989) *Maktens Natverk* (Stockholm: Carlssons).

Petracca, M. (1992) 'The Rediscovery of Interest Group Politics', in *The Politics of Interests: Interest Groups Transformed,* ed. M. Petracca (Boulder, CO and Oxford: Westview) pp. 3–31.

Pew Global Attitudes Project (2006) *America's Image Slips* (Washington, D.C.: Pew Research Center), http://pewglobal.org/reports/display.php?ReportID=252, accessed 17 June, 2006.

Pharr, S. and Putnam, R. (eds) (2000) *Disaffected Democracies: What's Troubling The Trilateral Countries?* (Princeton, NJ: Princeton University Press).

Philip, G. (2003) *Democracy in Latin America* (Cambridge: Polity and Malden, MA: Blackwell).

Phillips, A. (1995) *The Politics of Presence* (Oxford and New York: Oxford University Press).

Pierre, J. and Peters, B. Guy (2000) *Governance, Politics and the State* (Basingstoke: Macmillan and New York: St Martin's Press).

Pierson, C. (1998) *Beyond the Welfare State? The New Political Economy of Welfare,* 2nd edn (University Park: Pennsylvania State University Press and Cambridge: Polity).

Pierson, C. (ed.) (2000) *The New Politics of the Welfare State* (Oxford and New York: Oxford University Press).

Pierson, P. (2004) *Politics in Time: History, Institutions and Social Analysis* (Princeton, NJ: Princeton University Press).

Plender, J. (2003) 'Wheezing Through the Fiscal Fog', *Financial Times,* 4 April, p. 17.

Poguntke, T. and Webb, P. (2005) 'The Presidentialization of Politics in Democratic Societies: A Framework for Analysis', in *The Presidentialization of Politics: A Comparative Study of Modern Democracies*, ed. T. Poguntke and P. Webb (Oxford and New York: Oxford University Press) pp. 1–25.

Poguntke, T. and Webb, P. (eds) (2005) *The Presidentialization of Politics: A Comparative Study of Modern Democracies* (Oxford and New York: Oxford University Press).

Polanyi, K. (1957) *The Great Transformation: The Political and Economic Origins of Our Time* (Boston, MA: Beacon Press).

Polidano, C. (1998) 'Why Bureaucrats Can't Always Do What Ministers Want: Multiple Accountabilities in Westminster Democracies', *Public Policy and Administration* (13) 35–50.

Political Studies Review (2006) 'Review Symposium of Steven Lukes, *Power: A Radical View*' (Basingstoke and New York: Palgrave Macmillan, 1974 [2005 edn]). (4) 115–75.

Pollitt, C. and Bouckaert, G. (2004) *Public Management Reform: A Comparative Analysis,* 2nd edn (Oxford and New York: Oxford University Press).

Polsby, N. (1975) 'Legislatures', in *The Handbook of Political Science*, vol. V, ed. F. Greenstein and N. Polsby (Reading, MA: Addison-Wesley) pp. 275–319.

Posusney, M. (2005) 'The Middle East's Democracy Deficit in Comparative Perspective', in *Authoritarianism in the Middle East: Regimes and Resistance*, ed. M. Posusney and M. Angrist (Boulder, CO and London: Lynne Rienner) pp. 1–20.

Posusney, M. and Angrsit, M. (eds) (2005) *Authoritarianism in the Middle East: Regimes and Resistance* (Boulder, CO and London: Lynne Rienner).

President of the United States (2002) *National Security Strategy of the United States of America* (Washington, DC), http://www.whitehouse.gov/nsc/nss.html, accessed 5 January, 2006.

President of Russia (2006) *President of Russia*, http://www.kremlin.ru/eng/, accessed 11 November, 2006.

Press Reference (2006) *Spain*, http://www.pressreference.com/Sa-Sw/Spain.html, accessed 12 December, 2006.

Pressman, J. and Wildavsky, A. (1973) *Implementation: How Great Expectations in Washington Are Dashed in Oakland; Or, Why It's Amazing that Federal Programs Work at All* (Berkeley, CA: University of California Press).

Preston, P. (2004) *Juan Carlos: Steering Spain from Dictatorship to Democracy* (New York and London: Norton).

Pridham, G. (ed.) (1995) *Transitions to Democracy* (Brookfield, VT and Aldershot: Dartmouth).

Prillaman, W. (2000) *The Judiciary and Democratic Decay in Latin America: Declining Confidence in the Rule of Law* (Westport, CT: Praeger).

Prosser, T. and Moran, M. (1994) 'Privatization and Regulatory Change: The Case of Great Britain', in *Privatization and Regulatory Change in Europe,* ed. M. Moran and T. Prosser (Buckingham and Bristol, PA: Open University Press) pp. 35–49.

Pryor, K. (2003) *A National State of Confusion* (New York: Salon.com), http://dir.salon.com/story/opinion/feature/2003/02/06/iraq_poll/index.html, accessed 2 May, 2006.

Przeworski, A. (1991) *Democracy and the Market: Political and Economic Reforms in Eastern Europe and Latin America* (Cambridge and New York: Cambridge University Press).

Przeworski, A. (1995) 'The Role of Theory in Comparative Politics', *World Politics* (48) 16–21.

Przeworski, A. and Teune, H. (1970) *The Logic of Comparative Inquiry* (New York: Wiley).

Przeworski, A. *et al.* (2000) *Democracy and Development: Political Institutions and Well-Being in the World, 1950–1990* (Cambridge and New York: Cambridge University Press).

Psephos (2005) *Kingdom of Denmark: Legislative Elections of 8 February* (Melbourne: Adam Carr's Election Archive), http://psephos.adam-carr.net/countries/d/denmark/denmark2005.txt, accessed 17 July, 2006.

Psephos (2006) *United Mexican States: 2006 Legislative Elections,* http://psephos.adam-carr.net, accessed 12 December, 2006.

Putnam, R. (1976) *The Comparative Study of Political Elites* (Englewood Cliffs, NJ: Prentice Hall).

Putnam, R. (1993) *Making Democracy Work: Civic Traditions in Modern Italy* (Princeton, NJ: Princeton University Press).

Putnam, R. (1995) 'Bowling Alone: America's Declining Social Capital', *Journal of Democracy* (6) 65–78.

Putnam, R. (2000) *Bowling Alone: The Collapse and Revival of American Community* (New York: Simon & Schuster).

Putnam, R. (2001) 'Civic Engagement in Contemporary America', *Government and Opposition* (30) 135–56.

Putnam, R. (ed.) (2002) *Democracies in Flux: The Evolution of Social Capital in Contemporary Society* (Oxford and New York: Oxford University Press).

Putnam, R. and Goss, K. (2002) 'Introduction', in *Democracies in Flux: The Evolution of Social Capital in Contemporary Society,* ed. R. Putnam (New York and Oxford University Press) pp. 3–20.

Putnam, R., Pharr, S. and Dalton, R. (2000) 'What's Troubling the Trilateral Countries?', in *Disaffected Democracies: What's Troubling the Trilateral Countries?,* ed. S. Pharr and R. Putnam (Princeton, NJ: Princeton University Press) pp. 3–30.

Pye, L. (1985) *Asian Power and Politics: The Cultural Dimensions of Authority* (Cambridge, MA: Harvard University Press).

Pye, L. (1995) 'Political Culture', in *The Encyclopaedia of Democracy,* ed. S. Lipset (London and New York: Routledge) pp. 965–9.

Q

Qualter, T. (1991) 'Public Opinion', in *The Blackwell Encyclopaedia of Political Science,* ed. V. Bogdanor (Oxford and Cambridge, MA: Blackwell) p. 511.

Qvortrup, M. (2005) *A Comparative Study of Referendums: Government by the People,* 2nd edn (Manchester: Manchester University Press).

R

Raadschelders, J. and Rutgers, M. (1996) 'The Evolution of Civil Service Systems', in *Civil Service Systems in Comparative Perspective,* ed. H. Bekke, J. Perry and T. Toonen (Bloomington, IN: Indiana University Press) pp. 67–99.

Rahman, F. (1982) *Islam and Modernity: Transformation of an Intellectual Tradition* (Chicago, IL: University of Chicago Press).

Ragin, C. (1987) *The Comparative Method: Moving Beyond Qualitative and Quantitative Strategies* (Berkeley, CA and London: University of California Press).

Ragin, C. (1994) 'Introduction to Qualitative Comparative Analysis', in *The Comparative Political Economy of the Welfare State,* ed. T. Janoski and A. Hicks (New York and Cambridge: Cambridge University Press) pp. 299–319.

Ragin, C., Berg-Schlosser, D. and de Meur, G. (1996) 'Political Methodology: Qualitative Methods', in *A New Handbook of Political Science,* ed. R. Goodin and H. Klingemann (Oxford and New York: Oxford University Press) pp. 749–68.

Rainer, H. and Siedler, T. (2006) 'Does Democracy Foster Trust?' *ISER Working Paper 2006–31* (Colchester: University of Essex).

Ramseyer, J. and Rasmusen, E. (2001) 'Why Are Japanese Judges so Conservative in Politically Charged Cases?', *American Political Science Review* (95) 331–44.

Rasch, B. (2004) 'Parliamentary Government', in *Nordic Politics: Comparative Perspectives,* ed. K. Heidar (Oslo: Universitetsforlaget) pp. 127–41.

Ravenhill, J. (ed.) (2005) *Global Political Economy* (Oxford and New York: Oxford University Press).

Regini, M. (2003) 'Tripartite Concertation and Varieties of Capitalism,' *European Journal of Industrial Relations* (9) 251–63.

Remington, T. (2004) 'Politics in Russia', in *Comparative Politics Today: A World View,* 8th edn, ed. G. Almond *et al.* (New York and London: Pearson Longman) pp. 366–417.

Remington, T. (2006) 'Parliamentary Politics in Russia', in *Developments in Russian Politics 6,* ed. S. White, Z. Gitelman and R. Sakwa (Basingstoke and New York: Palgrave Macmillan) pp. 40–60.

Reno, W. (2003) 'The Politics of Insurgency in Collapsing States', in *State Failure, Collapse and Reconstruction,* ed. J. Milliken (Malden, MA and Oxford: Blackwell) pp. 83–104.

Reynolds, A., Reilly, B. and Ellis, A. (2005) *Electoral System Design: The International IDEA Handbook* (Stockholm: International Institute for Democracy and Electoral Assistance), http://www.idea.int/publications/, accessed 11 June, 2006.

Rhodes, R. (1994) 'State-building Without a Bureaucracy: The Case of the United Kingdom', in *Developing Democracy: Essays in Honour of J. F. P. Blondel,* ed. I. Budge and D. McKay (Thousand Oaks, CA and London: Sage) pp. 165–88.

Rhodes, R. (1995) 'The Institutional Approach', in *Theory and Methods in Political Science*, ed. D. Marsh and G. Stoker (Basingstoke: Macmillan) pp. 42–57.

Rhodes, R. (1996) 'The New Governance: Governing without Government', *Political Studies* (44) 652–67.

Rhodes, R. (2006a) 'Policy Network Analysis', in *The Oxford Handbook of Public Policy*, ed. M. Moran, M. Rein and R. Goodin (Oxford and New York: Oxford University Press) pp. 424–47.

Rhodes, R. (2006b) 'Executives in Parliamentary Government', in *The Oxford Handbook of Political Institutions*, ed. R. Rhodes, S. Binder and B. Rockman (Oxford and New York: Oxford University Press) pp. 323–43.

Rhodes, R., Binder, S. and Rockman, B. (eds) (2006) *The Oxford Handbook of Political Institutions* (Oxford and New York: Oxford University Press).

Rich, R. (2001) 'Bringing Democracy into International Law', *Journal of Democracy* (12) 20–34.

Riches, W. (2004) *The Civil Rights Movement: Struggle and Resistance*, 2nd edn (Basingstoke: Palgrave Macmillan).

Ridley, F. (1975) *The Study of Government: Political Science and Administration* (London: Allen & Unwin).

Riesman, D. (1950) *The Lonely Crowd* (New Haven, CT: Yale University Press).

Riker, W. (1975) 'Federalism', in *The Handbook of Political Science*, Vol. 5, ed. F. Greenstein and N. Polsby (Reading, MA: Addison-Wesley) pp. 93–172.

Riker, W. (1996) 'European Federalism: The Lessons of Past Experience', in *Federalizing Europe? The Costs, Benefits and Preconditions of Federal Political Systems*, ed. J. Hesse and V. Wright (Oxford and New York: Oxford University Press) pp. 9–24.

Ripley, R. and Franklin, G. (1991) *Congress, the Bureaucracy and Public Policy*, 5th edn (Homewood, IL: The Dorsey Press).

Robertson, R. (1992) *Globalization: Social Theory and Global Culture* (London: Sage).

Rockman, B. (2000) 'Administering the Summit in the United States' in *Administering the Summit*, ed. B. Guy Peters, R. Rhodes and V. Wright (London: Macmillan) pp. 245–62.

Rohe, K. (1993) 'The State Tradition in Germany: Continuities and Change', in *Political Culture in Germany*, ed. D. Berg-Schlosser and R. Rytlewski (New York: St. Martin's Press) pp. 215–31.

Rokkan, S. (1970) *Citizens, Elections, Parties* (New York: McKay).

Romero, A. (1997) 'Rearranging the Deck Chairs on the Titanic: The Agony of Democracy in Venezuela', *Latin America Research Review* (32) 7–36.

Rose, L. (2004) 'Local Government and Politics', in *Nordic Politics: Comparative Perspectives*, ed. K. Heidar (Oslo: Universitetforlaget) pp. 164–82.

Rose, R. (1989) *Politics in England: Change and Persistence* (Basingstoke: Macmillan).

Rose, R. (1991) 'Comparing Forms of Comparative Analysis', *Political Studies* (39) 446–62.

Rose, R. (1999) 'Living in an Antimodern Society', *East European Constitutional Review* (8) 68–75.

Rose, R. (2000) *The Post-Modern President*, 2nd edn (Chatham, NJ: Chatham House).

Rose, R. (2004) *Learning Lessons in Comparative Public Policy* (London and New York: Routledge).

Rose, R. and Shin, D. (2001) 'Democratization Backwards: The Problem of Third-Wave Democracies', in *British Journal of Political Science* (31) 331–54.

Rosenau, J. (1992) 'Governance, Order and Change in World Politics', in *Governance without Government: Order and Change in World Politics*, ed. J. Rosenau and E. O. Czempiel (Cambridge and New York: Cambridge University Press) pp. 3–6.

Rosenbluth, F. and Thies, M. (2004) 'Politics in Japan' in *Comparative Politics Today: A World View*, 8th edn, ed. G. Almond *et al.* (New York: Pearson Longman) pp. 318–65.

Rosenfeld, G. (2005) *The World Hitler Never Made: Alternate History and the Memory of Nazism* (Cambridge and New York: Cambridge University Press).

Ross, M. (2001) 'Does Oil Hinder Democracy?' *World Politics* (53) 356–7.

Rossi, P., Freeman, H. and Lipsey, M. (1999) *Evaluation: A Systemic Approach*, 6th edn (Thousand Oaks, CA and London: Sage Publications).

Rotberg, R. (ed.) (2004) *When States Fail: Causes and Consequences* (Princeton, NJ: Princeton University Press).

Rothchild, D. (1997) *Managing Ethnic Conflict in Africa: Pressures and Incentives for Cooperation* (Washington, DC: Brookings Institution Press).

Rothstein, B. (2002) 'Sweden: Social Capital in the Social Democratic State', in *Democracies in Flux: The Evolution of Social Capital in Contemporary Society*, ed. R. Putnam (Oxford and New York: Oxford University Press) pp. 289–332.

Rousseau, D. (1994) 'The Constitutional Judge: Master or Slave of the Constitution?' in *Constitutionalism, Identity, Difference and Legitimacy: Theoretical Perspectives*, ed. M. Rosenfeld (Durham, NC and London: Duke University Press) pp. 261–83.

Rousseau, J.-J. (1762) [1913 edn] *The Social Contract* (London: Dent and New York: Dutton).

Roy, O. (1994) *The Failure of Political Islam* (London: I. B. Taurus).

Rubio, L. and Purcell, S. (eds) (2004) *Mexico under Fox* (Boulder, CO and London: Lynne Rienner).

Rueschmeyer, D., Rueschmeyer, M. and Wittrock, B. (1998) 'Contrasting Patterns of Participation and Democracy', in *Participation and Democracy: Comparisons and Interpretations*, ed. D. Rueschmeyer, M. Rueschmeyer and B. Wittrock (Armonk, NY and London: M. E. Sharpe) pp. 266–84.

Rueschmeyer, D., Rueschmeyer, M. and Wittrock, B. (eds) (1998) *Participation and Democracy: Comparisons and Interpretations* (Armonk, New York and London: M.E. Sharpe).

Rush, M. (2005) *Parliament Today* (Manchester: Manchester University Press).

Russell, B. (1938) *Power: A New Social Analysis* (London: Allen & Unwin).

Russell, M. (2000a) *Reforming the House of Lords: Lessons from Overseas* (Oxford and New York: Oxford University Press).

Russell, M. (2000b) 'A "More Democratic and Representative" Upper House? Some International Comparisons', *Representation* (37) 131–8.

Russell, M. (2001) 'What Are Second Chambers For?', *Parliamentary Affairs* (54) 442–58.

Rutland, P. (2005) 'Putin's Economic Record', in *Developments in Russian Politics 6*, ed. S. White, Z. Gitelman and R. Sakwa (Basingstoke and New York: Palgrave Macmillan) pp. 186–203.

S

Sabatier, P. (1999) *Theories of the Policy Process* (Boulder, CO: Westview).

Sabatier, P. and Jenkins-Smith, H. (1993) *Policy Change and Learning: An Advocacy Coalition Approach* (Boulder, CO: Westview).

Sachs, J. and Warner, A. (1995a) 'Economic Reform and the Process of Global Integration', *Brookings Papers on Economic Activity*, 1–118.

Sachs, J. and Warner, A. (1995b) 'Natural Resource Abundance and Economic Growth', *Working Paper 5398* (Cambridge, MA: National Bureau of Economic Research).

Sadurski, W. (2005) *Rights before Courts: A Study of Constitutional Courts in Postcommunist States of Central and Eastern Europe* (Dordrecht: Springer).

Safire, W. (1993) *Safire's New Political Dictionary* (New York: Random House).

Saich, A. (2004) *Governance and Politics of China,* 2nd edn (Basingstoke and New York: Palgrave).

Saikal, A. (2003) *Islam and the West: Conflict or Cooperation?* (Basingstoke and New York: Palgrave Macmillan).

Sait, E. (1938) *Political Institutions: A Preface* (New York: Appleton-Century).

Sakwa, R. (2002) *Russian Politics and Society*, 3rd edn (London and New York: Routledge).

Salamon, L. (2002) 'The New Governance and the Tools of Public Action: An Introduction', in *The Tools of Government: A Guide to the New Governance*, ed. L. Salamon (New York: Oxford University Press) pp. 1–47.

Salamon, L. (ed.) (2002) *The Tools of Government: A Guide to the New Governance* (New York: Oxford University Press).

Salmond, R. (2006) 'Proportional Representation and Female Parliamentarians', *Legislative Studies Quarterly* (31) 175–204.

Sandbrook R. (1985) *The Politics of Africa's Economic Stagnation* (Cambridge and New York: Cambridge University Press).

Sanderson, I. (2002) 'Evaluation, Policy Learning and Evidence-Based Policy Making', *Public Administration* (80) 1–22.

Sanderson, J. (1961) 'The National Smoke Abatement Society and the Clean Air Act (1956)', *Political Studies* (9) 236–53.

Santa-Cruz, A. (2005) *International Election Monitoring, Sovereignty and the Western Hemisphere: The Emergence of an International Norm* (London and New York: Routledge).

Sartori, G. (1976) *Parties and Party Systems: A Framework for Analysis* (Cambridge and New York: Cambridge University Press).

Sartori, G. (1987) *The Theory of Democracy Revisited,* Part II (Chatham, NJ: Chatham House).

Sartori, G. (1991) 'Comparing and Miscomparing', *Journal of Theoretical Politics* (3) 243–58.

Sartori, G. (1994) *Comparative Constitutional Engineering: An Inquiry into Structures, Incentives and Outcomes* (Basingstoke: Macmillan).

Scarrow, S. (2002a) 'Party Decline in the Parties State? The Changing Environment of German Politics', in *Political Parties in Advanced Industrial Democracies,* ed. P. Webb, D. Farrell and I. Holliday (Oxford and New York: Oxford University Press) pp. 77–106.

Scarrow. S. (2002b) 'Germany: The Mixed-Member System as a Political Compromise', in *Mixed-Member Electoral Systems: The Best of Both Worlds,* ed. M. Shugart and M. Wattenberg (Oxford and New York: Oxford University Press) pp. 5–69.

Scarrow, S. (ed.) (2002c) *Perspectives on Political Parties: Classic Readings* (Basingstoke and New York: Palgrave Macmillan).

Schain, M. (2004) 'Politics in France', in *Comparative Politics Today: A World View,* 8th edn, ed. G. Almond *et al.* (New York and London: Pearson Longman) pp. 206–59.

Scharpf, F. (1988) 'The Joint Decision Trap: Lessons From German Federalism and European Integration', *Public Administration* (66) 239–78.

Schattschneider, E. (1942) *Party Government* (New York: Farrar & Reinhart).

Schedler, A. (2005) 'From Electoral Authoritarianism to Democratic Consolidation', in *Mexico's Democracy at Work: Political and Electoral Dynamics,* ed. R. Crandall, G. Paz, and R. Roett (Boulder, CO and London: Lynne Rienner) pp. 9–38.

Schedler, A. (ed.) (2006) *Electoral Authoritarianism: The Dynamics of Unfree Competition* (Boulder, CO and London: Lynne Rienner).

Scheiner, E. (2006) *Democracy without Competition in Japan: Opposition Failure in a One-Party Dominant State* (Cambridge and New York: Cambridge University Press).

Schlesinger, Jr, A., (1998) *The Disuniting of America*, revised edn (New York: Norton).

Schmidt, V. (2002) *The Futures of European Capitalism* (New York and Oxford: Oxford University Press).

Schmieding, H. (1993) *Europe after Maastricht* (London: Institute of Economic Affairs).

Schmitter, P. (2004) 'The Ambiguous Virtues of Accountability', *Journal of Democracy* (15) 47–60.

Scholte, J. (2005) *Globalization: A Critical Introduction*, 2nd edn (Basingstoke and New York: Palgrave Macmillan).

Schumpeter, J. (1943) *Capitalism, Socialism and Democracy* (London: Allen & Unwin).

Scott, S. (1997) 'Australia and International Institutions', in *New Developments in Australian Politics,* ed. B. Galligan, I. McAllister and J. Ravenhill (South Melbourne: Macmillan) pp. 271–90.

Segal, J. and Spaeth, H. (2002) *The Supreme Court and the Attitudinal Model Revisited* (New York and Cambridge: Cambridge University Press).

Seligson, M. (2005) 'Democracy on Ice: The Multiple Challenges of Guatemala's Peace Process', in *The Third Wave of Democratization in Latin America: Advances and Setbacks,* ed. F. Hagopian and S. Mainwaring (New York and Cambridge: Cambridge University Press) pp. 202–34.

Senelle, R. (1996) 'The Reform of the Belgian State', in *Federalizing Europe? The Costs, Benefits and Preconditions of Federal Political Systems,* ed. J. Hesse and V. Wright (Oxford and New York: Oxford University Press) pp. 266–324.

Seyd, P. and Whiteley, P. (2002) *New Labour's Grassroots: The Transformation of the Labour Party Membership* (Basingstoke: Palgrave Macmillan).

Seznec, J. F. (2003) 'Stirrings in Saudi Arabia', in *Islam and Democracy in the Middle East*, ed. L. Diamond, M. Plattner and D. Brumberg (Baltimore, MD and London: Johns Hopkins University Press) pp. 76–83.

Shafritz, J., Hyde, A. and Parkes, S. (eds) (2003) *Classics in Public Administration*, 5th edn (Belmont, CA: Thomson Wadsworth).

Shapiro, M. (1964) [2002 edn] 'Political Jurisprudence', in *On Law, Politics and Judicialization,* ed. M. Shapiro and A. Stone Sweet (Oxford and New York: Oxford University Press) pp. 19–54.

Shapiro, M. (1987) 'Review of Rasmussen's "On Law and Policy in the European Court of Justice: A Comparative Study in Judicial Policy-making"', *American Journal of International Law* (81) 1007–11.

Shapiro, I. (2006) 'On the Second Edition of Lukes' Third Face', *Political Studies Review* (4) 146–55.

Shapiro, M. and Stone Sweet, A. (2002) *On Law, Politics and Judicialization* (Oxford and New York: Oxford University Press).

Sharlet, R. (1997) 'The Progress of Human Rights', in *Developments in Russian Politics 4,* ed. S. White, A. Pravda and Z. Gitelman (Basingstoke: Macmillan) pp. 129–48.

Sharlet, R. (2005) 'In Search of the Rule of Law', in *Developments in Russian Politics 6,* ed. S. White, Z. Gitelman and R. Sakwa (Basingstoke and New York: Palgrave Macmillan) pp. 130–47.

Shepherd, R. (2006) 'The Denim Revolt That Can Rid Europe of Tyranny', *Financial Times,* 17 March, p. 19.

Shirk, D. (2005) *Mexico's New Politics: The PAN and Democratic Change* (Boulder, CO and London: Lynne Rienner).

Shively, W. (2002) *Power and Choice: An Introduction to Political Science,* 8th edn (New York and London: McGraw-Hill).

Shively, W. (2006) *Power and Choice: An Introduction to Political Science,* 10th edn (New York and London: McGraw-Hill).

Shonfield, A. (1969) *Modern Capitalism* (Oxford and New York: Oxford University Press).

Shugart, M. and Carey, J. (1992) *Presidents and Assemblies: Constitutional Design and Electoral Dynamics* (Cambridge and New York: Cambridge University Press).

Shugart, M. and Wattenberg, M. (eds) (2000) *Mixed-Member Electoral Systems: The Best of Both Worlds* (Oxford and New York: Oxford University Press).

Sica, A. (ed.) (2006) *Comparative Methods in the Social Sciences,* four vols (London and Thousand Oaks, CA: Sage).

Silva, P. (ed.) (2001) *The Soldier and the State in South America* (London: Palgrave).

Simeon, R. (2002) 'Federalism and Intergovernmental Relations', in *The Handbook of Canadian Public Administration,* ed. C. Dunn (Don Mills, Ontario: Oxford University Press) pp. 204–24.

Simeon, R. and Cameron, D. (2002) 'Intergovernmental Relations and Democracy: An Oxymoron if ever there Was One', in *Canadian Federalism: Performance, Effectiveness and Legitimacy,* ed. H. Bakvis and G. Skogstad (Don Mills, Ontario and Oxford: Oxford University Press) pp. 278–95.

Simon, H. (1983) *Reason in Human Affairs* (Oxford and Cambridge, MA: Blackwell).

Sjolin, M. (1993) *Coalition Politics and Parliamentary Power* (Lund: Lund University Press).

Skinner, Q. (1978) *The Foundations of Modern Political Thought,* Vol. 1 (Cambridge and New York: Cambridge University Press).

Sklair, J. (1987) 'Political Theory and the Rule of Law', in *The Rule of Law: Ideal or Ideology?,* ed. A. Hutchinson and P. Monahan (Toronto: Carswell Legal Publications) pp. 1–23.

Skocpol, T. (1979) *States and Social Revolutions: A Comparative Analysis of France, Russia and China* (Cambridge and New York: Cambridge University Press).

Slaughter, A.-M. (1997) 'The Real New World Order', *Foreign Affairs* (76) 183–94.

Slaughter, A.-M. (2003) 'Governing the Global Economy through Government Networks', in *The Global Transformations Reader,* 2nd edn, ed. D. Held and A. McGrew (Cambridge and Malden, MA: Polity) pp. 189–203.

Slaughter, A.-M. (2004) *A New World Order* (Princeton, NJ: Princeton University Press).

Smith, A. (1776) [1993 edn] *An Inquiry into the Nature and Causes of the Wealth of Nations,* ed. K. Sutherland (Oxford and New York: Oxford University Press).

Smith, A. (1998) *Nationalism and Modernism: A Critical Survey of Recent Theories of Nations and Nationalism* (London and New York: Routledge).

Smith, A. (1999) *Myths and Memories of the Nation* (Oxford and New York: Oxford University Press).

Smith, B. (1996) *Understanding Third World Politics* (London: Macmillan).

Smith, M. (1995) *Pressure Politics* (Manchester: Baseline Books).

Smooha, S. (2002) 'The Model of Ethnic Democracy', *Nations and Nationalism* (8) 475–503.

Solomon, P. and Foglesong, T. (2000) *Courts and Transition in Russia: The Challenge of Judicial Reform* (Boulder, CO and Oxford: Westview).

Somit, A. (1994) '... And Where We Came Out', in *The Victorious Incumbent: A Threat to Democracy?,* ed. A. Somit *et al.* (Aldershot and Brookfield, VT: Dartmouth) pp. 11–18.

Sørensen, G. (1997) 'An Analysis of Contemporary Statehood: Consequences for Conflict and Cooperation', *Review of International Studies* (23) 253–70.

Sørensen, G. (2004) *The Transformation of the State: Beyond the Myth of Retreat* (Basingstoke and New York: Palgrave Macmillan).

Sotiropolilos, D. (2004) 'Southern European Public Bureaucracies in Comparative Perspective', *West European Politics* (27) 405–22.

South African Government Information (2006) *Preamble,* http://www.info.gov.za/documents/constitution/1996/96preamble.htm, accessed 11 December, 2006.

Spruyt, H. (2005) *Ending Empire: Contested Sovereignty and Territorial Partition* (Cornell, NY: Cornell University Press).

Statistics Canada (2001) *2001 Census of Canada,* http://www12.statcan.ca/english/census01/home/index.cfm, accessed 15 December, 2006.

Steen, A. (1995) *Change of Regime and Political Recruitment: The Parliamentary Elites in the Baltic States* (Bordeaux: ECPR Workshop on Political Recruitment).

Steen, A. (2004) 'The Welfare State: Still Viable?', in *Nordic Politics: Comparative Perspectives,* ed. K. Heidar (Oslo: Universitetsforlaget) pp. 207–27.

Steinmo, S. (2003) 'The Evolution of Policy Ideas: Tax Policy in the Twentieth Century', *British Journal of Politics and International Relations* (5) 206–36.

Stepan, A. (2001) *Arguing Comparative Politics* (Oxford and New York: Oxford University Press).

Stepan, A. and Skatch, C. (1993) 'Constitutional Frameworks and Democratic Consolidation: Parliamentarism versus Presidentialism', *World Politics* (46) 1–22.

Stern, N. (2007) *The Economics of Climate Change: The Stern Review* (Cambridge and New York: Cambridge University Press).

Stern Review (2006) *The Economics of Climate Change*, http://www.hm-treasury.gov.uk/media/999/76/CLOSED_SHORT_executive_summary.pdf, accessed 12 December, 2006.

Stevens, A. (2003) *Government and Politics of France*, 3rd edn (Basingstoke and New York: Palgrave Macmillan).

Stimson, J. (1991) *Public Opinion in America: Moods, Cycles and Swings* (Boulder, CO and Oxford: Westview Press).

Stimson, J. (2004) *Tides of Consent: How Public Opinion Shapes American Politics* (Oxford and New York: Oxford University Press).

Stone, D. (2001) *Policy Paradox: The Art of Political Decision Making*, rev. edn (New York: Norton).

Stone Sweet, A. (2000) *Governing with Judges: Constitutional Politics in Europe* (Oxford and New York: Oxford University Press).

Stone Sweet, A. (2002) 'Constitutional Courts and Parliamentary Democracy', *West European Politics* (25) 77–110.

Stonecash, J. (2005) *Political Parties Matter: Realignment and the Return of Partisan Voting* (Boulder, CO: Lynne Rienner).

Stouffer, S. (1966) *Communism, Conformity and Civil Liberties* (New York: Wiley).

Strange, S. (1994) *States and Markets* (London and New York: Pinter).

Strange, S. (1997) 'The Future of Global Capitalism; Or, Will Divergence Persist Forever?', in *Political Economy of Modern Capitalism: Mapping Convergence and Diversity*, ed. C. Crouch and W. Streeck (London and Thousand Oaks, CA: Sage) pp. 182–91.

Street, J. (2001) *Mass Media, Politics and Democracy* (Basingstoke and New York: Palgrave).

Sundberg, J. (2002) 'The Scandinavian Party Model at the Crossroads', in *Political Parties in Advanced Industrial Democracies*, ed. P. Webb, D. Farrell and I. Holliday (Oxford and New York: Oxford University Press) pp. 181–216.

Sunstein, C. *et al.* (2006) *Are Judges Political? An Empirical Analysis of the Federal Judiciary* (Washington, DC: Brookings).

Sweating, D. (2003) 'How Strong Is the Mayor of London?', *Policy and Politics* (31) 465–78.

T

Taagepera, R. and Recchia, S. (2002) 'The Size of Second Chambers and European Assemblies', *European Journal of Political Research* (41) 165–85.

Tálos, E. and Kittel B. (2002) 'Austria in the 1990s: The Routine of Social Partnership in Question?', in *Policy Concertation and Social Partnership: Lessons for the 21st Century*, ed. S. Berger and H. Compston (New York and Oxford: Berghahn) pp. 35–50.

Taras, R. (2003) 'Executive Leadership: Presidents and Governments', in *Developments in Central and East European Politics 3*, ed. S. White, J. Batt and P. Lewis (Basingstoke: Palgrave Macmillan) pp. 115–31.

Tardi, G. (2002) 'Departments and Other Institutions of Government', in *Canadian Public Administration*, ed. C. Dunn (Don Mills, Ontario: Oxford University Press) pp. 281–304.

Tarrow, S. (1998) *Power in Movement: Social Movements and Contentious Politics*, 2nd edn (Cambridge and New York: Cambridge University Press).

Tarrow, S. and McAdam, D. (2005) 'Scale Shifts in Transnational Contention', in *Transnational Protest and Global Activism*, ed. D. della Porta and S. Tarrow (Lanham, MD: Rowman & Littlefield) pp. 121–50.

Taylor, C. and Hudson, M. (1972) *World Handbook of Political and Social Indicators* (New Haven, CT: Yale University Press).

Tetlock, P. and Belkin, A. (1996) *Counterfactual Thought Experiments in World Politics* (Princeton, NJ and London: Princeton University Press).

Teune, H. (1995a) 'Preface', *Annals of the American Academy of Political and Social Sciences* (540) 8–10.

Teune, H. (1995b) 'Local Government and Democratic Political Development', *Annals of the American Academy of Political and Social Sciences* (540) 11–23.

Thomas, C. (ed.) (2001) *Political Parties and Interest Groups: Shaping Democratic Governance* (Boulder, CO and London: Lynne Rienner).

Thorlakson, L. (2003) 'Comparing Federal Institutions: Power and Representation in Six Federations', *West European Politics* (26) 1–22.

Tilly, C. (1975) 'Reflections on the History of European State-Making', in *The Formation of National States in Western Europe*, ed. C. Tilly (Princeton, NJ: Princeton University Press) pp. 3–83.

Tilly, C. (1978) *From Mobilization to Revolution* (Reading, MA: Addison-Wesley).

Tilly, C. (1997) 'Means and Ends of Comparison in Macrosociology', *Comparative Social Research* (16) 43–53.

Tilly, C. (2004) *Social Movements, 1768–2004* (Boulder, CO: Paradigm Publishers).

Tivey, L. (ed.) (1981) *The Nation-State: The Formation of Modern Politics* (London: Martin Robertson).

Tracey, M. (1998) *The Decline and Fall of Public Service Broadcasting* (New York and Oxford: Oxford University Press).

Transparency International (2005) *Global Corruption Report*, http://www.transparency.org/policy_and_research/surveys_indices/cpi/2005, accessed 28 February, 2006.

Tremewan, C. (1994) *The Political Economy of Social Control in Singapore* (Basingstoke: Macmillan).

Tripp, A. (2000) *Women and Politics in Uganda* (London: James Currey).

Trotsky, L. (1932/3) [1965 edn] *The History of the Russian Revolution*, Vol. 1, trans. M. Eastman (London: Gollancz).

Tschentscher, A. (2004) *China Constitution* (International Constitutional Law Project), http://www.oefre.unibe.ch/law/icl/ch00000_.html, accessed 16 August, 2006.

Tsebelis, G. and Garrett, G. (1997) 'Agenda Setting, Vetoes and the European Union's Co-Decision Procedure', *Journal of Legislative Studies* (3) 74–92.

Tsebelis, G. and Money, J. (1997) *Bicameralism* (Cambridge and New York: Cambridge University Press).

Turner, M. and Hulme, D. (1997) *Governance, Administration and Development* (London: Macmillan).

Twigg, J. (2005) 'Social Policy in Post-Soviet Russia', in *Developments in Russian Politics 6*, ed. S. White, Z. Gitelman and R. Sakwa (Basingstoke and New York: Palgrave Macmillan) pp. 204–20.

U

Uhr, J. (2006) 'Bicameralism', in *The Oxford Handbook of Political Institutions*, ed. R. Rhodes, S. Binder and B. Rockman (Oxford and New York: Oxford University Press) pp. 474–94.

Umbach, M. (ed.) (2002) *German Federalism: Past, Present, Future* (Basingstoke: Macmillan).

UNESCO (United Nations Educational, Scientific and Cultural Organization) (2002) *Universal Declaration on Cultural Diversity*, http://www.unesco.org/education/imld_2002/unversal_decla.shtml#2, accessed 14 April, 2006.

UNHCR (United Nations High Commission for Human Rights) (1966) *United Nations Covenant on Civil and Political Rights*, http://www.unhcr.ch, accessed 9 February, 2006.

United Nations (2005) *Growth in United Nations Membership, 1945–2005*, http://www.un.org/Overview/growth.htm, accessed 1 November, 2006.

United Nations Development Programme (UNDP) (2005) *Human Development Report*, http://hdr.undp.org/reports/global/2005/pdf/HDR05_HDI.pdf, accessed 3 April, 2006.

US Congress (2002) *Report of the Joint Enquiry into the Terrorist Attacks of September 11, 2001* (Washington, DC: US Congress), http://usinfo.state.gov/topical/pol/terror, accessed 12 April, 2006.

US Election Assistance Commission (2004) *Report of the U. S. Election Assistance Commission On Best Practices for Facilitating Voting by U.S. Citizens covered by the Uniformed and Overseas Citizens Absentee Voting Act*, http://www.eac.gov/docs/UOCAVA%20best%20Practices%20Summary.doc, accessed 7 June, 2006.

V

van Biezen, I. (2003) *Political Parties in New Democracies: Party Organization in Southern and East-Central Europe* (Basingstoke and New York: Palgrave Macmillan).

van Creveld, M. (1999) *The Rise and Decline of the State* (Cambridge and New York: Cambridge University Press).

van de Walle, N. (2003) 'The State and African Development', in *Beyond Structural Adjustment: The Institutional Context of African Development*, ed. N. van de Walle, N. Ball and V. Ramachandran (Basingstoke and New York: Palgrave Macmillan) pp. 1–34.

van der Meer, F., and Roborgh, R. (1996) 'Civil Servants and Representativeness', in *Civil Service Systems in Comparative Perspective*, ed. H. Bekke, J. Perry and T. Toonen (Bloomington, IN: Indiana University Press) pp. 119–33.

van Deth, J. (2000) 'Interesting but Irrelevant: Social Capital and the Salience of Politics in Western Europe', *European Journal of Political Research* (37) 115–47.

van Eijk, R. (1997) 'The United Nations and the Reconstruction of Collapsed States', *African Journal of International and Comparative Law* (9) 543–72.

van Geffen, S. (2001) *The Court Rules: Modelling and Testing Supreme Court Influence on Policy* (Assen: Van Gorcum).

van Woerkens, M. (2002) *The Strangled Traveler: Colonial Imaginings and the Thugs of India*, trans. C. Tihanyi (Chicago, IL: University of Chicago Press).

Vanhanen, T. (1997) *Prospects of Democracy: A Study of 172 Countries* (London and New York: Routledge).

Vartiainen, J. (2004) 'Scandinavian Capitalism at the Turn of the Century', in *Where are National Capitalisms Now?*, ed. J. Perraton and B. Clift (Basingstoke and New York: Palgrave Macmillan) pp. 111–32.

Vedung, E. (1998) 'Policy Instruments: Typologies and Theories', in *Carrots, Sticks, and Sermons: Policy Instruments and Their Evaluation*, ed. M.-L. Bemelmans-Videc, R. Rist and E. Vedung (New Brunswick, NJ: Transaction) pp. 21–52.

Verba, S. (1987) *Elites and the Idea of Equality: A Comparison of Japan, Sweden and the United States* (Cambridge, MA and London: Harvard University Press).

Verba, S., Scholzman, K. and Brady, H. (1995) *Voice and Equality: Civic Voluntarism in American Politics* (Cambridge, MA and London: Harvard University Press).

Veronis, Suhler and Stevenson (2005) *Communications Industry Forecast Highlights*, http://www.vss.com/pubs/pubs_cif_highlights.html, accessed 30 April, 2006.

Villordes, C. (2003) 'Intra-party Competition under Preferential List Systems: The Case of Finland', *Representation* (40) 55–66.

Volkswagen A G (2005) *Annual Report*, http://gb.volkswagen.com/index.php@id=831.html, accessed 17 May, 2006.

Volkswagen (2007) *Bodies: Working at Volkswagen*, http://www.vw-personal.de/content/www/en//arbeiten/organe/aufsichtsrat.html, accessed 26 February, 2007.

von Beyme, K. (2003) 'Constitutional Engineering in Central and Eastern Europe', in *Developments in Central and East European Politics 3*, ed. S. White, J. Batt and P. Lewis (Basingstoke and New York: Palgrave Macmillan) pp. 190–210.

von Mises, L. (1920) [1935 edn] 'Economic Calculation in a Socialist Commonwealth', in *Collective Economic Planning*, ed. F. Hayek (London: Routledge & Kegan Paul) Ch. 1.

W

Wade, R. (1990) *Governing the Market* (Princeton, NJ: Princeton University Press).

Wagstyl, S. (2006) 'Growth Figures Mask Nerves', *Financial Times*, 21 April, p. 2.

Wahlke, J. *et al.* (1962) *The Legislative System* (New York: Wiley).

Walker, J. (1991) *Mobilizing Interest Groups in America: Patrons, Professionals and Social Movements* (Ann Arbor, MI: University of Michigan Press).

Walpole, S. (1881) *The Electorate and the Legislature* (London: Macmillan).

Wang, X. (2002) 'The Postcommunist Personality: The Spectre of China's Market Reforms', *The China Journal* (47) 1–17.

Warber, A. (2006) *Executive Orders and the Modern Presidency: Legislating from the Oval Office* (Boulder, CO and London: Lynne Rienner).

Ware, A. (2002) *The Direct Primary in the United States: Party Institutionalization and Transformation in the American North* (Cambridge and New York: Cambridge University Press).

Waters, M. (2000) *Globalization*, 2nd edn (London and New York: Routledge).

Watt, E. (1982) *Authority* (London: Croom Helm).

Wattenberg, M. (2000) 'The Decline of Party Mobilization', in *Parties Without Partisans*, ed. R. Dalton and M. Wattenberg (Oxford and New York: Oxford University Press) pp. 64–76.

Watts, R. (2005) 'Comparing Forms of Federal Partnerships', in *Theories of Federalism: A Reader*, ed. D. Karmis and W. Norman (New York and Basingstoke: Palgrave Macmillan) pp. 233–54.

Weaver, R. and Rockman, B. (eds) (1993) *Do Institutions Matter? Government Capabilities in the United States and Abroad* (Washington: The Brookings Institution).

Web Japan (2006) *Governmental Structure*, http://www.web-japan.org/factsheet/index.html, accessed 28 December, 2006.

Webb, P. and Kolodny, R. (2006) 'Professional Staff in Political Parties', in *Handbook of Party Politics*, ed. R. Katz and W. Crotty (London and Thousand Oaks, CA: Sage) pp. 337–47.

Webb, P., Farrell, D. and Holliday, I. (eds) (2002) *Political Parties in Advanced Industrial Democracies* (Oxford and New York: Oxford University Press).

Weber, M. (1905) [1930 English translation] *The Protestant Ethic and the Spirit of Capitalism* (London: Allen & Unwin).

Weber, M. (1918) [1990 edn] 'The Advent of Plebiscitarian Democracy', in *The West European Party System,* ed. P. Mair (Oxford and New York: Oxford University Press) pp. 31–7.

Weber, M. (1922) [1957 edn] *The Theory of Economic and Social Organization* (Berkeley, CA: University of California Press).

Weber, M. (1923) [1946 edn] 'The Social Psychology of the World Religions', in *From Max Weber: Essays in Sociology,* ed. and trans. H. Gerth and C. Wright Mills (Oxford and New York: Oxford University Press) pp. 267–301.

Weber, M. (1921–22) [1978 edn] *Economy and Society: An Outline of Interpretive Sociology*, ed. G. Roth and C. Wittich (Berkeley, CA: University of California Press).

Wedeen, L. (1999) *Ambiguities of Domination: Politics, Rhetoric and Symbolism in Contemporary Syria* (Chicago, IL: University of Chicago Press).

Wehner, J. (2006) 'Assessing the Power of the Purse: An Index of Legislative Budget Institutions', *Political Studies* (54) 767–85.

Weiler, J. (1994) 'A Quiet Revolution: The European Court of Justice and its Interlocutors', *Comparative Political Studies* (26) 519–34.

Weiss, L. (1998) *The Myth of the Powerless State: Governing the Economy in a Global Era* (Cambridge: Polity).

Weiss, L. (2004) 'Developmental States Before and After the Asian Crisis', in *Where Are National Capitalisms Now?*, ed. J. Perraton and B. Clift (Basingstoke and New York: Palgrave Macmillan) pp. 154–68.

Weissberg, R. (1998) *Political Tolerance: Balancing Community and Diversity* (Thousand Oaks, CA and London: Sage).

Weissberg, R. (2002) *Polling, Policy and Public Opinion: The Case Against Heeding 'The Voice of the People'* (London and New York: Palgrave Macmillan).

Wellman, B. (2001) 'Does the Internet Increase, Decrease or Supplement Social Capital? Social Networks, Participation and Community Commitment', *Research Bulletin* (6) (Toronto: Centre for Urban and Community Studies, University of Toronto), http://www.urbancenter.utoronto.ca/pdfs/researchbulletins/06.pdf, accessed 27 April, 2006.

West, D. and Orman, J. (2003) *Celebrity Politics* (Upper Saddle River, NJ: Prentice Hall).

Wheare, K. (1963a) *Federal Government,* 4th edn (Oxford and New York: Oxford University Press).

Wheare, K. (1963b) *Legislatures* (Oxford: Oxford University Press).

White, S. (2005a) 'The Political Parties', in *Developments in Russian Politics 6*, ed. S. White, Z. Gitelman and R. Sakwa (Basingstoke and New York: Palgrave Macmillan) pp. 80–95.

White, S. (2005b) 'Russia: The Authoritarian Adaptation of an Electoral System', in *The Politics of Electoral Systems*, ed. M. Gallagher and P. Mitchell (Oxford and New York: Oxford University Press) pp. 313–32.

White, S., Batt, J. and Lewis, P. (eds) (2003) *Developments in Central and East European Politics 3* (Basingstoke: Palgrave Macmillan).

White, S., Gitelman, Z. and Sakwa, R. (eds) (2005) *Developments in Russian Politics 6* (Basingstoke and New York: Palgrave Macmillan).

White House (2006) *National Security Strategy, March 2006*, http://www.whitehouse.gov/nsc/nss/2006/, accessed 24 August, 2006.

Wiarda, H. (ed.) (2004a) *Authoritarianism and Corporatism In Latin America – Revisited* (Gainesville, FL: University Press of Florida).

Wiarda, H. (ed.) (2004b) *Comparative Politics: Critical Concepts in Political Science,* 6 vols (London and New York: Routledge).

Wiener, A. and Diez, T. (eds) (2004) *European Integration Theory* (Oxford and New York: Oxford University Press).

Wigbold, H. (1979) 'Holland: The Shaky Pillars of Hilversum', in *Television and Political Life*, ed. A. Smith (London: Macmillan) pp. 191–231.

Wildavsky, A. (1979) *The Art and Craft of Policy Analysis* (Boston, MA: Little, Brown).

Wilde, R. (2007) *Territorial Administration by International Organizations* (Oxford and New York: Oxford University Press).

Wilensky, H. (1984) *The Welfare State and Equality* (Berkeley, CA: University of California Press).

Willerton, J. (1997) 'Presidential Power', in *Developments in Russian Politics*, ed. S. White, A. Pravda and Z. Gitelman (Basingstoke: Macmillan) pp. 35–60.

Willerton, J. (2005) 'Putin and the Hegemonic Presidency', in *Developments in Russian Politics 6*, ed. S. White, Z. Gitelman and R. Sakwa (Basingstoke and New York: Palgrave Macmillan) pp. 18–39.

Williams, P. (1970) *Wars, Plots and Scandal in Post-War France* (Oxford: Oxford University Press).

Williams, R. (1962) *Communications* (Harmondsworth and New York: Penguin).

Wilson, A. (2006) *Ukraine's Orange Revolution* (New Haven, CT: Yale University Press).

Wilson, G. (1990) *Interest Groups* (Oxford and Cambridge, MA: Blackwell).

Wilson, G. (2003) *Business and Politics: A Comparative Introduction,* 3rd edn (Basingstoke: Macmillan).

Wilson, J. (1989) *Bureaucracy: What Government Agencies Do and How They Do It* (New York: Basic Books).

Wilson, W. (1885) *Congressional Government* (Boston, MA: Houghton Mifflin).

Wilson, W. (1887) 'The Study of Administration', *Political Science Quarterly* (2) 197–222.

Winham, G. (2005) 'The Evolution of the Global Trade Regime', in *Global Political Economy*, ed. J. Ravenhill (Oxford and New York: Oxford University Press) pp. 87–115.

Winter, L. and Brans, M. (2003) 'Belgium: Political Professionals and the Crisis of the Party State', in *The Political Class in Advanced Democracies*, ed. J. Borchert and J. Zeiss (Oxford and New York: Oxford University Press) pp. 45–66.

Wise, L. (2003) 'Representative Bureaucracy', in *Handbook of Public Administration,* ed. B. Guy Peters and J. Pierre (London and Thousand Oaks, CA: Sage) pp. 343–53.

Wood, G. (1993) 'Democracy and the American Revolution', in *Democracy: The Unfinished Journey: 508 BC to AD 1993*, ed. J. Dunn (Oxford and New York: Oxford University Press) pp. 91–106.

Worger, W. and Clark, N. (2003) *The Rise and Fall of Apartheid* (Harlow, Longman).

World Bank (1997) *World Development Report: The State in a Changing World* (Oxford and New York: Oxford University Press).

World Bank (2006a) *Country Groups*, http://web.worldbank.org/WBSITE/EXTERNAL/DATASTATISTICS/0,,contentMDK:20421402~pagePK:64133150~piPK:64133175~theSitePK:239419,00.html, accessed 21 August, 2006.

World Bank (2006b) *Doing Business: Economy Rankings*, http://www.doingbusiness.org/EconomyRankings/, accessed November 19, 2006.

WRI (World Resources Institute) (2007) *Earthtrends*, http://earthtrends.wri.org, accessed 9 January, 2007.

Wright, V. (ed.) (1994) *Privatization in Western Europe: Pressures, Problems and Paradoxes* (London and New York: Pinter).

Wright, V. (1997) 'La Fin du Dirigisme?', *Modern and Contemporary France* (5) 151–5.

Wright, V., Peters, B. Guy and Rhodes, R. (eds) (2000) *Administering the Summit: Administration of the Core Executive in Developed Countries* (Basingstoke: Macmillan).

Y

Yang, D. (1996) *Calamity and Reform in China: State, Rural Society and Institutional Change since the Great Leap Forward* (Stanford, CA: Stanford University Press).

Yanow, D. and Schwartz-Shea, P. (eds) (2006) *Interpretation and Method: Empirical Research Methods and the Interpretive Turn* (Armonk, New York and London: M. E. Sharpe).

Yin, R. (2003) *Case Study Research: Design and Methods,* 3rd edn (Thousand Oaks, CA and London: Sage).

Yin, R. (ed.) (2004) *The Case Study Anthology* (Thousand Oaks, CA and London: Sage).

Z

Zakaria, F. (2003) *The Future of Freedom: Illiberal Democracy at Home and Abroad* (New York and London: Norton).

Zartman, W. (ed.) (1995a) *Collapsed States: The Disintegration and Restoration of Legitimate Authority* (Boulder, CO and London: Lynne Rienner).

Zartman, W. (1995b) 'Posing the Problem of State Collapse' in *Collapsed States: The Disintegration and Restoration of Legitimate Authority*, ed. W. Zartman (Boulder, CO and London: Lynne Rienner) pp. 1–14.

Zaslavsky, K. and Brym, J. (1978) 'The Functions of Elections in the USSR', *Soviet Studies* (30) 362–71.

Ziller, J. (2003) 'The Continental System of Administrative Legality' in *Handbook of Public Administration*, ed. B. Guy Peters and J. Pierre (London and Thousand Oaks, CA: Sage) pp. 260–8.

Zirakzadeh, C. (1997) *Social Movements in Politics: A Comparative Study* (London and New York: Longman).

Index

Note: entries in red indicate a definition.

Q

R